Alaska
a Lonely Planet travel survival kit

Jim DuFresne

Alaska

5th edition

Published by
Lonely Planet Publications
Head Office: PO Box 617, Hawthorn, Vic 3122, Australia
Branches: 155 Filbert St, Suite 251, Oakland, CA 94607, USA
                 10 Barley Mow Passage, Chiswick, London W4 4PH, UK
                 71 bis rue du Cardinal Lemoine, 75005 Paris, France

Printed by
Craft Print Pte Ltd, Singapore

Photographs by
Alaska Division of Tourism (ADT), Camp Denali (CD), Jim DuFresne (JD), Kenai Fjords Tours (KFT),
Carl Palazzola (CP), Donna Pietsch (DP), Robert Strauss (RS), Deanna Swaney (DS), National Park
Service (NPS), Jeff Williams (JW), Pattie Zwers (PZ)

Front cover: Moose in the morning mist; Paul McCormick, The Image Bank

First Published
June 1983

This Edition
May 1997

National Library of Australia Cataloguing in Publication Data

DuFresne, Jim
    Alaska – a travel survival kit

    5th ed.
    Includes index.
    ISBN 0 86442 414 0.

    1. Alaska – Guidebooks.
    1. Title. (Series: Lonely Planet travel survival kit).

917.98045

text © Jim DuFresne 1997
maps & illustrations © Lonely Planet 1997
photos © photographers as indicated 1997

Jim DuFresne

Jim is a former sports and outdoors editor of the *Juneau Empire* and the first Alaskan sportswriter to win a national award from Associated Press. He is presently a freelance writer, specializing in outdoor and travel writing. His previous books include the Lonely Planet guides *Tramping in New Zealand* and *Backpacking in Alaska*. He has also written wilderness guides to Isle Royale, Voyageurs and Glacier Bay national parks.

From the Author

My deepest appreciation goes to my old Alaskan mates Jeff & Sue Sloss, Ken Leghorn & Susan Warner, Larry Persily and Ed Fogel. Thanks also to the legion of Lonely Planet travelers who went to Alaska with this book in hand and then took the time to drop me a line.

I received considerable assistance from: Ken Morris of the Anchorage Convention & Visitor Bureau; Anne Shepard of the Sitka Convention & Visitor Bureau; Suzi Bock of the Matanuska-Susitna Convention & Visitor Bureau; Lois Wirtz of the Nome Convention & Visitor Bureau; Ileen Ellison of the Kodiak Convention & Visitor Bureau; Rebecca Godek of the Kenai Peninsula Tourism Marketing Council; Cyndy Dickson of the Seward Chamber of Commerce; Carol Rushmore, economic development planner for the City of Wrangell; Sharon Syverson of the City of Unalaska; Grace Norton of the City of Kotzebue; Connie McKenzie of the Juneau Convention & Visitor Bureau; and Tyson Verse, tourism director for the City of Haines.

Also lending me an invaluable hand were Linda Mickle of the Alaska Marine Hwy; Carol Waddell of Reeve Aleutian Airways; John Beiler of the Alaska Division of Tourism; and Barabara Kagerer of Kenai Fjords Tours.

Most of all I thank my traveling partners Nadine Caisley, Samantha Thompson, Alistair Davidson, Bob Storey, Pattie Zwers and Donna Pietsch, each of whom I've watched become captivated by the aura of Alaska.

We'll all meet again, I'm sure, in the Land of the Midnight Sun.

From the Publisher

This book was edited at the Lonely Planet office in Melbourne, Australia, by Chris Wyness with the help of Lindsay Brown, Lyn McGaurr and Kate Hoffman. Craig MacKenzie helped take the book through layout and Anthony Phelan was responsible for the mapping, design and layout of this edition. The cover was designed by Simon Bracken. Marcel Gaston produced the climate charts and Michael Signal the back cover map.

Thanks

Many thanks to the travellers who used the last edition and wrote to us with helpful hints, useful advice and interesting anecdotes:

Christine Agnitti, Ori Aphek, Wendy Bell, Richard Bond, Ian Brown, Mat Bruce, Alex Carter, Tom Choate, Jennifer Craig, Keigo Fukatsu, Lorraine Grave, Linda Greenfield, Gavin Hardy, Nigel Harper, Ian Harrison, Patricia Hunt, L Hunter, Belinda Johnson, Hermann Koerbel, Nonna Kokayeff, JM MacPherson, Nina McKenna, Renie Norton, Brian & Mary Raybould, Phyl Shimeld, Heather Tregoning, Rachel Yee Quill.

Warning & Request

Things change – prices go up, schedules change, good places go bad and bad places go bankrupt – nothing stays the same. So, if you find things better or worse, recently opened or long since closed, please tell us and help make the next edition even more accurate and useful.

We value all of the feedback we receive from travellers. Julie Young coordinates a small team who read and acknowledge every letter, postcard and email, and ensure that every morsel of information finds its way to the appropriate authors, editors and publishers.

Everyone who writes to us will find their name in the next edition of the appropriate guide and will also receive a free subscription to our quarterly newsletter, *Planet Talk*. The very best contributions will be rewarded with a free Lonely Planet guide.

Excerpts from your correspondence may appear in updates (which we add to the end pages of reprints); new editions of this guide; in our newsletter, *Planet Talk*; or in the Postcards section of our Web site – so please let us know if you don't want your letter published or your name acknowledged.

Contents

Boxed Asides

Map Legend

BOUNDARIES

International Boundary

Regional Boundary

ROUTES

Highway

Highway - Unsealed

Major Road

Major Road - Unsealed

Minor Road

City Road

City Street

Railway

Railway - Underground Section

Walking / Bicycle Track

Walking Tour

Canoeing / Kayaking Route

Ferry Route

AREA FEATURES

Parks

Built-Up Area

Market

Forest

Cemetery

Mud Flats

Glacier

Rocks

HYDROGRAPHIC FEATURES

Coastline

River, Creek

Intermittent River or Creek

Rapids, Waterfalls

Lake, Intermittent Lake

River Flow

Swamp

SYMBOLS

✪	CAPITAL	National Capital
◉	Capital	Regional Capital
⬤	CITY	Major City
●	City	City
•	Town	Town
•	Village	Village
■ ▼		Place to Stay, Place to Eat
		Cafe, Pub or Bar
✉ ☎		Post Office, Telephone
❶ ❸		Tourist Information, Bank
● ᴾ		Transport, Parking
⛫ ⌂		Museum, Youth Hostel
⛺ ⚑		Caravan Park, Camping Ground
⛪ ✚		Church, Cathedral
⚓ ⛵		Canoeing / Kayaking, Shelter
✛ ★		Hospital, Police Station

◔ ᴾ		Embassy, Petrol Station
✈ ✚		Airport, Airfield
⬛ ✿		Swimming Pool, Gardens
❖ 🐘		Shopping Centre, Zoo
⌒ ⛶		Mountain Range, Picnic Area
← A25		One Way Street, Route Number
⛫ ♟		Stately Home, Monument
⌒ ⌂		Cave, Cabin
▲ ☀		Mountain or Hill, Lookout
⛫ ❶		Stately Home, Toilet
)(◎		Pass, Spring
⚐ ⚐		Ski Field, Trail Head
∴		Archaeological Site or Ruins
		Building
		Cliff or Escarpment, Tunnel
		Railway Station

Note: not all symbols displayed above appear in this book

Alaska Map Index

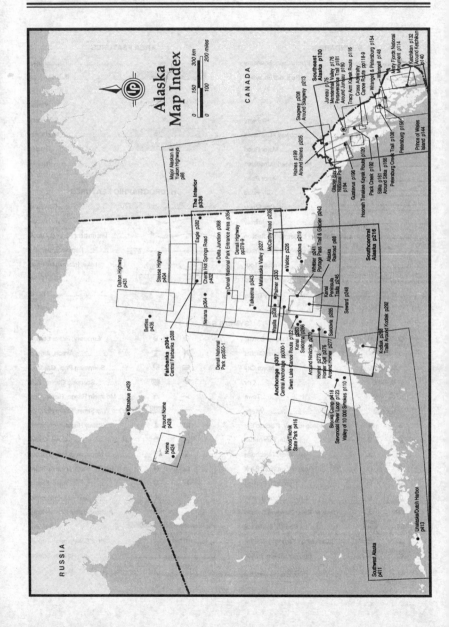

Introduction

It isn't the mountains, sparkling lakes or glaciers that draw travelers to Alaska every year but the magic in the land, an irresistible force that tugs on those who dream about the north country.

No area in the USA possesses the mystical pull that this land has. It ignites the imagination of people who live in the city but long to wander in the woods. Its mythical title of the 'Final Frontier' is as strong today as it was in the past when Alaska's promise of adventure and the lure of quick wealth brought the first invasion of miners to the state. Today, they have been replaced by travelers and backpackers but the spirit of adventure is still the same.

Travelers, drawn to Alaska by its colorful reputation, are stunned by the grandeur of what they see and often go home penniless.

There are mountains, glaciers and rivers in other parts of North America but few are on the same scale or as overpowering as those in Alaska. To see a brown bear rambling up one side of a mountain valley or to sit in a kayak and watch a five-mile-wide glacier continually calve ice off its face are experiences of natural beauty that permanently change your way of thinking.

If nature's handiwork doesn't affect you, then the state's overwhelming size will. Everything in Alaska is big – that is, everything except its population. There are 550,043 residents and almost half of them live in one city, Anchorage. Yet the state is huge at 591,004 sq miles which makes it a fifth of the size of the USA; as big as England, France, Italy and Spain put together; bigger than the next three largest

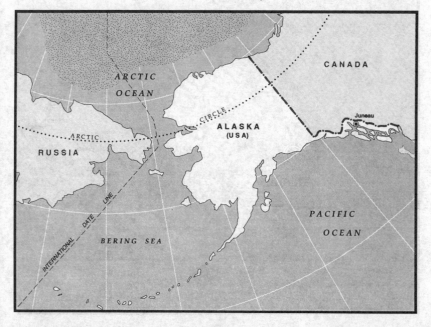

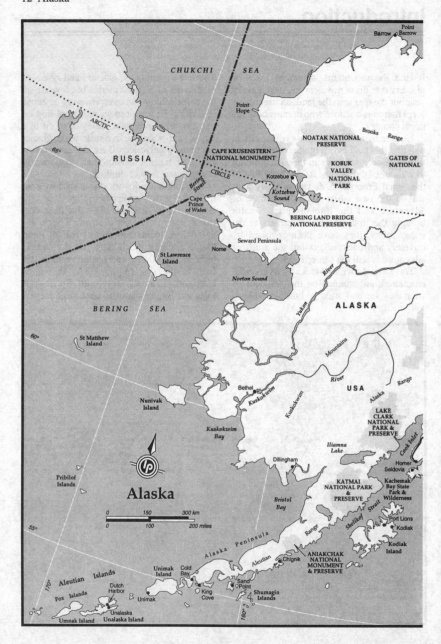

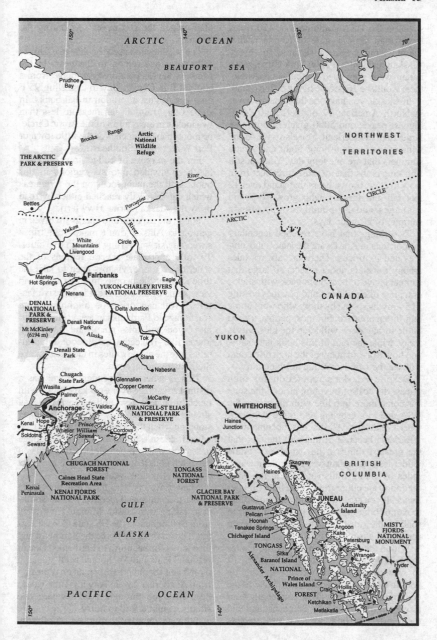

states in the USA combined; or 120 times larger than the US state of Rhode Island. There is more than a sq mile for every Alaskan resident – if New York City's Manhattan were populated to the same density there would be 16 people living on the island.

In Alaska, you have the third longest river in North America; 17 of the country's 20 highest peaks; and 5000 glaciers, with one larger than Switzerland. You also have Arctic winters that are one long night and Arctic summers that are one long day. You can still find king crabs that measure three feet from claw to claw, brown bears that stand over 12 feet tall and farmers who grow 70-pound cabbages and 30-pound turnips after a summer of 20-hour days.

Two things that have reached legendary proportions in Alaska are the state's mosquitoes and its prices. There are always tales among travelers about insects so large that campers have to beat them back with sticks; or a plate of eggs, toast and potatoes costing $15 – myths spread by those who went home bug-bitten or broke. For most people, a good bottle of bug dope will keep the mosquitoes away, while the aim of this book is to show you how to avoid many of the high prices and still see the wonders of the north country.

Despite Alaska's reputation for high prices, the cost of traveling around the state has come more into line with the rest of the USA due to a growing and more stabilized tourist industry. Alaska has become very affordable because of that and the fact that the greatest things it has to offer – prime wilderness, abundant wildlife, clear water, miles of hiking trails (in general the great outdoors) are either free or cost little to experience. If you are low on funds but are willing to camp, hike or sit on a mountain peak to soak up the sunshine and scenery, then you can afford a trip to Alaska.

Within the state, which ranges 1400 miles from north to south and 2400 miles from east to west, are several regions making up Alaska's character, each as distinctive as the countries in Europe. You can begin your travels in the rainy, lush Southeast and end them in the Arctic tundra – a vast, treeless plain where the sun never sets during the summer.

The weather and scenery change dramatically from one region to the next. In the summer, the temperatures can range from a cool 50°F in Glacier Bay to a sizzling 95°F on a hot August afternoon in Fairbanks. In some years, rainfall can measure less than two inches in areas north of the Arctic Circle, or more than 300 inches at the little town of Port Walter in the Southeast.

For the purpose of budget travel, Alaska has been divided into six regions in this book, with the main focus on the five areas which can be easily reached either by road or by the Alaska Marine Hwy ferries.

For all the expense and energy involved in getting to Alaska, don't make your trip a seven-day/six-night fling through five cities. To truly appreciate several regions of the state, or even one, visitors need to take the time to meet the people, hike the trails and view some of nature's most impressive features. You can drive or hitchhike from Anchorage to Fairbanks in a day, but in your hurry you will miss small and interesting towns like Talkeetna or outdoor opportunities like the canoe routes in the Nancy Lake State Recreational Area.

This is where independent travel has a distinct advantage over a package tour – with much time and few obligations, you can slowly make your way through the state, stopping when it pleases you and moving on when it doesn't. Often a quaint little village or sea port will be especially inviting and you can pitch your tent along the beach for a few days or even a few weeks.

Many travelers who have less than three weeks to spare spend it entirely in the Southeast, taking the Alaska Marine Hwy ferry from Bellingham in the US state of Washington. Those who want to see the Southeast and then move further north to Fairbanks, Denali National Park and Anchorage need at least a month and should possibly plan on returning from Anchorage by air. Any less time would be a rush job through a land where one simply cannot afford to hurry.

With an increasing number of nonstop

flights being offered today from such cities as Reno, Detroit and Minneapolis, it's possible, and affordable, to fly to Anchorage and complete a tour of that city, Denali National Park and Fairbanks in three weeks.

But what's important is to keep in mind that the ever-increasing popularity of Alaska has not only stabilized the tourist industry but also made Alaska a painfully crowded destination at times.

Today travelers are shocked to head into the Kenai Peninsula area and find campground after campground filled in July. Denali National Park can be a zoo in August and often finding a bed in towns like Valdez and Seward at the height of the tourist season is a near impossible task. There are times when the George Parks Hwy between Anchorage and Fairbanks is just an endless line of RVs heading south.

The solution to that is to pack in more days to escape further off the beaten path and to try to make as many arrangements in advance of your trip as possible, especially if you plan to visit such popular areas as Denali or Katmai national parks or hope to secure passage for your vehicle on the ferries. (There isn't a day that goes by during the summer without a motorist being stunned to find out in Valdez that you need a reservation to transport a car to Whittier.)

One last thing for those who have seemingly been dreaming forever about Alaska. It's wise to start your trip at the beginning of the summer in case you want to extend your stay another month or even longer. One of the most common stories among residents is how somebody came to visit Alaska for six weeks and ended up staying six years. Once there, Alaska is a hard land to leave.

Facts about Alaska

HISTORY

Alaska's history is a strange series of spurts and sputters, booms and busts. Although today Alaska is viewed as a wilderness paradise and an endless source of raw materials, it has often in the past been regarded as a frozen wasteland, a suitable home only for Inuit and polar bears. When some natural resource was uncovered, however, a short period of prosperity and exploitation followed: first there were sea-otter skins; then gold, salmon and oil; and most recently, untouched wilderness. After each resource was exhausted, some would say raped, the land slipped back into oblivion.

The First Alaskans

The first Alaskans migrated from Asia to North America from 30,000 to 40,000 years ago during an Ice Age that lowered the sea level and gave rise to a 900-mile land bridge spanning Siberia and Alaska. The nomadic groups were not bent on exploring the new world but on following the animal herds that provided them with food and clothing. Although many tribes wandered deep into North and South America, four ethnic groups – the Athabascans, Aleuts, Inuit and the coastal tribes of Tlingits and Haidas – remained in Alaska and made the harsh wilderness their homeland.

The First Europeans

Thanks to the cold and stormy North Pacific, Alaska was one of the last places in the world to be mapped by Europeans. This lead to several countries exploring the region and then attempting to lay a claim to the land and its resources by establishing a fort or two. Spanish admiral Bartholeme de Fonte is credited by many for making the first trip into Alaskan waters when, in 1640, he sailed from Mexico up the West Coast of the USA to Alaska. There he explored a network of rivers looking for the Northwest Passage before returning south.

The first written record of the state was made by Virtus Bering, a Danish navigator sailing for the tsar of Russia. Bering's trip in 1728 proved that America and Asia were two separate continents, and 13 years later, commanding the ship *St Peter*, he went ashore near Cordova to become the first European to set foot in Alaska.

Bering and many of his crew died from scurvy during that journey, but his lieutenant (aboard the ship *St Paul*) sailed all the way to the site of present-day Sitka before turning around. Despite all the hardships, the survivors brought back fur pelts and tales of fabulous seal and otter colonies – Alaska's first boom was under way. Russian fur merchants wasted little time in overrunning the Aleutian Islands and quickly established a settlement on Kodiak Island. Chaos followed as bands of Russian hunters robbed and murdered each other for furs while the peaceful Aleutian Indians, living near the hunting grounds, were almost annihilated.

By the 1790s, Russia had organized the Russian-American Company to regulate the fur trade and ease the violent competition. However, tales of the enormous wealth to be gained in the Alaskan wildlife trade brought representatives of several other countries to the frigid waters. Spain claimed the entire North American west coast, including Alaska, and sent several explorers to the Southeast region. These early visitors took boat loads of furs but left neither settlers nor forts, only a few Spanish names.

The British arrived when Captain James Cook also began searching the area for the Northwest Passage between the Pacific and Atlantic oceans. From Vancouver Island, Cook sailed north to Southcentral Alaska in 1778, anchoring at what is now Cook Inlet for a spell, before continuing on to the Aleutian Islands, Bering Sea and even the Arctic Ocean. The French sent Jean de La Perouse, who in 1786 made it as far as Lituya Bay on the southern coast of Alaska. The wicked tides within the long, narrow bay caught the exploration party off guard, capsizing three longboats, killing 21 sailors and discouraging the French from colonizing the area.

It was Cook's shipmate, George Vancouver, returning on his own in the 1790s, who finally charted the complicated waters of the Southeast's Inside Passage. Aboard his ship, HMS *Discovery*, Vancouver surveyed the coastline from California to Alaska's Panhandle, producing maps so accurate they were still being used a century later.

Having depleted the fur colonies in the Aleutians, Alexander Baranof, who headed the Russian-American Company, moved his territorial capital from Kodiak to Sitka in the Southeast.

After subduing the Tlingit Indians in his ruthless manner, he proceeded to build a stunning city, 'an American Paris in Alaska', with the immense profits from furs. At one point, Baranof oversaw, or some would say ruled, a fur empire that stretched from Bistol Bay to northern California but when the British began pushing north into Southeast Alaska, he built a second fort near the mouth of the Stikine River in 1834. That fort, which was named St Dionysius at the time, eventually evolved into the small lumbering and fishing town of Wrangell.

George Vancouver charted the Southeast's Inside Passage in the 1790s.

When a small trickle of US adventurers began to arrive, four nations had a foot in the Panhandle of Alaska: Spain and France were squeezed out of the area by the early 1800s while the British were reduced to leasing selected areas from the Russians.

The Sale of Alaska

By the 1860s, the Russians found themselves badly overextended. Their involvement in Napoleon's European wars, a declining fur industry and the long lines of shipping between Sitka and the heartland of Russia were draining their national treasury. The country made several overtures to the USA for the sale of Alaska and fishers from Washington State pushed for it.

The American Civil War delayed the negotiations and it wasn't until 1867 that Secretary of State William H Seward, with extremely keen foresight, signed a treaty to purchase the state for $7.2 million – less than two cents an acre.

By then the US public was in an uproar over the 'Frozen Wasteland'. Newspapers called it 'Seward's Ice Box' or 'Walrussia', while one senator heatedly compared Alaska to a 'sucked orange' as little was left of the rich fur trade.

On the Senate floor, the battle to ratify the treaty lasted six months before the sale was approved. On 18 October 1867, the formal transfer of Alaska to the Americans took place in Sitka, while nearby Wrangell, a town both the Russians and the British controlled at one time, changed flags for the third time in its short existence.

Alaska remained a lawless, unorganized territory for the next 20 years, with the US Army in charge at one point and the US Navy at another.

This great land, remote and inaccessible to all but a few hardy settlers, remained a dark, frozen mystery to most people. Eventually its riches were uncovered one by one. First it was whales, taken mostly in the Southeast and later in the Bering Sea and the Arctic Ocean.

Next the phenomenal salmon runs were tapped, with the first canneries being built in

1878 at Klawock on Prince of Wales Island. Both industries brought a trickle of people and prosperity to Alaska.

Gold

What brought Alaska into the world limelight, however, was gold. The promise of quick riches and the adventure of the frontier became the most effective lure Alaska ever had. Gold was discovered in the Gastineau Channel in the 1880s and the towns of Juneau and Douglas sprang up overnight, living off the very productive Treadwell and Alaska-Juneau mines. Circle City in the Interior suddenly emerged in 1893 when gold was discovered in nearby Birch Creek. Three years later, one of the world's most colorful gold rushes took place in the Klondike of the Yukon Territory (Canada).

Often called 'the last grand adventure', the Klondike gold rush took place when the country and much of the world was suffering a severe recession. Thousands of people quit their jobs and sold their homes to finance a trip through Southeast Alaska to the newly created boom town of Skagway. From this tent city, almost 30,000 prospectors tackled the steep Chilkoot Trail to Lake Bennett, where they built crude rafts to float the rest of the way to the goldfields; an equal number of people returned home along the route, broke and disillusioned.

The number of miners who made a fortune was small, but the tales and legends that emerged were endless. The Klondike stampede, though it only lasted from 1896 to the early 1900s, was Alaska's most colorful era and earned Alaska the reputation of being the country's last frontier.

Statehood

By the 1900s, the attention of the miners shifted from the Klondike to Nome and then to Fairbanks, a boom town that was born when Felix Pedro discovered gold 12 miles north of the area in 1902. The gold mines and the large Kennecott copper mines north of Cordova also stimulated the state's growth and the 1900 census estimated the state's population to be 60,000, including 30,000

non-indigenous people. Alaskans, who moved their capital from Sitka to Juneau that year, began to clamor for more say in their future. The US Congress first gave them a nonvoting delegate to Washington in 1906 and then assisted in setting up a territorial legislature that met at Juneau in 1913. Three years later, the territory submitted its first statehood bill to Congress.

Statehood was set aside when many of Alaska's residents departed south for high-paying jobs that were created by WWI. Ironically, it took another war, WWII, to push Alaska firmly into the 20th century.

The USA experienced its only foreign invasion on home soil when the Japanese attacked the Attu Islands and bombed Dutch Harbor in the Aleutian Islands during WWII. Congress and military leaders panicked and rushed to develop and protect the rest of Alaska. Large army and air-force bases were built throughout the state at places including Anchorage, Fairbanks, Sitka, Whittier and Kodiak and thousands of military personnel were sent to run them. But it was the famous Alcan (also known as the Alaska Hwy) that was the single most important project of the military build-up. The 1520-mile road was a major engineering feat and became the only overland link between Alaska and the rest of the USA.

At the time, Japan and Germany, allied with Italy, looked all but unbeatable while the only countries with sufficient resources and armies to confront the aggressors (Britain, the Soviet Union and the USA) had but one common border – the Bering Strait, that narrow neck of water separating Alaska and Siberia. There was a need both to supply military hardware to Russia and to protect America's north-west flank, neither of which could be accomplished by sea after Japan bombed Pearl Harbor in December 1941.

An overland route, far enough inland to be out of range of aeroplanes carried by Japanese aircraft carriers, was the obvious answer. The US Army Corps of Engineers were sent to build the wilderness route and used seven regiments, three of which were Black, to finish the project at breakneck pace. In eight months and 12 days, the soldiers felled trees, put down gravel and built pontoon bridges until the Alcan was opened on 25 October 1942.

The road was built by the military but it was the residents who benefited as it stimulated the development of Alaska's natural resources. The growth lead to a new drive for statehood to fix what many felt was Alaska's status of '2nd-class citizenship' in Washington, DC. Early in 1958, Congress approved a statehood act which Alaskans quickly accepted, and on 3 January 1959, President Dwight Eisenhower proclaimed the land the 49th State of the Union.

The Modern State

Alaska entered the 1960s full of promise and then disaster struck: the most powerful earthquake ever recorded in North America (registering 9.2 on the Richter scale) hit Southcentral Alaska on Good Friday morning in 1964. More than 100 lives were lost and the damage was estimated at $500 million. In Anchorage, office buildings sank 10 feet into the ground and houses slid more than 1200 feet off a bluff into Knik Arm. A tidal wave virtually wiped out the entire community of Valdez. In Kodiak and Seward, 32 feet of the coastline slipped into the Gulf of Alaska, while Cordova lost its entire harbor as the sea rose 16 feet.

If the natural catastrophe left the newborn state in a shambles, then it was a gift from nature that rushed it to recovery and beyond. Alaska's next boom took place in 1968 when Atlantic Richfield discovered massive oil deposits underneath Prudhoe Bay in the Arctic Ocean. The value of the oil doubled after the worldwide Arab oil embargo of 1973 but the oil couldn't be touched until there was a pipeline to transport it to the warm-water port of Valdez. The pipeline, in turn, couldn't be built until the US Congress, which still administered most of the land, settled the intense controversy between industry, environmentalists and Native Alaskans with historical claims.

The Alaska Native Claims Settlement Act of 1971 was an unprecedented piece of legislation that opened the way for a group of oil companies to undertake the construction of the 789-mile pipeline. The oil began to flow in 1977, but during the brief years of pipeline construction Anchorage developed into a fully fledged modern city and Fairbanks burst at the seams as the transport center for much of the project. Along with four-digit weekly salaries, there was an astronomical rise in prices for basic items such as housing and food in Fairbanks, which some residents feel never came down with the wages.

For a decade or more, oil gave Alaska an economic base that was the envy of every other state. In the explosive growth period of the mid-1980s, Alaskans enjoyed the highest per-capita income in the country. The state's budget was in the billions and legislators in Juneau transformed Anchorage into a stunning city with sports arenas, libraries and performing-arts centers, while virtually every Bush town has a million-dollar school. From 1980 to 1986, this state of only a half-million residents generated revenue of $26 billion. For most Alaskans it was hard to see beyond the gleam of the oil dollar.

Their first rude awakening came in 1986 when world oil prices dropped. Their second dose of reality was even harder to swallow when in March 1989 the biggest oil spill in US history occurred in their state. The accident occurred after the *Exxon Valdez*, a 987-foot Exxon Oil supertanker, rammed Bligh Reef a few hours out of the port of Valdez. The ship spilled almost 11 million gallons of North Slope crude into the bountiful waters of Prince William Sound and then the oil quickly spread 600 miles from the grounding. Alaskans and the rest of the country watched in horror as the spill quickly became far too large for booms to contain the oil. Within months, miles of tainted coastline began to appear throughout the Gulf of Alaska as currents dispersed streamers of oil and tar balls.

State residents were shocked as oil began to appear from the glacier-carved cliffs of Kenai Fjords to the bird rookeries of Katmai National Park, and from lonely Cook Islet

Alaska's Permanent Fund

Nothing amazes visitors to Alaska more than a resident telling them that the state 'actually gives them money' every year just for living there. The annual checks date back to 1976 when residents approved a constitutional amendment for an Alaska Permanent Fund, money set aside from a percentage of all mineral-lease royalties. Prudhoe Bay oil made this fund so lopsided that in 1980 the state legislature created a Permanent Fund dividend payment program and two years later began handing out the interest from the fund, usually around $900 per resident annually.

The Permanent Fund is close to $12 billion and if it was a Fortune 500 company, it would be in the top 5% for income earned. It's estimated that by the year 2000 the fund will be earning more revenue for the state than Prudhoe Bay, and it is already the largest pool of money in the USA.

The problem is as Prudhoe Bay oil dries up, so does the amount of money that is funneled into the state's general operating budget. In recent years some politicians have advocated reducing the annual dividend or even doing away with it altogether in an effort to balance the budget. Others have proposed installing a state income tax to help pay for public programs. Either one leaves a sour taste in the mouth of most Alaskans who have always distrusted government and have come to love that dividend check in the middle of the winter. ■

beaches to the salmon streams on Kodiak Island. The spill eventually contaminated 1567 miles of shoreline; scientists estimated between 300,000 and 645,000 birds were killed, while the 1013 sea otters found dead in the oil represented only 20% of the total killed.

Valdez experienced another boom as the center of the clean-up effort which employed 10,000 workers, 800 boats and 45 oil skimmers. But the best this highly paid army could do was scrape 364 miles of shoreline before the on-coming winter weather shut down the effort in September. Only 14% of the oil was ever recovered by the crews. The rest either evaporated, sank to the bottom of the sea or broke down into components and chemicals on the beaches or in the water. Exxon walked away from the country's worst oil spill after agreeing to pay a $900 million settlement to the US and Alaska governments.

In the end, the oil, like every other resource that has been exploited in the past, is simply running out. That pot of gold called Prudhoe Bay began its decline in production in 1989 and in 1995 alone North Slope oil output decreased by more than 4%. This resulted in Acro, the state's second largest employer, laying off almost a third of its 2350 employees in Alaska. Other related companies, which move the oil and maintain

the Trans-Alaska Pipeline, also began to slash jobs. The end of the Cold War and the subsequent downsizing of the US military in the early 1990s was more economic bad news for Alaska. Fort Greely, Delta Junction's largest employer, was closed in 1994 with more Alaskan bases on the chopping block. Alaskan state revenues, once the envy of the governors of every other state in the country, went tumbling along with the declining oil royalties and forced Govenor Tony Knowles in Juneau to slash services and programs as he tried to balance the budget.

Many Alaskans see another North Slope oil field as the solution to their problems. Large mining projects and the logging of Tongass National Forest are being pushed as Alaska faces its greatest debate – the exploitation of its remaining wilderness. The issue first emerged moved to center stage when industry, conservationists and the government came head to head over a single paragraph in the Alaska Native Claims Settlement Act, known simply as 'd-2', that called for the preservation of 80 million acres of Alaskan wilderness. To most residents this evoked the entire issue of federal interference with the state's resources and future.

The resulting battle was a tug of war about how much land the US Congress would preserve, to what extent industries such as mining and logging would be allowed to develop, and what permanent residents would be allowed to purchase. The fury over wilderness reached a climax when, on the eve of his departure from office in 1980, President Jimmy Carter signed the Alaska Lands Bill into law, setting aside 106 million acres for national parks and preserves with a single stroke of the pen.

The problems of how to manage the USA's remaining true wilderness areas are far from over and presently the debate is centering on the Arctic National Wildlife Refuge (ANWR). Oil-company officials and Alaskan politicans in particular are pushing hard to open up this 1.5-million-acre refuge, one of the last great wilderness areas in the USA, to oil and gas drilling. A bill to open up the refuge in the US Congress, backed by President George Bush, was believed to be headed for passage when the *Exxon Valdez* ran aground in 1989.

After several years of hibernation, the effort was revived again when the Republicans took control of the US Congress in 1992 and members of Alaska's long-term Republication delegation suddenly had key leadership roles.

President Bill Clinton has vowed to veto any bill opening up the ANWR to pipelines and oil rigs. But many believe it's only a matter of time before the inevitable happens in a state where 85% of the revenue comes from the oil industry.

At the core of the dispute are issues of both 'locking up the land' and federal interference in the livelihood of Alaskans. Largely as the result of their remoteness, Alaskans have always been extremely independent, resenting anyone who traveled north with a book of rules and regulations. To most Alaskans, Washington, DC, is a foreign capital.

Today's Alaskans tend to be young (the median age is between 26 and 28 years) and spirited in work and play. They are individualistic in their lifestyles, following few outside trends and adhering only to what their environment dictates. They are lovers of the outdoors, though they don't always seem to take care of it, and generally extend a warm welcome to travelers. Occasionally you might run into an Alaskan who is boastfully loud, spinning and weaving tales of unbelievable feats while slapping you on the back. In this land of frontier fable, that's not being obnoxious – that's being colorful.

GEOGRAPHY
Southeast
Also known as the Panhandle, Southeast Alaska is a 500-mile coastal strip that extends from Dixon Entrance, north of Prince Rupert, to the Gulf of Alaska. In between are the hundreds of islands (including Prince of Wales Island, the third largest island in the USA) of the Alexander Archipelago and a narrow strip of coast separated from Canada's mainland by the glacier-filled Coastal Mountains.

Winding through the middle of the region is the Inside Passage waterway, the lifeline for the isolated communities as the rugged terrain prohibits road building. High annual rainfall and mild temperatures have turned the Southeast into rainforest which is broken up by majestic mountain ranges, glaciers and fjords that surpass those in Norway.

The area has many small fishing and lumbering towns as well as the larger communities of Ketchikan, Sitka and Juneau (the state capital considered by many to be the most scenic city in Alaska). Other highlights of the region include the wilderness areas of Glacier Bay, Admiralty Island, Misty Fjord and Tracy Arm, and the White Pass Railroad built in the days of the Klondike gold rush. Because the Alaska Marine Hwy connects the Southeast to Bellingham (USA) and Prince Rupert (Canada), the Southeast is the cheapest and often the first area visited by travelers.

Southcentral
This region curves 650 miles from the Gulf of Alaska, past Prince William Sound to Kodiak Island. Like the Southeast, it is a mixture of rugged mountains, glaciers, steep fjords and virgin forests, and includes the Kenai Peninsula, a superb recreational area for backpacking, fishing and boating. To the

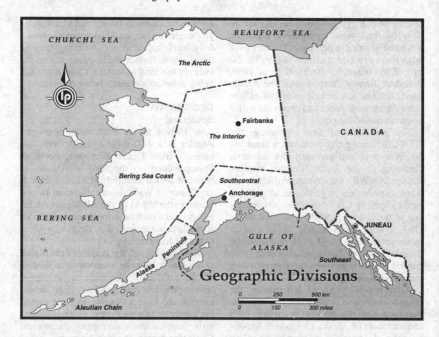

Geographic Divisions

south-west is Kodiak Island, home to much of Alaska's crab industry and the Kodiak bear, the largest species of brown bear in the state. To the east of the Kenai Peninsula is Prince William Sound, a bay that is famous for the Columbia Glacier and College Fjord and is still a mecca for kayakers and adventurers despite the Exxon oil spill.

The weather along the coastline can often be rainy and stormy but the summers are usually mild and have their share of sunshine. The peninsula is served by road from Anchorage and by the Alaska Marine Hwy which crosses Prince William Sound and runs to Kodiak.

Highlights of the region are the historical and charming towns of Homer, Seward, Cordova and Hope, while backpackers will find many opportunities for outdoor adventure in the wilderness areas of the Chugach National Forest, Kenai National Wildlife Refuge and the outlying areas around Kodiak, Cordova and Valdez.

Anchorage

Because of the city's size and central location, Anchorage has to be viewed as a separate region: one that is passed through whether you want to deal with an urban area or not. At first glance, Anchorage appears to be like any other city – billboards, traffic jams, fast-food restaurants and what seem like hordes of people. Among this uncontrolled urban sprawl, however, is a city that in recent years has blossomed on the flow of oil money. While older cities in the Lower 48 often worry about decaying city centers, Anchorage has transformed its city center with such capital projects as a sports arena, performing-arts center and 122 miles of bike paths.

Anchorage also has a feature most other cities don't have – wilderness at its doorstep. The nearby Chugach State Park, Turnagain and Knik arms, and the Matanuska Valley (home of the softball-size radishes) make Anchorage an area worth spending a little time in, if for no other reason than you'll have to arrive in, depart from or pass through it at some stage.

The Interior

This area includes three major roads – the George Parks, Glenn and Richardson highways – that cut across the center of the state and pass a number of forests, state parks and recreational areas, including Denali National Park & Preserve, Alaska's number one attraction. The heartland of Alaska offers warm temperatures in the summer and ample opportunities for outdoor activities in some of the state's most scenic and accessible areas. With the Alaska Range to the north, the Wrangell and Chugach mountains to the south and the Talkeetna Mountains cutting through the middle, the Interior has a rugged appearance matching that of either Southeast or Southcentral Alaska but without much of the rain and cloudy weather.

Fairbanks

The boom town of both the gold-rush days and later the construction of the pipeline to Prudhoe Bay has settled down a little, but it still retains much of its colorful and hardcore Alaskan character. A quick trip through Fairbanks is often a disappointment to most travelers, as Alaska's second largest city is very spread out. Located in the flat valley floor formed by the Tanana and Chena rivers, with the Alaska Range and Mt McKinley far off in the distance, Fairbanks lacks the dramatic setting many other areas offer.

However, the true delights of this freewheeling frontier town are revealed if sufficient time is spent here. In the summer, Fairbanks can be an unusually warm place with temperatures often reaching from 80°F to 90°F, and the midnight sun only setting for a few hours.

The surrounding area, especially the White Mountains, Circle, Eagle and the Dalton Hwy to Prudhoe Bay, has some of the most interesting backcountry areas accessible by road. Fairbanks is also the transport center for anybody wishing to venture north of the Arctic Circle or into the Brooks Range, site of many national parks and wildlife refuges.

The Bush

This region covers a vast area that includes the Brooks Range, Arctic Alaska, Western Alaska on the Bering Sea, and the Alaska Peninsula and Aleutian Islands which make up the out-reaching western arm of the state. The Bush is larger than the other five regions put together and is separated from them by great mountains and mighty rivers.

Occasionally, there are ways of beating the high cost of getting to the far reaches of the state, but for the most part traveling to the Bush involves small chartered aircraft, or 'bush planes'. These aeroplanes are a common method of travel through much of the state but, unfortunately, are prohibitively expensive for many budget travelers.

Except for the larger communities of Nome, Kotzebue and Barrow, independent

Shopping by Mail

No one knows the advantages of shopping by mail better than Alaskans, the kings and queens of catalogs. Thanks to the lack of national chains in most towns and the fact that many residents live in isolated rural areas, Alaskans tend to rank near the top in ordering merchandise by flipping the glossy pages of a catalog.

It's estimated that half of the adults in the USA shop by mail at one time or another but in Southcentral Alaska that rate is closer to seven out of 10 adults, and in rural bush communities it's even higher. JC Penny, the number one catalog nationally with more than $3.5 billion in sales, said the average Alaskan spends 50% more than a typical customer elsewhere in the country. What are they ordering? Women's clothes top the list followed by books, CDs, tapes and sporting goods. ■

travel in Bush villages is difficult unless you have a contact. If you have just stepped off a chartered aeroplane, the small and isolated villages may appear closed, unfriendly and have very limited facilities.

For those who do make an effort to leave the roads, Bush Alaska offers a lifestyle that is rare in other areas of the USA and, for the most part, is unaffected by the state's booming summer tourist industry. The climate in the summer can range from a chilly 40°F in the treeless and nightless Arctic tundra to the wet and fog of the Bering Sea coast, where the terrain is a flat land of lakes and slow-moving rivers.

CLIMATE & THE 24-HOUR DAY

It makes sense that a place as large and diverse as Alaska would have a climate to match. The effects of oceans surrounding 75% of the state, the mountainous terrain and the low angle of the sun give Alaska an extremely variable climate and daily weather that is famous for being unpredictable.

The Interior can top 90°F during the summer, yet six months later in the same region the temperature can drop to -60°F. Fort Yukon holds the state record for maximum temperature at 100°F in June 1915, yet it once recorded a temperature of -78°F.

For the most part, Southeast and Southcentral Alaska have high rainfall with temperatures that only vary 40°F during the year. Anchorage, shielded by the Kenai Mountains, has an annual rainfall of 15 inches and averages from 60° to 70°F from June to August. Juneau averages 57 inches of rain or snow annually, while Ketchikan gets 154 inches a year, most of which is rain, as the temperatures are extremely mild even in the winter.

Residents will tell you, however, that averages don't mean a thing. There have been summers when it has rained just about every day, and there have been Aprils when every day has been sunny and dry. A good week in Southcentral and Southeast Alaska during the summer will include three sunny days, two overcast ones and two when you will have to pull your rain gear out or duck for cover.

In the Interior and up around Fairbanks, precipitation is light but temperatures can fluctuate by more than 100°F during the year. In summer, the average daytime temperature

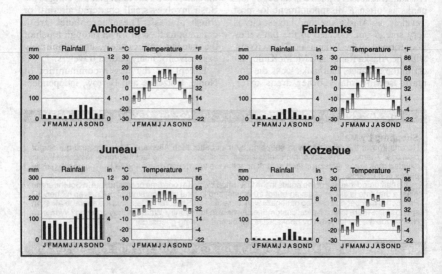

can range from 55 to 75°F with a brief period in late July to early August where it will top 80°F or even 90°F. At night, temperatures can drop sharply to 45°F or even lower, and freak snowfalls can occur in the valleys during July or August, with the white stuff lasting a day or two.

The climate in the Bush varies. The region north of the Arctic Circle is cool most of the summer with temperatures around 45°F, and annual rainfall is less than four inches. Other areas such as Nome in Western Alaska or Dillingham in Southwest Alaska aren't much warmer and tend to be foggy and rainy much of the summer.

In most of Alaska, summers are a beautiful mixture of long days and short nights, making the great outdoors even more appealing. At Point Barrow, Alaska's northernmost point, the sun never sets for 2½ months from May to August. The longest day is on 21 June (equinox), when the sun sets for only two hours in Fairbanks, for four hours in Anchorage and from five to six hours in the Southeast.

Even after the sun sets in late June and July, it is replaced not by night, but by a dusk that still allows good visibility. The midnight sun allows residents and visitors to undertake activities at hours undreamed of in most other places – six-mile hikes after dinner, bike rides at 10 pm or softball games at midnight. It also causes most people, even those with the best window shades, to wake up at 4 or 5 am.

No matter where you intend to travel or what you plan to do, bring protection against Alaska's climate. This should include warm clothing, rain gear and a covering if you are camping out. Alaska's weather is unpredictable and often changes when least expected – don't be left out in the cold.

ECOLOGY & ENVIRONMENT

Due to its size and the huge tracts of remaining wilderness, Alaska's environmental concerns are not just regional conflicts but, more often than not, national debates. Whether to open up the coastal plain of the Arctic National Wildlife Refuge to oil drilling is one of the most prominent issues.

One of the most heated controversies in recent years was over the state's decision in 1993 to embark on a program of 'wolf management' in a Connecticut-size chunk of spruce forests and foothills south of Fairbanks. This is the home of the Delta herd of caribou which has been steadily decreasing in numbers. Local hunters successfully urged the state to undertake the snaring and shooting of up to 80% of the wolves in the area as a way to build up the herd. One state official even suggested that wolves could be killed more efficiently by using helicopters and automatic weapons.

The outrage by Alaskan environmentalists and national organizations like the Sierra Club turned the issue into a national debate and lead to a brief tourism boycott on Alaska. The program was finally suspended in December 1994, after photographs of a biologist repeatedly shooting wolves that had been trapped live appeared in papers across the country. The wolf-management program was permanently cancelled in 1995.

A new concern for environmentalists is a bill being kicked around in the US Congress which mandates faster timber cuts in Tongass National Forest, a vast temperate rain forest in Southeast Alaska. The bill calls for a 50% increase in annual timber harvest in some of the most environmentally sensitive areas of the national forest. Ironically, most of the timber would be exported to Asia, particularly Japan, as raw logs, pulp and chips, where it would be used to make cellophane, diapers, paper cups and other such items. Despite heated debate from environmentalists, forest managers, local residents and even the governor, Tony Kowles, the bill has gained support in Congress.

FLORA & FAUNA
Flora
The flora of Alaska, like everything in the state, is diverse, changing dramatically from one region to the next. There are 33 native species of trees, the fewest of any state in the

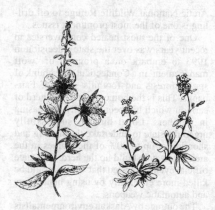

The brilliant fireweed (left) and Alaska's State flower, the forget-me-not

USA, and only 12 of these are classified as large trees (more than 70 feet in height). Not surprisingly, nine of these species are found in the coastal regions of Southeast and Southcentral Alaska.

In these areas, mild temperatures in winter and summer and frequent rains produce lush coniferous forests of Sitka spruce (the state tree) and western hemlock. Any opening in the forest is often a bog or filled with alder or spiny devil's club, a mildly poisonous plant that often causes a rash on contact. The tree line is often at an altitude between 2000 and 3000 feet where thick alder takes over until finally giving way to alpine meadows.

In the Interior, the large area of plains and hills between the Alaska Range and the Brooks Range is dominated by boreal forest of white spruce, cottonwood and paper birch, while on north-facing slopes and in moist lowlands you'll find a stunted forest of scrawny black spruce. Continue traveling north and you'll enter a zone known as taiga, characterized by muskeg, willow thickets and more stunted spruce, before entering the tundra of the Arctic coastal region.

The Arctic tundra is a bizarre world, a treeless area except for a few small stands on gravel flood plains of rivers. Plant life hugs the ground – even willow trees that only grow six inches in height still produce pussy willows. Other plants, including grasses, mosses and a variety of tiny flowers, provide a carpet of life for a short period in July and August despite little precipitation and a harsh climate.

Tundra can make for tough hiking for those who travel this far north in Alaska. Wet and moist tundra is underlain by permanently frozen ground known as permafrost. The tundra thaws in the summer but remains waterlogged because the permafrost prevents drainage. The caribou get around these soggy conditions because their dew claws and spreading cleft hooves help support their weight on the soft ground. Hikers are not so lucky.

Wild Berries Perhaps the flora that interests hikers and visitors most is Alaska's wild berries. Blueberries are found throughout much of the state while in the Southeast you'll encounter huge patches of huckleberries and salmonberries. Other species include blackberries, raspberries, highbush cranberries and strawberries. If you plan to feast on berries, take time to learn which ones are inedible. The most common poisonous one is the baneberry, found in the Southeast and the Interior, which often appears as a white berry.

Fauna

From the road, most visitors see more wildlife in Alaska than they do in a lifetime elsewhere. From the trail, such encounters are often the highlight of the entire trip; you can spot an animal, watch it quietly and marvel at the experience when the creature moves on leisurely.

Moose & Deer Moose are improbable-looking mammals: long-legged to the extreme, short-bodied, with a huge rack of antlers and a drooping nose. Standing there, they look uncoordinated until you watch them run, or better still, swim – then their speed and grace is astounding. They are the largest member of the deer family in the world and the Alaskan species is the largest of all moose. A newborn weighs in at 35 pounds and can grow to more than 300 pounds within five months. Cows range from 800 to 1200 pounds and bulls from 1000 to over 1500 pounds.

In the wild, moose may reach more than 20 years in age and often travel from 20 to 40 miles in their effort to find their main forage of birch, willow, alder and aspen saplings. In the spring and summer, you often encounter them feeding in lakes and ponds with that huge nose below the water as they grab for aquatic plants and weeds.

The population ranges from an estimated 120,000 to 160,000 animals and historically moose have always been the most important game animal in Alaska. Athabascan Indians survived by utilizing the moose as a source of food, clothing and implements while market hunting boomed in the 19th century, with professional hunters supplying moose meat to mining camps. Today some 35,000 Alaskans and nonresidents annually harvest 9000 moose or a total of five million pounds of meat during the hunting season.

Moose are widespread throughout the state and range from the Stikine River in the Southeast to the Corville River on the Arctic slope. They're most abundant in the second-growth birch forests, timberline plateaus and along major rivers of Southcentral Alaska and the Interior. Moose are frequently sighted along the Alcan, and Denali National Park is an excellent place to watch them. But the best place to see the biggest moose is the Kenai Peninsula, especially if you take time to paddle the Swanson River or Swan Lake canoe routes in Kenai National Wildlife Refuge. The refuge even maintains a Moose Research Center 50 miles from Soldotna where visitors can often see the animal.

The Sitka black-tail deer is a native to the coastal rainforests of Southeast Alaska but its original range has since been expanded to Prince William Sound and Kodiak Island. The deer is a favorite target of hunters but is not the abundant source of meat that the moose is. The largest black-tail deer weighs

212 pounds but most weigh an average of 100 pounds and bucks about 150 pounds.

The summer coat is reddish-brown and replaced by gray in the winter. The antlers are small, normal development is three points on each side, and its tail is indeed black. Sitka black-tail deer respond readily to calls. Most 'calls' are a thin strip of rubber or plastic between two pieces of wood held between the teeth and blown on. It produces a high-pitched note simulating a fawn's cry and can stop a deer in its tracks and turn it around. Some old time hunters can make the call by simply blowing on a leaf.

Caribou Caribou, of which there are an estimated 600,000 living in Alaska's 13 herds, are more difficult to view as they travel from the Interior north to the Arctic Sea. Often called the 'nomads of the north', caribou range in weight from 150 pounds to more than 400 pounds for a large bull. They migrate hundreds of miles annually between their calving grounds, rutting areas and winter area. In the summer, they feed on grasses, grass-like sedges, berries and small

A large bull caribou can weigh more than 400 pounds.

shrubs of the tundra. In the winter, they eat a significant amount of lichen called 'reindeer moss'.

The principal predators of caribou are wolves and some packs on the North Slope have been known to follow caribou herds over the years, picking off the young, old and victims of disabling falls caused by running in tightly massed herds. Bears, wolverines, foxes and eagles will also prey on calves while every year several thousand nonresident hunters come to Alaska in search of a bull. The caribou, however, are most important to the Inuit and other Native Alaskans who hunt more than 30,000 a year in their subsistence lifestyle.

The best place for the average visitor to see caribou is Denali National Park, where they are occasionally seen from the park road. But perhaps one of the greatest wildlife encounters left in the world today is the migration of the Western Arctic herd of barren ground caribou, North America's largest at 300,000 animals. The calving area of the herd is along the North Slope and in late August many of the animals begin to cross the Noatak River on their journey southward. During that time the few visitors lucky enough to be on the river are often rewarded with an awesome experience of watching 20,000 or more caribou crossing the tundra towards the Brooks Range.

Mountain Goats & Dall Sheep The mountain goat is the single North American species of the widespread group of goat-antelopes. All are characterized by short horns and a fondness for the most rugged alpine terrain. Although Captain Cook obtained goat hides in the 1700s, very little was known about the animal due to its remote habitat.

Although goats are often confused with dall sheep, they are easily identified by their longer hair, black horns and deep chest. They are quite docile, making them easy to watch in the wild, and their gait, even when they're approached too closely, is a deliberate pace. In the summer, they are normally found in high alpine meadows, grazing on grasses and herbs, and in the winter they often drop down to the tree line. In Alaska, they range throughout most of the Southeast, north and west into the coastal mountains of Cook Inlet as well as the Chugach and Wrangell mountains. Good places to spot them include Glacier Bay National Park, Wrangell-St Elias National Park and from many of the alpine trails in Juneau. But you have to climb to spot them.

Dall sheep are more numerous and widespread than mountain goats. They number close to 80,000 in Alaska and are found principally in the Alaska, Wrangell, Chugach and Kenai mountain ranges. Often sheep are spotted in Denali National Park when the bus crosses Polychrome Pass on its way to Wonder Lake.

Rams are easy to spot by their massive curling horns which grow throughout the life of the sheep, unlike deer antlers which are shed and regrown annually. The horns, like claws, hooves and your fingernails, grow from the skin and as rams mature the horns continue their ever-increasing curl, reaching a three-quarters curl in four to five years and a full curl in seven years.

It's spectacular to watch two rams in a horn-clashing battle but, contrary to popular belief, they are not fighting over a female, just for social dominance. Dall sheep do not clash as much as their big-horn cousins to the south but you can spot the activity throughout the summer and into fall. The best time to spot rams and see them clash is right before the rut, which begins in November. At that time they are moving among bands of ewes and often encountering other unfamiliar rams.

Bears Bears and visitors to Alaska have this love-hate relationship. Nothing makes you more afraid in the backcountry than the thought of encountering a bear, but you would hate leaving the state without having seen a bear in the wild. After a handful of bear encounters, most people develop a healthy respect for these magnificent animals. There are three species of bear in

Grizzlies are brown bears found in inland regions.

Alaska – brown, black and polar bears – with brown bears having the greatest range.

At one time brown and grizzly bears were listed as separate species but now both are classified as *Ursus arctos*. The difference isn't so much genetics but size. Browns live along the coast where abundant salmon runs help them reach a large size (often exceeding 800 pounds) while the famed Kodiak brown bear has been known to stand 10 feet tall and tip the scales at 1500 pounds. Grizzlies are browns found inland, away from the rich salmon runs, and normally a male ranges in weight from 500 to 700 pounds. Females weigh half to three-quarters as much.

The brown bear can be any color from almost black through to blond and resembles the black bear in shape. One way biologists tell them apart is to measure the upper rear molar – seriously. The length of the crown of this tooth in a brown is always more than an inch and a quarter. Perhaps a better way is to look for the prominent shoulder hump, easily seen behind the neck when a brown bear is on all fours.

Brown bears occur throughout Alaska except for some islands in the Frederick Sound in the Southeast, the islands west of Unimak in the Aleutian chain and some Bering Sea islands. There are more than 40,000 brown bears in Alaska and the most noted place to watch them is McNeil River, where a permit is needed in advance. Brown bears are also commonly seen in Denali National Park, on Admiralty Island in the Southeast and in Wrangell-St Elias National Park.

Though black bears are the most widely distributed of the three bear species in America, their range is more limited in Alaska than that of their brown cousins. They are usually found in most forested areas of the state but not on the Seward Peninsula, or north of the Brooks Range or on many large islands, most notably Kodiak and Admiralty.

The average male weighs from 180 to 250 pounds and can range in color from black to a rare creamy white color. A brown or cinnamon black bear is often seen in Southcentral Alaska, leaving many backpackers confused about what the species is. Beyond measuring that upper rear molar, look for the straight facial profile to confirm it's a black bear.

Both species are creatures of opportunity when it comes to eating. Bears are omnivorous and common foods include berries, grass, sedge, salmon runs and any carrion they happen to find in their travels. Browns occasionally fill the role of predator but only in the spring when the young are most vulnerable.

Bears don't hibernate; rather they enter a stage of 'dormancy', basically a deep sleep while denning up during the winter. Browns and black bears enter their dens usually in November or December and re-emerge in April or May. In the more northern areas of the state, some bears may be dormant for as long as seven or eight months a year.

Polar bears have always captured our interest because of their large size and white color but plan on stopping at the zoo in Anchorage if you want to see one in Alaska. (Polar bears occur only in the Northern Hemisphere and almost always in association with Arctic sea ice. They fall under the jurisdiction of only five nations – Russia, Norway, Denmark (Greenland), Canada and the USA – and past studies have shown there is only limited denning of polar bears along the north Alaska coast.)

A male usually averages between 600 and 1200 pounds but occasionally tops 1400 pounds. Adaptations to a life on the sea ice by polar bears include a white coat with water-repellent guard hairs and dense under fur, specialized teeth for its carnivorous diet primarily of seals, and hair almost completely covering the bottom of its feet.

Wolves While the wolf is struggling in numbers throughout most of the USA, its natural distribution and numbers still seem to be unaffected by human undertakings in Alaska. In fact, expanding wolf packs caused the Alaska Board of Game to schedule an aerial kill of 700 wolves in a 43,000-acre region between Anchorage and Fairbanks in 1993 because 'some hunters feel they are being short-changed'.

Throughout history no animal has been more misunderstood than the wolf. Alaska has roughly 8000 wolves scattered in packs throughout the state except for some islands in the Southeast, Prince William Sound and the Aleutian chain. Unlike the hunters, who seek out the outstanding physical specimens, wolves can usually only catch and kill the weak, injured or young, thus strengthening

About 8000 wolves are scattered in packs throughout Alaska.

the herd they are stalking. A pack of wolves is no match for a healthy 1200-pound moose.

Most adult males average from 85 to 115 pounds in weight and their pelts can be gray, black, off-white, brown, yellow or even have tinges approaching red. Wolves travel, hunt, feed and operate in the social unit of a pack and are very much carnivores. In the Southeast their principal food is deer, in the Interior it's moose and in Arctic Alaska it's caribou.

Even if you're planning to spend a great deal of time away from the road wandering in the wilderness, your chances of seeing wolves are rare. You might, however, find evidence of them either in their dog-like tracks, their howls at night or the remains of a wild kill.

Other Land Mammals In the lowlands, hikers have a chance to view red fox, beaver, pine marten, snowshoe hare, red squirrel, and on very rare occasions wolverines. Around lakes and rivers you have a good chance of spotting land otters and beavers. Both are found throughout the state with the exception of the North Slope, and are large animals. Otters range from 15 to 35 pounds; beavers weigh between 40 and 70 pounds, although 100-pound beavers have been recorded in Alaska.

Marine Mammals The most commonly spotted marine mammals are seals, often seen basking in the sun on an ice floe. There are three species of seal in Alaska but most visitors will encounter only harbor seals, the only seal whose range includes the Southeast, Prince William Sound and the rest of the Gulf of Alaska. The average weight of a male is 200 pounds – reached on a diet of herring, flounder, salmon, squid and small crabs.

The other two species, ringed and bearded seals, occur for the most part in the northern Bering, Chukchi and Beaufort seas where sea ice forms during the winter. Although travel on land or ice is laborious and slow, seals are renowned divers. During a dive their heartbeat may slow from a normal 55

to 120 beats per minute to 15. This allows them to stay under water for more than five minutes, often reaching depths of 300 feet or more. Harbor seal dives of 20 minutes or longer have been recorded by biologists.

Porpoises and dolphins are also commonly seen, even from the decks of the ferries. Harbor porpoises are often sighted but occasionally ferry travelers are treated to a pod of killer whales, or Orcas, whose high black and white dorsal fin makes them easy to identify from a distance. Orcas, which can exceed 20 feet in length, are actually the largest member of the dolphin family, which also includes the beluga or white whale. Belugas range in length from 11 to 16 feet and often weigh more than 3000 pounds, traveling in herds of more than 100. Their range includes the Arctic waters north of Bristol Bay but also Cook Inlet, where most visitors will spot them, especially in Kenai, where there is a beluga observation area.

The two most common whales seen in coastal waters are the 50-foot-long humpback, with its hump-like dorsal fin and long flippers, and the smaller minke whale. Other marine mammals include sea lions, sea otters and walruses.

The best known destination for witnessing marine mammals, particularly whales, is

Walruses are seal-like mammals that live in large herds.

Glacier Bay National Park in the Southeast. If you can spare a few days to kayak the glaciated sections of the bay, your chances of seeing a whale will be increased. Kayak and boat tours in Prince William Sound, particularly around Kenai Fjords National Park out of Seward, should result in encounters with marine mammals. Just a trip on the ferry from Seward to Kodiak will provide an opportunity to see a colony of sea lions.

Salmon The salmon runs (when thousands of fish swim upstream to spawn) are another of Alaska's most amazing sights and are common throughout much of the state. From late July to mid-September, many coastal streams are choked with salmon. You won't see just one here and there, but thousands – so many that they have to wait their turn to swim through narrow gaps of shallow water.

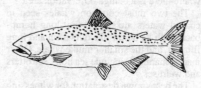

The king or chinook salmon

The sockeye or red salmon

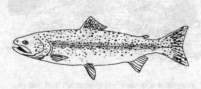

The rainbow trout

The salmon are famous for their struggle against the current, their magnificent leaps over waterfalls, and for covering stream banks with carcasses afterwards. There are five kinds of salmon in Alaska: sockeye (also referred to as red salmon), king (chinook), pink (humpie), coho (silver) and chum.

Birds More than anything, Alaska is a haven for winged wildlife. Biologists have identified 437 species of bird in the state and only 65 of them are accidental visitors. The Pribilof Islands in the Bering Sea attract birders (once called bird-watchers) from around the world. If you can't afford that, visit Potter Marsh south of Anchorage, a sanctuary that attracts more than 100 species annually.

The most impressive bird in Alaska's wilderness is the bald eagle, whose white tail and head, and wingspan that often reaches eight feet, have become the symbol of a nation. While elsewhere the bird is on the endangered list, in Alaska it thrives. The eagle can be sighted almost daily in most of the Southeast and is common in Prince William Sound. It also migrates once a year in a spectacle that exceeds even the salmon runs. As many as 1500 bald eagles gather along the Chilkat River north of Haines from late October to December. They come to feed on the late chum-salmon run and create an amazing scene during the bleakness of early winter. Bare trees, without a leaf remaining, support 80 or more white-headed eagles, four or five to a branch.

The state bird of Alaska, however, is the ptarmigan, a cousin of the prairie grouse. The species is found throughout the state in high treeless country and birds are easy to spot during the summer as their wings remain white while their head and chest turn brown. In the winter they have pure white plumage.

If you're serious about birding while traveling the state, the best bird book to pick up is *Guide to the Birds of Alaska* by Robert H Armstrong (Alaska Northwest Books, 22026 20th Ave SE, Bothell, WA 98021; 344 pages). The guide indexes 372 species and includes color photos and field identification marks.

GOVERNMENT & POLITICS

The government sector in Alaska is very strong, especially in Juneau, the capital city. Statewide, one in every three people is paid for government work, while in Juneau it's estimated that two-thirds of the residents work for either the federal, state or city government. The result is a lopsided pay scale with workers in the private sector rarely having a salary comparable with government workers.

All this government is most obvious when the state legislature and its army of aides and advisers convene in Juneau for the annual session. From across Alaska, 40 state representatives and 20 state senators arrive and take up temporary residence in the city until April to draw up a budget, spend the oil money and pass bills. Potential legislation is then passed onto the governor, who either signs it into law or vetoes the measures. The best way to understand Alaska's state politics and its colorful history is to join one of the free tours offered at the Alaska State Capitol in Juneau.

Alaska, like three other states in the USA, has only one US state representative and two US senators because of its small population. Local government consists of 1st, 2nd and 3rd-class boroughs and cities along with hundreds of unincorporated villages, the category that most Bush communities fall into. Although the populations may be small, many cities and boroughs can be quite large in area. Juneau, with more than 3000 sq miles within its jurisdiction, is the largest city in the country land-wise.

Although the governor, Tony Knowles, is a member of the Democratic political party, Alaskans often vote Republican, especially in presidential elections, and have grown more conservative in their attitudes since the 1970s.

ECONOMY

Alaska's economy, fueled by oil, is presently in a balancing act. The revenues from oil and gas still account for 80% of the gross state product annually and Alaska is behind only Texas as the country's top oil producer,
accounting for more than 25% of US production. But Prudhoe Bay, the largest oil field in North America, is drying up and not expected to have much of a life in the 21st century.

Alaskans must not only deal with the increasing layoffs in the oil industry but also the dwindling mineral royalities that paid for most of their government programs, from state parks to subsidized ferry travel. Thanks to North Slope crude, there are no state taxes in Alaska on income, sales or inheritance. But as the state government entered 1996 awash red ink, programs were cut, user fees were increased and talk of an income tax was heard in the legislature.

Commercial fishing is the second largest industry in the state as the Alaskan fleet contributes almost 25% of the country's annual catch, including nearly all canned salmon produced in the USA. The 970 million pounds of salmon caught in 1995 by Alaskan fishers was a record harvest while the herring fisheries have also come on strong in recent years with large catches and high prices.

But like the oil industry, commercial fishing is also in a transitional phase. Most crab stocks throughout the state are declining with harvest quotas at an all-time low. The huge salmon harvest, especially the stunning red salmon catch from Bristol Bay, only contributed to an already glutted Japanese market in 1995, sending the prices spiraling down. Alaska also finds itself competing against huge government-subsidized salmon farming operations in countries such as Norway and Chile.

By far the most serious conflict the industry faces is in Southeast Alaska where the stalled US-Canada Pacific Salmon Treaty Talks have crippled commercial fishers in that region.

The issue of how to divide the king salmon catch there became so heated in 1995 that the Canadian government tried to tax US fishing boats sailing from Washington to Southeast Alaska. British Columbia fishers attacked the Alaska Marine Hwy ferry *Taku* with spray paint, beer bottles and ball bearings flung from sling shots. How these two countries can resolve splitting a fishery and the related issue of Native Alaskans taking salmon under subsistence rights will surely plague the Alaskan fishing industry in the future.

Balancing this bad economic news is the fact that tourism in Alaska is booming. Tourism is the state's third largest industry and growing rapidly. A record 1.2 million visitors came to Alaska in 1995, an increase of more than 5% from just the year before. In part this is due to the popularity of *Northern Exposure*, the now cancelled TV series based on the fictional city of Cicely. Alaskan tourism injects more than $1.6 billion into the economy annually and employs a work force as large as the oil industry. The problem, however, is that while the average oil worker earned $7100 a month in 1994, the averaged hotel pay check was only $1500.

Mining is also on the upswing as $44 million was spent for mineral exploration in Alaska in 1995, an increase of 34%. There are almost 30,000 active federal mining claims, the vast majority of them lode and placer claims. Although gold holds the lure of riches, zinc is actually the state's most valuable non-fuel mineral.

Alaska is the top zinc producing state in the country with the Red Dog Mine, 90 miles north of Kotzebue, the largest such operation in the world. Alaska is the only state that produces platinum and it ranks second in the USA for gold production and third for silver. The future of mining in Alaska also looks rosy, much to the horror of environmentalists. Near Fairbanks the Fort Knox Gold Mine is under construction while near Juneau the Greens Creek Mine is set to reopen after closing due to falling silver prices.

Other industries include logging and to a very small degree commercial farming, which takes place almost exclusively in the Matanuska Valley around Palmer and the Tanana Valley between Fairbanks and Delta. These areas are home to the 70-pound cabbages and softball-size radishes but the top agricultural product for Alaskan farmers is milk.

POPULATION & PEOPLE

Alaska, the largest state in the USA, has the second smallest population (after only Wyoming) but it is the most sparsely populated. Permanent residents, not including the large influx of seasonal workers in the fishing and tourist industries, number 550,043 in a state of 591,004 sq miles. There is more than a sq mile for every resident but Alaska is actually even more sparsely populated when you consider that almost half of its population lives in the Anchorage Bowl area.

It is estimated that only 30% of the state's population were born in Alaska while 25% have moved there in the last five years. This means that the average resident is young (aged between 26 and 28 years), mobile and mostly from the US west coast. Inuit and other indigenous groups make up only 15% of the total population while ethnic groups of Japanese, Filipinos and Blacks represent less than 5%.

Bye-Bye to Bunny Boots

Few things symbolize Alaskan fashion better than bunny boots. The oversized, white rubber boots with the unique vapor-barrier system made your feet look like they belonged in a Walt Disney cartoon movie. But they kept your toes warm even when it was -60°F in Prudhoe Bay, and in Alaska that's all that matters.

Unfortunately the boot's sole manufacturer, Bata Shoe Company, discontinued production in 1994 when its biggest customer, the US Army, decided to switch to cheaper, mass-marketed boots. Only the Good Friday Earthquake of 1964 was more shocking to Alaskans.

A panic set in and stores in Anchorage and Fairbanks sold as many 100 pairs in one day. Customers included oil and construction companies from around the world, anticipating winter drilling projects on Alaska's North Slope. And some retailers, in the tradition of turn-of-the-century gold rushes and the pipeline boom of the mid-1970s, jacked up the price of the boots by as much as $20 a pair. ■

The five largest cities in Alaska are Anchorage (pop 248,296), Fairbanks (pop 82,428), Juneau (pop 28,791), Kodiak (pop 15,245) and Ketchikan (pop 14,276).

Native Alaskans

Long before Bering's journeys to Alaska, other groups of people had made their way there and established a culture and lifestyle in one of the world's harshest environments. The first major invasion, which came across the land bridge from Asia, was by the Tlingits and the Haidas (who settled throughout the Southeast and British Columbia), and the Athabascans (a nomadic tribe which lived in the Interior). The other two major groups were the Aleuts of the Aleutian Islands and the Inuit (Eskimos) who settled on the coast of the Bering Sea and the Arctic Ocean; both groups are believed to have migrated only 3000 years ago but were well established by the time the Europeans arrived.

The Tlingit and Haida cultures were advanced, as the tribes had permanent settlements including large clan houses. They were noted for their excellent woodcarving, particularly poles, called *totems*, which can still be seen today in most Southeast communities. The Tlingits were spread throughout the Southeast in large numbers and occasionally went as far south as Seattle in their large dugout canoes. Both groups had few problems gathering food, as fish and game were plentiful in the Southeast.

Not so for the Aleuts and the Inuit. With much colder winters and cooler summers, both groups had to develop a highly effective sea-hunting culture to sustain life in the harsh regions of Alaska. This was especially true for the Inuit, who could not have survived the winters without their skilled ice-hunting techniques. In the spring, armed with only jade-tipped harpoons, the Inuit stalked and killed 60-ton bowhead whales in skin-covered kayaks called *bidarkas* and *umikaks*.

The Aleuts were known for some of the finest basket weaving in North America, using the highly prized Attu grass of the

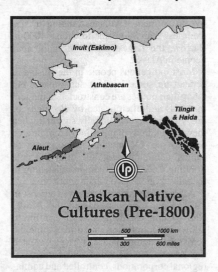

Alaskan Native Cultures (Pre-1800)

Aleutian Islands. The Inuit were unsurpassed carvers of ivory, jade and soapstone; many support themselves today by continuing the art.

The indigenous people, despite their harsh environment, were numerous until the White people brought guns, alcohol and disease that destroyed the Native Alaskans' delicate relationship with nature and wiped out entire villages. At one time, there were an estimated 20,000 Aleuts living on almost every island of the Aleutian chain. It took the Russians only 50 years to reduce the population (mainly through forced labour) to less than 2000. The whalers who arrived at Inuit villages in the mid-19th century were similarly destructive, introducing alcohol that devastated the lifestyles of entire villages. Even when the 50th anniversary of the Alcan was celebrated in October 1992, many Native Alaskans and Canadians called the event a 'commemoration' and not a 'celebration' due to the things that the highway brought (disease, alcohol and a cash economy) that further changed a nomadic lifestyle.

There are more than 85,000 indigenous people (half of whom are Inuit) living in Alaska. They are no longer tribal nomads but live in permanent villages ranging in size from less than 30 people to almost 4000 in Barrow, the largest center of indigenous people in Alaska.

Most indigenous people in the Bush still depend on some level of subsistence, but today their houses are constructed of modern materials and often heated by electricity or oil. Visitors are occasionally shocked when they fly hundreds of miles into a remote area only to see TV antennas sticking out of cabins, community satellite dishes, people drinking Coca-Cola or children listening to the latest pop songs on their boom box.

All indigenous people received a boost in 1971 when Congress passed the Alaska Native Claims Settlement Act in an effort to allow oil companies to build a pipeline across their traditional lands. The act created the Alaska Native Fund and formed 13 regional corporations, controlled and administered by the local tribes, that invested and developed the $900 million and 44 million acres received for their historical lands.

Today, all indigenous people hold stock in their village corporations and receive dividends when there's a profit. Although a few have floundered and lost money, others have done extremely well. The Arctic Slope Regional Corp, based in Barrow, has become the largest Alaskan-owned corporation in the state. The company, headed by Jacob Adams, an Inupiat whaling captain, has revenue of more than $460 million, thanks in part to the North Slope oil industry which lies on its home turf.

Native Alaskans face serious challenges, however, as they approach the 21st century. Many live at or below the poverty level as creating sustainable economic opportunities and jobs in small, isolated communities is especially difficult. Drug and alcohol abuse in rural Alaska is also rampant leading to a high death rate. The rate of suicide for Native males is seven times higher than the national average while it's estimated that one Native Alaskan dies every 12 days directly from alcohol abuse. This has led to a Native sobriety movement in recent years and tempers have raged over whether communities should be dry or not. In Barrow, residents overturned its successful alcohol ban in 1995 by a mere seven votes and in Tanana the murder of a sobriety activist by her alcoholic boyfriend stunned the state.

EDUCATION

Alaska has almost 500 public schools throughout the state, offering education from kindergarten for five-year-olds through 12th grade. The schools range in size from 2000-student high schools in Anchorage to

---

The Right to Subsist

One of the most explosive issues in Alaska is over subsistence, the right of rural residents to enjoy longer hunting seasons and bigger harvests of wild game in an effort to maintain their traditional lifestyle. Until recently most people living in Bush Alaska did not have access to stores or could not afford the high prices. Bush residents, particularly Native Alaskans, depended on a variety of game, from caribou and moose to salmon and walruses, for their protein. And they needed to hunt whenever they could because electricity was not always available to make freezing a method of food storage.

Subsistence is now a battle between the federal government, whose laws give rural residents priority to fish and game, and the state of Alaska, whose constitution gives all residents equal access to game and fish. In effect, this has pitted Native Alaskans against commercial fishers and sport hunters; in western Alaska it's salmon which are caught by both villagers and commercial fishers, in the Nelchina basin near Glennallen it's a dwindling herd of caribou, and in the Kenai Peninsula a proposed subsistence moose hunt brought the controversy to a boiling point in 1996.

Partly at issue is Alaska's changing society. There is now a growing number of Native Alaskans living in non-rural areas who still qualify as subsistence users. As one Alaskan who wrote to the *Anchorage Daily News* put it, 'Why should someone in Barrow making $50,000 a year get subsistence rights and not someone in Palmer making $10,000 a year?' ∎

one-teacher, one-room schools in the rural areas. Alaskan teachers are generally the highest paid in the country.

Because of the remote nature of Alaska, however, any student can elect to study at home through a unique state-operated Centralized Correspondence School. This option has been available to Alaskans since 1939 and presently up to 3000 students a year are enrolled in the program.

The University of Alaska is the largest college in the state and maintains campuses at a half-dozen cities. The largest campuses are in Fairbanks and Anchorage while the most scenic is in Juneau where the school is on the banks of Auke Lake with snow-capped mountains looming overhead. Travelers who will be in the Anchorage area for awhile might check into the outdoor classes offered by the University of Alaska-Anchorage, which range from canoeing and sea-kayaking to rafting and backpacking. Most courses include class time and a field trip. For more information and a schedule of the courses call UA-A's Alaska Wilderness Studies (☎ (906) 786-4066).

ARTS

Alaska's indigenous people are renowned for their traditional arts and crafts primarily because of their ingenious use of the natural materials around them which in the case of many groups, like the Inuit, were often limited. Roots, ivory tusks, birch bark, grasses and soapstone were used creatively to produce ceremonial regalia and other art work.

Thanks to a flourishing arts market, prompted by the increased tourism to the state, Native Alaskan arts have become an important slice of the economy in many Bush communities. The Inupiat and Yup'ik Inuit, with the fewest resources to work with, made their objects out of sea-mammal parts; and their ivory carving and scrimshaw work is world renowned. Only Native Alaskans are allowed to possess unworked ivory, and they can only sell it after it is handcrafted. Other crafts produced by the Natives of Northern Alaska include hide and whale-

bone masks, which often are sold for up to $1000.

The Aleuts of the Aleutian Islands are known for their bentwood hats and visors; the Athabascan Indians make decorative clothing with elaborate beadwork; and the Tlingit, Haida and Tsimshian of Southeast Alaska are among the carvers who ranged south into British Columbia and Washington and were responsible for the great totems and clan houses.

But perhaps no single item represents indigenous art better than Alaskan basketry. Each group produces stunning baskets in very distinctive styles based solely on the materials at hand. Athabascans of the Interior weave baskets from willow roots or produce them from birch bark. The Tlingits use cedar bark; the Inuit use grasses and baleen, a glossy hard material that hangs in slats from the jaw of certain species of whales.

The Aleuts are perhaps the most renowned basket weavers. Using rye grass, which grows abundantly in the Aleutian Islands, the Aleuts are able to work the pliable and very tough material into tiny, intricately woven baskets. The three styles of Aleut baskets (Attu, Atka and Unalaska) are named after the islands on which they originated. These baskets carry a steep price whenever they are sold on the open market.

The best known examples of the Native Alaskan craft skills are the totems of Southeast Alaska. Although most tourists envision totems as freestanding poles, totemic art is also used on houses and other clan structures. Totem poles are carved from huge cedar trees and are used to preserve family history or make a statement about a clan. They invariably were raised during a 'potlatch', a ceremony in which a major event was held designed to draw clans from throughout the region. The totem was erected to commemorate the event. There probably isn't a community in Southeast Alaska without a totem or two. But Ketchikan has by far the most impressive collections of them located at both the Totem Heritage Center in town and Saxman Totem Park and Totem Bight State Park out of town.

SOCIETY & CONDUCT
Traditional Culture

Despite the modernization of their lifestyles and the rapid advances of communications into what has been a remote region of the world, Native Alaskans still cling to their culture and practice traditional ceremonies. In recent years there has even been a movement to resurrect Native languages before they are forever lost with the few elders that still speak them. Of the 20 Native languages, 16 are in danger of becoming extinct.

Perhaps the best known Native ceremony is the potlatch, a village gathering to celebrate a major passage in a family's life. Usually the focal point of Native society, potlatches often involved the host family giving away most of its possessions in an effort to demonstrate wealth to the rest of the village. A funeral potlatch would result in the family giving away the deceased's worldly possessions. Both the USA and Canada outlawed potlatches in the 1880s, which resulted in a disintegration of all aspects of Native culture. That law was repealed in 1951.

The most commercialized Native custom is the blanket toss. Originally groups of villagers would grab a walrus hide in a circle to basically form a trampoline. This would allow hunters to be tossed high in the air in an effort to spot game on the flat, treeless terrain of the Arctic tundra. Depending on the number of people gripping the blanket, a hunter could be thrown 20 feet or higher. Today the ceremony is a popular one with tour-bus groups.

Travelers interested in experiencing a slice of Native culture should plan on attending the World Eskimo-Indian Olympics, held annually on the second-last weekend in July in Fairbanks. The four-day competition attracts several hundred Native athletes from both Alaska and other circumpolar nations, who compete in such events as ear-weighted pull, knuckle hop, fish cutting, blanket toss and dancing. Most of it is done in authentic Native costumes. For information write to World Eskimo-Indian Olympics, PO Box 2433, Fairbanks, 99707.

Dos & Don'ts

As with the indigenous people in any country, Native Alaskans deserve the respect of travelers, who basically are trespassing through their traditional homeland. Try to understand their culture and the delicate situation their society faces as it confronts the growing influence of modern society.

Don't just pick out a village and fly to it. It is wise to either have a contact there or travel with somebody who does. Although Native Alaskans, especially the Inuit, are very, very hospitable people, there can be much tension and suspicion of strangers in small, isolated Bush communities.

Also be conscious of the most widespread problem, the rip-off of Native arts which have become extremely valuable as well as a lucrative business with tourists. The problem is that much of what is being passed on as authentic art has in reality been mass produced in China, Taiwan or Bali. If you're considering purchasing Native art, try to search out a legitimate shop and look for the *Authentic Native Handicraft from Alaska* symbol (see the Things to Buy in the Facts for the Visitor chapter). If the price of a soapstone carving seems too good to be true, it probably is.

RELIGION

For the most part every religion that mainstream America practices in the Lower 48 can be found in Alaska. One of the most interesting, however, is represented by the Russian Orthodox Church, the most enduring aspect of a unique period in Alaska's history. After Russian merchants and traders had decimated indigenous populations in the mid to late 18th century, missionaries arrived as Russia's answer to the brutal subjugation.

They managed to convert the indigenous people of Southwest, Southcentral and Southeast Alaska to a new religious belief. These beliefs are as strong today as they have ever been, and one only has to look at the familiar onion domes of the Russian Orthodox churches in communities such as Juneau, Sitka, Kodiak or Unalaska to realize this.

Facts for the Visitor

PLANNING
When to Go

Because most travelers like to avoid minus-degree temperatures, Alaska's traditional travel season has been from June through August with the peak season from early July to mid-August, when visiting places like Denali National Park or the Kenai Peninsula can be a dismal experience due to crowds. The reality of the situation is there are an awful lot of tourists trying to see Alaska in a very short period of time.

Consider traveling during part of the 'shoulder season'. May and September offer not only mild weather but also a good chance for off-season discounts on accommodation and transportation. For the most part the Alcan can be driven throughout September and early October without too much fear of being holed up by a three-day blizzard. But if you arrive early or stay late, just make sure you equip yourself for some cold, rainy weather.

Arriving in Alaska in late April is possible in the Southeast and the Kenai Peninsula but in much of the Interior you could still be running into spring break-up, a time of slush and mud. Stay during October and in the Southeast and Southcentral regions you're guaranteed rain most of the time, while in the Interior and Fairbanks there will be snow.

In recent years, the state has been actively promoting winter travel in Alaska. Guiding companies that offer dog-sled trips are on the increase and a new downhill ski resort will soon appear next door to Anchorage's Alyeska Ski Resort. Even Fairbanks is now marketing winter travel to its frigid location

---

Alaska in April

Next to November and early December, April is often considered to be one of the worst times of the year to be traveling in Alaska. It's too late to go skiing, too early to start hiking and most of the state is in the middle of spring break-up, a time of melting rivers, dirty snow banks and bottomless mud puddles.

Or is it? For those who are content with simply seeing the grandeur of Alaska, late April and early May can be a delightful time for exploring Anchorage and the Kenai Peninsula via a rental car. Pack your parka, because the weather can be cloudy and rainy at this period of the year, but you will also enjoy a few sunny days when the temperature easily breaks 50˚F degrees and the snow-laden mountains are never more beautiful than when they are framed by that blue Alaskan sky. Depending on the previous winter, much of the city and the Kenai Peninsula will be free of snow cover by late April, when the days are already long with the sun not setting until 10 or 10.30 pm.

Alaska is also a bargain in April. You'll save considerably on airline tickets to the state. Once in Anchorage, you can pick up a subcompact from any of the discount car rental agencies for as little as $22 a day, whereas summer travelers will be paying close to $40. The price of motels and hotels is embarrassingly low. Chelsea Inn in Anchorage charges $97 for a single in the summer, $37 in April. The Kenai Princess Lodge, overlooking the Kenai River in Cooper Landing, will give you a private bungalow with a wood stove, a mountain view and an outdoor hot tub, for $79 a night from March through May. In July it's $175. You can discount anywhere from $20 to $40 for most room rates priced in this book during April.

Denali National Park is off limits unless you want to ski in, but in Kenai Fjords National Park the grey whale migration takes place in April. Kenai Fjords Tours, and other cruise-boat operators in Seward, offer two to three-hour trips to spot the whales for $49. Other boat tours to spot wildlife can be arranged in Homer.

But the best reason to visit Alaska in April is to meet Alaskans themselves. You'll find locals more friendly and willing to chat with you then than at almost any other time of the year. And why not? They have just endured another long, dark winter but are yet to be burned out by the approaching tourist season. ■

---

in February, using the Northern Lights as the draw, while not talking too much about the -50° F temperatures.

What Kind of Trip?

Independent travel to the 49th state is easy, in fact it's easier than in most other states in the USA thanks mainly to the booming tourist industry. There are various forms of public transportation to practically every accessible corner of the state, even to Prudhoe Bay at the north end of the Dalton Hwy.

Package tours also are offered by a variety of companies while luxury cruise lines are the fastest-growing segment of Alaskan tourism. Most of them, however, are too limiting and too much of a rush job to justify the high cost. Even if you only have a couple of weeks you'll do better sticking in one region of the state (see Suggested Itineraries below) and planning your own trip, the reason no doubt you purchased this book.

It's best to travel with somebody if possible, especially if you are planning to focus on wilderness adventures, hiking or backpacking. But every summer thousands of people arrive by themselves and then spend a good deal of time traveling solo throughout the state. It's just the spirit of adventure that Alaska evokes in all of us.

Maps

Unlike many places in the world, there are no shortages of accurate maps of Alaska, even if most of it is still wilderness. In fact, the state will give you a map...for free. When you call the Alaska Division of Tourism (☎ (907) 465-2010) you can request a free state highway map on the recorded message and one will be mailed out in advance of your trip. Once you arrive, every tourist office will have free maps of its town and surrounding area.

Drivers often swear that *The Milepost* has the best set of road maps you can obtain for Alaska. But an even more detailed collection of maps can be found in the *Alaska Atlas & Gazetteer* (☎ (800) 227-1656; DeLorme, PO Box 298-7200, Freeport, MA 04032; 156 pages, paperback). This atlas contains more than 100 maps that cover the state and includes some other unique features like an index of physical landmarks (want to find a certain mountain? Just look it up in the index). Its drawback, especially for backpackers and others living out of a suitcase, is its size – 11 by 15 inches. When driving, I find the road maps in the free publications handed out at every visitor center to be more than adequate to get you from one town to the next. When trekking in the backcountry and wilderness areas, the US Geological Survey (USGS) topographic maps are worth the $2.50 per quad you pay for them. USGS topographic maps come in a variety of scales but hikers prefer the smallest scale of 1:63,360, where each inch equals a mile. Canoers and other river runners can get away with the 1:250,000 map. The maps of Tongass and Chugach national forests produced by the USFS will not do for any wilderness adventure, as they lack the detail that backpackers rely on.

USGS maps can be purchased at the Public Lands Information centers in Anchorage, Tok and Fairbanks (see the regional chapters for addresses and phone numbers), but they tend to carry only the maps for their area of the state. It's best to stop at the main USGS offices in Alaska either in Fairbanks (Federal Building at 101 12th Ave) or Anchorage (Gambell Building on the Alaska Pacific University campus). These USGS sales offices have topos and other maps to cover the complete state. You can also order maps in advance by writing and asking for a free index of maps for Alaska from the main office, USGS Western Distribution Branch, Denver Federal Center, PO Box 25286 Denver, CO 80225.

What to Bring

Clothes With nights that freeze and days that fry, layering is the only way to dress for Alaskan summers without having to take a pair of shipping containers. It's an accepted fact in the north country that several light layers of clothing are warmer than a single heavy layer. With layers you trap warm air near the body to act as an insulation against the cold. Layers are also easy to strip off when the midday sun begins to warm you up.

Instead of a heavy coat, pack a long-sleeved jersey, or woollen sweater, and a wind-breaker/parka; they are easier to pack and more versatile for Alaska's many changes of weather. A woollen hat and mittens are necessary items to fend off the cold night air, freak snowfalls or the chilly rain of the Southeast. Leave the umbrellas at home. Your parka is your protection against rain, wind or snow and, if you can afford it, should be made of a high quality fabric that 'breathes'. If you plan to go on a lot of wilderness trips then you should also pack along overpants. Gore-Tex is the best known of the materials that breathe, but others are available. Such a set will cost $300 to $500 but for those who spend a great deal of time outdoors it is a worthwhile investment.

The number of luxury restaurants, hotels and entertainment spots is growing in the large Alaskan cities. Along with having to dress up, these places have high prices. For the most part, Alaska is still a land of jeans, hiking boots (or brown rubber boots in the Southeast) and woollen shirts – the acceptable attire for the majority of restaurants, bars and hotels throughout this state. If you are going to backpack around the north on a budget, there is no reason to take anything that isn't comfortable, functional in the harsh environment, and easy to pack and wash.

Hiking Boots Most recreational hikers and backpackers today opt for the new lightweight nylon boots made by sporting-shoe companies like Nike, Vasque and Hi-Tech. These are lighter to pack and easier on the feet than leather boots, while providing the foot protection and ankle support needed on most trails and wilderness trips when carrying a medium-weight pack. Others turn to leather boots when heavy loads must be shouldered or a trek involves off-trail trekking or scrambling over boulders or ridges or glacial streams. Normal tennis shoes are not enough for the trails but are handy to have as a change of footwear at night or for

fording rivers and streams. All boots should either be waterproof or well greased.

Day-Hike Equipment Too often, visitors undertake a day hike with little or no equipment and then, three hours from the trailhead, get caught in bad weather wearing only a flimsy cotton jacket. Along with your large, framed backpack, take a soft day pack or rucksack with you to Alaska. These small knapsacks are ideal for day hikes and should contain waterproof clothing, woollen mittens and hat, a knife, high-energy food (like chocolate), matches, map and compass, a metal drinking cup and insect repellent.

Hikers should not only carry a compass onto any trail but should also have some basic knowledge of how to use it correctly. You should also have the correct USGS map for the area in which you are planning to travel (see the Maps section earlier in this chapter for details).

Expedition Equipment For longer treks and adventures into the wilderness, backpackers should double-check their equipment before they leave home, rather than scurry around some small Alaskan town trying to locate a camp stove or a pair of glacier goggles. Most towns in Alaska will have at least one store with a wall full of camping supplies, but prices will be high and by mid to late summer certain items will be out of stock.

You don't need to arrive with a complete line of the latest Gore-Tex, but then again, that $4.95 plastic rain suit probably won't last more than a few days in the woods. Bring functional and sturdy equipment to Alaska and you will go home after a summer of wilderness adventures with much of it intact.

Along with a tent (see the Accommodation section later in this chapter), you need a sleeping bag. This is a good item to bring whether you plan on camping or not, as it is also very useful in hostels, on board the State Marine Ferry and in seedy hotels when you're not sure what's crawling in the mattress. There has been many an all-night discussion among backpackers on the qualities of down versus synthetic fibres. What can't be argued about though is down's quality of clumping when wet – in rainy Southeast and Southcentral Alaska, this means trouble during most wilderness trips. For a summer in Alaska, choose a three-season bag with a temperature range of -10°F to 40°F or close to that.

Also seriously consider bringing an insulated foam pad to sleep on – it will reduce much of the ground chill. In the Interior, you will often be sleeping just inches away from permafrost or permanently frozen ground. If you'll be spending a considerable amount of time sleeping in the wilderness, skip the foam and invest in a self-inflating sleeping pad such as the Thermarest. It may cost $70 to $90 but once you're out there you'll be thankful for having purchased it.

A reliable backpacker's stove will make life much simpler in the wilderness. Rain, strong winds and a lack of available wood will hamper your efforts to build a fire, while some preserves like Denali National Park won't even allow campfires in the backcountry.

There are many brands of stove on the market today but ones like MSR Whisper Lite, which can be 'field repaired', are the most dependable you can take along. Remember, you cannot carry white gas or other camp-stove fuels on an airline flight but just about every small town or park visitor center will stock them.

SUGGESTED ITINERARIES

The trip you take to Alaska depends on your time, money and how you like to travel. The mistake most people make is trying to see too much in too little time. Alaska is huge and if your days are limited to less than three weeks, give serious consideration to exploring only one region of the state.

If travel by ferry appeals to you, a popular two-to-three-week adventure is to fly to Seattle and then cruise Southeast Alaska on the Alaska Marine Hwy ferry out of Bellingham, Washington, stopping at a handful of towns for a few days each. The same type of trip can be done on the ferry in Prince William Sound and could include stops at Homer and Seward on the Kenai Peninsula as well as Kodiak Island.

Travel exclusively by train is also possible by flying into Anchorage and then using the Alaska Railroad to see parts of the Kenai Peninsula to the south or Denali National Park, Fairbanks and the towns in between to the north.

I advocate seeing the state by car even if you have no desire to drive the Alcan. An excellent two-week trip is to fly into Anchorage and rent a vehicle from one of the discount car-rental shops away from the airport. Subcompacts will run anywhere from $30 to $40 a day with 100 miles. A 10-day rental gives you 1000 miles to play with and that's enough to thoroughly explore the Kenai Peninsula or drive the Glenn and Richardson highways loop to Valdez.

The classic Alaska trip is to begin in the Southeast and move north into Anchorage, Denali National Park and Fairbanks, using a variety of public transportation. Plan at least a month for that and more time if you are planning to undertake any wilderness adventure along the way.

Finally, if you are bent on driving the Alcan, keep in mind that the Alaska Hwy is a trip in itself.

The mistake most travelers make is they rush past the sights, parks and history found along this legendary highway on their way to Alaska. If that's the case, why drive it? For anybody coming from the midwest or east coast of the USA, it's an eight to 10-day drive just to reach Alaska by road. Plan at least six weeks for this type of trip, although it's better to have two months.

HIGHLIGHTS

There is much to do and see in Alaska. The following are my favorite 10 attractions, but there are many others. Twenty-two outstanding wilderness trips are listed in the Hiking and Paddling sections of the Wilderness chapter.

1. Riding the shuttle bus along the Denali National Park & Preserve road to view the wildlife (Interior chapter)

2. Taking a passage on one of the special State Marine Ferry runs from Kodiak to Dutch Harbor on the Alaska Peninsula (Bush chapter)
3. Flying into a USFS cabin for a few days (Wilderness chapter)
4. Viewing the northern lights from the University of Alaska campus in Fairbanks (Fairbanks chapter)
5. Traveling to Tenakee Springs aboard the State Marine Ferry and soaking in the village's hot springs (Southeast chapter)
6. Taking a glacier cruise on Prince William Sound, either to Kenai Fjords, to College Fjord or on the State Marine Ferry past Columbia Glacier (Southcentral chapter)
7. Taking in the show and Robert Service poetry at the Malamute Saloon in Ester (Interior chapter)
8. Riding the White Pass & Yukon Route from Skagway (Southeast chapter)
9. Viewing the midnight sun on or near 21 June (the summer solstice) from Eagle Summit off the Steese Hwy (Fairbanks chapter)
10. Traveling to and spending a night in McCarthy (Southcentral chapter)

TOURIST OFFICES

The first place to write to while planning your adventure is the Alaska Division of Tourism (Dept 901, PO Box 110801, Juneau, AK 99811-0801; ☎ (907) 465-2010, fax (907) 586-8399) where you can request a copy of the *Alaska State Vacation Planner*, a 120-page annually updated magazine, a state highway map, and schedules for the Alaska Marine Hwy and the Alaska Railroad.

Travel information is easy to obtain once you are on the road as almost every city, town and village has a tourist contact center whether it be a visitor center, a chamber of commerce or a hut near the ferry dock. These places are good sources of free maps, information on local accommodation, and directions to the nearest campground or hiking trail.

If you are planning to spend a considerable amount of time in Anchorage, contact the Anchorage Convention & Visitors Bureau (1600 A St, Ste 200, Anchorage, AK 99501-5160; ☎ (907) 276-4118 or fax (907) 278-5559) and request its city guide which is published twice a year for travel in summer and winter.

VISAS & DOCUMENTS
Passport

If you are traveling to Alaska from overseas, you will need a passport. Only US and Canadian citizens can cross the borders to Alaska without one. Even they should have valid identification on them such as a driver's license and a voter registration card. Often a driver's license or a social security card alone is not enough to satisfy some customs officials.

Make sure your passport does not expire halfway through the trip and if traveling with children it's best to bring a photocopy of their birth certificate.

Visas

Overseas travelers also need at least one visa, possibly two. Obviously a US visa is needed, but if you're taking either the Alcan or the State Marine Ferry from Prince Rupert in British Columbia then you will also need a Canadian visa. The Alcan begins in Canada, requiring travelers to pass from the USA into Canada and back into the USA again.

Travelers from Western Europe and most Commonwealth nations do not need a Canadian visa and can get a six-month travel visa to the USA without too much paperwork or waiting. All visitors must have an onward or return ticket to enter the USA and sufficient funds to pass into Canada. Although there is no set amount that constitutes 'sufficient funds' most customs officials suggest around $500 and surely anybody arriving at the Canadian border with less than $250 will be turned back.

Vaccinations are not required for either country and only people who have been on a farm during the previous 30 days will be detained by immigration officials.

A word of warning: overseas travelers should be aware of the procedures to re-enter the USA. Occasionally visitors get stuck in Canada because they had a single-entry visa into the USA and used it passing through the Lower 48. Canadian immigration officers often caution people who they feel might have difficulty returning to the USA. If you are unsure about visa or other requirements for entering the USA, check out the US Department of State Home Page on the World Wide Web (http://dosfan.libuic. edu/dosfan.html) which among other things lists foreign embassies and consulates in the USA. You can also email them questions from this site.

Photocopies

A smart precaution for overseas travelers is to photocopy vital documents and then store the copies in a separate place. Copy your passport data, birth certificate, credit cards, airline tickets, other travel documents and a list of your travelers' checks' serial numbers. Add some emergency stash to this, maybe a $50 bill, and store it in a safe place. A copy of these documents left at home with somebody is also a smart precaution.

Driver's License & Permit

Next to your passport, a picture driver's license is the best piece of identification you can carry. Most national driver's licenses are valid in Canada or you can obtain an international driving permit before leaving home. If you plan to take a vehicle rented in the USA into Canada make sure the company issues you a rental contract that stipulates its use in Canada.

Americans traveling extensively through Canada to reach Alaska should look into obtaining a Canadian Nonresident Interprovincial Motor Vehicle Liability Insurance Card. Such a card provides proof of insurance and can be obtained in the USA through insurance companies.

Hostel & Student Cards

Occasionally in Alaska, especially around the University of Alaska campuses in Anchorage and Fairbanks, there are discounts for students in which case your university identification or Hostelling International card is a handy thing to have – especially the hostel card as there is a growing number of businesses that are feeding off the Alaskan hostels (see the Accommodation section later in this chapter) by targeting such travelers with discounts.

In the USA, you can get a Hostelling International membership by contacting Hostelling International, Ste 840, 733 15 St, NW, Washington, DC 20005; ☎ (202) 786-6161. Adults' memberships are $25 a year or $250 for a lifetime.

Seniors' Cards

The best card to carry is the one issued by the American Association of Retired Persons (AARP), which can be obtained for $8 if you're over the age of 50 (doesn't even matter if you're not retired) by writing to AARP, P.O. Box 199, Long Beach, CA 90801.

FOREIGN CONSULATES

There are no embassies in Alaska but there are a dozen foreign consulates in Anchorage to assist overseas travelers with unusual problems. They include:

Belgium
     1031 West 4th Ave, Room 400, Anchorage, AK 99501-7502 (☎ (907) 276-5617)
Canada
     3512 Campbell Airstrip Rd, Anchorage, AK 99504-3838 (☎ (907) 333-1400)
Denmark and France
     3111 C St, Ste 100, Anchorage, AK 99503-3915 (☎ (907) 279-7611)
Finland
     1529 P St, Anchorage, AK 99501-4923 (☎ (907) 279-7670)
Germany
     425 G St, Ste 650, Anchorage, AK 99501-2176 (☎ (907) 274-6537)
Italy
     12840 Silver Spruce Dr, Anchorage, AK 99516-2603 (☎ (907) 762-7664)
Japan
     550 West 7th Ave, Suite 701, Anchorage, AK 99510-3559 (☎ (907) 279-8428)
Korea
     101 West Benson Blvd, Suite 304, Anchorage, AK 99503-3997 (☎ (907) 561-5488)
Norway
     203 West 15th Ave, Ste 105, Anchorage, AK 99501-5128 (☎ (907) 279-6942)
Sweden
     The corner of Northern Lights Blvd and C St (PO Box 100600), Anchorage, AK 99510-0600 (☎ (907) 265-2927)

UK
    3211 Providence Dr, Room 362, Anchorage, AK
    99508-4614 (☎ (907) 786-4848)

CUSTOMS

Travelers are allowed to bring all personal goods (including camping gear or hiking equipment) into the USA and Canada free of duty, along with food for two days and up to 50 cigars, 200 cigarettes and 40 ounces of liquor or wine.

There are no forms to fill out if you are a foreign visitor bringing a vehicle into Alaska whether it is a bicycle, motorcycle or a car; nor are there forms for hunting rifles or fishing gear. Hunting rifles (handguns and automatic weapons are prohibited) must be registered in your own country and you should bring proof of this. There is no limit to the amount of money you can bring into Alaska but anything over $5000 must be registered with customs officials.

Keep in mind that there are endangered-species laws prohibiting transporting products made of bone, skin, fur, ivory etc through Canada without a permit. Import and export of such items into the USA is also prohibited. If you have any doubt about a gift or item you want to purchase, call the US Fish & Wildlife Service office in Anchorage at ☎ (907) 786-3311.

Hunters and anglers who want to ship home their salmon, halibut or the rack of a caribou can easily do so. Most outfitters and guides will make the arrangements for you which include properly packaging the game. In the case of fish, most towns have a storage company that will hold your salmon or halibut in a freezer until you are ready to leave Alaska. When frozen, seafood can usually make the trip to any city in the Lower 48 without spoiling.

MONEY
Costs

Alaskans use the same currency as the rest of the USA, American dollars, only they tend to use a little more of it. The state is traditionally known for having the highest cost of living in the country, though places like southern California, and San Francisco and New York City have caught up with Alaska if not surpassed it. There are two reasons for the high prices in Alaska: the long distances needed to transport everything and the high cost of labor.

To buy a dozen eggs in Fairbanks will cost you more than in other parts of the USA (from around $1.50 to $1.90), but to walk into a cafe and have two eggs cooked and served is where the high prices slap you in the face like a July snowfall. In the restaurants, not only are the transport costs added to the price, but so are the high salaries of the chef, waitress and busboy who put the sunny-side-up plate of eggs on your table. Also keep in mind that tourism in Alaska has basically a three-month season. If the prices seem inflated, they have to be to cover the other nine months when many restaurants, motels and other businesses are barely scraping by.

The trick to budget travel, or beating the high prices, is to either travel out of season or avoid the labor cost. If you just can't get yourself to take a vacation in Fairbanks in February when it is -40°F then try to avoid the labor cost. Buy your own food in a market and cook it at the hostel or camp site. Use public transport; sleep in campgrounds and enjoy your favorite brew around a campfire at night. It is the restaurants, bars, hotels and taxi companies, with their inflated peak-season prices, that will quickly drain your money pouch.

A rule of thumb for Alaskan prices is that they are lowest in Ketchikan and increase gradually as you go north. Overall, the Southeast is generally cheaper than most places in the Interior or elsewhere because barge transport from Seattle (the supply center for the area) is only one to two days away. Anchorage, and to a lesser extent Fairbanks, are the exceptions to the rule as they have competitive prices due to their large populations and business communities. Anchorage, which also receives most of its goods on ocean-going barges, can be extremely affordable if you live there, outrageous if you are a tourist. Gas prices often hover around $1.30 a gallon and apples in a supermarket could cost less than 90 cents a pound. But it's hard to find a motel room under $80 and the price of other tourist-related services such as taxis and restaurants, seems to be inflated as well.

When traveling in the Bush, on the other hand, be prepared for anything. The cost of fresh food, gasoline or lodging can be two or three times what it is anywhere else in the state. It is here that the tales of $25 breakfasts were conjured up, and in some isolated Bush villages these stories might not be too mythical.

Outside of Anchorage, a loaf of bread will cost from $2 to $2.50, a can of tuna fish from 90 cents to $1.60, apples from $1.50 to $2 per pound and a hamburger anywhere from $2 per pound in the large cities to over $4 per pound in outlying communities. Generally the cost of dairy products, even in Anchorage, will get you to swear off them forever or at least until the end of your trip. A gallon of milk will be priced anywhere from $3.75 to over $5 (in Bettles it will cost $8). When buying fresh fruit and vegetables take the time to look over them closely, especially in small town markets. It is not too uncommon to buy a stalk of celery and later discover the middle of it is spoiled.

The cost of gas here is surprisingly reasonable, far cheaper than it is in Canada. A gallon in Anchorage will cost anywhere from $1.25 to $1.35 while in many secondary cities, such as Seward and Valdez, it will cost $1.50 or so. Only at some deserted station will you pay more than $2.50 a gallon. A single in the cheapest motels or hotels costs from $60 to $70 per night while many state and federal campgrounds charge $6 per tent site and privately owned campgrounds charge anywhere from $10 to $15 a night.

An inexpensive restaurant in Alaska is one where two people can have breakfast, coffee and leave a tip for under $15. For dinner, it's a challenge for two travelers to leave most restaurants, apart from fast-food chains, for under $25. If you need to obtain your main meal at a restaurant, look for the many places that now serve lunch buffets until late in the

afternoon. Chinese restaurants (every major town has one) are notorious for this. Often until 3 pm you can enjoy an all-you-can-feed-on feast of fried rice, chow mein and egg rolls for around $7.

Carrying Money
Due to a lack of large cities, Alaska is a relatively safe place in terms of carrying your money, credit cards and travelers' checks. Still you want to be careful when moving through normally busy places like airport terminals. Don't flaunt your money when making a purchase and avoid placing a wallet in your back pocket. Always keep some money stashed away in another location in case you do lose your wallet or purse.

Cash
Cash works. It may not be the safest way to carry funds but nobody will hassle you when you purchase something with US dollars. Most businesses along the Alcan in Canada will also take US dollars and, to a lesser degree, many merchants in Alaska will accept Canadian money. Keep in mind, however, they often burn you on the exchange rate.

Credit Cards
There are probably cases of a store or a hotel in some isolated Bush community somewhere in Alaska that doesn't accept any type of credit card, but not many. Like in the rest of the USA, Alaskan merchants are geared and willing to accept just about all major credit cards. Visa and MasterCard are the most widely accepted cards by far but American Express and Discovery are not far behind.

Tesoro is one of the most widespread chains of gasoline stations in Alaska and has its own form of plastic money. But practically all stations, Tesoro included, will accept one of the big four cards mentioned above.

In short, having some plastic money is good security for the unexpected on any major trip and some travelers say it's now even better to take a credit card than haul a wad of travelers' checks.

Travelers' Checks

Other ways to carry your funds include the time-honored method of travelers' checks. The popular brands of US travelers' checks such as American Express and VISA are widely used around the state and will be readily cashed at any store, motel or bank in the major tourist areas of Alaska.

ATMs

In 1995, the National Bank of Alaska (NBA) embarked on a pilot program called Delivering Banking To Rural Alaska. Basically, it put an automatic teller machine (ATM) in Unalakleet, a small native village south of Nome on the Bering Sea. I suspect it won't be long until there's an ATM in every town and village in Alaska with more than 100 residents.

For this reason, you might also consider bringing your ATM card from home to access such machines in Alaska as a way of receiving funds. Not only will you have easy access to your money, but you will save money. According to Money Magazine, using ATMs saves 3.5% when compared to exchanging travelers' checks. The NBA, which has offices throughout the state, is connected to both the Plus and Cirrus ATM networks. Chances are that any bank in the USA is connected to one or the other.

Wire Transfers

You can also have money wired to Alaska through Western Union. Money transfers can also be sent and usually received in 15 minutes at any Western Union branch office in the state. If you're in Alaska, call ☎ (800) 325-6000 to locate the nearest office.

Bank Accounts

If you're spending several months in the state or think you might end up staying there for good, open an account at the NBA. With such an account, you will have access to your money at virtually every major town and village and 24 hours a day via ATMs. But keep in mind that you'll usually end up paying some banking fees.

Currency

All prices quoted in this book are in US dollars unless otherwise stated. The following currencies convert at these approximate rates:

Australia	A$1	=	$0.85
United Kingdom	UK£1	=	$1.59
Canada	C$1	=	$0.78
New Zealand	NZ$1	=	$0.75
Germany	DM1	=	$0.70
Japan	Yen100	=	$0.96

Changing Money

The NBA is the largest bank in the state with offices in most towns on the heavily traveled routes. The NBA can meet the needs of most visitors, including changing currency. Though opening hours vary from branch to branch, you can usually count on their being open from 10 am to 3 pm Monday to Friday with evening hours on Wednesday and Friday.

Tipping

Tipping in Alaska, like in the rest of the USA, is expected. The going rate for restaurants, hotels and taxi drivers is about 15%.

POST & COMMUNICATIONS

Planning to write home or to friends? Send your mail 1st class by sticking a 32-cent stamp on the envelope or by using a 50-cent aerogram for overseas destinations. Surface mail, slow anywhere in the USA, can take up to a month moving to or from Alaska.

To receive mail while traveling in Alaska, have it sent c/o General Delivery to a post office along your route. Although everybody passes through Anchorage (zip code 99501), it's probably better to choose smaller towns like Juneau (99801), Ketchikan (99901), Seward (99664), Tok (99780) or Delta Junction (99737). Post offices are supposed to keep letters for 30 days before returning them, although smaller places may keep letters longer, especially if your letters have 'Please Hold Forever!!' on the front written in big red crayon. If you are planning to stay at hostels, theirs are the best addresses to leave with letter writers.

For travelers, especially those from overseas, tripping through Canada into Alaska, it's best to wait until you're in the USA to mail home packages. Generally you'll find the US postal service is half the cost and twice as fast as its Canadian counterpart.

Telephone

Telephone area codes are simple in Alaska: the entire state shares 907 except Hyder which uses 604.

There are public pay phones in every little town and village in Alaska that you can use to call home if you have a phone credit card or a stack of quarters. The best way to make international calls is to first purchase a phone debit card. The cards are sold in amounts of $5, $10 and $20 and are available at airports, in many drug stores or shipping companies like Mail Boxes.

BOOKS

The following publications will aid travelers heading north to Alaska. A few of the more popular ones can be found in any good bookstore but most are available only in Alaska or by writing to the publisher. A better alternative, however, is to request a catalog from the Alaska Natural History Association (ANHA, Mail Order Services, 605 West 4th Ave, Ste 85, Anchorage, AK 99501; ☎ (907) 274-8440), which distributes more than 50 Alaskan titles. Most of the following books can also be ordered through Wild Rose Guidebooks, PO Box 240047, Anchorage, AK 99524.

Lonely Planet Guides

Backpacking in Alaska by Jim DuFresne (Lonely Planet Publications, PO Box 617, Hawthorn, Victoria 3122, Australia; 250 pages, maps, photos). This is a new addition to the Lonely Planet trekking series. The book covers almost 40 trails around the state with maps, day-by-day descriptions of the routes and information on getting to and from the trailheads. The treks range from day

hikes to week-long adventures and they are scattered from Ketchikan to Fairbanks, including several routes in Denali National Park. Dozens of other trails are also covered in every region of the state. The hikes mentioned in this book are covered in greater detail in *Backpacking in Alaska*.

Travel Guides

The Milepost (Vernon Publications, 3000 Northup Way, Bellevue, WA 98004-1446; 640 pages), unquestionably the most popular travel guide, is put out every year. While it has good information, history and maps of Alaska and western Canada, its drawbacks include its large size – at eight by 11 inches it is impossible to slip into the side pocket of a backpack – and that its listings of hotels, restaurants and other businesses are limited to advertisers.

The Alaska Wilderness Milepost (Vernon Publications, 3000 Northup Way, Bellevue, WA 98004-1446; 454 pages) used to be a slim section in *The Milepost* but is now the most comprehensive guide to Bush Alaska, the parts of Alaska that can't be reached by road. This *Milepost* covers more than 250 remote towns and villages in a much smaller format.

Adventuring in Alaska by Peggy Wayburn (Sierra Club Books, 530 Bush St, San Francisco, CA 94108; 375 pages) is a good general guidebook to the many new national parks, wildlife preserves and other remote regions of Alaska. It also contains excellent 'how-to' information on undertaking wilderness expeditions in the state, whether the mode of travel is canoeing, kayaking or hiking.

Alaska's Southeast: Touring the Inside Passage by Sarah Eppenbach (Globe Pequot Press, PO Box 833, Old Saybrook, CT 06475; 308 pages) offers some of the most comprehensive accounts of the Southeast's history and culture, although it lacks detailed travel information.

Alaska's Wilderness Highway by Mike Jensen (Epicenter Press, PO Box 82368, Kenmore Station, Seattle, WA 98026; 114 pages) is a guide to traveling the Dalton

Hwy, which climbs over the Brooks Range enroute to Prudhoe Bay on the Artctic Sea. The book includes a history of the area, a primer for those driving the road and then a mile-by-mile description of the road itself.

Alaska's Parklands, The Complete Guide by Nancy Simmerman (The Mountaineers, 1011 SW Klickitat Way, Suite 107, Seattle, WA 98134; 336 pages) is the encyclopaedia of Alaskan wilderness, covering over 110 state and national parks and wilderness areas. It lacks detailed travel information and guides to individual canoe and hiking routes but does a thorough job of covering the scenery, location and activities available in each preserve.

Hiking Guides

55 Ways to the Wilderness in Southcentral Alaska by Helen Nienhueser & John Wolfe (Mountaineer-Books, 1001 SW Klickitat Way, Ste 201, Seattle, WA 98134; 176 pages) is a hiking guide covering popular trails around the Kenai Peninsula, the Anchorage area and from Palmer to Valdez.

Juneau Trails by the USFS (60 pages) is a bible for Juneau hikers as it describes 26 trails around the capital city – perhaps the best area for hiking in Alaska. The guide-book includes basic maps, distances, rating of the trails and location of trailheads along with brief descriptions of the route.

Sitka Trails by the USFS (72 pages) is similar to *Juneau Trails* and covers 30 hiking trails around Sitka and its nearby coastline.

Petersburg Hiking Trails by the USFS (72 pages) is the newest USFS trail guide for Southeast Alaska. The Petersburg booklet covers more than 20 trails and a handful of portages that kayakers would use when pad-dling Kuiu Island.

Discover Southeast Alaska with Pack and Paddle by Margaret Piggott (Mountaineer-Books, 1001 SW Klickitat Way, Ste 201, Seattle, WA 98134; 238 pages), a longtime guidebook to a dozen water routes and 58 trails of the Southeast, was out of print for years before the author finally updated the first edition in 1990. Its downfall is the weak, hand-drawn maps. Make sure you pack the topos.

Backcountry Companion for Denali National Park by Jon Nierenberg (Alaska Natural History Association, 605 West 4th Ave, Anchorage, AK 99501; 94 pages, maps, photos) is a general guide to wilderness trek-king in the popular national park. It's not a trail guide, but rather provides short synop-ses to each of Denali's backcountry zones to assist backpackers to pick the right area to travel in.

Katmai by Jean Bodeau (Alaska Natural History Association, 605 West 4th Ave, Anchorage, AK 99501; 206 pages, photos) is a general guide to Katmai National Park on the Alaska Peninsula. It will assist you in understanding this special park and help you arrange a trip here but not necessarily lead you through the Valley of 10,000 Smokes.

Chilkoot Pass by Archie Satterfield (Alaska Northwest Books, 130 2nd Ave South, Edmonds, WA 98020; 224 pages, photos) is a historical guide for hikers fol-lowing Alaska's most famous gold rush trail. The book includes both a mile-by-mile description of the trail and history and stories of every segment of the route that Klondike stampeders followed at the turn of the century.

Paddling Guides

The Kenai Canoe Trails by Daniel Quick (Northlite Publishing Co, HC-3, PO Box 5751, Soldotna, AK 99669; 167 pages, maps, photos) covers the Swanson River and Swan Lake canoe trails in the Kenai National Wildlife Refuge although most paddlers don't need such an in-depth and expensive guide to an area so easily explored.

A Guide to Alaska's Kenai Fjords by David Miller (Wilderness Images, Anchor Cove, PO Box 1367, Seward, AK 99664; 1987, 116 pages) is a coastal paddling guide to the Kenai Fjords National Park with route descriptions and maps. The author provides an overview of the area plus specific infor-mation about protected coves, hikes, fishing tips and protected areas for kayakers to arrange drop-offs and pick-ups.

Glacier Bay National Park: A Backcountry Guide to the Glaciers and Beyond by Jim DuFresne (Mountaineer-Books, 1001 SW Klickitat Way, Ste 201, Seattle, WA 98134; 160 pages) is a complete guide to Glacier Bay's backcountry. Along with introductory material on the park, the book contains information on kayak rentals, transport up the bay and detailed descriptions of water and land routes; maps are included.

Alaska Paddling Guide by Jack Mosby & David Dapkus (J&R Publishers, PO Box 140264, Anchorage, AK 99514; 1986, 113 pages) is a statewide guide which covers 110 possible water trips, many having road access. Descriptions of the journeys are brief but practical, with information such as access points, trip length and a rough map.

The Alaska River Guide by Karen Jettmar (Alaska Northwest Books, 2208 NW Market St, Seattle, WA 98107; 302 pages, maps, photos) is the most complete river guide for Alaska, covering more than 100 possible trips with two or three pages of description and a general map. The rivers range from the Chilkat in the Southeast to Colville on the Arctic slope.

Fast & Cold: A Guide To Alaska Whitewater by Andrew Embick (Valdez Alpine Books, PO Box 1889, Valdez, AK 99686; 292 pages, maps, photos) a companion to *The Alaska River Guide*, this book is dedicated to experienced whitewater kayakers and rafters looking to enjoy the state's top rivers. The author covers 79 rivers and discusses difficulty, gradient, character of the trip and permits among other topics.

General & History

Alaska by James A Michener (Fawcett Books, New York, NY) – whether you love or hate him as an author, just about everybody agrees that James Michener leaves no stone unturned in writing about a place. He usually begins with the creation of the mountains and rivers, and 1000 pages later brings you to the present; his novel of Alaska is no different. It's a bit wordy for my literary taste but many others rave about the book.

Coming into the Country by John McPhee

(The Noonday Press, 19 Union Square West, New York, NY 10003; 438 pages) takes a mid-1970s look at Alaska in a book that is 600 pages shorter and considerably lighter than Michener's effort. McPhee's experiences included a kayak trip down the Kobuk River in the Brooks Range, living in the town of Eagle for a while and spending time in Juneau during the height of the capital move issue. All of the stories provide an excellent insight into the state and the kind of people who live there.

Mount McKinley: Icy Crown of North America by Fred Beckey (The Mountaineers, 1011 SW Klickitat Way, Suite 107, Seattle, WA 98134; 320 pages) is the history and lore of Alaska's tallest mountain and it's most popular natural attraction. Beckey, a climber himself, uses stories and a unique narrative style to bring the famed peak to life. He begins with the natural forces that created it, covers the fascinating race of the first successful attempt at the summit and looks at what climbers go through to climb Mt McKinley.

Alaska Almanac (Alaska Northwest, PO Box 10306, Portland, OR 97210; 224 pages) covers just about every topic imaginable, from what a potlatch is to the state's heaviest snowfall (974.4 inches).

City Visitor Guides

Various large and small newspapers around the state put out special visitor guides at the beginning of the summer. All are filled with local history, information, things to do and trails to hike in the area where the newspaper circulates. Look for the free guides at restaurants, bars, hotels and tourist offices or write to the papers in advance:

Anchorage
  Visitors Guide, Anchorage Daily News, PO Box 149001, Anchorage, AK 99514
Fairbanks
  Interior & Arctic Alaska Visitors' Guide, Fairbanks Daily News Miner, PO Box 710, Fairbanks, AK 99707
Haines
  Haines Sentinel, Chilkat Valley News, PO Box 630, Haines, AK 99827

Homer
> *Homer Tourist Guide*, The Homer News, 3482 Landing St, Homer, AK 99603

Juneau
> *Juneau Guide*, Juneau Empire, 235 2nd St, Juneau, AK 99801

Ketchikan
> *Ketchikan Visitors' Guide*, Ketchikan Daily News, PO Box 7900, Ketchikan, AK 99901

Kodiak
> *Kodiak Visitors' Guide*, Kodiak Daily Mirror, 1419 Selig St, Kodiak, AK 99615

Petersburg
> *Viking Visitor Guide*, Petersburg Pilot, PO Box 930, Petersburg, AK 99833

Skagway
> *Skagway Alaskan*, The Skagway News, PO Box 1898, Skagway, AK 99840

Sitka
> *All About Sitka*, Sitka Daily Sentinel, PO Box 799, Sitka, AK 99835

Valdez
> *Valdez/Cordova Visitors' Guide*, Valdez Vanguard, PO Box 157, Valdez, AK 99686

Wrangell
> *The Wrangell Guide*, Wrangell Publishing Inc, PO Box 798, Wrangell, AK 99929

Nature

Guide to the Birds of Alaska by Robert H Armstrong (Alaska Northwest Books, 22026 20th Ave SE, Bothell, WA 98021; 344 pages). To ornithologists, Alaska is the ultimate destination. More than 400 species of birds have been spotted in the state and the above guide has information on identification, distribution and habitat of 335 of them. Along with text, the book contains color photographs of the species, drawings and a bird checklist.

A Guide to Alaskan Seabirds by the Alaska Natural History Association (2525 Gambell St, Anchorage, AK 99503; 40 pages) is a thin guide to the birds that thrive in coastal Alaska. It has excellent drawings for easy identification.

Alaska-Yukon Wild Flowers Guide (Alaska Northwest Books, 130 2nd Ave South, Edmonds, WA 98020; 224 pages, illustrations, photos) uses both illustrations and color photos to help you identify what's blooming.

Wild, Edible & Poisonous Plants of Alaska by Dr Christine Heller (Alaska Natural History Association; 88 pages), a handy little guide, is an excellent companion on any hike, as it contains both drawings and color photos of Alaskan flora, including edible plants, berries and wildflowers.

Animal Tracks of Alaska by Chris Stall (Mountaineer-Books, 1001 SW Klickitat Way, Ste 201, Seattle, WA 98134; 112 pages) is a must for anybody who plans to do a fair amount of hiking or beachcombing in Alaska. You'll see wildlife tracks everywhere.

A Guide to Wildlife Viewing in Alaska (Alaska Department of Fish & Game; 1983, 170 pages) describes the best opportunities to view wildlife by regions and seasons. The first chapter explains how to find wildlife and the following chapters cover Alaska's 14 different types of wildlife habitats.

ONLINE SERVICES

Highly computer literate, extremely remote: Alaska was made for the Internet and electronic mail. Small, isolated schools in the Bush were some of the first in the country to get online in the classroom and use the Internet for a peak at the outside world.

As a traveler, you can access a great deal of information about the state if your computer at home is online. Although many Alaskan Web pages are university and government sites, there is a large number dedicated to travel in the state. Try the Alaskan Center (http://alaskan.com/) which features background on the state as well as bus, ferry, air and train schedules. The Alaskan Center also serves as a link to many other Web pages, including The Juneau Web, Alaskan Visitors and Information Center and the State of Alaska page.

There is also the Alaska Internet Travel Guide (http://www.Alaska-Online.com/travel/) which includes lists of accommodation throughout the state. Some of the B&Bs have their own home page with photos of the house but most of the lodging information is simply an address and phone number. The Alaska Internet Travel Guide covers many of the attractions in Southcentral Alaska, and

Juneau has a page relating to tourism (http://www.neosoft.com/citylink/juneau/).

You can also retrieve Alaskan information from the travel forums of the major commercial online services. In its Travel forum, American Online has Outdoor Adventure Online. This site includes message boards which allow you to post questions about Alaskan trails or parks, or search out partners or outfitters for wilderness adventures. In Compuserve there is GO OUTFOR for the Great Outdoors Forum and GO USTOUR for the US Tourism Forum.

The information is easy to obtain but I have found a great deal of it misleading or simply incorrect. That includes one person extolling the great 'backpacking trails in Mt McKinley National Park' which is now called Denali and has always been a trail-less wilderness.

Other Web sites and email addresses will appear throughout this guidebook, allowing you to contact everything from a B&B in Anchorage and a wilderness outfitter in Bettles to Alaska Airlines, all for the cost of a local phone call.

FILMS & TV SHOWS

Occasionally Alaska becomes the setting for a major motion picture but not very often. What really gave the state a boost was the TV show *Northern Exposure*.

The Emmy-winning TV series was about a New York City doctor who had to repay the state of Alaska for financing his education by working in the fictional town of Cicely. Others in the cast played eccentric and free-spirited townspeople.

The show was a hit in the mid-1990s and some towns in Alaska, most notably Talkeetna, promoted themselves as the 'Cicely of Alaska'. Unfortunately the TV series was cancelled by CBS in the spring of 1995 and was never actually filmed in Alaska but rather the town of Roslyn in the state of Washington.

NEWSPAPERS & MAGAZINES

There are more than 30 daily, weekly and trade newspapers in Alaska, though most contain eight pages of local news, softball scores and advertising. The largest daily in the state with a circulation of almost 61,000 is the *Anchorage Daily News*, a top-rate newspaper that captured the Pulitzer Prize in the 1970s with its stories on the Trans-Alaska Pipeline.

The Sunday edition of the *Daily News* can make for particularly interesting reading, especially its 'Dispatch: Alaska' column which features news from around the state, and the in-depth features in its *We Alaskans* magazine.

Looking for Love in Alaska

There it was in the Sunday singles page of the *Anchorage Daily News*: 'Need a Woman!!! SWM, late 40s, with 30 sled dogs, looking for SWF to warm up the cabin and help feed the team'. Looking for love? If you're a woman, the odds are in your favor in Alaska. It is estimated in some small communities, such as Skagway in the Southeast, that in the winter there are five to seven single men to every single woman. The *Daily News*, meanwhile, prints an entire page of letters from 'desperately seeking' men every Sunday.

You can browse through the ads on the Internet at http://www.mva.com or hear their message by calling ☎ (900) 288-1870. Simply remember what one Alaskan woman said about men and love in the Last Frontier: 'The odds are good, but the goods are odd'. ■

The next biggest daily and an equally outstanding publication is the *Fairbanks Daily News Miner*, while the largest paper in the Southeast is the *Juneau Empire*.

The Empire, however, is owned by a rather detached company which is based in Georgia. That has given rise to *The Paper*, a new and highly entertaining weekly that began publication in Juneau in 1995. The *Seattle Post-Intelligencer* is flown into the Southeast daily and the usual news magazines, *Time* and *Newsweek*, are available, though they are a week old by the time they reach the newsstand.

RADIO & TV

Because of its small, isolated communities, public broadcasting is more important to Alaska than almost any other state. But both the Alaska Public Radio Network and the Rural Alaska Television Network, which provides a mix of commercial and regional TV programs to the Bush, are under the knife due to the state's recent attempt to balance its budget. In 1996 the state legislators were attempting to cut the public broadcasting's $6 million budget in half, which some observers predicted would reduce 12 public radio stations in such towns as Ketchikan, Valdez, Kotzebue and Barrow to little more than local access repeaters with no news operations of their own.

Still, if you are driving around the state you'll find a wide range of radio stations, a lot of them playing country music. If possible, search for a public radio station like Homer's KBBI (AM 890). A daily staple for most of them is 'bushlines' when messages are passed back and forth to isolated residents on the airwaves. It provides an interesting glimpse of life in Alaska. Where else could you hear, 'Ben, meet me at the cabin Tuesday. I'll have a chainsaw and the dog', but in rural Alaska.

VIDEO SYSTEMS

Overseas visitors who are thinking of purchasing videos should remember that the USA uses the National Television System Committee (NTSC) color TV standard. This system is not compatible with other standards used in Africa, Europe, Asia and Australasia unless it is converted, which can be expensive to have done.

PHOTOGRAPHY & VIDEO
Film & Equipment

The most cherished items you can take home from your trip are pictures and slides of Alaska's powerful scenery. Much of the state is a photographer's dream and your shutter finger will be tempted by mountain and glacier panoramas, bustling waterfronts, and diverse wildlife encountered during paddling and hiking trips. Even if you have never toted a camera before, seriously consider taking one to Alaska.

A small, fixed-lens, so-called 'no-mind' (just point and shoot!) 35-mm camera is OK for a summer of backpacking in the north country. A better step up, however, is to purchase a 35-mm camera with a fixed zoom lens. The Nikon Zoom-Touch 500 series is such a camera, providing a lens that zooms from a 35-mm-wide angle to an 80-mm telephoto. The camera is still compact and easy to use but will greatly increase your variety of shots.

If you want to get serious about photography you need a full 35-mm camera with a couple of interchangeable lenses and maybe even a second body. To photograph wildlife in its natural state, a 135-mm or larger telephoto lens is needed to make the animal the main object in the picture. Just remember any lens larger than 135 mm will probably also require a tripod to eliminate camera shake, especially during low-light conditions. A wide-angle lens of 35 mm, or better still 28 mm, adds considerable dimension to scenic views while a fast (f1.2 or f1.4) 50-mm 'normal' lens will provide you with more opportunities for pictures during weak light.

If you want simplicity, check out today's zoom lenses. They are much smaller and compact than they have been in the past and provide a sharpness that's more than acceptable to most amateur photographers. A zoom from 35 mm to 105 mm would be ideal.

Photographers find that Kodachrome ASA 64 or Fujichrome ASA 100 are the best all-around films for slides, especially when you're photographing glaciers or snowfields where the reflection off the ice and snow is strong. A few rolls of high-speed film (ASA 200 or 400) are handy for nature photography as the majority of wildlife will be encountered at dusk and dawn, periods of low light. For print film, try to use Kodacolor 100 or Fujicolor 100.

Bring all your own film if possible; in the large cities and towns it will generally be priced around $9 to $11 for a roll of Kodachrome (36 exposures), while in smaller communities you may have a hard time finding the type of film you want.

Technique

If you take enough shots, you're bound to end up with a few good ones. But here are a few tips to shooting better pictures in Alaska:

- Take time to compose your shots; don't just point and shoot. Experiment with different distances and angles – vertical, hortizontal or from the ground shooting up.
- Get close to your subject and avoid what professional photographers call middle-distance shots; photos with too much foreground and clutter.
- Be aware that the best light for the most vivid colors is just after sunrise and before sunset. Shooting at midday with its harsh light is not as bad in Alaska as it would be in a place like Arizona, but you still want to take advantage of afternoon sunlight.
- If shadows are inevitable, make use of your flash (even in daytime) to brighten objects in the shade. You might also consider bracketing your photos by reducing or adding to the exposure time over several frames to ensure that one picture is at the right setting. Remember that film is cheap when compared to the cost of your trip to Alaska.
- Don't try to hand-hold a camera for an exposure time longer than the focal length of your camera. If you're shooting with a 200-mm lens, any exposure longer than 1/200 second will require a tripod. Consider purchasing a mini-tripod for the trip, one that will easily fit into a side pocket of a backpack but features a Velcro strap so you can attach it to a tree for an extended exposure or self portrait.

Weather & Airport Security

Keep in mind the rainy weather that you'll encounter on your trip; a waterproof camera bag is an excellent investment, especially if a great deal of your time will be spent in the woods.

When flying to and around Alaska, pack your film in your carry-on luggage and have it hand-inspected. Security personnel at US airports are required by law to honor such requests and are usually very accommodating if you have the film out and ready. I've only ever met a handful who made me uncap all 48 rolls of film I was hauling along. Scanning machines are supposed to be safe for film, but why take the chance? Remember

the higher the speed of film, the more susceptible it is to damage by scanners.

TIME

With the exception of four Aleutian Island communities and Hyder, a small community on the Alaska/British Columbia border, the entire state shares the same time zone, Alaska Time, which is one hour earlier than Pacific Standard Time – a zone in which Seattle (Washington) falls. When it is noon in Anchorage, it is 9 pm in London, 4 pm in New York and 7 am the following day in Melbourne, Australia.

ELECTRICITY

Voltage in Alaska is 110/120 V – the same as everywhere else in the USA.

WEIGHTS & MEASURES

Alaska uses the imperial system of measurement. Weight is measured in ounces (oz) and pounds (lb), volume is measured in pints and gallons, and length in inches, feet, yards and miles etc. A conversion table is provided at the back of this book for people more comfortable with metric measurement.

LAUNDRY

Virtually every town with more than 100 residents in Alaska has a laundromat, the place to go to clean your clothes or take a shower. A small load of clothes is going to cost from $3, plus you'll need another $1 to dry them in the dryer. A shower and clean towel is around $3. You'll find many hostels and a few motels also provide laundry facilities for a fee.

HEALTH
Predeparture Preparations

Health Insurance The cost of health care in the USA is extremely high and Alaska is no exception. A travel insurance policy to cover theft, loss and medical problems is therefore a wise idea. There is a wide variety of policies and your travel agent will have recommendations. The international student travel policies handled by the Student Travel Association (STA) or other student travel organizations are usually good value. Some policies offer lower and higher medical expenses options but the higher one is chiefly for countries like the USA which have extremely high medical costs. Check the small print.

Medical Kit A small, straightforward medical kit is a wise thing to carry, especially if you plan to venture away from populated areas. A possible kit list includes:

• Paracetamol (called acetominophen in North America) – for pain or fever
• Antihistamine (such as Benadryl) – useful as a decongestant for colds, for allergies, to ease itching from insect bites or stings, or to help prevent motion sickness
• Antibiotics – useful if you're traveling in the wilderness, but they must be prescribed and you should carry the prescription with you
• Loperamide (eg Imodium) or Lomotil for diarrhoea; prochlorperazine (eg Stemetil) or metaclopramide (eg Maxalon) for nausea and vomiting. Antidiarrhoea medication should not be given to children under the age of 12
• Rehydration mixture – for treatment of severe diarrhoea, this is particularly important if traveling with children
• Antiseptic and antibiotic powder, or similar 'dry' spray – for cuts and grazes
• Calamine lotion – to ease irritation from bites or stings
• Bandages and Band-aids – for minor injuries
• Scissors, tweezers and a thermometer – mercury thermometers are prohibited by airlines
• Insect repellent, sunscreen, suntan lotion, chap stick and water purification tablets

Water Purification

Tap water in Alaska is safe to drink but it is wise to purify surface water that is to be used for cooking and drinking. The simplest way of purifying water is to boil it thoroughly. Technically this means boiling it for 10 minutes. Remember that at high altitude water boils at a lower temperature, so germs are less likely to be killed.

If you cannot boil water, it can be treated chemically. Chlorine tablets (Puritabs, Steritabs or other brand names) will kill many pathogens but not those pathogens causing giardia and amoebic dysentery. Iodine is very effective in purifying water

and is available in tablet form (such as Potable Aqua), but follow the directions carefully and remember that too much iodine can be harmful.

If you are trekking in the wilderness, all this can be handled easily by investing in a high-quality filter. Filters such as First Need or MSR's Waterworks are designed to take out whatever you shouldn't be drinking, including *Giardia lamblia* (see the following section). They cost between $45 and $80 and are well worth it.

Water from glacial rivers may appear murky but you can drink it, if necessary, in small quantities. The murk is actually fine particles of silt scoured from the rock by the glacier and drinking too much of it has been known to clog up internal plumbing.

Medical Problems & Treatment

Giardia Giardiasis, commonly known as Giardia and sometimes called 'beaver fever', is caused by an intestinal parasite *(Giardia lamblia)* present in contaminated water. The symptoms are stomach cramps; nausea; a bloated stomach; watery, foul-smelling diarrhoea and frequent gas. Giardia can appear several weeks after you have been exposed to the parasite. The symptoms may disappear for a few days and then return; this can go on for several weeks. Metronidazole, known as Flagyl, or Tinidazole, known as Fasigyn, are the recommended drugs for treatment.

Sunburn & Windburn Alaska has long hours of sunlight during the summer and the sun's rays are even more intense when they are reflected off snow or water. Sunburn and windburn should be primary concerns for anyone planning to spend time trekking or paddling. The sun will burn you even if you feel cold and the wind will cause dehydration and skin chafing. Use a good sunscreen and a moisture cream on exposed skin, even on cloudy days. A hat provides added protection, and zinc oxide or some other barrier cream for your nose and lips is recommended for people spending any time on the ice or snow.

Reflection and glare off ice and snow can

cause snow blindness, so high-protection sunglasses, known by many locals as 'glacier goggles', should be considered essential for any sort of visit on or near glaciers.

Hypothermia Perhaps the most dangerous health threat in the Arctic regions is hypothermia. Hypothermia occurs when the body loses heat faster than it can produce it and the core temperature of the body falls. It is surprisingly easy to progress from very cold to dangerously cold due to a combination of wind, wet clothing, fatigue and hunger, even if the air temperature is above freezing point.

It is best to dress in layers – silk, wool and some of the new artificial fibers are all good insulating materials. A hat is important, as a lot of heat is lost through the head. A strong, waterproof outer layer is essential, as keeping dry is vital. Carry basic supplies, including food containing simple sugars to generate heat quickly and lots of fluid to drink.

Symptoms of hypothermia are exhaustion, numb skin (particularly toes and fingers), shivering, slurred speech, irrational or violent behavior, lethargy, stumbling, dizzy spells, muscle cramps and violent bursts of energy. Irrationality may take the form of sufferers claiming they are warm and trying to take off their clothes.

To treat hypothermia, first get the victim out of the wind and/or rain, remove their clothing if it's wet and replace it with dry, warm clothing. Give them hot liquids – not alcohol – and some high-calorie, easily digestible food. This should be enough for the early stages of hypothermia, but if it has gone further it may be necessary to place victims in warm sleeping bags and get in with them. Do not rub victims, instead allow them to slowly warm themselves.

Motion Sickness Since a great deal of travel in Alaska is done by boat and much of the overland travel is over rough, unsurfaced roads, motion sickness can be a real problem for those prone to it.

Eating lightly before and during a trip will reduce the chances of motion sickness. If you are prone to motion sickness, try to find a place that minimizes disturbance – near the wing on aircrafts, close to midships on boats and near the center of buses. Fresh air or watching the horizon while on a boat usually helps; reading or cigarette smoke doesn't. Commercial antimotion-sickness preparations, which can cause drowsiness, have to be taken before the trip commences; when you're feeling sick it's too late. Ginger (available in a capsule) and peppermint (including mint-flavored sweets) are natural preventatives.

Rabies Rabies is found in Alaska, especially among small rodents such as squirrels and chipmunks in wilderness areas; it is caused by a bite or scratch from an infected animal. Any bite, scratch or even lick from a mammal should be cleaned immediately and thoroughly. Scrub with soap and running water, and then clean with an alcohol or iodine solution. If there is any possibility that the animal is infected, medical help should be sought immediately.

Even if the animal is not rabid, all bites should be treated seriously as they can become infected or can result in tetanus. A rabies vaccination is now available and should be considered if you are in a high-risk category – for instance, handling or working with animals.

HIV & AIDS The human immunodeficiency virus (HIV), may develop into acquired immune deficiency syndrome (AIDS). HIV is a major problem in many countries. Any exposure to blood, blood products or bodily fluids may put the individual at risk. In many developing countries transmission is predominantly through heterosexual sexual activity. This is quite different from the situation in industrialised countries where transmission is mostly through contact between homosexual or bisexual males, or via contaminated needles shared by intravenous drug users. Apart from abstinence, the most effective preventative is always to practice safe sex using condoms. It is impossible to detect the HIV-positive status of an otherwise healthy-looking person without a blood test.

HIV/AIDS can also be spread through infected blood transfusions; some developing countries cannot afford to screen blood for transfusions. It can also be spread by dirty needles – vaccinations, acupuncture, tattooing and ear or nose piercing can be potentially as dangerous as intravenous drug use if the equipment is not clean. If you do need an injection, ask to see the syringe unwrapped in front of you, or better still, take a needle and syringe pack with you overseas – it is a cheap insurance package against infection with HIV.

Fear of HIV infection should never preclude treatment for serious medical conditions. Although there may be a risk of infection, it is very small indeed.

WOMEN TRAVELERS

Perfumes or scented cosmetics, including deodorants, should not be worn in areas where you are likely to encounter bears as the smell will attract them. Women who are menstruating should also be cautious. Women should also be alert to the dangers of hitchhiking, especially when they are traveling alone – use common sense and don't be afraid to say no to lifts.

In general, women should feel safe traveling, hiking and camping in Alaska. The combination of a booming tourist industry, low crime rate and small towns and cities allow women to have fewer worries traveling without male companions in Alaska than in almost any other state in the USA.

GAY & LESBIAN TRAVELERS

There are gay people everywhere in the USA and Alaska is no exception. But the gay community here is far smaller and less open than in such cities as San Francisco or New York. In Anchorage, the only city in Alaska with any real size, you have Identity, Inc and its Gay & Lesbian Helpline (☎ (907) 258-4777), a Gay & Lesbian Student Association at the University of Alaska campus and even an openly gay dance bar, the *Blue Moon Bar*,

at 530 E 5th Ave. But none of the other cities have such an active gay community and in rural Alaska gay travelers should think twice before openly showing their sexual preference.

DISABLED TRAVELERS

Thanks to the American Disabilities Act, many state and federal parks are installing wheelchair-accessible sites and restrooms in their campgrounds. You can call the Alaska Public Lands Information Center (☎ (907) 271-2737) to receive a map and campground guide to such facilities. The Alaska State Marine Ferry, the Alaska Railroad, many bus services and cruise ships are also equipped with wheelchair lifts and ramps that make their facilities easier to access.

In advance of planning your trip, call Access Alaska (☎ (907) 248-4777) for a free packet of information on accessible services and sites within the state.

You might also consider Alaska Snail Trails (☎ (800) 348-4532). This company offers 10-day tours for the mobility impaired on specially designed mini-buses that include such popular attractions as Denali National Park and whale watching in Kenai National Park.

SENIOR TRAVELERS

Seniors, mostly in the form of RVers or passengers of cruise-ship lines, love Alaska. They can also receive discounts on admission to most museums, parks and other attractions with an identification card. What they will quickly discover, however, is the 10% discount at motels and the 'early bird dinner specials' at restaurants for seniors is not the widespread practise it is elsewhere in the USA. The reason is simple economics; the tourist season is too short and competition for rooms too high for most places to give seniors a discount.

DANGERS & ANNOYANCES
Paralytic Shellfish Poisoning

In recent years paralytic shellfish poisoning (PSP) has become a problem in Alaska. In 1995, more than a half-dozen cases of PSP were reported, one of which resulted in death. State officials warned people not to eat mussels, clams or snails gathered from unmonitored beaches in Alaska. PSP is possible anywhere in Alaska and within 12 hours of consuming the infected shellfish victims experience symptoms of tingling or numbness in the lips and tongue that can spread to the fingers or toes as well as loss of muscle coordination, dizziness, weakness and drowsiness. To get an update on the PSP situation, or to find out which beaches in the state are safe to clam, call the Division of Environmental Health (☎ (907) 465-5280).

Insects

Alaska is notorious for its biting insects. In the cities and towns you have few problems, but out in the woods you'll have to contend with a variety of insects, including mosquitoes, black flies, white-socks, no-see-ums and deer flies. Coastal areas, with their cool summers, have smaller numbers of insects than the Interior. Generally, camping on a beach where there is some breeze is better than pitching a tent in the woods. In the end, just accept the fact that you will be bitten.

Mosquitoes can often be the most bothersome pest. They emerge from hibernation before the snow has entirely melted away, peak in late June and are around until the first frost. You can combat mosquitoes by wearing light colors, a snug-fitting parka and by tucking the legs of your pants into your socks or boots.

The best protection by far is a high-potency insect repellent; the best contain a high percentage of Deet (diethyltoluamide), the active ingredient. A little bottle of Musk Oil or Cutters can cost $6 or $7 (they contain 100% Deet) but it's one of the best investments you will make.

Unfortunately, repellents are less effective, and some people say useless, against black flies and no-see-ums. Their season runs from June to August and their bite is far more annoying. The tiny no-see-um bite is a prolonged prick after which the surrounding skin becomes inflamed and itches intermittently for up to a week or more. Unlike the mosquito, these insects will crawl into your hair and under loose clothing in search of bare skin.

Thus, the best protection and a fact of life in Alaska's backcountry are long-sleeved shirts, socks that will allow you to tuck your pants into them and a snug cap or woollen hat. You also see many backcountry travelers packing head nets. They're not something you wear a lot, as it drives you crazy looking through mesh all day, but when you really need one they're a lifesaver.

Other items you might consider are bug jackets and an after-bite medication. The mesh jackets are soaked in insect repellent and kept in a zip-lock bag until you wear them and some people say they are the only effective way to keep no-see-ums at bay. After-bite medications contain ammonia and are rubbed on; while this might drive away your tent partner, it does soothe the craving to scratch the assortment of bites on your arms and neck.

Bears

The fact is, as one ranger put it, 'no matter where you travel in Alaska, you'll never be far from a bear'. But too often travelers decide to skip a wilderness trip because they hear a local tell a few bear stories. Your own equipment and outdoor experience should determine whether you take a trek into the woods, not the possibility of meeting a bear on the trail. As the Alaska Department of Fish & Game points out, the probability of being injured by a bear is one-fiftieth of the chance of being injured in a car accident on Alaskan highways.

The best way to avoid bears is to follow a few common-sense rules. Bears do not roam the backcountry looking for hikers to maul; they only charge when they feel trapped, when a hiker comes between a sow and her cubs or when they are enticed by food. It is a good practise to sing or clap when traveling through thick bush so you don't bump into a bear. That has happened, and usually the bear feels threatened and has no choice but to defend itself. Don't camp near bear food sources or in the middle of an obvious bear path. Stay away from thick berry patches, streams choked with salmon or beaches littered with bear scat.

Leave the pet at home; a frightened dog only runs back to its owner and most dogs are no match for a bear. Set up your 'kitchen' – the spot where you will cook and eat – 30 to 50 yards away from your tent. In coastal areas, many backpackers eat in the tidal zone, knowing that when the high tide comes in all evidence of food will be washed away.

At night try to place your food sacks 10 feet or more off the ground by hanging them in a tree, placing them on top of a tall boulder or putting them on the edge of a rock cliff. In a treeless, flat area, cover up the food sacks with rocks. A bear is not going to see the food bags, it's going to smell them. By packaging all food items in zip-lock plastic bags, you greatly reduce the animal's chances of getting a whiff of your next meal. Avoid odoriferous foods such as bacon or sardines in areas of high concentrations of bears.

And please, don't take food into the tent at night. Don't even take toothpaste, hand lotion, suntan oils or anything with a smell. If a bear smells a human, it will leave; anything else might encourage it to investigate.

If you do meet a bear on the trail, *do not* turn and run. Stop, make no sudden moves, and begin talking calmly to it. Bears have extremely poor eyesight and speaking helps them understand that you are there. If it doesn't take off right away, back up slowly before turning around and leaving the area. A bear standing on its hind legs is not on the verge of charging, only trying to see you better. When a bear turns sideways or begins a series of woofs, it is only challenging you for space – just back away slowly and leave. But if the animal follows you, *stop* and hold your ground.

Most bear charges are bluffs, with the animal veering off at the last minute. Experienced backpackers handle a charge in different ways. Some throw their packs three feet in front of them, as this will often distract the bear long enough for them to back away. Others fire a hand-held signal flare over the bear's head (but never at it) in an attempt to

use the noise and sudden light to scare it away. If an encounter is imminent, drop into a foetal position, place your hands behind your neck and play dead. If a black bear continues biting you after you have assumed a defensive posture, then you must fight back vigorously.

Some people carry a gun to fend off bear charges. This is a skilled operation if you are a good shot, a foolish one if you are not. With a gun, you must drop a charging bear with one or two shots as it will be extremely dangerous if only wounded. Others are turning to defensive aerosol sprays which contain capsicum (red pepper extract). These cost $40 a piece and have been used with some success for protection against bears. These sprays are effective at a range of six to eight yards but must be discharged downwind. If not, you will just disable yourself.

Be extremely careful in bear country, but don't let the bears' reputation keep you out of the woods.

LEGAL MATTERS

At one time marijuana was technically legal in Alaska when it was used in the privacy of your home. The legalization came about in 1975 after the state Supreme Court ruled that the health threat from marijuana was insufficient to warrant government intrusion on the privacy of residents. For 16 years, Alaskans showed their fierce individual character and distrust of government regulations, as Alaska was the only state in the country where you could legally smoke pot.

That all changed in 1991 when the voters approved a new drug law that made possession of small amounts of marijuana a misdemeanor punishable by up to 90 days in jail and a $1000 fine. The Alaska Civil Liberties Union has vowed to challenge the new law but regardless of the status of pot in Alaska, it is foolhardy for any visitor to carry it when hitchhiking or driving along the Alcan as you have to pass through the close inspection of immigration officers at two borders. The use of other drugs is also against the law, resulting in severe penalties, especially for cocaine which is heavily abused in Alaska.

Alcohol abuse is also a problem in Alaska and if you are caught driving under the influence of alcohol (DWI) this can be a serious problem. The maximum penalty for a DWI is loss of your license, a $5000 fine and one year in jail. For most people with no prior record a DWI usually results in a loss of license, a $250 fine and 72 hours in jail.

BUSINESS HOURS
Banks and post offices in Alaska are generally open from 9 am to 5 pm from Monday to Friday. Other business hours are variable but many shops are open until 10 pm during the week, from 10 am to 6 pm Saturday and from noon to 5 pm on Sunday.

PUBLIC HOLIDAYS & SPECIAL EVENTS
Alaskans do their fair share of celebrating, much of it during the summer. One of the biggest celebrations in the state is the Summer Solstice on 21 June, the longest day of the year. Fairbanks holds the best community festival, with a variety of events including midnight baseball games (played without the use of artificial light) and hikes to local hills to view the midnight sun. Nome stages a week-long Midnight Sun Festival while Barrow stages a 'Sun will not set for 83 days' Festival. If you are in Anchorage or the Kenai Peninsula, head over to Moose Pass to its Summer Solstice Festival, where the chicken-barbecue dinner alone is worth the trip.

Independence Day (4 July) is a popular holiday around the state when the larger communities of Ketchikan, Juneau, Anchorage and Fairbanks sponsor well-planned events. Perhaps even more enjoyable during this time of year is a visit to a small settlement such as Gustavus, Seldovia or McCarthy, where you cannot help but be swept along with the local residents in an afternoon of old-fashioned celebrating that usually ends with a square dance in the evening.

Salmon and halibut derbies that end with cash prizes for the heaviest fish caught are regular events around the coastal regions of Alaska, with Juneau and Seward having the largest. Although most travelers are ill prepared to compete in such fishing contests, watching the boats returning to the marina with their catch makes for an interesting afternoon.

State fairs, though small compared to those in the Lower 48, are worth attending if for no other reason than to see what a 70-pound cabbage, a 20-pound stalk of celery or a 200-pound pumpkin looks like. The fairs all take place in August and include the Alaska State Fair at Palmer, the Tanana Valley Fair at Fairbanks, the Southeast State Fair at Haines and smaller ones at Kodiak, Delta Junction and Ninilchik.

State & National Holidays
The public holidays for Alaska include:

January
    New Year's Day
    Martin Luther King Day
February
    President's Day
March
    Seward's Day
April
    Easter
May
    Memorial Day
July
    Independence Day
September
    Labor Day
October
    Columbus Day
    Alaska Day
November
    Veteran's Day
    Thanksgiving
December
    Christmas Day

Special Events
The regional festivals and celebrations in Alaska include:

April
    Piuraagiaqta Spring Festival – Barrow
    Spring Ski Splash – Girdwood
    Alaska Folk Festival – Juneau
    Tanner Crab Roundup – Unalaska

May
   Prince William Sound Regatta of Ships –
   Cordova, Valdez and Whittier
   Crab Festival – Kodiak
   Polar Bear Swim – Nome
   Little Norway Festival – Petersburg
   Miner's Day Celebration – Talkeetna
June
   Alaska Renaissance Festival – Anchorage
   Nalukataq (Whaling Festival) – Barrow
   Summer Solstice, Great Tanana River Raft
   Classic – Fairbanks
   Summer Solstice Festival – Moose Pass
   Nenana River Days – Nenana
   Midnight Sun Festival – Nome
   Summer Music Festival, All Alaska Logging
   Championships – Sitka
   Whitewater Weekend – Valdez
July
   Bear Paw Festival – Chugiak/Eagle
   Summer Arts Festival, Golden Days – Fairbanks
   Forest Faire – Girdwood
   Summer Festival – North Pole
   Mount Marathon Race – Seward
   Soapy Smith's Wake – Skagway
   Progress Days – Soldotna
   Moose Dropping Festival – Talkeetna
August
   Tanana Valley Fair – Fairbanks
   Southeast Alaska State Fair – Haines
   Blueberry Arts Festival – Ketchikan
   St Herman's Pilgrimage – Kodiak
   Kenai Peninsula State Fair – Ninilchik
   Alaska State Fair – Palmer
   Silver Salmon Derby – Seward
September
   Oktoberfest, Equinox Marathon – Fairbanks
   Taste of Homer – Homer
   State Fair & Rodeo – Kodiak
   Great Bathtub Race – Nome
   Blueberry Festival – Seldovia
   Trading Post Potato Festival – Willow
October
   October Arts Festival – Petersburg
   Alaska Day Celebration – Sitka

WORK

Opportunities for astronomical wages for jobs on the Trans-Alaska Pipeline and other high-paying employment are, unfortunately, either exaggerated or nonexistent today. Except for brief hiring booms, like during the Exxon oil spill clean-up, the cold reality is that Alaska has one of the highest unemployment rates in the country, averaging 11% annually and often reaching 20% during the winter.

Many summer travelers arrive thinking they will get work on a fishing boat after hearing of someone earning $10,000 in six weeks by getting a percentage of the catch on a good boat. After discovering they lack the deck-hand experience necessary for any kind of position on a fishing vessel, they end up cleaning salmon on the 'slim line' in a cannery for $8 to $11 per hour.

July is the month to be hanging around the harbors looking for a fishing boat desperate for help and the best cities to be in are Kodiak, Cordova and Dillingham. Boats from these places work fish runs in Prince William Sound and Bristol Bay, or Ketchikan, Petersburg and Pelican in the Southeast. Most canneries (many of which are based in the Seattle area) fill their summer employment needs during the winter. If you really want to work in a cannery instead of touring Alaska, contact them by February. Otherwise just show up during the season and hope they are hiring. Finding work is possible as most cannery positions don't require experience and burn-outs are common in this trade.

Other summer employment in Alaska is possible but be realistic about what you will be paid and look in the right places. In the USA, workers are required to have a social security number, a birth-right for anybody born in the country. For foreigners and others who don't have a social security card, the law stipulates that you apply for a green card, which involves a long bureaucratic process that rarely can be accomplished in a summer.

If you lack the proper documentation, then search out tourist-related businesses such as hotels, restaurants, bars and resorts which need additional short-term help to handle the sudden influx of customers. The smaller the business, the more likely the employer will be to pay you under the table. Other cash-paying jobs, whether house cleaning or stocking shelves, can sometimes be found by checking bulletin boards at hostels or the student unions at the various University of Alaska campuses.

If you do have your number, finding some kind of work during the summer is usually not a problem. Retailing is booming in such cities as Anchorage, Fairbanks and Juneau and in 1994 the average wage for the retail trade was $10.36 an hour. Tour companies also hire a large number of seasonal help in the form of bus drivers, raft guides, sales representatives and program coordinators. Companies you can contact in advance include:

Alaska Travel Adventures, 9085 Glacier Hwy, Ste 205, Juneau, AK 99801 (☎ (907) 789-0052)

Denali Park Resorts, 106 Railroad Plaza, 241 West Ship Creek Ave, Anchorage, AK 99501 (☎ (907) 272-9653)

Princess Tours, 519 West 4th Ave, Anchorage, AK 99501 (☎ (907) 276-7711)

Westmark Hotels, 880 H St, Ste 101, Anchorage, AK 99501 (☎ (907) 272-9403)

Gray Line of Alaska, 745 West 4th Ave, Ste 200, Anchorage, AK 99501 (☎ (907) 277-5581)

Alaska Wildland Adventures, PO Box 389, Girdwood, AK 99587 (☎ (907) 783-2928)

Alaska Sightseeing, 513 West 4th Ave, Anchorage, AK 99501 (☎ (907) 276-1305)

You can also check out the regional offices of the USFS and national parks, which hire a number of temporary workers during the summer. But be aware that these federal agencies, like many canneries, recruit their workers during the winter and have little if anything to offer someone passing through in June or July.

In short, those people whose sole interest is working for a summer in Alaska rather than traveling should begin looking for work the winter before. Start by contacting regional offices of the USFS, national parks or the chambers of commerce in fishing communities such as Petersburg, Kodiak or Cordova. You can also get some information from the Alaska State Employment Service (PO Box 3-7000, Juneau, AK 99802) though it tends to do everything it can to discourage Outsiders from seeking jobs in Alaska.

Volunteer Positions

The other option is volunteer work. Although you won't get a wage, you are often provided with room and board and get to work in a spectacular setting. Most volunteer positions are with federal or state agencies. The Bureau of Land Management (BLM) uses almost 300 volunteers annually, people who do everything from office work and maintaining campgrounds to even working on the famous Iditarod Trail. For more information on volunteer work with the BLM begin making enquiries in the winter by writing to BLM-Alaska (Public Affairs, 222 West 7th Ave, Anchorage, AK 99513).

The USFS maintains the largest volunteer program in the state, each year recruiting hundreds of people and providing their room and board and, at times, even transportation costs. Begin making enquiries in the winter by writing to USFS (Pacific Northwest Region, Volunteer Coordinator, PO Box 3623, Portland, OR 97208). Next, write to the individual area offices around the state (see the Wilderness chapter for addresses).

At state parks, summer volunteers fill many positions ranging from trail crew members and research assistants to campground hosts. To receive a booklet on the positions contact the Volunteer Coordinator, Alaska Division of Parks and Recreation (☎ (907) 269-8708), 3601 C St, Ste 1200, Anchorage, AK 99503-5921.

You might also consider contacting the Student Conservation Association (SCA) during the winter. The non-profit New Hampshire-based organization places more than 1000 college students and adults annually in expenses-paid internships which allow the volunteers to live and work with professionals in the conservation and natural resources field. Many of these positions are in Alaska. Write to the SCA (PO Box 550, Charlestown, NH 03603) or call ☎ (603) 543-1700.

ACCOMMODATION

It's important to remember that when booking a room at a B&B, hotel, lodge or even the youth hostel, you will most likely be hit with a city tax and possibly a bed tax. Almost every town of any size in Alaska has them and they can range from as low as 4% to Seward which adds 9% for both city tax and bed tax and Ketchikan which has an

11.5% tax. Bed prices in this book do not include the taxes but towns with the highest taxes are clearly noted.

Camping

Bring a tent – then you will never be without inexpensive accommodation in Alaska. There are no cheap B&Bs like those in Europe and the number of hostels is limited but there are state, federal and private campgrounds from Ketchikan to Fairbanks. Nightly fees range from $6 for the walk-in Morino Campground in Denali National Park to $25 to park your 30-foot RV in some of the more deluxe private campgrounds.

It is also a widely accepted practise among backpackers to just wander into the woods and find a spot to pitch a tent. With the exception of Anchorage, Fairbanks and a few cities, you can walk a mile or so from most towns and find yourself in an isolated wooded area.

Your tent should be light (under five pounds) and come complete with a good rain fly; if it has been on more than its fair share of trips, consider waterproofing the rain fly and tent floor before you leave for Alaska. Make sure the netting around the doors and windows is bug proof and will prevent you from turning into a nightly smorgasbord for mosquitos. The new free-standing dome tents work best, as in many areas of the state the ground is rocky and difficult to sink a peg into.

Hostels

The once-struggling Alaska Council of American Youth Hostels is now a lot more stable and most of its 11 hostels scattered around the state have been in operation for years at the same location. The mainstays of the system are the hostels in Anchorage, Juneau, Ketchikan, Sitka, Seward and Tok. The first hostel you check into is the best source of information on which hostels are open and which need reservations in advance. You should always plan reserving your bed at Anchorage, Juneau and Ketchikan.

The hostels range from a huge house in Juneau (four blocks from the capitol building) with a common room with a fireplace, cooking facilities and showers to remote Bear Creek Camp in Haines and a church basement in Ketchikan. Perhaps the most important hostel for many budget travelers is the Anchorage International (AYH) Hostel, which is now closer to the city center and the bus terminal.

The hostel fees range from $10 for members for a one-night stay to $18 for non-members. Some hostels accept reservations and others don't; each hostel's particulars will be discussed later in this guide. Be aware that hosteling means separate male and female dormitories, house parents, chores assigned for each day you stay and curfews. Also, the hostels are closed during the day – even when it rains. The hostels are strict about these and other rules such as no smoking, no drinking and no illegal drugs. Still, hostels are the best bargains for accommodation in Alaska and the best place to meet other budget travelers and backpackers.

For more information on Alaska's hostels before you depart on your trip, write to or call Hostelling International – Anchorage (☎ (907) 276-3635 or 276-7772 for a machine message), 700 H St, Anchorage, AK 99501.

Backpacker's Hostels Long overdue, Alaska is finally getting some offbeat hostels that offer cheap bunkroom accommodation but without all the rules and regulations of an official youth hostel. Check them out in Anchorage, the Denali Park area, Fairbanks and Homer. More are sure to spring up in the near future.

B&Bs

It is now possible to stay in a B&B from Ketchikan to Anchorage, in Cordova, in Fairbanks, and as far away as Nome and Bethel. What was once a handful of private homes catering to travelers in the early 1980s is now a network of hundreds. One B&B owner estimated there are now more than

1000 such places in Alaska with several hundred in Anchorage alone.

For travelers who want nothing to do with a sleeping bag or tent, B&Bs can be an acceptable compromise between sleeping on the ground and high-priced motels and lodges. Some B&Bs are bargains and most have rates below those of major hotels. Still, B&Bs are not cheap and you should plan on spending anywhere from $60 to $100 per couple per night for a room.

Some B&Bs are in small, out-of-the-way communities such as Angoon, Gustavus, McCarthy or Talkeetna where staying in a private home can be a unique and interesting experience. All recommend making reservations in advance but it is often possible, in cities like Anchorage, Juneau and Fairbanks where there are many B&Bs, to obtain a bed the day you arrive by calling around. Many visitor centers now have sections devoted entirely to the B&Bs in their area and even courtesy phones for booking a room. Details about B&Bs will be covered in the regional chapters. For more information or to make reservations contact the following statewide B&B associations in Alaska:

Southeast Alaska
Alaska Bed & Breakfast Association, 369 South Franklin, Ste 200, Juneau, AK 99801-1353 (☎ (907) 586-2959) Send $5 for a catalog of accommodation.
Ketchikan Reservation Service, 412 D-1 Loop Rd, Ketchikan, AK 99901 (☎ (800) 987-5337).
Statewide
Alaska Private Lodging, PO Box 200047, Anchorage, AK 99520-0047 (☎ (907) 258-1717). Send $5 for a descriptive directory.
Accommodation in Alaska, PO Box 110624, Anchorage, AK 99511-0624 (☎ (907) 345-4279). Send a large self-addressed-stamped envelope for a brochure.
Mat-Su Region
Mat-Su Chapter of Bed and Breakfast Association of Alaska, PO Box 873507, Wasilla, AK 99687 (☎ (800) 401-7444).
Fairbanks
Fairbanks Bed & Breakfast, PO Box 73334, Fairbanks, AK 99707-3334 (☎ (907) 452-7700).

Roadhouses
Roadhouses, found along the highways, are another option. The authentic roadhouses that combine cabins with a large lodge/dining room are slowly being replaced by modern motels, but some places can still offer rustic cabins and sleep from two to four people for $40 to $70 per night. A few of the roadhouses, those with a roaring blaze in the stone fireplace and an owner who acts as chef, bartender and late-night storyteller, are charming. A classic roadhouse and one of the state's oldest is located in Copper Center.

Hotels & Motels
Hotels and motels are the most expensive lodgings you can book. Although there are a few bargains, the average single room in an 'inexpensive' hotel costs from $50 to $60 and a double costs from $60 to $70 (these are the places down by the waterfront with shared bathrooms). Better hotels in each town will be even more costly, with Anchorage's best places charging close to $200 per night.

The other problem with hotels and motels is that they tend to be full during much of the summer. Without being part of a tour or having advance reservations, you may have to search for an available bed in some cities. In small villages, you could be out of luck as they may only have one or two places to choose from.

USFS Cabins
Built and maintained by the US Forest Service (USFS), these cabins are scattered throughout the Tongass National Forest (practically the entire Southeast), the Chugach National Forest on the Kenai Peninsula and in Prince William Sound. For the most part, the cabins are rustic log cabins or A-frames with wood-burning stoves, plywood bunks, pit toilets and often a rowboat if the cabins are on a lake.

A few cabins can be reached by hiking, but for most a bush plane or chartered boat has to drop you off and then return for you. Staying in the cabins is an ideal way to sneak into the woods and separate yourself from the world without having to undertake rigorous backcountry travel.

Top: The humpback whale sometimes surfaces in a spectacular fashion (KFT)
Bottom: A pair of horned puffins, Kenai Fjords National Park (NPS)

Top left: Husky (RS)
Top right: Black bear (JD)

Middle right: Arctic poppies, Chugiak (DS)
Bottom: Moose (without antlers) (JD)

USFS cabins cost $25 per night to rent but can comfortably hold parties of six or more people. You can reserve the cabins 179 days in advance by sending the total payment and the dates you want to stay to the various Forest Service offices which administer the cabins.

During the summer, the cabins are heavily used by both locals and travelers, and stays are limited to seven consecutive nights per party or three days if it is a hike-in cabin.

The cabins provide excellent shelter from bad weather but you have to bring your own bedding (sleeping bag and ground pad), food and cooking gear, including a small backpacker's stove for when the wood pile is wet. Other items that come in handy are insect repellent, matches, candles, water filter and a topographic map of the surrounding area.

Of the 190 USFS public-use cabins, almost 150 of them are in the Southeast and are accessible from Ketchikan, Petersburg, Juneau or Sitka. If you don't make reservations but have a flexible schedule, it is still possible to rent one. During the summer, USFS offices in the Southeast maintain lists of the cabins and dates still available. There are always a few cabins available for a couple of days in the middle of the week, although they will most likely be the remote ones requiring more flying time (and thus money) to reach.

In the regional chapters, a description of selected cabins is given under the names of towns they are most accessible from. These cabins are special because they can either be reached in 30 minutes or less by bush plane or have some intriguing feature nearby, such as natural hot springs or a glacier.

For a complete list of cabins in the Southeast, write to the following USFS offices in Alaska, which will forward a booklet describing each cabin in its district along with details about the surrounding terrain and the best way to travel to it.

Sitka Ranger District
    201 KatlianSt, Ste 109, Sitka, AK 99835
    (☎ (907) 747-4220)

Forest Service Information Center
    101 Egan Dr, Juneau, AK 99801 (☎ (907) 586-8751)
Ketchikan Ranger District
    3031 Tongass, Ketchikan, AK 99901 (☎ (907) 225-2148)
Stikine Area Supervisor
    PO Box 1328, Petersburg, AK 99833 (☎ (907) 772-3871)

The Chugach National Forest in Southcentral Alaska has 39 cabins, including seven along the Resurrection Trail and three on the Russian Lakes Trail. There are also a couple of cabins in the Cordova area that can be reached by foot, but the rest are accessible only by air or boat. For a complete list of cabins and for bookings in the Chugach National Forest, write to the following Alaska Public Lands Information Center or USFS district offices in Alaska:

Alaska Public Lands Information Center
    605 West 4th Ave, Ste 105, Anchorage, AK 99501-5162 (☎ (907) 271-2737)
Cordova Ranger District
    PO Box 280, Cordova, AK 99574 (☎ (907) 424-7661)
Seward Ranger District
    PO Box 390, Seward, AK 99664 (☎ (907) 224-3374)

Wilderness Lodges

These are off the beaten path and you usually require a bush plane or boat to reach them. The vast majority of places need advance booking and offer rustic cabins with saunas and ample opportunities to explore the nearby area by foot, canoe or kayak (they provide the boats). The lodges are designed for people who want to 'escape into the wilderness' without having to endure the 'hardship' of a tent, freeze-dried dinners or a small camp stove. The prices range from $150 to $250 per person per day and include all meals.

FOOD

The local supermarket will provide the cheapest food whether you want to live on fruit and nuts or cook full meals at a hostel. The larger cities will have several markets which offer competitive prices and a good selection of fruit and vegetables during the summer.

While strolling down the aisles also keep an eye out for fresh Alaskan seafood, especially in Southeast and Southcentral markets. Local seafood is not cheap but it is renowned throughout the country for its superb taste. The most common catches are king salmon steaks at $10 per pound, halibut filets at $6 per pound, whole Dungeness crab at $4 to $5 per pound and prawns, which are large shrimp, at $9 to $10 per pound. The larger markets will also have halibut, smoked salmon and cooked king crab.

Alaska is no longer so remote that the US fast-food (and cheapest) restaurants have not reached it. Back in the late 1970s only Anchorage and Fairbanks had a McDonald's franchise. Now you can order a Big Mac in Ketchikan, Juneau and Kodiak, Homer and Eagle River while other chains such as Pizza Hut, Burger King, Wendy's and Taco Bell are almost as widespread. There is even a Burger King in Nome.

Much of the state, however, is safe from the fast-food invasion and the smaller towns you pass through will offer only a local coffee shop or cafe. Breakfast, which many places serve all day, is the best bargain; a plate of eggs, toast and hash browns will cost from $5 to $7 while a cup of coffee will cost from 75 cents to $1.

An influx of Oriental people immigrating to Alaska has resulted in most mid-size towns having at least one Chinese restaurant if not two. Some towns, like Homer (population 3900) support three. All of these places have a lunch buffet that runs from 11 am to 3 pm or so and is an all-you-can-eat affair that costs from $6 to $8. Eat a late lunch here and you can make it through to breakfast the next morning.

One popular eating event during the summer in most of the state, but especially the Southeast, is the salmon bake – a dinner costs from $15 to $20 but it is worth trying at least once. The salmon is caught locally, grilled, smothered with somebody's home-made barbecue sauce and often served all-you-can-eat-style. One of the best bakes is at Alaskaland in Fairbanks.

DRINKS
Coffee
Espresso Shops The coffee craze that began in Seattle and the Northwest has extended into Alaska. Espresso shops are everywhere – even in towns as small as McCarthy you can find somebody with an espresso machine. In Anchorage there are dozens of these places.

Alcohol
The legal drinking age in Alaska is 21 years and only the churches outnumber the bars. Except for 70 Native Alaskan towns like Bethel or Angoon, where alcohol is prohibited, it is never very difficult to find an open bar or liquor store. That and the long, dark winters explain why Alaska has the highest alcoholism rate in the USA, especially among the indigenous people. Bar hours vary but there are always a few places that open their doors at 9 am and don't close until 5 am.

Bars in the larger cities vary in their décor and many offer live entertainment, music and dancing. The bars in smaller towns are good places to have a brew and mingle with people from the fishing industry, loggers or other locals passing through. All serve the usual US beer found in the Northwest (Miller, Rainier) and usually one or two places have that fine Canadian brew, which is darker and richer than US beer, costing around $4 for a 12-ounce bottle. There is also a growing number of Alaskan microbreweries with the largest being Juneau's Alaskan Brewing Co. Its Alaska Ambler is now seen all over the state and sold in stores for around $7 a six-pack.

ENTERTAINMENT
You won't find Broadway in Alaska or stadium rock concerts. But the state does have a lively arts community that organizes events that are both affordable and well worth an evening out. Many theater groups feast on the summer tourists by offering

plays that combine music, a little local history and a lot of comedy. These events are staged in bars, the Lions Clubs and hotels and generally range in admission price from $5 to $10 a show. The two shows not to be missed are the 'Days of '98 Show' in Skagway and the show at Ester's Malamute Saloon.

Alaskan Bars

Alaskans work hard, play hard and, ultimately, drink hard. Their bars reflect that. Great Alaskan bars are saloons where an extensive menu might be peanuts, popcorn *and* pretzels, the floors are often covered by sawdust, the walls are decorated with an assortment of junk, including somebody's 50-pound king salmon, and the clientele might include commercial fishers, loggers or a hard-bitten miner.

Here are eight classic Alaskan bars not to be missed:

Salty Dawg Saloon
    The ramshackle lighthouse in Homer is now a great place to have a drink.
Red Dog Saloon
    This is Juneau's most famous drinking hole, but come late to miss the cruise-ship crowds snapping pictures.
Red Onion Saloon
    This former brothel now serves drinks in Skagway.
Rosie's Bar & Grill
    This is a classic fishers' hangout in Pelican.
Howling Dog Saloon
    This is a rock 'n' roll bar north of Fairbanks where they play volleyball on outside courts all night long...without any lights.
Malemute Saloon
    Located just south of Fairbanks, this is the best place to tip a glass to the verses of Yukon poet Robert Service.
Chilkoot Charlie's
    This is Anchorage's liveliest bar...and there's a lot of them in this city.
Fairview Inn
    This historic hotel in Talkeetna was built in 1923 as an overnight stop for the Alaska Railroad. Its bar was once the setting for a 'Women of Talkeetna' photostory in Playboy magazine.

SPECTATOR SPORT

The biggest spectator sport in Alaska is the Iditarod. The 1100-mile dog-sled race from Anchorage to Nome is held in the first two weeks of March, when the temperatures are usually in the low teens and the snow coverage is good. In Anchorage, the start of the race at 4th Ave and E St is mostly ceremonial as the 60-plus mushers run their teams only a few miles and then truck them up to Wasilla for the re-start of the event. Still thousands of spectators come out in Anchorage for what is a lively weekend of events.

Not planning to come up to Alaska in March? Then spectator sports in the summer are few. But there is the great American pastime of baseball in the form of the Alaska League. Several towns, including Fairbanks, Anchorage and North Pole, sponsor these semi-pro teams of highly regarded college players trying to get a jump on the major leagues. Among the hall-of-famers who have played in Alaska are pitcher Tom Seaver and slugger Dave Winfield. See the regional chapters for where the teams play and when.

THINGS TO BUY

As far as things to buy go, Alaska abounds with gift shops, with items often much too tacky for my taste. Authentic Native Alaskan carving, whether in ivory, jade or soapstone, on the other hand, is exquisite and highly prized, thus expensive. A six-inch carving of soapstone, a soft stone that indigenous people in western Alaska carve and polish, runs from $150 to more than $300 depending on the carving and the detail. Jade and ivory will cost even more. When shopping for such artwork be especially conscious of who you

Check products for these logos to ensure they are authentic Alaskan items.

are purchasing it from. Non-Native art, sometimes carved in places as far away as Bali, is often passed off and priced as Native-produced. If you're considering investing in Native art, here is what you should know and do:

Ask lots of questions. Is the product made in Alaska? Is it made by a Native artist? What is his or her name and where is he or she from? If you make a purchase, have the seller write the name and details on your receipt.

Watch out for the wiggle words. Carvings may be labeled 'Alaska fossil ivory', but just because the raw material is from Alaska it doesn't mean the work was done in the state.

Look for the 'Silver Hand' label. This state-run program is intended to guarantee that the tagged handicrafts are made by a Native Alaskan artist. Just keep in mind the Silver Hand is not widely used, and plenty of legitimate crafts do not display the Silver Hand.

Be especially wary of soapstone carving. Almost all soapstone is imported; it is not a traditional material used by Native Alaskans.

It is estimated that only 10% of the soapstone castings in the state are made by Native artists and the rest are made by Outsiders.

Shop around and learn about the item you want to buy. Check out art books, museums or other collections for information. Purchasing Native Alaskan art is an investment that should not be taken lightly.

Moose nuggets will be seen from one end of the state to the other. But even if they are varnished, you have to wonder who is going to wear ear rings or a necklace made of the scat of an animal. More interesting, and much more affordable than gold-nugget jewelry, is what is commonly called Arctic opal. The blue and greenish stone was uncovered in the Wrangell Mountains in the late 1980s and now is set in silver in a variety of earrings, pins and other pieces.

Want a keepsake T-shirt or jacket? Avoid the gift shops in Anchorage and Fairbanks and head for the bookstores at the University of Alaska campuses which have an interesting selection of clothing that you won't find anywhere else.

Getting There & Away

Many travelers from the Lower 48 mistakenly think that a trip to Alaska is like visiting another state of the USA. It isn't; getting to the north country is as costly and complicated as traveling to a foreign country. Plan ahead and check around for the best possible deal, especially on airline flights.

If you are coming from the US mainland, there are three ways of getting to Alaska: by the Alcan (also known as the Alaska Hwy), the Inside Passage waterway, or flying in from a number of cities.

If you are coming from Asia or Europe, it is no longer as easy to fly direct to Anchorage, via the polar route. Many international airlines, British Airways and Japan Air Lines to name but two, have dropped their service to Anchorage. Now most international travelers come through gateway cities including Seattle, Los Angeles, Detroit and Vancouver to pick up a second flight to Anchorage.

AIR

The quickest and easiest way to reach Alaska is to fly there. A number of major US domestic carriers and a few international airlines offer regular service to Alaska, primarily to Anchorage international airport. As a result of the deregulation of the US airline industry in 1979, fares tend to fluctuate wildly due to airline ticket wars and travel promotions. This also has resulted in an alarming number of airlines going belly up, including MarkAir. Once the largest Alaska-based airline, MarkAir shut down its operations in 1995 and turned to the US Bankruptcy Court to hold off its creditors.

This turned out to be both good and bad for travelers to Alaska. In the all-important Seattle-to-Anchorage market, discount airlines Reno Air and America West stepped in to fill the MarkAir void and the added competition brought down the price of that ticket. But on intrastate routes, such as Anchorage to Nome, Alaska Airlines is now your only

choice which, ultimately, means higher prices.

The other significant change in Alaska air travel is the marketing agreement that Seattle-based Alaska Airlines and Northwest Airlines entered in late 1995. This means convenience for travelers more than a price reduction in tickets. You now can call either airline and book a ticket from virtually any city in the USA and many in Asia and Europe to virtually any town in Alaska. Another plus is that frequent-flyer miles on one airline are now good for tickets with the other.

Anchorage International Airport

The vast majority of visitors to Alaska fly into Anchorage international airport. At one time Anchorage was the 'Air Crossroads of the World' and practically every great foreign carrier made a stop here to refuel. But due to new long-range, intercontinental jets that didn't require a midway refueling stop, the international airlines began dropping the stopover in the mid-1980s. The only international airlines that serve Alaska from the east are Aeroflot, China Airlines and Korean Air while Swissair has a nonstop flight from Zurich, the only such flight from Europe.

International flights arrive at the north terminal, while domestic flights arrive at the south terminal, and there is a complimentary shuttle service between the two terminals and all the various parking lots. You'll find taxis and car rental companies at both terminals.

The airport has the usual services of any major center including gift shops, restaurants, bars, pay phones, ATMs, currency exchange, and baggage storage – $3 a day per bag (ground level of south terminal; ☎ (907) 248-0373).

The following airlines have scheduled services into and out of Anchorage. The numbers are either local Anchorage numbers or toll-free numbers good for anywhere in the USA:

Aeroflot	(☎ (907) 248-8400)	Reno Air	(☎ (800) 736-6247)
Alaska Airlines	(☎ (800) 426-0333)	Reeve Aleutian Airways	(☎ (907) 243-4700)
American West Airlines	(☎ (800) 235-9292)	Swissair	(☎ (800) 322-5247)
China Airlines	(☎ (907) 248-3603)	United Airlines	(☎ (800) 241-6522)
Continental	(☎ (800) 525-0280)		
Delta Airlines	(☎ (800) 221-1212)		
ERA Aviation	(☎ (800) 426-0333)		
Korean Air	(☎ (800) 438-5000)		
Northwest Air	(☎ (800) 225-2525)		
PenAir	(☎ (800) 448-4226)		

Buying Tickets

Airfare Report once tracked down 58 different published fares for a Northwest flight between Detroit and Los Angeles and several

---

Air Travel Glossary

Baggage Allowance This will be written on your ticket; you are usually allowed one 44-pound item to go in the hold, plus one item of hand luggage. Some airlines which fly transpacific and transatlantic routes allow for two pieces of luggage (there are limits on their dimensions and weight).

Bumped Just because you have a confirmed seat doesn't mean you're going to get on the plane – see Overbooking.

Cancellation Penalties If you have to cancel or change an Apex or other discount ticket, there may be heavy penalties involved; insurance can sometimes be taken out against these penalties. Some airlines impose penalties on regular tickets as well, particularly against 'no show' passengers.

Check In Airlines ask you to check in a certain time ahead of the flight departure (usually two hours on international flights). If you fail to check in on time and the flight is overbooked, the airline can cancel your booking and give your seat to somebody else.

Confirmation Having a ticket written out with the flight and date on it doesn't mean you have a seat until the agent has confirmed with the airline that your status is 'OK'. Prior to this confirmation, your status is 'on request'.

Consolidators Also known as bucket shops (UK), these are unbonded travel agencies specialising in discounted airline tickets.

Lost Tickets If you lose your airline ticket, an airline will usually treat it like a travelers' check and, after inquiries, issue you with a replacement. Legally, however, an airline is entitled to treat it like cash, so if you lose a ticket, it could be forever.

No Shows No shows are passengers who fail to show up for their flight for whatever reason. Full-fare no shows are sometimes entitled to travel on a later flight. The rest of us are penalised (see Cancellation Penalties).

Open Jaw Tickets These are return tickets which allow you to fly to one place but return from another, and travel between the two 'jaws' by any means of transport at your own expense. If available, this can save you backtracking to your arrival point.

Overbooking Airlines hate to fly with empty seats, and since every flight has some passengers who fail to show up (see No Shows), they often book more passengers than they have seats available. Usually the excess passengers balance those who fail to show up, but occasionally somebody gets bumped. If this happens, guess who it is most likely to be? The passengers who check in late.

Reconfirmation You must contact the airline at least 72 hours prior to departure to 'reconfirm' that you intend to be on the flight. If you don't do this, the airline can delete your name from the passenger list and you could lose your seat.

Standby This is a discounted ticket where you only fly if there is a seat free at the last moment. Standby fares are usually only available directly at the airport, but sometimes may also be handled by an airline's city office. To give yourself the best possible chance of getting on the flight you want, get there early and have your name placed on the waiting list. It's first come, first served.

Transferred Tickets Airline tickets cannot be transferred from one person to another. Travelers sometimes try to sell the return half of their ticket, but officials can ask you to prove that you are the person named on the ticket. This may not be checked on domestic flights, but on international flights, tickets are usually compared with passports.

Travel Periods Some officially discounted fares, Apex fares in particular, vary with the time of year. There is often a low (off-peak) season and a high (peak) season. Sometimes there's an intermediate or shoulder season as well. At peak times, when everyone wants to fly, both officially and unofficially discounted fares will be higher, or there may simply be no discounted tickets available. Usually the fare depends on your outward flight – if you depart in the high season and return in the low season, you pay the high-season fare. ■

more that weren't published. A seat in the coach section ranged from a high of $629 for a normal round trip to as low as $129 for senior-citizen travel based on a coupon booklet. The Minneapolis-based newsletter said that on any given flight few passengers have paid the same price for their seats.

Keep all this in mind when purchasing a ticket. Even if you are using a travel agent, comparison shop by calling some of them to see who comes up with the best price.

Basically tickets fall into two groups: regular fares, which no budget traveler would ever be caught purchasing; and Advance Purchase Excursion (Apex) or 'Supersavers' as they are known domestically that require round-trip tickets to be booked 14 to 30 days in advance and have a maximum number of days you can stay. The wide variety of prices is caused by promotional gimmicks that the airlines say are necessary to remain competitive. US domestic airlines may offer a special price to passengers traveling on Tuesday and Wednesday – off-peak days for the airline industry – and most have off-season rates for travel to Alaska between December and May.

Many airlines offer senior citizens and students a 10% discount but they have to ask for it when booking the ticket. The information is rarely volunteered. Ticket consolidators, such as Nonstop Air Service and ValuTravel, receive wholesale rates from airlines that fly to Alaska, including Reno Air and America West, then pass on the savings to travel agents.

Often the lowest prices are for 'non-refundable' tickets. This is great if you make the flight, bad if there is a change in plans after you booked it. At Northwest, you have to use the value of that ticket within a year of booking it you will not receive a refund if the value of the new ticket you are purchasing is less and you will be charged a $50 fee.

The Lower 48

Domestic air fares are constantly moving up and down and will vary with the season, the days you want to travel, the length of stay and how rigid the ticket is in terms of changes and refunds after being purchased. Many tickets allow you to stay in Alaska

from three months up to a year. Some even allow a stay of 21 days or less which makes it challenging when you're planning week-long treks into the Alaska wilderness.

The air fare to Alaska is far more affordable now than it was 10 or 15 years ago and occasionally now you can pick up a round-trip ticket from the US midwest or east coast to Anchorage for under $500. But most of those 'economy fares' either have tight restrictions, are for off-season travel or have a limited number of seats available. The summer travel season in Alaska is short and demand for seats on the plane is high. Airlines don't offer economy fares during July.

Seattle (Washington) is the traditional departure point within the USA for air travel to Alaska, but now you can book a nonstop flight to Anchorage from a number of cities including San Francisco, Salt Lake City, Detroit, Minneapolis, Portland, Chicago, Denver and Los Angeles. Northwest flies round-trip nonstop between Minneapolis and Anchorage for a fare that usually falls between $450 and $550 for an advance purchase ticket and $550 to $800 for a similar ticket from Detroit. Delta Airlines flies from Salt Lake City to Anchorage for a round-trip fare of $774. United Airlines has two daily, non-stop flights from Chicago to Anchorage for $660 and similar flights from Denver for $646. A cheaper fare from Chicago is often possible through Northwest with a change of planes in Minneapolis. Continental offers a one-stop flight with no change of planes from Houston to Anchorage for $766 during the summer if booked 14 days in advance. From Boston, you can fly to Anchorage with one or two stops on Delta, United, Northwest or Continental, which often has the lowest fare. Still a round-trip, advance-purchase ticket will usually exceed $800.

Thanks to the arrival of American West Airlines and Reno Air to Anchorage, there have been some bargain air fares to Alaska recently. American West began service in 1996 and offered a Phoenix-to-Anchorage, round-trip fare for under $300, while from Columbus, Ohio, another hub for the relatively new airline, the same fare was $493.

The other strategy is to look for a cheap flight to Seattle with such discount carriers as Southwest Airlines (☎ (800) 444-5660) or American West and then book a second ticket with a different airline to Anchorage. Alaska Airlines is by far the largest carrier of travelers to Anchorage with 20 daily flights from Seattle as compared to two for United, Reno Air and Continental and one for Delta. During the off season and shoulder seasons (May and September) Alaska Airlines has non-refundable return fares from Seattle to Anchorage for as low as $218. The only requirement is that you book 21 days in advance, stay over at least one Saturday and return within a year. You might get a similar fare during the summer by requesting a 'red eye' flight with Reno Air, Delta or Alaska Airlines; these depart at between 9 pm and 2 am. Otherwise expect to pay between $300 and $350 for such a ticket during the high season of July and August.

Similar return fares between Seattle and Juneau on Alaska Airlines are $250, and between Seattle and Fairbanks are between $400 and $480. During the profitable summer season you can add $100 to $150 to that ticket for every stop you make along the way.

Alaska Airlines has a Web site on the Internet (http://www.alaskaair.com). It was still under construction in 1996 yet you could already check fares and book a reservation on it.

In short, air travel is the best way to go if you plan to spend three weeks or less touring Alaska or have the funds to afford the flight. But if you are planning to spend a month or more venturing through the state, you see more and pay less by combining the State Marine Ferry out of Bellingham with a bus ride into the rest of the state from Haines.

Canada

Canadian Airlines does not service Alaska but will fly you to Seattle where you can pick up a domestic US carrier for the second leg of your journey. The round-trip fare from Toronto to Seattle, for a ticket purchased 14 days in advance, is US$562.

The airline also has a marketing agreement with Alaska Airlines so it can book the US portion of your trip as well. A Toronto-to-Seattle-to-Juneau flight with both Canadian and Alaska Airlines is between US$800 and US$900. You can contact Canadian Airlines toll-free at ☎ (800) 665-1177 from throughout Canada and ☎ (800) 426-7000 in the USA.

Another option in Canada is to fly from Vancouver to Whitehorse on Canadian Airlines and then take an Air North Flight into either Juneau or Fairbanks. You can book through Canadian Airlines and such a round-trip flight to Juneau would be between US$500 and US$536. A round-trip Air North flight from Whitehorse to Juneau is US$155 and to Fairbanks between US$300 and US$350. The Whitehorse-based airline also offers a Klondike Explorer Pass for US$470. This allows unlimited air travel for 21 days between the five cities it serves: Juneau, Whitehorse, Dawson City, Old Crow and Fairbanks. In Alaska call Air North (☎ (800) 764-0407); in northern British Columbia and the Yukon Territory call ☎ (403) 668-2228.

The UK

British Airways no longer flies into Anchorage. It does have nonstop flights from London (Heathrow) to Seattle where you can pick up a domestic carrier to continue north. The round-tip fare is US$984 and the ticket must be booked 21 days in advance and your stay in the USA cannot exceed 45 days.

Northwest has a London-to-Anchorage flight that begins at Gatwick airport and changes planes in Detroit. A round-trip Apex fare is US$1312. Both Delta (Gatwick) and United Airlines (Heathrow) offer similar flights.

Continental Europe

The usual route to Anchorage from Europe is to head west with a stop in New York and then Seattle. From Paris, Continental offers a daily flight to Anchorage that changes planes in Houston and then makes an additional stop before reaching Alaska. A round-trip fare, purchased 14 days in advance, is US$1222. Northwest also has a

Air Shipping a Bicycle

A bicycle is a handy thing to haul up to Alaska, especially if your itinerary includes a lot of travel on the state ferry system. If set up to carry your equipment, a bike will allow you to easily explore the many small ports the ferries connect and then in the evening ride out of the towns to stay at campgrounds that are usually cheaper and much more scenic than those found in the town centers.

You have to pay extra for shipping a bike on the airlines (Alaska Airlines charges $45 each way) but this is usually far cheaper than renting one a handful of times during a trip. In the few towns where you can rent a quality bicycle, you can expect to pay anywhere from $20 to $35 a day.

The first step to air shipping your two-wheeler is to obtain a cardboard bike box. Most airlines will sell you one for around $10, but you can usually get one for free at your local bicycle shop. You will also need some bubble wrap, twine, duct tape, and a small block of wood or fork spacer.

Begin by removing and wrapping the seat and seatpost as a unit and then removing and wrapping both pedals. Open both brake quick releases and remove the handlebars and stem as a unit, then remove the front wheel. Place the small block of wood or spacer between the front-fork dropouts and then rotate the fork so that it faces backwards. You can protect the frame with the bubble wrap before placing the front wheel next to it and tying it in place. Align the handlebars-and-stem unit along the top tube with the stem inside the main frame triangle if you can, and then secure with the twine. Wrap the rear derailleur where it is likely to contact the box as well as any loose parts (pedals, seat and seatpost, etc). You can secure the parts in the box below the down tube. Lower the bike into the box and make sure nothing is loose or rattling around.

Reinforce the outside of the box with the duct tape and make sure all previous addresses and shipping labels are blacked out. Finally write your name and address all over the box. This is one piece of luggage you don't want to end up in Albuquerque instead of Anchorage. ∎

---

daily Paris-to-Anchorage flight that changes planes in Detroit. The round-trip fare is US$1250 but the ticket must be booked 21 days in advance, can only be used in July and August and the maximum stay in Alaska would be 30 days. You also have to travel between Monday and Thursday.

Similar flights can also be arranged from Frankfurt through Delta and Northwest and United Airlines. Northwest charges US$1769 for a round trip with a 21-day advance purchase ticket but allows you to stay up to three months. Travel must take place between Monday and Friday. Delta offers a similar ticket for US$1703. Balair/CTA, a line of Swissair, offers a nonstop Zurich-to-Anchorage flight every Wednesday May through September for US$1100 round-trip.

Asia

There are daily flights from Tokyo to Anchorage. None are direct, nonstop flights but several fly into Seattle or Los Angeles and then on to Alaska.

Keep in mind the fares with US-based airlines like Northwest and Delta fluctuate wildly with the rise and fall of the dollar against the yen.

Northwest flies into Seattle and onto Anchorage daily on an Apex round-trip fare of US$2356. Delta offers a daily flight that changes at Salt Lake City and has no requirements for length of stay; the round-trip fare is US$1813.

Japan Air Lines has discontinued its service to Anchorage and does not fly into Seattle. On JAL the best you can do is fly to San Francisco and then pick up an Alaska Airlines flight to Anchorage.

There is also daily service from Seoul to Anchorage which is far cheaper than departing from Tokyo. United Airlines offers a daily flight with a change of planes at San Francisco. Or you can fly nonstop four days a week with Korean Air. Its round-trip fare is US$1242 and requires only a four-day advance purchase.

There is also nonstop service between Taipei, Taiwan and Anchorage with China Air and daily service with United Airlines with a change of planes in San Francisco.

Australia & NZ

In Australia, STA and Flight Centres are major dealers in cheap air fares. They have branches in all the major cities. Otherwise, check the travel agents' ads in the Yellow Pages and ring around. Qantas Airways has flights from Sydney to Los Angeles with direct connections on Alaska Airlines to Anchorage. Several excursion (round-trip) fares are available. A return advance purchase ticket will cost from A$2822 and will allow you to stay up to two months in Alaska.

Air New Zealand has a similar agreement with Alaska Airlines. Most flights between the USA and New Zealand are to/from the USA's west coast and go through Los Angeles where you pick up an Alaska Airlines flight. Such a round-trip ticket is NZ$2736 if purchased 14 days in advance and is good for up to two months of travel.

Round-the-World Tickets

Round-the-World tickets allow you to fly on the combined routes of two or more airlines in one direction for a more economic journey around the globe. Several major airlines, including TWA and Continental, offer such tickets but unfortunately Anchorage is not one of the possible stopovers.

LAND – THE ALCAN

What began in April 1942 as an unprecedented construction project during the heat of WWII ended eight months later as the first overland link between the Lower 48 and Alaska, known formally as the Alaska-Canada Military Hwy and affectionately as the Alcan. Today, the Alcan (also known as the Alaska Hwy) is a road through the vast wilderness of north-west Canada and Alaska. It offers a spectacular drive enjoyed by thousands of travelers each summer who take their time to soak up the scenery, wildlife and clear, cold streams along the way.

For those with the time, the Alcan is a unique way to travel north. The trip is an adventure in itself; the 1520-mile road is a legend among highways and to complete the journey along the Alcan is a feather in any traveler's cap. *Mile 0* of the Alcan is at

Dawson Creek in British Columbia, while the other end is at Delta Junction.

The Alcan is now entirely asphalt-paved, and although sections of jarring potholes, frost heaves (the rippling effect of the pavement caused by freezing and thawing) and loose gravel still prevail, they offer nothing like the rough conditions it was famous for 20 years ago. The era of lashing spare fuel cans to the side of the car and gasoline stations every 250 miles is also gone. Food, gas and lodging can be found every 20 to 50 miles along the highway, with 100 miles being the longest stretch between fuel stops.

There are several ways to get to the Alcan: you can begin in the US states of Washington, Idaho or Montana and pass through Edmonton or Jasper in Alberta or Prince George in British Columbia, Canada. There are also several ways of traveling the highway: bus, car, a combination of State Marine Ferry and bus or the cheapest of all – hitchhiking.

Bus

A combination of buses will take you from Seattle via the Alcan to Anchorage, Fairbanks, Skagway or Haines for a moderate cost. There are no direct bus services from the Lower 48 to Alaska; travelers have to be patient as services here are more limited than in the rest of the country. Keep in mind, however, that a round trip on a bus from Seattle to Anchorage will end up costing you more than flying.

Greyhound The closest you can get to Alaska on this giant among bus companies is Whitehorse in British Columbia and this involves purchasing two tickets. You begin at the Greyhound station in the center of Seattle on the corner of 8th Ave and Stewart St where you can buy a one-way ticket to Vancouver for $25. The bus departs at least five times a day, more often if the demand is high during the summer. Call the station (☎ (206) 628-5530) to double-check exact departure days and times. You switch to a Greyhound Lines of Canada bus at Pacific

Central Station on Main St in Vancouver, and continue your journey north with a two-hour layover at Prince George and another at Dawson Creek, in British Columbia. The bus departs at 7.30 am on Monday, Wednesday and Friday and you arrive in Whitehorse at 4.30 am, 44 hours later – beat to hell most likely. The one-way fare from Vancouver to Whitehorse is C$292.

When planning your trip, remember that most Greyhound special offers, such as Ameripass (unlimited travel for seven days), do not apply to Yukon or Alaska destinations. Also keep in mind that if you plan to continue your travels on an Alaska Direct bus and don't want to overnight in Whitehorse, you have to pick up the Monday 7.30 am bus from Vancouver.

There is also a more pleasant way to reach Alaska than spending two days on a Greyhound bus. Once in Vancouver, you can also pick up a ticket to Prince Rupert, where you can then hop on a delightful Alaska Marine Hwy ferry. There are three buses a day, at 7.30 am, and 6 and 8.45 pm, and they arrive in Prince Rupert 12 hours later. The one-way fare is C$85. Call Greyhound Lines of Canada (☎ (604) 662-3222) for information.

Alaskon Express Once you've reached Whitehorse, you change to an Alaskon Express bus for the next leg of the journey. Gray Line of Alaska operates these buses from May to September, from either Westmark Whitehorse, at 2nd Ave and Steele St, or the Greyhound Bus Terminal at the north end of 2nd Ave.

Buses depart the Yukon capital for Anchorage on Tuesday, Thursday and Sunday at noon, stay overnight at Beaver Creek in the Yukon and then continue to Anchorage the next day, reaching the city at 7.30 pm. You can also get off the bus earlier at Tok, Glennallen or Palmer. On Monday, Wednesday and Saturday buses depart Whitehorse at noon for Haines, reaching the Southeast Alaska town and ferry terminal port at 6.30 pm.

As a testimony to the popularity of the Chilkoot Trail, an Alaskon Express bus

departs daily from Whitehorse at 4.30 pm for Skagway, stopping along the way to pick up backpackers coming off the popular trek.

You can also go overland to Fairbanks, something that was hard to do in the past. An Alaskon Express bus departs at noon on Tuesday, Thursday and Sunday for Fairbanks with a stopover in Beaver Creek. A nice thing about these buses is that you can flag them down along the road or in a small town, which is good if you have been sitting around for most of the morning trying to thumb a ride out of a town like Haines Junction. Can you imagine doing that to a Greyhound bus in the Lower 48?

The one-way fare from Whitehorse to Anchorage is $190, to Fairbanks $165, to Haines $85 and to Skagway $54; these fares do not include lodging at Beaver Creek. In Whitehorse, call ☎ (403) 667-2223 for current bus information. If you are still in the planning stages of your trip, call the toll-free US number for Gray Line of Alaska, ☎ (800) 544-2206, or fax (206) 281-0621; by January it can provide schedules, departure times and rates for the following summer.

Alaska Direct Busline Much smaller and slightly cheaper than Gray Line's Alaskon Express is Alaska Direct Busline based in Anchorage. On Tuesday, Friday and Sunday an Alaska Direct bus departs Whitehorse at 7 am, reaching Tok around 3 pm where you can continue on to Fairbanks or transfer to a bus for Anchorage.

The one-way fare from Whitehorse to Tok is $80, to Fairbanks $120 and Anchorage $145. In Alaska or the USA call Alaska Direct at ☎ (800) 770-6652; in Whitehorse call ☎ (403) 668-4833. Make sure you call to find out what hotel the pick-up point is or even if the company is still in business.

Norline Coaches This was the Canadian bus company that used to provide the final link between Whitehorse and Alaska but now runs between Whitehorse and Dawson City to the north. From June to September, buses depart from the Whitehorse bus terminal on Monday, Wednesday and Friday at 9 am and cover the 335 miles to Dawson City, arriving at 3.30 pm. The bus then turns around and repeats the trip the same day. The one-way fare is C$72.

While many feel this is the more scenic and adventurous route into Alaska, there is no bus transport beyond Dawson City and the hitch across the border through Chicken and down to Tok can be a long wait at times. For current rates and schedules call the Whitehorse Bus Terminal at ☎ (403) 668-3355, which handles information for Norline, Greyhound Lines of Canada and Alaska Direct.

AlaskaPass

A concept which has been hugely popular in Europe for years arrived in the North Country in 1989 when a small company in Haines (of all places) organized nine major carriers and offered an unlimited travel pass. AlaskaPass Inc, now with headquarters in Seattle, offers the only all-inclusive ground transportation pass that will get you from Washington through Canada into Alaska and even as far north as Dawson City in the Yukon for a set price.

You purchase your pass, choosing the number of days you want to travel, then, armed with a list of schedules of various carriers, make your own reservations or arrangements.

The carriers include Alaska Marine Hwy, Greyhound Lines of Canada, Island Coach Lines, British Columbia Rail and British Columbia Ferries to move you north from Bellingham or Vancouver. You can continue on Alaskon Express, Norline Coaches or the Alaska Railroad to reach Alaska and then travel around the state. Each time you pick up a ticket you simply flip them your AlaskaPass.

On the plus side, you can save money with such a pass. On the down side you have to plan carefully to do so and the pass does not include any air travel.

The passes are offered for either continuous or flexible travel which allows travel on a number of days during a time period. The latter is a much better choice as it leaves you

time to enjoy an area or take side trips before moving on.

The eight-day pass is $499 but there is a $50 surcharge if you use it in Bellingham to board the Alaska Marine Hwy ferry. The longest is the 30-day pass at $899. Still better over the long haul is the 12/21-day pass (travel 12 out of 21 days) for $669 and the 21/45 for $949. There are discounts for children, aged between three and 11 years, and for an off-season pass for travel from October to April.

You can purchase a pass ahead of time from most travel agents or directly from the company by calling ☎ (800) 248-7598 or from the UK at ☎ (800) 89-82-85. You can receive information by faxing them at (800) 488-0303.

Driving the Alcan

Without a doubt, driving your own car to Alaska allows you the most freedom. You can leave when you want, stop where you feel like it and pretty much make up your itinerary as you travel along. It's not exactly cheap driving to Alaska, and that's not even considering the wear and tear and thousands of miles you'll clock up on your vehicle.

If you're contemplating this car trip, remember that the condition of your tires is most important. The Alcan may be paved but it's constantly under repair and stretches of frost heaves and pot holes are common, especially on the Canadian side; worn tires don't last long here.

Even your spare, and you *must* have one, should be fairly new. You should also avoid the newer 'space-saver' spares, and carry a full-size spare as your extra tire.

Replace windshield wipers before you depart and carry an extra set along with a gallon of solvent for the windshield-washer reservoir. Dust, dirt and mud make good visibility a constant battle while driving. Also bring a jack, wrenches and other assorted tools, spare hoses, fan belts and a quart of oil or two; even an extra headlight or air filter is not being too extreme. Carry them and hope you never have to use them.

Some travelers use an insect screen, others

put plastic headlight covers or a wire-mesh screen over the headlights, and others place a rubber mat or piece of carpet between the gas tank and securing straps. All this is to protect the vehicle from the worst danger on the road – flying rocks that are kicked up by truck-and-trailer rigs passing you.

By far the worst problem on the Alcan and many other roads in Alaska and the Yukon is dust – that's why even on the hottest days you see most cars with their windows up. To control dust in an RV or trailer, reverse the roof vent on your rig so it faces forward. Then keep it open a few inches while driving, creating air pressure inside to combat the incoming dust.

Those traveling the route in small or compact vehicles often face another problem – an overloaded car. Stuffing the trunk and the backseat and then lashing on a car-top carrier in order to take along extra boxes of macaroni-and-cheese dinners could do you in, miles from anywhere. It's been said that the biggest single cause of flat tires and broken suspension systems along the Alcan is an overloaded car.

Since almost 80% of the Alcan is in Canada, it's best to brush up on the metric system or have a conversion chart taped to the dashboard. On the Canada side you'll find kilometer posts (as opposed to the mileposts found in Alaska) which are placed every five km with the zero point in Dawson Creek.

With more than 1000 vehicles passing through this town en route to Alaska daily during the summer, it's the one place where you might want to book a room or a camp site in advance. Most Alcan veterans say 300 miles a day is a good pace – one that will allow for plenty of stops to check out scenery or wildlife.

The best stretch? That's tough but some will argue it's the 330 miles from Fort Nelson (British Columbia) to Watson Lake (Yukon). This is the day you cross the Rockies and along with the hairpin turns and granite peaks, you'll enjoy panoramas of the mountains; enjoy rest areas overlooking Summit Lake and stand a good chance of spotting wildlife, especially if you leave early in the morning.

It's always good to have Canadian currency on hand to purchase gasoline or plan on using a major credit card, which will also result in an accurate exchange rate. One or two of the major gasoline credit cards also come in handy, especially if you have a major breakdown. The other thing to keep in mind is that Tourism Yukon operates a number of visitor reception centers that provide a wealth of information and maps for drivers. The ones along the Alcan are:

Watson Lake
> Alaska Highway Interpretive Center, at the junction of the Alcan and Campbell St (☎ (403) 536-7469)

Whitehorse
> Visitor Center near Milepost 886, adjacent to the Transportation Museum (☎ (403) 667-2915)

Haines Junction
> Visitor Center, at Kluane National Park Headquarters (☎ (403) 634-2345)

Beaver Creek
> Visitor Center, at Mile 1202 of the Alcan in the heart of Beaver Creek (☎ (403) 862-7321)

Books The following two guidebooks will make interesting reading as you bump and rattle your way through the North Country. The books can be obtained through Alaska Natural History Association (☎ (907) 274-8440), Mail Order Services, 605 West 4th Ave, Ste 85, Anchorage, AK 99501.

Roadside Geology of Alaska by Cathy Connor & Daniel O'Haire (Mountain Press Publishing, Missoula, Montana; 250 pages, $14) does an excellent job of covering the geology of Alaska you see from the road and explaining how it shaped the state's history and development. Every road and sea route is covered, even dead-end roads in the Southeast. Along the way you learn what happened during the Good Friday Earthquake and why miners turned up gold on the beaches of Nome – not dull reading by any means.

Wildflowers along the Alaska Highway by Verna Pratt (Alaskakrafts, 7446 East 20th Ave, Anchorage, AK 99504; 240 pages, $20.00). Written for the amateur botanist, this guide to the wildflowers of the Alcan has species keyed by color and includes 497 color photographs and a check list for each 300-mile section of the road.

Hitching the Alcan

Hitching is probably more common in Alaska than it is in the rest of the USA, and more so on the rural dirt roads such as the McCarthy Rd or the Denali Hwy than the major paved routes. But this doesn't mean it's a totally safe way of getting around. Just because we explain how it works doesn't mean we recommend it. If you are properly prepared and have sufficient time, thumbing the Alcan can be an easy way to see the country, meet people and save money.

The Alcan seems to inspire the pioneer spirit in travelers who drive it. Drivers are good about picking up hitchhikers, much better than those across the Lower 48 – the only problem is that there aren't as many of them. In some places along the route you may have to wait 30 minutes or longer before a car passes by. During the summer, the number of vehicles increases significantly, but if you're attempting the trip in early spring or late fall, be prepared to wait hours or even overnight at one of a handful of junctions along the way.

All hitchhikers should be self-sufficient with a tent, some food, water, warm clothing and a good book or two. Hitchhikers must be patient and not over-anxious to reach their destination. Moving through the USA and southern Canada, you will get the usual short and long rides from one city to the next. Once you make it to Dawson Creek it will probably only take you one or two longer rides to reach your destination.

Any part of the Alcan can be slow, but some sections are notorious. The worst can be Haines Junction, the crossroads in the Yukon where southbound hitchhikers occasionally have to stay overnight before catching a ride to Haines in Southeast Alaska. Longer waits may also occur if you are heading home in late summer or early fall and thumbing out of Glennallen, Tok or Delta Junction back into Canada and the Lower 48. A sign with your destination on it helps, as does displaying your backpack, which tells drivers you're a summer traveler.

The hardest part of the trip for many is crossing the US-Canadian border. Canadian officials usually pull cars over if the passengers are not of the same nationality as the driver, and they will ask to see proof of sufficient funds. Anybody without prearranged transport is required to have $80 per day to travel through Canada or a total of $200 to $250.

The Canadians are not hassling hitchhikers when they do this, they're just making sure that visitors don't get stuck somewhere for a week because they've run out of money. On the way to Alaska, most travelers will have these funds; on the way back, however, it may be difficult if you are at the end of your trip and without money.

Three places to make contacts for a ride back to the Lower 48 are the Anchorage International Hostel; the Wood Center in the middle of the University of Alaska campus in Fairbanks, which has a noticeboard for students offering or needing rides; and the Chamber of Commerce hospitality center in Tok, where the free coffee pulls in many drivers before they continue into Canada. If you are heading north, the noticeboard outside the tourist office in Dawson Creek is worth checking as it often contains messages from people looking for somebody to help with fuel costs.

With luck, it can take you less than a week to hitchhike from Seattle to Fairbanks or Anchorage, but to be on the safe side, plan on the trip taking from seven to eight days. The route from Seattle to Alaska is good as it is the most direct and has the most traffic to Dawson Creek. This combines hitching along the Interstate 5 in Washington to the Canadian border, the Trans Canada Hwy 1 to Cache Creek, and Hwy 97 north to Dawson Creek and the Alcan.

An alternative to hitching the entire Alcan is to take the Alaska Marine Hwy ferry from Bellingham in Washington to Haines and start hitching from there, cutting the journey in half but still traveling along the highway's most spectacular parts. Haines, however, is a town of about 1150 people and traffic is light on the road to the Alcan at Haines Junction. It is best to hustle off the ferry and begin thumbing as vehicles unload, so that you can try to catch a driver heading north. Or seek out a lift while you are still on the boat by taping a notice outside the ship's cafeteria or showers.

SEA
The Inside Passage
As an alternative to the Alcan or to avoid doubling back on the highway, you can travel the Southeast's Inside Passage, a waterway made up of thousands of islands, fjords and mountainous coastlines. To many, the Southeast is the most beautiful area in the state and the Alaska Marine Hwy ferries are the country's best public transport bargain.

The large 'blue canoes' of the Alaska Marine Hwy are equipped with observation decks, food services, lounges and solariums with deck chairs. You can rent a stateroom for overnight trips but most backpackers head straight for the solarium and sleep in one of the deck chairs or on the floor with a sleeping pad. On long-distance hauls from Bellingham, travelers even pitch their dome tents.

With its leisurely pace, travel on the ferries is a delightful experience. The midnight sun is warm and, apart from the scenery, the possibility of sighting whales, bald eagles or sea lions keeps most travelers at the side of the ship. This is also an excellent way to meet other independent travelers heading for a summer in the north country.

Bellingham, Washington Bellingham is the southern terminus of the Alaska Marine Hwy and includes an information center, a ticket office, luggage lockers and an outdoor seating area with a nice view of Bellingham Bay and the surrounding hills. It's 10 minutes north of the Bellingham international airport in the historic Fairhaven shopping district, 87 miles north of Seattle. From the Interstate 5 Hwy, you depart west on Fairhaven Parkway (exit 250) for 1.1

miles and then turn right onto 12th St where signs will direct you to the terminal at the end of Harris Ave.

The ferries are extremely popular during the peak season from June to August. Reservations are needed for cabin or vehicle space and for walk-on passengers on departures from Bellingham. Space for summer sailings from Bellingham is often filled by April, forcing walk-on passengers to wait stand-by for an available spot.

If you plan to depart Bellingham in June or July, it is best to make reservations. The Alaska Marine Hwy's reservation office will take written requests any time and telephone requests from the first working day of January for summer sailings. As telephone lines are jammed most of the time after the first day of the year, it is wise to send in a written request as soon as you can figure out your itinerary. When writing or faxing in the reservation provide port of embarkation; names and ages of all travellers; width, height and overall length of vehicle including trailers; mailing address; telephone numbers; alternative travel dates; and the date you will be leaving home.

The summer sailing schedule comes out in December and you can obtain one by contacting the Alaska Marine Hwy (☎ (907) 465-3941), PO Box 35535, Juneau, AK 99802-5535. There is now a toll-free telephone number (☎ (800) 642-0066 from the Lower 48) to handle schedule requests and reservations but you'll often find it nonstop busy, which forces you to pay for the call anyway. You can also choose to fax in your reservation at (907) 277-4829 or look at fares or even the current schedule located on the Internet at http://www.dot.state.ak.us/external/amhs/home.html.

The ferries to Alaska stop first at Prince Rupert in British Columbia, and then continue on to Ketchikan in Alaska. Most ferries then depart for Wrangell, Petersburg, Sitka, Juneau, Haines and Skagway before heading back south. A trip from Bellingham to Juneau takes from 2½ to four days depending on the route. Most ferry terminals are a few miles out of town and the short in-port time doesn't allow passengers to view the area without making a stopover.

If you intend to use the ferries to view the Southeast, obtain a current schedule and keep it handy at all times. The ferries stop almost every day at larger centers like Juneau, but the smaller villages may only have one ferry every three or four days and many places won't have a service at all.

There are six ships working Southeast Alaska; four of them are larger vessels that sail the entire route from Bellingham to Skagway. The *Columbia*, *Malaspina*, *Matanuska* and *Taku* all have cabins, lounges, eating facilities and public showers for both walk-on passengers and cabin renters.

The other two ships are smaller and serve out-of-the-way villages from Juneau or Ketchikan. In the summer, the *Aurora* sails between Ketchikan, Metlakatla, Hollis, Hyder and Prince Rupert. The *Le Conte* stops at Juneau, Hoonah, Angoon, Sitka, Kake, Tenakee Springs, Skagway, Haines and Petersburg, and makes a special run to Pelican once a month.

It's important when you book a passage on the ferry that you have an idea of what ports you want to visit along the route. Stopovers are free but you must arrange them, with exact dates, whenever you make the reservation or purchase the ticket. By doing so, a Bellingham-to-Haines ticket would then allow you to leave the boat at a handful of cities including Ketchikan, Petersburg and Juneau at no additional cost. Once on the boat you can still arrange a stopover but will be charged an additional fee. If you plan to spend a good deal of time or the entire summer in the region, purchase a ticket to Juneau and then use that as your base, taking shorter trips to other towns on the *Le Conte*. The fare for walk-on passengers from Bellingham to Haines is $240, while the ticket from Bellingham to Juneau is $226.

One way to save money is to take a bus or hitchhike to Prince Rupert in British Columbia where the dramatic mountain scenery begins, and hop on the ferry from there. The fare from Prince Rupert to Haines is $118 and to Juneau $104.

The *Alaska Marine Highway Schedule* is now a magazine with not only departure times and fares but also ads, blurbs on each port and a section entitled 'What to Expect on Board'. Here are a few tips they don't tell you. When boarding in Bellingham, it is best to scramble to the solarium and either stake out a lounge chair or at least an area on the floor. The solarium and observation deck are the best places to sleep as the air is clean and the night-time peace is unbroken. The other places to crash out are the indoor lounges, which can be smoky, noisy or both.

Backpackers are still allowed to pitch free-standing tents outside the solarium and the ferry staff even designate the correct area for doing so. Bring duck tape to attach the tent to the floor but remember that during a busy summer tents tend to take up more space than two people really need in an already popular and crowded section of the ship.

Food on board is reasonably priced compared to what you will pay on shore, with breakfast and lunches costing around $4 to $6 and dinner $7 to $10. Still it's cheaper to bring your own grub and eat it in the solarium or the cafeteria. Some backpackers bring their own tea bags, coffee or instant soup and then just purchase the cup of hot water. The pursers, however, do not allow any camp stoves to be used on board and are very strict about enforcing this.

The only things cheaper than the food on board are the showers. They're free on all ferries except the MV *Tustumena* and then only cost 25 cents for 10 minutes. They are the best bargain you'll find in Alaska.

There is a tariff for carrying on bicycles or kayaks, but compared to the cost of bringing a car or motorcycle it is very reasonable. The cost is only $39 to take what ferry officials call an 'alternative means of conveyance' from Bellingham to Haines. A bicycle can be a handy way to see at least part of a town without disembarking for a few days, while a summer (or even a lifetime) can be spent using the ferry system to hop from one wilderness kayak trip to another.

All fares listed in the book are for adults (consider to be anybody 12 years and older).

You'll find the fares for children aged from two to 11 years about half the price of an adult fare and children under two years travel free. The ferry system also offers 50% discount passes to both senior citizens and disabled persons. Both are restricted to travel between Alaskan ports when space is available and can be used only for the *Le Conte*, *Aurora*, *Bartlett* and *Tustumena*. Applications for a disabled pass must be filed in advance by writing to: Alaska Marine Highway System, Pass Desk, PO Box 25535, Juneau, AK 99802-5535.

Above all else, when using the Alaska Marine Hwy system, check and double-check the departures of ferries once you have arrived in the Southeast. It is worth a phone call to the terminal to find out actual arrival and departure times; the ferries are notorious for being late or breaking down and having their departures cancelled. It's something that happens every summer without fail.

Prince Rupert, British Columbia (Canada) If the Alaska Marine Hwy ferries are full in Bellingham, one alternative is to begin your cruise in Seattle, utilizing two ferry systems before switching to the Alaska line in Prince Rupert.

From Pier 69 in the heart of Seattle off Alaskan Way, catch the *Victoria Clipper* to Victoria on Vancouver Island. During the summer, boats depart at least four times daily at 7.30, 8 and 9 am and 4 pm for a trip that takes from 2½ to three hours. The one-way fare for walk-on passengers is $55. For pretrip planning or reservations call ☎ (800) 888-2535 when you are in the USA.

Once you land on Vancouver Island, head north to Port Hardy and catch the BC Ferries to Prince Rupert. From this Canadian city, you have a much better chance of boarding the Alaska Marine Hwy ferry because there are five vessels that connect Prince Rupert to Southeast Alaska. Port Hardy can be reached by bus from Victoria on Pacific Coast Lines (☎ (604) 385-4411), which leaves once a day at 6.20 am for a one-way fare of C$78. The bus depot is at 700 Douglas St, behind the Empress Hotel in the center of Victoria.

At Port Hardy, the BC Ferries dock at Bear Cove is about five miles from town but there is a shuttle van service from the Island Coach Line bus terminal on Main St. At Bear Cove the *Queen of the North* departs at 7.30 am and reaches Prince Rupert at 10.30 pm on one day and returns to Vancouver Island the next, maintaining this every-other-day schedule from June to the end of September. The trip is scenic and the daylight voyage takes 15 hours; the one-way fare for walk-on passengers is C$100. The same ship also makes a stop once a week at the isolated town of Bella Bella in British Columbia.

More information and complete schedules for the BC Ferries can be obtained by calling or writing to BC Ferries (☎ (604) 386-3431), 1112 Fort St, Victoria, British Columbia, Canada V8V 4V2. In Vancouver call ☎ (604) 669-1211 for detailed ferry information and reservations.

Hyder If for some strange reason you can't catch an Alaska Marine Hwy ferry at Prince Rupert, there's a last alternative. Make your way east along the Yellowhead Hwy from Prince Rupert and then head north along the Cassiar Hwy. You travel 99 miles along the scenic Cassiar Hwy and then turn off at Kitwanga for Stewart. You can either hitch this route or catch a Greyhound bus to Kitwanga, basically the junction of Hwy 16 and Hwy 37 reached an hour before the town of Terrace. At the Petro-Can Service Station, a Seaport Limousine Service bus (☎ (604) 636-2622) stops by daily at 4 pm from Monday to Friday and for C$21 will take you to Stewart. Across the border from Stewart is Hyder, a Southeast Alaska hamlet of about 100 people with cafes, bars and gift shops.

During the summer, the Alaska Marine Hwy ferry *Aurora* usually departs from here two Tuesdays a month at 3.45 pm for Ketchikan, where you can continue north on one of several other boats. The one-way fare from Hyder to Ketchikan is $40.

Note It is vital to double-check the departure time for the Hyder ferry as it may leave on Pacific Time as opposed to Alaska Time.

ORGANIZED TOURS

The land of the midnight sun is also the land of the package tour. Every cruise-ship line and sightseeing company loves Alaska and the draw it has on travelers, especially older tourists with lots of disposable income but not a high sense of adventure.

Actually, package tours can often be the most affordable way to see a large chunk of Alaska if your needs include the better hotels in each town and a full breakfast every morning. Just keep in mind they move quickly and rarely offer enough extra time to undertake such activities as a wilderness trek or a paddle into Glacier Bay National Park. A thumbnail sketch of just the largest tour companies follows.

Gray Line

You see this company so often throughout the state that it seems to practically own Alaska. Seattle-based Gray Line offers 19 package tours into the Far North that begin in various cities, including Seattle, Vancouver and Anchorage. The All Alaska Air Tour is an 11-day trip that includes Juneau, Anchorage, Denali, Fairbanks and part of the Alcan for $2150 per person based on double occupancy – if this is Thursday, this must be Tok.

It also has a number of shorter ones that begin and end in Alaska such as the Denali/ Prince William Sound Discovery, seven-day tour from Anchorage that includes Fairbanks, Denali and Columbia Glacier for $1275 per person. Or the Prince William Sound Tour, a two-day bus and cruise-ship journey past the Columbia Glacier for $295 per person. Most of its tours within the state are covered in detail in the regional chapters. If you're interested in a complete package tour throw away this book and call Gray Line at ☎ (800) 628-2449 to get its slick brochure.

American Sightseeing

Another biggie in Alaska, this company offers dozens of itineraries, including cruises/tours out of Seattle, and Alaska land tours that begin in Anchorage. A cruise tour on the company's *Spirit of Discovery* begins at $2494 during the peak season for an eight-day trip out of Seattle through Southeast Alaska, including Glacier Bay National Park. The company's Prince William Sound & Denali Park land tour is a six-day trip that includes Columbia Glacier, Denali National Park and Fairbanks for $1145. It begins and ends in Anchorage and doesn't include air fare to Alaska. Call Alaska Sightseeing at ☎ (800) 426-7702.

Knightly Tours

This company offers budget package tours for independent travelers; in other words you're not being herded around with 100 others. It does the bookings and reservations for you, from the Alaska State Marine Ferry system and side tours with American Sightseeing to all your hotels along the way. Knightly Tours also offers a varied selection of other tours that cover the state in a fashion that's similar to Gray Line. For its complete brochure call ☎ (800) 426-2123.

Natural Habitat Adventures

This tour company specialises in animal-watching adventures around the world including several in Alaska. Most tour members sign up for the opportunity to photograph the wildlife, which in Alaska could include brown bears, moose, whales, sea lions, caribou and bald eagles. An 11-day tour that includes whale watching in Glacier Bay and viewing giant brown bears on Kodiak Island is $3995. All tours include accommodation but air fare to Anchorage is extra. For a catalog call the company at ☎ (800) 543-8917.

Green Tortoise

At the other end of the spectrum is Green Tortoise Alternative Travel, the company with recycled buses whose seats have been replaced with foam-covered platforms, sofas and dinettes.

When not sleeping on the bus during night drives, Green Tortoise groups use state and federal campgrounds for accommodation and make an effort to include hiking, rafting and other outdoor activities on their itinerary. Food is not included in the fare but the bus travelers pool their funds to purchase goods in bulk and then prepare food in group cookouts.

On Green Tortoise tours, group interaction is a large part of the experience. Everybody pitches in during meal time and spontaneous volleyball matches or Frisbee games are frequent activities during rest breaks. Beer and wine are allowed on the bus and people are encouraged to bring musical instruments. Although passengers could be any age, the vast majority of people are in their 20s or early 30s.

This type of travel is not for everybody, especially if you suddenly discover you don't get along with half the people on the bus.

Some readers have also complained about a general 'lack of organization' about the trips and 'dictatorial drivers'.

Still there's no cheaper tour then Green Tortoise. The company runs a pair of four-week tours through Alaska in June and then again in July which includes cruising through Southeast Alaska on the State Marine Ferry as well as stops in the Yukon Territory, Fairbanks, Denali National Park, Kenai Peninsula and then returning home along the Alcan. The bus can be picked up in San Francisco (California), Eugene and Portland (Oregon) or Seattle (Washington). The fare ($1500) covers everything except food and side trips.

For more information write to Green Tortoise (☎ (415) 821-0803 or (800) 867-8647), PO Box 494 Broadway, San Francisco, CA 94133.

Cruises

The biggest growth in Alaskan tourism during the past few years has been the number of cruise lines now sailing up the Inside Passage and beyond.

In 1995, nine lines deployed 22 major ships in Alaskan waters during the May-through-September season that included the 1075-passenger *Rotterdam* and the 1590-passenger *Regal Princess*. There also are a dozen smaller vessels, which can hold 49 to 100 passengers each, sailing around the state.

Actually an Alaskan cruise can be a bargain with an early booking and a budget cabin. Two people sharing a cabin can often get a seven-day Alaskan cruise for $700 to $800 a person if they book it by February or March. That covers your food, lodging and transportation. Not bad if you want to zip through a portion of Alaska in seven days. Keep in mind just about everything else, including drinks on the boat, entertainment and on shore activities and tours, is an additional fee.

If that's what you're looking for throw away this book and contact a travel agent. Some of the large-vessel leaders of the Alaskan flotilla are Cunard Line (☎ (800) 221-4770), Regency Cruises (☎ (800) 388-5500), Norwegian Cruise Line (☎ (800) 327-7030) and Princess Cruises (☎ (800) 421-5522).

DEPARTURE TAXES

When you leave Alaska, there are no additional state or airport departure taxes to worry about.

WARNING

The information in this chapter is particularly vulnerable to change: prices for international travel are volatile, routes are introduced and cancelled, schedules change, special deals come and go, and rules and visa requirements are amended. Airlines and governments seem to take a perverse pleasure in making price structures and regulations as complicated as possible. You should check directly with the airline or a travel agent to make sure you understand how a fare (and ticket you may buy) works. In addition, the travel industry is highly competitive and there are many lurks and perks.

The upshot of this is that you should get opinions, quotes and advice from as many airlines and travel agents as possible before you part with your hard-earned cash. The details given in this chapter should be regarded as pointers and are not a substitute for your own careful, up-to-date research.

Getting Around

Touring Alaska on a budget means not departing from the roads and not traveling in areas without a ferry dock. Travelers on a strict budget, however, shouldn't worry because although the roads and the marine highway (the cheapest ways to travel) cover only a quarter of the state, this quarter comprises the most popular regions of Alaska and includes the major attractions, parks and cities.

Even if there is a road to your destination, travel around Alaska is unlike travel in any other state in the country. The overwhelming distances between regions, and the fledgling public transport system make getting around almost as hard as getting there. Any long visit to Alaska usually combines transport by car, bus, marine ferry, train and often a bush plane for access into the wilderness.

AIR
Bush Planes

When you want to see more than the roadside attractions, you go to a dirt runway or small airfield outside town and climb into a bush plane. With 75% of the state not accessible by road, these small single-engine planes are the backbone of intrastate transport. They carry residents and supplies to desolate areas of the Bush, take anglers to some of the best fishing spots in the country and drop off backpackers in the middle of prime, untouched wilderness.

The person at the controls is a bush pilot, someone who might be fresh out of the US Air Force or somebody who arrived in Alaska 'way bee-fore statehood' and learned to fly by trial and error. A ride with such a person is not only transport to isolated areas and a scenic view of the state but it also can include an earful of flying tales – some believable, some not.

Don't be alarmed when you hear that Alaska has the highest number of aeroplane crashes per capita in the country – it also has the greatest percentage of pilots. One in

every 58 residents has a license, and one resident in almost 60 owns a plane. That's six times more pilots and 16 times more planes per capita than any other state in the USA. Bush pilots are safe flyers who know their territory and its weather patterns; they don't want to go down any more than you do.

A ride in a bush plane is essential if you want to go beyond the common sights and see some of Alaska's most memorable scenery. In the larger cities of Anchorage, Fairbanks, Juneau and Ketchikan it pays to check around before chartering. In most small towns and villages, however, you will be lucky if there is a choice. In the following regional chapters, air-taxi services are listed under the town or area from which they operate.

Bush aircraft include float planes that land and take off on water and beach-landers with oversized tires that can use rough gravel shorelines as air strips. Other aircraft are equipped with skis to land on glaciers, sophisticated radar instruments for stormy areas like the Aleutian Islands, or boat racks to carry canoes or hard-shell kayaks.

The fares differ with the type of plane, its size, the number of passengers and the amount of flying time. On the average, a Cessna 185 that can carry three passengers and a limited amount of gear will cost up to $250 to charter for an hour of flying time. A Cessna 206, a slightly larger plane that will hold four passengers, costs up to $300 and a Beaver, capable of hauling five passengers with gear averages $400 for an hour of flying time. Keep in mind that when chartering a plane to drop you off at an isolated USFS cabin or for a wilderness trek, you must pay for both the air time to your drop-off point and for the return to the departure point.

As a general rule, if Alaska Airlines has a flight to your destination, it will be the cheapest way of flying there. There is a huge difference between a one-way fare and a round-trip fare that is purchased 14 days in advance and includes staying over on a Saturday. A sample of Alaska Airlines round-trip Apex fares for intrastate flights is: Anchorage to Fairbanks \$140 to \$168; Juneau to Anchorage \$200 to \$250; Anchorage to Nome \$350; Anchorage to Kodiak \$200; Juneau to Cordova \$253; Juneau to Sitka \$98; and Juneau to Petersburg \$151.

Before chartering your own plane, check out all the possibilities. Most air-taxi companies have regularly scheduled flights to small towns and villages in six to nine-seater aircraft with single-seat fares that are a fraction of the cost of chartering an entire plane. Others offer a 'mail flight' to small villages. These flights are run on a regular basis with one or two seats available to travelers.

Even when your destination is a USFS cabin or some wilderness spot, check with the local air-taxi companies. It is a common practise to match up a party departing from the cabin with another that's arriving, so that the air-charter costs can be split by filling the plane on both runs.

Booking a plane is easy and often can be done the day before or at the last minute if need be. Double-check all pick-up times and places when flying to a wilderness area. Bush pilots fly over the pick-up point and if you are not there, they usually return, call the USFS and still charge you for the flight.

When flying in and out of bays, fjords or coastal waterways, check the tides before determining your pick-up time. It is best to schedule pick-ups and drop-offs at high tide or else you may end up tramping a half-mile through mud flats.

Always schedule extra days around a charter flight. It's not uncommon to be 'socked in' by weather for a day or two until a plane can fly in. Don't panic: they know you are there. Just think of the high school basketball team in the mid-1960s which flew to King Cove in the Aleutians for a weekend game – they were 'socked in' for a month before they could fly out again.

When traveling to small Bush towns, a scheduled flight or mail run is the cheapest way to go. Don't hesitate, however, to charter a flight to some desolate wilderness

Skipping the Alcan

Upon reaching Haines, many independent travelers continue their Alaskan adventure by heading north through Canada's Yukon Territory to the Alcan (Alaska Hwy). They drive, hitchhike or bus the famous highway to the state's interior, viewing Denali National Park and possibly Fairbanks before heading south towards Anchorage.

For travelers who were enchanted by the Southeast and the Alaska Marine Hwy and want to avoid the long days on the Alcan, there is a pleasant and cheaper alternative from Juneau. For slightly less than the price of a Haines-to-Anchorage bus ticket, you can fly one-way on Alaska Airlines from Juneau to Cordova (\$181), another remote coastal fishing town. From Cordova you can jump on the southwest system of the Alaska Marine Hwy to explore Southcentral Alaska to the west. Known by many as the Gulf Coast region, this area is really a continuation of Alaska's rugged coastal playground that begins in Ketchikan. ■

spot on your own; the best that Alaska has to offer is usually just a short flight away.

BUS

Regular bus services within Alaska are limited, but they are available between the larger towns and cities for independent travelers (as opposed to package tours) at reasonable rates. The only problem is that as one bus company goes under another appears, so the phone numbers, schedules, rates and pick-up points change drastically from one summer to the next. It pays to call ahead after arriving in Alaska to make sure that buses are still running to where you want to go.

Alaskon Express

These buses are the Gray Line motorcoaches which mainly serve travelers needing transport along the last leg of the Alcan from Whitehorse into Haines, Skagway, Anchorage or Fairbanks (see the Land – The Alcan section in the Getting There & Away chapter). You can also use the bus line to travel from Anchorage to Glennallen (\$59),

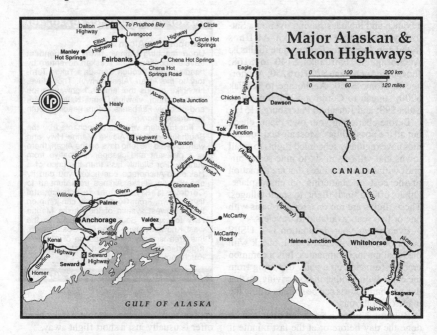

from Anchorage to Seward ($39) or from Tok to Fairbanks ($67).

From Haines, you can book a passage on Alaskon Express for the two-day run to Anchorage which leaves every Tuesday, Thursday and Sunday at 8.15 am for $185. The service is offered from mid-May to mid-September and the fare does not include overnight lodging at Beaver Creek. The same is true for Skagway where there is an Alaskon Express bus departing at 7.30 am on the same days, overnighting at Beaver Creek and reaching Anchorage at 7.30 pm. The reverse routes are also possible.

Local passenger boarding points, departure times and phone numbers are given in later chapters. For information or reservations while planning your trip, contact Gray Line of Alaska (☎ (800) 544-2206), 300 Elliott Ave West, Seattle, WA 98119.

Alaska Direct Bus Line

Alaska Direct offers affordable transporta-

tion from Anchorage to the rest of the state on a number of routes. On Monday, Wednesday and Saturday a bus departs Anchorage at 6 am and reaches Whitehorse at midnight. The next day there is a van service to Skagway. The one-way fare from Anchorage to Skagway is $180.

A bus also departs Fairbanks on Monday, Wednesday and Saturday at 9 am for a similar run to Skagway. The one-way fare from Fairbanks to Tok is $40, to Skagway $155.

Buses stop at the major hotels in Anchorage for passengers or you can pick them up at the company office at 125 Oklahoma on the north end of town. For more information call Alaska Direct Bus Line at ☎ (907) 277-6652 or (800) 770-6652.

Seward Bus Lines

This company provides services between Anchorage and Seward and used to run buses to Kenai and Homer but dropped that portion of its bus route in 1995. A bus leaves Seward daily at 9 am, reaches Anchorage at noon and then departs at 2.30 pm for the return run, arriving at Seward at 5.30 pm; the one-way fare is $30. Pick up these buses at 1915 Seward Hwy just north of Seward and at Alaska Samovar Inn, 720 Gambell St in Anchorage. Call ☎ (907) 224-3608 for current schedules and rates.

Denali National Park Van Service
A number of small companies offer van transport between Denali National Park and both Anchorage and Fairbanks. They come and go with a great regularity but generally offer the cheapest transport to the popular park and usually get you there well ahead of the train, an important consideration if you are hoping to arrange shuttle-bus rides, campground sites or backpacking permits.

In Anchorage, try Moon Bay Express (☎ (907) 274-6454) which departs daily from the hostel at 8 am and reaches the park at 1 pm. The one-way fare is $35, round-trip $60. There is also Alaska Backpacker Shuttle (☎ 344-8775) and Parks Highway Express (☎ 479-3065). In Fairbanks, there is Fireweed Express (☎ (907) 452-0521) which departs from the Fairbanks Visitor Center at 8 am, reaches the park at 10.30 am and charges $25 one way, $45 round-trip.

TRAIN
In a state the size of Alaska, the logistics of building a railroad were overwhelming at the turn of the century; many private companies tried but failed, leading to federal government intervention in 1912. Three years later, construction began on a route from the tent city of Anchorage to the boom town of Fairbanks. The line cut its way over what were thought to be impenetrable mountains, across raging rivers and through a wilderness as challenging as any construction crew had faced in the history of American railroading.

No wonder it took them eight years to build the Alaska Railroad. Today, it stretches 470 miles from Seward to Fairbanks and provides a good, though rarely the cheapest, means of transport for travelers. The scenery on each route, however, is spectacular. You'll save more money bussing the George Parks Hwy, but few travelers, even those counting their dimes, regret booking a seat on the Alaska Railroad and viewing one of the world's most pristine wilderness areas from the train's comfortable cars.

Anchorage to Fairbanks
The Alaska Railroad operates a year-round service between Fairbanks and Anchorage, and summer services from late May to mid-September between Anchorage and Whittier on Prince William Sound, and from Anchorage to Seward. Although the 114-mile trip down to Seward is a spectacular ride, unquestionably the most popular run is the 336-mile trip from Anchorage to Fairbanks with a stop at Denali National Park. Heading north, at *Mile 279* the train passes within 46 miles of Mt McKinley, a stunning sight from the train's viewing domes on a clear day, and then slows down to cross the 918-foot bridge over Hurricane Gulch, one of the most spectacular views of the trip.

North of the Denali National Park the train hugs the side of the Nenana River Canyon, passes numerous views of the Alaska Range and, 60 miles south of Fairbanks, crosses the 700-foot Mears Memorial Bridge (one of the longest single-span bridges in the world) over the Tanana River. Before the bridge was completed, this was the end of the line in both directions as people and goods were then ferried across the river to waiting cars on the other bank.

From late May to mid-September, two express trains run daily between Anchorage and Fairbanks with stops at Wasilla, Talkeetna, Denali National Park and Nenana. The express trains are geared for out-of-state travelers as they offer vista-dome cars for all passengers to share, reclining seats and a full dining and beverage service. You can also take your own food and drink on board, which isn't a bad idea as dinner on the train can cost between $13 and $16.

The northbound train departs Anchorage

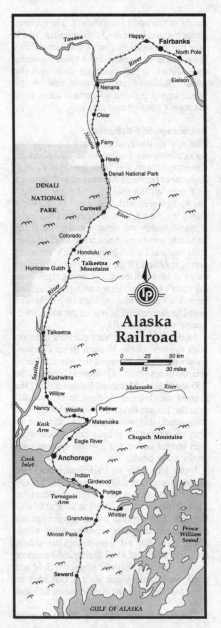

Alaska Railroad

daily at 8.30 am, reaches Denali National Park at 4 pm and Fairbanks at 8.30 pm. The southbound train departs Fairbanks at 8.30 am, reaches Denali National Park at 12.15 pm and Anchorage at 8.30 pm. The one-way fare from Anchorage to Denali National Park is $95, and to Fairbanks $135; from Fairbanks to Denali it is $50. From mid-May to early June and in the first two weeks of September is the railroad's 'Value Season' when $20 is cut from the Anchorage-Denali fare and $27 from the Anchorage-Fairbanks fare.

From late September to mid-May the schedule changes to one train per week, which departs Anchorage at 8.30 am on Saturday and then leaves Fairbanks at 8 am on Sunday for the return trip.

The Alaska Railroad still makes a 'milk run' in which a train stops at every town and can even be flagged down by backpackers, anglers and mountain climbers emerging from their treks at the railroad tracks. The run used to extend all the way to Fairbanks but now stops at Hurricane Gulch, where it turns around and heads back to Anchorage the same day. Still, the trip takes you within view of Mt McKinley and into some remote areas of the state and allows you to mingle with more local residents than you would on the express train.

During the May to mid-September summer season, this diesel train departs Anchorage at 6.30 am and returns by 4.30 pm on Wednesday and Saturday. On Sunday, it departs at noon and returns by 10.30 pm. The rest of the year it only makes the trip on the first Thursday of the month, departing Anchorage at 8.30 am; a round-trip ticket is $88.

There are a few things to keep in mind when traveling by train from Anchorage to Fairbanks. Arrive at the depot at least 15 minutes before departure as the express trains leave on time. Sit on the east side of the train if you want to see the mileposts, and for the best scenery sit on the west side for the stretch from Anchorage to Denali and then on the east side north of there.

The windows in all carriages are big but

taking pictures through them is less than satisfactory due to their distorting curves and the dust on them. To avoid this, step outside to the platform between cars to shoot photos.

Finally, it pays to book early on this popular train; in Anchorage call ☎ (907) 265-2494. Before your trip call Alaska Railroad on the toll-free number, ☎ (800) 544-0552, fax (907) 265-2323, email ☎ akrr@Alaska.net or write to Alaska Railroad, PO Box 107500, Anchorage, AK 99510-7500.

Anchorage to Whittier

There is rail service from Portage and Whittier during the summer. One run is timed to meet the arrivals and departures of the Alaska Marine Ferry, MV *Bartlett*, which crosses Prince William Sound to Valdez on a scenic cruise past the Columbia Glacier.

If you don't have a car, then the first leg is from Anchorage to Portage via a van shuttle service through Alaska Backpackers Shuttle (☎ (907) 344-8775 or (800) 266-8625). It runs a van to meet all trains and charge a one-way fare of $17.50. Gray Line's Alaskon Express also makes a daily run to Portage, charging an outrageous $29 for the trip.

To catch the ferry you need to pick up the 1.20 pm train out of Portage to arrive in Whittier at 2 pm and board the MV *Bartlett* by 2.45 pm. The train then departs Whittier at 3.30 pm. Reservations for the train and ferry are highly recommended as this is a popular excursion. Even if you don't plan to take the marine ferry across Prince William Sound, the trip to Whittier can be a fun day trip as it is a scenic and interesting town. The train ride, although only 40 minutes long, includes two tunnels, one of which is 13,090 feet long. The train shuttle makes several round trips daily; the round-trip fare from Portage to Whittier is $16 per passenger and $70 for most cars, which includes driver fare.

There are four runs from Portage on Wednesday and Thursday at 10.15 am and 1.20, 5 and 7.30 pm, and six trains during the rest of the week at 7.25 and 10.15 am and 1.20, 5, 7.30 and 10 pm. Tickets for the Whittier shuttle can be purchased from con-ductors at Portage. No reservations are taken for the rail service between Anchorage and Whittier, but passengers with confirmed ferry tickets have priority on boarding the 1.20 pm train from Portage. Call ☎ (907) 265-2607 for pre-recorded information about fares and schedules.

Anchorage to Seward

Some say the ride between Anchorage and Seward is one of the most spectacular train trips in the world, rivaling those in the Swiss Alps or the New Zealand train that climbs over Arthur's Pass in the Southern Alps. From Anchorage, the 114-mile trip begins by skirting the 60-mile-long Turnagain Arm on Cook Inlet where travelers can study the bore tides. After leaving Portage, the train swings south and climbs over mountain passes, across deep river gorges and comes within half a mile of three glaciers: Spencer, Bartlett and Trail. The trip ends in Seward, a quaint town that is surrounded by mountains on one side and Resurrection Bay on the other.

The service is offered daily from late May to early September with a train departing Anchorage at 6.45 am and reaching Seward at 11 am. It departs Seward the same day at 6 pm and reaches Anchorage at 10 pm; the round-trip fare is $80. The Seward run does not include a baggage car, like northbound trains to Denali, and ticket agents will warn you of 'hand-carried luggage only'. But don't despair if you have a hefty backpack or even a Klepper kayak. The train is rarely full and extra luggage can be stored in the empty seats.

White Pass & Yukon Route

The White Pass & Yukon Railroad, a historic narrow-gauge railroad, was built in 1898 and connected Skagway to Whitehorse. It was the first railroad to be built in Alaska and at that time the most northern line in North America.

The railroad was carved out of the rugged mountains by workers who, in places, had to be suspended by ropes from vertical cliffs in order to chip and blast the granite away. It followed the 40-mile White Pass Trail from

Skagway to Lake Bennett where the miners would build rafts to float the rest of the way to Dawson City on the Yukon River. The line reached Whitehorse in 1900 and by then had made the Chilkoot Trail obsolete.

The railroad also played an important role in building the Alcan during WWII and was then used for transporting ore by mining companies in the Yukon Territory. In 1982, after world metal prices fell and the Canadian mines closed, operation of the White Pass & Yukon Railroad was suspended. But it has always been a popular tourist attraction, especially with big cruise ships, and in 1988, under the name of White Pass & Yukon Route, the railroad resumed limited service.

It's still the incredible ride it must have been for the Klondike miners. The White Pass & Yukon Railroad has one of the steepest grades in North America as it climbs from sea level in Skagway to 2885 feet at White Pass in only 20 miles. The mountain scenery is fantastic, the old narrow-gauge cars intriguing, and the trip is a must for anyone passing through Southeast Alaska.

The train operates from late May to mid-September and offers a one-day summit excursion and a scheduled through-service for travelers who actually want to use it as a means of transport to Whitehorse and the Alcan. Northbound trains depart Skagway daily at 12.40 pm and arrive in Fraser at 2.40 pm, where passengers transfer to buses which arrive in Whitehorse at 6 pm (Pacific Time). Southbound buses depart Whitehorse at 8.15 am (Pacific Time), and the train leaves Fraser at 10.20 am, arriving in Skagway at noon. The one-way fare from Skagway to Whitehorse is $95.

Knowing the history of this train, reservations wouldn't be a bad idea and can be made before your trip by calling the toll-free number ☎ (800) 343-7373, or writing to the White Pass & Yukon Route (☎ (907) 983-2217) PO Box 435, Skagway, AK 99840.

CAR
Car Rental
Having your own car in Alaska, as in any other place, provides freedom and flexibility that cannot be obtained from public transport. Car rental, however, is a costly way to travel for one person but for two or more people it can be an affordable way out of Anchorage, which has the best car rental rates by far. In Alaska, it isn't the charge per day for the rental but the mileage rate and the distances covered that make it so expensive. Outside Anchorage and Fairbanks, drivers will find gas 20 to 30 cents per gallon more expensive than in the rest of the USA.

The Alaska tourist boom of the 1980s has produced a network of cheap car-rental companies that offer rates considerably lower than those of national firms such as Avis, Hertz and National Car Rental. The largest of these is Practical Car Rental (☎ (800) 426-5243)(it used to be Allstar and in Alaska it still refers to itself as such), which has offices in seven Alaskan towns but unfortunately not Anchorage or Fairbanks. It does have branches in Ketchikan, Petersburg, Juneau, Wrangell and Sitka, Klawock on Prince Wales Island and Bethel. Its rates change from city to city as its branches are independently owned, but most charge around $40 to $45 a day for a subcompact with 100 free miles.

Other companies include Rent-A-Wreck, which has an outlet in Anchorage (☎ (907) 562-5499), at 541 West International Airport Rd. The smallest subcompacts at Rent-A-Wreck are $39 a day during the summer but before June and after August are considerably less, sometimes as low as $26 a day. In Fairbanks, there is a Rent-A-Wreck (☎ (907) 452-1606) with the same rates and a 150 free miles a day for a subcompact.

These used cars, though functional, are occasionally stubborn about starting up right away. However, if there are three or four people splitting the cost, car rental is far cheaper than taking a bus and allows you total freedom to stop when you want.

All the used-car rental companies will be listed in the regional chapters under the towns where they maintain offices. You can also try Affordable Car Rental (☎ (907) 243-3370) or U-Save (☎ (800) 272-8728 or (907) 272-8728).

Motorhome Rental

Want to be a road hog? You can also rent a motorhome in Alaska if that's the way you like to travel. And many people do. RVers flock to the land of the midnight sun in numbers that are astounding. There are some roads, like the George Parks Hwy, that are almost nothing but an endless stream of trailers, pop-ups and land cruisers.

More than a dozen companies, almost all of them based in Anchorage, will rent you a motorhome, ranging from 20 to 35 feet in length, that accommodates up to six people. The price can vary from $100 to $150 per day but again you have to consider all the extra charges. Many places offer 100 free miles per day then charge 15 to 25 cents per mile for any additional mileage.

You also have to pay for insurance and possibly even a 'housekeeping kit' – pots, pans and sheets etc. It's best to anticipate a daily fee of between $150 and $200 and remember that full-hook-up campgrounds cost from $15 to $20 a night. Still, when divided between four to six people the cost comes to around $28 to $35 a day per person for both transport and a soft bed. Not a bad deal if you can round up several other people who want to share the same itinerary. Other costs include gasoline, food and camp sites.

You almost have to reserve a motorhome well in advance to be assured of securing one when you arrive during the summer months. A few of the larger Anchorage rental companies are Great Alaskan Holidays (☎ (800) 642-6462) which does not charge extra for housekeeping packages, cleaning or insurance and has 20-footers with prices that begin as low as $122 a day for a rental of seven days or more; Alaska Motorhome Rentals (☎ (800) 254-9929) which offers a seven-day rental with housekeeping package and 350 free miles with a 21-footer for $795; Clippership Motorhome Rentals (☎ (800) 421-3456); and ABC Motorhome Rentals (☎ (800) 421-7456).

BICYCLE

For those who want to bike it, Alaska offers a variety of cycling adventures on paved roads during long days with comfortably cool temperatures. Most cyclists hop on the Alaska Marine Hwy ferries, carrying their bike on for an additional fee ranging anywhere from $7 up to $38 for the longest run from Bellingham to Skagway. The individual Southeast communities are good places to gear up for the longer rides up north.

From Haines, you can catch an Alaskon Express bus to Tok or Anchorage in the heart of Alaska. There is no charge for the bike but be prepared to have it stored in the luggage compartment under the bus. You can also take your bike on Alaska Airlines for a $45 excess-baggage fee each way.

Summer cyclists have to take some extra precautions in Alaska. There are few towns with comprehensively equipped bike shops so it is wise to carry not only metric tools but also a tube-patch repair kit, brake cables, spokes, brake pads and any other parts that might be needed during the trip.

Due to high rainfall, especially in the Southeast, waterproof saddle bags are useful, as are tire fenders. Rain gear is a must, and storing gear in zip-lock plastic bags within your saddle bags is advised. Warm clothing, mittens and a woollen hat should be carried, along with a tent and rain tarpaulin.

Some roads do not have much of a shoulder – the Seward Hwy between Anchorage and Girdwood for example – so cyclists should utilize the sunlight hours to pedal when traffic is light in such areas. It is not necessary to carry a lot of food, as you can easily restock on all major roads.

Most cyclists avoid gravel, but biking the Alcan (an increasingly popular trip) does involve riding over some short gravel breaks in the paved asphalt. When riding along gravel roads, figure on making 50% to 70% of your normal distance and take spare inner tubes – flat tires will be a daily occurrence.

Mountain bikers, on the other hand, are in heaven with such gravel roads as the Denali Hwy in the Interior, the logging roads on Prince of Wales Island in the Southeast and the park road in Denali National Park. Mountain bikers are even pedaling the Dalton Hwy to Prudhoe Bay.

Within Anchorage is the Arctic Bicycle Club which sponsors a variety of road-bike and mountain-bike tours during the summer. Call the club's Information Hotline (☎ (907) 249-9700) for a recorded message of upcoming tours.

The following cities and towns in Alaska also have bike shops that offer a good selection of spare parts and information on riding in the local area. However, by the end of the summer many are low on, or completely out of, certain spare parts.

Anchorage
    The Bicycle Shop, 1035 West Northern Lights Blvd (☎ (907) 272-5219)
    Gary King Sporting Goods, 202 East Northern Lights Blvd (☎ (907) 279-7454)
    REI Co-op, 1200 West Northern Lights Blvd (☎ (907) 272-4565)
Girdwood
    Girdwood Ski & Cycle, Alyeska Access Rd (☎ (907) 783-2453)
Fairbanks
    Beaver Sports, 2400 College Rd (☎ (907) 479-2494)
Juneau
    Adventure Sports, 8345 Old Dairy Road (☎ (907) 789-5696)
    Mountain Gears, 210 North Franklin St (☎ (907) 586-4327)
Sitka
    Southeast Diving & Sport Shop, 203 Lincoln St (☎ (907) 747-8279)
Skagway
    Sockeye Cycle, 5th Ave and Broadway St (☎ (907) 983-2851)
Kodiak
    52 Degrees North, 326 Center Ave, Ste 90-D (☎ (907) 486-6249)

Bicycle Routes

The following are the more common long-distance trips that can be undertaken by cyclists during the summer in Alaska.

Anchorage to Fairbanks This ride can be done comfortably in five to six days along the George Parks Hwy, and is 360 miles of generally flat road with scattered sections of rolling hills. Highlights are the impressive views of Mt McKinley and an interesting side trip into Denali National Park where cyclists can extend their trip with a ride along the gravel park road. Keep in mind the stretch from Anchorage to Denali National Park is a busy road with heavy traffic most of the summer. To avoid this, many cyclists take the Alaska Railroad part of the way and then bike the rest; there is an excess-baggage charge for carrying your bicycle on the train.

Anchorage to the Kenai Peninsula There is an endless number of possible bike trips or combinations of biking and hiking adventures in the Kenai Peninsula. You can also utilize the Southwest runs of the Alaska Marine Hwy. A common trip is to cycle from Anchorage to Homer, take the ferry to Kodiak, then return via Seward and pedal back to Anchorage.

This is a seven to 12-day trip depending on how much time you spend in Homer and Kodiak; the distance by bike is 350 miles with an additional 400 miles by ferry. Bikes can also be used to hop from one hiking trail to another in some of Alaska's most pleasant backcountry. Or, you can cycle to Portage, combine the rail and ferry transport across Prince William Sound to Valdez and then head north. The Kenai Peninsula can also be a nightmare of heavy traffic for bikers while the Seward Hwy from Anchorage to Girdwood is narrow with little shoulder in many places. The best bet is to begin with a bus trip at least to Portage.

Fairbanks to Valdez This is perhaps one of the most scenic routes cyclists can undertake and also one of the hardest. The six to seven-day trip follows the Richardson Hwy from Delta Junction to Glennallen and then goes onto Valdez – a total of 375 miles. It includes several hilly sections and tough climbs over Isabel Pass before Paxson, and Thompson Pass at 2771 feet, 25 miles east of Valdez.

New brake pads are a must, along with rain gear and warm clothing, as the long ride downhill from Thompson Pass is often a cold and wet one. From Valdez, you can take a ferry across Prince William Sound and head back to Anchorage, or backtrack to the Glenn Hwy and eventually to Anchorage.

North Star Bicycle Route This 3400-mile ride is a summer-long adventure that begins in Missoula (Montana) and ends in Anchorage. Along the way you cross the Canadian Rockies, pick up the Alcan in British Columbia, pedal through the Yukon Territory and follow Alaskan highways from Tok to Anchorage.

Although the Alcan is now paved, miles of rough surface still exist due to construction work, making this a trip only for experienced cyclists looking for a grand adventure. The trip can be reduced significantly by either bussing part of the route in Canada (see the Bussing the Alcan section in the Getting There & Away chapter) or by utilizing the Alaska Marine Hwy from Bellingham. It is 446 miles from Haines to Tok, and 328 miles from Tok to Anchorage, a ride that can be done comfortably in five days.

Those interested in this route could pick up bicycle maps of the route from Missoula north to Jasper, Alberta, from Adventure Cycle Association (☎ (406) 721-1776), PO Box 8308, Missoula, MT 59807. *Great Parks North*, a two-map set, costs $16.50. This non-profit bicycle association also organizes a North Star Ride every summer that usually departs in June. The 73-day cycling adventure is a tour from Missoula to Anchorage, averaging between 30 to 85 miles a day of pedaling, depending on the terrain. This is definitely for advanced bikers. The cost is $2650 and includes three meals a day and all your camping fees.

Cycling Books

You might also consider the *Alaska Bicycle Touring Guide* by Pete Praetorius & Alys Culhane (The Denali Press, PO Box 021535, Juneau, AK 99802-1535; 1989, 328 pages, maps, photos, $17.50), which is the first guide put together for touring Alaska on two wheels. It's been called the 'bicycling equivalent of *The Milepost*' for its thorough description of routes throughout the state, including two that go north of the Arctic Circle.

Mountain Bike Alaska by Richard Larson (Glacier House Publications, PO Box 201901, Anchorage, AK 99520; 1991, 120 pages, maps, $14) is a guide to 49 trails for mountain bikers. They range from the Denali Hwy and the Denali park road to many of the traditional hiking trails situated on the Kenai Peninsula.

BOAT
Alaska Marine Hwy

In the Southeast, the Alaska Marine Hwy replaces bus services and operates from Juneau or Ketchikan to Skagway, Haines, Hoonah, Tenakee Springs, Angoon, Sitka, Kake, Petersburg, Hyder and Hollis, with an occasional special run to the tiny fishing village of Pelican (see the Inside Passage section in the Getting There & Away chapter for more details).

There are also marine ferry services in Southcentral and Southwest Alaska, where the MV *Bartlett* and the MV *Tustumena* connect towns along Prince William Sound and the Gulf of Alaska.

The Southwest marine ferry does not connect with the Southeast line, but you can get around that by picking up an Alaska Airlines flight from Juneau to Cordova to continue your ferry trip around the Alaskan coast.

The MV *Bartlett* sails from Cordova and Valdez to Whittier across Prince William Sound, passing the Columbia Glacier along the way. The MV *Tustumena* provides a service between Seward, Homer and Seldovia on the Kenai Peninsula; Port Lions

---

The Business of Ferrying
The Alaska Marine Hwy is not only an enjoyable way to travel but it's big business for the state. The eight vessels in the fleet travel 3500 miles of waterways, from Dutch Harbor to Ketchikan, visiting 30 communities. The ferries are responsible for bringing one in every 12 visitors to Alaska, or about 60,000 people in a summer. The Alaska Marine Hwy annually pumps $150 million into the Alaskan economy by carrying more than 400,000 travelers and 100,000 vehicles. ■

and Kodiak on Kodiak Island; and Valdez on the eastern shore of Prince William Sound.

In 1993, the Alaska Marine Hwy instituted a direct service from Whittier to Cordova, on board the MV *Bartlett*. From May to September, the ship leaves Whittier at 2.45 pm on Monday, reaching Cordova seven hours later. On Wednesday the ship departs Cordova at 7 am and sails to Whittier. This makes the charming town of Cordova a nice three-day sidetrip from Anchorage.

Also six times during the summer – in mid-May, June, July, August and twice in September – the MV *Tustumena* also makes

a special run to Sand Point, King Cove, Cold Bay and Dutch Harbor at the end of the Alaska Peninsula. The cruise is six days (round trip) from Kodiak and is clearly the cheapest way to see part of Alaska's stormy arm (see the Southwest section in the Bush chapter).

Here are some sample fares for ferry travel along the Southwest routes for walk-on passengers: Valdez to Cordova, $30; Valdez to Whittier, $58; Valdez to Seward, $58; Seward to Kodiak, $54; Homer to Kodiak, $48; Kodiak to Unalaska, $202; Homer to Seldovia, $18.

The Wilderness

Alaska is many things, but first and foremost it is the great outdoors; you go there for the mountains, the trails, the wildlife and the camping – the adventure of it all. If retrieving the morning newspaper is all the fresh air you can handle, Alaska can be a dull place. But if you're a camper, hiker, backpacker or someone who likes to spend a lot of time at scenic lookouts, the north country has two things for you – extensive wilderness areas and long days to enjoy them in.

Compared to the cost of getting there, the cost of enjoying most of the backcountry is relatively low. Hiking is free and even the most expensive camping fee is cheap compared to what motels will charge. Camping areas across Alaska range from places with cosy lounges and heated bathrooms to out-of-town clearings.

The different adventures available in Alaska vary as much; you can take a three-hour hike on a well-maintained trail that begins from the center of Juneau or a week-long trek in Wrangell-St Elias National Park where there are no trails at all.

The best way to enter the state's wilderness is to begin with a day hike the minute you step off the ferry or depart from the Alcan. Once having experienced a taste of the woods, many travelers forgo the cities and spend the rest of their trip taking long-term adventures into the backcountry to make the most of Alaska's immense surroundings.

THE WILDERNESS EXPERIENCE

Alaska, which covers over 550,000 sq miles, is serviced by only 5000 miles of public highway. Most of the recent tourist boom is centered around these roads and visitors tend to cling to them. Ironically, this causes the state, with all its space, to have its share of over-crowded parks and campgrounds.

Residents of Alaska know this and tend to stay away from heavily touristed places such as Denali National Park during the middle of

summer. They also know how to escape into the backcountry – those wearing Sierra Club T-shirts call it a 'wilderness experience'. Others throw a backpack together and say they're 'going out the road for a spell'. It's all the same – a journey into the woods, away from the city, neighbors, TV and other signs of human existence. That is the greatest enjoyment Alaska can offer anyone – a week of nothing but nature in all its splendor.

You have to be careful on such adventures. In a true wilderness experience, you are completely on your own. But don't let the lack of communication with the civilized world prevent you from venturing into the wilderness – it's the best part. On an ideal trip, you won't meet another person outside your party, see a boat or hear the hum of a bush plane.

In this perfect tranquillity, all the worries and pressures of day-to-day living are cast aside and you begin to discover yourself in the natural setting. More enjoyment and satisfaction can be derived from a few days in the wilderness than from a three-week bus tour. Some people, once they enter the wilderness, never get it out of their blood.

Local hiking trails and camping areas are covered in the regional chapters. The 23 trips described in this chapter are popular wilderness excursions that backpackers can do on their own if they are properly equipped and have sufficient outdoor experience. These are either maintained trails or natural paddling routes enjoyed by backpackers every year. Some trips cannot provide a true 'wilderness experience' as they are too popular during the summer, but many are in isolated areas and offer a glimpse of pristine backcountry.

Those people who didn't come to Alaska with the right gear or who lack camping knowledge can still escape into the woods and return safely. There are two ways of doing this. The first is to join a guided expedition where equipment, group organization

WILDERNESS

Exploring Alaska Parks Online
At home you're only a few keystrokes away from any of Alaska's 13 national parks, which went online in 1996. By typing http://www.nps.gov/dena you can enter the Denali National Park site where there is up-to-date information on fees, activities in the park and natural and cultural notes. Here are the Internet addresses for the rest of the parks:

Wrangell-St Elias:
    http://www.nps.gov/wrst
Aniakchak:
    http://www.nps.gov/ania
Bering Land Bridge:
    http://www.nps.gov/bela
Gates of the Arctic:
    http://www.nps.gov/gaar
Glacier Bay:
    http://www.nps.gov/glba
Katmai:
    http://www.nps.gov/katm
Klondike Gold Rush:
    http://www.nps.gov/klgo
Kenai Fjords:
    http://www.nps.gov/kefj
Cape Krusenstern, Kubuk and Noatak:
    http://www.nps.gov/noaa
Lake Clark:
    http://www.nps.gov/lacl
Sitka:
    http://www.nps.gov/sitk
Yukon-Charley:
    http://www.nps.gov/yuch

and knowledge of the area are supplied. Guided expeditions, which cover the state, range from half a day to three weeks and cost between $150 and $175 per person per day (a list of guide companies is provided in the Tours section at the end of this chapter). The other way to sample the wilderness, without enduring a 20-mile hike or hiring the services of a tour guide, is to rent a Forest Service cabin (see the Accommodation section in the Facts for the Visitor chapter).

GENERAL INFORMATION
Who Controls What
With almost three-quarters of the state locked up, it's good to know which federal or state agency administers the land you want to hike on. Almost all of the recrea-

tional areas, parks and forests, including the campgrounds and trails in them, are controlled by one of five agencies.

US Forest Service This federal bureau handles the Tongass and Chugach national forests which cover practically all of the Southeast and Eastern Kenai Peninsula, including Prince William Sound. The US Forest Service (USFS) can provide detailed information on the 190 public-use cabins it maintains, along with hiking, kayaking, canoeing and other recreational opportunities in its domain. Most USFS campgrounds charge from $6 to $8 per day, depending on the facilities, and have a 14-day limit. The addresses for the main USFS offices are given in the Accommodation section in the Facts for the Visitor chapter but there are also smaller offices in Craig, Wrangell, Hoonah and Yakutat.

In the Southeast, each USFS office has a copy of the *Southeast Alaska Community Opportunity Guide* which is put together by the Forest Service and contains information about camping, trails, fishing areas and cabins throughout Tongass National Forest. If you plan to spend any time in a Southeast town, it is well worth your while to venture to the USFS office and thumb through this reference guide.

National Park Service The National Park Service administers Denali, Glacier Bay and Katmai national parks and preserves, all of which have maintained campgrounds and are accessible by either an Alaska Airlines flight or by road. The seven campgrounds in Denali National Park are scattered across the park. Morino Campground at the entrance to the park is a no-frills area for backpackers without vehicles with sites for $6 per person per night.

Two other national parks, Kenai Fjords and Wrangell-St Elias, also have roads leading into them but their facilities are not nearly as well developed for visitors as the first three national parks mentioned – of course many people consider that a plus. Without the visitor centers, camper van

Top: Train on the Alaska Railroad heading to Fairbanks (DP)
Middle: Matanuska Ferry cruising the waters of Southeast Alaska (CP)
Bottom: Kayakers in Katmai National Park (DP)

Top: Chilkat dancers performing in Haines (ADT)
Bottom left: Totem fronting a clan house in Totem Bight State Park, near Ketchikan (JD)
Bottom right: A tall totem in downtown Sitka (PZ)

hook-ups, hot showers and expensive lodges, these national parks escape the mid-summer crush of tourists that the other parks suffer.

There are three other national parks (Gates of the Arctic, Kobuk Valley and Lake Clark) and three national preserves (Aniakchak National Monument & Preserve, Noatak and Yukon-Charley Rivers national preserves) that are administered by the National Park Service. All of them are only accessible by bush plane or boat and offer no facilities within the park. Most visitors reach them through guide companies which venture into the wilderness areas by raft, kayak or foot. In fact, Kobuk Valley National Park is North America's least visited national park receiving only 2,781 visitors a year compared with Yosemite's four million visitors.

The National Park Service also maintains numerous national monuments and national historical parks for a total of 54 million acres. For addresses and more information on the individual parks, check the regional chapters. For general information on all parks, contact the main National Park Service offices: Alaska Public Lands Information Center (☎ (907) 271-2737), 605 West 4th Ave, Suite 105, Anchorage, AK 99501-2231; and the National Park Service (☎ (907) 586-7137), 709 West 9th St, Juneau, AK 99801.

Bureau of Land Management The Bureau of Land Management (BLM) is the federal agency that maintains much of the wilderness around and north of Fairbanks. It has developed 25 camping areas and a dozen public-use cabins in the Interior as well as two popular trails (Pinnell Mountain and White Mountain), both off the highways north of Fairbanks. Most of the cabins are in the White Mountains National Recreation Area whose trails are primarily winter routes and are often impassable during the summer. Camping, free in most BLM campgrounds, is handled on a first-come-first-serve basis. The cabins are $20 a night and most of them are within 100 miles of Fairbanks.

The BLM offices have good publications on the Taylor Hwy, a secondary road that is

an adventure in itself, and national wild rivers such as the Gulkana, Fortymile and Delta. For more information contact the BLM District Office (☎ (907) 474-2200), 1150 University Ave, Fairbanks, AK 99709; or the BLM District Office (☎ (907) 822-3217), PO Box 147, Glennallen, AK 99588.

US Fish & Wildlife Service This arm of the Department of the Interior administers 16 wildlife refuges in Alaska that total more than 77 million acres. The largest, Yukon Delta that surrounds Bethel in Western Alaska, covers almost 20 million acres.

The purpose of wildlife refuges is to protect habitats; visitor use and developed recreational activities are strictly an after-thought. Most of the refuges are in remote areas of the Bush with few, if any, developed facilities – guide companies are the only means by which most travelers visit them. The one exception is Kenai National Wild-life Refuge, which can be reached by road from Anchorage. This preserve has 15 camp-grounds, of which the Kenai-Russian River Campground is by far the most popular, and over 200 miles of hiking trails and water routes, including the popular Swanson River Canoe Route.

The Kodiak National Wildlife Refuge, although considerably more remote and more expensive to reach than Kenai, does offer nine wilderness cabins similar to USFS cabins for $15 per night. For more informa-tion about individual areas, see the regional chapters. For general information contact the Regional Office (☎ (907) 786-3487), US Fish & Wildlife Service, 1011 East Tudor Rd, Anchorage, AK 99503.

Alaska Division of Parks The Alaska Divi-sion of Parks & Outdoor Recreation controls more than 100 areas in the Alaskan state park system, ranging from the 1.5-million-acre Wood-Tikchik State Park, north of Dillingham on Bristol Bay, to small wayside parks along the highway. The areas also include state trails, campgrounds, wilderness parks and historic sites, all maintained by the state.

Among the more popular parks which offer a variety of recreational opportunities are Chugach, Denali State Park south of Mt McKinley, Nancy Lake Recreational Area just south of Willow, Captain Cook State Recreation Area on the Kenai Peninsula and Chilkat State Park south of Haines. Most campgrounds cost $8 a night with a couple of the more popular ones charging $15 a night.

For travelers planning to spend a summer camping in Alaska, a state park camping pass, allowing unlimited camping for a year, is a wise investment at $100 for non-residents. The state parks division also rents out recreational cabins in the Southeast, the Southcentral and the Interior regions for $30 a night. To obtain an annual Alaska Camping Pass in advance, send a check or money order to one of the following offices: Alaska Division of Parks (☎ (907) 269-8400), 3601 C St, Ste 200, Anchorage, AK 99503-5929, or the Alaska Division of Parks (☎ (907) 465-4563), 400 Willoughby Center, Juneau, AK 99801.

TOURS
Guide Companies
Most of Alaska's wilderness is not accessible to the first-time visitor; travelers either don't know about wilderness areas or don't know how to get to them. This is where guide companies are very useful.

Guides are not only for novice campers. Their clients can be experienced backpackers who want to explore the far reaches of Alaska's wilderness but don't have the time or money to put together an expedition on their own. Guides can arrange the many details of a large-scale trip into the backcountry – everything from food and equipment to air charter.

Trips can range from a day hike on a glacier to a 12-day raft trip or a three-week ascent of Mt McKinley, and costs range from $175 to more than $250 per day, depending upon the amount of air travel involved. Expeditions usually have five to 12 clients; guide companies are extremely hesitant to take larger groups because of their environ-

mental impact. The tour season extends from late May to September, while a select group of companies specialize in winter expeditions of Nordic (cross-country) skiing or dog-sledding.

Guided expeditions cost money, and most budget travelers prefer unguided trips. However, many guide companies offer adventures to areas that are only visited by a few people each year and there is something inviting about that.

Although most companies begin taking reservations in April, don't hesitate to call one after you've arrived in Alaska. Often you can score a hefty discount of 30% to 50% in the middle of the summer as guide companies are eager to fill any remaining places on a scheduled trip.

The following is a list of recreational guide companies in Alaska. Don't get them confused with hunting or fishing guides whose main interest is to make sure that their client gets a trophy to hang on the wall of the family room.

Also be careful not to confuse expeditions with fishing camps or wilderness lodges. The camps and lodges are established rustic resorts in the wilderness where you spend a week with many of the comforts of home, but see little beyond the immediate area.

Southeast Southeast Exposure (☎ (907) 225-8829), PO Box 9143, Ketchikan, AK 99901, rents kayaks and offers guided trips to Misty Fjords National Monument and Barrier Islands, a wilderness area on Prince of Wales Island. A four-day paddle to the heart of Rudyerd Bay, the most scenic part of Misty Fjords, along with Manzanita Bay and Behm Canal is $655 per person and includes boat transport from Ketchikan. A six-day trip that includes Walker Cove is $895 per person while an eight-day expedition into Barrier Islands and the west coast of Prince of Wales Island is $1200.

Alaska Discovery (☎ (800) 586-1911 or email akdisco@alaska.net), 5449 Shaune Drive, Ste 4, Juneau, AK 99801, was organized in 1972 and today is one of the oldest and largest guide companies in Alaska. It used to operate mainly in the Southeast but has since expanded with raft trips down the Kongakut River in the Arctic National Wildlife Refuge. Still, kayak trips in Glacier Bay and Russell Fjord, home of Hubbard Glacier, are its specialty. Among its expeditions are an eight-day paddle in Glacier Bay for $1890 per person and a three-day Hubbard Glacier adventure for $880 per person. It also offers 10 to 12-day raft trips down the spectacular Tatshenshini River for $1975. The company maintains a Web site at http://www.gorp.com.ak.

Chilkat Guides (☎ (907) 766-2491), PO Box 170, Haines, AK 99827, offers a handful of raft trips from its base in Haines as well as a 10-day canoe trip down the Stikine River, using 31-foot Voyageur canoes. The small guiding company is best known for its raft trips down the Tatshenshini and Alsek rivers. Both are extremely spectacular trips past dozens of glaciers. The 'Tat' is a 10-day float which costs $2150 per person and the Alsek, which involves helicopter time in bypassing Turnback Canyon, is a 13-day trip for $2475.

Alaska Cross Country Guiding & Rafting (☎ (907) 767-5522), PO Box 124, Haines, AK 99827, runs trips around the Chilkat Bald Eagle Preserve. The outfitter's best trip begins with a flight to remote DeBlondeau Glacier Cabins just outside Glacier Bay National Park for a night and then continues with a float down to the Chilkat River back to Haines. This two-day adventure is $650 per person, which includes the air charter.

Spirit Walker Expeditions (☎ (907) 697-2266 or (800) 529-2537, or email 72537.555@Compuserve.com), PO Box 240, Gustavus, AK 99826, is based near Glacier Bay and offers sea kayaking trips along the coastline of Chichagof Island just south of the national park, as well as to Hubbard Glacier near Yakutat. The company prides itself of sighting whales and on providing memorable dinners that range from halibut kebabs to fresh dungeness crabs. Prices range from $663 for a two-night paddle to $2172 for a seven-day trip along Chichagof Island.

Anchorage Area & Southcentral Adventures & Delights (☎ (907) 276-8282 or (800) 288-3134, or email AFJLV@acad2.alaska.edu), 414 K St, Anchorage, AK 99501, specializes in sea-kayak adventures in Prince William Sound and Kenai Fjords National Park. A three-day paddle into Resurrection Bay from Seward is $575 per person, a three-day trip into Kenai Fjords is $795. The company also rents kayaks in Seward and can arrange drop-off and pick-up service.

Hugh Glass Backpacking Co (☎ (907) 344-1340), PO Box 110796-LP, Anchorage, AK 99511, is a long-established guide company which offers a wide range of trips into Prince William Sound, Kenai Fjords National Park, the Arctic National Wildlife Refuge, Katmai National Park, Brooks Range, and the Wrangell and St Elias mountains. Trips may include trekking, canoeing, rafting or sea kayaking, and can be designed as photography or fishing adventures. Among its expeditions are a 10-day kayak expedition into Katmai National Park for $1595 per person and a seven-day trek in Wrangell-St Elias National Park for $1195.

Alaska River Adventures (☎ (907) 276-3418), *Mile 48.2* Sterling Hwy, Cooper Landing, AK 99572, offers guided tours all year round. In summer, it runs boating trips ranging from an overnighter along the Kenai River for $149 to three days of whitewater paddling through the Talkeetna Canyon and five days on Lake Creek, south of Mt McKinley, for $1695. There are also longer expeditions to the Alagnak River and the Kanektok River in the Bristol Bay region and sea kayaking on Prince William Sound and Kenai Fjords (six days for $1795).

Adnadyr Adventures (☎ (907) 835-2814), PO Box 1821, Valdez, AK 99686, offers trips, paddling classes and kayak rentals for use in Prince William Sound. Guided trips range from one-day paddles and a three-day trip to the Columbia Glacier for $585 per person to an eight-day tour in the Sound that includes charter boat drop-off for $1925.

Alaska Wildtrek (☎ (907) 235-6463), PO Box 1741, Homer, AK 99603, offers guided tours throughout the state from the Brooks

Range to the Alaska Peninsula. Directed by Chlaus Lotscher, a German 'transplant' in Alaska, the company caters almost entirely to Europeans, especially Germans. Among the wilderness trips he offers is a 10-day rafting adventure down the Hulahula River in the Arctic National Wildlife Refuge for $2290 and a six-day float along the Chilikadrotna in Lake Clark National Park for $1695.

Mt McKinley & the Interior St Elias Alpine Guides (☎ (907) 277-6867), PO Box 111241, Anchorage, AK 99511-1241, specializes in mountaineering and glacier-skiing adventures at Wrangell-St Elias National Park. It also offers a 13-day trip down the Copper River to Cordova for $1975 and an 11-day backpacking trip around Chitistone Canyon of the Wrangell-St Elias National Park for $1873. Want to climb a mountain? The 17-day ascent of Mt Blackburn (elevation 16,390 feet) is only $2675.

Denali Raft Adventures (☎ (907) 683-2234), Drawer 190, Denali Park, AK 99755, offers a variety of day rafting trips down the Nenana River near Denali National Park; some are in calm waters while others involve two hours of whitewater rafting. Prices range from $42 to $62 per person for two to five-hour trips. It also has a full-day trip.

Osprey Expeditions (☎ (907) 683-2734), PO Box 209, Denali National Park, AK 99755, is another raft company based near Denali National Park but offers multi-day floats. They range from a three-day float on the Nenana River for $525 and a five-day trip on the Talkeetna for $1275 to an eight-day expedition on the Fortymile River near the Canadian border for $1500.

Nova (☎ (907) 745-5753), PO Box 1129, Chickaloon, AK 99674, specializes in river rafting. Its trips range from a day run down the Matanuska River for $60 per person to a three-day journey along the Talkeetna River that involves flying to the heart of the Talkeetna Mountains and grade IV whitewater for $875 per person. The company runs trips to the Kobuk River in the Brooks Range

(10 days for $2800 per person) and the Copper River in Wrangell-St Elias National Park (six days for $1100).

River Wrangllers (☎ (907) 822-3967), PO Box 146, Gakona, AK 99586, is a relatively new outfitter that floats the rivers of Wrangell-St Elias Mountain National Park as well the Gulkana, Klutina and Tazlina rivers of Interior Alaska. It offers day trips and extended outings such as a four-day float of the Gulkana River for $500 per person as well as rent rafts.

Fairbanks & Brooks Range Alaska Fish & Trails Unlimited (☎ (907) 479-7630), 1177 Shypoke Dr, Fairbanks, AK 99701, runs backpacking, kayaking and canoeing trips in the Gates of the Arctic National Park, that include a 14-day backpack and raft trip from Anaktuvuk Pass in the Brooks Range to Bettles for $1800. It also offers an unguided raft-and-backpack trip from Summit Lake along the Koyukuk River for $1000.

Arctic Treks (☎ (907) 455-6502), PO Box 73452, Fairbanks, AK 99707, is a family operation that also specializes in treks and rafting in the Gates of the Arctic National Park as well as the Arctic National Wildlife Refuge. A 10-day backpacking trip to the high mountain valleys of the Brooks Range is $2275 per person, while a float of the Hulahula River through the Arctic North Slope for 10 days costs $2575.

Sourdough Outfitters (☎ (907) 692-5252, or email sour@niga.sourdough.com), PO Box 90, Bettles, AK 99726, runs canoe, kayak and backpacking trips to the Gates of the Arctic National Park, Noatak and Kobuk rivers and other areas.

The outfitters also provide unguided trips for individuals who have the experience to make an independent journey but want a guide company to handle the logistics (such as trip planning, transport and canoe or raft rental) of a major expedition. Unguided trips throughout the Brooks Range are priced from $400 to $900 per person depending on the number of people in your party. Guided trips include an eight-day backpacking trek in the Gates of the Arctic National Park for

Alaska by Dog Sled

There is a wilderness guide who will you take into almost any region of Alaska or down any river. But the growth of the guiding industry in the past few years has been dog mushing. There are now more than two-dozen outfitters from Bettles to Homer who will set you up with a team and then lead you into a winter wilderness.

Some outings are only three or four hours long, others are an eight-day journey into the Brooks Range with your own team. The best time for such an adventure is late February through early April, when the days are long, the temperatures are much more agreeable but the snow base is still deep. You do not need previous experience with dog teams or mushing but you should be comfortable with winter camping and have cold-weather clothing and gear. Accommodation on such trips ranges from wall tents with small stoves and remote cabins to mountain lodges. Interested? Here is a sampling of outfitters now using dog mushing to attract travelers to Alaska in the winter.

Chugach Express Dog Sled Tours, PO Box 261, Girdwood, AK 99587, (☎ (907) 783-2266), is located in Girdwood and offers rides that last from 30 minutes to three hours in the Alyeska area of Chugach National Forest. A three-hour ride is $85 but there is also a three-day package where you mush each day but return to a comfortable lodge at night for $675.

Outback Kachemak Dog Sled Tours, PO Box 1797, Homer, AK 99603, (☎ (907) 235-6333), explores the backcountry around Homer and often combines dog mushing with skijoring, where a dog pulls a cross-country skier. An hour of mushing is $40, and two-day packages are $350 including lodging.

Denali West Lodge, PO Box 12, Lake Minchumina, AK 99757, (☎ (907) 674-3112) has a five-day package, where you stay at the lodge but mush each day in and around Denali National Park, for $1500.

Brooks Range Wilderness Trips, PO Box 80121, Fairbanks, AK 99708, (☎ (907) 488-6787) is based in Fairbanks and offers three to 10-day trips, mushing 20 to 30 miles a day, in the White Mountains north of the city. The cost is $300 a day per person or $400 for two people.

Sourdough Outfitters, PO Box 90, Bettles, AK 99726, (☎ (907) 692-5252) is based in Bettles, the unofficial capital of dog-mushing outfitters. The handful of companies all offer long-term expeditions that range from six to 14 days and allow groups to travel extensively into Brooks Range and Gates of the Arctic National Park. You mush your own team, travel 15 to 25 miles a day and usually sleep in large wall tents. Sourdough Outfitters provides several different trips including an eight-day excursion for $1500 per person. ∎

$1300 per person, a 10-day canoe trip along the Noatak River for $1950 and a five-day paddle of the Wild River in the Brooks Range for $1100.

ABEC's Alaska Adventures (☎ (907) 457-8907), 1550 Alpine Vista Court, Fairbanks, AK 99712, is another outfitter that concentrates on trips in the Arctic National Wildlife Refuge and Gates of the Arctic National Park. Its 12-day Hulahula River raft trip is $2400 while a 12-day backpack trek to witness the caribou migration is $1800.

Wilderness Alaska (☎ (907) 345-3567), PO Box 113063, Anchorage, AK 99511, although based in Anchorage does exclusively float and backpacking trips in the Brooks Range and the Arctic National Wildlife Refuge. Among its more interesting trips is a 10-day float trip of the Porcupine River in September to watch the caribou ($2150) and a five-day Arctic Refuge Base Camp for those seeking a shorter and more relaxing outing into the Brooks Range ($1985). At the other extreme, the company offers 20-day trips that combine rafting and backpacking and cost more than $3600 per person.

Hiking

Camping, hiking and backpacking in Alaska are more dangerous than in most other places. The weather is more unpredictable, the climate harsher, and encounters with wildlife a daily occurrence. Unpredictable situations such as getting lost, snow storms in the middle of the summer or being 'socked in' by low clouds and fog for days while waiting for a bush plane happen annually to hundreds of backpackers in Alaska.

If you're planning to wander beyond roadside parks, don't take your adventure lightly. You must be totally independent in the wilderness – a new experience for most city dwellers. You need the knowledge and equipment to sit out bad weather, endure an overturned boat or assist an injured member of your party. For that information consult a survival manual such as *Walking Softly in the Wilderness* by John Hart (Sierra Club Books). It cannot be stressed enough that the most important thing about Alaska wilderness is to be prepared before you enter the woods.

See the What to Bring section in the Facts for the Visitor chapter on what expedition equipment to bring. Keep in mind, it's best to stock up on food and supplies at the last major town you pass through before entering

such wilderness areas as Glacier Bay, Denali or Katmai national parks.

The trips described in this section are along routes that are popular and well developed. Backpackers still need the proper gear and knowledge but can undertake these adventures on their own without the services of a guide. Always check with the offices or park headquarters listed for current trail conditions. A few of the trails have USFS cabins along the way, but these must be reserved well in advance. Bring a tent on any wilderness trek.

For more detailed descriptions of the hikes see Lonely Planet's *Backpacking in Alaska*.

Backcountry Conduct

It is wise to check in with the USFS office or National Park headquarters before entering the backcountry. By letting them know your intentions, you'll get peace of mind knowing that someone knows you're out there. If there is no ranger office in the area, the best place to advise of your travel plans is the air charter service responsible for picking up your party.

Do not harass wildlife while traveling in the backcountry. Avoid startling an animal, as it will most likely flee, leaving you with a short and forgettable encounter. If you flush a bird from its nest, leave the area quickly, as an unattended nest leaves the eggs vulnerable to predators. Never attempt to feed wildlife; it is not healthy for you or the animal.

Finally, be thoughtful when in the wilderness as it is a delicate environment. Carry in your supplies and carry out your trash, never litter or leave garbage to smoulder in a fire pit. Always put out your fire and cover it with natural materials or, better still, don't light a fire in heavily traveled areas. Use biodegradable soap and do all washing away from water sources. In short, practice low-impact no-trace camping and leave no evidence of your stay. Only then can an area remain a true wilderness.

Wilderness Camping

Choosing a spot to pitch a tent in a campground is easy, but in the wilderness the choice is more complicated and should be made carefully to avoid problems in the middle of the night. Throughout much of Alaska, especially the Interior, river bars are the best place to pitch a tent. Strips of sand or small gravel patches along rivers provide good drainage and a smoother surface than tussock grass on which to pitch a tent.

Take time to check out the area before unpacking your gear. Avoid animal trails (whether the tracks be moose or bear), areas with bear scat, and berry patches with ripe fruit. In late summer, it is best to stay away from streams choked with salmon runs.

In the Southeast and other coastal areas of Alaska, search out beaches and ridges with southern exposures; they provide the driest conditions in these rainy zones. Old glacier and stream outwashes (sand or gravel deposits) make ideal camp sites as long as you stay well above the high-tide line. Look for the last ridge of seaweed and debris on the shore and then pitch your tent another 20 to 30 yards above that to avoid waking up with salt water flooding your tent. Tidal fluctuations along Alaska's coast are among the largest in the world – up to 30 feet in some places.

CHILKOOT TRAIL

Denali National Park may be the most popular park in Alaska, but the Chilkoot is unquestionably the most famous trail and often the most used during the summer. It is the same route as that used by the Klondike gold miners in the 1898 to 1900 gold rush and walking it is not so much a wilderness adventure as a history lesson.

The well-developed and well-marked trail is still littered with artefacts of the era – everything from entire ghost towns and huge mining dredges to a lone boot lying next to the trail. The trip is from 33 to 35 miles long (depending on where you exit) and includes the Chilkoot Pass – a steep climb up loose rocks to 3550 feet, where most hikers use all fours to scramble over the loose rocks. The trail can be attempted by anyone in good physical condition with the right equipment and enough time. The hike normally takes

three to four days, though it can be done in two days by experienced trekkers.

Traditionally one of the more popular highlights of the hike was riding the White Pass & Yukon Railroad (WP&YR) back to Skagway but in 1996 the historic railroad suspended Lake Bennett service for trekkers due to high operating costs on that portion of the track. That's too bad because experiencing the Chilkoot and returning on the WP&YR was probably the ultimate Alaska trek, combining great scenery, a first-hand view of history and an incredible sense of adventure. Now you would have to hike or bus a portion of the Klondike Hwy south to Fraser in British Columbia to pick up the narrow-gauge train for its run through White Pass Summit to Skagway.

Information

Stop at the National Park Service visitor center in the refurbished railroad depot on the corner of 2nd Ave and Broadway St, Skagway, for current weather and trail conditions, exhibits and films on the area's history, and hiking maps. There is also a 13-minute video on hiking the Chilkoot for those who are not sure if they're up for the adventure. For more information contact the National Park Service (☎ (907) 983-2921) at PO Box 517, Skagway, AK 99840.

RESURRECTION PASS TRAIL

Located in the Chugach National Forest, this 39-mile trail was carved by prospectors in the late 1800s and today is the most popular hiking route on the Kenai Peninsula. It also becoming an increasing popular trail for mountain bikers, who can ride the entire route in one long Alaskan day. For those on foot, the trip can be done in three days by a strong hiker but most people prefer to do it in five to seven days to make the most of the immense beauty of the region and the excellent fishing in Trout, Juneau and Swan lakes.

There is a series of eight USFS cabins along the route for $25 per night. They have to be reserved in advance at the USFS office in Anchorage and, being quite popular, are fully booked for most of the summer which makes last-minute reservations almost impossible. Most hikers take a tent and a camp stove, as fallen wood can sometimes be scarce during the busy summer. See the Kenai Peninsula Hiking Trails map in the Southcentral Alaska chapter.

Information

For more information on the trail or reserving cabins along it, contact the Seward Ranger District, 334 Fourth Ave, Seward, AK 99664; (☎ (907) 224-3374).

RUSSIAN LAKES TRAIL

This 21-mile, two-day hike is an ideal alternative for those who do not want to over-extend themselves in the Chugach National Forest. The trail is well traveled, well maintained and well marked during the summer, and not too demanding on the legs. Most of the hike is a pleasant forest walk broken up by patches of wildflowers, ripe berries, lakes and streams.

The walk's highlights include the possibility of viewing moose or bears, the impressive glaciated mountains across from Upper Russian Lake or, for those carrying a fishing pole, the chance to catch your own dinner. The trek offers good fishing for Dolly Varden, rainbow trout and salmon in the upper portions of the Russian River; rainbow trout in Lower Russian Lake, Aspen Flats and Upper Russian Lake; and Dolly Varden in Cooper Lake near the eastern trailhead.

If you plan ahead, there are three USFS cabins on the trail for $25 per night but you need to reserve them in advance. One is on Upper Russian Lake, nine miles from the Cooper Lake trailhead. Another is at Aspen Flats, and another is three miles north-west along the trail or 12 miles from the western trailhead. See the Kenai Peninsula Hiking Trails map in the Southcentral Alaska chapter.

Information

For more information on the trail or to reserve cabins by mail, contact the Seward Ranger District, 334 Fourth Ave, Seward, AK 99664; (☎ (907) 224-3374).

JOHNSON PASS TRAIL

In the same area as the Resurrection Pass and Russian Lakes trails, and nearly as popular, is the Johnson Pass Trail, a two-day and 23-mile hike over an alpine pass 1500 feet in elevation. The trail was originally part of the Old Iditarod Trail blazed by prospectors from Seward to the golden beaches of Nome, and later was used as part of the old Seward mail route.

Most of the trail is fairly level, which makes for easy hiking and explains the growing numbers of mountain bikers seen on it. Anglers will find arctic grayling in Bench Lake and rainbow trout in Johnson Lake. Plan to camp at either Johnson Lake or Johnson Pass, but keep in mind that these places are above the tree line, making it necessary to carry a small stove. There are no cabins on this trail. See the Kenai Peninsula Hiking Trails map in the Southcentral Alaska chapter.

Information

The best USFS office for information is the Seward Ranger District, 334 Fourth Ave, Seward, AK 99664; (☎ (907) 224-3374).

COASTAL TRAIL

Caines Head State Recreation Area is a 6000-acre park on Resurrection Bay south of Seward. This area has long been favored by boat and kayak enthusiasts who go ashore to explore the remains of Fort McGilvray and the South Beach Garrison, old WWII outposts that were built as a result of the Japanese attack on the Aleutian Islands. Along with the remains of an army pier, firing platforms and the 'garrison ghost town' at South Beach, the park also has much natural beauty including a massive headland that raises 650 feet above the water and provides sweeping views of Resurrection Bay.

The Coastal Trail is a 4.5-mile one-way hike from Lowell Point to North Beach, where you can continue along old army roads to Fort McGilvray and South Beach. Along the way you pass a walk-in campground, vault toilets and a picnic shelter at

Tonsina Point; and a campground, picnic shelter and ranger station at North Beach. There is also a state cabin ($35, reservations) that can be rented at Derby Cove. This hiking trail makes an excellent overnight trip, combining history with great scenery and an opportunity to climb a spur trail into alpine areas; it's also affordable as the trailhead is an easy walk from Seward. See the Kenai Peninsula Hiking Trails map in the South-central Alaska chapter.

Information
For a brochure on the park, contact Division of Parks and Outdoor Recreation, PO Box 1247, Soldotna, AK 99669; ☎ (907) 262-5581.

CHENA DOME TRAIL
Fifty miles west of Fairbanks in the Chena River State Recreation Area, this 29-mile trail makes for an ideal three-day backpacking trip with you ending up where you began. The trail circles the entire Angel Creek drainage area and for the first three miles cuts through forest and climbs to the timberline. It ends that way as well but the vast majority of the hike follows tundra ridgetops where the route has been marked by rock cairns.

For those who enjoy romping in the alpine area, this route is a treat. Four times you reach summits that exceed 3000 feet and in between you are challenged with steep climbs and descents.

Chena Dome is the highest point on the trail, a flat-topped ridge at 4,421 feet that provides awesome views. Other highpoints of the hike are the wildflowers in July; the blueberries in August; wildlife, including bears, at anytime of the year and a public-use cabin that can be rented in advance. See the Chena Hot Springs Road map in the Fairbanks chapter.

Information
For a trail information sheet or to reserve the Angel Creek Cabin contact Alaska Division of Parks & Recreation (☎ (907) 451-2695), 3700 Airport Way, Fairbanks, AK 99709.

PINNELL MOUNTAIN TRAIL
The midnight sun is the outstanding sight on the Pinnell Mountain Trail, a 27.3-mile trek, 85 miles north-east of Fairbanks on the Steese Hwy. From 18 to 25 June, the sun never sets on the trail, giving hikers 24 hours of light each day. The polar phenomenon of the sun sitting above the horizon at midnight can be viewed and photographed at several high points on the trail, including the Eagle Summit trailhead.

The route is mostly tundra ridgetops that lie above 3500 feet and can be steep and rugged at times. Water is scarce in the alpine sections so you need to bring your own. The other highlight of the trip is the wildflowers (unmatched in much of the state) which carpet the Arctic-alpine tundra slopes, beginning in late May and peaking in mid-June. Hikers may spot small bands of caribou along with grizzly bears, rock rabbits and an occasional wolf in the valleys below but you need binoculars to really see any wildlife. The views from the ridge tops are spectacular, with the Alaska Range visible to the south and the Yukon Flats to the north. See the Steese Highway map in the Fairbanks chapter.

Information
For trail conditions or a free trail map, contact the Bureau of Land Management office in Fairbanks by writing to BLM District Office (☎ (907) 474-2302), 1150 University Ave, Fairbanks, AK 99709-3844.

WHITE MOUNTAINS SUMMIT TRAIL
The Bureau of Land Management (BLM), which maintains the Pinnell Mountain Trail, also administers the White Mountains trail network, including the Summit Trail. This 22-mile, one-way route was especially built for summer use and includes boardwalks over the wettest areas. The route winds through dense spruce forest, traverses scenic alpine ridgetops and Arctic tundra, and ends at Beaver Creek in the foothills of the majestic White Mountains.

On the banks of the creek is the Borealis-Le Fevre Cabin which can be reserved for

$25 a night. Reservations aren't really necessary as the last 2.5 miles of this trail drops off the ridgeline and descends into muskeg where hikers must ford up to four streams. The cabin receives little use during the summer as most parties end the day camping above the tree line as opposed to dealing with the low-lying swamp.

Hiking in for a night at the cabin is a five-day adventure. Even stopping short of the cabin, the hike still requires two or three days to camp near the highest point along the route. The trailhead is at *Mile 28* of the Elliott Hwy, 31 miles north of Fairbanks. You need to bring water which is scarce in the alpine sections. Highlights of the trek are the views from the top of Wickersham Dome – it's possible to see Mt McKinley, the White Mountains and the Alaskan Range.

Don't confuse the White Mountains Summit Trail (also called Summer Trail), which was made for hikers, with the Wickersham Creek Trail, that also departs from the trailhead (but leads more to the north-east). The Wickersham Creek or Winter Trail was cut primarily for snow machines, cross-country skiers and people using snow shoes, and leads through swampy, muskeg lowlands. See the Steese Highway map in the Fairbanks chapter.

Information

The BLM District Office in Fairbanks (☎ (907) 474-2200), 1150 University Ave, Fairbanks, AK 99709-3844, can supply a free map that lacks topographic detail but contains plenty of information on the trail. The office will also have current information on trail conditions and the availability of water, and is the place to reserve the Borealis-Le Fevre Cabin.

DENALI NATIONAL PARK – MT EIELSON CIRCUIT

Not the budget destination it once was, Denali National Park & Preserve is still a paradise for backpackers. The combination of terrain, outstanding scenery and wildlife that will make your heart pound make this park a popular attraction with all visitors.

However, only backpackers equipped to depart from the park road can escape the crowds that descend on Denali National Park from July to September. There is information about the park in the Denali National Park section in the Interior chapter.

The reserve is divided into 43 backcountry zones and only a regulated number of overnight hikers, usually from two to 12, are allowed into each zone with the exceptions of a few unregulated zones west of Wonder Lake. In the height of the summer, it may be difficult to get a permit for the zone of your choice and other zones will be closed off entirely when the impact of visitors is too great for the wildlife. The number of visitors tapers off dramatically in late August. Many people consider the end of August to mid-September as the prime time to see the park, as the crowds and bugs are gone and the fall colors are setting in.

There are many treks in the park. If time allows, begin by taking a ride on the shuttle bus and doing a day hike to get acquainted with a trail-less park, fording streams and rivers, and reading your topographic map accurately; then plan an overnight excursion. The Mt Eielson Circuit, 14 miles long, is a leisurely two-day walk, or a three-day trek if a day is spent scrambling up any of the nearby peaks.

The hike offers an excellent opportunity to view Mt McKinley, Muldrow Glacier and an abundance of wildlife. The route begins and ends at the Eielson Visitor Center and involves climbing 1300 feet through the pass between Mt Eielson and Castle Peak. The most difficult part of the walk, however, is crossing the Thorofare River, which should be done wearing tennis shoes and with an ice axe or sturdy pole in hand.

From Eielson Visitor Center, *Mile 66* of the park road, you begin the route (heading south-east) by dropping down the steep hill to Gorge Creek, crossing it and continuing south to the Thorofare River. Follow the tundra shelf along the east side of the river until you cross Sunrise Creek, which flows into the Thorofare River.

After fording Sunrise Creek, you must

then ford Thorofare River. Search the braided river in this area for the best crossing place and then proceed with extreme caution. Once you're on the west bank of the river, continue hiking south until you reach the confluence of Contact Creek and the Thorofare River. The creek flows almost due west from Bald Mountain Summit and leads up to the pass between Mt Eielson and Castle Peak. The pass, at an elevation of 4700 feet, is a good place to spend the night, as views of Mt McKinley are possible in clear weather.

From the pass, follow the rock cairns west to pick up Intermittent Creek. The creek leads to the gravel bars of Glacier Creek on the south-west side of Mt Eielson. This section of the river makes for easy hiking or a good camp site for those who want to tackle Mt Eielson from the west side, its most manageable approach. Head north along Glacier Creek until you reach the flood plain with the many braids of Camp Creek and the Thorofare River woven across it. Cross the channels and proceed north-east towards the Eielson Visitor Center. See the Denali National Park & Reserve map in the Interior chapter.

Information

For a shoebox full of free information about the park, contact the Denali National Park & Preserve (☎ (907) 683-2294 or (907) 683-9640 for a recorded message), PO Box 9, Denali Park, AK 99755. If you are in Anchorage, contact the National Park Service center for information about Denali or any national park in Alaska at the Alaska Public Lands Information Center (☎ (907) 271-2737), 605 West 4th Ave, Anchorage, AK 99501.

DEER MOUNTAIN TRAIL

Located in Ketchikan, the Deer Mountain Trail is often the first hike visitors do in the north country, and it rarely disappoints them. The trail is a steady but manageable climb to the sharp peak above the city, with incredible views of the Tongass Narrows and the surrounding area.

What many backpackers don't realize is that the Deer Mountain Trail is only part of a challenging, overnight alpine trail system. This 11-mile trip, which could include spending the night in a USFS cabin, begins with the three-mile Deer Mountain Trail and leads into the Blue Lake Trail. This path is a natural route along an alpine ridge extending four miles north to John Mountain. Here, hikers can return to the Ketchikan road system by taking the John Mountain Trail for two miles to Upper Silvis Lake and then following an old access road from the hydroplant on Lower Silvis Lake to the parking lot off the South Tongass Hwy.

Deer Mountain is a well-maintained and heavily used trail during the summer. Even though it is a steady climb, the hike to the summit is not overly difficult. A quarter of a mile before the summit you pass the junction to Blue Lake and the posted trail to the Deer Mountain USFS Cabin. The cabin, located above the tree line, sleeps eight people and used to be free. But it was improved and now the USFS rents it out for $25 per night. The Blue Lake Trail crosses alpine country with natural but good footing, although in rainy weather it may be difficult to follow. The scenery from the trail is spectacular.

Within two miles from the junction of the Deer Mountain Trail, you arrive at the shore of Blue Lake. This lake, at 2700 feet, is above the tree line in a scenic alpine setting.

If you are going to trek along the John Mountain Trail, it is marked by a series of steel posts and has 20% grades on the first mile from Upper Silvis Lake. After this it passes through alpine country. The John Mountain Trail is a fairly difficult track to follow and presents hikers with a challenge in reading their topographic maps and choosing the right route. See the Around Ketchikan map in the Southeast Alaska chapter.

Information

The cabins and trails are maintained by the USFS, which has its main headquarters and visitor center in the Federal Building on Stedman St in Ketchikan. You can contact them for trail conditions or more information at USFS Office (☎ (907) 225-3101), Federal Building, Ketchikan, AK 99901.

PETERSBURG CREEK TRAIL

A short hop across the Wrangell Narrows from the fishing community of Petersburg is Petersburg Creek Trail and Portage Mountain Loop that can be combined for a trek to two USFS cabins (reservations, $25 a night).

The Petersburg Creek Trail is well planked and provides backpackers with a wilderness opportunity and access to a USFS cabin without expensive bush-plane travel. Those planning to continue onto Portage Bay or Salt Chuck along Portage Mountain Loop should keep in mind that the trails are not planked or maintained and at best only lightly marked. The seven-mile trek to Portage Cove is very challenging and involves crossing wet muskeg areas or stretches flooded out by beaver dams.

Bring a fishing pole, as there are good spots in the creek for Dolly Varden and cut-throat trout. In August and early September there are large coho salmon runs throughout the area that attract anglers and bears.

The trek begins across Wrangell Narrows from Petersburg at the Kupreanof Island public dock. From the dock a partial boardwalk leads south for two miles past a handful of cabins and then turns north-west up the tidewater arm of the creek, almost directly across Wrangell Narrows from the ferry terminal. A well-planked trail goes from the saltwater arm and continues along the northern side of the freshwater creek to the Petersburg Lake USFS Cabin on the eastern end of the lake. From the cabin, Portage Mountain Loop continues north to Portage Bay.

The only hitch to this trip is getting across Wrangell Narrows to the public dock on Kupreanof Island. The USFS office above the post office in Petersburg provides a list of charter-boat operators, or contact Lodge Across the Bay (☎ (907) 772-9214) which

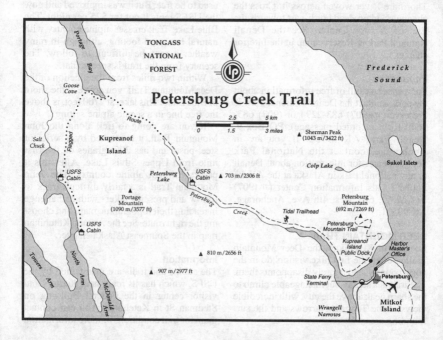

runs trekkers over to the lodge for $10 per person.

The cheapest way to get across Wrangell Narrows is to hitch a ride with one of the boats that cross the narrows every day. Go to the skiff float in the North Harbor (Old Harbor) near the Harbor Master's Office on the waterfront and ask around for boats crossing. A small population lives on the other side of the narrows so boats are constantly crossing, though at times you might have to wait a bit.

Those who arrive at Petersburg with their own kayak can paddle to the creek during high tide to avoid much of the hike along the tidewater arm. This is one trip that you'll want good waterproof clothing and rubber boots. Bring a tent or plan on reserving the cabins at least two months in advance, even earlier if you want to tackle the route in August during the salmon runs.

Information
The Petersburg District USFS office is on the 2nd floor of the post office along Main St. Make sure you contact the office before embarking to double-check on trail conditions and the status of the new trail from Salt Chuck to Petersburg Lake. Write or call Petersburg Ranger District (☎ (907) 772-3871), PO Box 1328, Petersburg, AK 99833.

DAN MOLLER TRAIL
Across the Gastineau Channel from the center of Juneau is the Dan Moller Trail. It was originally built during the 1930s for downhill skiers and at one time had three warming huts and two toll ropes along it. Today, the skiers continue along the North Douglas Hwy to the Eaglecrest Ski Area, while the Dan Moller Trail has become a popular access to the alpine meadows in the middle of Douglas Island.

The trail is 3.3 miles long and leads to a beautiful alpine bowl where the USFS has restored the remaining ski cabin. As with all USFS cabins, you have to reserve it in advance ($25 per night) but from 10 am to 5 pm it's shared by everybody as a warming hut.

Even if you can't secure the cabin, don't pass up this trail. Camping in the alpine bowl is superb and an afternoon or an extra day can be spent scrambling up and along the ridge that surrounds the bowl and forms the backbone of Douglas Island. From the ridge, there are scenic views of Douglas Island, Admiralty Island and Stephens Passage. See the Around Juneau map in the Southeast Alaska chapter.

Information
Contact the USFS office in Juneau for trail conditions and to reserve the Dan Moller USFS Cabin: Forest Service Visitor Information Center (☎ (907) 586-8751), Juneau Centennial Hall, 101 Egan Dr, Juneau, AK 99801.

KATMAI NATIONAL PARK – VALLEY OF 10,000 SMOKES
Katmai National Park & Preserve, an expensive side trip, is an intriguing place for a long-term wilderness adventure. A series of volcanic eruptions in 1912 left the area with unique land formations, including the popular Valley of 10,000 Smokes with its eerie, barren landscape. Wildlife is plentiful, with the brown bear the most prominent animal. Moose live in most parts of the park and the fishing is often said to be among the best in Alaska, as Katmai is an important spawning area for salmon.

The Valley of 10,000 Smokes is the most popular route for backpacking in Katmai, even though none of the famed '10,000 smokes' are active today. It begins with a short trail from Three Forks Overlook Cabin at the end of the park road to Windy Creek on the floor of the valley. A well-defined route then leads 12 miles south-east across the valley to some old US Geological Survey cabins on the side of Baked Mountain.

The hike is considered fairly challenging and includes some steep trekking along the foothills of the Buttress Range, followed by a drop down to the River Lethe, a major fording. From the river, you head for the divide between Broken Mountain (3785 feet) and Baked Mountain (3695 feet). You

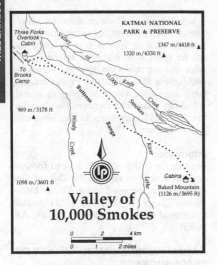

KATMAI NATIONAL PARK & PRESERVE

Three Forks Overlook Cabin

To Brooks Camp

1347 m/4418 ft ▲
1320 m/4330 ft ▲

969 m/3178 ft ▲

1098 m/3601 ft ▲

Knife Creek

Valley of 10,000 Smokes

Windy Creek

Buttress Range

River Lethe

Cabins ▲
Baked Mountain (1126 m/3695 ft)

0   2   4 km
0   1   2 miles

then head south-east to climb the short but steep slope of Baked Mountain to the cabins.

Getting Started

Turn to the Katmai National Park section in the Bush chapter for travel information for getting to and from Katmai National Park, but be prepared to pay around $350 to $450 for a return trip from Anchorage, 290 miles away. The only developed facilities in the park, apart from a couple of expensive wilderness lodges, are at Brooks Camp, the summer headquarters of the park.

At Brooks Camp there is lodging, a restaurant and a park store which sells limited quantities of freeze-dried food, topographic maps and white gas for camp stoves. The park store also rents tents, canoes, camp stoves and fishing rods among other things. It is best to stock up on food and fishing tackle in Anchorage to avoid emptying your entire money pouch here. Also keep in mind that the campground is free but you must reserve a site in advance of your trip as competition is extremely heavy (see the Bush chapter).

Like Denali National Park, Katmai has a shuttle bus that travels the park road daily. A

return trip on the bus costs $60 and a spot should be reserved the night before. Hikers who have a week in the park can skip the bus fare by walking the 23 miles out to Three Forks Overlook from Brooks Camp or take the bus just one-way and pay $30. The weather in the area can be consistently poor even by Alaskan standards; the skies are clear for only 20% of the summer and from September onwards strong winds are fairly frequent.

Information

In Anchorage, contact the Alaska Public Land Information Center (☎ (907) 271-2737), on the corner of 4th Ave and F St, for information about Katmai National Park. If you're planning to visit the park, it is best to write ahead for information to Katmai National Park (☎ (907) 246-3305), PO Box 7, King Salmon, AK 99613. Trail sections and distances follow:

Section	miles
Brooks Camp to Three Forks via Park Rd	23
Three Forks to Windy Creek*	1
Windy Creek to River Lethe via the Buttress Range*	7
River Lethe to Baked Mountain Cabins*	4

* Marked distances are rough estimates only.

WRANGELL-ST ELIAS NATIONAL PARK – DIXIE PASS

Even by Alaskan standards, Wrangell-St Elias National Park is a large tract of wilderness. At 13.2 million acres it's the largest US national park, contains the most peaks over 14,500 feet in North America and has the greatest concentration of glaciers in the continent. The park is a mountainous wilderness with three mountain chains (Wrangell, St Elias and Chugach) converging here. Wildlife in the park includes dall sheep, moose, three herds of caribou and, of course, lots of bears. The rivers are full of grayling, while trout thrive in the lakes.

The most common trek is to spend a day hiking up to Bonanza Mine or Root Glacier (see the Wrangell-St Elias National Park section in the Southcentral chapter). Dixie

Pass offers a longer, more rugged and more authentic wilderness adventure into the interior of this park. The trek up to Dixie Pass and back is 24 miles, but plan to camp there at least one or two extra days to take in the alpine beauty and explore the nearby ridges. This itinerary requires three or four days and is of moderate difficulty.

The trip begins from McCarthy Rd by hiking 2.5 miles up the Nugget Creek/Kotsina Rd and then another 1.3 miles along Kotsina Rd after Nugget Rd splits off to the north-east. The Dixie Pass trailhead is posted on the right-hand side of Kotsina Rd usually as a pile of rocks with a stick in it. It's a definite trail but easy to miss. The route begins as a level path to Strelna Creek, reached in three miles, and then continues along the west side of the creek for another three miles to the first major confluence.

After fording the creek, you continue along animal trails, fording the creek when necessary to avoid rock bluffs. It's five to six miles to the pass and along the way you cross two more confluences and hike through a interesting gorge. The ascent to the pass is a fairly obvious route. Dixie Pass offers superb scenery, good camping and opportunities to spend an extra day or two hiking the ridges.

The vast majority of people backtrack but the more adventurous return along the Kotsina Trail Loop. This trail begins by descending the pass and following Rock Creek north 5.5 miles to the Upper Kotsina River drainage area. The route involves hiking along the west side of the creek and then fording it at Pass Creek to avoid a canyon. Where Rock Creek merges into Kotsina River, you can pick up Kotsina Rd for the final 25 miles back to the Dixie Pass trailhead. In all, the Kotsina Trail Loop is a 45-mile hike that requires from five to seven days and that you have experience in wilderness travel. See the McCarthy Road map in the Southcentral Alaska chapter.

Information

For more information, contact the Wrangell-St Elias National Park headquarters (☎ (907) 822-5235, fax (907) 822-7216), PO Box 29,

Glennallen, AK 99588. During the summer there is also a ranger station (☎ (907) 823-2205) at Chitina.

Paddling

Bluewater Paddling

Bluewater in Alaska refers to the coastal areas of the state that are characterized by extreme tidal fluctuations, cold water temperatures and the possibility of high winds and waves. Throughout Southeast and Southcentral Alaska, the open canoe gives way to the kayak, and bluewater paddling is the means of escape into the beauty of the coastal wilderness.

Don't confuse whitewater kayaking with ocean touring. River running in light, streamlined kayaks wearing helmets, wet suits and executing Eskimo rolls has nothing to do with paddling coastal Alaska in ocean-touring kayaks. Every year, hundreds of backpackers with canoeing experience arrive in the north country and undertake their first bluewater kayak trip in such protected areas as Muir Inlet in Glacier Bay National Park or Tracy Arm Fjord, south of Juneau.

Tidal fluctuations are the main concern in bluewater areas. Paddlers should always pull their boats above the high-tide mark and secure them by tying a line to a rock or tree. A tide book for the area should be in the same pouch as the topographic map – paddlers schedule days around the changing tides, traveling with the tidal current or during slack tide for easy paddling. Check with local rangers for the narrow inlets or straits where rip tides or whirlpools might form, and always plan to paddle these areas during slack tides.

Cold coastal water, rarely above 45°F in the summer, makes capsizing more than unpleasant. Even with a life jacket, survival time in the water is less than two hours; without one it is considerably less. Plan your trip to run parallel with the shoreline and arrange your schedule so you can sit out rough weather without missing your pick-up date. If you do flip, stay with the boat and attempt to right it and crawl back in. Trying to swim to shore in Arctic water is risky at best.

Give a wide berth to marine mammals such as sea lions, seals and especially any whales that are seen while paddling. Glacial ice should also be treated with respect. It is unwise to get closer than a half a mile to a glacier face as icebergs can calve suddenly and create a series of unmanageable waves and swells. Never try to climb onto floating icebergs as they are extremely unstable and can roll without warning.

Framed backpacks are almost useless in kayaks; gear is better stowed in duffel bags or small day packs. Carry a large supply of assorted plastic bags, including several garbage bags. All gear, especially sleeping bags and clothing, should be stowed in plastic bags, as water tends to seep in even when you seal yourself in with a cockpit skirt. For getting in and out of kayaks as well as pulling them across muddy tidal flats, over-the-calf rubber boots, so-called Southeast sneakers, is the best footwear to have. You might also want to invest in a pair of felt liners to help keep the toes warm. Other equipment for any bluewater paddling include an extra paddle, a large sponge for bailing the boat, sunglasses and sunscreen, extra lines and a repair kit of duct tape and a tube of silicon sealant for fiberglass cracks.

Whitewater Paddling

Throughout Alaska's history, rivers have been the traditional travel routes through the rugged terrain. Many rivers can be paddled in canoes; others, due to extensive whitewater, are better handled in rafts or kayaks. If access is available by road, hardshell canoes and kayaks can be used. If not, you might have to arrange for a folding boat, such as a Klepper kayak, or an inflatable canoe or raft. Either that or pay for an additional bush flight so a hardshell can be carried in on the floats.

Alaska's rivers vary from one end of the state to the other but you will find they share characteristics not found on many rivers in the Lower 48. Water levels tend to change rapidly in Alaska. Due to temperature changes, rainfall and other factors, a river's depth and character can change noticeably even within a day. Many rivers are heavily braided and boulder-strewn and require a careful eye in picking out the right channel to avoid spending most of the day pulling your boat off gravel. And count on there being cold water, especially in any glacial-fed river where the temperatures will be in the mid-30s (°F). You can survive flipping your canoe in an Alaskan river but you'll definitely want a plan of action in case you ever do.

North Slope rivers in the Arctic tend to be extremely braided, swift and free flowing by mid-June. They remain high and silty for several weeks after that, but by mid-July even the sea ice is open enough to permit coastal lagoons.

Rivers flowing from the south slope of the Brooks Range are moving by early June and have good water levels through mid-August, while rivers in Fairbanks and Interior areas can usually be run from late May to mid-September. Further south around Anchorage and the Southcentral region, the paddling season lasts even longer – from May to September.

Much of the equipment for canoers is the same as it is for bluewater paddlers. You want all gear in dry storage bags, especially extra clothing, sleeping bag and tent. Tie everything into the canoe, you never know when a whirlpool or a series of standing waves will be encountered. Wear a life jacket at all times.

Many paddlers stock their life jacket with insect repellent, waterproof matches and other survival gear in case they flip and get separated from their boat.

Always make a float plan before you depart and leave it with either the bush pilot who flies you in or the nearest BLM or USFS office. Most importantly, research the river you want to run and make sure you have the ability to handle whatever class of water it's rated. Descriptions of paddling conditions follow:

Class I – easy
The river ranges from flatwater to occasional series of mild rapids.

Class II – medium
The river has frequent stretches of rapids with waves up to three-feet high and easy chutes, ledges and falls. The best route is easy to identify and the entire river can be run in open canoes.

Class III – difficult
The river features numerous rapids with high, irregular waves and difficult chutes and falls that often require scouting. These river are for experienced paddlers who either use kayaks and rafts or have a spray cover for their canoe.

Class IV – very difficult
Rivers with long stretches of irregular waves, powerful back eddies and even constricted canyons. Scouting is mandatory and rescues can be difficult in many places. Suitable in rafts or whitewater kayaks with paddlers equipped with helmets.

Class V – extremely difficult
Rivers with continuous violent rapids, powerful rollers and high, unavoidable waves and haystacks. These rivers are only for whitewater kayaks and paddlers who are proficient in the Eskimo roll.

Class VI – highest level of difficulty
These rivers are rarely run except by very experienced kayakers under ideal conditions.

MISTY FJORDS

The Misty Fjords National Monument, which encompasses 2.3 million acres of wilderness, lies between two impressive fjords – Behm Canal, 117 miles long, and Portland Canal, 72 miles long. The two natural canals give the preserve its trademark of extraordinarily deep and long fjords with sheer granite walls that rise thousands of feet out of the water. Misty Fjords is named after the rainy weather that seems to hover over it much of the year; the annual rainfall is 14 feet!

But don't let the rain put you off, Misty Fjords is an incredible place to spend a few days paddling. Lush forests, dramatic waterfalls plunging out of granite walls and diverse wildlife make the monument a kayaker's delight.

The destination for many kayakers are the smaller but equally impressive fjords of Walker Cove and Punchbowl Cove in Rudyerd Bay, off Behm Canal. The vegetation featured in this monument area is dense spruce-hemlock rainforest, while the abundant wildlife includes sea lions, harbor seals, killer whales, brown and black bears, mountain goats, moose and bald eagles.

Ketchikan is the departure point for most trips into Misty Fjord. Several tour boats run day trips into the area and there are the usual expensive sightseeing flights on small bush planes. Kayakers can either paddle out of the city (a seven to 12-day trip for experienced paddlers only) or utilize one of the tour boats to drop you off deep in Behm Canal near Rudyerd Bay and protected water.

Those contemplating paddling all the way from Ketchikan have to keep in mind that the currents around Point Alava and Alava Bay are strong and tricky, often flowing in unusual patterns.

Rounding the point into Behm Canal should be done at slack tide, which means leaving the city at high tide. The three to four-mile crossing of Behm Canal should also be done with caution, as northerly winds can create choppy conditions.

The Misty Fjords National Monument, which is administered by the US Forest Service, has 15 cabins (reservations needed, $25 rental fee) and 15 miles of trails. Two of the cabins, at Alava Bay and Winstanley Island, are right on Behm Canal and allow kayakers to end a day of paddling at the doorstep of a cabin. Many of the others are a short hike inland.

Getting Started

Alaska Cruises, a Ketchikan tour company, offers many services for kayakers to Misty Fjords, including a variety of boat and plane trips into the monument. The company will drop you off and pick you up at the entrance of Rudyerd Bay, one of the most scenic areas, for $175; a boat leaves on Tuesday, Thursday, Saturday and Sunday. For $225 you can be dropped or picked up at other locations along the route. This allows inexperienced paddlers to avoid much of the open water of Behm Canal and to experience only the protected and spectacular areas.

To rent a kayak contact Southern Exposure Sea Kayaking. This guiding company

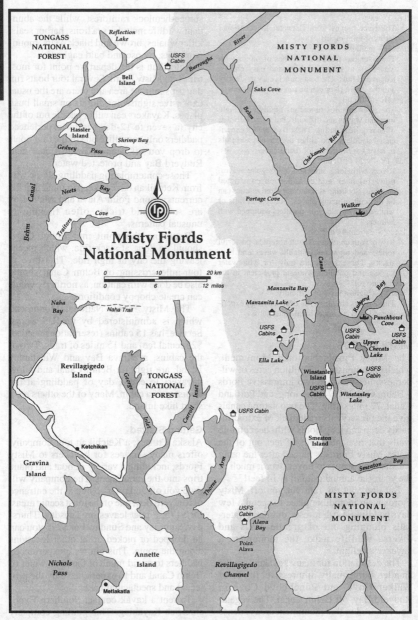

Misty Fjords
National Monument

0   10   20 km
0   6   12 miles

TONGASS
NATIONAL
FOREST

Reflection
Lake

USFS
Cabin

Burroughs   River

MISTY FJORDS
NATIONAL
MONUMENT

Bell
Island

Saks Cove

Behm

Chickamin River

Hassler
Island

Shrimp Bay

Gedney   Pass

Portage Cove

Walker   Cove

Neets   Bay

Traitors   Cove

Canal

Rudyerd   Bay

Naha
Bay

Naha Trail

Manzanita Bay

Manzanita Lake

USFS
Cabins

Punchbowl
Cove

USFS
Cabin

Ella Lake

USFS
Cabin

Upper
Checats
Lake

USFS
Cabin

Revillagigedo
Island

George   Inlet

TONGASS
NATIONAL
FOREST

Carroll   Inlet

Winstanley
Island

USFS
Cabin

USFS
Cabin

Winstanley
Lake

USFS Cabin

Smeaton
Island

Ketchikan

Gravina
Island

Thorne   Arm

Smeaton   Bay

MISTY FJORDS
NATIONAL
MONUMENT

USFS
Cabin

Alava
Bay

Nichols
Pass

Metlakatla

Annette
Island

Point
Alava

Revillagigedo
Channel

will rent a double fiberglass kayak for $50 per day and a single for $35 per day for one to three days. Rent it six or more days and the rate drops.

If possible, plan ahead and reserve your kayaks before the summer. Contact Southeast Exposure (☎ (907) 225-8829) at PO Box 9143, Ketchikan, AK 99901. Alaska Cruises (☎ (907) 225-6044) is at PO Box 7814, Ketchikan, AK 99901.

You cannot do this trip without good rain gear or a backpacker's stove, as wood in the monument is often too wet for campfires. Be prepared for extended periods of rain and have all gear sealed in plastic bags.

Either order your maps ahead of time or hope that the sections you want are in stock at the Tongass Trading Company, 203 Dock St in Ketchikan.

Then take the maps to the USFS office and have somebody point out the camping spots in the area where you are going to paddle. Since much of the monument is steep-sided fjords, good camp sites are scarce in many areas.

Information

For information or hand-outs on the monument, either visit the USFS office in the Federal Building in Ketchikan or contact the monument office at Misty Fjords National Monument (☎ (907) 225-2148), 3031 Tongass Hwy, Ketchikan 99901. Canoe-route sections and distances follow:

Section	miles
Ketchikan to Thorne Arm	13
Thorne Arm to Point Alava	9
Point Alava to Winstanley Island	21
Winstanley Island to Rudyerd Bay	9
Rudyerd Bay to Walker Cove	10

TRACY ARM

Tracy Arm, like Glacier Bay, is another fjord in the Southeast that features tidewater glaciers and steep 2000-foot granite walls that rise straight out of the water. This 30-mile arm was an ideal choice for novice kayakers as calm water is the norm here due to the protection the steep and narrow fjord walls provide.

Recently, however, the Arm has become a major attraction for tour ships and other motorized boats which takes away some of the wilderness experience many paddlers are seeking. If you have more experience as a kayaker, consider exploring the other fjords that adjoin Tracy Arm at Holkam Bay. Just to the south, is Endicott Arm, another 30-mile fjord that was carved by Dawes and North Dawes glaciers. It is the icebergs from these glaciers, some as large as three-story buildings, that often make it into the main shipping lanes of Stephens Passage, delighting travelers on the state ferries.

The other advantage of paddling Endicott Arm over Tracy Arm is there are considerably more places to pitch a tent at night. The only other camping spots in the first half of Tracy Arm are two valleys almost across from each other, eight miles north along the fjord, and a small island at the head of the fjord.

Extending from Endicott Arm is Fords Terror. This narrow water chasm was named after a US sailor who, in 1889, found himself battling surging rapids, whirlpools and grinding icebergs for six terrifying hours when he tried to row out against the incoming tide. Endicott Arm, Tracy Arm and Fords Terror together make up the Tracy Arm-Fords Terror Wilderness Area, a 653,000-acre preserve, where you can easily spend seven days paddling.

Getting Started

The departure point for Tracy Arm-Fords Terror Wilderness Area is Juneau. Kayaks can be rented for $35/45 a single/double per day from Juneau Outdoor Center (☎ (907) 586-8220), located in a warehouse in Douglas Harbor. As the rental shop is on Douglas Island figure on spending another $10 each way for transportation of the kayaks to the tour boats downtown. Try Adventure Bound Alaska (☎ (800) 228-3875), which charges only $125 per person for drop-off and pick-up. Wilderness Swift Charters (☎ (907) 463-3466) offers drop-offs at the entrance of Endicott Arm for $85 per person. Add another $85 if you want to

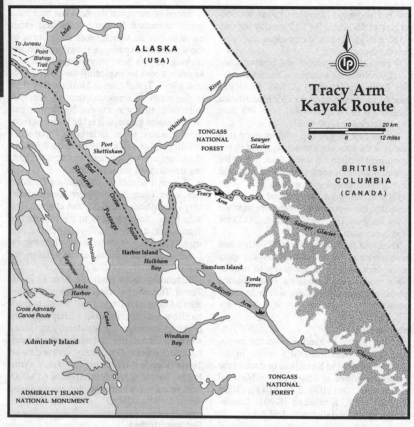

Tracy Arm Kayak Route

be picked up later. This makes the trip considerably easier as it is a two or three-day paddle in open water to either Endicott or Tracy Arm.

It is a pleasant two to three-day paddle from one end of the arm to the other. Most kayakers camp on Harbor Island, near the entrance of Tracy and Endicott arms, for at least one night even though level ground for a tent is difficult to find.

Purchase topographic maps from the Big City Bookstore at 100 North Franklin St in Juneau and then head over to the USFS Information Center in Centennial Hall at 101

Egan Drive for location of places to camp inside the arms. Also get a tide book, available in town, and plan your paddle with the tides for an easier trip.

Information

Tracy Arm Wilderness Area is managed by the USFS, which can be contacted for more information or hand-outs at USFS Juneau District (☎ (907) 581-8800), 8465 Old Dairy Rd, Juneau, AK 99801.

CROSS ADMIRALTY ISLAND

Admiralty Island National Monument, 50

miles south-west of Juneau, is the site of one of the few canoe routes in the Southeast. This preserve is a fortress of dense coastal forest, ragged peaks, and brown bears outnumbering anything else on the island including humans. The island also supports one of the largest bald-eagle nesting areas, and Sitka black-tailed deer can be seen throughout the monument.

The Cross Admiralty Canoe Route is a 32-mile paddle that spans the center of the island from the village of Angoon to Mole Harbor. Although the majority of it consists of calm lakes connected by streams and portages, the 10-mile paddle from Angoon to Mitchell Bay is subject to strong tides that challenge even experienced paddlers.

Avoid Kootznahoo Inlet as its tidal currents are extremely difficult to negotiate; instead, paddle through the maze of islands south of it. Leave Angoon at low tide, just before slack tide so that the water will push you into Mitchell Bay, and keep a watchful eye out for tidal falls and whirlpools. When paddling to Angoon, leave Salt Lake four hours before the slack tide, after high tide.

From the west end of Salt Lake there is a 3.5-mile portage to Davidson Lake, which is connected to Lake Guerin by a navigable stream. Between Lake Guerin and Hasselborg Lake is a 1.7-mile portage followed by a half-mile portage on the east side of Hasselborg Lake to Beaver Lake.

Canoeists can paddle from Beaver Lake to the east end of Lake Alexander, where they can take a 2.5-mile trail to Mole Harbor. This is the most common route followed, but there are numerous trails in the area including portages to Thayer Lake and a route along Hasselborg Creek that connects Salt Lake with Hasselborg Lake.

There are good camping spots at Tidal Falls on the eastern end of Salt Lake, on the islands at the south end of Hasselborg Lake and on the portage between Davidson Lake and Distin Lake. The USFS also maintains three-sided shelters (no reservations or rental fee) at the south end of Davidson Lake, at the east end of the Hasselborg Lake portage and at Mole Harbor. Finally, for those who can

plan in advance, there are several USFS cabins (reservations needed, $25 per night) along the route, including those on Hasselborg Lake, Lake Alexander and Distin Lake.

Getting Started
Juneau is the departure point for this four to seven-day trip, though you will probably have to pass through the small village of Angoon, a port of call on the State Marine Highway, which greatly reduces your transport costs as the one-way fare between Juneau and Angoon is $24. The problem is what to do at Mole Harbor, the east end of the trail. You can charter a bush plane to pick up your party and the boats, but that is an expensive exercise for those on a tight budget.

The best alternative is to backtrack to Angoon and return to Juneau on the ferry, which charges only $9 for canoes or kayaks. This means setting up your trip around the ferry schedule, but the savings are enormous.

Renting a boat for this trip is an even bigger challenge. You can rent a kayak at Juneau Outdoor Center (☎ (907) 586-8220) in Douglas, but it's a hassle to portage across the trails.

The preferred boat is a canoe. In Angoon, Favorite Bay Inn (☎ (907) 788-3123) has canoes for rent for $50 a day, less if you rent it for six days or more. But that means paddling a return trip to the small village. Purchase your topographic maps in Juneau and then take them to the USFS information center in Centennial Hall to have someone point out where strong tidal currents exist.

Information
This is a USFS-maintained preserve and information or a Cross Admiralty Island Canoe map ($3) can be obtained from the information center in the Juneau Centennial Hall or by writing to the Admiralty Island National Monument (☎ (907) 586-8790), 8461 Old Dairy Rd, Juneau, AK 99801. Canoe-route sections and distances follow:

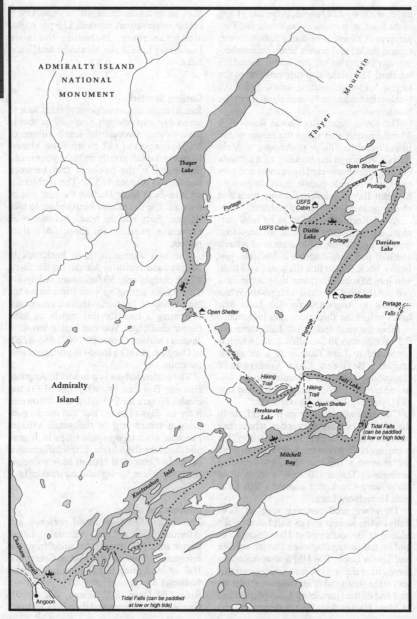

ADMIRALTY ISLAND
NATIONAL
MONUMENT

Thayer Mountain

Thayer
Lake

Open Shelter

Portage

Portage

USFS
Cabin

USFS Cabin

Distin
Lake

Portage

Davidson
Lake

Admiralty
Island

Portage

Open Shelter

Portage
Falls

Open Shelter

Salt Lake

Portage

Hiking
Trail

Hiking
Trail

Open Shelter

Freshwater
Lake

Tidal Falls
(can be paddled
at low or high tide)

Kootznahoo Inlet

Mitchell
Bay

Chatham Strait

Angoon

Tidal Falls
(can be paddled
at low or high tide)

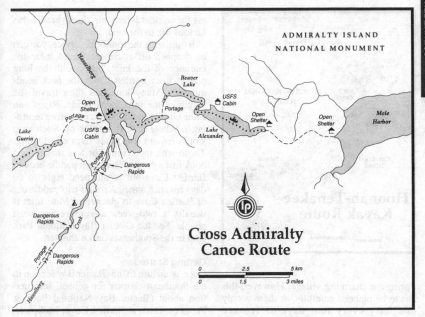

Cross Admiralty Canoe Route

Section	miles
Angoon to Salt Lake Tidal Falls	10.0
Tidal Falls to Davidson Lake portage	2.5
portage to Davidson Lake	3.5
Davidson Lake to Hasselborg Lake portage	6.0
portage to Hasselborg Lake	1.7
Hasselborg Lake to Beaver Lake portage	2.0
portage to Beaver Lake	0.5
Beaver Lake to Mole Harbor portage	3.0
portage to Mole Harbor	2.5

HOONAH TO TENAKEE SPRINGS

This 40-mile paddle follows the shorelines of Port Frederick and Tenakee Inlet from Hoonah to Tenakee Springs and includes a short portage of 100 yards or so. You pass an ever increasing number of clear cuts, especially around Hoonah and up Port Frederick, but there are few other signs of civilization along the route once you are beyond the two villages.

The area is part of the Tongass National Forest and consists of rugged and densely forested terrain populated by brown bears,

which are often seen feeding along the shoreline.

It is important to carry a tide book and to reach the portage at high tide. Boot-sucking mud will be encountered along the portage, but take heart, it is just a short walk over a low ridge to the next inlet. Highlights of the trip include the scenic south shore of Tenakee Inlet with its many bays and coves. The village of Tenakee Springs has a public bath house around its natural hot springs that will soothe any sore muscles resulting from the paddle.

Getting Started

This adventure is within the grasp of many backpackers on a budget as there is a ferry service to both Hoonah and Tenakee Springs from Juneau. The one-way fare from Juneau to Hoonah is $20 (to Tenakee Springs $22), with a $7 charge for kayaks.

The best way to start the paddle is from Hoonah in order to end the trip in Tenakee

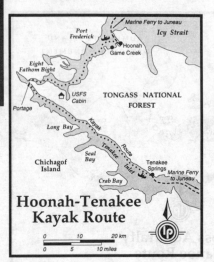

Hoonah-Tenakee
Kayak Route

Springs, a charming village. However, this has to be planned carefully, as there is only one ferry every four days to Tenakee Springs. Kayaks ($35/45 a single/double per day) can be rented from Juneau Outdoor Center (☎ (907) 586-8220), located in a warehouse in Douglas Harbor. Staff will also transport you and your boat to the Auke Bay Ferry Terminal for an additional $25.

More Information

For more information about the route or the surrounding area, contact the USFS office in the Hoonah Ranger District (☎ (907) 945-3631), PO Box 135, Hoonah, AK 99829.

GLACIER BAY NATIONAL PARK – MUIR INLET

More than anything else, Glacier Bay is a kayaker's paradise. When you combine the stunning alpine scenery of the Fairweather Mountains with more than a dozen glaciers and the marine wildlife, you can understand the attraction for bluewater paddlers, despite the high costs of getting there. Those with some extra change in their pocket and a few spare days can put together a paddle past three tidewater glaciers in Muir Inlet, includ-

ing the one that John Muir 'discovered' in his famous trip to the area.

By utilizing the tour-boat service, you can be dropped off at Sebree Island, near the entrance of the inlet, and avoid the long paddle from Bartlett Cove, the park headquarters. Many kayakers then travel the length of the inlet to McBride, Riggs and Muir Glacier at the north end before returning to Sebree Island for a pick-up. Such a trip would require five to six days of paddling. Those with more time but less money, can book just a drop-off and then paddle back to Bartlett Cove but would need eight to 10 days for such a trip. A round-trip paddle out of Bartlett Cove to glaciers of Muir Inlet is usually a two-week adventure for most people. See the Glacier Bay National Park map in the Southeast Alaska chapter.

Getting Started

Once again turn to the Glacier Bay section in the Southeast chapter for general information about Glacier Bay National Park & Preserve. Once at Bartlett Cove, backpackers can stay in the free campground while preparing for their excursion up the bay. Call at the visitor center to obtain a backcountry permit and to purchase the proper topographic maps.

It's best to arrange both kayak rental and tour boat passage in advance. Glacier Bay Sea Kayaks (☎ (907) 697-2257) in Gustavus will rent two-person kayaks for $50 a day or $40 for a rental five days or longer. The company also has singles for $40 a day or $35 for more than five days. The price includes paddles, lifevests, spray covers and loading the kayaks on the tour boat. The *Spirit of Adventure* will provide drop-off and pick-up at Sebree Island from mid-May to late September. One-way drop-offs are $88 per person, round-trip $174 per person.

You must pack waterproof clothing (pants, parka) and a camp stove. Stock up on supplies in Juneau to avoid having to purchase anything in Gustavus. To reserve a kayak, and you almost have to in July and August, contact Glacier Bay Sea Kayaks at PO Box 26, Gustavus, AK 99826.

The alternative is to rent a kayak in Juneau (see Juneau in Southeast chapter) and then use either Auk Nu Tours (☎ (907) 586-1337) or Kayak Express (☎ (907) 780-4591) for transport to Gustavus. Auk Nu is considerably cheaper but still it would cost $135 round trip to get you and your boat over to the Gustavus Dock.

Information

In Juneau, the USFS office in the Centennial Hall supplies information on Glacier Bay along with maps and hand-outs. For information before you depart, contact the National Park Service (☎ (907) 697-2230), Glacier Bay National Park, PO Box 140, Gustavus, AK 99826-0140. Route sections and distances follow:

Section	miles
Sebree Island to Wachusett Inlet	16
Wachusett Inlet to Riggs Glacier	9
Riggs Glacier to Muir Glacier	8
Muir Glacier to Sebree Island	33

SWANSON RIVER & SWAN LAKE

In the northern lowlands of the Kenai National Wildlife Refuge there is a chain of rivers, lakes, streams and portages (of course) that make up the Swanson River and nearby Swan Lake canoe routes. The trips are perfect for novice canoeists as rough water is rarely a problem and portages do not exceed half a mile on the Swan Lake system or one mile in the Swanson River area.

Fishing is good for rainbow trout in many of the lakes and wildlife is plentiful; a trip on either route could result in sightings of moose, bears, beavers or a variety of waterfowl. Both routes are popular among Anchorage canoeists. They are well marked and maintained, with open shelters along the way.

The Swanson River system links more than 40 lakes and 46 miles of river, and a one-way trip is 80 miles that ends at Cook Inlet in Captain Cook State Park. It's a more challenging trip than the Swan Lake paddle, especially when the water is low, but also a more popular one. More than 1,500 paddlers float the river annually because of the numer-

ous moose in the area, the silver salmon run in late summer and the lack of portages.

The easier Swan Lake route connects 30 lakes with forks of the Moose River; the one-way trip is 60 miles. A common four-day trip on Swan Lake begins at the west entrance of the canoe route and ends at Moose River Bridge on the Sterling Hwy.

Getting Started

To reach either the Swan Lake or Swanson River canoe routes, travel to *Mile 84* of the Sterling Hwy east of Soldotna and turn north on Robinson Lake Rd, just west of Moose River Bridge. Robinson Lake Rd turns into Swanson River Rd and leads to Swan Lake Rd 17 miles north from the Sterling Hwy. East on Swan Lake Rd are the entrances to both canoe systems, with the Swanson River route beginning at the very end of the road. The west entrance for Swan Lake is at Canoe Lake and the east is another six miles beyond at Portage Lake; both are well marked.

During the summer, the Great Alaska Fish Camp, a lodge at *Mile 81.7* of the Sterling Hwy where it crosses the Moose River, rents out canoes and runs a shuttle bus service to the head of Swan Lake Canoe Trail. You conveniently end up back at Moose River Bridge and the camp to eliminate any need for a pick-up. The rental fee for a canoe is $35 per day, and it costs $75 to have your boat and yourself shipped to the western entrance or the eastern entrance of the trail. The same outfitter also rents tents, camp stoves and sleeping bags to spur-of-the-moment wilderness adventurers. Contact the Great Alaska Fish Camp (☎ (907) 262-4515; (800) 544-2261 in the winter), PO Box 218, Sterling, AK 99672.

You can also rent canoes in Soldotna from Ronland's Sports Den (☎ (907) 262-7491), PO Box 2861, Soldotna, AK 99669; or The Fishing Hole (☎ (907) 262-2290), 139 B Warehouse, Soldotna, AK 99669, which also provides drop-off service.

Information

The visitor center for the Kenai National Wildlife Refuge is situated at *Mile 97.9* of

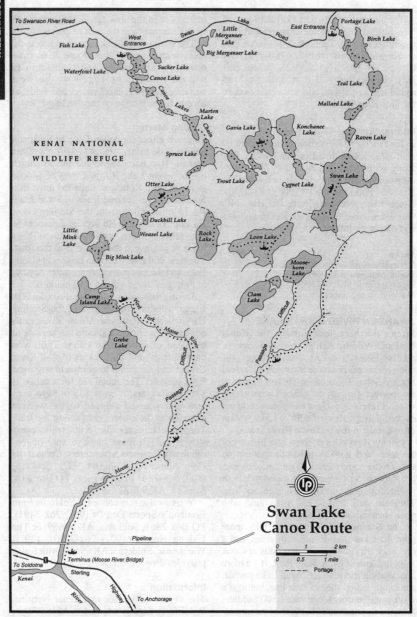

To Swanson River Road

West Entrance

Swan Lake Road

East Entrance

Portage Lake

Birch Lake

Fish Lake

Little Merganser Lake

Big Merganser Lake

Waterfowl Lake

Sucker Lake

Canoe Lake

Teal Lake

Canoe Lakes

Marten Lake

Mallard Lake

KENAI NATIONAL

Gavia Lake

Konchanee Lake

Raven Lake

WILDLIFE REFUGE

Spruce Lake

Trout Lake

Cygnet Lake

Swan Lake

Otter Lake

Duckbill Lake

Weasel Lake

Rock Lake

Loon Lake

Little Mink Lake

Moose-horn Lake

Big Mink Lake

Clam Lake

Camp Island Lake

West Fork Moose River

Grebe Lake

Difficult

Passage

Difficult Passage

Moose River

Moose River

Swan Lake
Canoe Route

Pipeline

Terminus (Moose River Bridge)

To Soldotna

Kenai

Sterling Highway

To Anchorage

0   1   2 km

0   0.5   1 mile

--- --- Portage

the Sterling Hwy, two miles south of Soldotna. You can also get information before your trip from the Refuge Manager, Kenai National Wildlife Refuge (☎ (907) 262-7021), PO Box 2139, Soldotna, AK 99669.

KATMAI NATIONAL PARK – SAVONOSKI RIVER LOOP

This route begins and ends at Brooks Camp (the summer headquarters of Katmai National Park) and takes paddlers into more remote sections of the preserve, offering the best in wilderness adventures without expensive bush-plane travel.

The complete circuit is an 80-mile, six to eight-day paddle, depending on weather and wind conditions.

The trip is long and moderately difficult. No whitewater is encountered but the 12-mile run of the Savonoski River can be a challenging paddle because of its braided nature and many deadheads and sweepers.

You also have to carry your boat across a mile-long portage that during most summers is a mud-hole of a trail. The first section from Brooks Camp to the Bay of Islands is especially scenic and well protected at the end where you dip in and out of the Bay of Islands. Here the water is deep and clear and offshore islands provide superb camp sites.

It takes two to three days to paddle through Naknek Lake and the Bay of Islands to the Lake Grosvenor portage. From this portage, it is a 14-mile paddle along the south shore of Lake Grosvenor to the Grosvenor River. The Grosvenor is a slow-moving clear-water river where paddlers often spot moose, bears, beavers and river otters. It flows into the Savonoski River, a prime brown-bear habitat, especially when the salmon are running. For this reason, park rangers often recommend paddling the 12 miles of the Savonoski in a single day and not camping along the river.

Canoeists also have to keep a sharp eye

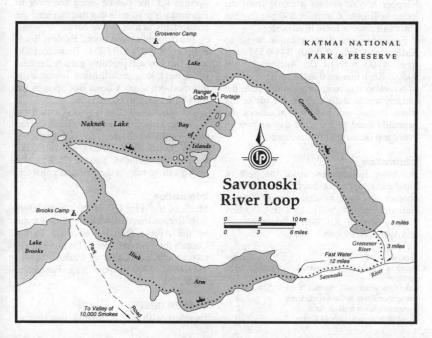

out for obstructions and sand bars that may develop in the river. The last leg is the 20-mile paddle along the south shore of the Iliuk Arm back to Brooks Camp.

Getting Started

See the Katmai National Park section in the Bush chapter for information on getting to and from the park; also check the section on the Valley of 10,000 Smokes in this chapter for the special backcountry needs of the preserve. Paddlers have to remember that Katmai is famous for its sudden and violent storms, some that last for days. Good waterproof clothing is essential and all gear should be sealed in plastic bags. It is unwise to paddle too far from shore, as it leaves you defenceless against sudden storms or high winds.

Getting a canoe or hard-shell kayak into the park is now possible as there is a jet-boat service from King Salmon to Brooks Camp. But most visitors either haul in a folding Klepper Kayak or rent a canoe from the lodge in Brooks Camp for $30 per day but you can't reserve them in advance.

For more rental information write to Katmailand Inc (☎ (800) 544-0551, toll free), 4700 Aircraft Dr, Anchorage, AK 99502. Keep in mind that the preferred mode of travel on this route is a kayak due to the sudden winds and rough nature of the big lakes. People still paddle it in canoes but generally need to sit out a day or two on every trip because of foul weather.

Information

For more information about the park or hand-outs covering backcountry travel, contact the park headquarters at Katmai National Park (☎ (907) 246-3305), PO Box 7, King Salmon, AK 99613. Route sections and distances follow:

Section	miles
Brooks Camp to Lake Grosvenor portage	30
portage	1
Lake Grosvenor to Grosvenor River	14
Grosvenor River to Savonoski River	3
Savonoski River to Iliuk Arm	12
along Iliuk Arm to Brooks Camp	20

CHENA RIVER

The Chena River is one of the finest rivers for canoeing in the Fairbanks area and a longtime favorite among local residents. It flows through a landscape of rolling forested hills with access to alpine tundra above 2800 feet. The river features no whitewater and paddlers only have to watch out for the occasional sweeper or log jam.

Wildlife in the area includes brown bears, moose, red foxes, beavers and river otters, while the fishing is excellent for grayling and northern pike. With the Interior's long, hot summer days, this trip can be an outstanding wilderness adventure.

Getting Started

Chena Hot Springs Rd provides access to the river at *Mile 27.9* east of Fairbanks, *Mile 28.6*, *Mile 29.4*, *Mile 33.9* at Four Mile Creek and *Mile 39.6* at North Fork Chena River where there is a state *campground* (20 sites, $6 fee). From *Mile 39.6* of Chena Hot Springs Rd, the paddle along the river to Fairbanks is a 70-mile trip that can be done comfortably in four to five days.

You can rent canoes from 7 Bridges Boats & Bikes (☎ (907) 479-0751). Boats cost $30 a day but you will probably get a better deal for a week-long rental. More importantly, transport out along Chena Hot Springs Rd for a $1 a mile can be provided.

The other alternative is to rent a used car in Fairbanks (see the Getting Around section in the Fairbanks chapter), drop off the canoe, return the car to Fairbanks and hitchhike back to the trailhead. See the Cheena Hot Springs Road map in the Fairbanks chapter.

Information

Much of the river lies in the Chena River State Recreation Area, which is administered by the Alaska Division of State Parks. Contact the Fairbanks office for more information at the Division of Parks (☎ (907) 451-2695), 3700 Airport Way, Fairbanks, AK 99709.

BEAVER CREEK

Travelers with lots of time, a yearning to

paddle through a roadless wilderness but not a lot of funds for bush-plane travel, will find Beaver Creek the ultimate adventure. The moderately swift stream, characterized by long clear pools and frequent rapids, is rated Grade I in difficulty and can be handled by novice canoers with previous expedition experience. The BLM manages the 111-mile creek, as part of the White Mountains National Recreation Area, where it flows through rolling hills forested in white spruce and paper birch and past the jagged peaks of the White Mountains.

The scenery is spectacular, the chances of seeing another party remote and you'll catch so much grayling you'll probably never want to eat another one after the trip. If you take a day off at Victoria Creek and scale the 5000-foot high Victoria Peak, you should see wildlife such as moose, bears and mountain sheep. You can also spend a night in the Borealis-Le Fevre Cabin, a BLM cabin on the banks of Beaver Creek.

The trip begins from *Mile 58* of the Steese Hwy at Nome Creek where nine times out of 10, due to low water, you'll be forced to line your boat 10 miles to its confluence with Beaver Creek. Most paddlers then plan on seven to 10 days to reach Victoria Creek, a 127-mile trip, where gravel bars nearby are used by bush planes to land and pick paddlers up.

From the confluence with Nome Creek to Victoria Creek is a 90-mile paddle along Beaver Creek through the White Mountains where the stunning scenery includes limestone towers, buttes and spires. Large gravel bars provide plenty of places to pitch a tent along the river here which generally poses few technical difficulties.

A day's paddle beyond Victoria Creek, Beaver Creek spills out of the White Mountains into Yukon Flats National Wildlife Refuge where it slows down and meanders through a marshy area. Eventually it flows north into the Yukon River, where after two or three days, you'll pass under the Yukon River Bridge on the Dalton Hwy, thus avoiding another air fare if arrangements have been made to be picked up. This is a 395-mile

paddle and a three-week expedition – the stuff great Alaska adventures are made of. See the Steese Highway map in the Fairbanks chapter.

Getting Started

You can rent a canoe and get transport through 7 Bridges Boats & Bikes (see the previous Chena River section). Transport through 7 Bridges would be almost $250 at $1 a mile as the start of the paddle is at *Mile 58* of the Steese Hwy where a rough 4WD track, US Creek Rd, leads down to Nome Creek. The end of the paddle for many is the Yukon River Bridge on the Dalton Hwy, 175 miles north of Fairbanks.

Also check into Interior Canoe and Outfitting (☎ 479-9697) on the Parks Hwy towards Ester. Keep in mind that Steven's Village is half a day's paddle from the Yukon River Bridge on the banks of the river. Spending a night in this small village is a cultural experience in itself and you could use its one radio-telephone to contact your driver and arrange an exact pick-up time for the next day.

You can also check with the Fairbanks Visitors Bureau for any tour company running trips up the Dalton Hwy.

Information

For more detailed information contact the Steese-White District of the BLM (☎ (907) 474-2200), at 1150 University Ave, Fairbanks, AK 99709.

Other Activities

Wilderness Fishing

Many people have a 'fish-per-cast' vision of angling in Alaska. They expect every river, stream and lake, no matter how close to the road, to be bountiful but often go home disappointed when their fishing efforts produce little to brag about. Serious anglers visiting Alaska carefully research the areas to be fished and are equipped with the right gear and tackle. They often pay for guides or book a room at remote camps or lodges where rivers are not 'fished out' by every passing motorist.

If, however, you plan to undertake a few wilderness trips, by all means pack a rod, reel and some tackle. It's now possible to purchase a backpacking rod that breaks down into five sections and has a light reel; it takes up less room than soap, shaving cream and wash rag. In the Southeast and Southcentral regions, backpackers can catch cutthroat trout, rainbow trout and Dolly Varden (a fish similar to the other two). Further north, especially around Fairbanks, you'll get grayling, with its sail-like dorsal fin, and arctic char; during August, salmon seem to be everywhere.

If angling is just a second thought, load an open-face spinning reel with light line, something in the four to six-pound range, and take along a small selection of spinners and spoons. After you arrive, you can always purchase the lures used locally, but in most wilderness streams I've rarely had a problem catching fish on Mepps spinners, sizes No 1 to No 3. Other lures that work well are Pixies, Dardevils and Krocodiles.

For fly fishing a No 5 or No 6 rod with a matching floating line or sinking tip is well suited for Dolly Vardens, rainbows and grayling. For species of salmon a No 7 or No 8 rod and line are better choices. For ease of travel, rods should break down and be carried in a case.

Here is a brief synopsis of the most common non-salmon species you find in lakes and streams all summer long.

Rainbow Trout This is without a doubt the best fighting fish and thus the most sought after by most anglers. Fishing from shore in lakes is best in late spring and early summer, just after ice break-up, and again in the fall when water temperatures are cooler. During the height of the summer, rainbows move into deeper water in lakes and you usually need a boat to fish them.

Fish them at dawn and dusk when, on calm days, they can be seen surfacing for insects. Turn to spinners, size No 1 to No 3, and

flashy spoons but avoid treble hooks (or clip one or two of the hooks on them) as they make releasing fish hard. The workhorse fly is the lake leech, in either purple or olive, fished with a slow retrieve on sinking-tip lines.

Cutthroat Trout The cutthroat picks up its name from reddish-orange slash along the inner edge of the fish's lower jaw. Outside Southeast Alaska, most traveling anglers end up casting for resident cutthroats that spend their entire lives in the streams and lakes as opposed to larger anadromous (those migrating upstream to breed) cutthroats that migrate to saltwater where food is more abundant. This trout likes to stay around submerged logs, aquatic vegetation or near other cover and is an aggressive feeder.

In most lakes, you can take them on small spinners, size No 0 up to No 2, but they also will hit on larger spoons, especially red-and-white Dardevils. For fly fishing, a floating line with a nine-foot leader and a slowly twitching mosquito-larva fly can be very effective. The best time to fish is early morning and at dusk when light is low and cutthroats are often cruising the shallows for food.

Dolly Varden This is one of the most widespread varieties of fish in Alaska and their aggressive behavior makes them easy to catch. Dolly Varden are often caught near the entrances of streams or along weed beds near shore, making them accessible to backpacking anglers. With spinning gear, use spinners in sizes No 1 and No 2 or small spoons. Fly fishers often use a blue smolt fly on a sinking-tip line and a short leader and use an erratic strip retrieve. Other streamers work as well, while a pin-head muddler and a floating line is often used in shallow rivers or when Dolly Varden are holding in shallow water.

Arctic Char A closely related cousin to the Dolly Varden, the arctic char is not quite as widespread in Alaska. Often anglers will confuse the two species. Arctic char will be encountered predominantly in the Alaska Peninsula and Bristol Bay areas, on Kodiak Island, in some lakes in the Kenai Peninsula and in the Brooks Range and to the north. Spawning male char turn brilliant red or gold with red or orange spots while Dolly Varden are just as brightly colored but only on their lower body. For the most part, anglers use the same tackle and techniques for catching both species.

Grayling There's no mistaking the grayling, its long dorsal fin allows travelers to identify the fish even if they have never hooked one before. Grayling in streams feed at the surface or in mid-water drift and almost exclusively on insects or larvae. In other words, they are a fly fisher's dream. They are extremely receptive to dry flies and rarely are so selective as to choose one pattern over another. Generally small flies (sizes No 16 to No 18) will produce more rises than larger ones. Even if you have spinning gear, tie on a clear plastic bubble four to six feet above a dry fly and fish for grayling with that.

Fishing License A nonresident's fishing license costs $50 a year (compared with only $15 for residents) or you can purchase a three-day license for $15 or a 14-day one for $30; every bait shop in the state sells them.

Books The Alaska Department of Fish & Game puts out a variety of material including the *Recreational Fishing Guide*. You can obtain the 72-page guide ($5) by writing to the Department of Fish & Game (☎ (907) 465-4112), PO Box 25526, Juneau, AK 99802-5526.

Perhaps the most comprehensive angler's guide to the state is *Alaska Fishing* by Gunnar Pedersen and Rene Limeres (Foghorn Press, 555 De Haro St, San Francisco, CA 94107; 640 pages, photos, drawings). The authors begin with a detailed look at the different species of Alaska fish, including the best techniques used, and then follow with a review of each region and

major river system throughout the state. To order directly from the publisher call ☎ (800) 364-4676.

Equally good for fly fishing is *Flyfishing Alaska* by Anthony Route (Johnson Books, 1880 S. 57th Court, Boulder, CO 80301; 230 pages). Route writes a fly fishing column for the *Anchorage Daily News* and does a particularly good job covering the species found in Alaska's rivers, streams and lakes and the tackle and equipment you need to catch them.

For those who want to combine a cabin rental with fishing there is *Fishing Alaska on Dollars a Day* by Christopher & Adela Batin (Alaska Angler Publications, PO Box 83550, Fairbanks, AK 99708; 352 pages, maps, photos, ☎ (800) 455-8000 to order). The book is based on Forest Service cabins that can be rented for $25 a day. The guide describes each cabin, fishing in the immediate area and gateway city.

Watching Wildlife

The BLM says to avoid being disappointed by not seeing wildlife in Alaska, the first thing you have to do is to not pack high expectations. Every year visitors arrive thinking they will see herds of wildlife, only to go home with a photo of a squirrel that was raiding their picnic table.

To see a variety of wildlife you have to leave the roads, travel into the backcountry and learn how to 'watch wildlife'. Here's what the BLM recommends:

- KEEP YOUR DISTANCE
  Don't try to get too close with camera in hand. Most wild animals react with alarm when approached by humans on foot or in vehicles. Repeated disturbances may cause animals or birds to leave the area for good. Also learn animal behavior patterns that will tip you off when you are too close. Mammals often raise their heads high with ears pointed in the direction of the observer if you are closing in too fast. They might also exhibit signs of skittishness or display aggressive behavior. You are too close to birds if they also seem skittish or raise their heads to watch you. They may preen excessively, give alarm calls, flush repeatedly or even feign a broken wing when felt threatened by your presence.

WILDERNESS

Mink   Black Bear   Dall Sheep   Snowshoe
                                   Hare

Wolf   Lynx   Mountain   Caribou
                 Goat

Moose   Brown Bear   Wolverine   Human

Human and wildlife tracks

- **DON'T HURRY**
  The more time you take in the backcountry, the greater the opportunity to observe wildlife. Instead of moving camp every day, set up a base camp and do nothing at dawn or dusk but scan areas for wildlife.
- **USE PROPER EQUIPMENT**
  You will see more by carrying high-quality binoculars or even a spotting scope. If you're set on photographing wildlife, make sure you have the telephoto lens, tripod and the right film for low-light conditions to deliver those close-up shots.
- **BLEND IN**
  Wear muted colors, sit quietly and even avoid using scented soaps and perfumes.
- **LOOK FOR WILDLIFE SIGNS**
  There's added enjoyment in recognizing animals by their tracks, droppings or vocalizations. To do that you might want to carry a field guide or two (see the Books section in the Facts for the Visitor chapter).

Southeast Alaska

The north country begins in Southeast Alaska, as do the summer adventures of many visitors to the state, and for good reasons. The Southeast is the closest part of Alaska to continental USA; Ketchikan is only 90 minutes away by air from Seattle or two days on the Alaska Marine Hwy ferry from Bellingham.

The Southeast, affected greatly by warm ocean currents, has the mildest climate in Alaska and offers warm summer temperatures averaging 69°F, with an occasional heat wave that sends temperatures to 80°F. Similarly, the winters are equally mild and subzero day temperatures are rare. Residents who have learned to live with an annual rainfall of 60 to 200 inches call the frequent rain 'liquid sunshine'. The heavy precipitation creates the dense, lush forests and numerous waterfalls most travelers come to cherish.

Travel to and around the Southeast is easy. The Alaska Marine Hwy connects this roadless area to Bellingham in the US state of Washington and provides transport around the area, making it the longest (and many think the best) public ferry system in North America. Relaxing three-day cruises through the maze of islands and coastal mountains of the Southeast's Alexander Archipelago are a pleasant alternative to the long and often bumpy Alcan (Alaska Hwy). The ferry connects 14 ports and services 64,000 residents, of which 75% live in Juneau, Ketchikan, Sitka, Petersburg and Wrangell.

However, the best reason to begin and end your trip in the Southeast is its scenery. Few places in the world have the spectacular views found in the Southeast. Rugged snow-capped mountains rise steeply from the water to form sheer-sided fjords, decorated by cascading waterfalls. Ice-blue glaciers that begin among the highest peaks, fan out into a valley of dark-green Sitka spruce trees, and melt into wilderness waters that support

HIGHLIGHTS

- Gaze at the totems and shoreline scenery of Sitka National Historical Park
- Soak in the hot springs at the Tenakee Springs bathhouse
- See Mendenhall Glacier from above by hiking the West Glacier Trail in Juneau
- View icebergs, glaciers and sea life on a boat tour of Tracy Arm Fjord
- Hiss and boo at Alaska's most beloved villain, Soapy Smith, at the *Days of '98* show in Skagway
- Experience stunning mountain scenery as you ride the historic narrow gauge White Pass & Yukon Railroad

whales, sea lions, harbor seals and huge salmon runs.

At one time the Southeast was the heart and soul of Alaska, and Juneau was not only the capital but the state's major city. However, WWII and the Alcan shifted the state's growth to Anchorage and Fairbanks. Much of the region lies sleepily in the Tongass National Forest which, at 16 million acres, is the largest national forest in the USA.

In recent years, the Southeast has experienced an incredible boom in summer tourism, but there is still room to breathe. The population density is about 2.5 people per sq mile and will probably stay that way as much of the region is federal monuments

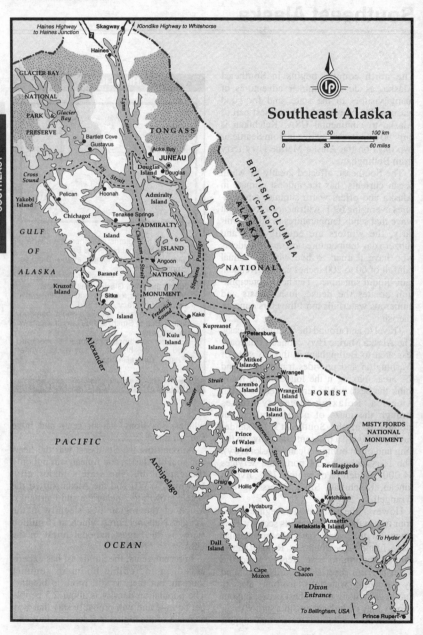

and preserves such as the spectacular Glacier Bay National Park & Preserve, Admiralty Island and Misty Fjords national monuments, Klondike National Historical Park, Tracy Arm and Fords Terror wilderness.

More than anywhere else in Alaska, each community in the Southeast clings tightly to its own character, color and past. There is Norwegian-influenced Petersburg and Russian-tinted Sitka. You can feel the gold fever in Skagway, see lumberjacks and fishers in Ketchikan or venture to Juneau for a hefty dose of government, glaciers and uncontrolled growth.

The best way to visit the Southeast is to purchase a ferry ticket from Bellingham to Skagway ($246 one way) with lengthy stops at a handful of towns. To rush from the Lower 48 to Juneau and then fly to Anchorage is to miss some of the best things that Alaska has to offer.

Ketchikan

Ketchikan, otherwise known as the First City, has a population of almost 14,000 and is on the south-west side of Revillagigedo (ra-vee-ah-ga-GAY-doh) Island, only 90 miles north of Prince Rupert. It is the first stop the ferry makes in Alaska so tourists pile off the boat for their first look at the north country, and rarely does Ketchikan disappoint them.

History

The town grew around salmon canneries and sawmills. The first cannery was built in 1883, and at one time Ketchikan was proclaimed the 'Salmon Capital of the World', a title that reappeared in 1996 with a new welcome arch across Mission St. A sawmill was built in the center of Ketchikan in 1903, and in 1954 the huge Ketchikan Pulp Mill was constructed at Ward Cove. However, in the 1970s over-fishing nearly collapsed the salmon fisheries while strikes began to mar the logging industry.

Just as Ketchikan began to recover from

hard times, the sawmill in the city center was subject to a strike in 1983 that resulted in Louisiana-Pacific closing the mill. Two years later the historical downtown mill was razed for a parking lot. In 1984, Louisiana-Pacific shut down the Ward Cove Pulp Mill, the area's major employer, for six months, and the population of Ketchikan decreased during the hard times of the early 1980s.

The city and the people survive, a credit to their frontier spirit. Although the First City's industries include government services and, increasingly, tourism, fishing and timber are still its trademark. Fishing provides almost 20% of the city's economy and 230 commercial fishers are based in Ketchikan. The timber industry (consisting of logging, a sawmill and a pulp mill) account for almost 15% of the jobs. These industries have given the city its rough-and-tumble character and on a Saturday night Ketchikan bars are full, loud and lively.

If you stay in Ketchikan longer than an hour, chances are good that it will rain at least once, if not several times. The average annual rainfall is 162 inches, but has been known to be more than 200 inches. Despite all the rain, the only people with umbrellas are tourists. First City residents never seem to use them, nor do they let the rain interfere with their daily activities, even outdoor ones, whether it be fishing, hiking or having a softball game. If they stopped everything every time it drizzled, Ketchikan would cease to exist.

Orientation

The city is spread out – it is several miles long and never more than 10 blocks wide. Ketchikan is centered around one road, Tongass Ave, which runs along the shores of Tongass Narrows and sometimes over it, supported by pillars. Crossroads appear mostly in the city center and the area surrounding the ferry terminal known as West End. There were no traffic signals in Ketchikan until 1984, and the first one was installed despite the objections of many residents. Many businesses and homes are suspended above the water or cling to the

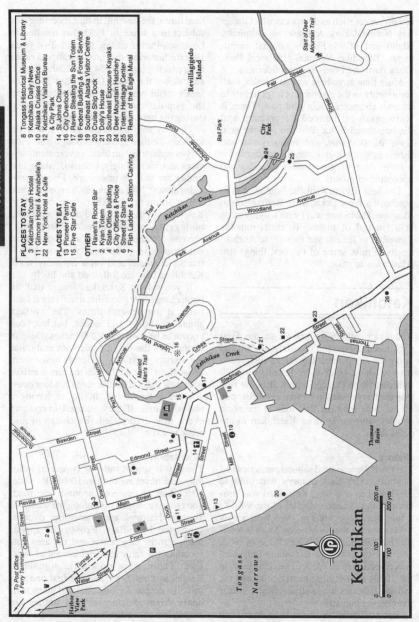

PLACES TO STAY
3 Ketchikan Youth Hostel
11 Gilmore Hotel & Annabelle's
22 New York Hotel & Cafe

PLACES TO EAT
13 Pioneer Pantry
15 Five Star Cafe

OTHER
1 Raven's Roost Bar
2 Kyan Totem
4 State Office Building
5 City Offices & Police
6 Street of Stairs
7 Fish Ladder & Salmon Carving

8 Tongass Historical Museum & Library
9 Ketchikan Daily News
10 Alaska Cruises Office
12 Ketchikan Visitors Bureau & City Park
14 St Johns Church
16 City Overlook
17 Raven Stealing the Sun Totem
18 Federal Building & Forest Service
19 Southeast Alaska Visitor Centre
20 Dolly's House
21 Cruise Ship Dock
23 Southeast Exposure Kayaks
24 Deer Mountain Hatchery
25 Totem Heritage Center
26 Return of the Eagle Mural

Ketchikan

hillside and have winding staircases or wooden streets leading to their front doors.

On a clear day – and there are a few during the summer – Ketchikan is a bustling community. It is backed by forested hills and surrounded by a waterway that hums with float planes, fishing boats, ferries and large cruise ships; to the south is the distinctively shaped Deer Mountain. Whether basked in sunshine or painted with a light drizzle, Ketchikan is an interesting place to start an Alaskan summer.

Information
Tourist Offices The Ketchikan Visitor Bureau (☎ 225-6166) on the City Dock can supply general information about Ketchikan and the city bus system. The bureau is open Monday to Friday from 8 am to 5 pm and when the cruise ships are in on Saturday and Sunday.

For information about hiking trails, cabin reservations or other outdoor opportunities, head to the trip-planning room of the Southeast Alaska Visitor Center (☎ 228-6214) on the corner of Bawden and Mills streets. Managed by the USFS, the room contains reference guides, topo maps and a huge selection of videos to watch. Hours are 8.30 am to 4.30 pm daily in the summer.

Money National Bank of Alaska has an office downtown on Main St (☎ 225-2184) and a branch in the Plaza Mall (☎ 225-4141).

Post The main post office is near the ferry terminal on Tongass Ave.

Travel Agencies Ketchikan Travel (☎ 225-4400) has a location downtown on Main St and an office in the airport.

Bookshops The best place to purchase Alaska books is at the Southeast Alaska Visitor Center. There is also a Waldenbooks in the Plaza Mall.

Library Near the corner of Park Ave and Dock St is the Centennial Building housing the Ketchikan Public Library (☎ 225-3331).

It is open daily and until 8 pm Monday through Wednesday. Often the library has used books for sale.

Laundry Highliner Laundromat (☎ 225-5308), which also has showers, is at 2703 Tongass Ave while The Mat Laundry & Showers (☎ 225-0628) is at 989 Stedman St.

Medical Services Ketchikan General Hospital (☎ 225-5171) is at 3100 Tongass Ave, between the ferry terminal and the downtown area.

Things to See
The best way to explore Ketchikan is on foot with a three-hour, two-mile walk around the city center. Start at the Visitor Bureau, a brown building on the busy City Dock, and pick up a free *Ketchikan Walking Tour Map* which has a two-mile tour that takes about two hours to cover. Begin by heading up Mission St and swinging (south-west) over to Mill St. Within three blocks, on the corner of Mills and Bawden streets, is the new **Southeast Alaska Visitor Center**, built in 1995 and managed by the USFS. The minute you step inside you are impressed with the facility. Three huge totems greet you in the lobby while a school of more than two-dozen silver salmon, suspended from the ceiling, lead you into the exhibit hall and a slice of rainforest. Admission to the theater and exhibit hall is $3, the book shop and impressive trip-planning room are free. Hours are 8.30 am to 4.30 pm daily in the summer.

By turning right (south-west) on Stedman St, you cross Ketchikan Creek and come to **Creek St**, not so much a street as a boardwalk built on pilings. This was the famed red-light district in Ketchikan for half a century until prostitution became illegal in 1954. During its heyday, Creek St supported up to 30 brothels. The first house, with its bright red doors and windows, is **Dolly's House**, the parlor of the city's most famous madam, Dolly Arthur.

The house has since been turned into a museum dedicated to this infamous era and is open only when there are tour ships in port

Creek St once was the famed red-light district of Ketchikan.

– almost daily during summer. For a $3 admission fee you can see the brothel, including its bar that was placed over a trap-door to the creek for quick disposal of bootleg whiskey. There are another 20 buildings on Creek St including small shops and a restaurant. Perhaps the best attraction on this unusual street is free – watching the salmon swim up Ketchikan Creek to spawn.

Across from Creek St (to the south) is **Thomas Basin**, one of three boat harbors in the city. It is impossible to stay in Ketchikan and not spend any time at the waterfront. The lifeblood of this narrow city is found in its collection of boat harbors, float planes and fishing fleets that stretch along the lapping waters of the Tongass Narrows.

Thomas Basin, along with Thomas Street (another boardwalk built on pilings) is the most picturesque harbor. An hour or so spent at the docks will acquaint you with Ketchikan's fishing fleet and the three kinds

of fishing boats – gillnetters, power trollers and seiners. You may even end up at the colorful Potlatch Bar on Thomas St having a brew with someone from the fishing fleet.

Head east onto Deermont St to reach the **Totem Heritage Center**, where totem poles salvaged from deserted Tlingit communities are brought to be restored to their original condition. The total collection, the largest in Alaska, numbers more than 30. Five of the poles are on display in the central gallery along with indigenous art and a Southeast Alaskan fish camp from the 1920s. Guided tours are scheduled around the times when the large cruise ships are in port. The center (☎ 225-5900) is open daily from 8 am to 5 pm in the summer; admission is $3.

A bridge from the Totem Heritage Center crosses Ketchikan Creek to the **Deer Mountain Hatchery** (☎ 225-6760), a fascinating place where biologists annually raise 150,000 king salmon and an equal number of coho salmon and then release them into the nearby stream. Observation platforms, outdoor displays and friendly workers provide an interesting lesson in the salmon's life cycle. In July or later, you'll see not only the salmon fry but returning adult fish swimming upstream to spawn. Hours are 8 am to 4.30 pm daily and admission is $3, which includes a performance of Alaska Native dancers and a sample of smoked salmon in the gift shop. A ticket to both the hatchery and Totem Center is $5.

Next to the hatchery is **City Park**, a quiet spot with numerous small streams, each, it seems, with its own wooden bridge and bench. The park is a pleasant place to escape from the bustling crowds and tour groups that fill the city when a cruise ship is in town.

From the hatchery head down Park Ave, cross Ketchikan Creek again and on the other side of the road you will soon see the Upland Way stairs. A climb up the stairs takes you to a viewing platform overlooking the city center, Thomas Basin and Creek St. Beyond Upland Way on Park Ave you will arrive at another bridge crossing Ketchikan Creek, with a fish ladder at the creek's falls. The ladder enables salmon to reach upstream spawning gravels; it's a magnificent sight when these fish leap against the current during the late-summer migration. Next to the bridge is one end of **Married Man's Trail**, a delightful boardwalk that leads back to Creek St.

Park Ave curves south towards the city center and ends near Dock St and the Centennial Building which houses the **Tongass Historical Museum** as well as the library. The museum features a small collection of local and indigenous artefacts, many of them tied in with Ketchikan's fishing industry. Hours are 8 am to 5 pm daily and admission is $2. Near the Centennial Building is the 'Raven Stealing the Sun' totem, which was commissioned by the city in 1983.

Head west along Dock St, and alongside the Ketchikan Daily News Building is Edmond St. This is the 'Street of Stairs', as it leads to a system of long staircases. Back along Dock St, the next crossroad to the west is Main St which leads north to the Ketchikan (AYH) Hostel on the corner of Grant St and to the huge Kyan Totem another block beyond that.

Hiking

There is a variety of hiking adventures in the Ketchikan area, but the majority are either out of town or the trailhead must be reached by boat. The one exception is the Deer Mountain Trail, a 3.1-mile climb which begins near the city center and provides access to a USFS cabin ($25 a night, reserve in advance) and two other alpine trails (see the Hiking section in the Wilderness chapter).

This trail is extremely well maintained and is a great way to escape the masses from the cruise ships that overtake the downtown area. There is an excellent lunch spot and viewpoint of Ketchikan just two miles up.

Ward Lake Nature Walk This is an easy trail around Ward Lake that begins near the shelters at the far end of the lake. The trail is 1.3 miles of flat terrain with information signs. To reach the lake, follow North Tongass Hwy seven miles out of the city to the pulp

mill on Ward Cove, turn right on Ward Lake Rd and follow it for a mile.

Perseverance Trail This trek is a 2.2-mile walk from Ward Lake Rd to Perseverance Lake through mature coastal forest and muskeg. The view of the lake with its mountainous backdrop is spectacular, while the hiking is easy as the trail consists mainly of boardwalks and steps. The trailhead is 1.5 miles from the start of Ward Lake Rd.

Talbot Lake Trail This trail starts from Connell Lake Rd which is a gravel road that heads east, three miles from the start of Ward Lake Rd. The 1.6-mile trail is a mixture of boardwalk and gravel surface and leads north from the Connell Lake Dam to Talbot Lake, where it ends at private property. The more adventurous, however, can cross a beaver dam at the south end of the lake and hike eastward onto the north ridge of Brown Mountain to eventually reach its 2978-foot summit. Keep in mind this is steep country with no established trail.

Cycling

Ketchikan has two bicycle trails along Tongass Ave. The most scenic is the 2.5-mile trail that follows the water from the downtown area to Saxman Totem Park. The other follows North Tongass Hwy to Ward Lake Recreation Area, a one-way ride of 6.4 miles. You can rent bikes at The Pedalers (☎ 723-1088) in the Spruce Mill Center next to the Visitor Bureau. Rentals are $25 for a half day, $40 for a full day.

Paddling

Many short and long-term kayak trips begin in Ketchikan and range from an easy paddle in well-protected waters to a week-long trip to Misty Fjords National Monument and back (see the Paddling section in the Wilderness chapter). Kayaks can be rented from Southeast Exposure (☎ 225-8829) at 507 Stedman St and transported to some areas through Alaska Cruises (☎ 225-6044). Double kayaks rent for $50 a day or $45 for six days or more. There are also singles available. Before any trip, purchase the topographic map that covers the area from Tongass Trading Company at the north end of City Dock, or from Murray Pacific at 1007 Water St.

If you just want to try your hand kayaking without the rigors of an overnight paddle on your own, Southeast Exposure has two great paddling tours. The first is a three-hour waterfront day trip where a guide leads you past the historic downtown area of the city. The cost is $50 per adult and includes all equipment. The second is an extended day trip to a number of areas including Carroll Inlet, George Inlet or Naha Bay. The cost is $70 for six hours of paddling.

Naha River Trail From the end of the North Tongass Hwy, it's an eight-mile paddle to the trailhead for the Naha River Trail, a 6.5-mile path that follows the river and leads to three USFS cabins and two lakes. The trailhead is on Naha Bay, a body of water that leads into Roosevelt Lagoon through a narrow outlet. Kayakers trying to paddle into the lagoon must enter it at high slack tide, as the narrow pass becomes a frothy, roaring chute when the tide is moving in or out. The current in the salt chuck actually changes directions depending on the tide.

The trail is a combination of boardwalk, swing bridges and an uphill walk to Naha River, Jordan and Heckman Lake cabins. All three cabins ($25 per night) must be reserved in advance at the USFS office in Ketchikan. This is an interesting side trip as locals fish these waters for salmon and trout, while in August it's often possible to see bears catching salmon at a small waterfall two miles up the trail from the Roosevelt Lagoon.

Wolf Creek Trail An even easier paddle is the five-mile trip from the end of North Tongass Hwy to the trailhead for the Wolf Lake Trail at Moser Bay. The 2.5-mile trail passes through timber slopes and over muskeg to a three-sided shelter (no reservation or rental fee) at the outlet of Wolf Lake. A steep hill is encountered near the salt water but this should not discourage the average hiker.

George & Carroll Inlets At the end of South Tongass Hwy past Herring Bay, you are already in George Inlet, which makes this three to four-day paddle an easy one in water that is calm most of the time. North winds do occasionally whip down George Inlet but both waterways are protected from southwesterlies, the prevailing winds in the Ketchikan area.

While not on the same dramatic scale as Misty Fjords, the two inlets are scenic and it's an easy way to explore some of Ketchikan's backcountry. The return trip from Herring Bay to the end of George Inlet is a 25-mile paddle.

Organized Tours
Need a tour of the city? Ketchikan, being the cruise ship port that it is, has a bundle of different tours you can sign up for. Tour giant Gray Line is here but for something a little personal, and cheaper, try the local companies. Little Red Riding Tours (☎ 225-0411) uses a small red bus for a two-hour tour that includes Totem Heritage Center, Creek St and even a short walk through a rainforest for $20 per person. City Tour (☎ 225-9465) has a non-stop, one-hour tour for $15 and a two-hour tour that includes Totem Bight State Park for $25. Rainbird Deluxe Tours (☎ 254-0647) uses 25-passenger coach buses to show you the sights downtown, Saxman Village and a rainforest walk in a two-hour tour for $20. You can book any of these at the Visitor Bureau on the City Dock.

Special Events
Ketchikan has three major festivals during the summer, of which the 4 July celebration is the biggest and the best. It includes a parade, contests and softball games, an impressive display of fireworks over the channel and a logging show sponsored by the Alaska Loggers Association.

On a smaller scale is the Blueberry Festival that takes place in the lower floor and basement of the State Office Building and

Main Street Theater in mid-August. The festival consists of an arts & crafts show, singers and musicians, and food stalls that serve blueberries in every possible way.

Places to Stay

When booking a bed in the city, be prepared for an additional 11.5% in city tax and bed tax or $6 to $9 above the prices quoted here.

USFS Cabins There are 30 cabins in the Ketchikan area; most need to be reserved in advance and cost $25 per day. With the exception of Deer Mountain Cabin, which you can hike to, the rest require charter air time. The following cabins are close to the city, which reduces air-charter time, the biggest cost factor in using them. There are numerous bush-plane operators in Ketchikan; two of the more reliable ones are Taquan Air (☎ 225-8800 or (800) 770-8800), 1007 Water St, Ketchikan, AK 99901 and Ketchikan Air Service (☎ 225-9888 or (800) 656-6608), 1600 Airport Terminal Bldg, Ketchikan, AK 99901.

Alava Bay Cabin is on the southern end of Behm Canal. It provides ample opportunity for hiking and beachcombing along the coast, freshwater fishing and viewing wildlife such as black bear and Sitka deer. The cabin is 20 air miles from Ketchikan.

Fish Creek Cabin is connected by a short trail to Thorne Bay. You can either paddle to it (a three to four-day trip) or fly in, as it is only 18 air miles from Ketchikan. There is a trail to nearby Low Lake; fishing for cutthroat trout, rainbow trout and Dolly Varden is possible in the creek.

Patching Lake Cabins (there are two cabins) on Patching Lake are 20 air miles from Ketchikan. At either one there is good fishing for cutthroat trout and grayling.

Camping There are four public campgrounds in Ketchikan and unfortunately, none of them is close to town. *Settler's Cove* (12 sites, $6 fee) is 16 miles north of the ferry terminal and worth the hassle of getting there. The state recreation area features a scenic beach and coastline, picnic shelters

and a quarter mile trail to a waterfall and observation deck. This far out, it's not nearly as busy as the campgrounds situated at Ward Lake.

The other three campgrounds are on Ward Lake Rd. Take North Tongass Hwy four miles north of the ferry terminal and then turn right onto Ward Lake Rd just before the pulp mill on Ward Cove. The first campground is *Signal Creek* (19 sites, $8), a mile up the road. It is followed by *CCC Campground* (four sites, $8) a quarter of a mile further up and *Last Chance Campground* (25 sites, $10), another 1.8 miles along Ward Lake Rd.

The entire area is known as the Ward Lake Recreational Area and a night spent here is worth all the effort it takes to reach it. Along with the campgrounds there are four scenic lakes and three trails that dip back into the surrounding lush rainforest. Just keep in mind how close the pulp mill is; when the wind is right you'll know it's nearby.

Hostels The *Ketchikan (AYH) Hostel* (☎ 225-3319) is in the basement of the United Methodist Church on the corner of Grant and Main streets in the center of the city. It's open from Memorial Day to Labor Day and provides kitchen facilities, showers and a space on the floor with a mat to sleep on. The hostel is interesting because it always seems full with travelers heading north for a long trip. Since Ketchikan is their first Alaskan stop, they fill the recreation room with travel talk and much excitement in the evenings. The fee is $7 per night for hostel members and $10 per night for non-members. If you're arriving at night, call the hostel to check whether space is available.

The *Rain Forest Inn* (☎ 225-7246) is at 2311 Hemlock St, 0.7 miles from the ferry terminal and half a block from the bus stop on the corner of Tongass Ave and Jefferson St. The Inn offers dormitory bunks for $25 per night and provides showers, laundry facilities and a guest lounge. Head to the hostel if you can, this place is, at best, rundown.

B&Bs Ketchikan Reservation Service (☎ 247-5337 or (800) 987-5337) will book a room in a B&B in advance for you. B&Bs in the city have the full 11.5% tax, those outside the city limits have only the 6% bed tax. You might consider *The Great Alaska Cedar Works* (☎ 247-8287) which was at one time the foreman of a salmon cannery's house. Eleven miles north of the city on a beach, this B&B offers cottages for $55 for single or double or $100 for four people.

B&Bs within easy walking distance of downtown include *Captain's Quarters* (☎ 225-4912) at 325 Lund St, which has singles or doubles for $75 and *Innside Passage* (247-3700), a half mile north of the city center with rooms for $60/75. Almost four miles south of downtown is *House of Stewart* at 3725 South Tongass Hwy with two rooms for $50 for a single or a double.

Hotels Avoid the Union Rooms Hotel, a flophouse on Mill St. The *Gilmore Hotel* (☎ 225-9423) at 326 Front St used to be another run-down place before undergoing major renovations, giving it a historical flavor. Rooms begin at $70/75 for single or double. Nearby is the *Ingersoll Hotel* (☎ 225-2124), 303 Mission St with singles/doubles for $84/94. Also downtown is the *New York Hotel* (☎ 225-0246), above the Thomas Basin Boat Harbor at 207 Stedman St, a charming eight-room hotel with a view of the waterfront. Singles or doubles are $69.

Further out there's also *Super 8 Motel* (☎ 225-9088) situated a half-mile south of the ferry terminal at 2151 Sea Level with singles/doubles for $76/83. The *Best Western Landing* (☎ 225-5166 or (800) 428-8304) is located across from the airport ferry at 3434 Tongass Ave and has singles or doubles for $86.

Places to Eat

There's a good choice of places to eat in Ketchikan, but all places reflect the expensive Alaskan prices that usually send the newly arrived visitor into a two-day fast. If

this is your first Alaskan city, don't fret – it gets worse as you go north!

Downtown For breakfast in the city center, there is the *Pioneer Pantry* at 124 Front St, that opens at 7 am and where three eggs, potatoes and toast costs $7. In the Gilmore Mall on Front St is *Annabelle's*, a chowder house and saloon with a 1920s décor. Chowder of the day is $4, sourdough-bowl chowder is $8 and an excellent selection of salads cost from $7 to $10. A stack of sourdough pancakes in the morning will only set you back $4. Equally charming is the *New York Cafe*, where you can get a window-side table overlooking Thomas Basin Harbor.

The best restaurant for vegetarian dishes and other 'healthy stuff' is *The Five Star Cafe*, a pleasant restaurant with a variety of art on display in the Star Building on Creek Street. The menu ranges from home-made soups and baked goods to a nice variety of sandwiches for around $6, salads and espresso drinks. Try the PNTHB (Peanut Butter, Tahini with Honey and sliced Bananas).

Elsewhere There is a *McDonald's* at Plaza Mall on Tongass Ave if you have a Big Mac attack. Nearby on Tongass Ave is *Harbor Lights Pizza*, which features mediums with one item for $12, subs and $6 pasta dinners as well as a view of the boat harbor and even tables outside if it's not raining.

Closer to downtown is *Sea Breeze Cafe*, overlooking a float-plane dock at 1287 Tongass. The cafe has an adjoining bar, outdoor deck and opens at 6 am for breakfast. Sandwiches and burgers are $6 to $8, seafood dinners $15 to $24.

Next door to the Plaza Mall is *Carr's*, with an excellent salad bar for $3 a pound, espresso bar, deli and ready-to-eat items including stir fry. It's open 24 hours and has a seating area inside that overlooks the Tongass Narrows.

Entertainment

After hiking all day, if you're still raring to go, try the *1st City Saloon*, 803 Water St, a sprawling bar with giant TV screens, pool tables, a cigar shop, live music, small dance floor and an impressive selection of beers. Edgar Winter once played here (obviously at the end of his career). There is a cover charge. More live music is featured a couple nights a week at *Raven's Roost* on Tongass Ave at the north end of the tunnel.

The *Sourdough Bar* at the north end of the City Dock has walls covered with photos of fishing boats while ship bells, ring floats and other fishing memorabilia hang from the ceiling. Just up Tongass Ave before the tunnel is *Arctic Bar*, a quiet little place where you can go for an afternoon brew on a hot summer day. The bar is built on pillars above the water and has a sun deck that overlooks Tongass Narrows. Here you can enjoy the sea breeze while watching the float planes take off and land, as Taquan Air is next door and moors its planes at the dock right below the deck.

The longtime fisher's pub is the *Potlatch Bar* on Thomas St just above the Thomas Basin Boat Harbor. For cheap beer without all the fixings, try the *Eagles Club* on Creek St, where pints are under $3 and small pitchers $5.

Getting There & Away
Air Alaska Airlines (☎ 225-2141) flies to Ketchikan with stops at other major Southeast communities as well as Anchorage and Seattle. There are several flights between Ketchikan and Juneau, including one that locals call the 'milk run', as it stops at Petersburg, Wrangell and Sitka and is little more than a series of take-offs and landings.

Boat It's an exceptional day when there isn't a ferry departing from Ketchikan for other Southeast destinations or Bellingham. The one-way fares from Ketchikan to Wrangell are $24, Petersburg $38, Juneau $74, Sitka $54 and Haines $88.

The MV *Aurora* provides service to Metlakatla and Hollis on Prince of Wales Island. The trip runs almost daily during the summer and the one-way fare to Hollis is $20

and to Metlakatla $14. For exact sailing times call the ferry terminal (☎ 225-6181).

Getting Around
The Airport The Ketchikan airport is on one side of Tongass Narrows and the city is on the other. To go from one to the other you can hop on the airport ferry that leaves the airport 15 and 45 minutes past the hour to a ramp next to the ferry terminal. The fare is $2.50 one way for walk-on passengers. There is also the Airporter bus that will take you to the downtown area for $12, ferry fare included.

Bus The city bus system consists of small buses that hold up to 30 passengers and follow a circular route from the ferry terminal in the West End to the area south of Thomas Basin, circling back by the Totem Heritage Center and within a half mile of the Deer Mountain trailhead. The route does not include Saxman Totem Park or anything north of the ferry terminal. Buses run from 5.30 am to 9.30 pm during the week and less on Saturday and Sunday. Fare is $1.

Car Alaska Car Rental (☎ 225-5000 or (800) 662-0007) with an office in the airport terminal and another at 2828 Tongass Ave, rents vehicles for $45 a day with unlimited mileage. For two to four people, this is a good way to spend a day seeing the sights out of town. There is also Practical Car Rental (☎ 225-8778) with the same rates.

AROUND KETCHIKAN
Saxman Totem Park
For a look at the world's largest standing collection of totem poles, head 2.3 miles south of Ketchikan on South Tongass Hwy to Saxman Totem Park. The park's 24 poles were bought here from abandoned villages around the Southeast and were restored or recarved in the 1930s.

At the entrance to the park is the impressive **Sun & Raven totem**, probably the most photographed one in Alaska, and the rest of

SOUTHEAST

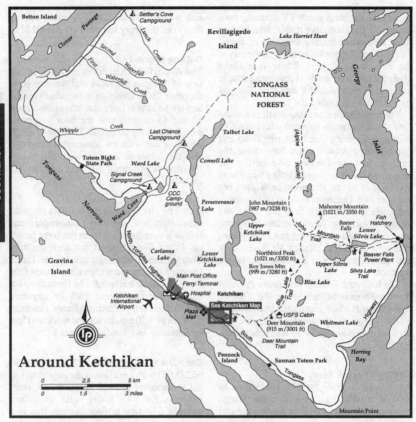

Around Ketchikan

the park is uphill from there. Among the collection is a **replica of the Lincoln Pole**; the original is in the Alaska State Museum in Juneau. This pole was carved in 1883 to commemorate the first sighting of white people, using a picture of Abraham Lincoln.

Saxman Totem Park, an incorporated Native Alaskan village of more than 300 residents, also has a community hall, clan house and theater where you can see a slide and sound show about the park and Tlingit culture. This cultural center (☎ 225-5163) is open daily in the summer with the hours depending on when the cruise ships are in

port. Most people see the village through an organized tour. You can book one at the Visitor Bureau or call the center but expect to pay $20 for a two-hour tour. If you can do without the slide show and cultural performances, just head down to the park and wander around.

From Saxman, South Tongass Hwy continues another 12 miles. Although there are no stores, restaurants or campgrounds here, this is a very scenic stretch, more scenic I believe, than driving North Tongass Hwy. You end up at Beaver Falls Hatchery where the trailhead for Silvis Lake Trail is located.

The Rise and Fall of Totems

Ironically Europeans both stimulated and then almost ended the art of carving totems by Native Alaskans in the Southeast region. Totems first flourished in the late 18th century after clans had acquired steel knives, axes and other cutting tools through the fur trade with White explorers.

Between 1880 and the 1950s the art form was almost wiped out when a law forbidding potlatches took effect and banned the Native ceremony for which most totems were carved. When the law was repealed in 1951 a revival of the totem carving took place and still continues.

The oldest totems generally are 50 to 60 years old. After they reach this age the heavy precipitation and acidic muskeg soil of Southeast Alaska takes its toll on the cedar pole until the totem finally tumbles due to the wood rotting. ■

North Tongass Hwy

Totem Bight Ten miles north of Ketchikan, is a state historical park (no entry fee) which contains 14 restored or recarved totems and a colorful community house. Just as impressive as the totems is the park's wooded setting and the coastline. A viewing deck overlooks the Tongass Narrows. The North Tongass Hwy ends 18 miles north of Ketchikan at Settler's Cove State Campground, another scenic coastal area with a lush rainforest bordering a gravel beach and rocky coastline.

Misty Fjords National Monument

This spectacular national monument, which begins just 22 miles east of Ketchikan, is best noted for its sea cliffs, steep-sided fjords and rock walls that jut 3000 feet straight out of the ocean. Walker Cove, Rudyerd Bay and Punchbowl Cove (the most picturesque areas of the preserve) are reached via Behm Canal, the long inlet that separates Revillagigedo Island from the Coastal Mountains on the mainland.

Wildlife at Misty Fjords includes brown or black bears, mountain goats, Sitka deer,

bald eagles and a multitude of marine mammals. As the name suggests, the monument can be a drizzly place with an average annual rainfall of 150 inches, but many people think the real beauty of Misty Fjords lies in the granite walls and tumbling waterfalls wrapped in a veil of fog and mist.

The preserve is popular with kayakers (see the Paddling section of the Wilderness chapter), while less adventurous visitors view it on day cruises or sightseeing flights. Viewing Misty Fjords from a charter plane costs $130 per person for 1½ hours and most charter companies in town offer the trip, including Taguan Air (☎ 225-8800). The time actually spent viewing the monument is short, however, and the area's peaceful atmosphere is lost when the pilot has to yell at you over the roar of the bush plane. The best deal is probably through Island Wings (☎ 225-2444), a one-plane, one-pilot company. Michelle Masden offers a three-hour tour, that includes a hour-long stopover and picnic lunch for $150. She also has an hour flight into the area for $90 per person.

Tour ships offer a more dramatic perspective of the preserve while letting you view it at a much more leisurely pace. Alaska Cruises (☎ 225-6044) offers an 11-hour cruise for $140 that departs from Hansen float, adjacent to the tunnel. The boat leaves at 8 am every Tuesday, Thursday, Saturday and Sunday, and the cruise includes three meals. A shorter seven-hour trip in which you return aboard a bush plane costs $185. If you can plan ahead, the best way to experience Misty Fjords is to rent one of the 15 USFS cabins (reservations needed, $25 per night) in the area.

Metlakatla

This small Native Alaskan community used to be a common day trip out of Ketchikan until the ferry *Chilkat* was taken out of service. Metlakatla is now served four times a week by the *Aurora*; on Saturday the ferry visits the community twice, making it possible to do a day trip from Ketchikan. The rest of the week the ferry stays in port only as long as it takes to unload, generally half an hour, which means viewing the town requires either staying overnight or flying back to Ketchikan.

Metlakatla, 12 miles south-west of Ketchikan on the west coast of Annette Island, is a well-planned community in the heart of the Annette Island Indian Reservation, the only reservation in Alaska. The village (pop 400) bustles during the summer as its boat harbor overflows with fishing vessels and its cold storage plant and cannery, which has been operating continuously since 1901, is busy handling the fleet's catch.

Things to See While on board the ferry or from the shore near the terminal, you can see one of the community's four fish traps, a large collection of logs and wire with a small hut off to one side. The fish traps, illegal everywhere else in Alaska, catch salmon by guiding the fish through a series of funnels, keeping them alive until they're ready to harvest.

The main attraction in town is **Father Duncan's Cottage**, now preserved as a museum. Metlakatla was founded when

William Duncan, a Scottish-born minister, led several hundred Tsimshian Indians here from British Columbia in 1887 after a dispute with church authorities. In 1891, Congress granted reservation status to the entire island and under Duncan's supervision the tribe prospered after building a salmon cannery and sawmill. Duncan lived in the cottage until his death in 1918 and it now features the minister's personal artefacts and many photographs of turn-of-the-century Metlakatla. The museum is open Monday to Friday from 10 am to noon; there is a small admission.

A traditional **Tribal Loghouse**, down by the small boat harbor, has displays of log carvings and indigenous art, and is the site of the community salmon bake whenever a cruise ship is in port.

Hiking The hike to Yellow Hill provides good views of the western side of the island. Walk south along Airport Rd for 1.5 miles and look for the boardwalk on the right; it's an easy 30-minute walk to the top. Another hike in the area is the three-mile Purple Lake Trail, 1.8 miles down Purple Mountain Rd. You can reach Purple Mountain Rd by traveling 2.7 miles south on Airport Rd. This trail involves a steep climb to the mountainous lake area.

Places to Stay & Eat At the *Metlakatla Hotel* (☎ 886-3456) a single/double is $75/95 while in the back a small cafe overlooks the cannery. Keep in mind the town is 'dry' and camping on the island is discouraged. In the end, it's better and much cheaper to visit Metlakatla on Saturday, bring your own lunch and plan on spending the night back in Ketchikan.

Getting There & Away Four days a week the ferry MV *Aurora* makes a single run to Metlakatla but on Saturday it visits the community twice. The first run departs Ketchikan at 6.15 am, arriving in Metlakatla in about an hour. The second run leaves Metlakatla at 8.45 pm, giving you almost a full day on the island. Since the ferry terminal is only a mile east of town, there's enough time to walk to Metlakatla for an interesting and cheap trip. The one-way ferry ticket from Ketchikan to Metlakatla is $14.

You can also fly to Metlakatla. Taquan Air (☎ 225-9668) provides daily, regularly scheduled flights for $36 round trip. Metlakatla Tour (247-8737 or (800) 643-4898) offers a 2½-hour tour, which includes the flight over, a salmon bake and tribal dance performance, for $89 per person. You can book this at the Visitor Bureau in Ketchikan.

Hyder

Hyder is a ferry port at the head of Portland Canal on the fringe of Misty Fjords National Monument. Nass Indians regularly visited the area to hunt birds, pick berries and more often than not to hide from the aggressive Haida tribes. In 1896, Captain DD Gailland explored the Portland Canal for the US Army Corps of Engineers and built four stone storehouses, the first masonry buildings erected in Alaska, which still stand today.

But Hyder and its British Columbia neighbor Stewart, didn't boom until Yukon gold-rush prospectors began settling in the area at the turn of the century. Major gold and silver mines were opened in 1919 and Hyder, enjoying its heyday, became the supply center for more than 10,000 residents. It's been going downhill ever since and the population has now shrunk to around 90 year-round residents, leading to its title 'the friendliest ghost town in Alaska'.

Because of Hyder's isolation from the rest of the state, and the country for that matter, residents are almost totally dependent on the much larger Stewart (pop 2000) just across the Canadian border. They use Canadian money in Hyder, set their watches to Pacific time (not Alaska time), use a British Columbia area code and the children go to school in Canada. All this can make a side trip here a little confusing.

The most famous thing to do in Hyder is drink at one of its 'friendly saloons'. The historic *Glacier Inn* is the best known and features an interior papered in signed bills,

creating the '$20,000 Walls' of Hyder. Next door is *First and Last Chance Saloon* and both bars hop at night.

Stewart has a museum on the corner of 6th and Columbia streets that is open afternoons from Monday to Friday and features local artefacts and mining relics. Or you can head five miles north of town to Fish Creek and watch bears feed on chum salmon runs from late July to September. There are hiking trails in the area and during the summer the US Forest Service sets up an office in the Hyder Community Building, which also contains a post office and the town's library.

Places to Stay In Stewart, you can pitch a tent at the *Bear River RV Park* (☎ (604) 636-9205) for $10 per night for two people or secure a bed at the *King Edward Hotel* for $55/65 for single/double and the *King Edward Motel* (☎ (604) 636-2244) on 5th and Columbia streets. In Hyder, you don't have to pay the 7% city tax that you do in Stewart so at the *Grand View Inn* (☎ (604) 636-9174), a mile from the ferry terminal, a single/double is $45/50.

Getting There & Away Hyder is a possible side trip from Ketchikan because twice a month the ferry MV *Aurora* departs Ketchikan at 1.45 am on a Tuesday and reaches Hyder at 1 pm. It then departs Hyder at 3.45 pm and reaches Ketchikan at 1.30 am the next day, giving you three hours to explore the town (or drink in the bars). The one-way fare is $40 and the trip includes cruising scenic Portland Canal. If you want to stay overnight, you might have to charter a flight there. Taquan Air (☎ 225-8800) charges $194 for round-trip fare between Hyder and Ketchikan.

Prince of Wales Island

If time is no problem and out-of-the-way places or different lifestyles intrigue you, then this accessible island with Native Alaskan villages and logging camps can be

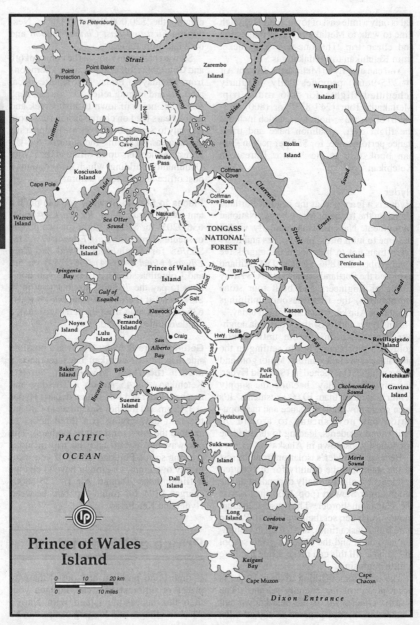

Prince of Wales Island

an interesting jaunt. At 135 miles long and covering more than 2230 sq miles, Prince of Wales Island is the third largest island in the USA after Kodiak and Hawaii.

The island's landscape is characterized by steep forested mountains, deep U-shaped valleys, lakes, salt-water straits and bays that were carved out by glaciers long ago. The mountains rise to 3000 feet and the spruce-hemlock forest is broken up by muskeg and, unfortunately, more clear cuts than most visitors ever dreamed they would see. The 900-mile coastline has numerous bays, coves, inlets and protective islands, making it a kayaker's delight.

You can take the ferry from Ketchikan to Hollis. From this village (pop 475) there is access to a 500-mile network of roads, the most extensive network in the Southeast – in fact more roads than in the rest of the Southeast put together. Some stretches in the center of the island are now paved but the vast majority are rough dirt roads. The logging roads connect Hollis with remote backcountry and the villages of Craig, Klawock, Thorne Bay and Hydaburg. For someone carrying a mountain bicycle through Alaska, a week on Prince of Wales Island is worth all the trouble of carting the bike around.

Information

Tourist Offices In Craig there is the Prince of Wales Chamber of Commerce (☎ 826-3870) and a USFS office (☎ 826-3271) on 9th St near the boat harbor. There is also a USFS office in Thorne Bay (☎ 828-3304).

Money Craig has two banks, including a National Bank of Alaska (☎ 826-3040) on Main St.

Post Major communities such as Craig, Hydaburg and Klawock have a post office.

Laundry In Craig there is TLC Laundry & Rooms and in Klawock you can do a wash at P&P Laundromat.

Medical Services Most of the communities have a small medical clinic such as the Craig Family Medical Clinic (☎ 826-3257) in Craig.

Craig

Craig (pop 2000), 31 miles south-west of Hollis, is the most interesting community to visit, and on a Saturday night you can rub elbows with loggers and fishers in lively Alaskan fashion at the Craig Inn. The town was originally called Fish Egg and was founded as a salmon canning and cold-storage site in 1907. Fishing still accounts for more than half of its employment but it was the timber industry that sparked Craig's growth in the 1980s, which explains the clear cuts around Craig.

Other than a totem pole that washed up on a beach and was erected in front of the old school gym, there are no 'attractions' in Craig. The reason you come here is to experience an Alaskan town that doesn't turn itself inside out for tourists every summer.

Camping is permitted in the city park overlooking the ocean. The park is a short hike from town and can be reached by following Hamilton Dr onto Graveyard Island, or just ask any local for directions to the ball field. Other accommodation includes *Ruthann's Hotel* (☎ 826-3378) which has 10 rooms from $90 per night, *Haida Way Lodge* (☎ 826-3268) with singles/doubles for $90/100 and *TLC Laundry & Rooms* (☎ 826-2966) for a bunkroom bed and shared bathrooms for $30 a night. There are also several restaurants, including *Lacey's Pizza* in the Thibodeau Mall, *Submarina* on Water St, and *Thompson House Grocery*. Just want a cold beer? Not to worry. Craig has three bars and three liquor stores.

There are several fishing lodges on Prince of Wales Island with one of the largest being *Waterfall Resort* (☎ (800) 544-5125), a restored cannery built southwest of Craig in 1912. Such lodges sell only package stays that include lodging, meals and charter fishing. At Waterfall Resort the cheapest packages begin at $2600.

SOUTHEAST

Klawock

Klawock (pop 890) is a Tlingit village 24 miles north-west of Hollis and only six miles north of Craig. The town was the site of the first cannery in Alaska (built in 1878) but is better known today for its collection of 21 totem poles. Totem Park, in the center of the village, features 21 totems that were both replicas and originals that were found in the abandoned Native Alaskan village of Tuxekan in the 1930s.

The best place to stay is half a mile up Big Salt Road at *Log Cabin Campgrounds* (☎ 755-2205 or (800) 544-2205) which offers tent space and showers for $6 per night per person and rustic cabins along the beach for $40 for two people. It also rents canoes for $20 per day that can be used in either Big Salt Lake or Klawock Lake. Within town there is *Fireweed Lodge* (☎ 755-2930) with single or double for $95 a night and *Dave's Diner* (☎ 755-2986) for the cheapest meals.

Hydaburg

Hydaburg (pop 450) was founded in 1911 when three Haida villages were combined. Today, most of the residents are commercial fishers but subsistence is still a necessary part of life. Located 36 miles south-west of Hollis, Hydaburg was only connected to the rest of the island by road in 1983.

This scenic village is known for an excellent collection of restored totems in **Totem Park** near the school that was developed in the 1930s. On the way to Hydaburg, you can view **Dog Salmon Fishpass**. At the junction of the paved road to Craig, head south almost nine miles on the unpaved Hydaburg Rd and then east on Polk or No 21 Rd. The fishpass is reached in 16.7 miles and was built in 1989 as an Alaskan steeppass type of fish ladder. Between July and September you can see salmon using the fishpass, as well as black bears, from an observation platform.

Lodging and meals are available at *Sanderson's Boarding House* (☎ 285-3244) and *Marlene Edenshaw Boarding House* (☎ 285-3254) which charges $90 for a bed and three meals. There is also a grocery store,

Sandwiches, Etc. restaurant and gasoline station in town.

Thorne Bay

Thorne Bay (pop 632) was established in 1962 when Ketchikan Pulp Company moved its main logging camp here from Hollis. Some say the town still looks like a logging camp but it lies in a picturesque setting 59 miles north-east of Hollis.

Just after turning east on Thorne Bay Road, you pass the *Eagles Nest Campground* overlooking a pair of lakes. The 11-site facility is also a canoe launching place on Balls Lake and features almost a half-mile boardwalk along the shore. The fee is $5 a night. Continuing east, the *Gravely Creek Picnic Area* is reached after 13 miles. The facility has fireplaces, pit toilets and an open shelter. Less than a mile away, the Thorne River offers excellent fishing for cutthroat trout, Dolly Varden, rainbow trout and steelhead. Another scenic spot, just six miles north of Thorne Bay on Forest Rd 30, is *Sandy Beach Picnic Area* with tables, pit toilets and fireplaces. It's a great place to set up camp as there are spectacular views of Clarence Strait.

In Thorne Bay, supplies can be obtained at *Thorne Bay Market* while *McFarland's Floatel* (☎ 828-3335) has beach-front log cabins that sleep four for $180 a night. There is a US Forest Ranger Office (☎ 828-3304) in town for recreational information on the area.

Northwest of Thorne Bay or a 94-mile drive from Hollis, is a pair of caves that have become increasingly popular with travelers in recent years. **El Capitan Cave**, 11 miles west of Whale Pass on Forest Road 15, is so popular that the USFS erected a gate across the entrance to prevent further damage to its formations. You can descend into the cave during a free, two-hour tour that the USFS conducts Wednesday through Sunday in the summer. Tours are limited to six people and involve a 370-step stairway trail. Call the Throne Bay USFS Office (☎ 828-3304) for the times of the tours and to reserve a spot in one. The other cave, **Cavern Lake Cave**, is nearby and can be entered on your own but is not nearly as impressive as El Capitan.

Getting There & Away
The ferry *Aurora* makes a daily run, expect on Friday, from Ketchikan to Hollis during the summer, including two trips on Saturday. The one-way fare from Ketchikan to Hollis is $20. Once you're at Hollis, where there are few visitor facilities and no stores or restaurants, getting around the island is a little more difficult.

Getting Around
Bus Prince of Wales Transporter (☎ 755-2348) runs a minivan between Hydaburg and Klawock, stopping at Craig along the way, for $25 one way. Ask the ticket agent at the ferry terminal as soon as you arrive for information on minivan departures.

Car If there are three or four of you, an ideal way to get around is to rent a vehicle at Ketchikan's Alaska Rental (☎ 225-2232 in Ketchikan) and take it over on the ferry for an additional $26 one way. Or rent a car through Wilderness Rent-A-Car in Craig (☎ 826-2205) or Klawock (☎ 755-2205). This allows you to explore the far reaches of the island and to fish the highly productive streams (accessible by road) for cutthroat trout, Dolly Varden and salmon. Two of the 22 USFS cabins, Stanley Creek Cabin and Red Bay Lake Cabin (reservations, $25 per night), can be reached from the road; check with the USFS information center in Ketchikan for availability.

Bicycle With a mountain bike you can explore the island and its network of logging roads. The main roads are gravel surface and stretch between the communities of Hollis, Klawock, Craig, Hydraburg, and Thorne Bay. The rest are logging roads and their condition depends on the weather and the amount of traffic on them. It's not unusual to find a culvert missing or a section washed out completely and passable only by 4WD vehicles – in other words, a mountain biker's

dream come true. The fare to carry a bike over on the ferry is $8 one way but invest another $3 for a copy of the *Prince of Wales Road Guide* that can be purchased at the US Forest Service office in Ketchikan or Craig.

Hitchhiking You can always hitchhike as there is a small amount of traffic to Craig and Klawock after the arrival and departure of each ferry, but keep in mind that most of the boats arrive at 9 pm.

Wrangell

The next major town north along the ferry route is Wrangell (pop 2600). The community's claim to history is that it is the only Alaskan fort to have existed under three flags – Russian, British and American. Its strategic location near the mouth of the Stikine River has given it a long and colorful history.

History
The Russians founded the town when they arrived in 1834 and built a stockade they called Redoubt St Dionysius. The town's purpose then was to prevent encroachment by the Hudson's Bay traders working their way down the Stikine River. But in 1840, the Russians leased it to the British, who renamed it Fort Stikine.

The Americans gained control of the center when they purchased Alaska, and in 1868 changed the name to Fort Wrangell. Wrangell thrived as an important supply center for fur traders and later for gold miners, who used the Stikine River to reach gold rushes in both British Columbia and the Klondike fields in the Yukon.

Today, the town is still considered colorful by Southeast residents but for different reasons. Wrangell is a proud, traditional and sometimes stubborn community that clings to age-old Alaskan beliefs of independence from excess government and of using the land and natural resources to earn a living.

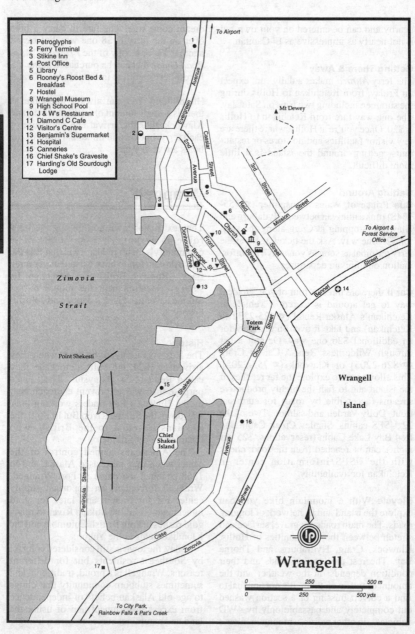

1 Petroglyphs
2 Ferry Terminal
3 Stikine Inn
4 Post Office
5 Library
6 Rooney's Roost Bed & Breakfast
7 Hostel
8 Wrangell Museum
9 High School Pool
10 J & W's Restaurant
11 Diamond C Cafe
12 Visitor's Centre
13 Benjamin's Supermarket
14 Hospital
15 Canneries
16 Chief Shake's Gravesite
17 Harding's Old Sourdough Lodge

To Airport

Mt Dewey

Zimovia

Strait

Point Shekesti

Wrangell

Wrangell Island

To Airport & Forest Service Office

Chief Shakes Island

Totem Park

To City Park, Rainbow Falls & Pat's Creek

Wrangell

0   250   500 m
0   250   500 yds

SOUTHEAST

As the rest of the state is pushed into the 21st century with heavy regulations on industries such as mining, logging and fishing, Wrangell often finds itself lagging behind economically while resisting the new ideas of preserving the environment and setting aside the wilderness. It's not that the town lynches environmentalists every Saturday night, but the issues surrounding timber sales in the Tongass National Forest hit Wrangell and its residents harder than most other towns in the Southeast.

When Alaska Pulp Corp closed its mill here in 1994, the company eliminated 250 of the best paying jobs in the area. The sawmill provided 20% of the jobs in the town and 30% of the payroll. Wrangell is still staggering from the closure with a 20% unemployment rate that is triple the state average.

Whether the new compromise plan for the Tongass National Forest will provide enough timber to re-open the mill remains to be seen.

Meanwhile, Wrangell residents try to survive on a limited fishing fleet, government jobs and tourism in the summer.

Information

Tourist Offices The Wrangell Visitor Center (☎ 874-3901) is an A-frame hut on Outer Dr in front of City Hall. During the summer it's open weekdays 8 am to 5 pm, Saturday mornings and Sunday afternoons. Nearby is the Wrangell Sentinel on Lynch St, which publishes the free *Wrangell Visitors Guide*, the best source of information for the area.

The US Forest Service office (☎ 874-2323), 0.75 miles north of town at 525 Bennett St, is open Monday to Friday from 8 am to 5 pm. It is the source of information for USFS cabins, trails and campgrounds in the area.

Money First Bank (☎ 874-3363) is on Brueger St across from Benjamin's Supermarket.

Loggers, Greenies & the Tongass National Forest

The Tongass National Forest, the largest in the USA at 16.9 million acres, sprawls across an archipelago of islands and a strip of coast from below Ketchikan to north of Yakutat. It is the last intact portion of a vast coastal rain forest that once ranged from northern California to Kodiak Island. It breeds immense hemlock, spruce and red and yellow cedar, which is the reason it has become an intense battle ground between lumber companies, loggers, commercial fishermen, Native Alaskans and environmentalists.

In 1990 the US Congress enacted the Tongass Timber Reform Act that provided additional protection to the forest by ending special subsidies for loggers in the form of road building and timber management. In effect, US citizens, including Alaskans, were paying Japanese-owned sawmills to clear-cut their most prized old-growth forests and ship much of the raw timber back to Japan at below market rates. Native Alaskan corporations were no easier on the forest. They began logging their lands almost as soon as the Alaska Native Claims Settlement Act was signed in 1971 and continue to do so at an alarming rate. To arrive at Hoonah, where Native corporations have logged off almost every tree in the area surrounding the village, is a shocking experience.

The entire issue reached a boiling point after Republicans took control of the US Congress in 1994 and Alaska's three-man delegation, all Republicans, began to work on legislation to repeal much of that act.

The question isn't whether logging should be permitted in the Tongass National Forest, but how much land should be open to timber harvest and how much should be protected. Southeast towns need the high paying jobs that timber brings to their residents. One only has to look at Wrangell to see how much an entire community suffers when a sawmill is closed and that income is lost.

On the other hand, commercial fishermen have long complained that extensive clear-cutting and road building trigger mudslides which in turn choke salmon streams and thus reduce the runs. Many Native Alaskans say the liquidation of their settlement land by their own Native corporations for short-term logging profits is antithetical to Tlingit cultural values. And tourists riding the state ferry through Southeast Alaska are simply horrified at the sight of massive clear cuts leaving entire mountains and ridges treeless. ■

Post The post office is up Front St at the north end of town, and from its lawn there is a good view of Zimovia Strait.

Travel Agencies Tyee Travel (☎ 874-3383) is on Front St near the City Dock.

Bookshop & Library BB Brock's Bookstore is also on Front St next to the City Dock. The Irene Ingle Public Library is on 2nd St behind the post office and features several totems in front of it.

Medical Services Wrangell General Hospital (☎ 874-3356) is on Airport Rd, next to the elementary school.

Things to See

Wrangell is one of the few places in the Southeast where the ferry terminal is in the heart of town. If you're not planning to spend a night here, you can still disembark for a quick look around. To get a good view of Wrangell, including a stroll out to the petroglyphs along the shoreline, you'll need about two hours.

The **Wrangell Museum** (☎ 874-3770) was moved to an interim site on Church St between the Presbyterian Church and the high school in 1994 when its original building, the town's first schoolhouse, deteriorated beyond repair. The collection features indigenous artefacts, petroglyphs, local relics and photographs from Wrangell's past. There is also a collection of Alaska art that includes a Sidney Laurence painting. The museum is open in the summer Monday to Friday from 10 am to 5 pm and Saturday from 1 to 4 pm; there is a $2 admission.

Front St is the heart of Wrangell's business district and the eastern (uphill) side of the street is a historical area featuring buildings with quite distinctive false fronts. Also on Front St is **Kiksadi Totem Park**, which was dedicated in 1987 by Sealaska Native Corporation with the first traditional totem raising in Wrangell in more than 40 years. Four totems are now in place.

Front St heads south through town and becomes Shakes St, leading to the bridge to

Chief Shakes Island, Wrangell's most interesting attraction. A mile from the ferry terminal, the island is in the town's Inner Boat Harbor and features an impressive collection of totem poles (duplicates of the originals that were carved in the late 1930s) and the **Shakes Community House**. The community house is an excellent example of a high-caste tribal house and contains tools, blankets and other cultural items. It is open at various times to accommodate the cruise ships in town and there is a $2 donation to see it. Call the Wrangell Museum (☎ 874-3770) to find out when a tour is scheduled. Just as impressive as the tribal house is the view of bustling Wrangell Harbor from the island.

From Shakes St (heading north) you can turn right onto Case Ave and follow it for two blocks to Wrangell Shipyard. Across the street on the hillside is **Chief Shakes' gravesite** enclosed by a Russian-style picket fence topped by two killer-whale totems.

Petroglyphs

An interesting afternoon can be spent looking for petroglyphs – primitive rock carvings believed to be 8000 years old. The best set lies three quarters of a mile from the ferry terminal and can be reached by heading

Petroglyphs (top) and other forms of rock art are commonly found in the Southeast.

north on Evergreen Rd or, as the locals call it, Old Airport Rd. Walk past Stough's Trailer Court and proceed to a marked wooden walkway. Follow the boardwalk to the beach and then turn right and start walking north towards the end of the island. With your back to the water, look for the carvings on the large rocks.

Many of the petroglyphs are spirals and faces, and there are about 20 in the area but most are submerged during high tide. Check a tide book before you leave and remember that the entire walk takes an hour or two – too long for the ferry stopover. People used to rub the images with paper but archaeologists now strongly discourage the practice as it damages the ancient carvings.

Anan Bear Observatory

The most interesting USFS cabin in the area (see the Places to Stay section for information on other cabins) is on the mainland at Anan Bay, 28 air miles from Wrangell. Near the Anan Bay Cabin is a mile trail that leads to a bear observation & photography platform. The observatory is on the creek from Anan Lake and in July and August can be used to safely watch black bears and a few browns feeding on the salmon runs. The cabin is a 50-minute flight from Wrangell or a 31-mile paddle.

Even if you don't have access to the cabin for a night, the Anan Creek Bear Observatory can still be visited and, in late July to early August, a fascinating day can be spent photographing the bears and eagles feeding on the salmon. A number of charter companies including Breakaway Adventures (☎ 874-2488) and Stikine Wilderness Adventures (☎ (800) 874-2085) will take you, via jet boat, to the trailhead. Trips range from five to eight hours and generally cost $140 per person with four people chartering the boat.

Hiking

Mt Dewey Trail This half-mile trail winds its way up a hill to an observation point overlooking Wrangell and the surrounding waterways. From Mission St, walk a block and turn left at the first corner, 3rd St. Follow

the street past a brown and red A-frame house with a white balcony. The trail, marked by a white sign, begins 50 yards past the house on the right. Once you're at the trailhead, the hike is 15 minutes or so to the top, but it is often muddy. John Muir fanatics will appreciate the fact that the great naturalist himself climbed the mountain in 1879 and built a bonfire at the top, alarming the Tlingits living in the village below.

Rainbow Falls Trail The trailhead for the Rainbow Falls Trail is signposted 4.7 miles south of the ferry terminal on the Zimovia Hwy. The trail begins directly across from the Shoemaker Bay Recreation Area and just before the Wrangell Institute Complex.

From the trailhead it is a mile hike to the waterfalls and then another 2.5 miles to an observation point overlooking Shoemaker Bay on Institute Ridge, where the USFS has built a three-sided shelter. The lower section can be soggy at times so it is best hiked in rubber boots, while upper sections are steep. The views are worth the hike and a pleasant evening can be spent on the ridge. A return trip to the ridge takes four to six hours.

Thoms Lake Trail At the end of the paved Zimovia Hwy is a dirt road, known officially as Forest Rd 6290, that extends 30 miles south along Wrangell Island. On this road, 23 miles south of Wrangell, is the Thoms Lake Trail, which leads 1.2 miles to a state park recreation cabin and a skiff on the lake. Since there is no state park office in Wrangell, you have to reserve the cabin through the Division of Parks office in Juneau (☎ 465-4563). Keep in mind that this trail cuts through muskeg and during wet weather can get extremely muddy. It is a 1½-hour hike to the cabin.

Long Lake Trail The trailhead for the Long Lake Trail is 27 miles south-east of Wrangell on Forest Rd 6270. This pleasant hike is only 0.6 miles long and is planked the entire way. It leads to a shelter, skiff and outhouses on the shores of the lake. Plan a half hour for the trek into the lake or out.

Highbush Lake Trail This very short (300-foot) path leads to the lake where there's a skiff and oars. Fishing is fair and the surrounding views excellent. The parking lot for the trailhead is 29 miles from Wrangell on Forest Rd 6265 and Forest Rd 50040.

Paddling

The beautiful, wild Stikine River is characterized by a narrow, rugged shoreline and the mountains and hanging glaciers that surround it. It is the fastest navigable river in North America and is highlighted by the Grand Canyon, a steep-walled enclosure of the waterway where churning whitewater makes river travel impossible.

Trips from below the canyon are common among rafters and kayakers; they begin with a charter flight to Telegraph Creek in British Columbia and end with a 160-mile float back to Wrangell.

Travelers who arrive at Wrangell with their own kayak but not enough funds for the expensive charter of a bush plane can undertake a trip from the town's harbor across the Stikine Flats, where there are several USFS cabins, and up one of the three arms of the Stikine River. By keeping close to shore and taking advantage of eddies and sloughs, experienced paddlers can make their way 30 miles up the Stikine River to the Canadian border

or even further, passing 12 USFS cabins and the two bathing huts at Chief Shakes Hot Springs along the way. But you must know how to line a boat upstream and navigate a highly braided river and, while in the lower reaches, accept the fact there will be a considerable amount of jet-boat traffic.

The USFS office in Wrangell can provide information on the Stikine River, including a very helpful brochure and map entitled *Stikine River Canoe & Kayak Trips*. There are no places in Wrangell to rent a canoe or kayak so if you are still intrigued by the Stikine River, plan to rent a boat in Juneau.

Guide companies no longer offer boat trips down the Stikine, probably due to a lack of demand. Several charter captains will run up the river but usually only for a day of fishing or sightseeing. Call Stikine Wilderness (☎ (800) 874-2085) or Breakaway Adventures (☎ 874-2488) for such a trip and expect to pay $135 for a five to seven-hour ride up the river.

Special Events

The only major event during the summer, other than the local salmon derby, is the 4 July celebration. All of Wrangell, like most small Alaskan communities, gets involved in the festival, which features a parade, fireworks, logging show, street games, food booths and a salmon bake in town.

Garnet Sellers of Wrangell

Located eight miles north-east of Wrangell on the mainland is Garnet Ledge, which has been mined for more than a century, including by the first all-women corporation in the USA. The all-woman Alaska Garnet Mining and Manufacturing Co was based in Minneapolis and operated at the ledge from 1912 to 1922, using the garnets to make hatpin heads, watch fobs and other such jewelry of the day. In 1962 former mayor Fred Hanford deeded the ledge to the children of Wrangell and placed the ledge in the care of the local Boy Scout Council. Now only children are allowed to sell garnets.

Garnets grow out of minerals that undergo crystal-forming changes brought about by heat and pressure, and Wrangell garnets have long been recognized for their faceted, luminous beauty. But their structure and color make them difficult to cut into attractive stones for jewelry. Still, they are a popular souvenir and young garnet sellers meet most cruise ships that dock in Wrangell.

To collect garnets on your own, first obtain a $10 permit through the Wrangell Museum (☎ 874-3770) and contact a charter operator, through the visitors center, for a trip to the ledge. When you return from the ledge you must donate 10% of your garnet collection to the museum. The revenue from the sale of the garnets help to support the local Boy & Girl Scout troops in town. ■

Places to Stay

Wrangell has a 7% city tax and a $3 bed tax for hotels, B&Bs and even the hostel.

USFS Cabins The 20 USFS cabins in the Wrangell Ranger District are not as busy as those around Juneau or Ketchikan. Six of them (Binkley Slough, Koknuk, Little Dry Island, Sergief Island and two on Gut Island) lie on the Stikine River flats, 12 to 15 miles from Wrangell. The cabins can be paddled to or are a 30-minute bush-plane flight.

Camping The nearest campground to town is the *City Park*, 1.8 miles south of the ferry terminal on Zimovia Hwy. This waterfront park is immediately south of the cemetery and city ball field and provides picnic tables, shelters and rest rooms. Camping is free but for tents only and there is a one-night limit.

Further out of town is the *Shoemaker Bay Recreation Area*, 4.7 miles south of the ferry terminal on Zimovia Hwy and across from the trailhead to the Rainbow Falls Trail. Camping is provided in a wooded area near a creek, and there is a 10-day limit but no fees for tents. The fee for RVs is $5 to $8.

Still further south is *Pat's Creek* at *Mile 11* of Zimovia Hwy where it becomes a narrow Forest Service road. There are two dirt roads heading off to the left; the first is to the lake and the second is to the campground, which is basically just a clear spot to park vehicles. Near the campground there is a trail along the creek that leads back to Pat's Lake, where you'll easily locate some excellent spots to go fishing for cutthroat trout and Dolly Varden.

Hostel The *Wrangell (AYH) Hostel* (☎ 874-3534) was organized in Wrangell in 1994 in the First Presbyterian Church, the oldest continuously operating Protestant Church in Alaska, dating back to 1877. Located at 220 Church St, the hostel provides affordable accommodation as well as kitchen facilities. The rate is $10 a night.

B&Bs If staying in a private home interests you, there are a handful of B&Bs in the area,

including several downtown. You can get a complete list from the Visitor Bureau or try *Rooney's Roost* (☎ 874-2026) three blocks from the ferry terminal at 206 McKinnon St. Singles/doubles are $45/55 and airport pick-up is available. There's also *The Anchor B&B* (☎ 874-2078) at 325 Church with singles/doubles for $57/67.

Hotels The cheapest hotel in town is the *Thunderbird Hotel* (☎ 874-3322), at 110 Front St, with rooms at $55/65. A step up is *Stikine Inn* (874-3388), near the cruise ship dock at 107 Front St, with rooms for $65/75. A mile south of town is *Hardings Old Sourdough Lodge* (☎ 874-3613) with 20 rooms, a sauna, steambath and free transport from the ferry or airport. Rooms are $55 for single or double and meals are available.

Places to Eat

The cheapest place for a meal is undoubtedly *Diamond C Cafe* located on Front St, in the Kadin Building. The restaurant is open daily and has breakfasts for around $5, sandwiches and hamburgers for around $6 and local seafood. Nearer to the ferry terminal and open later at night is *J&W's* at the City Dock, which sells fish sandwiches and shrimp burgers. Pizza is best purchased at *Maggie's & Sons* on Front St where a large is around $13.

The top place to eat, featuring local shrimp and other seafood, is the *Dockside Restaurant* in the Stikine Inn, with its excellent view of the boat harbor. Dinners range from $15 to $20 or you can just tackle the salad bar for under $5.

Benjamin's on Outer Dr is the largest supermarket, featuring an in-store bakery and ready-to-eat items in its deli. *Jitterbugs* on Front St serves espresso drinks.

Entertainment

It is often the case that the town's bars are the location for the true spirit of Wrangell to come shining through. Mingle with locals at the *Totem Bar* on Front St or with people from the fishing industry at the *Marine Bar* on Shakes St near Chief Shakes Island.

SOUTHEAST

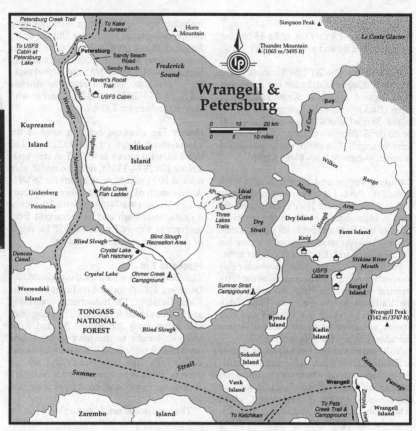

During a night run on the ferry, you have time to get off for a beer at the *Stikine Inn Lounge*, which has live music and the only dance floor in Wrangell.

Getting There & Away

Air Alaska Airlines (☎ 874-3308) provides a year-round jet service to Wrangell with a daily northbound and southbound flight. Many claim that the flight north to Petersburg is the 'world's shortest jet flight', since the 11-minute trip is little more than a take-off and landing with the huge aircraft seeming to skim the waterway.

Boat There is an almost daily northbound and southbound ferry service from Wrangell in the summer. The next stop north is Petersburg via the scenic Wrangell Narrows. The ferry terminal in Wrangell is open 1½ hours before each ferry arrival and from 2 to 5 pm on weekdays. There's a recorded message (☎ 874-3711) for 24-hour ferry information.

Getting Around

You can rent a car through Practical Rent-A-Car (☎ 874-3975) which is located at the airport. You can rent a road or mountain bike from Sea Cycle Rental (☎ 874-3015).

Petersburg

When the ferry heads north from Wrangell, it begins one of the most scenic and exciting sections of the Inside Passage trip. After crossing over from Wrangell Island to Mitkof Island, the ferry threads its way through 46 turns of Wrangell Narrows, a 22-mile narrow channel that is only 300 feet wide and 19 feet deep in places. At one point the sides of the ship are so close to the shore that you can almost gather firewood for the evening.

At the other end of this breathtaking journey lies Petersburg (pop 3350), one of the hidden gems of Southeast Alaska. This busy little town, an active fishing port during the summer, is decorated by weathered boathouses on the waterfront, freshly painted homes along Nordic Dr and the distinctive Devil's Thumb peak and other snow-capped mountains on the horizon.

History

Peter Buschmann arrived in the area in 1897 and found a fine harbor, abundant fish and a ready supply of ice from nearby Le Conte Glacier. He built a cannery and enticed his Norwegian friends to follow him there, and the resulting town was named after him. Today, a peek into the local phone book will reveal evidence of the strong Norwegian heritage which unifies Petersburg.

Petersburg is the youngest community in the Southeast but boasts of having the largest home-based halibut fleet in Alaska, some say the world. The economy has blossomed on fishing as the town processes more than $40 million of seafood annually through four canneries and two cold-storage plants that draw an army of summer workers from the Lower 48. Several of the canneries are sitting above the water on pilings overlooking boat harbors bulging with vessels and a constant flow of barges, ferries and sea planes. Even at night you can see small boats trolling the nearby waters for somebody's dinner.

Without the heavy dependency on timber,

Petersburg enjoys a healthier economy than Wrangell or Ketchikan. This partly explains why the town doesn't go out of its way for tourists. The other reason is that it lacks a deep water port for large cruises ship to dock. For independent travelers this is good and bad. On one hand you're not overrun by masses of tourists pouring out of the Love Boat. On the other the lack of a youth hostel and viable camping areas near town often leaves you little choice but to book a $80 room for the night.

Information

Tourist Offices The Petersburg Visitor Center (☎ 772-3646) is on the corner of Fram and 1st streets and has both community and USFS information. It's open daily until 5 pm during the summer.

For information about hiking, paddling, camping or reserving cabins, head over to the US Forest Service office (☎ 772-3871) upstairs in the Federal Building on Nordic Dr. The office is open weekdays from 8 am to 5 pm.

Money National Bank of Alaska (☎ 772-3833) has an office at 201 Nordic Dr.

Post The post office is in the first level of the Federal Building on Nordic Dr.

Travel Agency Viking Travel (☎ (800) 327-2571) is on the corner of Harbor Way and Chief John Lott St.

Bookshop Sing Lee Alley Books, on Sing Lee Alley of course, is a delightful little bookshop with an impressive selection of Alaska material. You can purchase topographic maps at Diamante (☎ 772-4858), a gift shop on Nordic Dr.

Library The Petersburg Public Library is on the second level of the Municipal Building at Nordic Dr and Haugen Dr. It's open daily, including until 9 pm Monday through Thursday, and often has used books for sale.

SOUTHEAST

SOUTHEAST

1 Petersburg Fisheries	10 Clausen Memorial Museum
2 Swimming Pool	11 Scandia House
3 Laundromat	12 Helse Health Foods & Deli
4 Harbor Bar	13 Kito's Kave
5 Tides Inn	14 Forest Service & Post Office
6 Coastal Cold Storage	15 Le Conte RV Park
7 Harbor Master	16 Municipal Building
8 Visitor Center	17 Sons of Norway Hall
9 Medical Center	18 Harbor Lights Pizza

Petersburg

Wrangell
Narrows

Eagle's
Roost
Park

Mitkof
Island

To Sandy Beach Road

Laundry Glacier Laundry, on Nordic Drive, is open until 10 pm and has showers for $2.

Medical Services Petersburg Medical Center (☎ 772-4291), on the corner of 1st and Fram streets, is the local hospital.

Things to See

On the waterfront near the corner of Dolphin St and Nordic Dr is **Petersburg Fisheries**, founded in 1900 by Peter Buschmann and today a subsidiary of Icicle Seafoods of Seattle. On Harbor Way, at the end of Gjoa

St, is the long pier that leads out to **Chatham Strait Seafoods**. The canneries, the backbone of the Petersburg economy, are not open to the public and do not offer tours.

Continuing south, Harbor Way passes Middle Boat Harbor and turns into **Sing Lee Alley**. This was the center of old Petersburg and much of the street is built on pilings over Hammer Slough. The **Sons of Norway Hall**, begun by Buschmann in 1897 and finished in 1912, is the predominant large white building with the colorful rosemaling, a flowery Norwegian art form.

Hammer Slough provides photographers

with the most colorful images of Petersburg. Both Sing Lee Alley and Birch St follow the tidal area and wind past clusters of weathered homes and boathouses suspended on pillars above a shoreline of old boats, nets and crab pots. Sing Lee Alley crosses Hammer Slough and then joins Nordic Dr. To the south, Nordic Dr turns into Mitkof Hwy and heads out past the ferry terminal; to the north Nordic Dr heads back into the center of Petersburg.

Turn east up Fram St from Nordic Dr to the **Clausen Memorial Museum** on the corner of 2nd St. Outside the museum is the *Fisk*, an 11-foot bronze sculpture commemorating the town's life by the sea. Inside the museum is an interesting collection of local artefacts and relics, most tied in with the history of fishing in Petersburg. Included in the back room is the largest king salmon ever caught – 126 pounds. You'll also see the giant lens from the old Cape Decision Lighthouse. The museum is open daily during the summer until 4.30 pm. Admission is $2.

From the downtown area, Nordic Dr heads north and then curves east at **Eagle's Roost Park**, a small hilltop park where you can often see eagles perched on top of trees. A little further is Hungry Point View Area, where the Wrangell Narrows merges into Frederick Sound and finally **Sandy Beach Recreation Area**, two miles from downtown. The day use area features three enclosed shelters, a mile-long boardwalk trail out to Frederick Point and Tlingit petroglyphs that can be seen at low tide. Call the USFS office about interpretive walks at Sandy Beach to look at the petroglyphs.

Hiking

Frederick Point Boardwalk Near the downtown area is this mile-long boardwalk that begins off Nordic Dr next to Sandy Beach Recreation Area. The trail winds through rainforest, across muskeg and then crosses a salmon stream that is quite a sight during the peak spawning runs in August.

Raven's Roost Trail This four-mile trail begins at the water tower on the south-east side of the airport, accessible from Haugen Dr. A boardwalk crosses muskeg areas at the start of the trail, while much of the route is a climb to beautiful open alpine areas at 2013 feet; some of it is steep and requires a little scrambling. A two-story US Forest Service cabin (reservations, $25 per night) is above the tree line in an area that provides good summer hiking and spectacular views of Petersburg, Frederick Sound and Wrangell Narrows.

Petersburg Mountain Trail On Kupreanof Island, this trail ascends 2.5 miles from Wrangell Narrows behind Sasby Island to the top of Petersburg Mountain. There are outstanding views from here, the best in the area, of Petersburg, the Coastal Mountains, glaciers and Wrangell Narrows. Plan on three hours to the top of the mountain and two hours for the return. To get across the channel, go to the skiff float at the North Boat Harbor (Old Boat Harbor) and hitch a ride with somebody who lives on Kupreanof Island. From the Kupreanof Public Dock, head right on the overgrown road towards Sasby Island.

Petersburg Lake Trail This 10.3-mile trail, part of a trail system in the Petersburg Creek-Duncan Salt Chuck Wilderness on Kupreanof Island, leads to a USFS cabin (reservations, $25 per night). See the Hiking section in the Wilderness chapter for further details.

Three Lakes Trails These four short trails, connecting three lakes and Ideal Cove, are off Three Lakes Rd, a Forest Service road that heads east off Mitkof Hwy at *Mile 13.6* and returns at *Mile 23.8*. Beginning at *Mile 14.2* of Three Lakes Rd is a three-mile loop with boardwalks leading to Sand, Crane and Hill lakes, known for their good trout fishing.

On each lake there is a skiff and a picnic platform. Tennis shoes are fine for the trail but to explore around the lakes you need rubber boots. There is a free-use shelter on Sand Lake. From the Sand Lake Trail there is a 1.5-mile trail to Ideal Cove on Frederick Sound.

Blind River Rapids Boardwalk Starting at *Mile 14.5* of the Mitkof Hwy is this easy mile-long boardwalk that winds through muskeg before arriving at the rapids, a popular fishing spot during the summer.

Paddling

There is a variety of interesting trips in the Petersburg area, most of which are bluewater paddles requiring a week or more to undertake. Kayak rentals are difficult to come by in Petersburg. Try Tongass Kayak Adventures (☎ 772-4600), 106 North Nordic Dr, which offers a five-hour guided tour up Petersburg Creek for $45.

For transportation, there's Alaskan Scenic Waterways (☎ 772-3777) which makes runs to both Le Conte Glacier and Thomas Bay. There are also a dozen charter boats, including Scenic Day Charters (☎ 772-4615), that deal mostly in fishing trips, but will provide drop-off and pick-up services to remote areas. Contact the chamber of commerce office for a current list of them.

Le Conte Glacier The most spectacular paddle in the region is to Le Conte Glacier, 25 miles east of Petersburg and the southernmost tidewater glacier in North America. From town, it takes three to four days to reach the frozen monument, which includes crossing Frederick Sound north of Coney Island. The crossing should be done at slack tide as winds and tides can cause choppy conditions. If the tides are judged right, it is possible to paddle far enough into Le Conte Bay to camp within view of the glacier.

To skip the paddling but still see the glacier, check with Kupreanof Flying Service (☎ 772-3396) for a flightseeing trip, but expect to split $150 among three passengers for the trip. More worthwhile is a cruise to the glacier with Alaskan Scenic Waterways (☎ 772-3777), which has an office in Scandia House Hotel. A full-day cruise is $145 per person.

Thomas Bay Almost as impressive is Thomas Bay, 20 miles from Petersburg and north of Le Conte Bay on the east side of Frederick Sound. The bay features a pair of glaciers, including Baird Glacier where many paddlers spend a day hiking. The mountain scenery surrounding the bay is spectacular and there are three USFS cabins (reservations, $25 per night): Swan Lake Cabin, Spurt Cove Cabin and Cascade Creek Cabin. Paddlers need from four to seven days for the round trip out of Petersburg.

Kake to Petersburg Backpackers can take the ferry to the Native Alaskan village of Kake and paddle back to Petersburg. This 90-mile route follows the west side of Kupreanof Island through Keku Strait, Sumner Strait and up Wrangell Narrows to Petersburg. The highlight of the trip is Rocky Pass, a remote and narrow winding waterway in Keku Strait that has almost no boat traffic other than the occasional kayaker. Caution has to be used in Sumner Strait, which lies only 40 miles away from open ocean and has its share of strong winds and waves. Plan on seven to 10 days for the trip.

Special Events

Petersburg puts on its own 4 July celebration with the usual small-town festivities. The community's best event, and one that is famous around the Southeast, is the Little Norway Festival, held on the weekend closest to Norwegian Independence Day on 17 May, usually before most tourists arrive. If you are even near the area, hop over to Petersburg for it. The locals dress in old costumes, Nordic Dr is filled with a string of booths and games, and several dances are held in local halls. The best part of the festival is the fish feed, when the town's residents put together a pot-luck feast.

Places to Stay

Petersburg adds 9% to the price of any bed in town.

Camping It is difficult to camp near town. Petersburg has *Tent City* on Haugen Dr, half a mile or a 10-minute walk north-west of the airport. The city-operated campground provides wooden pads, each holding three to five tents, to avoid the wet muskeg. However, the facility was designed primarily for young cannery workers who invariably arrive in the early summer months and occupy an entire pad by building plastic shelters around them. By the time you come along, there are few, if any, spaces available to pitch a tent. The cost is $5 per night and there is a campground manager on site most evenings to collect it.

Within town, on the corner of 4th St and Haugen Dr, is *LeConte RV Park* (772-4680), which charges $6 for a tent site. Out of town at *Mile 22* of the Mitkof Hwy is the *Ohmer Creek Campground* (15 sites, no fee) with an interpretive trail, fishing in the creek and a scenic setting.

Backpackers have a couple of ways to avoid the lack of budget accommodation in Petersburg. There is no camping within the city limits, and if you pitch a tent at the Sandy Beach Recreation Area, on the corner of Sandy Beach Rd and Haugen Dr three miles north of town, local police will most likely kick you out in the middle of the night.

However, by hiking half a mile beyond the Sandy Beach Park out on Frederick Point, you can camp on the scenic beach. Bring drinking water and pitch your tent above the high-tide line. You can also camp up along the Ravens Roost Trail which begins near the airport, but you will have to walk more than a mile uphill before finding a site that isn't muskeg.

B&Bs Petersburg has a half-dozen B&Bs and practically all of them charge around $70/80 for a single/double. At *Nordic House* (☎ 772-3620), three blocks north of the ferry terminal, guests enjoy a spectacular view of the Narrows. *Water's Edge B&B* (☎ 772-3736) is north of town overlooking Frederick Sound and *Harbor Day B&B* (☎ 772-3971) is a half mile from either the ferry terminal or downtown at 404 Noseeum St. The Visitor Center has brochures for all of them.

Hotels There is no hostel in Petersburg, although this town desperately needs one. The cheapest hotel is *Narrows Inn* (☎ 772-4284) opposite the ferry terminal with singles/doubles for $55/65. A step up is *Tides Inn* (☎ 772-4288) on the corner of 1st and Dolphin streets. Singles/doubles are $70/85 but include a continental breakfast and some rooms have kitchenettes. *Scandia House* (☎ 772-4281), on Nordic Dr, is in the center of town and charges $75/85 for singles/doubles.

A delightful alternative is *Lodge Across the Bay* (☎ 772-9214), especially if you want to hike Petersburg Mountain or Petersburg Lake Trails. The lodge has five rooms for $60 per night per person including kitchen facilities and a boat ride across the Narrows.

Places to Eat
Locals eat at *Homestead Cafe* on Nordic Dr, which can be a little greasy at times but is open 24 hours and has breakfasts for $5 to $7. The hamburgers ($4 to $8) are served with a huge scoop of potato salad. *Harbor Lights Pizza* is diagonally opposite the Sons of Norway Hall on Sing Lee Alley and offers pasta dinners ($6), pizzas ($11 to $15), beer, wine and a good view of the busy boat harbor. The best pizza is at *Pelleritos Pizza*, on Nordic Dr near the ferry terminal, while good Chinese is enjoyed at *Joan Mei*, next door to the Narrows Inn. Dinners here range from $8 to $13.

Another interesting place in town is *Helse Health Foods & Deli* on Sing Lee Alley. The health-food store and restaurant is a pleasant place for tea during a rainy afternoon and features soups or seafood chowder with a thick slice of home-made bread for $5. The best seafood is at *Coastal Cold Storage*, downtown on Nordic Dr. You can purchase shrimp sandwiches and salads, live crab, oysters and clams, or takeaways such as halibut beer bits with french fries ($6).

Entertainment
To listen to the fisher's woes or to meet cannery workers, there is the *Harbor Bar* on Nordic Dr. For something livelier try *Kito's*

Kave on Sing Lee Alley. This bar and liquor store has live music and dancing most nights after 9 pm. When the boats are in it can be a rowdy place that hops until 2 or 3 am.

Getting There & Away

Air The Alaska Airlines (☎ 772-4255) milk run through the Southeast provides a daily northbound and southbound flight out of Petersburg. The airport is a mile east of the post office on Haugen Dr.

Boat The Alaska Marine Hwy terminal (☎ 772-3855) is about a mile along Nordic Dr from the southern edge of town. There is usually one northbound ferry arriving daily. Travelers continuing onto Juneau should consider taking the *Le Conte* on Tuesday if it fits into their schedule. This ship sails from Petersburg to Juneau but stops at Kake, Sitka, Angoon, Tenakee and Hoonah along the way; the one-way fare is $44.

Getting Around

Car You can rent a car at Practical Car Rental (☎ 772-5006) but during the summer you almost have to call ahead and reserve a vehicle. Rates are $45 per day.

Bicycle Northern Bikes Sports (☎ 772-3978), on Nordic Dr across the street from NBA, rents mountain bikes for $3 an hour or $20 for a day.

AROUND PETERSBURG

There are a few sights around Petersburg, although it's debatable whether it's worth the hassle of getting out to see them. Those without transport can either rent a vehicle or contact Tongass Traveller (☎ 772-4837) which offers a two-hour van tour. For $40, Patti Norheim takes you to a shrimp cannery, fish hatchery and a tree farm amongst other things, and then returns you to her home in town where you sit on her deck enjoying wine and a shrimp cocktail.

One of the best fishing spots in the area is at *Mile 14.5* of the Mitkof Hwy where a

0.3-mile boardwalk leads through a muskeg meadow to the **Blind River Rapids Recreation Area**. There is a small trail shelter along the river where anglers come to catch Dolly Varden, cutthroat trout and steelhead from mid-April to mid-May, king salmon in June and July, and coho salmon after mid-August.

The **Crystal Lake Fish Hatchery** at *Mile 17.5* of the Mitkof Hwy is a $2.2 million facility used to stock coho, king salmon and trout throughout the Southeast. No formal tours are offered, but hatchery personnel are pleasant and informative. It is open weekdays from 8 am to 4 pm. Nearby in Blind Slough Recreation Area is the **Trumpeter Swan Observatory**, designed to permit sheltered photography and viewing of this majestic bird.

On the way back to town, stop at the **Falls Creek Fish Ladder** at *Mile 13.7* of the Mitkof Hwy, an impressive sight in August when coho and pink salmon leap along its steps. At *Mile 9* of the highway is the **Heintzleman Nursery** operated by the USFS, which includes six greenhouses that produce a million seedlings of Sitka spruce per year. It is open to the public on an informal basis on weekdays from 8 am to 4.30 pm. Like at the hatchery, there is no admission charge.

Sitka

In a region of Alaska already strong in color and history, Sitka (pop 8600) is a gem in a beautiful setting. Facing the Pacific Ocean, the city is overshadowed to the west by Mt Edgecumbe, the extinct volcano with a cone similar to Japan's Mt Fuji. The waters offshore are broken up by a myriad of small, forested islands that are ragged silhouettes during the sunsets, while to the east the town is flanked by snow-capped mountains and sharp granite peaks. On a clear day Sitka, the only city in Southeast Alaska that actually fronts the Pacific Ocean, rivals Juneau for the sheer beauty of its surroundings.

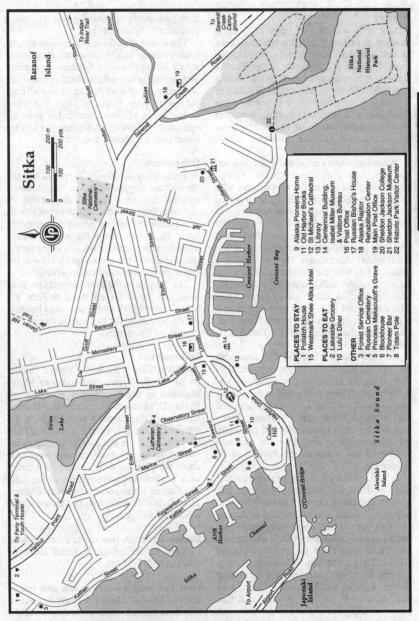

Sitka

To Sawmill
Creek Camp-
ground

Baranof
Island

Sitka
National
Historical
Park

Sitka
National
Cemetery

Crescent Harbor

Crescent Bay

Swan Lake

Sitka Sound

Aleutski
Island

ANB
Harbor

Japonski
Island

To Indian River Trail

River Road

Indian River

Sawmill Creek Road

Graven Hill Trail

Jeff Davis Street

College Street

Davis Street

Etolin Street

Baranof Street

Lincoln Street

Monastery Street

Groff Street

De Groff Street

Lake Street

Seward Street

Harbor Drive

Marine Street

Observatory Street

Lutheran
Cemetery

Russian
Cemetery

Erler Street

Kowanton Street

Kattian Street

Halibut Point Road

To Ferry Terminal &
Youth Hostel

O'Connell Bridge

To Airport

Airport Road

0   100   200 m
0   100   200 yds

PLACES TO STAY
1   Potlatch House
15 Westmark Shee Atika Hotel

PLACES TO EAT
10 Lakeside Grocery
14 Lulu's Diner

OTHER
3   Forest Service Office
4   Russian Cemetery
5   Princess Maksoutoff's Grave
6   Blockhouse
7   Pioneer Bar
8   Totem Pole
9   Alaska Pioneers Home
11 Old Harbor Books
12 St Michael's Cathedral
13 Library
14 Centennial Building,
     Isabel Miller Museum
     & Visitors Bureau
16 Post Office
17 Russian Bishop's House
18 Alaska Raptor
     Rehabilitation Center
19 Main Post Office
20 Sheldon Jackson College
21 Sheldon Jackson Museum
22 Historic Park Visitor Center

History

Along with its natural beauty, Sitka is steeped in history. The Russians may have landed in Sitka Sound as early as 1741 after two ships under explorer Vitus Bering became separated in a storm. While Bering was in Mt St Elias to confirm the presence of a continent, the other ship was much further south where it sent two longboats ashore in Sitka Sound in search of water. The boats never returned and the Russians wisely departed.

What the sailors undoubtedly encountered were members of two powerful Tlingit tribes: the Kiksadi and the Kogwanton, who over time had developed the most advanced culture of any group of Native Americans in Alaska. The Tlingits were still there in 1799 when the Russians returned and established the first non-indigenous settlement in the Southeast. Alexander Baranof built a Russian fort near the present ferry terminal to continue the rich sea-otter fur trade. He was in Kodiak three years later when Tlingits, armed with guns from British and American traders, overwhelmed the fort, burned it to the ground and killed most of its inhabitants.

Baranof returned in 1804, this time with an imperial Russian Navy warship, and after destroying the Tlingit fort, established a settlement called New Archangel at the present site of Sitka, making it the headquarters of the Russian-American Company. Sitka flourished both economically and culturally on the strength of the fur trade and was known as the 'Paris of the Pacific' in its golden era.

In 1867, Sitka picked up its present name after the USA took control of the town following the purchase of Alaska. After the territorial capital was transferred to Juneau in 1900, the city fell upon some hard times but boomed again during WWII when a military base was built on nearby Japonski Island. Today, the city is supported by a fishing fleet, cold-storage plants, several federal agencies that have offices in the area and, of course, tourism. A pulp mill that closed in 1993 hurt Sitka economically but didn't devastate the town as was the case a year later in Wrangell.

The charm of Sitka is not only its natural beauty but the way the residents cling to the area's strong Russian heritage and pride themselves on being the cultural center of the Southeast, if not of all Alaska. It seemed only natural to those living in Sitka that when author James Michener decided to write his epic novel *Alaska* he chose their town as his home base to conduct research.

Orientation

When arriving in Sitka by ferry, you will sail through the Sergius Narrows, a tight waterway that ships must navigate at slack tide. At any other time it is too hazardous for vessels to negotiate the fierce currents caused by the tides. This often forces the ferry to take a three-hour stop at Sitka while waiting for the tide and allows travelers a quick view of the city even if they're not disembarking.

The ferry terminal is seven miles north of town, too far to see anything on foot, but Sitka Tours (☎ 747-8443) does run a bus tour for those waiting for the ferry to depart (see Organized Tours later).

Information

Tourist Office The Sitka Visitor Bureau (☎ 747-5940) is part of the Isabel Miller Museum in the Centennial Building off Harbor Dr next to the Crescent Boat Harbor, and is open daily from 8 am to 6 pm in the summer. The US Forest Service office (☎ 747-6671), the place to go for trail information, cabin reservations and hand-outs about enjoying the wilderness, is in a three-story red building on the corner of Siginaka and Katlian streets, across from the Thomas Boat Harbor. The office is open on weekdays from 8 am to 5 pm.

Money There are two banks downtown on Lincoln St, including National Bank of Alaska (☎ 747-3226).

Post The main post office is a mile out of town on Sawmill Creek Rd. In the downtown area there is a substation in the MacDonald's

Bayview Trading Company building at 407 Lincoln St.

Travel Agency Totem Travel (☎ 747-3251) is at 903 Halibut Point Rd.

Bookshops & Library Books and topographic maps can be purchased at Old Harbor Books (☎ 747-8808) downtown at 201 Lincoln St. Next door to the Centennial Building is the city's impressive Kettleson Memorial Library (☎ 747-8708), an excellent rainy day spot that's open daily.

Laundry & Showers You can also get a shower for $2 at Homestead Laundromat, 713 Katlian St, behind Potlatch Motel or Duds 'n' Suds at 906 Halibut Point Rd.

Medical Services The Sitka Community Hospital (☎ 747-3241) is located just north of town, off Halibut Point Rd and Brady St, at 209 Moller Dr.

Things to See
Within the Centennial Building is the **Isabel Miller Museum** which has a collection of relics from the past, along with a model of the town as it appeared in 1867. Outside is a hand-carved Tlingit canoe made from a single log. The museum is open daily in the summer and there is a $1 donation.

At the heart of the city center is **St Michael's Cathedral** on Lincoln St, two blocks west from the Centennial Building. Built between 1844 and 1848, the church stood for over 100 years as the finest Russian Orthodox cathedral in Alaska until fire destroyed it in 1966. The priceless treasures and icons inside were saved by Sitka's residents, who built a replica of the original cathedral. The church is open daily from 1.30 to 5.30 pm on non-cruise ships day and longer if there is a boat in town. Admission is a $1 donation.

Continue west on Lincoln St for the walkway to **Castle Hill**. This was the site of an early stronghold of the indigenous Kiksadi clan and later the foundation of a succession of Russian buildings including

St Michael's in Sitka is a fine example of a Russian Orthodox cathedral.

Baranof's Castle, which housed the governor of Russian America in 1837. It was here on 18 October 1867 that the official transfer of Alaska from Russia to the USA took place.

More Russian cannons can be seen in Totem Square, near the end of Lincoln St. Next to it is the prominent, yellow **Alaska Pioneers Home**. Built in 1934 on the old Russian Parade Ground, the home is for elderly Alaskans. Visitors are welcome to meet the 'old sourdoughs' and listen to their fascinating stories of gold-rush days or homesteading in the wilderness. There is a gift shop in the basement that sells handicrafts made by the residents. The 13-foot bronze prospector statue in front of the state home was dedicated on Alaska Day in 1949 and is modelled on longtime Alaskan resident William 'Skagway Bill' Fonda.

Another part of Sitka's Russian past can be seen on the hill west of the Alaska Pioneer Home. On the corner of Kogwanton and Marine streets is the replica **blockhouse** of the type the Russians used to guard their stockade and separate it from the Indian village. Originally, there were three on a wall that kept the Tlingits restricted to an area along Katlian St. Adjacent to the wooden blockhouse, in the Lutheran Cemetery, is

Princess Maksoutoff's Grave, marking the exact spot where the wife of Alaska's last Russian governor is buried. There are more old headstones and Russian Orthodox crosses at the end of Observatory St in the **Russian Cemetery**.

The **Russian Bishop's House**, the oldest intact Russian building in Sitka, is the first of many sights at the east end of town. The soft-yellow structure on Lincoln St across from the west end of Crescent Harbor was built in 1842 and is one of the few surviving examples of Russian colonial architecture in North America. Bishop Ivan Veniaminov, who eventually was canonized St Innocent, was the first resident of the home which he later used as a school, chapel and office.

The National Park Service has renovated the building to its 1853 setting with a museum dedicated to its Russian occupants on the 1st floor. The 2nd floor has been restored as the bishop's personal quarters and the Chapel of the Annunciation. Hours are from 9.30 am to 3 pm daily in the summer.

Further east along Lincoln St, past the boat harbor, is Sheldon Jackson College, where Michener stayed and worked for much of the three summers he spent in Alaska. Among the buildings on campus is the octagonal **Sheldon Jackson Museum**. Constructed in 1895, it's the oldest cement building in Alaska and today houses one of the best indigenous-culture collections in the state.

The artefacts were gathered by Dr Sheldon Jackson, general agent for education, from 1880 to 1900, making the collection the oldest in the state. It features an impressive display of indigenous masks, hunting tools and baskets from such peoples as the Inuit, Tlingit, Haida and Aleut. Hanging from the ceiling, and equally impressive, is the collection of boats and sleds used in Alaska – from reindeer sleds and dog sleds to kayaks and umiaks. The museum (☎ 747-8981) is open daily from 8 am to 5 pm in the summer; admission is $3.

For a lot of visitors, Sitka's most colorful area is **Katlian St**, which begins off Lincoln St at the west end of town. The road is a classic mixture of weather-beaten houses, docks and canneries where there always seem to be fishing boats unloading their catch. Katlian St portrays the sights and sounds of the busy Southeast fishing industry. Even the vacant yards along it reflect dependence on the sea, as they have discarded fishing nets or stacks of crab pots. In short, it is a colorful, bustling place and a photographer's delight.

Sitka National Historical Park Sitka's most noted attraction is maintained by the National Park Service and lies further east at the end of Lincoln St. This 107-acre park, half a mile east of the city center, features a trail that winds past 15 totem poles that were once displayed in the Louisiana Exposition in St Louis in 1904 and now stand in a beautiful forest setting next to the sea.

The park is at the mouth of the Indian River where the Tlingit Indians were finally defeated by the Russians in 1804 after defending a wooden fort for a week. The Russians had arrived with a warship and three other ships to revenge a Tlingit Kiksadi clan raid on a nearby outpost two years earlier. But despite their cannons, they did little damage to the walls and, when they stormed the structure with the help of Aleuts, they were repulsed in a bloody battle. It was only when the Tlingits ran out of gunpowder and flint and slipped away at night that the Russians were able to enter the deserted fort.

Begin at the park's visitor center (☎ 747-6281) where there are displays of Russian and indigenous artefacts, and where carvers demonstrate traditional arts. A mile-long self-guided loop leads past the totems to the site of the Tlingit fort near Indian River. The fort is long gone but its outline can still be seen and is marked by posts. Admission is free and the visitor center is open daily from 8 am to 5 pm in the summer.

Nearby on Sawmill Creek Rd, just beyond the Indian River Bridge is **Alaska Raptor Rehabilitation Center**. A raptor is a bird of prey and at ARRC you'll see eagles, hawks and owls that are sick or injured and are undergoing treatment intended to enable

The famous bald eagle can be seen at the Alaska Raptor Rehabilitation Center.

them to survive in the wild. There are also more than a dozen bald eagles and you can watch the exercise sessions that are staged several times a week in a nearby muskeg areas. Here the birds are secured by a loose line and are encouraged to fly from one stand to the next.

The center offers tours ($10 per person) only when cruise ships are in, generally most mornings. Call the ARRC (☎ 747-8662) about tours, times and when the birds will be exercised.

Also at the east end of town and a place of interest mostly to history buffs is the **Sitka National Cemetery**. The plot is off Sawmill Creek Rd, just west of the Public Safety Academy, and can be reached from Sheldon Jackson College along Jeff Davis Rd. The area was designated a national cemetery by past president Calvin Coolidge and includes headstones of Civil War veterans, members of the Aleutian Campaign in WWII and many notable Alaskans.

Hiking

Sitka offers superb hiking in the beautiful but tangled forest that surrounds the city. Second only to Juneau for the variety and number of trails that can be reached on foot, Sitka has eight trails which start from its road system and total over 40 miles through the woods and mountain areas.

Indian River Trail This easy trail is a 5.5-mile walk along a clear salmon stream to the Indian River Falls, an 80-foot waterfall at the base of the Three Sisters Mountains. The hike takes you through a typical Southeast rainforest and offers the opportunity to view black bears, deer and bald eagles. The trailhead, a short walk from the center of town, is off Sawmill Creek Rd just east of the National Cemetery. Pass the driveway leading to the Public Safety Academy parking lot and turn up the dirt road with a gate across it. This leads back to the city water plant where the trail begins left of the pump house. Plan on four to five hours for a round trip to the falls.

Gavan Hill Trail Also close to town is the Gavan Hill Trail which ascends almost 2500 feet over three miles to the Gavan Hill peak. The trail provides excellent views of Sitka and the surrounding area. From the end of the trail, the adventurous hiker can then continue onto the peaks of the Three Sisters Mountains.

Gavan Hill is also linked to Harbor Mountain Trail and halfway across the alpine ridge is a free-use shelter. Built in 1991 by the USFS, the shelter is used on a first-come-first-gets-a-bunk basis and is 3.5 miles from the Gavan Hill trailhead or a hike of three to four hours.

From Lincoln St, head north up Baranof St for six blocks. The trailhead and a small parking area is reached just before the cemetery gate at the end of Baranof St. There is good camping in the alpine regions of the trail, but bring water and a camp stove, as drinking water and wood are not available above the tree line.

Harbor Mountain Trail This trail is reached from Harbor Mountain Rd, one of the few roads in the Southeast that provides access to a sub-alpine area. Head four miles northwest from Sitka on Halibut Point Rd to the junction with Harbor Mountain Rd. It is 4.5 miles up the rough dirt road to a parking area and nearby picnic shelter.

After another half-mile you reach the parking area at the end of the road and an unmarked trail begins on the east side of the

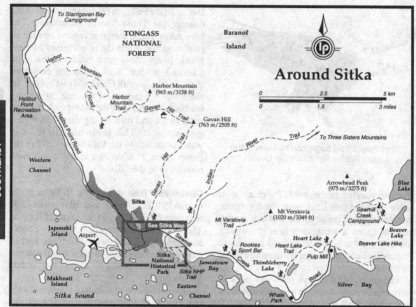

lot. The trail ascends for 1.5 miles to the alpine meadows, knobs and ridges above the road from where the views are spectacular. From here a recently cut trail follows the tundra ridge to the free-use shelter on the saddle between Harbor Mountain and Gavan Hill, where you can pick up the Gavan Hill Trail. Plan on spending two to four hours if just scrambling through the alpine area above Harbor Mountain Rd.

Mt Verstovia Trail This 2.5-mile trail is a challenging climb of 2550 feet to the 'shoulder', a small summit that is the most common end of the trail, although it is possible to climb to 3349 feet, the actual peak of Mt Verstovia. The view from the 'shoulder' on clear days is spectacular, undoubtedly the best in the area.

The trailhead is two miles east of Sitka along Sawmill Creek Rd. Once you reach Rookies Sports Bar on the left, look for the trailhead marked 'Mount Verstovia Trail'.

The Russian charcoal pits (signposted) are reached within a quarter of a mile and shortly after that the trail begins a series of switchbacks. Plan on a four-hour round trip to the 'shoulder'. From the 'shoulder', the true peak of Mt Verstovia lies to the north along a ridge that connects the two. Allow an extra hour each way to hike to the peak.

Beaver Lake Hike This short trail starts from Sawmill Creek Campground, which is reached from Sawmill Creek Rd, 5.5 miles east of Sitka. Across from the former pulp mill on Sawmill Creek Rd, turn left onto Blue Lake Rd for the campground; the trailhead is on the southern side of the campground.

Although steep at the beginning, the 0.8-mile trail levels out and ends up as a scenic walk through open forest and along muskeg and marsh areas to Beaver Lake which is surrounded by mountains. Plan on an hour for the round trip.

Mt Edgecumbe Trail The 6.7-mile trail begins at Fred's Creek USFS Cabin (reservations needed, $25 per night), and ascends to the top of the summit crater of this extinct volcano. Needless to say, the views from the summit are spectacular on a clear day. About three miles up the trail is a free-use shelter (no reservations required).

Mt Edgecumbe lies on Kruzof Island, 10 miles west of Sitka, and can only be reached by boat because large swells from the ocean prevent float planes from landing. Stop at the Sitka Visitor Bureau or call Alaska Adventures Unlimited (☎ (800) 770-5576) for a list of local operators who will drop off and pick up hikers for around $75 one way per party. Actual hiking time is from five to six hours one way, but by securing Fred's Creek USFS Cabin you can turn the adventure into a pleasant three-day trip with nights spent in two shelters.

Paddling

Sitka also serves as the departure point for numerous bluewater trips along the protected shorelines of Baranof and Chichagof islands. You can rent kayaks in town from Sitka Sound Ocean Adventures (☎ 747-6375) and Baidarka Boats (☎ 747-8996). Sitka Sound Ocean Adventures, which operates from a blue bus in the main harbor charges $30/40 a day for singles/doubles. Baidarka Boats rents rigid kayaks and folding doubles ($55/$315 a day/week) and both places offer guided day trips north of town.

Katlian Bay This 45-mile round trip, beginning from Sitka Harbor and ending at scenic Katlian Bay on the northern end of Kruzof Island, is one of the most popular paddles in the area. The route follows narrow straits and well-protected shorelines which are marine traffic channels, making it an ideal trip for less experienced bluewater paddlers who will never be far from help.

A scenic side trip is to hike the sandy beach from the Katlian Bay around Cape Georgiana to Sea Lion Cove on the Pacific Ocean. Catch the tides to paddle the Olga and Neva straits on the way north and return along Sukot Inlet, spending a night at the USFS cabin on Brent's Beach, if you can reserve it. Plan on four to six days for the paddle.

Shelikof Bay You can combine a 10-mile paddle to Kruzof Island with a six-mile hike across the island from Mud Bay to Shelikof Bay along an old logging road and trail. Once on the Pacific Ocean side you'll find a beautiful sandy beach providing opportunities for beachcombing and the Shelikof USFS Cabin (reservations needed, $25 per night).

West Chichagof The western shoreline of Chichagof Island is one of the best bluewater trips in Southeast Alaska for experienced kayakers. Unfortunately, the trip often requires other transport because as few paddlers have the experience to be able to paddle the open ocean around Khaz Peninsula which forms a barrier between the north end of Kruzof Island and Slocum Arm. Either rent a folding kayak and then book a floatplane or contact Southeast Alaska Ocean Adventures (☎ 747-5011) who will do kayak shuttle service on their 50-foot sailboat.

The arm is the southern end of a series of straits, coves and protected waterways that shield paddlers from the ocean's swells and extend over 30 miles north to Lisianski Strait. With all its hidden coves and inlets, the trip is a good two-week paddle. Those with even more time and some sense of adventure in their hearts could continue another 25 miles through Lisianski Strait to the fishing village of Pelican, where the ferry stops twice a month in the summer. Such an expedition would require at least two to three weeks.

Organized Tours

Sitka land tours include the ferry-stopover adventure by Sitka Tours (☎ 747-8443) for those waiting for the tide to switch. The tour briefly covers the major sites: Sitka National Historical Park, St Michael's Cathedral and Sheldon Jackson College. The cost is $8 per adult, half as much for children. The same company also offers an historical tour ($24 for three hours) which also includes Castle Hill and Russian Bishop's House.

You can also book marine wildlife tours in Sitka. Allen Tours (☎ 747-8100) offers a three-hour trip to view sea otters and other wildlife 25 miles north of Sitka for $80 per person, while Stellar Charters (☎ 747-0052) has a half-day trip in the Sitka Sound to spot whales and seabirds for the same price.

Special Events

Extending its reputation as the cultural center of the Southeast, the city sponsors the Sitka Summer Music Festival over three weeks in June at the Centennial Building. The emphasis of the festival is on chamber music and it brings together professional musicians for concerts and workshops. The highly acclaimed event is popular so it can be hard to obtain tickets to the twice-weekly evening concerts. However, rehearsals, open to the public, are easier to attend and usually free.

A bit of Russian culture is offered whenever a cruise ship is in port during the summer months. The New Archangel Russian Dancers take to the stage at the Centennial Building then for a half-hour show. It's $6 per person to see the performance of more than 30 dancers in Russian costumes.

On the weekend nearest 18 October, the city holds its Alaska Day Festival by re-enacting the transfer of the state from Russia to the USA with costumes (and even beard styles) of the 1860s. A parade highlights the three-day event.

Places to Stay

Sitka has a 5% city tax and a 4% bed tax so you can add a hefty 9% to the price of accommodation.

USFS Cabins There are a number of USFS cabins close to Sitka which require less than 30 minutes of flying time to reach. The following cabins, which cost $25 per night, should be reserved in advance through the USFS office in Sitka.

For information on Fred's USFS Cabin, Brent's Beach USFS Cabin and Shelikof USFS Cabin on Kruzof Island (the site of Mt Edgecumbe) see the Sitka Hiking and Paddling sections. Local air-service operators which can handle chartering requests are BellAir (☎ 747-3220) at 485 Katlian St, and Mountain Aviation (☎ 966-2288) in the airport terminal.

Redoubt Lake Cabin is an A-frame cabin at the north end of Redoubt Lake, a narrow body of water south of Sitka on Baranof Island. The cabin is a 20-minute flight from Sitka. You can also reach it by paddling to the head of Silver Bay from town and then hiking along a five-mile trail south to the cabin.

Baranof Lake Cabin is a favorite among locals, as it has a scenic, mountainous setting on the east side of Baranof Island with a mile trail to Warm Springs Bay. At the bay there is a bathhouse constructed around the natural hot springs which costs $2.50 to use. The cabin is a 20-minute flight from Sitka.

Lake Eva Cabin on Baranof Island has a skiff with oars, an outdoor fire pit and a wood stove inside. A trail from the lake outlet, which can be fished for Dolly Varden, cutthroat trout and salmon in late summer, leads down to the ocean. The cabin is a 20-minute flight from Sitka.

White Sulphur Springs Cabin is a 45-minute flight to the western shore of Chichagof Island and is popular with Southeasterners because of the hot springs bathhouse in front of it. The free hot springs are used by cabin renters as well as fishers and kayakers passing through.

Camping The nearest campground to the center of town is *Sealing Cove RV Parking* (☎ 747-3439), an overnight parking area for RVs at Sealing Cove Harbor on Japonski Island.

There are two USFS campgrounds in the Sitka area but neither is close to town. *Starrigavan Campground* is a 0.7-mile walk north of the ferry terminal at *Mile 7.8* of Halibut Point Rd. The campground (28 sites, $8 per night) is in a scenic setting adjacent to a saltwater beach and hiking trails, but the gate is locked at 10 pm, making it unavailable to late-night ferry arrivals. On your way to the area you'll pass Old Sitka State Park, which features trails and interpretive displays dedicated to the site of the original Russian settlement.

Sawmill Creek Campground (nine sites) is six miles east of Sitka on Blue Lake Rd off Sawmill Creek Rd and past the pulp mill. Although the area is no longer maintained by the USFS, it provides mountain scenery with an interesting trail to Blue Lake, a good fishing spot.

Hostels The *Sitka (AYH) Youth Hostel* (☎ 747-8356) is in the basement of the Methodist Church at 303 Kimsham Rd. Follow Halibut Point Rd north-west out of town and then turn right onto Peterson Rd, a quarter of a mile past the Lakeside Grocery Store. Once on Peterson Rd you immediately veer left onto Kimsham Rd. Facilities include a kitchen, lounge and eating area. Open only in the summer, the hostel is $7 for members and $10 for nonmembers. Shuttle buses from the ferry will drop you right at the door step.

B&Bs There are more than a dozen B&Bs in the Sitka area that offer rooms with a good meal in the morning for around $55/60 a single/double. Stop at the Sitka Visitor Bureau for an updated list of them or try *Creek's Edge Guest House* (☎ 747-6484) which overlooks Sitka Sound and Mt Edgecumbe and has rooms from $55 to $95. Downtown are *Karras B&B* (☎ 747-3978), at 230 Kogwanton St, with four rooms for $50/65 single/double, and *Abner's B&B* (☎ 747-8779), at 200 Seward St, with a single/double for $43/54.

If you have some extra funds and want a unique experience, call the *Rockwell Lighthouse* (☎ 747-3056), the last lighthouse built in Alaska. The three-minute skiff ride from town is provided and you'll not only get the whole lighthouse to yourself but will enjoy an excellent view of town and the rugged coastline around it. It's not cheap though at $150 a day per couple or $200 for four

people. You almost need to book this place a year in advance if planning to stay June through August.

Hotels There are six hotels/motels in Sitka. The cheapest is the *The Bunkhouse* (☎ 747-8796) at 3302 Halibut Point Rd with four rooms at $40 for a single or double. A small step up is *Potlatch House* (☎ 747-8611), at the end of Katlian St, near the intersection with Halibut Point Rd, with singles/doubles $75/85. Both tend to attract construction workers and commercial fishers.

There's also *Super 8 Motel* (☎ 747-8804), at 404 Sawmill Creek, with rooms beginning at $70 and the town's impressive *Westmark Shee Atika* (☎ 747-6241), right downtown, where you'll spend at least $110 a night.

Places to Eat

For just coffee in the morning, there is the *Coffee Express* on Lake St, near the fire station. It has limited seating inside, opens at 7 am on weekdays and offers a selection of coffees, lattes and teas, and sandwiches for around $6. There's also *Back Door Cafe*, accessed through Old Harbor Bookstore on Lincoln St, for sandwiches and espresso, and *The Kingfisher Cafe* at Totem Square for more espresso, sandwiches and baked delights.

Lulu's Diner, located next to the Sitka Hotel on Lincoln, is a local hangout with a 1950s décor and breakfast for $4 to $10 that is served all day. The biscuits and gravy will stay with you almost to dinner. The *Bayview*, upstairs in the MacDonald Bayview Trading Center across from Crescent Harbor, has a variety of hamburgers as well as a variety of fresh seafood dinners for $10 to $14. The Bayview also serves beer and wine in a setting which offers every table a view of the boat harbor across the street. The best hamburgers and some of the largest portions are at *Rookies Sports Bar* on Sawmill Creek Road at the Mount Verstovia trailhead.

Along Katlian St there is *El Dorado* for Mexican dishes and *Twin Dragon*, a Chinese restaurant with greasy décor but good food. Lunch specials begin at $6, dinners at $10.

The city's *McDonald's* is a mile out of town on Halibut Point Rd while *Subway* is on Seward St behind the Westmark Shee Atika Hotel.

For good local seafood, there is *Channel Club*, 2906 Halibut Point Road, and *Van Winkle & Daigler* at 228 Harbor Dr. The Channel Club also has the best steaks in town and a great salad bar. The more upscale Van Winkle & Daigler has an Alaska bouillabaisse of king crab, oysters, salmon and halibut. Expect to pay $12 to $25 at either for dinner.

Sitka's largest supermarket, *Sea Mart*, is at 1867 Halibut Point Road and features a bakery, deli, ready-to-eat items and a dining area overlooking Mount Edgecumbe. Closer to town at 705 Halibut Rd is *Lakeside Grocery* which has sandwiches, soups and a salad bar.

Entertainment

Sitka's most interesting night spot is the *Pioneer Bar*, the classic fisher's pub on Katlian St down by the waterfront. The walls are covered with photos of fishing boats and the scoreboard for the pool table often has 'help wanted' messages scrawled across it from fishers looking for black-cod crew or notes from somebody seeking work on a troller. Above the long wooden bar is a large brass bell, but put off the urge to ring it unless you want to buy a round of drinks for the house.

A more upscale bar is the lounge in the *Westmark Shee Atika*, and the only place with a dance floor in Sitka is at *Rookies Sports Bar* on Sawmill Creek Rd.

Getting There & Away

Air Sitka is served by Alaska Airlines (☎ 966-2266) with flights throughout the Southeast as part of the milk run. The one-way fare to Juneau is $90 while a round-trip ticket booked in advance is often under $100. The airport is on Japonski Island, 1.8 miles west of the town center. On a nice day it can be a scenic 20-minute walk from the airport terminal over the O'Connell Bridge to the heart of Sitka. Otherwise, the white airporter

minibus meets all jet flights and charges $2.50 for a ride to the city hotels.

Regularly scheduled flights by small air-charter companies include Sitka to Pelican for $95 one way with Bellair (☎ 747-3220) at 485 Katlian St, and Sitka to Tenakee Springs for $75 one way with Mountain Aviation (☎ 966-2288), located in the airport terminal.

Boat The Alaska Marine Hwy terminal (☎ 747-8737) is seven miles north of town on Halibut Point Rd, and there are north-bound or southbound departures almost daily.

Passage from Sitka to Juneau is $26, Sitka to Angoon $22, Sitka to Petersburg $26 and Sitka to Tenakee Springs $22. The Ferry Transit Bus (☎ 747-8443) meets all ferries for a trip into town. You can also catch the minibus out to the ferry terminal from the Westmark Shee Atika when it picks up hotel guests.

Getting Around

Car & Bicycle Allstar Rental (☎ 966-2552) can provide a subcompact vehicle for $40 per day with unlimited mileage. The dealer is adjacent to the airport terminal. J&B Bike Rentals (☎ 747-8279) at Southeast Diving & Sports, 203 Lincoln St, has hybrid bicycles for $5 an hour or $15 a day.

Secondary Ports

On the ferry runs between Sitka and Juneau there are a handful of secondary ports that you can stop at to escape the cruise ships and tourists found at the larger towns. Some are scenic, others are not, all are a cultural experience into rural Alaska.

KAKE

Kake is an Indian beachfront community (pop 700) on the north-west coast of Kupreanof Island. It is the traditional home of the Kake tribe of the Tlingit Indians and today the community maintains subsistence rights while also running commercial fishing, fish processing and logging enterprises to supplement its economy. Kake is known for having the tallest totem pole in Alaska (and some say the world), a 132-foot carving that was first raised at Alaska's pavilion in the 1970 World's Fair in Osaka, Japan.

The ferry *Le Conte* stops twice a week at Kake on its run between Petersburg and Sitka. The one-way fare from Petersburg to Kake is $20. Within town, 1.5 miles from the ferry terminal, are three general stores, a laundromat and the *Waterfront Lodge* (☎ 785-3472), where rooms are $70/89 for singles/doubles. Rough logging roads lead south from town and eventually reach scenic Hamilton Bay, 20 miles south-east of Kake.

Unless you want to spend three or four days in Kake, you can fly out on regularly scheduled flights with Wings of Alaska (☎ 785-6466) or LAB (☎ 785-6435) to Juneau, or with Bellair (☎ 785-6411) to Sitka. The one-way fare to either is around $90.

Tebenkof Bay Wilderness Kake serves as the departure point for bluewater trips into Tebenkof Bay Wilderness, a remote bay system composed of hundreds of islands, small inner bays and coves. The return paddle is a scenic 10-day adventure that can lead to sightings of bald eagles, black bears and a variety of marine mammals. Paddlers should have experience in ocean touring and be prepared to handle a number of portages. Kayaks can be rented in either Juneau or Sitka and then carried on board the ferry to Kake.

The most common route is to paddle south from Kake through Keku Strait into Port Camden, where at its western end there is a 1.3-mile portage trail to the Bay of Pillars. From the Bay of Pillars you encounter the only stretch of open water as you paddle three miles around Point Ellis to Tebenkof Bay. The return east follows Alecks Creek from Tebenkof Bay into Alecks Lake, where there is a 2.3-mile portage trail to No Name Bay. From here paddlers can reach Keku

Strait and paddle north to Kake via the scenic Rocky Pass.

TENAKEE SPRINGS

What began in the late 1800s as a winter retreat for fishers and prospectors on the east side of Tenakee Inlet has today evolved into a rustic village known for its slow and relaxed pace of life. At the turn of the century the springs were actually enlarged when the locals blasted out the surrounding rock. The Forest Service followed up by building a concrete container around them in 1915 to keep the hot water out and brushed back a path along the shoreline that for years served as the town's main street.

Tenakee Springs (pop 150) is slowly changing. It now has a dirt road called Tenakee Ave, a handful of three-wheel motorized carts and logging has begun in the area. But for the most part the settlement is still a ferry dock, a row of houses on pilings and the hot springs, the town's main attraction that comes bubbling out of the ground at 108°F. The alternative lifestyle is centered around the public bathhouse at the end of the ferry dock. The building there encloses the principal spring which flows through the concrete bath at seven gallons per minute. Bath hours, separate for men and women, are posted and most locals take at least one good soak per day, if not two.

Tenakee Springs can be an interesting, relaxed and inexpensive side trip, especially if you use the ferry *Le Conte*'s Friday night run from Juneau, thus saving accommodation expenses.

Places to Stay & Eat

The town's only restaurant is the *Blue Moon Cafe* while opposite the bathhouse at the foot of the ferry dock is the *Snyder Mercantile Company* (☎ 736-2205). Started by Ed Snyder in the late 1890s, the store has been in business ever since and in 1976 installed the town's first phone. Snyder's sells limited supplies and groceries, and also rents seven cabins, including several small ones at $40 a night for two people. To be sure of getting a cabin, you have to reserve them in advance

(PO Box 505, Tenakee Springs, AK 99841) and check in during store hours, Monday to Saturday from 9 am to 5 pm, and Sunday from 9 am to 2 pm. You also need a sleeping bag. The only other accommodation is a fishing lodge with week-long packages.

There is a chance your ferry will arrive in the middle of the night, in which case it's best to plan on camping out for the first evening. Either pitch your tent near the boat harbor or plan on hiking out of town a fair way before finding an available spot to camp.

The best place to pitch a tent, if you are planning to stay a few days, is at the rustic campground a mile east of town at the mouth of the Indian River. It's quiet, picturesque and equipped with several tables and a covered picnic shelter. Keep the camp clean, however, to discourage brown bears from investigating your site, especially during the salmon runs in late August.

Hiking & Paddling
There is good fishing in the local streams for trout, salmon and Dolly Varden, and day hikes begin at each end of town. The dirt road extends eight miles east of town, where it ends at an old cannery on Coffee Cove, and more than seven miles to the west of town, passing a few cabins in either direction.

Tenakee Springs is also one end of a common bluewater paddle from Hoonah (see the Paddling section in the Wilderness chapter); obtain supplies and a kayak from Juneau.

Whether paddling or hiking along the shore, always keep an eye out for marine mammals such as humpback whales, which are commonly sighted in Tenakee Inlet, along with killer whales and harbor porpoises. You may also see brown bears while paddling or hiking in the area as Chichagof Island is second only to Admiralty Island in the Southeast for the highest density of bears.

Getting There & Around
The ferry *Le Conte* stops at Tenakee Springs three to four times a week, connecting it to Angoon, Hoonah, Sitka, Juneau and occasionally even Haines and Skagway. Study the ferry schedule carefully to make sure you don't have to stay in the town longer than you want. The one-way fare from Tenakee Springs to Juneau or Sitka is $22.

Wings of Alaska (☎ 789-0790 in Juneau) has two flights from Juneau to Tenakee Springs from Monday to Saturday. The one-way fare is about $75.

HOONAH
As you head north on board the ferry *Le Conte*, the next stop after Tenakee Springs before reaching Juneau is Hoonah. It is the largest Tlingit village in Southeast Alaska, with a population of almost 1,000. The Huna, a Tlingit tribe, have lived in the Icy Strait area for hundreds of years and legend tells of their being forced out of Glacier Bay by an advancing glacier. A store was built on the present-day Hoonah site in 1883 and an established community has existed there ever since.

Hoonah's population is roughly 80% indigenous people. The town lacks the charm and friendliness – as well as the public bathhouse – of Tenakee Springs, and in recent years even its coastal beauty has been stripped due to intense logging of Port Frederick. The logging controversy is a sticky one because in this predominantly Native Alaskan village it's their own Native Alaskan corporation who are removing the timber and leaving behind barren mountainsides. As loggers cut the old growth trees, many local families wonder if their lifestyle is being diminished for quick cash. Except for a protected swath behind the town, Hoonah's Huna Totem Corp has logged or sold to be logged all of its commercially viable trees.

Like the streams and valleys north of Fairbanks that have been reduced to rubble by gold miners and sluice boxes, the naked hillsides around Hoonah can be a depressing sight for many visitors traveling to Alaska to enjoy its natural beauty.

Things to See
The most photogenic area lies a mile northwest of Hoonah, where the faded red

buildings of the old **Hoonah Packing Cannery** serenely guard Port Frederick. There is good fishing for Dolly Varden from this point.

In town, or actually on a hill overlooking Front St, is the **Cultural Center & Museum** (☎ 945-3545) which displays indigenous art and artefacts. The center, open Monday to Friday from 8 am to 4.30 pm, has no admission charge.

Hiking & Paddling
The **Spassky Trail**, a 3.3-mile walk, begins 3.5 miles east of Hoonah and winds to Spassky Bay on Icy Strait.

The **Pavlof Trail** is a three-mile walk along the Pavlof River, past two fish ladders between the lake and harbor of the same name. During mid to late August, the salmon runs can be impressive here. Originally the trail was accessed only by boat and plane but now you can link up with the trailhead from Forest Development Road 8515. Pick up a copy of *Hoonah Area Road Guide* ($3) from the USFS office if you want to go looking for this trail.

Hoonah lies south-east of Glacier Bay National Park across Icy Strait, but the paddle to the preserve is an extremely challenging trip for advanced kayakers only. An overnight kayak trip can be made to the Salt Lake Bay USFS Cabin, 14 miles from Hoonah on Port Frederick.

The cabin is rented out for $25 per night and needs to be reserved, but it is not heavily used. Originally a trapper's cabin, the structure is small but can still sleep four. There is a log-transfer facility across the bay and active logging in the area so be ready for clear cuts.

For more information about hiking or paddling in the area, contact the USFS office (☎ 945-3631) at PO Box 135, Hoonah, AK 99829.

Places to Stay & Eat
There is a small grocery store in Hoonah. You can occasionally purchase fresh seafood directly from the *Cold Storage Plant*. You'll find showers and a laundromat at the marina,

and accommodation and meals at the *Huna Totem Lodge* (☎ 945-3636), 1.4 miles from the ferry terminal. In town, there's *Mary's Inn Restaurant*.

Getting There & Away
The *Le Conte* docks in Hoonah three days a week on its route between Tenakee Springs and Juneau. The ferry terminal (☎ 945-3292), half a mile from town, is open two hours before the ferry arrives. Wings of Alaska (☎ 945-3275) and LAB Flying Service (☎ 945-3266) also maintain offices in Hoonah and provide daily services to Juneau.

PELICAN
If you time it right, you can catch a ferry to Pelican, a lively little fishing town on Lisianski Inlet on the north-west coast of Chichagof Island. The *Le Conte* makes a special run to Pelican (pop 209) twice a month, providing a unique day trip from Juneau for only $62.

The cruise through Icy Straits is scenic, the possibility of seeing humpback whales good and the hour and half in port is more than enough time to walk the length and even have a beer in one of the last true boardwalk communities in Southeast.

The town was established in 1938 by a fish packer and named after his boat. Fishing is Pelican's reason for being – it's the closest harbor to the rich Fairweather salmon grounds. Its population doubles during the summer when commercial fishers and cold-storage workers arrive for the trolling season from June to mid-September. Although its life blood, Pelican Seafoods, closed briefly in 1996, the company was since purchased by the Kake Native corporation and the town again seems economically stable.

Pelican is a photographer's delight as most of it is built on pilings over tidelands and its main street, dubbed Salmon Way, is a mile-long wooden boardwalk. There are only two miles of rough gravel road beyond that. The main attraction is *Rosie's Bar & Grill* (☎ 735-2265) where you can get a burger, a beer or even a bed – there are four

SOUTHEAST

rooms for rent for $65. This is a classic Alaskan fisherman's bar, though when legendary Rose Miller gave up the place in 1996, due to poor health, it lost some of its charm. Still you can mingle with trollers, longliners and Pelican Seafood workers or marvel at the half king salmon, half black tail deer mounted on the wall.

If you plan to stay over, there are a handful of places to secure a bed, including *Otter Cove B&B* (☎ 735-2259), a short walk from town where a single/double costs $55/65. Pelican also has a small library, another bar, the *Lisianski Inlet Cafe*, a laundromat, general store, a liquor store with adjoining steambaths and showers, and kayak rentals at Loken Air, which has an office on the boardwalk. Both Loken Air and Wings of Alaska (☎ 789-0790 in Juneau) has scheduled flights to Juneau for $90 one way.

Juneau

First appearances are often misleading, and Juneau (pop 30,000) is a case in point. Almost half of the northbound state ferries arrive in the capital city between midnight and 6 am at the Auke Bay Ferry Terminal, 14 miles from the city center, leaving disgruntled backpackers and tired travelers to sleepily hunt for transport and lodging. At this point you might be unappreciative of Juneau, but give it a second chance. Few cities in the USA and none in Alaska are as beautiful as Juneau. Residents claim it is the most scenic capital in the country, while others describe it as a 'little San Francisco'.

The city center, which hugs the side of Mt Juneau and Mt Roberts, has many narrow streets running past a mixture of new structures, old storefronts and slanted houses, all held together by a network of staircases. The bustling waterfront features cruise ships, tankers, fishing boats, a few kayakers and a dozen float planes buzzing in and out like flies. Overhead are the snow-capped peaks of Mt Juneau and Mt Roberts, which provide just a small part of the superb hiking found in the area.

History

Although the Gastineau Channel was a favorite fishing ground for local Tlingit Indians, the town was founded on gold nuggets. In 1880, Sitka mining engineer George Pilz offered a reward to any local chief who could lead him to gold-bearing ore. Chief Kowee arrived with such ore and Pilz sent Joe Juneau and Dick Harris, two vagabond prospectors, to investigate. The first time the prospectors arrived they found little that interested them in Gold Creek. But at Kowee's insistence, Pilz sent the two men back to the Gastineau Channel and this time they hacked their way through the thick rainforest to Snow Slide Gulch, the head of Gold Creek, and found, in the words of Harris, 'little lumps as large as peas and beans'. On 18 October 1880, the two men staked out a 160-acre townsite and almost overnight a mining camp appeared. It was not only the state's first major gold strike but within a year the camp became a small town, the first to be founded after Alaska's purchase from the Russians.

Initially the town was called Harrisburg and then Rockwell, then finally in 1881 the miners met and officially named it after Juneau. The post office was established shortly later and the name has stuck ever since. After the declining whaling and fur trade reduced the importance of Sitka, the capital of Alaska was moved to Juneau in 1906.

Almost 75 years later in 1974, Alaskans voted to move the state's capital again, this time to a small highway junction called Willow that lay in Anchorage's strong sphere of influence. The so-called 'capital move' issue hung over Juneau like a dark cloud, restricting its growth and threatening to turn the place into a ghost town, as 50% of the residents work for the federal, state or local government.

The issue became a political tug-of-war between Anchorage and the Southeast until the voters, faced with a billion-dollar price

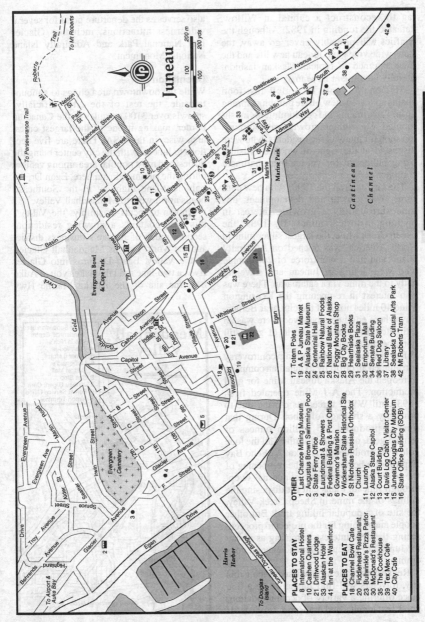

SOUTHEAST

Juneau

To Mt Roberts

Roberts Trail

To Mt Roberts

To Perseverance Trail

Basin Road

Evergreen Bowl & Cope Park

Gold Creek

Evergreen Cemetery

Harris Harbor

Juneau Douglas Bridge

To Douglas Island

To Airport & Auke Bay

Gastineau Channel

Marine Park

Egan Drive

PLACES TO STAY
8   International Hostel
10 Cashen Quarters
21 Driftwood Lodge
33 Alaskan Hotel
41 Inn at the Waterfront

PLACES TO EAT
18 Channel Bowl Cafe
20 Fiddlehead Restaurant
23 Bullwinkle's Pizza Parlor
30 McDonald's Restaurant
35 The Cookhouse
39 Tex Mex Cafe
40 City Cafe

OTHER
1   Last Chance Mining Museum
2   Augustus Brown Swimming Pool
3   State Ferry Office
4   Laundromat & Showers
5   Federal Building & Post Office
6   Governor's Mansion
7   Wickersham State Historical Site
9   St Nicholas Russian Orthodox
    Church
11 Laundry
12 Alaska State Capitol
13 Court Building
14 Davis Log Cabin Visitor Center
15 Juneau-Douglas City Museum
16 State Office Building (SOB)
17 Totem Poles
19 A & P Juneau Market
22 Alaska State Museum
24 Centennial Hall
25 Rainbow Natural Foods
26 National Bank of Alaska
27 Foggy Mountain Shop
28 Big City Books
29 Hearthside Books
31 Sealaska Plaza
32 Emporium Mall
34 Senate Building
36 Red Dog Saloon
37 Library
38 Sealaska Cultural Arts Park
42 Mt Roberts Tram

tag to reconstruct a capital at Willow, defeated the funding in 1982. Although the conflict will probably never go away, the state-wide vote gave Juneau new life and the town boomed in typical Alaskan fashion, literally bursting at its seams.

McDonald's and Taco Bell fast-food chains appeared, new office buildings sprang up and apartments and condominiums mushroomed. The sudden growth was too much too soon for many of the residents, who were disgusted at the sight of wooded hillsides being bulldozed for yet another apartment complex.

The city entered the 1990s with new concerns over growth and development, this time surrounding a growing interest in opening historical mines. By 1989, the Green Creek Mine, the largest silver mine in North America, was opened on Admiralty Island and had a workforce of 260 people who were living in Juneau and traveling daily to the mine via a catamaran. There was also interest in re-opening the Kensington Mine 40 miles north of the city near Berners Bay where engineers believed there was an estimated $855 million worth of gold still lying below the surface.

But the heart of the mining controversy surrounded an effort by a Canadian company to reopen the Alaska-Juneau Mine for gold production. The A-J Mine operated from 1893 until WWII forced its closure due to primarily a shortage of labor. During that time it produced 3.5 million ounces of refined gold, or about a fourth of all the lode gold ever produced in Alaska. As Echo Bay Exploration began to plot the re-opening of the A-J, environmental concerns swept through Juneau. Plans call for disposing the tailings of the mine in Sheep Creek Valley, the site of a popular hiking trail. But other people are pushing for the project to proceed, seeing the new interest in mining as a way for Juneau to lessen its dependency on government.

Regardless of the unique issues facing this city, travelers will find Juneau to be a fine place offering a variety of accommodation, good restaurants and transport services. It also serves as the departure point for several wilderness attractions, including Glacier Bay National Park and Admiralty Island National Monument.

Orientation

While the downtown area clings to a mountainside, the rest of the city 'officially' sprawls over 3100 sq miles to the Canadian border, making it one of the largest cities, area-wise, in the USA. There are five sections to Juneau, with the city center being the busiest and most popular area among visitors during the summer. From here, Egan Dr, the only four-lane highway in the Southeast, heads north-west to Mendenhall Valley.

Known to locals as simply 'the Valley', this area contains a growing residential section, much of Juneau's business district and the world-famous Mendenhall Glacier. In the Valley, Egan Dr turns into Glacier Hwy, a two-lane road that takes you to Auke Bay, the site of the Alaska Marine Hwy

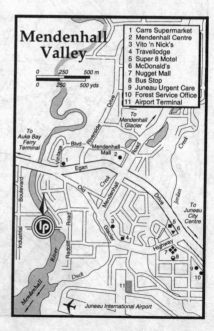

Mendenhall Valley

0   250   500 m
0   250   500 yds

1 Carrs Supermarket
2 Mendenhall Centre
3 Vito 'n Nick's
4 Travellodge
5 Super 8 Motel
6 McDonald's
7 Nugget Mall
8 Bus Stop
9 Juneau Urgent Care
10 Forest Service Office
11 Airport Terminal

terminal, more boat harbors and the last spot for purchasing food or gas until the end of the road at Echo Cove.

Across the Gastineau Channel is Douglas, a small town south-east of Juneau, which at one time was the area's major city. The road north out of this sleepy little town is Douglas Hwy which runs around Douglas Island to the fifth area of Juneau known to locals as North Douglas. Around here you'll find the Eagle Crest Ski Area, many scenic turn-offs, and a lot of half-hidden cabins and homes owned by people who work in Juneau but don't want to live in its hustle-bustle.

Information

Tourist Offices The main visitor center is the Davis Log Cabin (☎ 586-2201), at 134 3rd St, open daily until 5 pm during the summer. There are also smaller visitor information booths at the Juneau Airport terminal out in the Valley and at the Marine Park on the city waterfront.

For information about cabin rentals, hiking trails, Glacier Bay, Admiralty Island or any outdoor activity in the Tongass National Forest, stop at the information center (☎ 586-8751) in the Centennial Hall at 101 Egan Dr. The center is staffed by both US Forest Service and National Park personnel and is open from 8 am to 5 pm daily in the summer.

For state park information the Alaska Division of Parks and Outdoor Recreation (☎ 465-4563) also has an office in Juneau on

The Davis Log Cabin houses the Juneau Visitor Center.

the 3rd floor, 400 Willoughby Ave, which is open Monday to Friday from 8 am to 4.30 pm.

Money Juneau has almost a dozen banks. National Bank of Alaska (☎ 586-3324) has a branch downtown at the corner of Seward and 2nd streets and another towards the Valley at 9150 Glacier Hwy. Thomas Cook (☎ 586-5688) has a foreign exchange office in the Baranof Hotel at 127 North Franklin St. American Express (☎ 586-1235) is at 101 North Franklin St.

Post The main post office in Juneau is on the first floor of the Federal Building on the corner of 9th St and Glacier Ave.

Travel Agency Juneau Travel (☎ 586-6031) is at 14 Marine Way in the downtown area.

Bookshops There are two excellent book stores, practically next door to each other in the downtown area: Hearthside Books at 254 Front St, and Big City Books across from the Baranof Hotel on North Franklin St.

Library If nothing else, you should stop at Juneau's main public library (☎ 586-5249) at 292 Marine Way for the view. From the top of a parking structure, the windows of the library provide a panorama of downtown Juneau leading up to Mount Juneau. Open daily and until 9 pm Monday through Thursday, this excellent facility has used books for sale, a phone for free local calls and computers with Internet access.

Laundry Harbor Washboard (☎ 586-1133) at 1114 Glacier Avenue, across Egan Dr from the Small Boat Harbor, also has showers. In the basement of an apartment building on the corner of 4th St and North Franklin St is The Dungeon, a small laundromat with no attendant or showers. It's not well posted outside but the entrance is a stairway on North Franklin St.

Medical Services Bartlett Memorial Hospital (☎ 586-2611) is off Glacier Hwy, between the downtown area and Lemon Creek, and is a stop along the city bus route. Near Nugget Mall in the Valley is Juneau Urgent Care (☎ 790-4111), a medical clinic with walk-in service at 8505 Old Dairy Rd.

City Center

Much of your sightseeing time will be spent in the city center, where nothing more than a good pair of walking shoes is needed. Start at the **Marine Park**, a delightful waterfront park across from the Sealaska Building at the southern end of Egan Dr, where there is an information kiosk, open daily. Among the hand-outs they offer is a walking-tour map.

The tour leads from the park along Admiralty Way to **South Franklin St**, a historical district that underwent major renovation in 1985. The buildings along this stretch, many dating back to the early 1900s, have since been turned into bars, gift shops and restaurants and are stormed by mobs of visitors every time a cruise ship docks.

At Hearthside Bookstore, the tour veers left onto Front St and then continues onto Seward St, where it passes the **Davis Log Cabin**, a replica of the first public school in Juneau. The cabin is another information center and houses a small collection of local historical relics and objects.

Swing left (south-west) onto 3rd St and head uphill on Main St where first you'll pass an impressive lifesize bronze sculpture of a bear before reaching the **State Capitol**, though you might not recognize it as such. Built in 1929-31 as the territorial Federal Building, to many the capitol looks more like a high school than the Alaskan seat of government. Inside are the legislative chambers, the governor's office and offices for the hundreds of staff members who arrive in Juneau for the winter legislative session. Within the lobby is a visitors desk where free 30-minute tours of the building are offered every half hour daily during the summer from 9 am to 4.30 pm.

The walking tour returns to Seward St, climbs one block up and then turns right (north-east) on 5th St to the **St Nicholas Russian Orthodox Church**, probably the

most photographed structure in Juneau. The octagonally shaped building was built in 1894, making it the oldest church in the Southeast, and has exhibits of Russian icons, original vestments and religious relics. Tours are conducted during the summer from 9 am to 6 pm Monday to Saturday. Admission is a donation.

You backtrack to the corner of 4th and Main streets to reach the **Juneau-Douglas City Museum** (☎ 586-3572). Housed in the old Memorial Library building, the museum has local artwork, a large custom relief map of the area and audio-visual presentations. But its best exhibits are interpretive displays covering the gold-mining history of Juneau and Douglas. The museum is open Monday to Friday from 9 am to 6 pm and Saturday and Sunday from 10 am to 6 pm during the summer; the admission charge is $2.

Across from the museum is the **State Office Building**, or the SOB as it is known locally. Inside the SOB on the 8th floor is the grand court which features a century-old totem pole and a restored 1928 Kimball organ played for office workers and visitors each Friday at noon. The **Alaska State Library** is also off the grand court. The panoramic view of Juneau's waterfront and Douglas Island from the adjoining outdoor balcony is most impressive – an excellent place to have lunch on a sunny day.

Heading west from the SOB, 4th St curves north and becomes Calhoun Ave; in a block it reaches the six-pillar **Governor's Mansion**. Built and furnished in 1912 at a cost of $44,000, the structure has a New England appearance but is accented by a totem pole, carved in 1940 by Tlingit Indians and presented to the governor as a gift.

Behind the Governor's Mansion is Indian St which curves sharply into 9th St. Follow 9th St south-west to the **Federal Building**, where next to the main post office on the 1st floor is a 1994 time capsule with a collection that can be viewed through a pair of windows. The Federal Building is at the junction of 9th St and Glacier Ave, a major bus stop where you can pick up buses to the Valley or Douglas.

Glacier Ave curves east and becomes Willoughby Ave, and in a few blocks you reach Whittier St. Turn right (south) on Whittier St to the **Alaska State Museum**, an impressive white building. This outstanding museum provides Alaskans with a showcase of their past, including artefacts from all four indigenous groups: Athabascan, Aleut, Inuit and north-west coast people. There are also displays relating to the Russian period, major gold strikes in the state, and the Trans-Alaska Pipeline.

By far the most impressive sight is the full-size eagle's nest which sits on top of a tree that is as high as the 2nd floor of the museum. A circular staircase allows you to view the nest from all angles. The museum is open Monday to Friday from 9 am to 6 pm and Saturday and Sunday from 10 am to 6 pm; admission is $3.

From Whittier St you can turn left (east) onto Egan Dr to the **Centennial Hall**, where there is a USFS information center and exhibits. During the summer films and slide presentations are shown in the adjoining theater.

Continue east on Egan Dr, and then Marine Way to the **Sealaska Cultural Park**, which features a Native Alaska art gallery and the Naa Kahidi Theater, in distinctive traditional-style clan houses. The theater (☎ 463-4844) stages dramatizations of Native Alaskan oral literature and mythology in accordance with the cruise-ship schedule. The one-hour performances are $16, a little steep if you ask me.

Another made-for-the-cruise-ship attraction is the **Mt Roberts Tram** (☎ 463-3412), just down South Franklin St. The tram commenced operation in 1996 and takes passengers from the cruise ship dock to the treeline of Mount Roberts for $16. Once on top you can hike around all day. The tram was a sore point with most locals, who fear that hoards of out-of-shape visitors will now be dumped onto one of the city's most popular alpine trails.

On 7th St, at the top (northern end) of Main St is the **Wickersham State Historical Site** (☎ 586-9001), the historical home of

Judge James Wickersham, the pioneer judge and statesman of Alaska. The house was built in 1898 and was occupied by the judge who also served as Alaska's first delegate to Congress from 1928 to 1939. Inside are photographs, books and other memorabilia from the judge's colorful career. The house is supposed to be open Monday to Friday from 9 am to 4 pm, and Sunday from noon to 4 pm, but hours seem sporadic; call first. Admission is $2.50.

Gold Mines

Gold fever and gold mines built Juneau and today mining companies are staging a resurgence in and around the city. There are several interesting and free places which help you gain an idea of what must have been an incredible era in Alaska's history. First head to the Juneau-Douglas City Museum for its exhibit and pick up the *Perseverance Trail* booklet ($1) and *Treadwell Mine Historic Trail* brochure (25 cents).

A hike up Basin Rd to the start of Perseverance Trail, a two-mile walk from the city center, will take you to the remains of the compressor house for the Alaska-Juneau Mine on Gastineau Channel. Today the building is the **Last Chance Mining Museum** (☎ 586-5338), where you can view the impressive complex of railroad lines, ore cars and repair sheds. Hours are 9.30 am to 6.30 pm daily and admission is $3. To reach the area follow North Franklin St up the hill to its end and turn right (south-east) onto 6th St. Turn immediately left (north-west) on Gold St which turns into Basin Rd. The ruins are half a mile down this scenic road.

At the end of nearby Perseverance Trail (see the Juneau Hiking section) is the **Glory Hole**, a caved-in mine shaft that was connected to the Alaska-Juneau Mine, along with the remains of the **Silver Bowl Basin Mine**.

Perhaps the most interesting areas to explore are the **Treadwell Mine** ruins across the Gastineau Channel near Douglas. From the Capital Transit bus turnaround in Douglas, continue south towards the Sandy Beach Recreation Area, past the softball fields and Douglas Boat Harbor. The beach was made from the tailings of the Treadwell Mine and the old pilings from its shipping dock still stand.

Take one of the staircases from the beach to St Ann's St right above Sandy Beach and follow the street further south to Old Treadwell Rd. The dirt road leads to old foundations, the shells of boarding houses and the mine shaft, another glory hole, of the Treadwell Mining Community. The operation closed down in 1922 after a 1917 cave-in caused the financial collapse of the company. During its heyday at the turn of the century the mine made Douglas the major city on the channel with a population of 15,000.

Across the channel from Treadwell is the **Alaska-Juneau Mine** on the side of Mt Roberts. The mine closed down in 1944 after producing more than $80 million in gold, then valued at $20 to $35 an ounce. Today, the mine is the center of a controversial plan by a Canadian mining company to reopen it.

There is a natural fascination among visitors passing through the Southeast about gold-rush history and even an interest among many to try gold panning themselves. Any hardware store in Juneau will sell you a gold pan (black plastic ones are the cheapest and easiest to see those flecks of gold in) while the best public creeks to pan are Bullion Creek in the Treadwell Mine area, Gold Creek up by the Last Chance Basin, Sheep Creek on Thane Rd and Salmon, Nugget and Eagle creeks off Egan Dr and Glacier Hwy north of the city center.

Glaciers

Juneau is also known as the 'Gateway to the Glaciers'. There are several glaciers in the area including the Mendenhall Glacier, Alaska's famous drive-in glacier. The ice floe is 13 miles from the city center at the end of Glacier Spur Rd. Head out along Egan Dr and at *Mile 9* turn right onto Mendenhall Loop Rd, staying on Glacier Spur Rd when the loop curves north to head back to Auke Bay.

The Mendenhall Glacier flows 12 miles from its source, the Juneau Icefield, and has a 1.5-mile face. On a sunny day it's beautiful, with blue skies and snow-capped mountains in the background. On a cloudy and drizzly afternoon it can be even more impressive, as the ice turns shades of deep blue.

There is an interesting visitor center (☎ 789-0097) at the glacier. It's open from 8.30 am to 5 pm daily during the summer. Inside is a large relief map of the icefield and glaciers, an audio-visual room with slide presentations and films, and an information desk with trail information. There are several hiking trails in the area, including a half-mile nature trail, the East Glacier Trail or the Nugget Creek Trail (see the Juneau Hiking section).

The cheapest way to see the glacier is to hop on a Capital Transit bus in the city center and get off at the corner of Mendenhall Loop and Glacier Spur roads. The fare is $1.25 and buses depart from the State Capitol and the Federal Building every half an hour or so. From the Loop Rd, it is another mile to the visitor center. There is also Mendenhall Glacier Transport (☎ 789-5460), whose two-hour city tour includes 40 minutes at the glacier. The cost is $12.50 per person.

On your way out to Mendenhall Valley, look to your right, high in the mountains, when you pass Lemon Creek to see the remains of the Lemon Creek Glacier. By hiking, you can get a close and uncrowded look at Herbert Glacier on *Mile 27.5* of Glacier Hwy or Eagle Glacier at *Mile 28.4* (see the Juneau Hiking section).

One way to see all the glaciers and the icefield is to splurge on a sightseeing flight. They're not cheap, most cost around $100 per person for a 45-minute flight, but on a clear day can provide a spectacular overview of the icefield. All the air-charter companies run them. Wings of Alaska (☎ 789-0790) offer scenic flights during the summer from the International Airport and the Marine Park at the city waterfront when there is a cruise ship in port.

You can also marvel at the icefield and glaciers from a helicopter which includes landing on the sea of ice and spending about

15 minutes walking around. Temsco Helicopters (☎ 789-9501) offers such a tour that lasts almost an hour. The price to stand on ice? How about $142 per person.

Hiking

Few cities in Alaska have such a diversity of hiking trails as Juneau; it's the area's top attraction. Many of these hiking routes are shown on the later Around Juneau map.

For those who don't feel up to walking the trails on their own, Juneau Parks & Recreation (☎ 586-5226) holds adult hikes every Wednesday, and family hikes along easier trails every Saturday. The hikes begin at the trailhead at 10 am; on Wednesday there is often car-pooling to the trail with hikers meeting at Cope Park, a short walk from the hostel. Call Juneau Parks & Recreation for a schedule.

If you need to rent overnight equipment; tent, sleeping bag or a stove, call Alaska Rainforest Tours (☎ 463-3466) or Gearing Up (☎ 586-2549).

Perseverance Trail This trail system off Basin Rd is the most popular one in Juneau and includes the Perseverance, Mt Juneau and Granite Creek trails. Together, the trails can be combined into a rugged 10-hour walk for hardy hikers or an overnight excursion into the mountains that surround Alaska's capital city.

To reach the trailhead from the international hostel, take 6th St one block south-west to Gold St which turns into Basin Rd, a dirt road that curves away from the city into the mountains as it follows Gold Creek. After crossing a bridge over the creek look for the posted trailhead on the left.

From the Perseverance Trail it is possible to pick up the Granite Creek Trail and follow the path to the creek's basin, a beautiful spot to spend the night. From here, you can gain access to Mt Juneau by climbing the ridge and staying left of Mt Olds, the huge rocky mountain. Once on the summit of Mt Juneau, you can complete the loop by descending along the Mt Juneau Trail, which joins Perseverance Trail a mile from its beginning.

The hike to the 3576-foot peak of Mt Juneau along the ridge from Granite Creek is an easier but longer trek than the ascent from the Mt Juneau Trail. The alpine sections of the ridge are peacefully serene and on a clear day in the summer there are outstanding

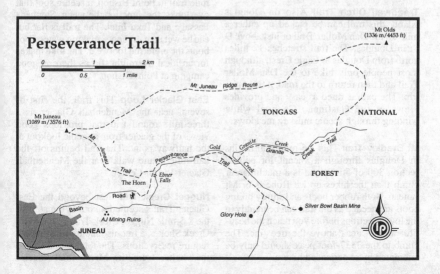

Perseverance Trail

0   1   2 km
0   0.5   1 mile

Mt Olds
(1336 m / 4453 ft)

Mt Juneau Ridge Route

Mt Juneau
(1089 m / 3576 ft)

TONGASS   NATIONAL

Gold   Granite   Creek

Granite   Creek   Trail

Mt Juneau Trail

Perseverance   Trail

Gold   Creek

FOREST

The Horn

Ebner Falls

Road

Basin

AJ Mining Ruins

JUNEAU

Glory Hole

Silver Bowl Basin Mine

views. From the trailhead for the Perseverance Trail to the upper basin of Granite Creek is a 3.3-mile one-way hike. From here it is then another three miles along the ridge to reach Mt Juneau.

Mt Roberts Trail This is the other hike that starts close to the international hostel. The trail is a four-mile ascent to the mountain above the city. The trail begins at a marked wooden staircase at the north-eastern end of 6th St and consists of a series of switchbacks with good resting spots. When you break out of the trees at Gastineau Peak you come across a wooden cross and the new tram station as well as good views of Juneau, Douglas and the entire Gastineau Channel. The Mt Roberts summit is a steep climb through the alpine brush to the north of the city.

Dan Moller Trail This 3.3-mile trail leads to an alpine bowl at the crest of Douglas Island where there is a USFS cabin (reservations needed, $25 per night). See the Trekking section in the Wilderness chapter for further details.

Treadwell Ditch Trail Also on Douglas Island, this trail can be picked up either a mile up the Dan Moller Trail or just above D St in Douglas. The trail stretches 12 miles north from Douglas to Eagle Crest, although most people only hike to the Dan Moller Trail and then return to the road, a five-mile trip. The path is rated as easy and provides views of the Gastineau Channel while winding through scenic muskeg meadows.

Mt Bradley Trail This 2.6-mile trail begins in Douglas through a vacant lot behind section 300 of 5th St and is a much harder climb than the hikes up Mt Roberts or Mt Juneau. Both rubber boots and sturdy hiking boots are needed as the trail can be muddy in the lower sections before you reach the beautiful alpine areas above the tree line. The climb to the 3337-foot peak should only be attempted by experienced hikers.

Cropley Lake Trail Another trail on Douglas Island is the 1.5-mile route to Cropley Lake. The trail was built primarily for cross-country skiing but in the summer it can be hiked to the alpine lake, which provides good scenery and camping. The start is up Fish Creek Rd, a short way past the Eagle Crest Ski Lodge in a creek gully to the right.

Sheep Creek Trail Southeast of Juneau along Thane Rd is the very scenic Sheep Creek Trail, a three-mile walk into the valley south of Mt Roberts where there are many historic mining relics. The trailhead is four miles from Juneau at a staircase on the gravel spur to a Snettisham Power Plant substation. The trail is fairly flat in the valley, from where you scramble up forested hillsides to the alpine zone. Many hikers follow the power line once they are above the tree line to reach the ridge to Sheep Mountain. You can continue from Sheep Mountain over Mt Roberts, returning to Juneau along the Mt Roberts Trail. This is a 10 to 12-hour day hike.

Point Bishop Trail At the end of Thane Rd, 7.5 miles south-east of Juneau, is this eight-mile trail to Point Bishop, a scenic spot that overlooks the junction between Stephens Passage and Taku Inlet. The trail is flat but can be wet in many spots, making waterproof boots the preferred footwear. The hike makes for an ideal overnight trip as there is good camping at Point Bishop.

East Glacier Loop This trail, the first of several near the Mendenhall Glacier, is a three-mile round trip that provides good views of the glacier from a scenic lookout at the halfway point. The trail begins off the half-mile nature walk near the Mendenhall Glacier Visitor Center.

Nugget Creek Trail Just beyond the East Glacier Creek lookout is the start of the 2.5-mile Nugget Creek Trail to the Vista Creek Shelter, a free-use shelter that doesn't require reservations. The total round trip to the shelter from the Mendenhall Glacier

Visitor Center is eight miles. Hikers who plan to spend the night at the shelter can continue along the creek towards Nugget Glacier, though the route is bushy and hard to follow at times.

West Glacier Trail This is one of the most spectacular trails in the Juneau area. The 3.4-mile trail begins off Montana Creek Rd past Mendenhall Lake Campground and hugs the mountainside along the glacier, providing exceptional views of the icefalls and other glacial features. It ends at a rocky outcrop but a rough route continues from here to the summit of Mt McGinnis, another two miles away. Plan on four to five hours for the West Glacier Trail; or plan on a long day if you want to tackle the difficult Mt McGinnis route.

Montana Creek & Windfall Lake Trails These two trails connect at Windfall Lake and can be combined for an interesting 13-mile overnight trip. It is easier to begin at Montana Creek and follow the Windfall Lake Trail out to the Glacier Hwy.

The 9.5-mile Montana Creek Trail, known for its high concentration of bears, begins near the end of Montana Creek Rd, close to the rifle range. The 3.5-mile Windfall Lake Trail begins off a gravel spur that leaves the Glacier Hwy just before it crosses Herbert River, 27 miles north-west of Juneau. The trail has been upgraded considerably in recent years and now is used by mountain bikers as well as hikers.

Spaulding Trail This trail's primary use is for cross-country skiing, but it can be hiked in the summer as it was upgraded in 1996. The three-mile trail provides access to the Auke Nu Trail that leads to the John Muir USFS Cabin (reservations needed, $25). The trailhead for the Spaulding Trail is at Glacier Hwy just past and opposite the Auke Bay Post Office, 12.3 miles north-west of Juneau. Check at the information center in the Centennial Building about the availability of the cabin.

Peterson Lake Trail This four-mile trail provides access to good Dolly Varden fishing in both Peterson Creek and Peterson Lake. The trailhead has been moved to avoid private property and is now 20 feet before the *Mile 24* marker on Glacier Hwy, north of the Shrine of St Terese. Wear rubber boots as it can be muddy during the summer. A USFS cabin (reservations needed, $25) is at Peterson Lake.

Herbert Glacier Trail This level trail extends 4.6 miles along the Herbert River to Herbert Glacier. The trail is easy, though wet in some places, and the round trip takes four to five hours. The trail begins just past the bridge over Herbert River at *Mile 28* of Glacier Hwy in a small parking lot to the left.

Amalga Trail Also known as the Eagle Glacier Trail, this level route winds 5.5 miles one way to the lake formed by Eagle Glacier, where there is now a USFS cabin (reservations needed, $25) 0.8 miles from its face. The view from the Eagle Glacier Cabin is well worth the effort of reserving it in advance. The trailhead is beyond the Glacier Hwy bridge across Eagle River, 0.4 miles past the trailhead for the Herbert Glacier Trail. Plan on a round trip of seven to eight hours to reach the impressive Eagle Glacier.

Paddling

Both day trips and extended three to five-day paddles are possible out of the Juneau area in sea kayaks. Boats can now be rented from several places in the area with the best being Juneau Outdoor Center (☎ 586-8220) near the Douglas Boat Harbor. Doubles are $45 a day, singles $35 and transportation to any location on the Juneau road system is available. There is also Adventure Sports (☎ 789-5696) on Old Dairy Road near the Forest Service office. Topographic maps can be obtained in Juneau at the Foggy Mountain Shop (☎ 586-6780), across from the Baranof Hotel on North Franklin St.

Guided Tours If unsure about kayaking, Alaska Discovery (☎ 800-586-1911) offers a guided day trip daily in Juneau where you get a chance to paddle the coastal islands of Lynn Canal. Tours are limited to 10 people and everything is provided including boats, lifejackets, rubber boots and transport from the downtown area. The cost is $95 per person. The guiding company also has a three-day paddle around Douglas Island for $495.

Auke Bay The easiest trip is to paddle out and around the islands of Auke Bay. You can even camp on the islands to turn the adventure into an overnight trip.

Taku Inlet This waterway is an excellent four to five-day trip highlighted by close views of Taku Glacier. Total paddling distance is 30 to 40 miles depending on how far you travel up the inlet. It does not require any major crossing, though rounding Point Bishop can be rough at times. It is possible to camp at Point Bishop and along the grassy area south-west of the glacier, where brown bears are occasionally spotted.

Berners Bay At the western end of Glacier Hwy, 40 miles from Juneau, is Echo Cove where kayakers put in for paddles into the protected waters of Berners Bay. The bay, which extends 12 miles north to the outlets of the Antler, Lace and Berners rivers, is ideal for an overnight trip or longer excursions up Berners River.

Oliver Inlet On the north-east coast of Admiralty Island is Oliver Inlet, where a 0.8-mile portage trail connects it to scenic Seymour Canal. The paddle to Oliver Inlet is 18 miles and involves crossing Stephens Passage, a challenging open-water crossing for experienced kayakers only. At the south end of the portage trail from Oliver Inlet is the Seymour Canal USFS Cabin (reservations needed, $25).

Organized Tours
City Tours A number of companies offer city tours through Juneau and the surrounding area for those travelers with limited time.

Gray Line (☎ 586-3773) departs from the Baranof Hotel at 127 North Franklin St and offers a 2½-hour Mendenhall Glacier tour with a few historic sights in town for $33. Much better is Mendenhall Glacier Transport (☎ 789-5460) which has basically the same thing for only $12.50.

Tracy Arm This steep-sided fjord, 50 miles south-east of Juneau, is highlighted by a pair of tidewater glaciers and a gallery of icebergs that float down the length of it. Tracy Arm makes an interesting day trip, especially if you don't have the time or funds for Glacier Bay. You're almost guaranteed of seeing seals inside the arm and there's a possibility of spotting whales on the way there.

A handful of tour boats make the run to the head of the fjord and they all take off from Marine Park and maintain a ticket office in the area. The trip is usually a full-day cruise, includes a light lunch, cash bar and costs $100. But Adventure Bound Alaska (☎ 463-2509 or (800) 228-3875) sells the trip to hostel members for $70. Also offering the cruise for $100 is Auk Nu Tours (☎ 586-8687.

For something different, call Wild Abandoned (☎ 463-4942). Lynn Schooler offers three and four-day outings for six passengers on his boat in which you camp on shore each night and bring your own food. The cost is around $400 per person and includes Admiralty Island's Pack Creek as well as Tracy Arm.

Special Events
Juneau's main festival during the summer is on 4 July when the celebrations include a parade, a carnival, fireworks over the channel, and a lot of outdoor meals from Sandy Beach in Douglas to Juneau's city center. In mid-April there is the week-long Alaska Folk Festival.

Places to Stay
Juneau tacks on 11% to the price of most lodging. Also keep in mind downtown hotels and B&Bs tend to be heavily booked during the summer tourist season.

USFS Cabins Numerous USFS cabins are accessible from Juneau but all are heavily used, requiring reservations in advance. If you're just passing through, however, check with the USFS information center in the Centennial Building, where the staff maintain a cabin update listing that shows which units are still available and when.

The John Muir, Peterson Lake and Dan Moller cabins and the new Eagle Glacier Cabin, accessible by foot from the Juneau road system; and Seymour Canal Cabin, at the southern end of the portage from Oliver Inlet, have already been mentioned in the Juneau Hiking and Paddling sections.

The following cabins are within 30 minutes' flying time from Juneau; the air charter costs range from $200 to $250 per person for return transport. Loken Aviation (☎ 789-3331) and Wings of Alaska (☎ 789-0790) can provide air services on short notice.

The *West Turner* cabin is one of the most scenic and by far the most popular cabin in the Juneau area. This unit is a 30-minute flight from Juneau on the western end of Turner Lake, where there is good fishing for trout, Dolly Varden and salmon. A skiff is provided.

The *Admiralty Cove* cabin is on a scenic bay and has access to Young Lake along a very rough 4.5-mile trail. The unit is a 30-minute flight from Juneau in a tidal area where float planes can land only during high tide. Brown bears frequent the area.

Young Lake has a USFS cabin at each end, and both cabins are provided with a skiff. The lake offers good fishing for cutthroat trout and land-locked salmon. An overgrown trail connects North Young Lake Cabin with Admiralty Cove. There is no trail between South and North Young Lake cabins.

Camping There are some fine campgrounds beyond Mendenhall Valley. *Mendenhall Lake Campground*, one of the most beautiful USFS campgrounds in Alaska, is 13 miles from downtown and five miles northeast of the Auke Bay Ferry Terminal. The campground (60 sites) has a separate seven-site backpacking unit and is on Montana Creek Rd, a dirt road that runs off Mendenhall Loop Rd. The tent sites are alongside a lake and many have spectacular views of the nearby glacier. The nightly fee is $8 per site.

The other USFS campground, *Auke Village*, is two miles from the ferry terminal on Glacier Hwy. The area (12 sites) provides shelters, tables, wood and an interesting beach to walk along. The fee is also $8 per night.

The city of Juneau now allows RV parking at the Norway Point Parking Area, near Aurora Basin off Egan Dr downtown, and Savikko Park in Douglas for $5 a night. There are no services or hook-ups at these areas but a trailer dump station and water are available at Savikko Park. There is also *Auke Bay RV Park* (☎ 789-9467), 1.5 miles east of the ferry terminal, a full-service campground that charges $16 per night.

Glacier Hwy ends 41 miles north of Juneau at a pleasant spot called Echo Cove. There are no developed facilities here, but it's a nice spot to camp for a while and a favorite among locals. There is usually good offshore salmon fishing in August. Other scenic but undeveloped areas are Eagle Beach on Glacier Hwy, and Fish Creek on North Douglas Hwy.

Hostels The *Juneau International Hostel* (☎ 586-9559) is one of the best hostels in Alaska. The large yellow house is on the corner of Harris and 6th streets in the colorful Starr Hill neighborhood. Its location is ideal – five blocks from the State Capitol, four blocks from the Mt Roberts Trail and two blocks from Basin Rd and the beginning of the scenic Gold Creek area.

The hostel has cooking and laundry facilities, showers, and a common room with a fireplace. Check-in time is from 5 to 11 pm, check-out is 9 am and reservations are accepted if accompanied by the first night's fee and sent with a self-addressed, stamped envelope. Fees are $10 a night. For reservations contact the Juneau International (AYH) Hostel, 614 Harris St, Juneau, AK 99801.

B&Bs Juneau has more than 50 bed & breakfasts with rates that range from $65 to $90 per couple per night. The only problem is securing a room after stepping off the ferry late at night. For that reason, it's wise to book ahead, even a day or two while traveling through the region. An easy way to do this is to contact the Alaska Bed & Breakfast Association (☎ 586-2959) which covers most of the Southeast, including Juneau, of course.

Downtown B&Bs include *Sally's B&B* (☎ 780-4708), next door to the Driftwood Inn at 465 Whittier St. There are six rooms with private baths and kitchenette for $70/75 for single/double. At 526 Seward St, just a block up from the State Capitol, is *The Mullins House* (☎ 586-3384) with rooms for $60/70. And at 326 6th St is *Devin House* (☎ 463-3704), a restored 19th-century home with two rooms for $75 a night.

In Douglas, there is *Windsock Inn* (☎ 364-2431), at 410 D St, with two rooms for $50/55. In North Douglas, try *Blueberry Lodge* (☎ 463-5886) which has five rooms near the Eaglecrest Ski Facility and a great view of the Gastineau Channel. A double is $85. Overlooking Auke Bay in a secluded location is *The Lost Chord* (☎ 789-7296), at 2200 Fritz Cove Rd.

Hotels The cheapest hotel is the *Alaskan Hotel* (☎ 586-1000), 167 South Franklin St, which has an historical décor in its lobby and rooms dating back to 1913. Rooms without bath are $55/65 a night for single/double. Just to the south at 455 South Franklin is the *Inn at the Waterfront* (☎ 586-2050), a small hotel where a single with a shared bath is $60 but includes a light breakfast. Another small hotel is *Cashen Quarters* (☎ 586-9863) at 303 Gold St with five rooms with baths and kitchens for $65/75 for single/double.

One of the best places to stay downtown is *Driftwood Lodge* (☎ 586-2280 or (800) 544-2239), near the Alaska State Museum. Rooms without kitchens are $68/78 for single/double and the motel has a courtesy van that runs out to both the airport and the ferry terminal.

Near the airport are several motels. *Super 8 Motel* (☎ 789-4858), next door to McDonald's on Trout St, has a van that meets flight and ferry arrivals, and rooms that begin at $87/97 for single/double. Even closer to the airport is *Travellodge* (☎ 789-9700), at 9200 Glacier Hwy, with single/doubles for $90/100.

Places to Eat

Juneau's size allows it to have an excellent range of restaurants that no other Southeast town could possibly support. There are more than 50 in the area, principally downtown, with a couple in Douglas and the rest in the Mendenhall Valley.

Salmon Bakes Juneau has a couple of salmon bakes with the best being *Thane Ore House* (☎ 586-3442), four miles south of town on Thane Road. The all-you-can-eat dinner of grilled salmon, halibut and ribs is $18.50 and includes a salad bar, corn, baked beans, the usual. At 6.30 pm is the Gold Nugget Revue and the show and dinner sets you back $27. Call if you need bus transport from the downtown area.

To combine flightseeing, glacier viewing and a salmon bake, there's *Taku Glacier Lodge* (☎ 586-8258), which is reached via a 15-minute floatplane flight up Taku Inlet. The tour last three hours but is a little pricey at $169 per person.

Cafes The cheapest place for breakfast or lunch is the *Federal Building Cafeteria* on the 2nd floor of the Federal Building, which also provides a nice view of the Gastineau Channel for its diners. Open from 7 am to 3.30 pm, the restaurant offers eggs, potatoes, toast and bacon for around $5, and hamburgers and sandwiches for under $4. The nearby *Channel Bowl Cafe*, a local hang-out on Willoughby Ave across from the A&P Juneau Market, is known for large portions and reasonable prices for breakfast. Try the Mt Jumbo, heaped plate of eggs, potatoes and peppers, onions and cheese for $7. It will keep you full until dinner.

Another interesting restaurant is *City Cafe*, on South Franklin St near the Mt

Roberts Tram. Breakfasts are $6 to $9 and include a recommended garden omelette. The cafe also has an interesting selection of Filipino and Indonesian dishes as well as cheap beer on tap; small pitchers are only $4.

Cheap dinners of pizza or sandwiches can be obtained at *Bullwinkle's Pizza Parlor* across from the State Office Building on Willoughby Ave. Good-sized sandwiches cost between $4 and $6, while medium pizzas begin at $10. There is also wine, a large selection of imported beer, and silent movies shown on the back wall at night. The best pizza downtown is at *Pizzeria Roma* in the Merchant's Wharf on Marine Way. The small restaurant has a full bar, beer on tap and medium thin crust pizzas for $14 to $20. Across Willoughby Ave from A&P Juneau Market is *Rick's Cafe* for hot subs and large salads.

On the 1st floor of the Emporium Mall is the *Heritage Coffee Co & Cafe*, Juneau's most popular coffee shop. Large, double-shot lattes are $3, huge bagels and cream cheese $2 and breakfast sandwiches $4. On Seward St is *Valentine's*, with expresso drinks and fresh baked goods. In Douglas, of the two restaurants on this side of the channel, I prefer the *Douglas Cafe*, next door to the Perseverance Theater on 3rd St. Breakfast begin at $4.50, almost 20 types of gourmet hamburgers are $6 to $8 and dinners are $13 to $16.

Restaurants Of the handful of Mexican restaurants in the city center, the best is *Armadillo Tex-Mex Cafe*, at 431 South Franklin St, where you can fill up on enchiladas, pollo loco (crazy chicken) or a vegetarian taco among other delights. Dinners with pinto beans and rice begin at $7 and most are under $10. If the place is full, and often it is, then head north on South Franklin Street to *El Sombrero*.

Longtime favorite *Fiddlehead Restaurant* on Willoughby Ave serves the best vegetarian cuisine in Juneau as well seafood. The food is excellent but dinners are $8 to $15 and just the bean burger is $7. The place is a good spot for afternoon tea and freshly baked

foods, while upstairs is the Fireweed Room for cocktails, fine dining and live music at night. On the corner of 2nd St and Seward St is *Rainbow Natural Foods*, a health food store.

Silverbow Inn (☎ 586-4146), at 120 2nd St, is one of Juneau's better restaurants for a splurge. Dishes range from seafood and tenderloin to vegetarian and Thai, prices from $18 to $24. Desserts are excellent as is the homemade ice cream. Equally acclaimed and in the same price range is *Summit Restaurant* (☎ 586-2050), on the main floor of the Inn on the Waterfront. Call ahead and make a reservation, both restaurants are small.

Giorgio at the Pier on South Franklin St near the tram is Juneau's newest restaurant and combines seafood with traditional Italian cuisine and a view of the waterfront. Next door to the Red Dog Saloon on Admiral Way is *The Cookhouse* which claims to serve the largest hamburger in Alaska, so big it feeds two. For $14 you can judge for yourself. The gold-rush theme restaurant is a bit touristy for me, but others find it fun. Full dinners of steak and prime rib are about $22.

Just north of the airport on Old Glacier Hwy is *Vito 'n' Nick's*, a small Italian restaurant. Deep dish pizzas begin at $11 for a medium, pasta dinners are under $9 and on Tuesday it's all the spaghetti you can consume for $8. Next door is *Valley Restaurant* which stays open to 4 am on Friday and Saturday for late ferry arrivals, serving the usual cafe food. Juneau has a second *McDonald's* on the corner of Egan Dr and Old Glacier Hwy across from the Nugget Mall. An excellent *Carr's* is at the corner of Egan Hwy and Vintage Blvd and has a salad bar, stir-fry counter, bakery and eating area. It's open 24 hours.

Supermarkets In the city center, *A&P Juneau Market* on Willoughby Ave across from the Federal Building has a good selection of local seafood, an espresso counter, salad bar for $3.50 a pound, ready-to-eat items and a small seating area. It's open 24 hours.

Entertainment

Bars & Pubs With a population that is larger, younger and a little more cultured than in most other Southeast towns, Juneau is able to support a great deal more nightlife. The most famous nightspot is the *Red Dog Saloon*, which is mentioned in every travel brochure and the first destination of every cruise ship passenger. The bar is interesting with its sawdust floor and relics covering the walls, but the Red Dog is not a place to spend an entire evening drinking unless you can put up with point-and-shoot cameras flashing at the stuffed bear.

South Franklin St as a whole is Juneau's drinking section. Many places are local hang-outs that will undoubtedly turn you off, which is fine with those leaning against the bar inside. The *Triangle Club*, however, is a pleasant little spot on the corner of Front and South Franklin streets. Although there is limited seating inside, the bar offers wide-screen television and a good hot dog to go along with a mug of beer. Hidden in the back of the *Alaskan Hotel* is a unique bar with an interior and cash register that matches the rest of the hotel's historical setting. Often there is folk or jazz music.

To sip a beer and watch the float planes take off and land on the Gastineau Channel, there's *The Hangar Pub & Grill* in the Merchant's Wharf, which also features a wide screen TV. For a view of the harbor, head to the *Breakwater Inn* on Glacier Ave, past the high school in west end of the downtown area. The bar is on the 2nd floor and overlooks the Aurora Basin Boat Harbor, an active place in the summer.

Out in the Valley, in the Airport Shopping Center on Glacier Hwy, is *Hoochie's Sports Pub*, Juneau's liveliest dance bar. There is live music almost nightly in the summer and until the band starts playing, large pitchers are only $8.

Theater Juneau is blessed with the *Perseverance Theater* (☎ 364-2421), an excellent local company that produces classic and original plays. The theater is on 3rd St in Douglas. Juneau's melodrama is *The Gold Nugget Revue*, a show of cancan dancers, music and local history. It's staged at the Thane Ore House (☎ 586-1462) and tickets, without the salmon bake, are $8.50.

Getting There & Away

Air Alaska Airlines (☎ 789-0600) has scheduled services to Seattle, all major Southeast communities, Glacier Bay, Anchorage, and Cordova from Juneau daily during the summer. Recent airfare wars have pushed the one-way fare from Juneau to Anchorage to as low as $110. The one-way fare from Juneau to Cordova, which allows you to continue traveling on the state ferries to Valdez, Seward, Homer and Kodiak, is $127 if purchased 21 days in advance. To Ketchikan the one-way fare is usually about $100. Delta Airlines (☎ 789-9771) has daily scheduled flights from Juneau to Anchorage, Fairbanks and Seattle, and Air North (☎ 789-2007) flies three times a week to Whitehorse.

The smaller air-service companies have a number of scheduled flights to small communities in the area that are considerably cheaper than chartering a plane there. LAB Flying Service (☎ 789-9160) flies to Hoonah for $50 one way and Haines for $65. Wings of Alaska (☎ 789-0790) offers a $70 flight to Tenakee Springs, $90 to Pelican and $75 to Angoon.

Skagway Air (☎ 789-2006) has daily flights to Skagway for $70 while Air Excursions (☎ 697-2375) can take you to Gustavus, the departure point for Glacier Bay National Park, for $100 round trip.

Boat The ferry arrives and departs from the Auke Bay Ferry Terminal, a hassle for budget travelers as it is 14 miles from the downtown area. There are daily ferry departures during the summer from Juneau to Sitka for $26, Petersburg $44, Ketchikan $74, Haines $20, and Skagway $26. A smaller ferry, the *Le Conte*, connects Juneau to Hoonah, Angoon and Tenakee Springs. The main ticket office for the ferry (☎ 465-3941 or 465-3940 for recorded information) is at 1591 Glacier Ave.

There are no state ferries to Gustavus, the

gateway to Glacier Bay, but Auk Nu Tours (☎ 586-1337 or (800) 820-2628) runs a 78-foot catamaran daily, departing from near the Auke Bay post office at 9.30 pm. The round-trip fare is $85, kayaks are an additional $25.

Getting Around

The Airport & Ferry Terminal Late-night arrivals at the ferry terminal are best off getting the Mendenhall Glacier Transport bus (☎ 789-5460) that meets all ferries and will take you to the airport or downtown for $5. There is also an airporter bus (☎ 780-4977) that makes hourly runs from major hotels to the airport for $7 a person. There are always taxis, of course, but expect to pay around $22 from the ferry terminal and $16 from the airport.

During the day, it is possible to walk to the nearest public bus stop for a $1.25 ride into town. From the ferry terminal, walk south along the Glacier Hwy for a little over a mile to Dehart's Grocery Store near the Auke Bay terminal. From the airport terminal, stroll to the backside of Nugget Mall, across the street from Mendenhall Auto, where there is a bus stop with a posted schedule.

Bus Capital Transit (☎ 789-6901), Juneau's public bus system, runs hourly during the week with alternating local and express services from 7 am until 6 pm and 9 am to 6 pm on Sunday. The main route circles the downtown area, stopping at the City Dock Ferry Terminal, Capitol Building, the Federal Building, and then heading out to the Valley and Auke Bay Boat Harbor via the Mendenhall Loop Rd, where it travels close to the Mendenhall Lake Campground. There is also a bus that runs every hour from city stops to Douglas. Fares are $1.25 each way. Grab a map and schedule the first time you board a bus.

Car There are almost a dozen car rental places in Juneau for those needing a vehicle – a great way for two or three people to see the sights out of the city or to reach a trailhead. Few hire companies have a mileage charge because all the roads in

Juneau don't total much more than 100 miles. For a $35 special call Rent-A-Wreck (☎ 789-4111) at 9099 Glacier Hwy, which provides pick-up and drop-off service. So does Allstar Rent-A-Car (☎ 790-2414 or (800) 722-0741) and Evergreen Ford (☎ 789-9386), which has compacts for around $40 a day.

Bicycle Juneau has several bike paths, including a nine-mile route from Auke Bay downtown to the Mendenhall Glacier, from the Juneau-Douglas bridge to Douglas and a new 2.5-mile path along Mendenhall River. Because of the steep nature of most of Juneau's trails, mountain biking is limited, but Perseverance, Windfall Lake and Peterson Lake trails are popular areas for off-road cyclists. You can rent bikes at Mountain Gears (☎ 586-4327), 210 North Franklin St, which charges $6 an hour or $25 a day. The bike shop also has organized cycling tours.

AROUND JUNEAU

Just three miles north of downtown at 2697 Channel Dr is **Gastineau Salmon Hatchery Visitor Center** part of the new $7 million, state-of-the-art Douglas Island Pink & Chum Hatchery (☎ 463-4810). The entire facility is a major producer of salmon for the northern region of Southeast Alaska and is geared for visitors with underwater viewing windows that allow you to see fish spawning, fish ladders and interpretive displays explaining the lifecycle of salmon and the different hatchery operations. The hatchery is close to a bus stop and tours are offered Sunday to Friday from 10 am to 6 pm, and Saturday from noon to 5 pm. Admission is $3 per person.

Other sights outside the city include the **Alaska Brewing Company** (☎ 780-5866) on Shaune Dr in the Lemon Creek area. Juneau's only brewery offers tours from Tuesday to Saturday every half-hour from 11 am to 4.30 pm and a free glass of suds at the end.

The **Auke Bay Marine Lab** is 12.5 miles north-west of Juneau and a mile south of the Alaska Marine Hwy terminal. The research

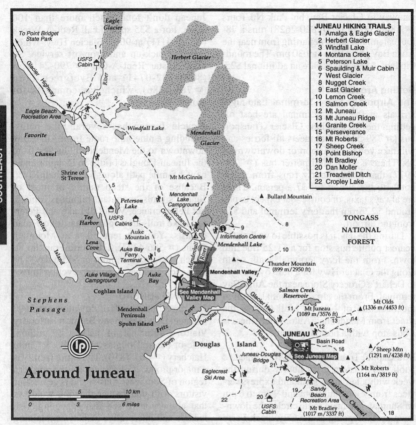

JUNEAU HIKING TRAILS
1 Amalga & Eagle Glacier
2 Herbert Glacier
3 Windfall Lake
4 Montana Creek
5 Peterson Lake
6 Spaulding & Muir Cabin
7 West Glacier
8 Nugget Creek
9 East Glacier
10 Lemon Creek
11 Salmon Creek
12 Mt Juneau
13 Mt Juneau Ridge
14 Granite Creek
15 Perseverance
16 Mt Roberts
17 Sheep Creek
18 Point Bishop
19 Mt Bradley
20 Dan Moller
21 Treadwell Ditch
22 Cropley Lake

Around Juneau

0   5   10 km

0   3   6 miles

facility has a self-guided tour of displays and saltwater tanks and is open from 8 am to 4.30 pm on weekdays. South of the lab on the shores of Auke Lake is the **University of Alaska (Juneau Campus)**, a small college in a beautiful setting. Among the many buildings are a student union and a bookstore while Egan Library features a Northwest Coast Native art collection of masks, baskets, hats and wooden panels.

At *Mile 23.3* of Glacier Hwy is the **Shrine of St Terese**, a natural stone chapel on its own island that is connected to the shore by a stone causeway. As well as being the site

of numerous weddings, the island is situated along the Breadline, a well-known salmon fishing area in Juneau. This is perhaps the best place to fish for salmon from the shore.

Juneau's only state park is **Point Bridget State Park**, a 2800-acre unit at *Mile 39* of Glacier Hwy. Point Bridget overlooks Berners Bay and Lynn Canal and features three trails that wander through rainforest, along a rugged shoreline and past two rental cabins (reservations needed, $35) that can be reserved by calling the state division of parks (☎ 465-4563).

Scenic viewing points include North

Douglas Rd for a look at Fritz Cove and Mendenhall Glacier from afar, and **Eagle Beach Recreation Area** at *Mile 28.6* of Glacier Hwy for stunning views of the Chilkat Mountains and Lynn Canal. Bird enthusiasts should stop at the scenic lookout at *Mile 6* of Egan Dr, which overlooks the **Mendenhall Wetlands & Refuge**. There's a viewing platform with signboards that explain the natural history of the refuge.

If the temperatures soar above 80°F, head over to **Sandy Beach** and watch the pale locals cram in as much suntanning as they can under the midnight sun.

Admiralty Island

Only 15 miles south-east of Juneau is Admiralty Island National Monument, a 955,747-acre preserve, of which 90% has been designated as wilderness. The Tlingit Indians, who know Admiralty Island as Kootznoowoo, 'the Fortress of Bears' (the name was well chosen), have resided on the 96-mile long island for more than 1000 years.

Admiralty Island has a wide variety of wildlife. Bays like Mitchell, Hood, Whitewater and Chaik contain harbor seals, porpoises and sea lions. Seymour Canal, the island's largest inlet, has one of the highest densities of nesting eagles in the world, and humpback whales often feed in the waterway. Sitka blacktail deer are plentiful and the streams choke with spawning salmon during August. But more than anything else Admiralty Island is known for its bears.

The island has one of the highest densities of bear in Alaska. It is estimated that 1500 to 1700 bears live here or about one bruin for every 1600 sq miles. Bears enjoy a good life on the island, roaming the drainage areas for sedges, roots and berries much of the year but feasting on salmon in August before settling into dens on the upper slopes to sleep away most of the winter.

Admiralty is a rugged island with forested mountains that rise to 4650 feet. The coastal rainforest of Sitka spruce and western hemlock are broken up only by numerous lakes, rivers and open areas of muskeg. Around 2500 feet, the tree line is reached and beyond that you'll find alpine-tundra and even permanent icefields.

Although you can fly in for a stay at a USFS cabin or an expensive lodge, most visitors to the monument are people looking for a wilderness experience and who take the Cross Admiralty Island Canoe Route (see the Paddling section in the Wilderness chapter) or spend time paddling Seymour Inlet and Mitchell Bay or one of many other bays.

Before arriving, secure supplies and information in Juneau. Most visitors arrive from Juneau and information can be obtained from the USFS office at Centennial Hall on Egan Dr or the Admiralty Island National Monument office (☎ 586-8790) at 8461 Old Dairy Road out in Mendenhall Valley.

ANGOON

The lone settlement on Admiralty Island is Angoon, a predominantly Tlingit community of 650 residents. Tlingit tribes occupied the site for centuries, but the original village was wiped out in 1882 when the US Navy, sailing out of Sitka, bombarded the indigenous people after they staged an uprising against a local whaling company.

Today, the economy is a mixture of commercial fishing and subsistence, while in town the strong indigenous heritage is evident in the painted fronts of the 16 tribal community houses. The old lifestyle is still apparent in this remote community and time in Angoon can be spent observing and gaining some understanding of the Tlingit culture. Tourism seems to be tolerated only because the village is a port-of-call for the ferry.

Angoon only has three miles of road. The village itself is at one end, perched on a strip of land between Chatham Strait on the west coast of Admiralty Island and turbulent Kootznahoo Inlet which leads into the interior of the national monument. The community serves as the departure point for many kayak and canoe trips into the heart of the monument, including the 32-mile Cross Admiralty Canoe Route to Mole Harbor.

Many people are content to just spend a few days paddling and fishing Mitchell Bay and Salt Lake. To rent a canoe in Angoon call Favorite Bay Inn (☎ 788-3123), which charges $50 a day, less for a rental six days or longer. Before undertaking such an adventure, stop at the USFS office (☎ 788-3166) in the Old City Office Building on Flagstaff Rd in Angoon for information on the tides in Kootznahoo Inlet and Mitchell Bay. The office is open Monday to Friday from 8 am to 5 pm. The tides here are among the strongest in the world; the walk between the airport and the town allows you to view the turbulent waters at mid-tide.

Places to Stay & Eat

By far the best place to stay in Angoon is the *Favorite Bay Inn* (☎ 788-3123 or (800) 432-3123), a large, rambling log home two miles from the ferry terminal. A bed and a hearty breakfast is $69/109 for a single/double. *Kootznahoo Lodge* (☎ 788-3501), with 10 rooms for $66/75, is on Kootznahoo Rd.

Angoon is a dry community and the only cafe in town is a hang-out for teenagers at night. Groceries and limited supplies can be picked up at the *Angoon Trading Company* (☎ 788-3111) on Kootznahoo Rd. There are also supplies at *Seaside Store* on Chatham St but it's best to come with a full supply of your own food.

Getting There & Away

There are approximately three southbound and two northbound ferries a week stopping at Angoon on the run from Sitka to Juneau during the summer. The one-way fare to Angoon is $24 from Juneau and $22 from Sitka. The ferry terminal is three miles from town.

Wings of Alaska (☎ 788-3530 in Angoon) has daily flights to Juneau for $75. Bellair, the Sitka air charter company, also has an office in Angoon (☎ 788-3501) and has scheduled flights between the two towns for about the same fare as flying to Juneau.

PACK CREEK BEAR REFUGE

On the eastern side of Admiralty Island, spilling into Seymour Canal, is Pack Creek. To the north of it is Swan Cove and to the south is Windfall Harbor. All three areas have extensive tide flats that draw a large number of bears to feed, thus making them favorite spots to observe and photograph the animals.

As Pack Creek has been closed to hunting since the mid-1930s, several bears have become used to the presence of humans. The bears are most abundant in July and August when the salmon are running, and most visitors are boaters who go ashore to view the animals and then camp somewhere else. At Pack Creek, you watch the bears from the Viewing Sand Spit or an observation tower along the creek reached by a mile-long trail. The only place to camp in the area is on the east side of Windfall Island, a half mile away, making a boat necessary for those who plan to spend more than a day in the area. To the south, there is a free, three-side shelter in Windfall Harbor.

A food cache is provided near the South Sand Spit as you should never enter the area with food in your pack. Do not leave the

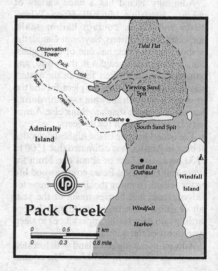

   Top: Floatplane dock, Ketchikan (JD)
Bottom: Colorful Creek Street, Ketchikan (JD)

Top: Downtown Juneau (JD)
Bottom left: St Nicholas Church, Juneau (JD)
Bottom right: Eklutna Russian Orthodox Cemetery (RS)

Viewing Sand Spit into the meadow to get closer to the bears. Stay on the spit, wait for the bears to move into range and use a telephoto lens for close-up shots.

In recent years, Pack Creek has become so popular that the area buzzes with planes and boats every morning from early July to late August. Anticipating this daily rush hour, most resident bears escape into the forest but a few adult females and cubs hang around to feed on salmon, having long since been habituated to the human visitors. Seeing five or six bears at one time would be a good viewing day at Pack Creek.

Permits

In the 1980s, the number of visitors to Pack Creek grew from 100 to more than a 1000, forcing the USFS and Alaska Department of Fish and Game to institute a permit system with a limit on visitors. Only 24 people are allowed per day from mid-June through August. One to three-day permits are issued in advance on a first-come, first-serve basis and are $10 per person per day. They are available from 1 March and are usually gone within two or three weeks. A handful are kept as spares, however, and handed out three days in advance at the monument office. Call the Admiralty Island National Monument (☎ 588-8790) in Juneau about obtaining one.

Getting There & Around

Experienced kayakers can rent a boat from Juneau Outdoor Center (☎ 586-8220) in Douglas and paddle to the refuge. The run down Gastineau Channel and around Douglas Island isn't bad, but the Stephens Passage crossing to reach Oliver Inlet has to be done with extreme care and a close eye on the weather. From the inlet, the Alaska Division of Parks & Outdoor Recreation operates the Oliver Inlet tramway that can be used to cross the mile-long portage into Seymour Canal. At the south end of the portage is the Seymour Canal Cabin (reservations needed) that can be rented for $25 per night by calling the State Division of Parks office (☎ 465-4563) in Juneau.

You can also arrange to be dropped off and picked up by Loken Aviation (☎ 789-3331), which departs daily at 8.30 am for Pack Creek and returns at 4 pm. It's $130 for the round trip. Alaska Discovery (☎ (800) 586-1911) rents canoes at Pack Creek ($50 a day) and offers guided trips into the area. The one-day tour includes flying over to Admiralty Island and then paddling canoes to Pack Creek, where you spend the day watching bears before returning to Juneau. The cost is $349 per person. There is also a five-day trip for $1400 per person.

Glacier Bay

Sixteen tidewater glaciers spilling out of the mountains and filling the sea with icebergs of all shapes, sizes and shades of blue have made Glacier Bay National Park & Preserve an icy wilderness renowned throughout the world.

When Captain George Vancouver sailed through the ice-choked waters of Icy Strait in 1774, Glacier Bay was little more than a dent in a mountain of ice. Less than a century later, John Muir made his legendary discovery of Glacier Bay and found that the end of the bay had retreated 20 miles from Icy Strait. Today, the glacier that bears his name is 60 miles from Icy Strait and in its rapid retreat has revealed plants and animals which have fascinated naturalists since 1916.

Apart from having the world's largest concentration of tidewater glaciers, Glacier Bay is the habitat for a variety of marine life, including whales – the humpbacks being by far the most impressive and acrobatic as they heave their massive bodies out of the water in leaps known as breaching. Adult humpbacks can often grow to 50 feet and weigh up to 37 tons. Other marine life includes harbor seals, porpoises, killer whales and sea otters, while other wildlife includes brown and black bears, wolves, moose, mountain goats and over 200 species of birds.

Glacier Bay is a park of contrasts. It is an

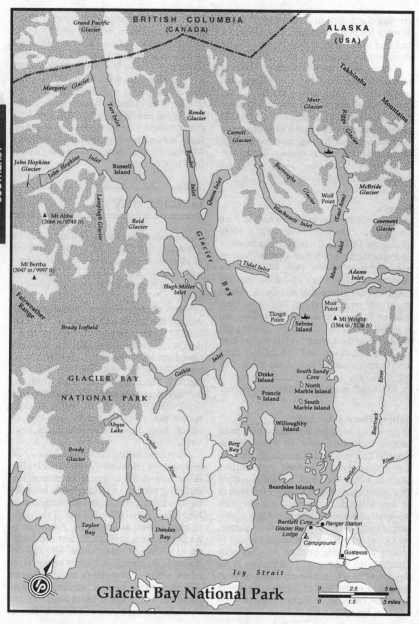

Glacier Bay National Park

The killer whale is one of several marine mammals to visit Glacier Bay.

area of lush spruce and hemlock forests, bare shores recently exposed by glaciers, steep fjords, the flat terrain around Gustavus and an inlet full of icebergs. It's also the site of a controversy that's brewing between the tourist industry, most notably the cruise-ship lines, and environmentalists. To the operators of the huge 10-story cruise ships, Glacier Bay is the jewel that attracts customers to these high-priced trips. To others, these floating resorts are the cause of the humpback whales' leaving the park while bringing smog – a big city problem – to the middle of the wilderness.

After the number of whales dropped dramatically in 1978, the National Park Service reduced ship visits from 103 to 79 during the three-month season. But eventually the industry lobbied US Congress (the US way of getting what you want) to increase the number to 184 a year or two a day during the season. Among the more bizarre problems the ships bring is smog, created when they park for an hour or so in front of a glacier and an air inversion leaves a haze hovering over the ice.

To kayakers and backcountry users, such a ship is a hotel on water, with 1000 passengers waving from the railing and a public-address system announcing happy hour. In an effort to separate the groups, the National Park Service has designated Muir

Inlet, or the East Arm, as wilderness waters prohibiting the large boats to sail there.

The park is many things to many people, but to no one is it a cheap side trip. Of the 216,000 annual visitors, over three-quarters arrive aboard a cruise ship and never leave the boat. The rest are a mixture of tour-group members who head straight for the lodge and backpackers who wander toward the free campground. Plan on spending at least $350 for a trip from Juneau to Glacier Bay, but remember that the cost per day drops quickly after you've arrived.

GUSTAVUS

The park is serviced by a small settlement called Gustavus, an interesting backcountry community of 400 residents. Among the citizens of Gustavus is a mixture of professional people – doctors, lawyers, former government workers and artists – who have decided to drop out of the city rat race and live on their own in the middle of the woods. Electricity only arrived in the early 1980s, and in some homes you still have to pump the water at the sink or build a fire before you can have a hot shower.

There is no 'town center' in Gustavus. The town is merely an airstrip left over from WWII and a road to Bartlett Cove, officially called Main Road and then Park Road but known to most locals as 'The Road'. They refer to every other road and dirt path in the area as 'The Other Road' regardless of which one they are talking about. Along The Road there is little to see, as most cabins and homes are tucked away behind a shield of trees. The heart of Gustavus is the bridge over the Salmon River; near it is Salmon River Park, the Gustavus Inn and the only grocery store in the area.

Places to Stay & Eat

The *Gustavus Inn* (☎ 697-2254) is a charming family homestead lodge that has 16 rooms and space for 26 people. The inn is mentioned in every travel book and brochure on Alaska and rooms are hard to obtain at the last minute. Nightly rates are $130 per person and include meals. The inn is really

SOUTHEAST

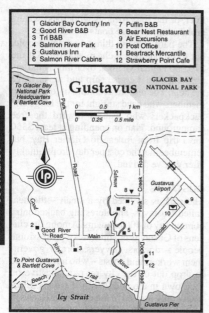

1 Glacier Bay Country Inn	7 Puffin B&B
2 Good River B&B	8 Bear Nest Restaurant
3 Tri B&B	9 Air Excursions
4 Salmon River Park	10 Post Office
5 Gustavus Inn	11 Beartrack Mercantile
6 Salmon River Cabins	12 Strawberry Point Cafe

known for its gourmet dinners which include home-grown vegetables and main courses of local seafood such as salmon, crab, halibut and trout served family style. Dinners cost $23 per person and you have to call ahead for a space at the table.

Another fine place is the *Glacier Bay Country Inn* (☎ 697-2288) which offers a room, three meals a day and all your transfers for $244 for two people. A cheaper alternative for lodging in Gustavus is the *Salmon River Cabins* (☎ 697-2245) on a road that heads north-east just before you cross the Salmon River Bridge from the airport. Cabins are $70 per night for two people and can accommodate up to four. Each has a wood-burning stove and a gas camp stove and bicycles can be rented.

Puffin B&B (☎ 697-2260) has five cabins with and without attached bathrooms near the Salmon River that range from $75 to $125 for two people, along with a laundromat and bicycles for guests. Other homes

with lodging include *Good River Bed & Breakfast* (☎ 697-2241), a spacious log home with free bicycles for guests and *Tri B&B* (☎ 697-2425), which offers individual cabins for $75 for two people.

A quarter mile south of the Salmon River Bridge on the way to the dock is the *Strawberry Point Cafe* and next door *Beartrack Mercantile*, where you can purchase groceries at outrageous prices, so it's best to purchase supplies before leaving Juneau. Across from Puffin B&B is *Bear Nest Restaurant* with vegetarian fare.

BARTLETT COVE

Bartlett Cove is the park headquarters and includes the Glacier Bay Lodge, a restaurant, a visitor center, a campground and the main dock where the tour boats depart for excursions up the bay. The cove lies within the Glacier Bay Park but is still 40 miles south (and another high-priced trip) of the nearest glacier. At the foot of the dock is the park's visitor center where you can obtain backcountry permits, seek out information or purchase a variety of books or topographic maps that cover the park.

Hiking

Glacier Bay is a mostly trail-less park, and in the backcountry foot travel is done along river banks, on ridges or across ice remnants of glaciers. The only developed trails are in Bartlett Cove.

Forest Trail This mile-long nature walk begins and ends near the Bartlett Cove Dock and winds through the pond-studded spruce and hemlock forest near the campground. There are daily ranger-led walks along this trail; enquire at the lodge.

Bartlett River Trail This 1.5-mile trail begins just up the road to Gustavus, where there is a posted trailhead, and ends at the Bartlett River estuary. Along the way it meanders along a tidal lagoon and passes through a few wet spots. Plan on two to four hours for the three-mile return trip.

Point Gustavus Beach Walk This walk along the shoreline south of Bartlett Cove to Point Gustavus and Gustavus provides the only overnight trek from the park headquarters. The total distance is 12 miles while the walk to Point Gustavus, an excellent spot to camp, is six miles. Plan on hiking the stretch from Point Gustavus to Gustavus at low tide, which will allow you to ford the Salmon River as opposed to swimming across it. Point Gustavus is an excellent place to sight killer whales in Icy Strait.

Paddling

Glacier Bay offers an excellent opportunity for people who have experience on the water but not a lot as kayakers. By utilizing the tour boat it is possible to skip the long and open paddle up the bay and enjoy only the well-protected arms and inlets where the glaciers are located.

Kayaks with skirts, paddles, life vests and foot-controlled rudders can be rented from Glacier Bay Sea Kayaks (☎ 697-2257), but reservations are strongly recommended for trips in July and August. Write to them before you leave at: Glacier Bay Sea Kayaks, PO Box 26, Gustavus, AK 99826. The rigid double kayaks cost $50 per day for one to four days, $40 a day for longer rentals. You can also rent singles for $40/35.

Transport is on the *Spirit of Adventure* which departs daily at 7 am and will put you ashore at Sebree Island where the East and West arms divide, Geikie Inlet near Hugh Miller Inlet, or Queen Inlet in the West Arm. The most dramatic glaciers are in the West Arm, but in recent years the upper areas of the arm have been off limits to campers and thus kayakers due to aggressive brown bears. Many paddlers, however, prefer Muir Inlet due to the lack of cruise ships and tour boats. Plan on a week to paddle from Sebree Island up the arm and return to the pick-up point, from eight to 10 days for a drop-off in the West Arm with a return paddle to Bartlett Cove.

Transport fares for kayakers (above and beyond your boat rental) are $88 per person

for a one-way drop-off and $175 return. A multi-drop pass which allows you to explore more than one area is an additional $24.

For paddlers who want to avoid the tour-boat fares but still long for a kayak adventure, there are the Beardslee Islands. While there are no glaciers to view, the islands (a day's paddle from Bartlett Cove) offer calm water, protected channels and pleasant beach camping. Wildlife includes black bears, seals and bald eagles, and the tidal pools burst with activity at low tide. The islands make for an easy three-day paddle.

Alaska Discovery also offers single-day guided trips that begin and end at Bartlett Cove. Kayaks, lifevests, rubber boots, paddles and rain gear are supplied. You supply $119. The paddles are only to Beardslee Islands, and not the glaciers, and it's best to reserve a spot on the trip at the Juneau office (☎ (800) 586-1911). Spirit Walker Expeditions (☎ 697-2266) has a single-day paddle to Pleasant Island outside of the park for $100.

Places to Stay

The *campground* is free and always seems to have space. It is a quarter of a mile south of the Glacier Bay Lodge in a lush forest just off the shoreline. It provides a bear cache, eating shelter and pleasant surroundings in which to pitch a tent. Coin-operated showers are available in the park, but there is no place that sells groceries or camping supplies.

Glacier Bay Lodge (☎ (800) 622-2042) has 55 rooms that cost $156 per night for a double. It also offers dormitory bunks at $28 a night but the campground is still a better place to spend the night. In the evening, there is a crackling fire in the lodge's huge stone fireplace while the adjoining bar usually hums with an interesting mixture of park employees, backpackers and locals from Gustavus. Nightly slide presentations, ranger talks and movies held upstairs cover the natural history of the park.

Getting There & Away

You can now fly or take a boat to Gustavus.

There is no ferry service to Gustavus but Au Nu Tours (☎ (800) 820-2628) has a boat that leaves Juneau's Auke Bay at 9.30 am daily and then departs Gustavus at 2 pm the same day for the return trip. Round-trip fare is $85.

Alaska Airlines departs Juneau daily at around 8 am and 5 pm for the 15-minute trip to Gustavus and the round-trip fare is $134. The cheapest flight is through Air Excursions (☎ 697-2375) which has three flights daily between the two towns and charges only $100 round trip.

Once at Gustavus Airport, you are still 10 miles from Bartlett Cove, the park headquarters. The Glacier Bay Lodge bus meets all airline flights, but charges $10 for the ride there. You can also hitchhike as there is always a stream of traffic shuffling between Gustavus and the park headquarters.

The other way to reach Glacier Bay is to book a total package tour out of Juneau, which usually includes return air fares and boat passage up the bay to view the glaciers. Such packages are offered by Glacier Bay Tours & Cruises (☎ (800) 451-5952). Several include your flight to Gustavus and then an overnight cruise up the bay on their boat *Wilderness Explorer*. A three-day/two-night package is $499 to $579 depending on the cabin you choose.

Tour Boats The *Spirit of Adventure*, a 220-passenger catamaran, departs Bartlett Cove for an nine-hour trip up the West Arm daily at 7 am. It returns at 4.30 pm where a waiting bus will whisk you away in time to catch the Alaska Airlines flight back to Juneau. The tour of the West Arm glaciers, the reason you've spent so much money to get here, is another $150. But that includes lunch – what a deal!

A much more personalized approach is offered by Gustavus Marine Charters (☎ 697-2233), which has overnight cruises into the bay. It's three day/two night trip is $900 per person and includes cabin, meals and opportunity to fish. It also has half-day whale-watching trips off Point Adolphus for $90 per person.

Haines

Haines (pop 2200) lies in the upper (northern) reaches of the Inside Passage and is an important access point to the Yukon Territory (Canada) and Interior Alaska. While the town itself may lack the charm of Sitka or Petersburg, the surrounding scenery is stunning. Travelers who arrive on the ferry will see Lynn Canal, the longest and deepest fjord in North America, close in on them. There's a mad scramble to the left side of the boat when the US Forest Service guide on board announces the approach of Davidson and Rainbow glaciers to the west.

Once in town, mountains seem to surround you on all sides. To the west, looming over Fort Seward, are the jagged Cathedral Peaks of the Chilkat Mountains; to the east is the Chilkoot Range; and standing guard behind Haines is Mt Ripinsky.

History
Haines is 75 miles north of Juneau on a wooded peninsula between the Chilkat and Chilkoot inlets. Originally it was a stronghold of the wealthy Chilkat Tlingit Indians who called the settlement Dtehshuh, meaning 'end of the trail'. The first White person to settle was George Dickinson of the Northwest Trading Company who arrived in 1878 and was followed by missionaries and a trickle of other settlers. Eventually, of course, the gold prospectors stampeded through the town.

In 1897, Jack Dalton, a gun-toting entrepreneur, turned an old Indian trade route into a toll road for miners seeking an easier way to reach the Klondike. He charged $2 per head of cattle. The Dalton Trail quickly became a heavily used pack route to mining districts north of Whitehorse, and Dalton himself reaped the profits until the White Pass & Yukon Railroad in Skagway put him out of business in 1900.

The army established Alaska's first permanent post at Haines in 1903 and named it Fort William H Seward after the secretary of

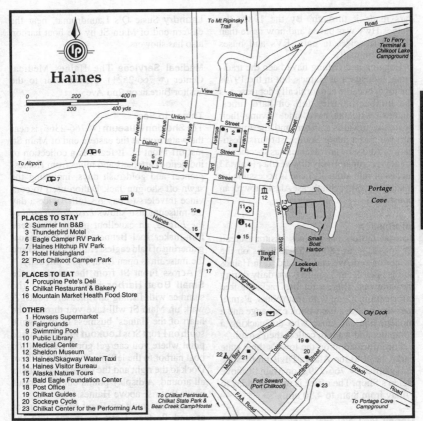

Haines

SOUTHEAST

0   200   400 m
0   200   400 yds

To Mt Ripinsky Trail

To Ferry Terminal & Chilkoot Lake Campground

To Airport

Portage Cove

Small Boat Harbor

Tlingit Park

Lookout Park

City Dock

PLACES TO STAY
2 Summer Inn B&B
3 Thunderbird Motel
6 Eagle Camper RV Park
7 Haines Hitchup RV Park
21 Hotel Halsingland
22 Port Chilkoot Camper Park

PLACES TO EAT
4 Porcupine Pete's Deli
5 Chilkat Restaurant & Bakery
16 Mountain Market Health Food Store

OTHER
1 Howsers Supermarket
8 Fairgrounds
9 Swimming Pool
10 Public Library
11 Medical Center
12 Sheldon Museum
13 Haines/Skagway Water Taxi
14 Haines Visitor Bureau
15 Alaska Nature Tours
17 Bald Eagle Foundation Center
18 Post Office
19 Chilkat Guides
20 Sockeye Cycle
23 Chilkat Center for the Performing Arts

To Chilkat Peninsula, Chilkat State Park & Bear Creek Camp/Hostel

Fort Seward (Port Chilkoot)

To Portage Cove Campground

state who negotiated the purchase of the state. It was renamed Chilkoot Barracks in 1922 to avoid confusing it with the town of Seward and for the next 20 years was the only army post in Alaska.

The fort was used as a rest camp during WWII and from there soldiers moved on to various points in the state where they formed the nucleus of new army installations. By 1946, the fort was deactivated and declared surplus.

WWII also led to the construction of the Haines Hwy, the 159-mile link between the Southeast and the Alcan (Alaska Hwy). By 1942, the Japanese had captured two Aleutian islands and were headed, many believed, towards a land war in Alaska. Military planners, seeking a second link to the sea and another possible evacuation route, chose to connect Haines to the Alcan. Construction began two months after the Alcan was completed and engineers merely followed Jack Dalton's trail. The route through the mountains is so rugged it would be 20 years before US and Canadian crews even attempted to keep the 'Haines Cut-off Road' open during the winter and, up until the early 1970s, a radio check system was used to make sure cars made it through. By the 1980s the Haines Hwy was paved and now more than 50,000 travelers in cars, RVs and buses follow it annually.

Logging and fishing have been the traditional industries of Haines, but in the 1970s the town became economically depressed as the lumber industry fell on hard times. Haines' residents have since swung their economy towards tourism and the town is surviving as a major Southeast tourist destination. And why not? Haines has spectacular scenery, comparatively dry weather (only 53 inches of rain annually) and is accessible by road. What other Southeast Alaska town can boost that?

Information

Tourist Office The Haines Visitor Bureau (☎ 766-2234 or (800) 458-3579) is on the corner of 2nd Ave and Willard St in Haines and is open from 8 am to 8 pm daily during the summer. The center has racks of free information, along with rest rooms, a small message board, a used-book exchange and a modem line for those who are packing a computer and want to collect their email.

For information on the town's three state parks, head to the Alaska Division of State Parks office (☎ 766-2292) on Main St above Helen's Shop. The office is open Monday to Friday from 8 am to 4.30 pm.

Money First National Bank of Anchorage (☎ 766-2321) is at the corner of 2nd Ave and Main St.

Post The post office is on the corner of the Haines Hwy and Mud Bay Rd near Fort Seward.

Travel Agency The Travel Connection Agency (☎ 766-2681) is on 2nd Ave across from the visitor's bureau.

Library South of Main St on 3rd Ave is the public library (☎ 766-2545), open daily and until 9 pm Monday through Thursday. The library provides free Internet access.

Laundry Susie Q's Laundromat, near the eastern end of Main St by the boat harbor, also has showers.

Medical Services The Haines Medical Center (☎ 766-2521) is next door to the Visitor Bureau on 2nd Ave.

Things to See

The **Sheldon Museum** (☎ 766-2366) is near the waterfront at the eastern end of Main St, just off Front St. It features a collection of indigenous artefacts and relics from Haines' pioneer and gold-rush days, including the sawn-off shotgun Jack Dalton used to convince travelers to pay his toll. Twice a day the museum also shows *Last Stronghold of the Eagles*, an excellent movie by Juneau film-maker Joel Bennett about the annual gathering of bald eagles. Admission is $3 and the museum is open from 1 to 5 pm daily.

Across Front St from the museum, the **Small Boat Harbor** bustles during the summer with fishing and pleasure boats. A walk up Main St will take you through the heart of the Haines' business district while south on Front St is **Lookout Park**, a vantage point where you can get good views of the boat harbor to the left (north), Port Chilkoot Dock to the right and the Coastal Mountains all around. A display points out the various peaks that rise above Haines.

Continue south on Front St as it curves around Portage Cove to merge into the Haines Hwy. If you head north on the highway, you'll past the post office and come to Haines' newest attraction, **American Bald Eagle Foundation** on 2nd Ave. The non-profit center opened in 1994 and features an impressive wildlife diorama with more than 100 species on display in their natural habitat. The middle of the hall is occupied by a tree full of eagles in every possible position, while a small video room shows the annual winter eagle congregation on the Chilkat River. Hours are 10 am to 5 pm daily and admission is by donation.

If you turn uphill (east) at the Front St, Haines Hwy junction, you reach **Fort Seward**. The old army fort was designated a national historical site in 1972 and is slowly being renovated. In the center of the fort are the parade grounds, while to the north is Building No 53, formerly the commanding officers' quarters and now the Hotel Halsingland. A walking-tour map of the fort is available in the lobby of the hotel.

Within the parade ground is **Totem Village**. Although not part of the original fort, it provides an interesting view of two tribal houses, totem poles and **Sea Wolf Art Studio** (☎ 766-2266), which features the work of Tresham Gregg, one of Haines' best known indigenous artists.

More art can be seen in Fort Seward at the **Alaska Indian Arts Center** (☎ 766-2160) in the former post hospital, and in the **Chilkat Center for the Performing Arts** – a refurbished cannery building and the site of nightly productions from the Chilkat Dancers and Lynn Canal Community Players. The skill center features indigenous artists carving totems, masks and war clubs or weaving Chilkat blankets; many of these items are available for purchase. The center is open from 9 am to noon and from 1 to 5 pm Monday to Saturday during the summer.

Hiking

There are two major trail systems near Haines: south of town are the Chilkat Peninsula trails which include the climb to Mt Riley; north of Haines is the path to the summit of Mt Ripinsky. Stop at the Visitor Bureau in town before hiking and pick up its brochure, *Haines is for Hikers*, which describes the trails in more detail.

Mt Ripinsky Trail The trip to the 3563-foot summit of Mt Ripinsky (also known as the South Summit) is an all-day hike with a sweeping view from Juneau to Skagway. The route which includes Peak 3920 and a descent from 7 Mile Saddle to Haines Hwy is either a strenuous 10-hour journey for experienced hikers or an overnight trip.

To reach the trailhead, follow 2nd Ave north to Lutak Rd (the road to the ferry terminal) and past the fire station. Leave Lutak Rd when it curves right and head up

the hill on Young St. Turn right along an old, buried pipeline and follow it for a mile to the start of the trail, just as the pipeline heads downhill to the tank farm.

The trail crosses a pair of streams, passes by an old reservoir and then ascends steadily through spruce and hemlock, reaching open muskeg at 1300 feet. After a second climb you come to Johnson's Creek at 2500 feet where there is drinking water and views of the Southeast's snowcapped mountains all the way to Admiralty Island. From here, the route goes from dwarfed hemlock to open slope where there is snow until late summer.

The North Summit has a benchmark and a high wooden surveyor's platform. You can camp in the alpine area between the two peaks and then continue the next day by descending the North Summit and hiking west along the ridge to Peak 3920. From here you can descend to 7 Mile Saddle and then to the Haines Hwy, putting you seven miles north-west of town. This is a 10-mile loop and a challenging overnight hike where the trail is steep in places and easily lost. The views, however, are spectacular.

Battery Point Trail This 2.4-mile trail is a flat walk along the shore to Kelgaya Point where there is a primitive camp site and a vault toilet. At Kelgaya Point, you can cut across to a pebble beach and follow it to Battery Point. The trail begins a quarter of a mile beyond Portage Cove Campground at the end of Beach Rd. Plan on about two hours for the return hike.

Mt Riley Trails This climb to a 1760-foot summit is considerably easier than the one to Mt Ripinsky, but it still provides good views in all directions, including Rainbow and Davidson glaciers. One trail up the mountain begins at a junction almost two miles up the Battery Point Trail out of Portage Cove Campground. From here, you hike 5.5 miles over Half Dome and up Mt Riley.

Another route, closer to town, begins at the end of FAA road which runs behind the Officers' Row in Fort Seward. From the road's end, follow the water-supply access route for two miles to a short spur which branches off to the right and connects with the trail from Mud Bay Rd. The hike is 3.8 miles one way and prevents you from having to find the three-mile ride out to Mud Bay Rd, the site of the third trailhead to Mt Riley. The trailhead off Mud Bay Rd is posted and this route is the steepest but most direct to the summit. Plan on five to six hours for a return hike to the summit.

Seduction Point Trail The trail begins at Chilkat State Park Campground and is a 6.5-mile, one-way hike to the point that separates Chilkoot and Chilkat inlets. The trail swings between inland forest and beaches and provides excellent views of Davidson Glacier.

If you have the equipment, it can be turned into an excellent overnight hike by setting up camp at the cove east of Seduction Point. Carry in water and check the tides before departing as the final stretch along the beach after David's Cove should be walked at low or mid-tide. The entire round trip takes most hikers from nine to 10 hours.

Rafting
Haines is also the departure point for numerous raft trips in the area. Chilkat Guides (☎ 766-2491) offers a four-hour float down the Chilkat River that provides plenty of opportunity to view bald eagles and possibly brown bears; there is little whitewater. The guide company runs the trip daily beginning from its shop on Beach Rd in Fort Seward. The cost is $75 for adults and $35 for children.

On a much grander scale of adventure is the exciting 10-day raft trip down the Tatshenshini/Alsek River system from Yukon Territory to the coast of Glacier Bay. Haines serves as the departure point for this river trip which is unmatched by any other Alaskan raft trip for its scenic mix of rugged mountain ranges and dozens of glaciers. Both Chilkat Guides and Alaska Discovery (☎ 586-1911) run the trip which costs around $2100 per person.

Special Events
Like every other Alaskan town, Haines has a 4 July celebration, but its biggest festival is the Southeast Alaska State Fair. Held in mid-August, the event includes parades, dances, livestock shows and exhibits and its famous pig races that draw participants from all Southeast communities. Coinciding with the state fair is the Bald Eagle Music Festival that brings together more than 50 musicians for five days of blues and bluegrass music.

In mid-November, Haines stages the Alaska Bald Eagle Festival, a three-day event at what is usually the peak time of the winter gathering of eagles.

Places to Stay
Camping Haines has several state campgrounds; the closest to town is *Portage Cove* (nine sites, $6). This scenic beach campground for backpackers and cyclists is only half a mile south-east of Fort Seward or two miles from the center of town and has water and pit toilets. Follow Front St south (which becomes Beach Rd as it curves around the cove near Fort Seward) and the campground is at the end of the gravel road. Five miles north of the ferry terminal on Lutak Rd is *Chilkoot Lake State Park* (32 sites, $10). The campground, which offers picnic shelters and good fishing for Dolly Varden, is on Chilkoot Lake, a turquoise-blue lake surrounded by mountain peaks.

If you have some spare time in Haines, spend a night at *Chilkat State Park* (33 sites, $6), seven miles south-east of Haines on Mud Bay Rd. The park, situated towards the end of the Chilkat Peninsula, has good views of Lynn Canal and of the Davidson and Rainbow glaciers that spill out of the mountains into the canal.

Within town is *Port Chilkoot Camper Park* (☎ 766-2755) where a tent site for those without a vehicle is $8.50 a night. The private campground is behind the Hotel Halsingland and has wooded sites, a laundromat and showers for $1.50. Other RV campgrounds include *Eagle Camper Park* (☎ 766-2335) on Union St and *Haines Hitch-up RV Park* (☎ 766-2882) on the corner of the Haines Hwy and Main St. Outside of town is *Salmon Run RV Campground* (☎ 766-3240), 1.8 miles north of the ferry terminal. Overlooking a mountainous stretch of Lutak Inlet, this campground features wooded sites, showers and a day lodge selling coffee and giant cinnamon rolls in the morning. A tent site is $12.50 a night.

Hostel *Bear Creek Camp & International Hostel* (☎ 766-2259) is 2.5 miles south of town. Follow 3rd Ave south onto Mud Bay Rd near Fort Seward. After a half-mile veer left onto Small Tract Rd and follow it for 1.5 miles to the hostel. There is room for 20 people in the hostel's dorms; the cost is $14 per night for hosteling members and $15 for nonmembers. There are also tent sites for $9 per night for two people (shower included) and two-person cabins for $37 per night. New owners have improved the rustic camp considerably by cleaning it up and adding a coin-operated laundry, free ferry pick-up, bike rentals and a hot tub.

B&Bs The *Summer Inn Bed & Breakfast* (☎ 766-2970), at 247 2nd Ave four miles from the ferry terminal, has five bedrooms with shared bath for $60/70 for single/double, most with a good view of Lynn Canal. There are several B&Bs in the historical buildings of the fort. *Fort Seward B&B* (☎ 766-2856) is in the former home of the army's surgeon where rooms with shared baths are $68/82. *Officers' Inn Bed & Breakfast* (☎ 766-2000 or (800) 542-6363) has some economy rooms for $50/55.

Hotels In Haines there are eight hotels and lodges of which the *Fort Seward Lodge* (☎ 766-2009 or (800) 478-7772), the former Post Exchange in the fort, is the cheapest with single/doubles beginning at $45/55. Also in the former fort is *Hotel Halsingland* (☎ 766-2000 or (800) 542-6363) where rooms cost $80/85, while near the entrance on Mud Rd is *Mountain View Motel* (☎ 766-2900 or (800) 478-2902) with rooms with kitchenettes at $59/64. In town there is *Thunderbird Motel* (☎ 766-2131 or (800) 327-2556) with rooms for $62/72.

Places to Eat

The popular place for breakfast among locals is the *Chilkat Restaurant & Bakery*, on the corner of Main St and 5th Ave, which opens at 7 am. A plate of eggs, potatoes and toast is $6, and you can get coffee and a warm muffin for around $2. On Friday night they have an all-you-can eat Mexican dinner for $12.

The *Commander's Room* in Fort Seward's Hotel Halsingland provides a historical setting (with a nice view of the surrounding mountains) in which to eat. The cost of breakfast is similar to the Chilkat Restaurant & Bakery and the portions are filling. At night, the restaurant serves a variety of seafood including prawns, scallops and salmon, with dinners ranging from $13 to $22. The best breakfast value in town is at the *Bamboo Room*, on the corner of 2nd Ave and Main St, where a plate of pancakes and a coffee costs $5.

For deli-type sandwiches or sourdough pizza by the slice try *Porcupine Pete's* deli across from the Bamboo Room on 2nd Ave. Vegetarian sandwiches and an espresso bar is found at *Mountain Market Health Food Store*, at 3rd Ave and Haines Hwy. Locally caught seafood ends up on a variety of menus in Haines. For Mexican food with a seafood twist, try halibut tacos ($3.50), shrimp burrito ($6.75) or an Alaskan shrimp nachos ($10) at *Bear-Rittos* next door to Susie Q Laundromat on Main St.

The town's salmon bake, *Port Chilkoot Potlatch*, takes place nightly from 5 to 8 pm at Totem Village in the center of Fort Seward. For $18 per person you can enjoy all the grilled salmon, salad and baked beans you can handle in one sitting. To take some salmon or crab back to your camp site, go to *Howsers Supermarket*, a distinctive store front with the large moose antlers, located on Main St.

Entertainment

For beer on tap and to rub elbows with the locals, stop at the *Fogcutter Bar* on Main St

SOUTHEAST

or the *Pioneer Bar* next to the Bamboo Room on the corner of 2nd Ave and Main St. Both spots can get lively and full at night as Haines is a hard-drinking town. At Fort Seward, the nights can get lively at the *Hotel Halsingland Pub*.

Other activities at night include performances by the Chilkat Dancers in full Tlingit costume at the Chilkat Center for the Performing Arts, situated in Fort Seward. The performances start at 8 pm on Monday, Wednesday and Saturday; the admission charge is $7. On Friday and Sunday at 8 pm you can see the melodrama *Lust for Dust*, performed by the Lynn Canal Community Players during the summer; tickets are $7.

Getting There & Around
Air There is no jet service to Haines, but several charter companies run regularly scheduled north and southbound flights. The cheapest service, Wings of Alaska (☎ 766-2030), has four daily flights to Juneau for $65, and four flights to Skagway for $35. Also check with Haines Airways (☎ 766-2646) or LAB Flying Service (☎ 766-2222). Any of them will arrange a sightseeing flight over Glacier Bay National Park; the park is only a 10-minute flight from Haines. For a 60 to 70-minute flight, which is enough air time to reach the park's famous glaciers, expect to pay $95 per person, two-person minimum for a flight. On a clear day it's money well spent.

Bus From Haines you can catch buses north to Whitehorse, Anchorage or Fairbanks. Alaskon Express has a bus departing Haines at 8.15 am Sunday, Tuesday and Thursday that overnights at Beaver Creek and then continues on to Anchorage, reaching the city at 7.30 pm the following day. The fare from Haines to Anchorage is $185 and does not include lodging.

On the same runs you can also make connections at either Haines Junction or Beaver Creek for Fairbanks, Whitehorse or Skagway, though why anybody would want to ride a bus instead of a ferry to Skagway is beyond me. The one-way fare to Fairbanks

is $180 and Whitehorse $85. The bus picks up passengers at Hotel Halsingland.

Boat State ferries arrive and depart almost daily from the terminal (☎ 766-2111) in Lutak Inlet north of town. The one-way fare north to Skagway is $14 and south to Juneau is $20.

Haines Taxi (☎ 766-3138) runs a ferry shuttle bus, meets all arrivals, and for $5 will take you the four miles into town. The bus also departs town 30 minutes before each ferry arrival and stops at the Hotel Halsingland and near the Visitor Bureau in town before heading out to the ferry terminal.

For a day trip to Skagway, contact Haines-Skagway Water Taxi (☎ 766-3395). The 40-passenger boat departs twice daily, the first at 8 am and then again at 5 pm, from the boat harbor in the heart of Haines; round-trip fare is $29, one-way is $18. Tickets can be purchased in advance on board the MV*Sea Venture* at the Haines Small Boat Harbor between noon and 4 pm.

Car To enjoy the sites out on the road, especially to visit the Chilkat Bald Eagle Preserve on your own, there are five car rental agencies in Haines. The best rates is with Affordable Cars at Captain's Choice Motel (766-3111) and Thunderbird Motel Car Rental (☎ 766-2131), which have compacts for $45 a day, 100 free miles and 35 cents a mile after that.

Bicycle Sockeye Cycle (☎ 766-2869) on Portage St in Fort Seward rents mountain bikes and road bikes by the hour, day or even weekly as well as selling parts. Rates are $6 an hour, $30 a day and discounts on two and three-day rentals. The shop also offers bike tours that range from one-hour to one-day journeys or will arrange van transport to those who want to cycle on their own.

AROUND HAINES
Alaska Chilkat Bald Eagle Preserve
In 1982, the state reserved 48,000 acres along the Chilkat River to protect the largest known gathering of bald eagles in the world.

Each year from October to January, more than 3500 eagles congregate here to feed on chum salmon. They come because an upswelling of warm water prevents the river from freezing and encourages the late run of salmon. It's a remarkable sight, hundreds of birds along the banks of the river sitting in the bare trees that line the river, with often six or more birds to a branch.

The eagles can be seen from the Haines Hwy, where lookouts allow motorists to park and view the birds. The best view is between *Mile 18* and *Mile 22* of the Haines Hwy and you really have to be here after November to enjoy the birds in their greatest numbers. Unfortunately, most travelers have long departed Alaska by then. Still there are more than 200 resident eagles which can be spotted throughout the summer.

The state park office in Haines can provide a list of state-authorized guides who conduct tours into the preserve. Among them is Alaska Nature Tours (☎ 766-2876) which conducts three-hour tours at 8.30 am and 1 pm. The tours cover much of the scenery around the Haines area but often concentrate on the river flats and river mouths where usually you see 40 to 50 eagles in the summer, many nesting. The tour is $45 per person.

Kluane National Park (Canada)

Kluane National Park, 120 miles north of Haines, is one of Canada's newest and most spectacular parks. The preserve encompasses 8649 sq miles of rugged coastal mountains in the south-western corner of the Yukon Territory. There are no roads in this wilderness park but the Haines Hwy runs along its eastern edge, providing easy access to the area. The 159-mile Haines Hwy, which follows Jack Dalton's gold-rush toll road, is paved and makes an extremely scenic and smooth drive ending at the Alcan in Haines Junction.

Amid the lofty mountains of Kluane National Park lies Mt Logan, Canada's highest peak at 19,636 feet and the most extensive nonpolar icefield in the world from which glaciers spill out onto the valley

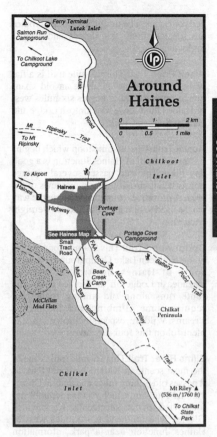

floors. Wildlife is plentiful and includes dall sheep, brown bears, moose, mountain goats and caribou.

The park's visitor center (☎ (403) 634-7207), in Haines Junction on the Alcan, is open from 8 am to 8 pm daily in the summer. Along with displays and a free slide show covering the area's natural history, the center can provide you with information, back-country permits and topographic maps for overnight hikes into the park.

The main activity in Kluane is hiking, and trails consist primarily of old mining roads, animal trails or natural routes along river beds or ridges. The trailheads for eight routes are located along the Haines and Alaska highways.

Alsek Pass Trail This 15-mile trail is a flat walk most of the way along an old abandoned mining road. It begins six miles west of Haines Junction at Mackintosh Lodge and ends at Sugden Creek.

Auriol Trail This 12-mile loop which begins 3.8-miles south of Haines Junction is a good day hike. The trail passes several vantage points which provide sweeping views of the area. A primitive campground along the way can be used to turn the walk into an overnight excursion.

Cottonwood Trail This 53-mile loop begins at the Kathleen Lake Campground, 12 miles south of Haines Junction. It ends at Dezadeash Lodge off the Haines Hwy. The route runs along old mining roads that require some climbing and fording of streams. Wildlife, especially brown bears, is plentiful on this four-day hike.

Slims River Trail This 16-mile trail is one of the most scenic in Kluane National Park as it passes old mining relics and ends at Observation Mountain, which you can scramble up for a view of the spectacular Kaskawulsh Glacier. The trailhead is 40 miles west of Haines Junction near a park information centre.

Skagway

Skagway (pop 800), a place of many names, much history and little rain, is the northern terminus of the Alaska Marine Hwy. The town lies in the narrow plain of the Skagway River at the head of the Lynn Canal and, at one time or another, has been called Skaguay, Shkagway and Gateway to the Golden Interior. It is also known as the Home of the North Wind, and residents tell visitors that it blows so much here you'll never breathe the same air twice.

But Skagway is also one of the driest places in what is often the soggy Southeast. While Petersburg averages over 100 inches of rain a year and Ketchikan a drenching 154 inches, Skagway only gets 26 inches of rain annually.

Much of Skagway is within the Klondike Gold Rush National Historical Park which extends from Seattle to Dawson in the Yukon Territory. The National Park Service is constantly restoring the old shop fronts and buildings so the town looks similar to the boom town it was in the 1890s, when the gold rush gave birth to Skagway.

History

The town and the nearby ghost town of Dyea were the start for over 40,000 gold-rush stampeders who headed to the Yukon by way of either the Chilkoot Trail or the White Pass Trail. The Chilkoot Trail, which started from Dyea, was the most popular as it was several miles shorter. The White Pass Trail, which began in Skagway and was advertised as a 'horse trail', was brutal. In the winter of 1897-98, some 3000 pack animals were driven to death by over-anxious owners and the White Pass was called the 'Dead Horse Trail'.

In 1887, the population of the town was two; 10 years later 20,000 people lived there and the gold-rush town was Alaska's largest city – a center for saloons, hotels and dance halls. Skagway became infamous for its lawlessness. For a time, the town was held under the tight control of Jefferson Randolph 'Soapy' Smith and his gang who conned and swindled naive newcomers out of their money and stampeders out of their gold dust. Soapy Smith was finally removed from power by a mob of angry citizens in a gunfight between him and city engineer Frank Reid. Both men died in the fight and Smith's reign as the 'uncrowned prince of Skagway' ended, having lasted only nine months.

At the height of the gold rush, Michael J Heney, an Irish contractor, convinced a group of English investors that he could build a railroad over the White Pass Trail to Whitehorse. Construction began in 1898 with little more than picks, shovels and blasting powder, and the narrow-gauge railroad reached Whitehorse, the Yukon capital, in July 1900. The construction of the White Pass & Yukon Railroad was nothing short of a superhuman feat, and the railroad became the focal point of the town's economy after the gold rush and during the military build-up of WWII.

The line was shut down in 1982 but was revived in 1988 to the delight of backpackers walking the Chilkoot Trail and cruise-ship tourists. Although the train hauls no freight, its rebirth was important to Skagway as a tourist attraction. Today, Skagway survives almost entirely on tourism as bus tours and more than 200 'Love Boat' cruise ships visit to turn this village into a modern-day boom town every summer. When two or three ships arrive on the same day, this is where Alaska can really get crowded. Keep in mind that Skagway has to make a living in three months but if the throngs of tourists are still too much for you, skip this town and depart the Southeast through Haines.

Information
Tourist Offices For information on the Chilkoot Trail, local trails and camping, contact the National Park Service Visitor Center (☎ 983-2921) on the corner of Broadway St and 2nd Ave. Hours are 8 am to 7 pm daily. For any other information, visit the Skagway Visitor Center (☎ 983-2854). While the historic City Hall is being renovated, the center is on 5th Ave, just west of Broadway St. By 1999, it should be back in the Arctic Brotherhood Hall, the driftwood building on Broadway St. Hours are 8 am to 5 pm daily.

Money National Bank of Alaska began in Skagway in 1916 and still maintains that first branch on Broadway St and 6th Ave. Thomas Cook has a foreign exchange booth on 2nd Ave and Spring St.

Post The post office in on Broadway St next door to the National Bank of Alaska.

Travel Agency Skagway Travel Service (☎ 983-2500) is located at the Westmark Inn on 3rd Ave.

Library & Bookshop The Skagway Library is at 8th Ave and State St and open daily except Sunday. Skagway News Depot is a small book store on Broadway Ave.

Laundry & Showers Service Unlimited is a gas station with a small laundromat on 2nd Ave and State St. For a shower, head to Pullen Park, where there are coin-operated showers ($1) in the RV campground and the Harbor Master's Office next door.

Medical Services Skagway Medical Clinic (☎ 983-2255) is situated on 11th Ave and Broadway St.

Things to See
Unlike most Southeast towns, Skagway is a delightful place to arrive at aboard the ferry. The dock and terminal are at the southwestern end of Broadway St, the main avenue in town. You step off the ferry right into a bustling town where half the people are dressed as if they are trying to relive the gold-rush days while the other half are obviously tourists off the luxury liners.

Near the dock, on the corner of Broadway St and 2nd Ave, is the visitor center for the **Klondike Gold Rush National Historic Park** in the White Pass & Yukon Railroad depot. The visitor center is open from 8 am to 7 pm daily and features displays, ranger talks and the movie *Days of Adventure, Dreams of Gold*, shown every hour. The 30-minute movie is narrated by Hal Holbrook and is the best way to slip back into the gold-rush days. The center also leads a 45-minute walking tour of the historic district daily at 9, 10 and 11 am and 2 pm.

A seven-block corridor along Broadway St, part of the historical district, is home to the restored buildings, false fronts and wooden sidewalks of Skagway's golden

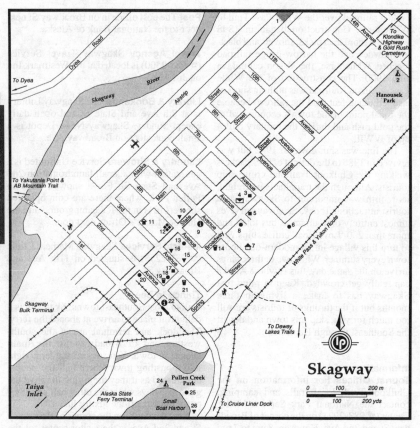

era. Diagonally opposite the NPS office is the **Arctic Brotherhood Hall**. The hall is hard to miss as there are about 20,000 pieces of driftwood tacked to the front of it, making it one of the most distinctive buildings in Alaska and probably the most photographed.

The hall presently houses the **Trail of '98 Museum**, which will move back to the City Hall when it is renovated. The museum is open daily in the summer from 9 am to 5 pm and charges $2 for admission. The money is well spent as the museum is jammed with gold-rush relics including many items devoted to the town's two leading characters,

'Soapy' Smith and Frank Reid. You can purchase a copy of the 15 July 1898 *Skagway News* that described all the details surrounding the colorful shoot-out.

Near the corner of 3rd Ave and Broadway St is the **Mascot Saloon**, the latest renovation project completed by the National Park Service. Built in 1898, the Mascot was one of just 70 saloons during Skagway's heyday as 'the roughest place in the world'. On the 1st floor are exhibits depicting the old saloon at the height of the gold rush; admission is free.

Just up Broadway St at 5th Ave is the

Corrington Museum of Alaska History
(☎ 983-2580). This private museum in the back of a gift shop covers the state's history, beginning with the Bering Land Bridge, on 40 pieces of scrimshaw, hand-carved ivory from walrus tusks. There is a small admission fee.

A block south-east of the museum on 5th Ave is **Moore's Cabin**, the oldest building in Skagway. Captain William Moore and his son built it in 1887 when they staked out their homestead as the founders of the town. Moore had to move his home to its present location, however, when gold-rush stampeders overran his homestead. The National Park Service has since renovated the building and in doing so discovered that the famous Dead Horse Trail that was used by so many stampeders actually began in the large lawn next to the cabin.

At the south-eastern end of 7th Ave is the **City Hall**, a granite building that was built in 1900 as McCabe College and later served as a US Court until the city obtained it in 1956.

For visitors who become as infatuated as the locals over Smith and Reid, there is the walk out to the **Gold Rush Cemetery**. From the ferry terminal, it is a 2.5-mile stroll to the graveyard north-east along State St, which runs parallel to Broadway St. Follow State St until it curves into 23rd Ave and look for the sign to Soapy's grave across the railroad tracks. A wooden bridge along the tracks leads to the main part of the cemetery, the site of many stampeders' graves and the plots of Reid and Smith. From Reid's gravestone, it is a short hike uphill to the lovely **Reid Falls** which cascade 300 feet from the mountainside.

In 1898, Skagway's rival city, **Dyea**, at the foot of the Chilkoot Trail, was on the shortest route to Lake Bennett where stampeders began their float to Dawson City. After the White Pass & Yukon Railroad was completed in 1900, Dyea quickly died. Today it is little more than a few old cabins, the pilings of Dyea Wharf and Slide Cemetery, where 47 men and women were buried after perishing in an avalanche on the Chilkoot Trail in April 1898.

Dyea Rd, a scenic drive, winds nine miles from Skagway to the ghost town but is filled with hairpin turns that are a headache for drivers of camper vans. **Skagway Overlook**, a scenic turn-off with a viewing platform, is 2.5 miles out of town along the Dyea Rd. The overlook offers an excellent view of Skagway, its waterfront and the peaks above the town. Just before crossing the bridge over the Taiya River, you pass the Dyea Camping Area (22 sites), a free campground where a NPS ranger is stationed in the summer to assist hikers on the Chilkoot Trail which starts near the campground.

Hiking
The Chilkoot Trail (see the Trekking section in the Wilderness chapter) is probably the most popular hike in Southeast, but there are other good treks around Skagway. There is no USFS office in Skagway, however the National Park Visitor Center on the corner of

Broadway St and 2nd Ave has an excellent brochure entitled *Skagway Trail Map*.

Dewey Lake Trail System This series of trails leads east of Skagway to a handful of alpine and subalpine lakes, waterfalls and historical sites. From Broadway St follow 3rd Ave south-east to the railroad tracks. On the east side of the tracks are the trailheads to Lower Dewey Lake, 0.7 miles; Icy Lake, 2.5 miles; Upper Reid Falls, 3.5 miles; and Sturgill's Landing, 4.5 miles.

Plan on taking an hour for the return hike to Lower Dewey Lake where there are picnic tables, camping spots and a trail that circles the lake. At the northern end of the lake is an alpine trail that ascends steeply to Upper Dewey Lake, 3.5 miles from town, and Devil's Punchbowl another 0.7 miles south of the upper lake.

The hike to Devil's Punchbowl is an all-day trip or an ideal overnight excursion, as the views are excellent and there is a free-use USFS shelter on Upper Dewey Lake that is in rough condition but does not require reservations. There are also camp sites at Sturgill's Landing.

AB Mountain Trail Also known as the Skyline Trail, this route ascends 5.5 miles to the 5100-foot summit of AB Mountain, named for the AB that appears on its south side in the form of a snow-melt every spring. The trailhead is on Dyea Rd about a mile from Skagway via the Skagway River footbridge off the north-west end of 1st Ave. The trail is very steep and requires a full day to complete.

Denver Glacier Trail This trail begins at *Mile 6* of the White Pass & Yukon Route, where the USFS has renovated a WP&YR caboose into a rental cabin (reservations, $25 per night). The trail heads up the East fork of the Skagway River for two miles then swings south and continues another 1.5 miles up the glacial outwash to Denver Glacier. Much of the trail is overgrown with brush but the second half is particularly tough hiking.

Laughton Glacier Trail At *Mile 14* of the White Pass & Yukon Route is a 1.5-mile hike to a USFS cabin (reservations, $25 per night). The cabin overlooks the river from Warm Pass but is only a mile from Laughton Glacier, an impressive hanging glacier between 3000-foot walls of the Sawtooth Range. The alpine scenery and possible ridge walks in this area is worth the $50 ticket WP&YR charges to drop off and pick up hikers. There are two excursion trains from Skagway so this could be a possible day hike. But it's far better to carry in a tent and spend a night in the area.

Organized Tours
Without a doubt the most spectacular tour from Skagway is the Summit Excursion on the White Pass & Yukon Route. The three-hour journey begins at the railroad depot where you board parlor cars for the trip to White Pass on the narrow-gauge line built during the 1898 Klondike gold rush.

This is only a small portion of the 110-mile route to Whitehorse but it contains the most spectacular scenery including crossing Glacier Gorge and Dead Horse Gulch, viewing Bridal Veil Falls and then making the steep climb to White Pass at 2885 feet, only 20 miles from Skagway. The tour is offered twice a day at 8.45 am and 1.15 pm. Tickets are $75 per person and can be purchased at the railroad depot (☎ 983-2217).

There are numerous tour companies in town with the most interesting being the Skagway Streetcar Company (☎ 983-2908), which uses eight-door, elongated White Motor Company vehicles from 1937. The problem is the $34, two-hour tours are pre-sold by the cruise ships so you usually need to book a seat a week in advance. Most other companies use vans or mini-buses, take you to Gold Rush Cemetery, White Pass Summit, Skagway Overlook and a handful of other sights in two to three hours and charge around $30. For such a tour call Frontier Excursions (☎ 983-2512), Southeast Tours (☎ 983-2990) or Gray Line (☎ 983-2241).

Other tours include bike tours through Sockeye Cycles (☎ 983-2851), a two-hour raft trip through the mild whitewater of Skagway River for $40 by Skagway Float Trips (☎ 983-3508) and kayak trips with Klondike Water Adventures (☎ 983-3769).

Special Events

Skagway's most unusual celebration is when locals and the cast of the Days of '98 show celebrate Soapy Smith's Wake on 8 July with a hike out to the grave and a toast of champagne, often sent up by Smith's great grandson from California. The 4 July celebrations feature a foot race, parade and fish feed.

Places to Stay

Skagway has an 8% bed tax that is applied to all lodging.

Camping The city manages two campgrounds that serve RVers and backpackers. On the corner of Broadway St and 14th Ave is *Hanousek Park* (☎ 983-3333), which provides tables, pit toilets and water in a wooded setting for $8 per tent site. Near the ferry terminal is *Pullen Creek Park Campground* (33 sites) on the waterfront by the Small Boat Harbor. Designed primarily for RVers, sites with electricity cost $18 per night.

For an informal but scenic camp site, go to the picnic area along Yakutania Point, two miles from the ferry terminal. Head northwest (left) on 1st Ave, cross the air strip and suspension bridge over Skagway River and then head west (left) along the path on the other side of the river. The path follows the river and leads to a picnic area that includes tables, grills and even a covered shelter. Nine miles north of Skagway is the free *Dyea Camping Area* (22 sites) which is operated on a first-come-first-to-set-up basis. There are vault toilets, tables and fire places but no water.

Hostel The *Skagway Home Hostel* (☎ 983-2131), a very pleasant and friendly place to stay, is a half-mile from the ferry terminal on 3rd Ave near Main St. Reservations are advised – call the hostel or write to the Home Hostel, Box 231, Skagway, AK 99840.

Along with a kitchen and baggage storage area, there are bikes for guests and laundry facilities. A bunk is $15, a couples room $40 a night.

B&Bs The *Skagway Inn* (☎ 983-2289 or (800) 478-2290 in Alaska) is in an 1897 Victorian home on the corner of Broadway St and 7th Ave. The B&B provides a full breakfast in the morning and free transport to the Chilkoot trailhead. Single/double is $60/75. At the corner of 7th Ave and State is *Gramma's Bed & Breakfast* (☎ 983-2312) with four rooms for $55/65.

Hotels *Miner's Inn* (☎ 983-3303), on Broadway St at 6th Ave, is the cheapest place with singles/doubles with shared baths for $45/60. The *Golden North Hotel* (☎ 983-2294), Alaska's oldest hotel on the corner of Broadway St and 3rd Ave, charges $60/75. *Sergeant Preston's Lodge* (☎ 983-2521), on 6th Ave and State St, has rooms with shared bath for $70/80, and the *Westmark Inn* (☎ 983-6000 or (800) 544-0970), on 3rd Ave between Broadway and Spring streets, has a special $75 rate on rooms with twins beds for two people when space is available.

Places to Eat

In the past few years the number of restaurants in Skagway have almost doubled. If you stumble off the ferry, head up Broadway Ave for an early breakfast at *Sweet Tooth Cafe*, which opens at 6 am. The coffee is weak but the breakfasts are agreeable and range from $6 to $8. At the corner of 4th Ave and State St is *Corner Cafe*, which also has a wide range of seafood; broiled, stuffed, poached or barbecued salmon or halibut dinners for around $14. When the weather is nice, there are few tables outside.

The best place for pizza is Pizzeria Roma, on 3rd Ave between State and Broadway St, where a 15-inch thin crust is $14 to $23. Pizza by the slice and a cold microbrew beer is available at *Broadway Bistro* on Broadway St while practically opposite at *Northern Lights Pizzeria* you get huge portions when

SOUTHEAST

ordering the pasta, Greek or Mexican dinners ($9 to $12).

There is also an assortment of espresso shops, lunch wagons and small delis in town and a couple of fine restaurants. The best is *The Stowaway Cafe* (☎ 983-3463), just past the Harbor Master's office. The small cafe has a handful of tables, a view of the boat harbor and excellent fish and Cajun-style steak dinners for $16 to $19.

Fairway Market, on the corner of 4th Ave and State St, has groceries for those camping or staying at the hostel while the *Skagway Sports Emporium*, nearby on 4th Ave, features a limited supply of freeze-dried food and white gas for hiking trips, along with topographic maps.

Entertainment

Bars For a town with only 800 permanent residents, there's a lot to do in Skagway at night. On the corner of Broadway St and 2nd Ave is the town's most unique bar, the *Red Onion Saloon,* which frequently features live music or at least a ragtime piano player. This former brothel, that was built in 1898, is now a gold-rush saloon complete with mannequins leering down at you from the 2nd story to depict those turn-of-the-century working girls. This is Skagway's liveliest bar. *Moe's Frontier Bar,* more of a local hangout down the street, can also be a lively spot late at night.

Theater Skagway has the best melodrama in the Southeast. Gambling for prizes and drinking begins in the back room of the *Eagle's Hall,* on the corner of Broadway St and 6th Ave, every night at 7.30 pm. This is followed at 8.30 pm by the lively production of *The Days of '98* which covers the gold-rush days of the town and the full story of 'Soapy' Smith in a truly entertaining manner. It is $14 for both the play and preshow entertainment.

Equally entertaining is 'Buckwheat' Donahue's performance of Robert Service ballads and other tall tales of the North at the *Clubhouse Theater,* across 2nd Ave from the WP&YR Depot nightly at 7.30 pm. Tickets

are $6 and the evening includes howling lessons.

Getting There & Away

Air There are regularly scheduled flights from Skagway to Juneau, Haines and Glacier Bay with LAB Flying Service (☎ 983-2471), Wings of Alaska (☎ 983-2442), and Skagway Air (☎ 983-2218) which generally offers the cheapest fares. Expect to pay $80 one way to Juneau and $40 to Haines.

Bus Northbound travelers will find that scheduled buses are the cheapest way to travel other than hitchhiking. Alaskon Express has a bus departing at 7.30 am daily that arrives in Whitehorse at 11.30 am. On Sunday, Tuesday, and Thursday, you can continue to Beaver Creek where the bus stops overnight and connections can be made to Anchorage or Fairbanks. Purchase tickets at the Westmark Inn (☎ 983-2241) on 3rd Ave. The one-way fare from Skagway to Whitehorse is $54 and to Fairbanks $205.

Alaska Direct Busline (☎ (800) 770-6652) departs Skagway daily 10 am for Whitehorse, where it's possible to move on to Fairbanks or Anchorage without that expensive overnight stop. The fare to Whitehorse is $35 and to Fairbanks $155. And finally, relatively new Evergreen Bus Line (☎ (800) 764-4502 in Alaska) departs for Whitehorse daily at 2.30 pm for only $22. Pick-up points include the Skagway Home Hostel.

Train Nowadays it's possible to travel to Whitehorse on the White Pass & Yukon Route with a bus connection at Fraser (British Columbia). The northbound train departs the Skagway depot (☎ 983-2217) daily during the summer at 12.40 pm and you arrive in Whitehorse on a bus at 6 pm. The one-way fare is $95, quite a bit more than the bus but the ride on the historic, narrow-gauge railroad is worth it.

Boat The Alaska Marine Hwy ferry (☎ 983-2941) departs daily during the summer from the terminal and dock at the south-west end of Broadway St. There are lockers in the terminal but the building is only open three hours prior to the arrival of a ferry and while the boat is in port.

There is also the Haines-Skagway Water Taxi. The 40-passenger boat departs the Skagway Small Boat Harbor twice daily for Haines with the first run at 9.45 am and the second at 6 pm. Round-trip fare is $29, one-way is $18 and you can purchase tickets on the boat.

Hitchhiking This is possible along the Klondike Hwy if you are patient and are hitching when a ferry pulls in. Backpackers contemplating hitchhiking north would do better, however, if they bought a $14 ferry ticket to Haines and hitchhiked along the Haines Hwy instead as it has considerably more traffic.

Getting Around

Taxi Just about every taxi and tour company in Skagway will run you out to Dyea and the trailhead for the Chilkoot Trail and the price hasn't gone up in years; $10 a head. Among them Chilkoot Express (☎ 983-2512) at Broadway St and 7th Ave, which has trips at 7 and 9 am, and 2 and 7 pm.

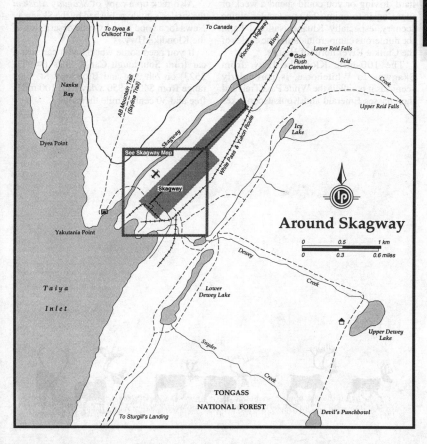

Bicycle There are several places in town to rent a bike, including Sockeye Cycle (☎ 983-2851) at 5th Ave and Broadway St. Rates are $6 an hour and $30 a day for the mountain bikes.

AROUND SKAGWAY

Golden Circle Route If you're not heading into the heart of Alaska but still want a taste of the interior, there is the Golden Circle Route, a 372-mile drive that forms a loop between Skagway, Whitehorse and Haines. It can be covered in as little as two days of hard driving or you could spend a week or more on it to enjoy the spectacular alpine scenery, especially Kluane National Park, the numerous campgrounds and the eagles of the Chilkat River north of Haines.

The 100-mile Klondike Hwy, from Skagway to Whitehorse, is particularly scenic as it parallels the White Pass Trail and then passes Emerald and Kookatsoon lakes near Carcross where there is a handful of campgrounds.

From Whitehorse you get to drive a 105-mile portion of the Alaska Hwy and then head south back into Alaska at Haines Junction on the Haines Hwy. The Alaska Marine Hwy would then complete the loop with transport back to Skagway or a return to Juneau.

Head to the Skagway Visitor Center for maps and information before staring out. In Whitehorse, stop at the Whitehorse Information Center (☎ (403) 667-2915) at 302 Steele St for material on the Yukon capital.

Also pick up a copy of *Skaguay Alaskan* the visitor's guide published by the Skagway News for a good mile-by-mile description of the Klondike Hwy.

If you need some wheels, you can rent a car from Sourdough Car Rentals (☎ 983-2523) on 6th Ave and Broadway St. Cars range from $40 to $50 a day with 100 miles free and 30 cents a mile thereafter.

Southcentral Alaska

Known by many as the Gulf Coast region, Southcentral Alaska is really a continuation of Alaska's rugged coastal playground that begins in Ketchikan. Both Southeast and Southcentral Alaska boast spectacular scenery with glaciers, fjords and mountain ranges half buried by icefields and covered at the base by lush forest; both areas are also affected by the Japanese Current causing a wet but mild climate. Fishing is an important industry to these regions and the Alaska Marine Hwy ferry is one of the main modes of transport.

But Southcentral (the region around Prince William Sound and the Gulf of Alaska) has one important feature that the Panhandle (Southeast) doesn't have – roads and traffic between many of the towns. This alone makes Southcentral one of the cheapest, most accessible and most popular areas in the state to visit.

Southcentral can be divided into three main areas. Prince William Sound, with its communities of Cordova, Valdez and Whittier, is characterized by towering mountains, glaciers and abundant marine wildlife.

To the west of the sound is the Kenai Peninsula and the towns of Seward, Kenai, Soldotna and Homer. This great forested plateau, bounded by the Kenai Mountains and the Harding Icefield to the east, is broken up by hundreds of lakes, rivers and streams, making it an outdoor paradise for hikers, canoeists and anglers...as well as RVers, tour groups and almost half of Alaska's population, which lives just to the north in Anchorage. Because of this easy accessibility, facilities and lodging in the Kenai can get surprisingly crowded during the short tourist season.

To the south-west is Kodiak Island and the city of Kodiak, the home of the largest fishing fleet in Alaska.

Though often caught in the rainy and foggy weather created on the Gulf of Alaska, Kodiak has a rugged beauty and isolated

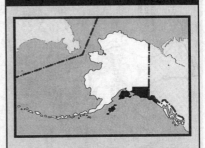

HIGHLIGHTS

- Marvel at Columbia Glacier from the state ferry, MV *Bartlett*, as it crosses Prince William Sound
- Enjoy breakfast on the porch of the *Kennicott Glacier Lodge* then visit the abandoned company town of Kennicott
- Take a boat tour to see glaciers, whales and seals in Kenai Fjords National Park
- Rent a shovel and dig for razor clams at Clam Gulch State Recreation Area
- Photograph the old Russian Church on a bluff at Ninilchik
- Camp in front of Grewingk Glacier at Kachemak Bay State Park

SOUTHCENTRAL

wilderness areas far fewer visitors make an effort to venture into.

YAKUTAT

On the flight to Cordova there is a stopover at Yakutat (pop 700), the most northern Southeast community. The town is isolated from the Alaska Marine Hwy because of the turbulent nature of the Gulf of Alaska. For travelers on a tight schedule, there is no reason to stop over in Yakutat but those who do will find the scenic setting of the Tlingit village stunning, even if the visitor facilities are limited and expensive.

The town is surrounded by lofty peaks, including Mt Elias at 18,114 feet to the west and Mt Fairweather at 15,388 feet to the east.

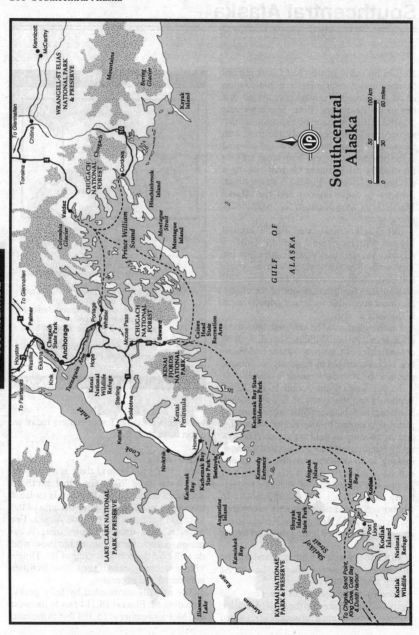

Southcentral Alaska

North-west of Yakutat lies the large **Malaspina Glacier**, the main attraction in the area, which can be viewed from sightseeing flights offered by Gulf Air Taxi (☎ 784-3240), the local air-charter operator based at the airport. A one-hour flight in a Cessna 185 would be enough to see both the Malaspina and Hubbard glaciers and would cost $215 for three people. For $430 for three passengers, you would get two hours in the air and that would be enough time to also include Mt Elias.

Other visitors come to beachcomb the miles of sandy beach that surround Yakutat, searching for Japanese glass balls (used as floats for fishing nets) blown onshore by the violent Pacific storms.

Places to Stay & Eat
The USFS, which maintains an office at Yakutat airport, administers 13 cabins in the area along with the Russell Fjord Wilderness to the north-east. None of the cabins is on the fjord or near Hubbard Glacier. Five of the 13 USFS cabins in the area can be reached from Forest Hwy 10, which extends east from Yakutat. It is best to rent the cabins from the USFS office in the Juneau Centennial Hall (☎ 586-8751 in Juneau) when you pass through the capital city. Rental information can also be obtained at the Yakutat USFS office (☎ 784-3359) in the Flight Service Building at the airport in Yakutat.

Camping in Yakutat is possible at *Cannon Beach*, a picnic area near town that is administered by the USFS. Yakutat has three lodges, an inn and a couple of B&Bs. The going rate seems to be $70 for a double, possible at *Glacier Bear Lodge* (☎ 784-3202) and *Silver Tip Lodge* (☎ 784-3533), which will also throw in breakfast. There is also a restaurant, and two grocery stores in town.

AROUND YAKUTAT
Yakutat was an obscure Alaskan town until 1986 when Hubbard Glacier captured national attention by galloping across Russell Fjord at an amazing speed, turning the long inlet into basically a lake. For much of the year scientists and geologists set up camp to monitor the unusual event while environmental groups debated whether man should interfere with Mother Nature by trapping and airlifting to the sea the doomed seals trapped inside Russell Fjord.

Eventually Hubbard receded to reopen the fjord but to this day the eight-mile-wide glacier remains one of the most active in Alaska. The rip tides and currents that flow between Gilberts Point and the face of the glacier, a mere 1000 feet away, are so wicked and strong they cause Hubbard to calve almost continuously at peak tides.

Kayakers often begin and end in the southern end of the fjord, a shorter and cheaper flight from Yakutat, and then paddle up to Hubbard Glacier. Such a trip requires a week or more of paddling. Gulf Air or Totem Air (☎ 784-3563 or (800) 352-3563) will drop off and pick up two kayakers and their equipment for $150 each way. Contact Lost Coast Adventures through Totem Air in regards to renting folding kayaks. Alaska Discovery (☎ (800) 586-1911) also has a three-day trip into the area that includes the flight in, kayaking near the face of Hubbard Glacier and hiking along the edge of it. The cost is $880 per person.

To experience this sight without paddling, you can be dropped off at the outwash gravel plain of Verigated Glacier which is adjacent to Hubbard at the north end of the fjord. Here you can camp for a few days and hike the outwash area to view Hubbard's turbulent nature. A wheel plane capable of landing on the gravel would be $230 per a party of two to three people for each drop-off or pick-up.

Prince William Sound

Prince William Sound, the northern extent of the Gulf of Alaska, rivals the Southeast for the steepest fjords and the most spectacular coastlines and glaciers. The Sound is a marvelous wilderness area of islands, inlets, fjords, lush rainforests and towering mountains. Flanked to the west by the Kenai

Mountains and to the north and east by the Chugach Mountains, Prince William Sound covers 15,000 sq miles and has abundant wildlife, including whales, sea lions, harbor seals, otters, eagles, dall sheep, mountain goats and, of course, bears.

Another trait the Sound shares with the Southeast is rain – lots of rain. There's an average of well over 100 inches of rain per year, with the fishing town of Cordova receiving 167 inches annually. Summer temperatures range from 54°F to 70°F.

At center stage of Prince William Sound is the Columbia Glacier. The bluish wall of ice, named after New York's Columbia University, is one of the most spectacular tidewater glaciers on the Alaskan coast, as it covers 440 sq miles. The glacier's face is three miles wide and in some places it is 262 feet high. When passing the glacier by boat, the stunning scene includes hundreds of seals sunning on the ice pack, a backdrop of mountains and usually the thunder of ice calving off its face.

Travelers who take the Alaska Airlines jet to Cordova can continue their journey across Prince William Sound by the Alaska Marine Hwy ferry. At Valdez, you have the option of returning to the road, but most travelers elect to stay on the ferry to Whittier on the west side of the sound as this section of the Alaska Marine Hwy includes passing the Columbia Glacier. From Whittier, there is a rail service to Anchorage (see the Getting Around chapter), and from Valdez you can reach Anchorage by bus.

CORDOVA

Nestled between Orca Inlet and Lake Eyak and overshadowed by Mt Eccles, Cordova is a beautiful little fishing town on the east coast of Prince William Sound and a place worth the extra time and expense needed to visit it due to the isolated nature. Not only is Cordova inaccessible by road, the reason for the lack of RVs, but it also has been bypassed by the large cruise-ship lines that spill thousands of tourists into every major town in the Southeast.

The community has 2600 permanent resi-

dents but its population doubles during the summer with fishers and cannery workers because the town's economy is centered around its fishing fleet and fish-processing plants. The area around Cordova is an outdoor paradise, and the town is a jumping-off point to 14 USFS cabins; some good alpine hiking; and the Copper River Delta, a staging and nesting area for millions of birds each year.

History

The area was first settled by nomadic Eyak Indians who were drawn down the Copper River by the enormous salmon runs and abundance of shellfish. Early US fishers built a cannery here in 1889 but modern-day Cordova was born when Michael J Heney, the builder of the White Pass & Yukon Railroad from Skagway to Whitehorse, arrived in 1906. At that point he had decided to transform the summer cannery site into the railroad terminus for his line from the Kennecott copper mines near McCarthy. Construction of the $23 million Copper River & Northwestern Railroad began that year and was completed in 1911 – another amazing engineering feat by the 'Irish Prince'.

Within five years, Cordova was a boom town with more than $32 million worth of copper ore passing through its docks. The railroad and town prospered until 1938, when labor strikes and the declining price of copper permanently closed the Kennecott mines. The railroad ceased operations and Cordova turned to fishing, its main economic base today, which is why the 1989 Exxon oil spill devastated the town.

Although most of the halibut and salmon swimming beneath the oil appear to have survived, the mishap cancelled or postponed the fishing seasons in 1989. Commercial fishing boats were left idle, while stories of lifelong fishers breaking down in tears as they steered their boats through the slick were common. The only saving grace for the industry was that Exxon was forced into leasing many of the commercial fishing

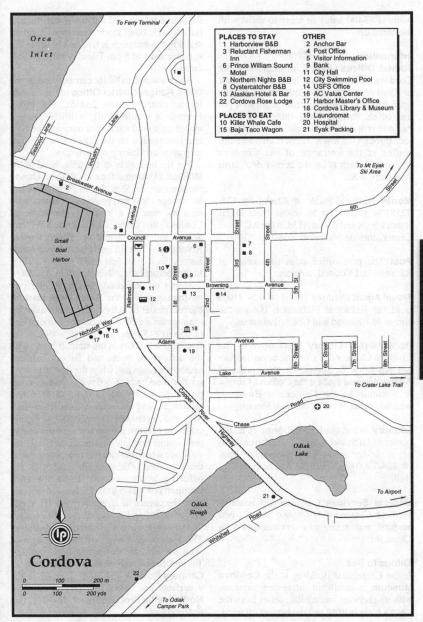

PLACES TO STAY
1   Harborview B&B
3   Reluctant Fisherman Inn
6   Prince William Sound Motel
7   Northern Nights B&B
8   Oystercatcher B&B
13 Alaskan Hotel & Bar
22 Cordova Rose Lodge

PLACES TO EAT
10 Killer Whale Cafe
15 Baja Taco Wagon

OTHER
2   Anchor Bar
4   Post Office
5   Visitor Information
9   Bank
11 City Hall
12 City Swimming Pool
14 USFS Office
16 AC Value Center
17 Harbor Master's Office
18 Cordova Library & Museum
19 Laundromat
20 Hospital
21 Eyak Packing

To Ferry Terminal

Orca Inlet

Seafood Lane

Industry

Breakwater Avenue

Railroad Avenue

Small Boat Harbor

Council Avenue

1st Street

Browning Avenue

2nd Street

Nicholoff Way

Adams Avenue

Copper River Highway

Chase

Whitshed Road

Odiak Slough

Odiak Lake

3rd Street

4th Street

5th St

5th Street

6th Street

7th Street

8th Street

6th Street

Mt Eyak Street

Lake Avenue

Avenue

To Mt Eyak Ski Area

To Crater Lake Trail

To Airport

To Odiak Camper Park

Cordova

0   100   200 m
0   100   200 yds

SOUTHCENTRAL

boats at $3400 a day or more to assist with the clean-up.

Information

Tourist Offices General information about Cordova can be obtained from the Chamber of Commerce (☎ 424-7260) on 1st St. It's open Monday to Friday from 8 am to 4 pm and offers, among other things, tape and cassette rentals for a 60-minute, self-guided tour through the town. There is also a visitor center at the entrance of the Cordova Museum, which is on the corner of Adams Ave and 1st St.

Money National Bank of Alaska (☎ 424-3258) is at 510 1st St across from Davis Super Foods and has an ATM in the AC Value Center store on Nicholoff Way.

Post The post office is at the corner of Railroad and Council avenues.

Travel Agent Cordova Travel (☎ 424-7102) is in the Reluctant Fisherman Inn on the corner of Railroad and Council avenues.

Bookshop & Library Next door to the Cordova Chamber of Commerce on 1st Ave is Orca Book & Sound. On the corner of Adams Ave and 1st St is the Cordova Library & Museum in the Centennial Building, which is open Tuesday through Saturday.

Laundry Whirlwind Laundromat is at the corner of 1st St and Adams Ave. You can also get a shower at the City Swimming Pool (☎ 424-7200) on Railroad Ave next to City Hall.

Medical Services Cordova Community Medical Center (☎ 424-8000) is a 22-bed hospital, with emergency services, and is on Chase Rd.

Things to See

In the Centennial Building is the **Cordova Museum**, a small but interesting museum with displays on marine life, relics from the town's early history and the Kennecott mine,

Russian artefacts and a three-seater bidarka (kayak-style boat) made with spruce and 12 sealskins. Admission is free and hours in the summer are 1 to 5 pm Tuesday through Saturday.

More natural exhibits can be seen at the **USFS Ranger District Office** in the historic former courthouse on 2nd St. The office features a whale skull, wildlife mounts including a bald eagle, sea otter and beaver, and information on the area's amazing bird migration and hiking opportunities.

For the best view of the area, head to the **Mt Eyak Ski Area** at the end of 6th St. During the summer, the Sheridan Ski Club operates its vintage chair lift, providing visitors with an easy ride to a stunning panorama of Cordova, this corner of the Prince William Sound and even a portion of the Copper River Delta. The lift itself has an interesting history as it was first used in Sun Valley, Idaho, before being shipped up to Alaska.

North on Railroad Ave from the city swimming pool is the **Small Boat Harbor**, the real center of activity in Cordova during the summer. In 1984, the harbor was doubled in size to 845 slips, and it is now one of the five largest harbors in the state. It hums with the activity of boats and fishers between season openings and when the fleet is in town on the weekends. Cordova's fleet is composed primarily of salmon seiners and gillnetters, and the season runs from mid-May into September. Dungeness and Tanner crabs are harvested for a few months during the summer and later in the winter.

To see where the catch is processed, ask at the chamber office which canneries are offering a tour or call **Eyak Packing Company** (☎ 424-5300). This small company is at the corner of Copper River Hwy and Whitshed Rd and is a smokery and cannery that specializes in mail-order canned salmon. The owners give tours of their set-up that even include salmon tasting opportunities. To purchase fresh seafood head over to **Cannery Row** (☎ 424-5920) located on the waterfront just before the ferry terminal or **North Pacific Processors** (☎ 424-7111) on Seafood Lane.

SOUTHCENTRAL

Hiking

There are more than 35 miles of trails accessible from the Cordova road system area with several of them leading to USFS cabins (see Places to Stay). As in much of the Southeast, the hiking in this area is excellent, combining a lush forest with alpine terrain, great views and glaciers. For transport to the trailheads, call Cooper River/Northwest Tours (☎ 424-5356) which offers hiker's drop-offs and pick-ups for $1 a mile.

Before venturing into the surrounding area, hikers should first stop at the USFS office (☎ 424-7661) on the corner of Browning Ave and 2nd St to pick up an assortment of free trail maps. Opening hours are 8 am to 5 pm Monday through Friday.

Mt Eyak Ski Hill After a quick scramble up the ski hill at the end of 6th Ave, hardy hikers can spend a day climbing from here to the top of Mt Eyak and down the other side to Crater Lake.

Crater Lake Trail This 2.5-mile hike begins on Eyak Lake, about half a mile beyond the Municipal Airfield on Eyak Lake Rd across from Skaters Cabin. The trail ascends steeply but is easy to follow as it winds through lush forest. At the top, it offers panoramic views of both the Copper River Delta and Prince William Sound. Plan on two to four hours for the round trip from the road to the open country around Crater Lake. Once at the lake, you can continue with a 5.5-mile ridge route to Power Creek Trail.

The entire loop would be a 12-mile trek or an ideal overnight backpack. You could also arrange for Copper River/Northwest Tours to drop you off at the Power Creek trailhead, a $12 charge from town, and then hike all the way back into town via the Mt Eyak Trail.

Lydic Slough Trail At *Mile 7.1* of Copper River Hwy is Lydic Slough Trail, which leads three miles along the Copper River Flats to a cabin on the Eyak River. The Eyak River offers excellent trout and salmon fishing as well as opportunities to view moose, brown bear and a wide range of waterfowl.

McKinley Lake Trail The 2.5-mile McKinley Lake Trail begins at *Mile 21.6* of Copper River Hwy and leads to the head of the lake and the remains of the Lucky Strike gold mine. Two cabins, McKinley Lake and McKinley Trail, are on this path, making them accessible by foot from the highway.

Pipeline Loop Trail At *Mile 21* of Copper River Hwy is this 1.8-mile trail past several small lakes. The trail provides access to good fishing holes for grayling and trout, and merges into the McKinley Trail, which can be followed back to make something of a loop. The entire walk provides excellent views of the surrounding Chugach Mountains but the muskeg areas can be very wet in places and rubber boots are recommended.

Sheridan Mountain Trail This trail starts at the end of Sheridan Glacier Rd, 17 miles south-east of town. Most of the 1.9-mile, one-way trail is a moderate climb that passes through mature forests before breaking out into an alpine basin. The view of mountains and Sheridan and Sherman glaciers from the basin is a stunning sight, and it only gets better when you start climbing the surrounding rim. During a dry spell, hiking boots are fine for the walk, otherwise you might want to tackle this one in rubber boots as well.

Saddlebag Glacier Trail This trail is accessed via a firewood-cutting road, at *Mile 25* of the Copper River Hwy. It's an easy walk of three miles through cottonwoods and spruce until you emerge at the outlet of Saddlebag Lake. The view is outstanding as the namesake glacier is at the far end of the lake and surrounded by peaks and cliffs. Often you can spot mountain goats residing here.

Special Events

Because of the economic importance of the fishing season, no events are planned during the summer in Cordova other than a small 4 July celebration and a couple of salmon

SOUTHCENTRAL

derbies. The town's biggest event is its Iceworm Festival in mid-February, when there is little else to do, while on the first weekend of May is the Copper Delta Shorebird Festival, celebrating the largest migration in North America.

Places to Stay

USFS Cabins Several of the trails accessible from the Cordova road system area lead to USFS cabins, all of which require reservations and cost $25 per day. There is a cabin at the end of the Lydic Slough Trail on Eyak River, and two cabins on the McKinley Lake Trail. For more information see the Cordova Hiking section or contact the USFS office in Cordova.

Camping There is no hostel in Cordova. The closest campground is the *Odiak Camper Park* (☎ 424-6200), half a mile from town on Whitshed Rd next to the recently covered and landscaped dump site. The gravel campground is primarily for RVers but there is a tent area. The tent rate is $6 per night and includes water, showers and restrooms. For RVers it's $12 for an electric hook-up. An unofficial spot for pitching a tent is up 6th St at the ski hill.

B&Bs There are now a dozen B&Bs operating in and around town. Check with the visitor center for a current list of B&Bs as they often change, and expect to pay around $60 per person for a room.

One of the oldest B&Bs, *Oystercatcher* (☎ 424-5154), is at 3rd St and Council Ave while nearby is *The Northern Nights Inn* (☎ 424-5356) with four rooms. Also in town are *Otter B'Here* (☎ 424-5863) with singles/doubles for $45/55 on Breakwater Ave and the *Harborview Bed & Breakfast* (☎ 424-5356) on Observation Ave with singles for $50. Further out of town is *Queen's Chair* (☎ 424-3000 or (800) 349-8489) near the Powder House Inn along the Copper River Hwy with a view of Eyak Lake. Singles/doubles with shared bath are $50/60 a night and the hosts will pick you up in town or at the ferry. Then there is *Cordova*

Rose Lodge (☎ 424-7673), a barge that was converted into a floating B&B. Docked, sort of, in Odiak Slough near the campground, the lodge has six rooms that run to $60/70 for a single/double with shared bath and a full breakfast.

Hotels Of the four hotels in town, the *Alaskan Hotel & Bar* (☎ 424-3288) on 1st St is the cheapest. A room with a shared bath costs $35 a night a double or single, while rooms with a private bath are $58. The Alaskan, like all hotels in Cordova, is booked solidly through most of the summer. Avoid the seedy Cordova Hotel on 1st St and instead book a room at the *Cannery Bunkhouse* (☎ 424-5920, above the Cookhouse Cafe on a dock on Orca Inlet. Singles/ doubles are $40/45. The *Prince William Sound Motel* (☎ 424-3201), on the corner of 2nd St and Council Ave, has singles/doubles for $70/80 while the *Reluctant Fisherman Inn* (☎ 424-3272), on the corner of Railroad and Council avenues, is usually booked solidly during the summer despite the cost of rooms beginning around $115 a night.

Places to Eat

Try the *OK Restaurant* near the museum for Chinese food with main meals ranging from $13 to $16, and *Baja Taco Wagon* in a converted school bus on Nicoloff Ave near the new boat harbor for $5 burritos or fish tacos. The *Ambrosia*, also on 1st St, specializes in pizza and Italian food with dinners around $15 and a slice of pizza for $2. The *Killer Whale Cafe* in the Orca Book & Sound Store is a delicatessen with sandwiches for around $7, good desserts, espresso and a view of the harbor.

Next to the ferry dock is *Cookhouse Cafe*, the centerpiece of an old working cannery. Once an old mess haul, the cafe is great for espresso drinks, sourdough pancakes and pastries. The seafood dinners ($12 to $15) are highly recommended as is the Sunday brunch. *The Powder House*, a little way from town at *Mile 1.5* of the Copper River Hwy, is a bar that serves sandwiches, chilli and barbecue dinners and has a deck overlooking Eyak Lake.

Places to pick up your own supplies include *Davis Super Foods*, a supermarket on 1st St, and *AC Value Center* on Nicholoff Way which has a bakery and deli as well as a grocery store.

Entertainment
The Powder House Bar, which earns its name because it lies on the site of the original Copper River & Northwestern Railroad powder house, is a fun place that features folk, bluegrass and country music at night. If you happen to be there on a rare evening when it isn't raining, there is a deck outside overlooking Eyak Lake.

In town, there is the *Club Bar* on 1st St with music nightly, or the *Anchor Bar* on Breakwater Ave, across from the Small Boat Harbor, for those who want to mingle with the fishers. The *Alaskan Hotel Bar* on 1st St usually has live music.

Getting There & Away
Air Alaska Airlines (☎ 424-7151) makes a daily stop at Cordova on its run to Seattle and its contract carrier, ERA, flies twice daily from Anchorage. An advance-purchased ticket is $119 round-trip from Anchorage, while a one-way ticket purchased three days in advance is $84.

Boat During the summer, the MV *Bartlett* stops at Cordova on Monday, Wednesday and Thursday from either Valdez or Whittier. This makes it possible to add on a side trip to the city without having to backtrack through Valdez. The fare from Cordova to Valdez is $30; it's $58 to Whittier. The ferry terminal (☎ 424-7333) is 1.5 miles north of town on Railroad Ave.

Getting Around
The Airport All jets arrive and depart from Cordova airport, 12 miles from town on Copper River Hwy. The airporter bus (☎ 424-5356) greets all arrivals and charges $9 for the trip into town. You can catch the

bus at the major hotels in town for a ride out to the airport.

AROUND CORDOVA
Copper River Highway
There are more than 50 miles of road extending out from Cordova, most of it centered around the Copper River Hwy. Built on the old railroad bed to the Kennecott mines, the road was originally going to connect Cordova with the Richardson Hwy and the rest of Alaska. Construction was halted in 1964 after the Good Friday Earthquake damaged the existing roadbeds and bridges, knocking out the fourth span of the famous Million Dollar Bridge in front of Childs Glacier.

At least a day should be spent exploring the Copper River Hwy, or take more if you want to include some time fishing and hiking. Stop at the USFS office in Cordova and pick up a copy of the brochure *Copper River Delta* which includes a map and milepost listings of trailheads, undeveloped camp sites, wildlife-viewing areas, and streams to cast a lure into.

Copper River Delta The highway provides access to the delta, a 60-mile arc formed by six glacial-fed river systems. Stretching for more than 700,000 acres, the delta is the largest continuous wetland on the Pacific Coast of North America. Its myriad tidal marshes, shallow ponds and outwashes are used by millions of birds and waterfowl as staging areas during the spring and fall migrations as well as nesting areas in the summer.

May is the prime month for birders, a period when as many as 20 million shorebirds rest and feed in the tidal flats, including seven-million western sandpipers and the entire population of west coast dunlins. Other species easily seen are arctic terns, dusty Canada geese, trumpeter swans, great blue herons and bald eagles. A drive along the highway at dawn or dusk can also provide you with views of moose, brown bears, beavers and porcupines, while on rare

SOUTHCENTRAL

occasions a lynx or wolverine can be seen from the roadside.

The wildlife is so abundant in this area that in 1962, the USFS, the US Fish & Wildlife and the state agreed to manage 33,000 acres of the delta as a game and fish habitat. The refuge has since been enlarged to 2.3 million acres and, in 1972, the delta on the east side of the Copper River Hwy was closed to off-road vehicles.

The area provides access to hiking (see the Cordova Hiking section), wildlife, birding, rafting on swift glacial rivers and angling. The streams and rivers along the highway are renowned for their fishing and can provide the ultimate angling experience – fishing an isolated stretch of river with mountains around you and wildlife just beyond the next bend. Sockeye-salmon fishing begins in mid-June and peaks around 4 July. Coho salmon run from August to September, and cutthroat trout and Dolly Varden can be caught throughout the summer and fall.

Glaciers The highway also provides access to a handful of glaciers that flow out of the Chugach Mountains. The first is the **Sheridan Glacier**, which you can view from the bridge over the Sheridan River 15 miles from Cordova or three miles beyond the Cordova Airport. One mile before the bridge, the Sheridan Glacier access road leads 4.3 miles to the north, ending at a picnic table with a partial view of the ice floe. From here there is a one-mile trail to the dirt-covered glacial moraine.

Several other glaciers can be seen spilling out of the mountains; by far the most impressive is **Childs Glacier** to the west of the Million Dollar Bridge, 48 miles from Cordova. A short side road leads from the highway to within 200 yards of the spectacular glacier's face. Periodic calving from the glacier almost stops Copper River's downstream momentum. From the Million Dollar Bridge you can view Childs Glacier, less than a mile downstream or **Miles Glacier**, five miles upstream.

Nearby you'll find a 15-foot-high viewing platform with an interpretive display on the history of the bridge and the start of the Childs Glacier Trail. The 1.2-mile trail follows an old road along the Copper River, passing superb views of the glacier. It ends at the Childs Glacier Recreation Area, featuring picnic tables, restrooms, and more interpretive displays and short trails.

Paddling The Copper River flows 287 miles, beginning at Copper Glacier near Slana in Alaska's Interior to the Gulf of Alaska east of Cordova. Most of the river is for experienced rafters as rapids, glaciers and narrow cannons give it a whitewater rating of Class II-III much of the way while Wood Canyon just below Chitina is considered by some as Class IV. The 20-mile stretch between the Million Dollar Bridge and Flag Point at *Mile 27* of the Copper River Hwy is considerably wider and slower. Here you're more concerned with tidal fluctuations than rapids. Experienced sea kayakers can run the river all the way through the Copper River Delta into the Gulf of Alaska. But keep in mind that below Flag Point the river becomes heavily braided which inevitably means dragging your boat through shallow channels.

Copper River/Northwest Tours (☎ 424-5356) will provide shuttle service for those who want to float the river from either Flag Point or the Million Dollar Bridge. The cost is $20 per person or $80 a trip for Flag Point and $30 per person or $120 a trip from the bridge. Contact Cordova Coastal Adventures (☎ 424-3842) in regards to renting kayaks. Singles are $24/250 for a day/week, while doubles are $65/315.

Getting Around The only problem in experiencing this area is transport. Hitching along the Copper River Hwy is slow going and renting a car in Cordova is expensive, if you can even obtain a vehicle. Imperial Cab Company (☎ 424-5982 or 424-3324) has vehicles for $55 a day with unlimited mileage. You can also try the Reluctant Fisherman Hotel (☎ 424-3272) which has basically the same rate but only 100 free miles each day.

Top: Fall in Eagle River valley (DS)
Bottom left: Moose warning sign on the Glenn Highway (JD)
Bottom right: Outhouse in 'downtown' Copper Center (DP)

Top: Sea kayaking in Blackstone Bay, Prince William Sound (DS)
Bottom: Trans-Alaska Pipeline workers' monument, Valdez (DS)

Copper River/Northwest Tours (☎ 424-5356) offers a six-hour tour out to the Million Dollar Bridge for $35 per person, with a minimum of four people per trip, and is by far the most reasonable way to see this road. The company uses a 25-passenger bus and serves a box lunch at the Childs Glacier Recreation Area.

Then there is Whiskey Ridge Cycle Shop (☎ 424-3354) on Breakwater Ave. It rents mountain bicycles for $25 a day and if you have three spare days an excellent bike trip can be managed, highlighted by day hikes and glacier watching. Cordova Coastal Adventures (☎ 424-3842) also has mountain bikes for rent at $20 a day and $100 a week.

VALDEZ

In the heart of Prince William Sound and less than 25 miles east of the Columbia Glacier is Valdez, the most northerly ice-free port in the western hemisphere and the southern terminus of the Trans-Alaska Pipeline.

History

The town and port were named after a Spanish naval officer by Spanish explorer Don Salvador Fidalgo in 1790. Valdez boomed in 1897-98 when 4000 gold-seekers arrived looking for what was being advertised in the Lower 48 as the 'All American Route' to Alaska's Interior and the Klondike gold fields. Talk about truth in advertising – what they found were a few tents set up above the tide line and one of the most dangerous routes to the Klondike.

Also known as the Valdez Trail, the route included a trek over two glaciers, beginning with the Valdez Glacier, as the key to crossing the Chugach Mountains. It was a suicidal trip at best and hundreds of lives were lost due to falls in crevasses, snowblindness and hypothermia. In the spring of 1899, Captain William Abercrombie arrived to find a devastated group of men, most of whom had scurvy and were short of supplies never having anticipated a lack of them in Valdez. The army captain soon set up a hospital and made arrangements for supplies and then began surveying a better route to the interior.

It was Abercrombie who found Keystone Canyon and Thompson Pass as a much more suitable place to cross the Chugach range. Eventually the gold miner's trail was improved into a wagon trail and then was paved in the 1920s to become the Richardson Hwy.

Valdez prospered briefly with a few mines of its own and as an outpost for the army. But by the early 1900s the town began a long decline when, in a bitter fight, it lost the Copper River & Northwestern Railroad to Cordova despite blasting tunnels in Keystone Canyon in anticipation of a line.

In 1964, Valdez lost even more than its role as the main cargo route to Interior Alaska. In four short minutes, the Good Friday Earthquake demolished the city. All of Valdez's history is dated either before or after the devastating catastrophe, as the city was one of the worst hit in Alaska with the epicenter only 45 miles to the west of town. The earthquake caused the land to ripple like water and a 4000-foot slice of waterfront to slide into the harbor. It also produced massive tidal waves that left few buildings undamaged in the town.

Afterwards, the residents voted to rebuild their city at a new site on more stable ground. The old town lies four miles east of Valdez on Richardson Hwy, but all that remains today is a vacant field and a plaque dedicated to those who lost their lives during the frightful event.

Valdez regained its role as the gateway to the Interior when it was chosen as the terminus of the Trans-Alaska Pipeline. Work began in 1974 and the $9 billion project was completed in 1977; the first tanker was filled with the black gold on 1 August 1977. Today, the city's economy depends heavily on oil and the taxes the oil company pays out.

Fishing and tourism also contribute to the economy, but oil has clearly made Valdez a rich city. Major projects completed in the early 1980s include a $50 million container terminal to enhance the city's reputation as the 'Gateway to the North' and the $7 million Civic Center. With oil money, the Chugach Mountains as a beautiful backdrop, and an

SOUTHCENTRAL

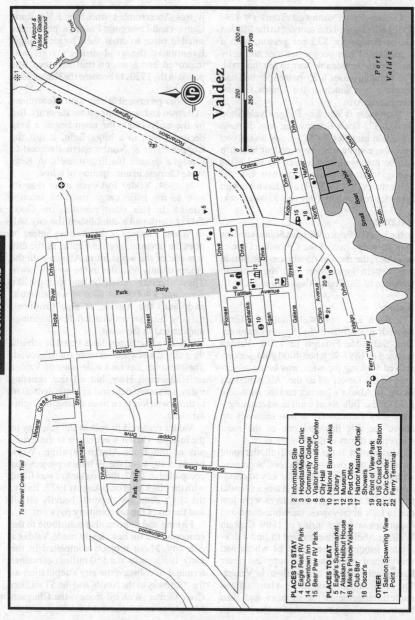

Valdez

PLACES TO STAY
4 Eagle Rest RV Park
14 Downtown Inn
15 Bear Paw RV Park

PLACES TO EAT
5 Eagle's Supermarket
16 Alaskan Halibut House
16 Mike's Palace/Valdez
      Club Bar
18 Oscar's

OTHER
1 Salmon Spawning View
      Point
2 Information Site
3 Hospital/Medical Clinic
6 Community College
8 Visitor Information Center
9 City Hall
10 National Bank of Alaska
11 Library
12 Museum
13 Post Office
17 Harbor Master's Office/
      Showers
19 Point of View Park
20 US Coast Guard Station
21 Civic Center
22 Ferry Terminal

ideal location in the middle of the Prince William Sound playground, Valdez and its 3700 residents seemed to have all a city could want.

However, a price was paid for the city's involvement in the oil industry when the *Exxon Valdez* rammed a reef and spilt 11 million gallons of oil into Prince William Sound in 1989. It was the worst oil spill in US history, and Valdez became the center of an environmental storm. Exxon directed the oil clean-up from Valdez during the first summer after the spill and created a money rush that hadn't been seen since the pipeline was built.

Thousands of people flocked to Valdez from all over the country in search of clean-up jobs that paid up to $20 an hour. Within a month the oil company had created an army of 9000 workers, many of whom spent their days at the oil-soaked beaches of Prince William Sound but their nights in Valdez, whose population jumped from 3000 to 12,000 with people living out of tents or in the back of pick-up trucks. Valdez is now a town where 30% of the population is employed in pipeline-related work. The only memorial to one of the worst oil spills in the country is a small exhibit in the museum.

Information

Tourist Office The Valdez Visitor Center (☎ 835-4636) is on the corner of Chenega Ave and Fairbanks Dr, diagonally opposite the library, and is open daily from 8 am to 8 pm in the summer. Ask about 1964 earthquake film that the visitor center shows throughout the summer. Admission to the films is $3.

Money There are two banks in Valedez with National Bank of Alaska (☎ 835-5762) at 302 Egan Dr.

Post The post office is at the corner of Galena St and Tatitlek Ave.

Travel Agency Easy Travel (☎ 835-3279) is in the Tatitlek Building on Fairbanks St.

Library Diagonally opposite the museum is the Valdez Library which runs a book and magazine swap for travelers on its lower floor. The library is open Tuesday to Thursday from 10 am to 8 pm, on Monday and Friday from 10 am to 6 pm, and Saturday from noon to 6 pm.

Laundry Like Home Laundromat is in the Valdez Mall on Egan Dr and has showers as well as coin-operated laundry machines.

Medical Services Valdez Community Hospital (☎ 835-2249) is at 911 Meals Ave while for walk-in care there is Valdez Medical Clinic (☎ 835-4811) next door.

Things to See

Valdez's bustling **Small Boat Harbor** is south of North Harbor Dr and features a long boardwalk with benches and ramps down to the various docks. With an impressive set of peaks in the background, the harbor is an excellent place to hang out in the evening, especially during July when you can watch lucky anglers weighing in 100 or 200-pound halibut right on the docks. From the west end of the harbor it is a short walk past the US Coast Guard Station to **Our Point of View Park**. The observation platform on the knoll is a good spot to view the old town site to the east, the pipeline terminal to the south and Valdez Narrows to the west. Nearby on the corner of Fidalgo Dr and Hazelet Ave is the **Civic Center** with more picnic tables and panoramas of the area.

From the Civic Center, head two blocks north on Hazelet Ave and turn right (east) on Egan Dr to the **Valdez Museum** (☎ 835-2764) in the Centennial Building. The museum is packed with displays that include a model of the Trans-Alaska Pipeline, a 19th-century saloon bar, an exhibit on glaciers that usually includes a cooler full of ice from the Columbia Glacier and a photo display on Valdez (the snow capital of Alaska – in 1989 the town received a record 46.7 feet of the stuff). Opposite each other are two exhibits connected with the town's most important dates in history (the 1964 earthquake and the

SOUTHCENTRAL

Exxon oil spill), including a piece of the ship's hull that was salvaged. In the summer, the museum is open daily from 8 am to 7 pm; a donation of $2 is requested.

To reach **Prince William Sound Community College**, follow Chenega Ave north from the museum and turn right (east) on Pioneer Dr. The small campus, a division of the University of Alaska, has three huge wooden carvings that are part of Peter Toth's collection of 50 sculptures dedicated to the Native Americans.

Pioneer Dr runs east into Richardson Hwy, and half a mile to the north is the **Crooked Creek Information Site**. The wooden platform, the site of the old hatchery, is a good spot to watch salmon spawn in July and August. USFS naturalists operate programs here throughout the summer.

Hiking

In an area surrounded by mountains and glaciers, you would expect good hiking around Valdez, but this is not the case. There are few developed trails in the area (though many are now being proposed), so reaching much of the surrounding alpine country requires considerable hacking through thick bush. There is no USFS office in Valdez and no nearby cabins.

Mineral Creek Trail The best walk away from town is the old road along Mineral Creek and the one-mile trail from its end to the old Smith Stamping Mill. The road can be in poor condition at times but most cars can usually manage it without bottoming out too many times.

To reach the trailhead, follow Hazelet Ave north 10 blocks from Egan Dr to Hanagita St and turn left (west); then turn right (north) onto Mineral Creek Rd. The road bumps along for 5.5 miles and then turns into a mile-long trail to the old stamping mill. Following the trail beyond the mill at Brevier Creek also requires considerable bush hacking. If you are hiking the entire road, the trip up the lush green canyon can be a pleasant 13-mile adventure that requires five to six hours.

Solomon Gulch Trail A newer trail is located across from the Solomon Gulch Fish Hatchery on Dayville Rd, off the Richardson Hwy. This 1.3-mile trail is a steep, uphill hike that quickly leads to splendid views of the Valdez Port and the city below. It ends at Solomon Lake, which is the source of 80% of Valdez's power.

Goat Trail The oldest trail in the area is Goat Trail, which originally was a Native Americans' route and then was discovered by Captain Abercrombie in his search of safe passage to the interior. Today you can pick up the posted trailhead at *Mile 13.5* of the Richardson Hwy, just past Horseshoe Falls in Keystone Canyon. The trail twists and turns for five miles as it follows the Lowe River until it stops at the original bridge over Bear Creek.

Paddling

Lowe River This glacial river cuts through the impressive Keystone Canyon and is a few miles outside Valdez. Lowe River has become a popular float trip during the summer. Keystone Adventures (☎ 835-2606 or (800) 328-8460) offers day trips on the river, carrying passengers six miles through whitewater and past the cascading waterfalls that have made the canyon famous. The guide company runs the 1½-hour trip five times daily (beginning at 10 am and ending with a run at 6 pm) and charges $30 per person.

Shoup Bay This bay off Valdez Arm is the location of a retreating tidewater glacier of the same name and is the destination of a popular overnight trip by kayak. The glacier features two tidal basins and is a protected area of icebergs, with harbor seals and other sea life. It's about 10 miles to the bay and another four miles up to the glacier but take a tide book. You must enter the bay two hours before the incoming tide to avoid swift tidal currents. Anadyr Adventures (☎ 835-2814) sets up shop and rents kayaks off North Harbor Dr across from the Small Boat Harbor from where you can launch. Singles are $45 a day, doubles $65 and there is a discount if you rent for more than two days. It also runs a day trip to the glacier that begins with a drop-off at the bay. The cost is $140 per person.

Columbia Glacier This is the largest tidewater glacier in Prince William Sound and a spectacular spot to spend a few days kayaking among the crackling ice watching seals and other wildlife. Only experienced paddlers should attempt to paddle the open water from Valdez Arm to the glacier. All others should arrange a drop-off and pick-up with one of the many tour boats that run cruises to the glacier such as Stan Stephens Cruises (☎ 835-4731 or (800) 992-1297). Many kayakers paddle Heather Bay to view the ice and camp on Heather Island. Rent a boat from Anadyr Adventures (☎ 835-2814) which also offers day trips to the glacier for $170 per person or overnight paddles for $295.

Special Events
Valdez has both a 4 July celebration and an end-of-summer festival called Gold Rush Days. The five-day festival takes place in mid-August and includes a parade, bed races, dances, a free fish feed and a portable jailhouse that is pulled throughout town by locals who go about arresting people without beards as well as other innocent bystanders.

Places to Stay
Cabins There aren't any USFS cabins near Valdez but there are a few opportunities to leave the city for a more wilderness setting in Prince William Sound. *Anadyr Adventures* (☎ 835-2814) rents a turn-of-the-century miner's cabin in Ellamar, a small outpost near the mouth of Valdez Arm. The cost is $25 per night per person and you need to bring along a sleeping bag, pad and food. Rent one of its kayaks to spend a day paddling Tatitlek Narrows and viewing sea otter pupping grounds.

Stan Stephens Cruises (☎ 835-4731), the giant tour boat company in Valdez, has large tents on platforms on Glacier Island in the vicinity of Columbia Glacier. The cost is $180 per night per person but includes an eight-hour cruise, accommodation and meals. Each additional night is $100.

Camping Valdez, the city of wealth and beauty, desperately lacks cheap accommodation for backpackers or a good public campground. There used to be a gravel camping area on the south side of the Small Boat Harbor for the seasonal cannery workers, nicknamed 'Hotel Hill', but that was closed by the city in 1996. Six miles out of town, past the airport in fact, is the *Valdez Glacier Campground* (101 sites, $10 per night) on Airport Rd. This campground isn't too bad, at least you get a private wooded site, but lacks the charm of the state campgrounds you've been passing along the highway all day.

A better deal are the private campgrounds in town. Downtown Valdez is full of RV campgrounds and you'll be amazed how they pack them in around the harbor. Two of the commercial campgrounds, however, also cater to those who arrive with a tent. *Bear Paw RV Campground* (☎ 835-2530), just off the Small Boat Harbor, has sites for $15 a night in a special wooded area just for tents. It's on a small knob above the City Dock and includes its own shower and laundry building. The rate for RVers here is about $22. *Eagle Rest RV Park* (☎ 835-2373), on the corner of Pioneer Dr and the Richardson Hwy, also has tent sites for $13 a night. It has showers, a laundry room and a few old-model bikes.

In recent years, Valdez has begun to restrict unauthorized camping within the city, especially on the hill overlooking the waterfront across Chitna St. The best place to find an unauthorized camp site is to hike a mile or so up Mineral Creek Rd.

B&Bs There are more than 30 B&Bs in and around town charging around $55/65 a single/double. They change often but the visitor center has a speed-dial phone outside with a bulletin board listing all the current B&Bs and their rates. Just pick a home and push a button. Or try *Mineral Creek Bed &*

Breakfast (☎ 835-4205), a cedar log cabin with a sauna, and mountain bikes to ride back into town.

Hotels

Rates in the city's six motel/hotels range from $95/100 a night for a single/double in the *Pipeline Inn* (☎ 835-4444), at 112 Egan Dr, to $130 at the top-of-the-range *Westmarks*. The best deal is *Downtown Inn* (☎ 835-2791 or (800) 478-2791 in Alaska only) which calls itself a B&B but in reality is more of a hotel, with 25 rooms. The inn is at 113 Galena Dr, near the post office, and has some rooms with shared bathrooms that begin at $80 for a single or a double. You also get a filling breakfast in the morning and there is a coin-operated washer and drier that cost half the price of those at the local laundromat. Call for a room in advance if you can.

Places to Eat

What used to be a Tastee Freez is now *Oscar's* and definitely a step up. On North Harbor Dr across from the Small Boat Harbor, the restaurant provides eggs-toast-potatoes for $4, hamburgers for $6 and, perhaps its best deal, home-made chowder served in a sourdough-bread bowl for $6. More local seafood can be enjoyed at *The Alaskan Halibut House*, on the corner of Meals Ave and Fairbanks Dr across from Village Inn, the closest thing Valdez has to a fast-food place. The restaurant has a salad bar and serves a fish & chip basket of halibut for $7 or catch-of-the-day (take your chances as to what they caught that day) for $5.

A little classier than the local hamburger joint is *Mike's Palace* on North Harbor Dr. The place specializes in pasta and local seafood, especially halibut, and dinners cost from $10 to $16, but you can pick up a small pizza that will easily feed two or three people for under $12. A short walk from the Small Boat Harbor is *Fu Kung* at 207 Kobuk St. The Chinese restaurant is in an old military hut but you wouldn't know it from the inside and the food is excellent. Dinners run from $10 to $14 but get there before 2.30 pm and

get a better deal with the lunch special: main dish, soup, fried rice and egg roll for $7.

Eagle's, on the corner of Pioneer Dr and Meals Ave, has the cheapest supermarket prices in town along with a bar serving salad, hot soup, and tacos, where $6 will get you a taco salad that will keep you filled until morning. It also serves breakfast in take-away trays from 6 to 10 am and for under $4 (unheard of almost anywhere else in Alaska) you can get your eggs, toast and hash browns.

Entertainment

Among the places you may want to try are *Sugarloaf Saloon* at the Village Inn, on the corner of Meals Ave and Richardson Hwy, or the *Valdez Club Bar* next door to Mike's Palace if you want to hang out with fishers.

There are usually numerous activities, including performances by traveling theater groups and movies shown on a large screen, at the Civic Center (☎ 835-4400) during the summer. The Prince William Sound Community College also runs a live theater that taps into the tourism season and sells its tickets at the Visitor Center (☎ 835-2984).

Getting There & Away

Air Alaska Airlines, through its contract carrier ERA Aviation (☎ 835-2636), provides five flights from Monday to Friday and three on Saturday and Sunday between Valdez and Anchorage from the Valdez Airport, five miles from town on Airport Rd. The one-way fare is $75 to $85.

Bus Alaskon Express (☎ 835-2357), operating out of the Westmark Hotel, departs Valdez at 8 am daily and reaches Anchorage at 6 pm that night. The one-way fare is $65. You can also get off at Glennallen and pick up a connecting bus to just about anywhere in the state, including Fairbanks for $149. For those who want to visit McCarthy and Wrangell-St Elias National Park, you pretty much have to take an Alaskon Express bus to Glennallen and then backtrack south via Backcountry Connection (☎ 822-5292 or

(800) 478-5292 in Alaska only) to the historic town.

Boat Taking the Alaska Marine Hwy ferry is by the far the cheapest way to view the Columbia Glacier and sometimes you can get almost as close to the thick ice pack as you would with most private tours. There is also a USFS naturalist on board pointing out sea otters, seals and sea lions and giving natural-history programs. Just keep in mind that private tours spend a great deal more time at the ice pack and observing wildlife – the ferry, on the other hand, has a schedule to keep.

The one-way Valdez to Whittier fare is $58. The ferry also connects Valdez to Cordova ($30), Seward ($58), Homer ($138) and Kodiak ($98), since both the MV *Bartlett* and MV *Tustumena* call at Valdez. Between the two ships there are runs to Whittier five times a week, two weekly sailings to Cordova and a weekly run to Seward, Homer and Kodiak. The ferry terminal (☎ 835-4436) in Valdez is at the southern end of Hazelet Ave and reservations for these popular runs are strongly recommended. If you don't have a confirmed space for you and your car, you can try your luck on standby. For the 7.15 am run to Whittier, the ferry terminal opens at 4.30 am and it's best to get there as early as you can to be at the front of the line of stand-by vehicles. Normally there is enough extra space for two or three cars.

AROUND VALDEZ

The **oil pipeline terminal**, the heart and soul of Valdez, lies across the bay on Dayville Rd, eight miles from town along Richardson Hwy. Dayville Rd is interesting as it branches off the highway and hugs the mountainside passing several eagle nests and the scenic **Solomon Gulch**.

The **Copper Valley Hydro Project** which supplies power for both Valdez and Glennallen has been completed at Solomon Gulch. Across the road is the **Solomon Gulch Hatchery**, which has a self-guided interpretive walk open to visitors from 8 am to 5 pm daily. Admission is $1. Dayville Rd

ends at the terminal's visitor center and a bronze monument dedicated to the construction workers who built the pipeline.

The terminal is nothing short of remarkable as it contains over 15 miles of pipeline, 18 oil-storage tanks and four tanker berths. Oil is pumped out of Prudhoe Bay on the Beaufort Sea in northern Alaska and travels 800 miles south through the pipeline to the terminal, where it is either stored or loaded into tankers. It is estimated that there are 9.6 billion barrels of oil under the North Slope and 1.7 million barrels flow out of the pipeline into tankers every day at the terminal.

Displays at the visitor center explain all this, and for many it's enough to stare at the facility from the entrance gate and then head back. If you want a closer look, Valdez Tours (☎ 835-2686) runs a two-hour tour that departs from the visitor center at the airport several times daily for $15 per person. During the tour you pass through a security check that's tougher than those you experience at most airports and you only step off the bus twice. Despite being total PR for big oil companies, the tour is interesting and unless you're a founding member of Greenpeace, you can't help but be a little impressed with all the security measures and safeguards here, especially in the wake of the *Exxon Valdez* oil spill.

COLUMBIA GLACIER

Columbia Glacier is the second largest tidewater glacier in North America and spills 40 miles out of the Chugach Mountains and ends with a three-mile-wide face.

Most travelers view this magnificent tidewater glacier while crossing Prince William Sound to or from Valdez. The MV *Bartlett* is the only ferry that passes a tidewater glacier and provides the cheapest way to sail between Whittier and Valdez. Because the glacier has been rapidly retreating for almost 10 years, it's difficult for any boat to get close to the face and subsequently there is now little difference between the ferry and the other cruise ships as far as the distance they travel up the bay. It's just too clogged with ice.

Privately-run cruise ships do spend considerably more time at the ice pack, threading their way through the icebergs, where you can often observe seals basking under the sun. At best the MV *Bartlett* turns up the bay and slows down but keeps chugging along and for many people that's all the glacial fix they need. Regardless of whether you are close to the 300-foot face or not, this sea of ice with the Columbia Glacier filling up the background is still an awesome sight and a photographer's delight.

Stan Stephens Charters (☎ 835-4731 or (800) 922-1297) is the largest tour operator, running five boats during the summer and six different cruises daily. A five-hour tour departs at 7 am on Monday and 12.30 pm the rest of the week and costs $67 per person. An eight-hour lunch cruise departs at 9.30 am and a similar dinner cruise departs at 1.30 pm. Both cost $94 per person. Stop at Bear Paw RV Park to purchase tickets or make reservations.

Also check with Glacier Charter Service (☎ 835-5141) which runs the *Lu-Lu Belle* and maintains an office on Kobuk Dr behind Totem Inn. The boat departs at 2 pm daily and during the height of the tourist season adds an 8 am cruise as well. The boat features a full bar and the cost of the five-hour cruise is $65 per person.

Smaller tour-boat operators come and go but it might pay to shop around by walking the docks of the Small Boat Harbor one night or carefully checking brochures at the visitor center.

RICHARDSON HIGHWAY TO MILE 115

The section of the Richardson Hwy from Valdez to Glennallen is an incredibly scenic route that includes canyons, mountain passes, glaciers and access to the massive Wrangell-St Elias National Park. Hitchhiking is fairly easy during the summer, making it convenient to stop often and enjoy the sights and campgrounds along the way.

The highway begins in the center of Valdez, but *Mile 0* is near the site of old Valdez, as the mileposts were erected before the Good Friday Earthquake and were never changed. The junction with Dayville Rd, which leads to the pipeline terminal, is 6.9 miles from town, and at this point Richardson Hwy swings north.

At *Mile 13* you reach **Keystone Canyon** with its many waterfalls and unusual rock formations high above the road. In the next mile, two magnificent waterfalls appear, first the Horsetail and then the Bridal Veil half a mile down the highway. The canyon wall is so sheer that the waterfalls appear to be cascading straight down and actually spray the road with mist.

At *Mile 14.8* of Richardson Hwy, the northern end of the canyon, there is an abandoned hand-drilled tunnel that residents of Valdez began but never finished when they were competing with Cordova for the railroad to the Kennecott mines. A historical marker briefly describes how nine companies fought to develop the short route from the coast to Kennecott copper mines, leading to the 'shootout in Keystone Canyon'.

The **Trans-Alaska Pipeline** can be seen at *Mile 20.4*. The short loop road to the first camping area, *Blueberry Lake State Recreation Site* (10 sites, $8 a night), is at *Mile 24* of Richardson Hwy. The recreational area offers 10 sites and four covered picnic shelters in a beautiful alpine setting with lofty peaks surrounding it. Often during the summer all the sites will be taken by RVers but it's easy for backpackers to find a spot to pitch their tent near the trails. There's good fishing in the nearby lakes for rainbow trout. In Summit Lake these fish can reach 18 inches long and are usually caught with flies, small spinners or salmon eggs. Keep in mind that above the tree line the weather can be windy and foul at times.

The highway continues to ascend until it reaches **Thompson Pass** at *Mile 26*. There are several scenic turn-offs near the pass (elevation 2771 feet) which in early summer is covered in wildflowers. This spot also holds most of Alaska's snowfall records, including 62 inches of snow in a 24-hour period in December 1955. That's the reason for the L-shaped poles along the highway. The snow is so deep here in the winter, snowplows need the poles to guide them over the pass.

At *Mile 28.6* of Richardson Hwy is the turn-off to the **Worthington Glacier State Recreation Area**, where it is possible to drive to the glacier's face on a short access road. Within this state recreation area are outhouses, picnic tables and a large covered viewing area.

Mile-long Worthington Glacier View Trail begins at the parking lot and follows the crest of the moraine. It's a scenic hike that follows the edge of the glacier, but the walk should be done with caution. Never hike on the glacier itself. Thompson Pass and the surrounding area above the tree line are ideal for tramping, as hikers will have few problems climbing through the heather.

The pipeline continues to pop into view as you travel north on Richardson Hwy and at one point it passes beneath the road. The next campground, the *Little Tonsina River State Recreation Site* (10 sites, $6 per night), appears at *Mile 65*. None of the sites is on the Little Tonsina River but a path leads down to the water where anglers will find fishing for Dolly Varden good most of the summer. The *Squirrel Creek State Campground* (14 sites, $8 per night) is at *Mile 79.4* of Richardson Hwy and offers a scenic little camping area on the banks of the creek. There are fishing opportunities for grayling and rainbow trout in Squirrel Creek, the reason, no doubt, why the campground is often filled. Nearby is a roadhouse for meals, while across the street is a small gas station and supplies.

The Edgerton Hwy junction that leads to the heart of the Wrangell-St Elias National Park is three miles past the campground while a lookout over **Willow Lake** is at *Mile 87.6*. The lake can be stunning on a clear day with the water reflecting the Wrangell Mountains, the 100-mile chain that includes 11 peaks over 10,000 feet. The two most prominent peaks visible from the lookout are Mt Drum, 28 miles to the north-east, and Mt Wrangell, Alaska's largest active volcano, to the east. Mt Wrangell is 14,163 feet and on some days a plume of steam is visible from its crater.

The Richardson Hwy now bypasses **Copper Center** (pop 449) which used to be at *Mile 101*. You now have to make a special effort to see the small village but you shouldn't hesitate. This town is a classic, especially compared with that dusty trailer park known as Glennallen to the north.

At the turn of the century, Copper Center was an important mining camp for the thousands of prospectors eyeing the gold fields in the Yukon and later in Fairbanks. Near the bridge over the Klutina River is the *Copper Center Lodge* (☎ 822-3245), which began in 1897 as the Blix Roadhouse and was the first lodge built north of Valdez. The lodge still serves as a roadhouse today. You can get a delicious plate of sourdough pancakes, reputedly made from century-old starter. The dining room is open from 7 am to 9 pm; double rooms range from $75 with shared bath to $85 with private bath.

Next door is the **George Ashby Museum**, open from 1 to 5 pm Monday to Saturday (no admission fee). Inside the log cabin are mining artefacts from the Kennecott mines as well as the record moose rack for Alaska. It's hanging over the door and, with a spread of almost 70 inches, you pray it doesn't fall when you leave. Also check out the Copper Center City Hall; it's good for a laugh.

Copper Center has gas, a store for supplies, a post office, and the *Silver Fox Drive Inn* which is an old bus that serves everything from hamburgers to tacos for under $6. Before you return to the Richardson Hwy you pass the **Wrangell-St Elias National Park Visitor Center**. During the summer the center is open to 6 pm daily and is the place to go for topo maps, trip suggestions and to leave your backpacking itinerary. Even if you don't plan to enter the park's backcountry, the center has a few displays and a small viewing area where they show videos on the area.

Just north of the town on Richardson Hwy is the **Chapel on the Hill**, built in 1942. During the summer the log chapel features a short slide presentation on the history of the Copper River Basin area; admission is free.

At *Mile 115* is the major junction between

the Glenn and Richardson highways. The Richardson Hwy continues north to Delta Junction and eventually Fairbanks (see the Interior chapter). The Glenn Hwy (see the Interior chapter) heads west to Glennallen, a short distance away, and on to Anchorage.

WRANGELL-ST ELIAS NATIONAL PARK

This national park, created in 1980, stretches north 170 miles from the Gulf of Alaska. It encompasses 13.2 million acres of mountains, foothills and river valleys bounded by the Copper River on the west and Canada's Kluane National Park to the east. Together, Kluane and Wrangell-St Elias national parks make up almost 20 million acres and the greatest expanse of valleys, canyons and towering mountains in North America, including the continent's second and third highest peaks.

This area is a crossroads of mountain ranges. To the north are the Wrangell Mountains; to the south, the Chugachs; and thrusting from the Gulf of Alaska and clashing with the Wrangells are the St Elias Mountains. There are so many mountains and so many summits in this rugged land that, as the park brochure says, 'you quickly abandon the urge to learn their names'.

Spilling out from the peaks are extensive icefields and over 100 major glaciers – some of the largest and most active in the world. The Bagley Icefield near the coast is the largest subpolar mass of ice in North America. The Malaspina Glacier, which spills out of the St Elias Range between Ice Bay and Yakutat Bay, is larger than the state of Rhode Island.

Wildlife in Wrangell-St Elias National Park is more diverse and plentiful than in any other Alaskan park. Species in the preserve include moose, black and brown bears, dall sheep, mountain goats, wolves, wolverines, beavers, and three of Alaska's 11 caribou herds.

The Richardson Hwy borders the northwest corner of the park and two rough dirt roads lead into its interior. The most popular access road by far is the McCarthy Rd with the historic mining towns of McCarthy and

Kennicott, serving as something of a visitor's area into the park. Whereas in the early 1980s a few hundred people would venture across the Kennicott River into McCarthy, today that many will show up on a good weekend and today both towns attract more than 20,000 visitors.

Despite the rebirth of McCarthy, Wrangell-St Elias is still a true wilderness park with few visitor facilities or services beyond the highway. An adventure into this preserve requires time and patience rather than money, but it can lead to a once-in-a-lifetime experience.

Information

The park's main headquarters (☎ 822-5235) is at *Mile 105* of Richardson Hwy, 10 miles before the junction with the Glenn Hwy. The office is open from 8 am to 6 pm daily during the summer and rangers can answer questions about the park as well as supply various hand-outs and rough maps of the area. During the summer, rangers are stationed in a log-cabin visitor center in Chitina (☎ 823-2205), at the end of Edgerton Hwy. There is also a new Slana ranger station at the start of the road to Nebesna.

The Road to McCarthy

Edgerton Hwy and McCarthy Rd combine to provide a 92-mile route into the heart of Wrangell-St Elias National Park, ending at the foot bridge across the Kennicott River to McCarthy.

The 32-mile Edgerton Hwy, fully paved, begins at *Mile 82.6* of Richardson Hwy and ends at Chitina. The town, which has 40 or so permanent residents, is the last place to purchase gas and to get a reasonably priced meal (that's 'reasonably' priced by Alaskan standards). Backpackers can camp along the three-mile road south to O'Brien Creek or beside Town Lake within Chitina. The best spot to stop, however, is 10 miles before you reach Chitina at *Liberty Falls State Recreation Site*. The campground has only three, maybe four, sites for RVs but there are another half-dozen spots for tents, including

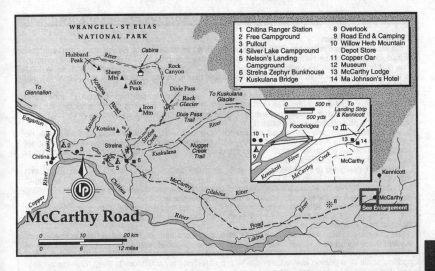

WRANGELL - ST ELIAS
NATIONAL PARK

Hubbard Peak
River
Cabins
Rock Canyon
Sheep Mtn
Alice Peak
Dixie Pass
To Glennallen
Iron Mtn
Rock Glacier
To Kuskulana Glacier
Edgarton
Highway
Kotsina
Kotsina
Kosina Road
Dixie Pass Trail
Strelna Creek
River
Chitina
Strelna
Kuskulana
Nugget Creek Trail
McCarthy
Gilahina River
River
McCarthy Road
Copper River
Chitina
River
Road
Lakina

1 Chitina Ranger Station
2 Free Campground
3 Pullout
4 Silver Lake Campground
5 Nelson's Landing Campground
6 Strelna Zephyr Bunkhouse
7 Kuskulana Bridge
8 Overlook
9 Road End & Camping
10 Willow Herb Mountain Depot Store
11 Copper Oar
12 Museum
13 McCarthy Lodge
14 Ma Johnson's Hotel

500 m
500 yds
To Landing Strip & Kennicott
Footbridges
10 11
9
13 14
12
Kennicott River
McCarthy Creek
McCarthy
Kennicott
McCarthy
See Enlargement

0   10   20 km
0   6   12 miles

four tent platforms right along rushing Liberty Creek. There is no piped-in water here but there is thundering Liberty Falls within the campground. Best of all the facility is free.

There is also a small campground with eight free sites next to the Copper River Bridge. It's maintained by the Alaska Department of Transportation and used primarily by dipnetters who descend on Chitina in July and August to scoop up reds and king salmon. Within Chitina there is a National Park Service ranger station, open from 9.30 am to 6 pm daily during the summer, and Spirit Mountain Artworks, a delightful gallery that also plugs flats for $8 a tire or patches them for $14. Art Koeninger loves his art but he undoubtedly makes a living repairing tires the McCarthy Rd chews up.

There is a grocery store, post office and two restaurants in town. Try *Chitina Cafe*, a good place to stop before the long drive out to McCarthy. The interior has – what else – miner's décor. Prices range from $5 to $10 for breakfast and $7 for a hamburger. Try the home-made biscuits and gravy for $5, guaranteed to keep you fueled until you've reached McCarthy.

From Chitina, McCarthy Rd – a rough dirt road that is not regularly maintained – follows the abandoned Copper River & Northwest Railroad bed that was used to transport copper from the mines to Cordova. It leads 60 miles or so further east to the Kennicott River. Your $40-a-day rental car can usually travel this stretch during the summer, but plan on three to four hours for the trip and if it's been raining hard don't plan it at all.

The road starts two miles west of Chitina and the first few miles offer spectacular views of the Chugach Mountains, the east-west range that separates the Chitina Valley lowlands for the Gulf of Alaska with peaks averaging 7000 to 8000 feet. You'll also cross the mighty Copper River where it is possible to see a dozen fish wheels or, if your timing is right, hordes of dipnetters. Just before *Mile 9* there is a pullout on the north side of the road that provides access to the half-mile trail to Strelna Lake. The lake is stocked with rainbow trout and silver salmon that anglers entice during the summer with salmon eggs.

Two commercial campgrounds with very limited services, gas not being one of them,

The McCarthy Tram

If the McCarthy Tram is still crossing the Kennicott River in 1997...use it. By the end of that year it is scheduled to be replaced with a foot bridge and when it is, a colorful bit of Alaskan history will be gone. The first bridge across the Kennicott was built by the Copper River & Northwestern Railway in 1911 to haul out the copper from the Kennecott Mines and that gave rise to McCarthy, a wild little railroad junction of saloons and bordellos.

The next bridge came in 1974 when the state built new bridges across the river's two channels and for a year you could actually drive to McCarthy. But high water partially destroyed the bridges the next spring, reducing them to rickety pedestrian crossings that were totally washed away in 1981. Two years later, a pair of trams were installed.

As a public utility, the trams had no agency responsible for them because McCarthy has no government. It's the Alaskan way of handling liability: nobody acknowledged it so nobody could get sued if a tourist fell off the open platform into the glacial waters below. Maintenance was spontaneous at best and usually done late at night.

Although designed to hold two passengers, as many as four or five locals, including two with mountain bikes, would jump on it to cross the river. It was cumbersome and slow due to it having to be pulled the 100 yards across the river by hand. During the summer 30 minutes was a normal waiting time and on the 4 July weekend, you could easily wait several hours.

But tourists loved it. After surviving the dusty drive in and crossing on the tram, you truly felt as if you had stepped back in time. Some residents also saw it as an effective way of preserving their isolated lifestyle in McCarthy.

By the early 1990s, when McCarthy was attracting more than 30,000 visitors a summer, it was evident the beloved tram would have to go. But a series of public hearings in 1995 over the type of crossing seriously divided the small town. Some wanted another tram, others a vehicle bridge, a few nothing at all. One person wanted a bridge with a gate that they could lock to keep 'Outsiders away' and this prompted a resident at the meeting to call out 'give the key (to the bridge) to someone in McCarthy and you'll have a gunfight'.

The state finally decided to build a modern, steel and girder foot bridge and construction began in the fall of 1996. When it is fully operational, in the late summer of 1997, the tram will be dismantled. In so doing, McCarthy will lose a little bit of its character but hopefully not its way of life. ■

JIM DUFRESNE

The McCarthy tram – one way of preserving an isolated lifestyle.

are quickly passed and then at *Mile 13.5* you come to the access road to the trailheads for the Dixie Pass, Nugget and Kotsina trails (see the Hiking section in the Wilderness chapter), across from the Strelna airstrip. For an interesting night or a different perspective on the National Park Service, head up the access road two miles and book a bed at the *Strelna Zephyr Bunkhouse*. Sandy Kasteler and her family run the quaint log cabin accommodations and inside you'll find four bunks, a wood-burning stove but no running water or electricity – they don't have it, why should you? Nearby is a log sauna. Bunks are $25 a night.

At *Mile 17* of McCarthy Rd is the Kuskulana River Bridge. This historic railroad bridge was built in 1910 with a 525-foot span across an impressive gorge that rises 238 feet above the river. From the time the road was opened to cars in the 1960s until the 1980s, this narrow, three-span railroad bridge was known as 'the biggest thrill on the road to McCarthy'. In 1988, however, the structure was completely upgraded by the state when they added guard rails and replanked it. Although it is no longer quite as thrilling, the view of the steep-sided canyon and rushing river from the middle of the bridge is mind-boggling, well worth the time to park at one end and walk back across it.

Two more bridges are crossed at *Mile 28.5* and *Mile 44* and at the first one you can still admire an impressive railroad trestle that was abandoned in the 1930s and left standing. At *Mile 57.3*, you come to an overlook on the south side of the road with a view of the town of McCarthy and glimpse of Kennicott Glacier through the forest of spruce and poplar.

To continue the final mile to McCarthy you have to leave the car behind and use the new foot bridge to cross the Kennicott River. Built in 1996, the bridge replaced the hand-pulled trams erected by the state when the original bridge was washed out in 1981. The trams, open platforms with two benches facing each other, were a classic way to enter McCarthy but as tourism began to boom they were viewed as neither very efficient nor even safe. On a busy Friday afternoon for instance, when you had waited an hour or two for a ride across the river, four or five people along with a mountain bike would be loaded on the tram. It was a crazy scene, that bit of Alaska most of us came looking for, and gave rise to the most popular saying in McCarthy: 'Everyday is Saturday once you cross over on the tram'.

McCarthy

With the exception of a lodge in Kennicott, all services are located in the mountainous hamlet of McCarthy, a scenic and funky little town. Its year-round population ranges from eight to 12 people depending on who is sticking out the winter but during the summer it swells to around 100. Once you've crossed the Kennicott River on the foot bridge, follow the road to the McCarthy River, which is also crossed on a foot bridge. On the other side the road leads half a mile to the **McCarthy & Kennicott Museum**, an old railroad depot that features old photographs and a few mining artefacts dating back to the mining days, along with a small coffee shop that serves giant muffins in the morning. From the museum take the right fork into the town of McCarthy (the left fork is the main road to Kennicott).

Kennicott was a company town, self-contained and serious. McCarthy, on the other hand, was created in the early 1900s for the miners as a place of 'wine, women and song'. In other words, it had several saloons, restaurants and a red light district. In its heyday the town had several hundred residents, its own newspaper and school. Today both O'Neill's Hardware Store and MotherLode Power House (the site of St Elias Alpine Guides) have been listed on the National Register of Historical Places.

Kennicott

In 1900, a pair of sourdough miners named Jack Smith and Clarence Warner stumbled up the east side of the Kennicott Glacier until they arrived at a creek and found traces of copper. They named the creek Bonanza and was it ever – the entire mountainside turned out to hold some of the richest copper deposits ever uncovered. In the Lower 48, mines were operating on ore that contained only 2% copper. Here the veins would average almost 13%, while some contained as much as 70%.

Eventually, a group of investors bought the existing stakes and formed the Kennecott Copper Corporation, named after a clerical worker misspelt 'Kennicott'. First the syndicate built its railroad, 196 miles of rails through the wilderness, including the leg that is now the McCarthy Rd and Cordova's famous 'Million Dollar Bridge'. The line cost $23 million before it even reached the mines in 1911.

Then the syndicate built the company town of Kennicott, a sprawling red-painted complex that included offices, the crushing mills, bunkhouses for the workers, company stores, a theater, wooden tennis courts and a school, all perched on a side of a mountain above the Kennicott Glacier. From 1911 until 1938 the mines operated 24 hours a day,

produced 591,000 tons of copper and reported a net profit of more than $100 million.

Then in November 1938, faced with falling world prices for copper, an uncertainty of how long the veins would play out and, most of all, a possible labor strike, the company managers decided to close the operation. They made the decision one night and then the next morning told the workers the mine was shut down and that they could stay or leave but that in two hours the last train out of Kennicott was leaving. The disgruntled miners left in what has to be one of the greatest exoduses from a town in the USA.

With the exception of two large diesel engines, everything was left behind and Kennicott was this perfectly preserved slice of US mining history. Unfortunately, when the railroad bed was converted to a road in the 1960s, Kennicott also became the biggest help-yourself hardware store in the country. Locals were taking windows, doors and wiring while tourists were picking the town clean of tools, spikes and anything they could haul away as a souvenir.

Despite the pillage, Kennicott is still an amazing sight for most travelers. The mill, where the ore was crushed and the copper

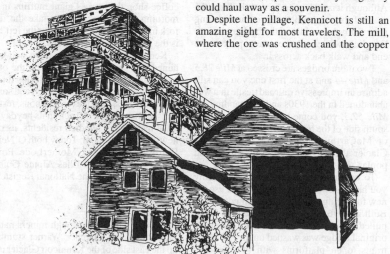

Mining ruins at Kennicott, abandoned in 1938

SOUTHCENTRAL

concentrated, towers above the surrounding buildings and still has tram cables leading up to the mountain mines. The rest of the buildings, including bunkhouses, train depot, worker's cottages and power plant, sit perched above the Kennicott Glacier surrounded by peaks.

Keep in mind that most, if not all, the buildings are privately owned and it is illegal to enter them. Eventually several of the larger ones, the mill and power plant among others, will probably be acquired and renovated by the NPS but that will take years. Until then, you have to be content with strolling through the center of town and admiring the mining history by peeping through the windows.

You can reach Kennicott from McCarthy by either walking the railroad grade, now the main road, or hiking up the Old Wagon Rd. The Wagon Rd is more of a trail for hiking or mountain bikes and is picked up from the main road at a junction marked with a 'To Glacier' sign. Either way it's a five-mile trek. Keep in mind there is also a van service in McCarthy and it's always possible to hitch a ride as during the summer there is a trickle of traffic between the two towns.

Hiking

Root Glacier From Kennicott, it's a 2.5-mile round trip past the mine ruins to Root Glacier, a sparkling white and blue floe of ice. Hike west of the town and continue west past an unmarked junction to the mines, reached in less than a quarter mile. Along the way you cross Jumbo Creek, where you will find a plank upstream for an easy ford in normal water conditions. Many people will climb the glacier upon reaching it but extreme caution should be used if you are inexperienced and lack the proper equipment (crampons, ice axe) for walking on ice.

Bonanza Mine Trail One of the best hikes from Kennicott is the alpine trek to Bonanza Mine. It's a round trip of almost seven miles to the mine and a steep uphill walk all the way. Plan on three to four hours to hike up if the weather is good, and half that time to get

back down. The trail is actually a rough dirt road to the tree line and is picked up just west of town at a junction that makes a sharp 180° turn up the mountain. Once above the tree line, a three-hour climb for most people, the view is stunning and you can clearly see the mountain valley where the mine still sits on the slope. To reach the mine you have to scramble up a scree slope to the remaining bunkhouse, shafts and tram platform.

There is water once you reach the top but carry at least a quart if the day is hot. For those who want to skip the long haul up but still enjoy the alpine portion of the hike, check at the Kennicott Lodge to see if anybody is driving hikers up. Normally a local will run you up to the tree line for $15 one way or $20 return. From there it's still a good 90-minute trek to the mine.

Rafting

Kennicott River Beginning near the glacier itself, rafting companies float the Kennicott River on half-day trips that features Class III whitewater. Copper Oar (☎ 522-1670 in Glennallen) maintains a small office on the west side of the river near the tram platform. The company offers a two-hour run down the Kennicott for $50 per person.

Nizina River For a full-day float, rafting companies combine the Kennicott with the Nizina and a portion of the Chitina River and then return you to McCarthy via a bush plane for a view of the mountains from above. The high point of the day is the run through the vertical-walled Nizina River Canyon. Both St Elias Alpine Guides in the MotherLode Power House and Copper Oar have a full-day three-rivers trip for $195.

Organized Tours

For a guided walk through Kennicott search out Chris Richards, the town's only legally registered voter. The year-round resident lives across the street from the Kennicott Glacier Lodge and has a call box along the street as Kennicott-McCarthy Wilderness Guides. He provides a colorful 1½-hour tour

SOUTHCENTRAL

of the mines for $12.50 per person as well as giving you an idea of what it's like to live in a one-person town in the winter (he reads a lot). The tour is well worth it.

St Elias Alpine Guides (☎ 277-6867 in Anchorage) located in the MotherLode Power House offers a variety of day trips out of McCarthy including a two-hour historical tour of the area for $25 per person. If you just want to wander through Kennicott on your own, stop at the McCarthy Museum and for $1 pick up a copy of its *Walking Tour of Kennicott*.

If the day is clear, splurge on a flightseeing tour of the surrounding mountains and glaciers. Both *McCarthy Air* and *Wrangell Mountain Air* offer a wide range of scenic flights, with a 30-minute flight beginning at around $40. But if you do fly, invest in an hour flight at $85 per person, giving you enough air time to fly around 16,930-foot Mt Blackburn and volcanic Mt Wrangell.

Places to Stay & Eat

The cheapest accommodation is camping along the west side of the Kennicott River. There are vault toilets and a $3 parking & camping fee but not piped-in water. On the weekends it can get crowded and dusty here.

It's hard to camp around either McCarthy or Kennicott due to private ownership of most of the land. Accommodation options in McCarthy change almost seasonally so it pays to walk around to see if anybody is renting out a cabin or has started up a B&B. For an affordable bunk, ask at the *McCarthy Country Store*.

Just down the street is the *McCarthy Lodge* (☎ 554-4402), full of mining relics and photographs of the era, and the place to get a bed, meal, shower or a cold beer in a frosty mug. The main lodge has a dining room where full dinners cost $17 to $22 and a lively bar with $4 beers. A lot for a beer maybe, but, hey, they're cold! Showers are $5 so skip the shower and have a beer. Across the street the lodge runs *Ma Johnson's Hotel*, built in 1916 as a boarding house and today totally renovated with rooms beginning at

$95/105 for a single/double, more if you want your meals included.

Next door to Ma Johnson's Hotel is *Tailor Made Pizza* where a pizza sets you back $14 and can be enjoyed with beer and wine. There's also *Nugget Gift Shop* with limited liquor, camping and food supplies.

In Kennicott, there is *Kennicott Glacier Lodge* (for reservations call ☎ (800) 582-5128 outside Alaska or (800) 478-2350 within the state) which offers beds, running water and electricity, but not a private bath, for $149/169 for a single/double. It also has a dining room and for $240 per couple you can get a bed, six meals and a guided walk of the mines. Even if you don't stay here, hike up in the morning and have breakfast on the long front porch. The meal is $11 but includes eggs, sourdough pancakes and sausage along with pitchers of juice and coffee, all enjoyed with a spectacular view of peaks and glaciers.

Getting There & Away

Air Several small air companies fly daily service between McCarthy and Glennallen. Ellis Air (☎ 822-3363 or (800) 478-3368 in Alaska) departs the Gulkana Airstrip at 9.45 am daily, arrives in McCarthy at 11 am and then turns around and heads back. The one-way fare is $62. Wrangell Mountain Air (☎ 345-1160 or 554-4440) also has service between McCarthy and Glennallen and even Chitina.

Bus Hitching McCarthy Rd is not nearly as challenging as it was 10 years ago but it still can be a wait at times. The alternative is Backcountry Connections (☎ 822-5292 or (800) 478-5292 in Alaska). The small tour company departs Caribou Motel on Glenn Hwy in Glennallen at 7 am on Monday through Saturday, reaching Chitina at 8.30 am and the McCarthy foot bridge at noon. After a five-hour layover, enough time to see McCarthy and ruins at Kennicott, the van backtracks to Glennallen, reaching the crossroads town at 9.15 pm. The round-trip fare for the same day is $70, though this is a lot of time to spend in a van. The round-trip fare on different days is $88 and one-way is $49.

Getting Around

Once you're in McCarthy, you can pick up a ride to Kennicott from either McCarthy Air or Wrangell Mountain Air which maintain log cabin offices in town. Both run vans up to the company town for $5 per person.

Mountain bikes clearly outnumber cars here as most locals and travelers use them as a means of getting around the area. In fact, those old mining roads and trails, which are tough on vehicles, are ideal for fat-tire bikes, turning McCarthy into something of a biker's paradise. If you have your own bike you can walk it across the foot bridge. If not, then St Elias Alpine Guides rents Diamond Back mountain bikes for $25 a day.

WHITTIER

On the day the military was cutting the ribbon that marked the completion of the Alcan, the army was also having a tunnel 'holing through' ceremony outside Whittier. WWII and the Japanese invasion of the Aleutian Islands brought the US military searching for a second warm-water port in Southcentral Alaska, one that would serve as a secret port. Whittier was chosen because it was well hidden between the high walls of the Passage Canal Fjord in which it lies, and for the consistently bad weather that hangs over it.

Work began immediately on two tunnels through the Chugach Mountains that would connect the port to the main line of the Alaska Railroad. The tunnels, though overshadowed by the Alcan, were another amazing feat of engineering. The first was drilled through almost a mile of solid rock, while the second, begun simultaneously from the other side of the mountain, required carving a route 2.5 miles long. When General Simon Buckner blasted open the second tunnel during the 'holing through' ceremony

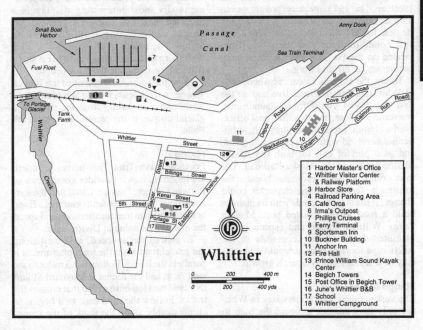

1	Harbor Master's Office
2	Whittier Visitor Center & Railway Platform
3	Harbor Store
4	Railroad Parking Area
5	Cafe Orca
6	Irma's Outpost
7	Phillips Cruises
8	Ferry Terminal
9	Sportsman Inn
10	Buckner Building
11	Anchor Inn
12	Fire Hall
13	Prince William Sound Kayak Center
14	Begich Towers
15	Post Office in Begich Tower
16	June's Whittier B&B
17	School
18	Whittier Campground

SOUTHCENTRAL

in 1942, the two tunnels missed perfect alignment by an eighth of an inch.

Whittier owes both its existence and its skyscraper appearance to the military. After WWII the port remained a permanent base due to the Cold War, and tall concrete buildings were constructed to house and serve the personnel. One building, the Begich Towers, is 14 stories tall. Nearby, the massive Buckner Building once housed 1000 people and had a bowling alley, a theater, cafes, a hospital, a pool and a jail. These skyscrapers look strange but their upward-pointing design greatly reduced the need for removal of snow which during some winters exceeds 14 feet.

The army declared the Whittier Post unnecessary in 1960 but maintained it until 1968, in part because of the extensive damage the town suffered from the Good Friday Earthquake. The quake caused more than $5 million in damage while 13 people died here and the harbor was destroyed by a tidal wave. Whittier was incorporated in 1969 and in 1973 the city bought seven military buildings and 97 acres for $200,000. Begich Towers was quickly converted into 198 condominiums and the city offices located on the 1st floor and the community businesses on the 2nd floor.

Today, the Begich Towers is where 60% of Whittier's 344 residents live and on the first two floors you'll find a laundromat, convenience store, beauty salon, post office, even a church. Since the military left, Whittier has survived with some fishing, tourism, and as a port of call for both the Alaska Marine Hwy and the Alaska Railroad. The town could receive an economic boost in the future, in fact its entire character could change, if the state proceeds with its plans to build a road to the isolated port. Making Prince William Sound, and especially the glaciated fjords, more accessible to the Anchorage tourism market would undoubtedly be a stimulus to Whittier's growth.

Things to See
The vast majority of travelers stay in Whittier only long enough to board the train to Anchorage or the ferry to Valdez. Although the town itself is nothing to brag about, even appearing dismal to many, the surrounding area is a scenic blend of mountains and glaciers and, on a rare clear day, an interesting spot to layover for the afternoon.

As soon as you disembark from the train you will spot the new **Whittier Visitor Center** (☎ 472-2379), housed in a rail car donated by the Alaska Railroad. It's part visitor center and part gift shop but the staff are friendly and will point you in the right direction. Due north is the **Small Boat Harbor** with fishing boats, private craft and the numerous tour vessels that work the Columbia Glacier route between Whittier and Valdez.

There is also a small museum in town on the 1st floor of the Begich Towers, down the hall from the post office. The **Whittier Historical Museum** is open from 1 to 5 pm Wednesday to Friday. It looks like a garage sale more than a museum and contains mostly historic photos and maritime specimens. Its most interesting display is a mounted wolf fish that a six-year-old girl caught while fishing in Prince William Sound. The mouth of this rare fish is filled with sharp teeth and molars used to eat shellfish and, on occasion, to attack people.

From the south-west corner of the Begich Towers, a track leads west to Whittier Creek, while above it, falling from the ridge of a glacial cirque, is the picturesque **Horsetail Falls**.

Hiking
Portage Pass Trail This makes a superb afternoon hike as it provides good views of Portage Glacier, Passage Canal and the surrounding mountains and glaciers. Even better, hike up in the late afternoon and spend the evening camping at Divide Lake.

To pick up the trailhead, walk west along the gravel road from the train platform as it parallels the tracks. Follow it 1.3 miles to the tank farm and the tunnel at Maynard Mountain, and turn left onto a road that crosses the tracks. Follow the right fork as it begins to climb steeply along the flank of the moun-

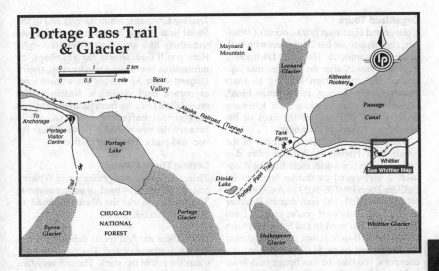

Portage Pass Trail & Glacier

To Anchorage

Portage Visitor Centre

Bear Valley

Maynard Mountain

Leonard Glacier

Kittiwake Rookery

Passage Canal

Alaska Railroad (Tunnel)

Tank Farm

Portage Lake

Divide Lake

Portage Pass Trail

Whittier

See Whittier Map

Trail

Byron Glacier

Portage Glacier

CHUGACH NATIONAL FOREST

Shakespeare Glacier

Whittier Glacier

0   1   2 km
0   0.5   1 mile

tain, until it goes through a small pond. Here you can climb a promontory (elevation 750 feet) for views of Portage Glacier or Passage Canal to the east.

Divide Lake is another half-mile southwest and by traveling left (south) around it you can head down the slope to the glacier. Plan on two hours to reach Divide Lake. The trip to the glacier and back to Whittier is an eight-mile hike.

Smitty's Cove From the front of the Sportsman Inn, Smitty's Cove lies a quarter of a mile down the road to the right (north-east). At low tide you can beachcomb all of the cove to the point east of it. Smitty's Cove is a favorite haunt of Alaska scuba divers and is occasionally referred to as Diver's Cove.

First Salmon Run This is a 0.8-mile walk along a dirt road to the First Salmon Run Picnic Area, so named because of the large king and silver salmon runs in the creek in June and late August.

From the north-east corner of the Buckner Building behind the Sportsman Inn, follow the road that leads up the mountain, staying

to the right at the first fork and to the left at the second fork.

The road leads into the picnic area, where you can cross a bridge over the stream and continue another three miles to Second Salmon Run. This walk, along what is known as Shotgun Cove Rd, is exceptionally scenic as you can see Billings Glacier most of the way.

Kayaking

Whittier is a prime location for sea kayakers as it is practically surrounded by glaciated fjords and inlets. Prince William Sound Kayak Center (☎ 562-2866 in Anchorage and 472-2452 in Whittier) operates out of Whittier during the summer and can outfit you with a rental kayak and gear. The center is not a shop here but rather is located in a fenced-in storage area just off Glacier St a block down from Begich Towers. It's best to make arrangements in advance at Anchorage as often the boats are rented during the summer. A single kayak is $40 a day, a double is $60. The company will also shuttle people out to Smitty's Cove or First Salmon Run for $5 per person.

Organized Tours

College and Harriman fjords, north of Whittier, contain not one but 26 glaciers with such academic names as Harvard, Dartmouth, Yale and Vassar, after the colleges that supported the expedition leading to their discovery. On the way to Harriman Fjord, cruise ships pass so close to a kittiwake rookery that you can see the eggs of the black-legged birds in their nests.

Various tour boats which sail out of the Small Boat Harbor in Whittier offer day cruises to this icy world, including the *Klondike*, a high-speed catamaran operated by Phillips Tours (☎ 276-8023 in Anchorage or (800) 544-0529). The boat departs Whittier at 11.15 am daily so if you're coming from Anchorage you need to catch the 10.15 am train. The 110-mile return trip lasts almost six hours and costs $119 per person; it's cheaper if you take the tour before mid-June.

Major Marine Tours offers a six-hour tour to the glaciers at the head of Blackstone Bay south of Whittier on board the 100-foot *Emerald Sea*. This boat, which includes a full bar, also departs daily during the summer at 11.15 pm. The difference between the two tours is Blackstone Bay is cheaper – only $99 per person – but visits fewer glaciers.

Places to Stay & Eat

There are two hotels in Whittier: the *Anchor Inn* (☎ 472-2354) and the *Sportsman Inn* (☎ 472-2352). Both sell groceries and have a dining room, public laundry, bar and rates of $65 for a single/double. The Anchor Inn appears to be not so run down. You can also book a bed in the Begich Towers through *June's Whittier Bed & Breakfast* (☎ 472-2396) which maintains three condos on the 5th, 8th and 15th floors. Rates begin at $75 for a single/double but jump to $90 if your room overlooks the bay and mountains.

Whittier Public Campground is primarily a gravel surface for RVers behind the Begich Towers but you can also set up a tent for $5 per night. Or you can pitch a tent just about anywhere near town by walking into the bush and away from the road.

For hamburgers, there is the *Hobo Bay Trading Company*, while the east end of the Small Boat Harbor has been developed into something of a strip mall – Whittier style. Here you'll find, among the gift shops, an information booth and a reindeer pen, *Irma's Outpost* where $7 will get you a hamburger or corned beef sandwich. Nearby is the quaint *Cafe Orca* for fresh pastries and a cup of gourmet coffee or espresso, while between the two places is *Tsunami Cafe* for beer and pizza. Take your choice.

Getting There & Away

There are two ways of getting out of Whittier and neither one is by road, or not yet anyhow. To go west you take the Alaska Railroad; to head east you take a boat.

Train There are four trains departing Whittier on Wednesday and Thursday, and six trains the rest of the week. The one-way fare from Whittier to Portage is $13. Once in Portage you can take a shuttle bus to Anchorage. Alaska Backpackers Shuttle (☎ (907) 344-8775 or (800) 266-8625) meets all trains and charges a one-way fare of $17.50. Alaskon Express also swings by Portage, charging $29 for the trip. If arriving by ferry, you need to catch the 6.15 pm train if you want to continue on to Anchorage that day. That's a three-hour layover in Whittier and for most people more than enough time for this town.

Boat The ferry MV *Bartlett* goes east six times a week at 2.45 pm from the ferry dock. On Monday the boat sails to Cordova, all other departures go to Valdez and cruise near the impressive Columbia Glacier. The one-way fare from Whittier to either Valdez or Cordova is $58.

Kenai Peninsula

Because of its diverse terrain, easy accessibility and close proximity to Anchorage, the Kenai Peninsula has become the state's top recreational area. It is well serviced, well

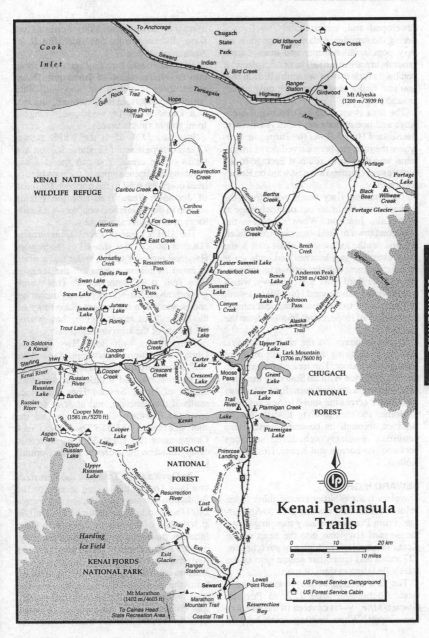

Kenai Peninsula Trails

SOUTHCENTRAL

developed and, unfortunately, well used during the summer. Although some trails are very popular all summer and many campgrounds are always filled to near capacity, if you hike a little further or climb a little higher you can find a tent space with only nature around you.

The area is serviced by two major highways and one minor one. From Anchorage, the Seward Hwy follows the Turnagain Arm where the road has been carved out of mountains, and then turns south at Portage to the picturesque community of Seward on Resurrection Bay.

The Sterling Hwy heads west from the Seward Hwy 90 miles out of Anchorage at Tern Lake Junction. When it reaches the crossroad town of Soldotna, near Cook Inlet, it turns south, follows the coast past some great clam-digging beaches and ends up at Homer, the most delightful town on the peninsula. The third road is Hope Hwy, which heads north from Seward Hwy, 70 miles out of Anchorage, to the small historical mining community of Hope, about 16 miles from the junction.

Traffic is heavy on the main highways, making hitchhiking an easy form of travel during the summer. The area is connected to the rest of Prince William Sound by the ferry MV *Tustumena* which runs from Cordova and Valdez across the sound to Seward, over to Homer and then south to Kodiak. Alaska Airlines, through its contract carrier, also provides regularly scheduled services between Anchorage and Kenai, Homer and Kodiak.

SEWARD HIGHWAY

Travelers from Whittier should think twice before immediately rushing back to Anchorage. From Portage it's easy traveling down the Seward Hwy and into the heart of the Kenai Peninsula. The highway stretches for 127 miles and is another scenic gem in the state's fledgling system of roads.

The first section of the Seward Hwy – from Anchorage, *Mile 127*, to Portage Glacier, *Mile 79* – is covered in the Anchorage chapter. When heading south keep in mind that the mileposts along Seward Hwy show distances from Seward, *Mile 0*, to Anchorage, *Mile 127*.

Near *Mile 68* the highway begins climbing into the alpine region of **Turnagain Pass**, where there is a roadside stop with litter barrels and toilets. In early summer, this area is a kaleidoscope of wildflowers ranging from purple violets to reds.

Just past *Mile 65* is the USFS *Bertha Creek Campground* (12 sites, $6) on the banks of the creek. You can spend a day climbing the alpine slopes of the pass here or head down the road to the northern trailhead of **Johnson Pass Trail** (see the Hiking section in the Wilderness chapter), a 23-mile route over another alpine pass.

The USFS *Granite Creek Campground* (18 sites, $6 fee) is at *Mile 63* of the Seward Hwy and provides tables, water and a place to camp for hikers coming off the Johnson Pass Trail at its northern end. This campground, about halfway between Anchorage and Seward, is a convenient place to spend the evening but recent logging has marred the beauty of the surrounding area.

The junction with Hope Hwy (see the Hope Hwy section in this chapter) is at *Mile 56.7*. From here the paved Hope Hwy heads 18 miles north, and a mile past the small hamlet of Hope. Seward Hwy continues south of this junction, and at *Mile 46* you cross the Colorado Creek Bridge and the short side road to the USFS *Tenderfoot Creek Campground* (28 sites, $6 fee), a scenic campground on the shores of Upper Summit Lake.

The **Devil's Pass Trail** (see the Resurrection Pass Trail in the Hiking section of the Wilderness chapter), a 10-mile hike over a 2400-foot gap to Resurrection Pass Trail, is at *Mile 39.4* of the Seward Hwy. Tern Lake Junction, the beginning of the Sterling Hwy, is at *Mile 37* and makes for an ideal place to stop and stretch the legs. Located at the junction is a USFS wildlife viewing area and from the platform that extends into the marshy north end of the lake you can usually spot common loons, bald eagles or arctic terns. In the lake look for beavers and river otters, while often feeding on the slopes of the surrounding mountains are dall sheep and mountain goats. For more wildlife head half a mile west from the junction to the USFS *Tern Lake Campground* (33 sites, $6 fee), where there is a salmon viewing platform on Dave's Creek. Occasionally brown and black bears come to the creek to feed on spawning salmon.

At *Mile 33* of the Seward Hwy is the **Carter Lake Trail**, a 2.3-mile trail that provides quick (but steep) access into subalpine terrain. The path, an old jeep trail, starts from a parking area on the west side of the highway and ascends steeply almost 1000 feet to Carter Lake.

From the lake, a trail continues another mile around the west side of the lake to Crescent Lake. There is good camping at the end of Carter Lake.

At *Mile 29.4* the Seward Hwy passes through the village of **Moose Pass** (pop 200) on the banks of the Upper Trail Lake. This small town has its roots in the Hope-Sunrise Gold Rush of the late 1800s but really came into its own when the original Iditarod Trail was cut around the lake in 1910-11. The abundance of moose in the area caused an early mail carrier to call the valley Moose Pass and the name stuck when the first post office opened in 1928.

Moose Pass has a general store & bar, post office, a handful of B&Bs and *Trail Lake Lodge* (☎ 288-3103). The lodge features a restaurant, 35 rooms that begin at $60 for single or double with a shared bath, showers, laundromat and a salmon bake on the shores of the lake during the summer. Just down the road is *Moose Pass RV Park* with sites that overlook the lake for $10 a night.

The best time to visit the area is during the Moose Pass Summer Festival on the weekend nearest the summer solstice on 21 June. This delightful little festival is spread over two days and includes a halibut barbecue, games for the kids, arts and crafts booths and a beer tent.

At *Mile 24* of the Seward Hwy is an obscure dirt road that leads west to the USFS *Trail River Campground* (63 sites, $6 fee), featuring many camp sites among the tall spruce along Kenai Lake and the Lower Trail River. Ptarmigan Creek Bridge is at *Mile 23* of the Seward Hwy. Right before it on the east side of the highway is the entrance to the USFS *Ptarmigan Creek Campground* (26 sites, $6 fee).

The 3.5-mile **Ptarmigan Creek Trail** begins in the campground and ends at Ptarmigan Lake, a beautiful body of water that reflects the mountains surrounding it. A four-mile trail continues around the north side of the lake, which offers good fishing for Dolly Varden at its outlet to the creek. Plan on five hours for a return hike to the lake, as some parts of the trail are steep. The **Victor Creek Trail**, at *Mile 19.7* on the east side of the highway, is the trailhead for a fairly difficult path that ascends three miles to good views of the surrounding mountains.

After crossing the bridge over South Fork Snow River at *Mile 17.2*, look west for the road that leads a mile to the USFS *Primrose Landing Campground* (10 sites, $6). This scenic campground is on the east end of the beautiful Kenai Lake and contains the trailhead to the Primrose Trail (see the Lost Lake Trail in the Seward Hiking section).

The **Grayling Lake Trail**, a two-mile hike to Grayling Lake, has side trails that connect it to Meridian and Leech lakes, a beautiful spot with good views of Snow River Valley. All three lakes have good fishing for grayling. The trailhead is in a paved parking lot at *Mile 13.2* on the west side of the Seward Hwy.

SEWARD

Seward (pop 3000) is a scenic town flanked by rugged mountains on one side and the salmon-filled Resurrection Bay on the other. It's the only town on the eastern side of the Kenai Peninsula and probably the only city of its size in Alaska without one of the fast-food chain restaurants. For that reason alone, you've got to love Seward.

History

The town was founded in 1903 when Alaska Railroad surveyors needed an ice-free port to

SOUTHCENTRAL

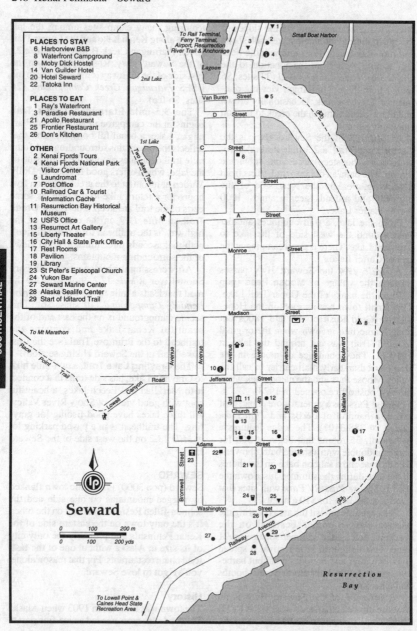

PLACES TO STAY
6 Harborview B&B
8 Waterfront Campground
9 Moby Dick Hostel
14 Van Guilder Hotel
20 Hotel Seward
22 Tatoka Inn

PLACES TO EAT
1 Ray's Waterfront
3 Paradise Restaurant
21 Apollo Restaurant
25 Frontier Restaurant
26 Don's Kitchen

OTHER
2 Kenai Fjords Tours
4 Kenai Fjords National Park
 Visitor Center
5 Laundromat
7 Post Office
10 Railroad Car & Tourist
 Information Cache
11 Resurrection Bay Historical
 Museum
12 USFS Office
13 Resurrect Art Gallery
15 Liberty Theater
16 City Hall & State Park Office
17 Rest Rooms
18 Pavilion
19 Library
23 St Peter's Episcopal Church
24 Yukon Bar
27 Seward Marine Center
28 Alaska Sealife Center
29 Start of Iditarod Trail

Seward

SOUTHCENTRAL

serve as the ocean terminal for the rail line. The first spike was driven in during 1904 and the line was completed in 1923. During that time Seward prospered as it served as the beginning of the Iditarod Trail to Nome and thousands of prospectors stampeded their way through town. Dog teams were used to haul supplies and mail along this 1200-mile route and return with the gold. In 1910, one of the largest shipments of Nome gold arrived when miner Bob Griffis mushed his dogs into Seward with his own armed guards. Griffis' gold bags would have been worth more than $6 million today.

Like most towns in Southcentral Alaska, Seward began a new era of history in 1964 after the Good Friday Earthquake (or Black Friday as Alaskans call it) caused fires and tidal waves that destroyed 90% of the town. At one point, a 3500-foot stretch of waterfront slid into the bay and Seward was completely cut off from the rest of the state.

The only reminder of the natural disaster is at the public library on the corner of 5th Ave and Adams St across from City Hall, where the slide show covering the earthquake, *Seward is Burning*, is shown from Monday to Saturday at 2 pm.

The town has completely rebuilt its fine Small Boat Harbor and waterfront facilities with a $10-million dock designed to be earthquake proof. Most of the area's residents either work at Seward Fisheries (the largest halibut-receiving station on the US west coast), fish, or are connected with the town's growing maritime industry.

Information

Tourist Offices If downtown, head over to the Seward Railroad Car on the corner of 3rd Ave and Jefferson St. Built as a dining car by Pullman Company in 1916, today it houses the Chamber of Commerce Information Cache where you can pick up maps, information or a guide with a walking tour of the city. Inside the car, you'll still find the original lunch counter and stools where you can sit back and enjoy a 25-cent cup of coffee. The center is open daily in the summer from 11 am to 5 pm.

If driving in, stop at the year-round visitor center in the Chamber office (☎ 224-8051) at *Mile 2* of the Seward Hwy. The center has racks of information, brochures on most of the B&Bs in the area and courtesy phones to book rooms or tours. During the summer the office is open from 8 am to 6 pm daily.

The Kenai Fjords National Park Visitor Center (☎ 224-3175) in the Small Boat Harbor has information on the nearby park and is open daily during the summer from 8 am to 7 pm. For information on Chugach National Forest trails, cabins and campgrounds, go to the USFS Ranger Station (☎ 224-3374) on the corner of 4th Ave and Jefferson St. The USFS office is open Monday to Friday from 8 am to 5 pm.

Money National Bank of Alaska (☎ 224-5283) is at the corner of 3rd and D streets.

Post The post office is open on the corner of 5th Ave and Madison St.

Bookshops Northland Books & Charts (☎ 224-3102), in the Orca Building at 201 3rd Ave, has Alaskan titles as well as USGS topographic maps.

Library The Seward Library (☎ 224-3646) is on the corner of 5th Ave and Adams St and often sponsors a used-book sale during the summer. Hours are noon to 8 pm Monday to Friday and until 6 pm on Saturday.

Laundry The closest place to Waterfront Campground is Seward Laundry on the corner of 4th Ave and B St near the Small Boat Harbor. Showers are $3.50.

Medical Services Seward General Hospital (☎ 224-5205) is on 1st Ave at the west end of Madison St. Family Medical Clinic of Seward (☎ 224-8911) is in the Seaview Plaza at 302 Railway Ave.

Walking Tour

From the Seward Railroad Car on 3rd Ave, the houses on the left are known as **Millionaires Row** and are the first stop on the local walking tours. They were built around 1905 by railroad officials and bankers who had just arrived in the newly created town. Nearby on the corner of Jefferson St and 3rd Ave is the **Resurrection Bay Historical Museum**, open daily from 11 am to 5 pm. The museum features artefacts and photographs of the 1964 earthquake, including a clock that stopped the instant the disaster struck. There are also exhibits on the Russian era in Resurrection Bay when a shipyard was established in 1793, and Seward's role in the Iditarod Trail. The admission charge is $1.

Head west to 1st Ave and follow it south to Lowell Canyon Rd to see the start of the trail to Mt Marathon (see the following Hiking section). Continue south to Adams St and then go east, where on the corner of 2nd Ave is **St Peter's Episcopal Church**. Built in 1906, the church contains the famous mural of the Resurrection by Dutch artist Jan van Emple who used Alaskan models and the nearby bay as the backdrop.

South-east on the corner of 3rd and Railway avenues is the **Seward Marine Education Center**, operated by the University of Alaska-Fairbanks. The center has aquariums featuring live Alaskan marine specimens as well as interesting displays and films on the sea life so important to the state. If you haven't witnessed a whale yet, you'll get a good idea of how large they are as a skull of a minke whale fills the middle of the room. Hours are from 10 am to 4 pm Tuesday through Sunday during the summer. Admission is by donation.

Proposed Alaska SeaLife Center

A more impressive display of marine wildlife will be at the Alaska SeaLife Center (☎ 224-3080) when it opens in 1998 in what used to be the ferry terminal at the foot of 4th Ave. The $49.5 million facility, funded in part by money from the *Exxon Valdez* oilspill settlement, will be both a research station for the rehabilitation of fish, marine mammals and sea birds and an interpretive area for visitors. The center will feature a bayside park with an artificial rookery in which marine mammals and sea birds will be viewed from several vantage points including underwater windows. Inside will be displays and hands-on exhibits that examine tidal pools, kelp forests and, of course, the effect the infamous oil spill had on wildlife in Resurrection Bay.

Small Boat Harbor

Not included on the walking tour but equally interesting is the Small Boat Harbor at the northern end of 4th Ave. The place hums during the summer with fishing boats, charter vessels and a large number of sailboats. It has also developed into a separate business district for Seward, especially as far as restaurants are concerned. The heart of the district is the Harbor Master's Office outside which, displayed in a square, is a pair of huge sea anchors and an equally impressive pile of chain. Nearby is the **Kenai Fjords National Park Visitor Center**. The center has both a bookshop and a few displays on the park. Most impressive is the oil-spill video it shows in a small theater. At the back there are picnic tables and a free sighting scope overlooking the harbor and the bay – it's a nice place to enjoy lunch.

Hiking

Race Point Trail The most popular trail near the town center is the trek towards the top of Mt Marathon, the mountain that sits behind the city. The route is well known throughout Alaska. In 1909, two sourdough miners wagered how long it would take to run to the top and back and then dashed off for the peak.

After that, it became an official event at the Seward 4 July celebrations and today attracts hundreds of runners with an equal number of spectators who line the streets to watch them race. The fastest time is 43 minutes and 23 seconds, set in 1981. Most runners come down the mountain in less than 10 minutes, usually by sliding halfway on their behinds.

Hikers, on the other hand, can take their time and enjoy the spectacular views of Seward and Resurrection Bay. The trail begins at the west end of Jefferson St (also known as Lowell Canyon Rd) up the Lowell Canyon. The trailhead is marked and is in a small gravel pit just past a pair of water tanks.

Scramble up the ridge to the right of the gully, and for fun return through the gully's scree. You never really reach Mt Marathon's summit, though you do reach a high point (known as Race Point) at 3022 feet on the broad east shoulder. Plan on three to four hours for the three-mile round trip.

Iditarod National Historic Trail Although most of the world knows the Iditarod as a sled-dog race from Anchorage to Nome, the legendary trail actually begins in Seward. There is a historical marker in Hoben Park at the foot of 4th Ave to mark *Mile 0* and from there a paved bike path heads north along the beach.

A far more interesting segment for hikers, however, is reached by heading east on Nash Rd just after the Seward Hwy crosses the Resurrection River. Within two miles you'll cross Sawmill Creek and arrive at a gravel parking lot on the north side of the road. From here you can follow the Iditarod Trail through the woods for the four-mile hike to Bear Lake.

Two Lakes Trail This easy one-mile loop goes through a wooded area, crosses a salmon-spawning creek and passes two small lakes at the base of Mt Marathon. Begin the hike near the first lake behind the Alaska Vocational & Training Center on the corner of 2nd Ave and B St and then use Hemlock St to loop back after you reach the second lake. Near the start of the trail is a scenic waterfall.

Resurrection River Trail This 16-mile trail, built in 1984, is the last link in a 70-mile system across the Kenai Peninsula from Seward to Hope. This continuous trail is broken only by the Sterling Hwy and provides the best long-term wilderness adventure on the peninsula, leading hikers through a diversity of streams, rivers, lakes, wooded lowlands and alpine areas.

The southern trailhead for the Resurrec-tion River Trail is eight miles up the Exit Glacier Rd which leaves the Seward Hwy at *Mile 3.7*. The northern trailhead joins the Russian Lakes Trail (see the Hiking section in the Wilderness chapter), five miles from Cooper Lake or 16 miles from the Russian River Campground off Sterling Hwy. The hike from Seward Hwy to Sterling Hwy is a 40-mile trip, including walking up Exit Glacier Rd.

There are two USFS cabins (reservations, $25 per night) along the trail; the *Resurrection River USFS Cabin* is 6.5 miles from the southern trailhead and the *Fox Creek USFS Cabin* is another 1.5 miles beyond it. Check with the USFS office in Seward about avail-ability of the cabins and the best places to camp along the trail, as good sites are scarce.

Lost Lake Trail This seven-mile trail to the alpine lake is one of the most scenic hikes the Kenai Peninsula has to offer in midsum-mer. The trailhead is in Lost Lake Subdivision, a quarter mile from *Mile 5.3* of Seward Hwy. At three miles you come to the summer trail that winds 1.5 miles south to Clemens Memorial Cabin (reservations, $25 per night, see Places to Stay). The final two miles of Lost Lake Trail are above the tree line, making the lake itself a glorious place to spend a night.

An alternative to returning is to continue around the east side of Lost Lake to the Primrose Trail, another USFS-maintained route. This eight-mile trail leads through alpine country and ends at *Primrose Camp-ground* at *Mile 17.2* of Seward Hwy. Plan on seven to 10 hours for the return trip to Lost Lake and bring a camp stove because there is no wood near the lake.

Caines Head State Recreation Area This 6000-acre preserve, 5.5 miles south of Seward on Resurrection Bay, contains mili-tary ruins, a 650-foot headlands and the Coastal Trail (see the Hiking section of the Wilderness Chapter). Even if you're not up for an overnight backpacking trip, the hike to Tonsina Point is an easy roundtrip of only three miles. At the point you can view the salmon spawning up Tonsina Creek if it's July or early August.

Kayaking

Kayaks can be rented from Adventure & Delights Eco Tours (☎ (800) 288-3134) at Lowell Point for $30/55 a day for singles/ doubles. The company also offers guided day trips which include morning kayaking instructions and then a paddle that departs and returns from Lowell Point three miles south of town. The cost is $95 per person. It also has an overnight tour from Seward for $395 and a three-day tour for $575.

Special Events

Seward holds two events each summer that have become popular with Alaskans throughout the Southcentral. The 4 July celebration is a big event in Seward, highlighted by the annual Mt Marathon Race, which draws runners from around the state. The city's most famous event, however, is the Silver Salmon Derby on the second Saturday of August.

Places to Stay

At the height of the summer season a last-minute room is hard to secure in Seward, which adds 9% tax to all room rates.

Wilderness Cabins Around Seward there are a handful of remote cabins, administered and maintained by a handful of agencies: the state Parks and Outdoor Recreation Division, the USFS and the National Park Service. Three of them can be reached on foot, saving the budget-minded trekker an expensive air-charter trip, but will not be nearly as secluded as the others.

Clemens Memorial ($25, reservations) is a six-bunk cabin that can be reached on foot with a 4.5-mile trek up the Lost Lake Trail (see the previous Hiking section) and is located at the tree line, providing spectacular views of Resurrection Peaks, Mt Ascension and Resurrection Bay.

Derby Cove is a state cabin located just off the tidal trail between Tonsina Point and North Beach in Caines Head State Recrea-

tion Area. From the trailhead at Lowell Point to the cabin is a four-mile trek that must be done during low tide. You could also rent kayaks (see Kayaking earlier) and paddle out to it. The cabin is actually situated on the backside of a marsh on Derby Cove away from the beach for a bit of privacy and the rate is $35 a night. Check its availability by calling the state Public Information Center (☎ 269-8400) in Anchorage or the Kenai Area Parks Office (☎ 262-5581) at Morgan's Landing. There is no longer a state park office in Seward.

In 1992, Kenai Fjords National Park built a series of wilderness cabins, which are reached either by air charter or kayak. The closest to Seward is *Aialik Bay* which is situated near one of the few beaches that you can hike in this portion of the bay. At low tide you can beachcomb for more than a mile to explore tidal pools or sight whales feeding in the area. The cabin is $30 a night and must be rented through Alaska Public Lands Information Center (☎ 271-2737) in Anchorage, not the National Park Service Visitor Center in Seward.

Located across the bay is *Holgate Arm Cabin*, which features a spectacular view of Holgate Glacier through its windows. This unit is also $30 and must be reserved through the Alaska Public Lands Information Center (☎ 271-2737) in Anchorage.

There are two USFS cabins on the Resurrection River Trail. For details see the Hiking section.

Camping Seward is one of the few towns in Alaska that has an excellent and affordable campground right in the heart of its downtown area.

The *Waterfront Campground*, managed by the city's Parks and Recreation Department (☎ 224-3331), is along Ballaine Blvd, overlooking the bay. Most of it is open gravel parking for RVers, but you'll also find a grassy tent area that even has a few trees and shrubs. There is a day-use area with grills, picnic tables and small shelters while running through the campground is a paved bike path. In 1996, the city even began adding full hook-ups for RVers. Best of all is the price: $6 a night for tents, $8 for RVers to park and $15 for full hook-up.

Forest Acres Campground is two miles north of town on the west side of Seward Hwy in a wooded area that tends to be a little buggy at times. It's $6 to pitch a tent and there is a 14-day limit. Further out of town still, but free, is the 12-site *Exit Glacier Campground*, a National Park Service facility for tents only, nine miles out at the end of Exit Glacier Rd.

Hostels *Snow River Hostel* always gets high marks from travelers but it's near Primrose State Campground 16 miles north of town on the Seward Hwy. The home hostel has 14 beds, a kitchen, laundry facilities, a storage area but no phone. The rate is $12 a night.

A bunkroom closer to town is at *Kate's Roadhouse* (☎ 224-3081) at *Mile 5.5* of the Seward Hwy. The roadhouse has seven beds for $17 a night as well as rooms and a cabin for rent. Within town is *Moby Dick Hostel* (☎ 224-7072) on 3rd Ave between Madison and Jefferson streets, which has 18 bunks for $15 a night.

B&Bs Downtown there is *Seward Waterfront Lodging* (☎ 224-5563) while *Harborview B&B* (☎ 224-3217) is on the corner of 3rd Ave and C St. Harborview is more of an inn than a B&B as all eight rooms have private entrances, full baths and color TV. The nightly rate for two is $85 and includes breakfast which is brought up to your room.

For most of the B&Bs you have to head up the Seward Hwy. Three miles north of town on Salmon Creek Rd is *The Farm B&B* (☎ 224-5691) which has a wide variety of accommodation. Rooms in the remodeled farmhouse range from $65 to $85 a night for two people. But there are also sleeping cottages for $75 a night complete with decks, and the House Boatel that sleeps four people for $40 a night. At the beginning of Exit Glacier Rd are several inns and B&Bs, including *Creekside Cabins* (☎ 224-3834) which has four cabins that overlook Clear Creek and range in price from $55 to $80 per

night. The resort also features a sauna, bathhouse and two secluded tent sites for $15 a night for two people.

Also off Exit Glacier Rd is *Le Barn Appetit* (☎ 224-8706), which is a B&B that also features Seward's only health food store. This funky lodge features several rooms (one with a king-size bed and mountain view is called the Passion Pit) and a genuine tree house with running water and private bath. Rates range from $60 to $90 for double occupancy.

Further out still is *Alaska's Treehouse* (☎ 224-3867) located in a wooded area at *Mile 7* of the Seward Hwy via Timber St and Forest Rd. Nightly rates are $70 to $95 for the B&B that features a sauna, espressos and lattes in the morning, and great views of Hearth Mountain and Mt Alice.

Hotels None of the hotels in town are cheap. Your best bet for a motel in the Small Boat Harbor area is *Breeze Inn* (☎ 224-5237) with singles/doubles at $95/105. *Murphy's Motel* (☎ 224-8090) nearby has singles/doubles for $75/85 a night, and the *Marina Motel* (☎ 224-5518) just up the highway also offers clean rooms in the same range but neither are as nice as Breeze Inn.

Downtown there is *Taroka Inn* (☎ 224-8687), a former officer's quarters during WWII, on the corner of 3rd Ave and Adams St. The nine rooms begin at $85 for a double but include kitchenettes.

The *Van Guilder Hotel* (☎ 224-3525), at 307 Adams St, was built in 1916 and placed on the National Register of Historical Places in 1980. Restored to its original Edwardian charm, the hotel has a few 'pension rooms' for $60 a night while double rooms with private bath start at $75. The nicest place in town is *Hotel Seward* (☎ 224-2378) on 5th Ave but singles and doubles are $168/178 and that's for a room without a view.

Places to Eat

Downtown *Don's Kitchen* at 405 Washington St is open 24 hours and probably has the cheapest fare; breakfasts begin at $4.35 and the Yukon Scrambler for $5.65 will keep you

SOUTHCENTRAL

going until late in the afternoon. It also has a half-pound halibut dinner for $11. Another local cafe with road food is the nearby *Main Street Cafe* on the corner of 4th Ave and Washington St.

For something nicer try the *Frontier* across Washington St from Don's, where you can enjoy a view of the bay from any table. Dinners begin at $13 but head over for a late lunch of seafood saute – halibut, scallops and shrimp sauted in white wine and herbs for $10. The *Harbor Dinner Club* is another upscale restaurant across 5th Ave from Hotel Seward, with a menu almost entirely of seafood and usually an 'inflation-fighter' special for under $10. If it has fresh halibut cheeks as an appetizer, skip dinner and just order these with a few beers.

Want Chinese? The *Peking Chinese Restaurant* is on the corner of 4th Ave and Jefferson St and is open until 10 pm daily. Dinners for two, which include egg rolls, two to four main dishes and fried rice, are $9.50 to $17 per person. Lunch specials are $6. If it's Greek or Italian you're craving, *Apollo* on 4th Ave has both with pasta dinners beginning at $8 and a gyro plate priced at $10. It also serves Alaskan seafood and pizza.

Small Boat Harbor This is home for Seward's cheap eats. Near the National Park Visitor Center is *Paradise Restaurant* for 'Chinese fast food'. It's fast and not that bad and best of all it's filling. Dinners run from about $7. *The Depot*, near the small shelter where the train drops you off, has sandwiches and hamburgers that begin at $5 and a pleasant solarium area overlooking the harbor.

Finally, there's *Ray's Waterfront* overlooking the boat harbor for excellent seafood including local salmon, halibut or pan-seared scallops. Try its cioppino, a spicy seafood stew served over linguini. It's one of Seward's nicer restaurants with dinners ranging from $16 to $21.

For something a little healthier than milkshakes and fried food, try *Le Barn Appetit* just off Exit Glacier Rd on Resurrection Rd past the first bridge. Seward's only health food store is also a restaurant and bakery offering deli sandwiches, crêpes, fresh-baked bread, quiche and other good things to eat. The vegetarian cuisine is about $7 for dinner.

Entertainment
Feel like pinning a few dollars to the ceiling? Head over to the *Yukon Bar* on the corner of 4th Ave and Washington St – Seward's most lively bar. You can order from a list of 20 imported beers or try a Yukon ice tea. From Wednesday to Saturday it somehow packs a band in and offers live music. Just down the street is the competition, *Tony's Bar*, which has live music on Friday and Saturday but not as much character.

If you don't like either one of these places there's another half-dozen bars on 4th Ave or the more upscale *Seward Saloon* on 5th Ave. For local color head up the Seward Hwy to *The Pit Bar* just pass Exit Glacier Rd. This place can get rolling on the weekend with pool, darts and shuffleboard inside and ping-pong and horseshoes outside. If you have a cast-iron stomach, have the bartender snare one of Chet's smoked pickeled eggs from the big jar behind the bar.

On the opposite end of the spectrum from The Pit Bar is *Resurrect Art Gallery and Coffee House* downtown on 3rd Ave. Located in an old church, the coffee house offers an interesting gallery of Native Alaskan art, block prints and pottery as well as a menu of espresso drinks, Italian sodas, teas and light snacks. At night there are often local musicians or story tellers or you can simply take your latte to the loft where there are stacks of books and board games.

Liberty Theater (☎ 224-5418), a great little movie theater on Adams St next door to the Van Gilder Hotel, shows movies nightly. The Seward Museum also has evening slide programs on Monday, Wednesday and Friday at 7 pm on either the history of Seward or the Iditarod Trail. Admission is $2.

Getting There & Away
Bus Seward Bus Lines (☎ 224-3608) provides a daily service to Anchorage during the

summer, with a bus departing from a small depot at 1915 Seward Hwy at 9 am. The bus departs Anchorage at 2.30 pm for the return trip to Seward; the one-way fare is $30.

Train From May to September, the Alaska Railroad provides passenger services to Seward with a daily run to Anchorage. Trains leave Seward at 6 pm daily for a spectacular route that includes glaciers, steep gorges and rugged mountain scenery. Even when departing that late you can still view the scenery thanks to those long Alaskan days. The one-way fare is $50. There's no depot in Seward so call the Anchorage terminal (☎ (800) 544-0552) for more information.

Boat In 1995 the ferry terminal (☎ 224-5485) was moved from the downtown waterfront to the Alaska Railroad Dock north of the Small Boat Harbor. From Seward Hwy, head east on Port Ave and follow the signs to the office. Ferries arrive in Seward twice a week, on Thursday and Friday, from Kodiak or Valdez and depart for the same communities before continuing on to other Southcentral ports. The fare to Valdez is $58, to Kodiak $54 and to Homer $96. The trip to Valdez includes passing the Columbia Glacier. The boat to Kodiak Island passes the Stellar sea lions on the Chiswell Islands near the mouth of Resurrection Bay.

Getting Around

Trolley To get around town, the Seward Trolley has a service that extends from the ferry terminal south to the downtown area for $1.50 per ride or $3 for a day pass. It runs from 10 am to 7 pm and stops at the library, museum, Harbor Master's Office and campgrounds.

KENAI FJORDS NATIONAL PARK

Seward serves as the departure point for most trips into the Kenai Fjords National Park, which was created in 1980 and thrust into the news during the Exxon oil spill. The park covers 587,000 acres and consists mainly of the Harding Icefield, the rugged coastline

where tidewater glaciers calve into the sea, and the offshore islands.

With its abundance of marine wildlife and glaciers, Kenai Fjords is a major tourist attraction, but unfortunately not an inexpensive one. That's why easy-to-reach Exit Glacier is its main attraction, drawing more than 100,000 visitors each summer.

For the adventurous, there is Harding Icefield. One of the largest icefields in North America, it remained undiscovered until the early 1900s when a map-making team realized several coastal glaciers belonged to the same massive system. The icefield is 50 miles long and 30 miles wide and in some places 200 inches deep. Eight glaciers reach the sea from it, while Exit Glacier is a remnant of a larger one that once extended into Resurrection Bay.

Hikers can reach the icefield's edge, via the Harding Icefield Trail, but only experienced mountaineers, equipped with skis, ice axes and crampons, can explore the 300 sq miles of ice. The many deep fjords and rich marine life also make the park a bluewater kayaker's dream, though you have to either paddle the sections exposed to the Gulf of Alaska to reach it or pay for a drop-off.

To the vast majority of visitors, however, the national park is either a quick trip to Exit Glacier or a splurge on a tour boat cruise to the coastal glaciers that cost up to $130 each.

Information

The Kenai Fjords National Park Visitor Center (☎ 224-3175), on 4th Ave overlooking Seward's Small Boat Harbor, is open daily from 8 am to 7 pm. There is also a ranger station at Exit Glacier, which is open daily during the summer from 10 am to 5 pm.

Exit Glacier

The three-mile-long Exit Glacier is fast becoming a frozen tourist attraction, ranking right up there with Portage Glacier and Juneau's Mendenhall. It picked up its name when explorers, crossing the Harding Icefield, found the glacier a suitable way to 'exit' the ice and mountains. It's believed that at one time the glacier extended all the way to Seward and today it is still active, only now it's retreating into the mountains.

You reach the ice on Exit Glacier Rd which leaves the Seward Hwy at *Mile 3.7* at a posted junction. The road first parallels the heavily braided Resurrection River, providing access to some unofficial but great camping spots on the surrounding gravel bars. Within seven miles you pass the trailhead to the Resurrection River Trail (see the Seward Hiking section) and then cross over the river on a bridge that was built only in 1985. At this point the view of the glacier fills your windshield and dominates the scenery for the remaining two miles.

At the end of the road there's a ranger station with a few displays and books for sale as well as the answers to any questions you might have. A ranger-led nature walk departs the station daily at 10 am and 2 pm for a short hike around the glacier. Every Saturday at 8 am there is a ranger-led trek up to the Harding Icefield that lasts a good part of the day.

A paved, wheelchair-accessible trail leads a quarter mile to the overlook of the glacier and information shelter. To continue further you have to take to the trails with the vast majority of people hiking the Lower Loop Trail so they can have their picture taken in front of the bluish ice.

Getting There & Away If you need transportation to Exit Glacier, call Seward Shuttle Service (☎ 362-3074), which offers tours daily during the summer at 9 am, 1 and 5 pm. The three-hour guided tours includes hiking the trails around the glacier and a little gold panning in the Resurrection River. The cost is $8 per person.

Hiking

Nature Trail A half-mile nature trail departs from the ranger station and winds through cottonwood forest, alder thickets and along old glacial moraines before emerging at the information shelter. It's a great way to return from the glacier if you're not up to facing the mass of humanity on the paved trail.

Exit Glacier Trails A network of loops provides close access to the ice itself from the information center. The Lower Loop Trail is an easy half-mile walk to the outwash plain in front of the ice. All around there's warning signs telling you to stay away from the face due to the danger of falling ice. Despite the signs, people are so determined to touch the ice or have their picture taken next to it, the park often posts a ranger out there to keep them away.

The Upper Loop Trail departs the first loop and climbs steeply to an overlook at the side of the glacier before returning. Both trails make for a hike not much more than a mile in length and sections may be closed at times due to falling ice. Don't skip the short spur to Falls Overlook, a scenic cascade off the upper trail.

Harding Icefield Trail Besides the nature trail from the ranger station to Exit Glacier, the only other developed hike in the glacier area is the trek to Harding Icefield. The hike to the icefield is a difficult ascent which follows a steep, roughly cut and sometimes slippery route on the north side of Exit Glacier, beginning at its base. It's a five-mile, one-way hike to the icefield at 3500 feet and for reasonably fit trekkers a good four-hour hike/climb.

The all-day trek is well worth it for those with the stamina, as it provides spectacular views of not only the icefield but of Exit Glacier and the valley below. The upper section of the route is snow covered for much of the year. You pick up the trailhead at the beginning of the Lower Loop Trail.

Kayaking

Bluewater paddles out of Resurrection Bay along the coastline of the park are challenges for experienced kayakers or involve a costly drop-off, pick-up fee but reward you with almost daily wildlife encounters and close-up views of the glaciers from a unique perspective. Adventures & Delights Eco Tours (☎ (800) 288-3134) rents out rigid kayaks from Lowell Point in Seward;

Top: McCarthy General Store, McCarthy (RS)
Bottom: Bonanza Mine, Wrangell-St Elias National Park (DS)

Top left: Kennicott ghost town, Wrangell-St Elias National Park (DS)
Top right: The picturesque Exit Glacier, near Seward (JD)
Bottom: Small boat harbor, Seward (DS)

singles/doubles are $30/55 a day and include skirts, paddles, lifejacket and storage bags.

The company books drop-off service for Fox Island Charters for those who want to skip the open water of the Gulf of Alaska. It's $200 to $230 for the round trip to Aialik Bay, depending how far up the bay you are dropped off, and $250 into the more remote Northwestern Lagoon.

Aialik Bay This is the more popular arm for kayakers to paddle. Many people are transported by the tour boats to near Aialik Glacier then take three or four days to paddle south past Pedersen Glacier and into Holgate Arm, where they are picked up. The highpoint of the trip is Holgate Glacier, an active tidewater one. Keep in mind, however, the glacier is also the main feature of all the boat tours.

Northwestern Lagoon This fjord is more expensive to reach but much more remote with not nearly as many tour boats entering it. The wildlife is excellent, especially the sea birds and sea otters, and there are more than a half-dozen glaciers that can be seen, including three tidewater ones. Plan on three to four days if you are being dropped inside the lagoon.

Boat Tours
For most visitors the best way to see the rugged fjords, glaciers and wildlife is on a tour boat. In the past few years, Kenai Fjords cruises have become Seward's main attraction and they all maintain a booth or office in the Small Boat Harbor, right next to the Harbor Master's Office. It always pays to shop around before booking but keep in mind there are Kenai Fjords tours and wildlife tours. The wildlife tours are just cruises inside Resurrection Bay that never get close to the glaciers and most of the wildlife is sea birds. If you want to view the national park, you're going to have to pay around $100.

Kenai Fjords Tours (☎ 224-8068 or (800) 478-8068 within Alaska) runs a six-hour tour of the park with boats departing at 8 and 11.30 am and 3 pm daily, and an eight-hour

trip along the same route at 10 am. The fare is $99 per person and tickets may be purchased at its office on the boardwalk in Seward's Small Boat Harbor. Likewise Mariah Charters & Tours (☎ 224-8623) has a nine-hour trip that departs at 8 am for $90, or there is Major Marine Tours (☎ 224-8030 or (800) 764-7300) for $99 with a departure at 10.30 am. All of these companies offer cruises to Aialik Bay, past several glaciers including Holgate and, if the sea gods are smiling on you that day, pass a variety of marine life including sea otters, a sea lion colony and even humpback or minke whales.

All three companies also offer a four-hour wildlife tour inside Resurrection Bay that includes swinging past Bear Glacier for around $50. Renown Charters (☎ 224-3806 or (800) 655-3806) does the run in 2.5 hours with departures at 8.30 and 11.30 am, and 2.30 and 5.30 pm.

Finally, Mariah and Kenai Fjords Tours offer a 10-hour tour into impressive Northwestern Lagoon. Mariah makes the run at 8 am and, if there is demand, at 10 am, charging $105. Kenai Fjords Tours departs at 9 am and charges $129 but throws in a deli lunch and beverages.

HOPE HIGHWAY
This paved road leads almost 18 miles north to the historical community of Hope and the northern trailhead for the Resurrection Pass Trail. Hope experienced a minor stampede in 1896 when news of a gold strike brought over 3000 prospectors to the cluster of cabins and to nearby Sunrise, a tent city. Within a few years the majority had left to look for gold elsewhere and today Hope is a small village with a summer population of 225. Nothing remains of Sunrise.

Even if you are not planning to hike the Resurrection Pass Trail, Hope is a great side trip; the town is tucked away in a very scenic area and lets you step back in time. Hitchhiking is not hard, but plan on at least two days for this trip rather than a rushed overnight stop.

At *Mile 16* of the Hope Hwy is the junction to Palmer Creek and Resurrection Creek roads. Turn left (south) onto Resurrection Creek Rd and in 0.7 miles Palmer Creek Rd branches to the left. Near the junction is the unattended Hope airstrip. Four miles down Resurrection Creek Rd is the northern trailhead of the Resurrection Pass Trail.

Palmer Creek Rd is a scenic drive that leads seven miles to the *Coeur d'Alene Campground*, a former USFS campground that has five rustic sites that are free. Beyond the campground, the road is not maintained but leads another five miles to alpine country above 1500 feet and ends at the ruins of the abandoned Swetmann mining camp. From the old mining buildings it is easy to scramble through the tundra to several small alpine lakes.

Hope

To reach the town of Hope, turn right on Hope Rd at *Mile 16.5* of Hope Hwy. Hope Rd first leads past the post office where across the street is the **Hope-Sunrise Mining Museum**, which was built in 1993. Then it winds past the many log cabins and some abandoned log structures that have become favorites among photographers. You end up near the waterfront at what is best described as 'downtown Hope'. Here you'll find a gift and mining shop, the Hope Social Hall and Seaview Cafe, all quaint buildings in a scenic setting.

Places to Stay & Eat Camp sites abound all around Hope but the USFS maintains the *Porcupine Campground* (24 sites, $6 fee), 1.3 miles beyond Hope at the end of Hope Hwy. The campground features the usual well spread out sites, a scenic overlook to watch the tide roll in and two trailheads to Hope Point and Gull Rock. Beware, the place is often filled on weekends and sometimes even in the middle of the week. Near the campground is *Davidson Enterprises*, a general store that sells groceries, gasoline and liquor.

Hope has a general store, laundromat and a couple of lodges and cafes. Near the junction to Resurrection Creek Rd on Hope Hwy, there is *Henry's One Stop* (☎ 782-3222)

where you can get a meal, a beer, a shower or even a room with a private bath for $50 a night for a single or a double. Next door is *Bear Creek Lodge* (☎ 782-3141), a scenic resort in the woods with a small restaurant, a scattering of cabins and even a replica of an old log cache. It's $75 a night for the five restored, hand-hewn log cabins along the creek.

The best meal in Hope is at *Discovery Cafe* at the intersection of Hope Hwy and Hope Rd. This is 'where the goldminers meet and eat' according to the cafe's proprietor, who serves large grilled cheese sandwiches and a heaping plate of french fries for under $4. You can also order a beer to wash it down or stop by for the weekday all-you-can-eat dinner specials.

Gold Panning

There are about 125 mining claims throughout the Chugach National Forest but most of today's prospectors are recreational miners out there for the fun, searching their pans or

Panning for a Fortune

When panning for gold the only piece of equipment that is absolutely necessary is a gravity-trap pan, one that measures 10 to 20 inches in diameter and can usually be bought at any good Alaskan hardware or general store. Those who have panned for a while also show up with rubber boots and gloves to protect feet and hands from icy waters, a garden trowel to dig up loose rock, a pair of tweezers to pick up gold flakes and a small bottle to hold their find.

Panning techniques are based on the notion that gold is heavier than the gravel it lies in. Fill your pan with loose material from cracks and crevices in streams or around large boulders where gold might have washed down and become lodged. Add water to the pan and rinse and discard larger rocks, keeping the rinsing in the pan. Continue to shake the contents towards the bottom by swirling the pan in a circular motion and wash off the excess sand and gravel by dipping the front into the stream.

You should be left with heavy black mud, sand and, if you are lucky, a few flakes of gold. Use tweezers or your fingernails to transfer the flakes into a bottle filled with water. ■

sluice box for a little color. Some of the more serious ones actually make money from their time spent along the creeks, but most are happy to take home a bottle with a few flakes of gold in it.

The Hope area provides numerous opportunities for the amateur panner, including a 20-acre claim that the USFS has set aside near the Resurrection Pass trailhead for recreational mining. There are usually some regulars out there who don't mind showing newcomers how to swirl the pan. Other panning areas include Sixmile Creek between *Mile 1.5* and *Mile 5.5* of the Hope Hwy, and many of the creeks along the Resurrection Pass Trail.

Hiking

Gull Rock Trail From Porcupine Campground there are two fine trails to scenic points overlooking the Turnagain Arm. The first is an easy 5.1-mile walk to Gull Rock, a rocky point 140 feet above the Turnagain shoreline. The trail follows an old wagon road built at the turn of the century, and along the way there are the remains of a cabin and a sawmill to explore. You also get an occasional view of the Turnagain Arm and even Mt McKinley on a clear day. The round trip to Gull Rock takes from four to six hours.

Hope Point This is not a trail but more of a route that follows an alpine ridge for incredible views of Turnagain Arm. Begin at the entrance sign to Porcupine Campground and follow an unmarked trail along the right-hand side of the small Porcupine Creek. After 0.3 miles, the trail leaves the side of the creek and begins to ascend a bluff to the right, reaching an outcrop with good views of Turnagain Arm in 45 minutes or so. From here you can follow the ridge above the tree line to Hope Point, elevation 3708 feet. Other than an early summer snowfield, there is no water after Porcupine Creek.

STERLING HIGHWAY TO KENAI NATIONAL WILDLIFE REFUGE

It is only 58 miles from Tern Lake Junction to Soldotna along the Sterling Hwy, not much more than an hour's drive. Yet the stretch contains so many hiking, camping and canoeing opportunities that it would take you a month to enjoy them all. Surrounded by the Chugach National Forest and Kenai National Wildlife Refuge, Sterling Hwy and its side roads pass a dozen trails, 20 campgrounds and an almost endless number of lakes, rivers and streams in which to fish or paddle.

More than anywhere else, this is Alaska's favorite playground. Despite all the campgrounds and facilities, the summer crowds that descend onto the area in July and August (both Alaskans and tourists) are crushing at times. Be prepared, if you're traveling by car at this time of year, to stop at a handful of campgrounds before finding an available site.

Mileposts along the highway show distances from Seward, making Tern Lake Junction, at *Mile 37*, the start of the Sterling Hwy. The first accommodation along the highway, eight miles west of Tern Lake, is the *Sunrise Inn* (☎ 595-1222) at *Mile 45*. The log lodge features a cafe and bar while next door is a 10-room motel where a single or double is $69. The inn also has a couple of rooms with a shared bath that are $50 a night for a single or a double. The first campgrounds are just past the Sunrise Inn down Quartz Creek Rd. Follow the road south 0.3 miles to the USFS *Quartz Creek Campground* (31 sites, $7 fee) on the shores of Kenai Lake or three miles to the USFS *Crescent Creek Campground* (9 sites, $7 fee).

The **Crescent Creek Trail**, about half a mile beyond the Crescent Creek Campground, has a marked trailhead and leads 6.5 miles to the outlet of Crescent Lake and a *USFS cabin* (reservations, $25 a night). The trail is an easy walk and is beautiful in September with the colors of fall; from the cabin there is access to the high country. Anglers can fish for arctic grayling in the lake during the summer. At the east end of the lake is the Carter Lake Trail to Seward Hwy with a rough path along the south side of the lake connecting the two trails.

Another half-mile west on Sterling Hwy

SOUTHCENTRAL

is a large lookout and observation point for dall sheep in the Kenai Mountains and mountain goats in the Cecil Rhode Mountains directly across Kenai Lake. Displays explain the life cycle of the animals. The Kenai River Bridge is at *Mile 47.8* and immediately after it is Snug Harbor Rd, which leads south 12 miles to Cooper Lake and the eastern trailhead to the Russian Lakes Trail (see the Hiking section in the Wilderness chapter).

Cooper Landing

After skirting the north end of Kenai Lake you enter scenic Cooper Landing (pop 400) at *Mile 48.4*. This service center was named after Joseph Cooper, a miner who worked the area in the 1880s. A school was built here in 1929 and the first post office was established in 1937, a year before the town was connected by road to Seward.

There is now a five-building national historic district that includes the post office and a handful of homesteader's cabins. It is situated right on the banks of the river and with the towering mountains overhead makes for a very photogenic stop.

Cooper Landing is best known, however, for red-salmon fishing in the Russian River and as the starting point for raft trips down the Kenai River. A number of companies run the trip, including Alaska Wildland Adventures (☎ (800) 478-4100) and the Alaska River Co (☎ 595-1226). Expect to pay around $40 for a three-hour, half-day trip or about $90 for a full day, which includes some Class III whitewater in the Kenai Canyon.

Even if you have no intention of baiting a hook, you can still enjoy the salmon runs on the Russian River. Head to the Russian River Campground at *Mile 52* of the Sterling Hwy and park at the Pink Salmon or Grayling day-use parking areas. From here steep stairs lead down to the river, where you can see sockeye spawn either in early June or during a second run in mid-July.

Places to Stay

Campgrounds At *Mile 50.7* of the Sterling Hwy is the USFS *Cooper Creek Campground* (27 sites, $6 fee) where there are camp sites on both sides of the highway. Several of those on the north side of the highway are scenically located on the Kenai River.

The final USFS campground before you enter the Kenai National Wildlife Refuge is at *Mile 52.6*, a half mile past Gwin's Lodge. The *Russian River Campground* (84 sites, $10) is a beautiful spot where the Russian and Kenai rivers merge and the most popular one by far. Both the Cooper Creek and Russian River campgrounds lie in prime red-salmon spawning areas and the camp sites tend to fill up by noon in late summer. The Russian River Campground is so popular that it charges $4 just to park and fish.

A mile down Russian River Campground Rd is the trailhead and parking area for the Russian Lakes Trail, while a quarter of a mile west of the campground on Sterling Hwy is the well-marked entrance to the Resurrection Pass Trail (see the Hiking section in the Wilderness chapter).

Lodges & Motels *Gwin's Lodge* (☎ 595-1266) at *Mile 52* of the Sterling Hwy is the classic Alaskan roadhouse. The log lodge was built in 1952 and features a cafe, bar and liquor store while next to it is the old Russian River ferry, preserved like a monument to the red salmon run that draws hundreds of anglers to the Russian River from June through July. The lodge also has log cabins at $89/94 for a single/double at peak season, and a fisher's cabin where a bunk is only $15 a night.

Closer to Cooper Landing is *Red Salmon Guest House* (☎ 276-3418), a delightful little resort where rooms are $79/99 for single/double and private cabins are $129. Every bed includes breakfast in a dining room overlooking the Kenai River. Both here and at Gwin's Lodge, guided fishing can be arranged for either spin or fly fishers. Most guides charge between $80 and $100 for a half-day trip on the river but will provide the drift boat, gear and lunch.

Other accommodation includes the lavish *Kenai Princess Lodge* (☎ (800) 426-0500), a Princess Cruises Hotel that charges $175 for a double, while at the other end of the spectrum is *Kaleidoscope* (☎ 595-1281), a bizarre B&B and art gallery on the shores of the Kenai Lake that charges between $70 and $90 for a double.

KENAI NATIONAL WILDLIFE REFUGE

Once west of the Resurrection Pass trailhead, you leave Chugach National Forest, administered by the USFS, and enter the Kenai National Wildlife Refuge, managed by the US Fish & Wildlife Service. The impressive populations of dall sheep, moose, caribou and bear found here have attracted hunters from around the world since the early 1900s. In 1941, President Roosevelt set aside 1.73 million acres as the Kenai National Moose Range and the 1980 Alaska Lands Act increased it to almost two million acres.

Along with an abundance of wildlife, good fishing and great mountain scenery, the refuge offers some of the least-used trails on the Kenai Peninsula. Hikers who want to spend a few days trekking here should first go to the Kenai National Wildlife Refuge Visitor Station at *Mile 58* of Sterling Hwy or the visitor center in Kenai for information on all the trails or an update on their condition.

The first campground in the refuge is *Kenai-Russian River Recreational Area* (180 sites, $6) at *Mile 55* of Sterling Hwy. West of the confluence of these two salmon-rich rivers, this campground is heavily used from mid to late summer by anglers and the fee applies whether you want to camp or just park.

A privately owned, 28-passenger ferry carries anglers to the opposite bank of the Kenai River here for $3, using cables and the current to propel it across the river in both directions. During the height of the salmon season a couple of hundred anglers will be lined up at 5 am to catch the first trip across the river.

The three-mile **Fuller Lakes Trail** begins at *Mile 57* of the Sterling Hwy and ends at Fuller Lake just above the tree line. The trail, an old road blocked by logs, is well marked along the highway and begins as a rapid climb. Halfway up the trail you reach Lower Fuller Lake, where you cross a stream over a beaver dam and continue over a low pass to Upper Fuller Lake. At the lake, the trail follows the east shore and then branches; the fork to the left leads up a ridge and becomes the **Skyline Trail**. This trail is not maintained and is unmarked above the bush line. It follows a ridge for 6.5 miles and descends to *Mile 61* of Sterling Hwy. Those who want to hike both trails should plan to stay overnight at Upper Fuller Lake, where there are several good camp sites.

Just past the Fuller Lakes trailhead on Sterling Hwy is the **Skilak Lake Loop Rd** junction at *Mile 58* and the **Kenai National Wildlife Refuge Visitor Station**. The log cabin is open daily from 10 am to 7 pm and is the source of hand-outs, maps and brochures on the refuge. The 19-mile loop road, a scenic side trip to an already scenic highway, is a popular and often crowded recreational avenue. There are six USFS campgrounds along the road. Some, like Hidden Lake and Upper Skilak, are $10 a night for RVers and $6 for a tent, while others are free. All these campgrounds are well marked and, from east to west, are:

Campground	No of Sites	Location
Jim's Landing	5	near the junction
Hidden Lake	44	Mile 3.6
Upper Skilak Lake	25	Mile 8.4
Lower Ohmer Lake	3	Mile 8.6
Engineer Lake	4	Mile 9.7
Lower Skilak Lake	14	Mile 14

The **Kenai River Trail**, 0.6 miles past the visitor station on the Skilak Lake Loop Rd, winds 5.1 miles to Skilak Lake and then turns into the **Hidden Creek Loop**. The 1.4-mile loop trail curves back to its beginning at *Mile 4.6* of Skilak Lake Loop Rd. Both trails are easy walks along level terrain.

The **Skilak Lookout Trail** begins at *Mile 5.5* of Skilak Lake Rd and ascends 2.6 miles to a knob at 1450 feet that offers a panoramic view of the surrounding mountains and lakes. Plan on four to five hours for the round trip and bring water as there is none on the trail.

The **Seven Lakes Trail**, a 4.4-mile hike to the Sterling Hwy, begins at *Mile 9.7* of Skilak Lake Loop Rd, at the spur to Engineer Lake. The trail is easy walking over level terrain and passes Hidden and Hikers lakes before ending at *Kelly Lake Campground* on a side road off Sterling Hwy. There is fair to good fishing in Kelly and Engineer lakes.

If you choose to stay on the Sterling Hwy past the Skilak Lake Rd junction, you pass the small *Jean Lake Campground* (three sites, free) at *Mile 60* and a side road at *Mile 69* that leads south to the *Peterson Lake Campground* (three sites, free) and *Kelly Lake Campground* (three sites, free) near one end of the Seven Lakes Trail. *Watson Lake Campground* (three sites, free) is at *Mile 71.3* and in another four miles down the highway is the west junction with Skilak Lake Rd.

At *Mile 81*, Sterling Hwy divides into a four-lane road and you arrive in the small town of **Sterling** (pop 1800), where the Moose River empties into the Kenai. Sterling meets the usual travelers' needs with restaurants, lodges, gas stations and grocery stores.

Beyond the town is the *Izaak Walton Recreation Site* (25 sites, $10 fee) at the confluence of the Kenai and Moose rivers. A display explains the nearby archaeological site where excavations suggest that the area was used by Inuit people 2000 years ago. The state recreational area is heavily used all summer, as anglers swarm here for the salmon runs, while paddlers end their Swan Lake canoe trip at the Moose River Bridge. Canoe rentals and transport are available at the bridge for the Swan Lake and Swanson River canoe trails (see the Paddling section in the Wilderness chapter).

At *Mile 85* of the Sterling Hwy, Swanson River Rd turns north for 18 miles, with Swan Lake Rd heading east for three miles at the end of it. The roads are accesses to the Swanson River and Swan Lake canoe routes and three campgrounds: *Dolly Varden Lake Campground* (12 sites, free) 14 miles up Swanson River Rd; the *Rainbow Lake Campground* (three sites, free) another two miles beyond; and the *Swanson River Campground* (four sites, free) at the very end of the

road. Even without a canoe, this is a good area to spend a day or two as there are trails to many of the lakes which offer superb fishing.

Across Sterling Hwy from Swanson River Rd is the entrance to Scout Lake Loop Rd, where the *Scout Lake Campground* (14 sites, $8) and *Morgans Landing State Recreation Area* (40 sites, $10) are located. Morgans Landing, a 3.5-mile drive from Sterling Hwy is a particularly scenic area as it sits on a bluff overlooking the Kenai River with the Kenai Mountains on the horizon. The Alaska Division of Parks and Outdoor Recreation Office (☎ 262-5581) for the Kenai Peninsula is located at the campground and has handouts, displays and information on both Kachemak Bay State Park to the south and Caines Head State Recreation Area in Seward. Hours are 8 am to 5 pm Monday through Friday.

KENAI

You have to leave the Sterling Hwy at *Mile 94.2* and head north on Kenai Spur Rd to reach Kenai (pop 6700). For that reason many people bypass it and instead stop in Soldotna, little more than a commercial crossroads without the scenic appeal or history of Kenai.

While Kenai does not have the charm of Seward or Homer, it offers good views of the active volcanoes across the inlet along with a little Russian history. The town itself is at the mouth of the Kenai River on Cook Inlet, where you can view Mt Redoubt (the volcano that erupted steam and ash in December 1989) to the south-west, Mt Iliamna at the head of the Aleutian Range and the Alaska Range to the north-west.

History

Kenai is the second-oldest permanent settlement in Alaska and the largest city on the peninsula. It was established by Russian fur traders, who arrived in 1791 with 300 settlers and set up camp near a Dena'ina Indian village of Skitok. The next most important year in Kenai's history is probably 1957 when Alaska's first oil discovery was made

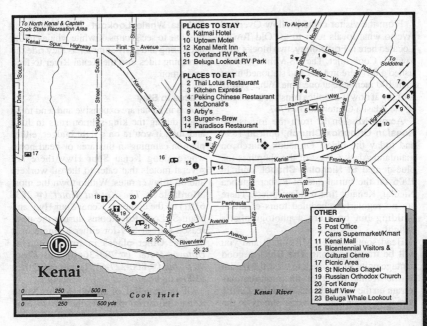

at Swanson River. Today the North Kenai industrial district around *Mile 19* of the Kenai Spur Rd is the largest concentration of oil industry infrastructure outside of Prudhoe Bay while across the inlet are 15 oil platforms, pumping out 42,000 barrels a day.

Information

Tourist Office The impressive Kenai Bicentennial Visitors Center (☎ 283-1991) was built in 1991 to mark the city's 200th anniversary. The center, on the corner of Main St and Kenai Spur Hwy, has racks of brochures on most of the B&Bs in the area and is open daily during the summer.

Money Bank of America (☎ 283-3369) is inside the Carrs Supermarket on Kenai Spur Hwy.

Post The post office is on Caviar St just north of Kenai Spur Hwy.

Library The library is on Main Street Loop, near Willow St, and is open Monday through Saturday.

Laundry Beluga Lookout RV Park, at Mission St and Main St, has showers and laundry facilities.

Medical Services See Soldotna's Medical Services section.

Things to See & Do

Inside the Bicentennial Visitor Center is the **Kenai Cultural Center**, featuring historical exhibits on the city's Russian heritage, wildlife displays and an audio-visual room with daily showings of videos on the state. The wildlife room should not be missed as it includes dozens of mounts, including 13 eagles, wolverines, brown bears and a beluga whale. The center and museum are open daily during the summer. Admission is free.

From the visitor center, follow Overland Ave to what locals refer to as 'Old Town'. Located here is **Fort Kenay**, two blocks west towards Cook Inlet. The US Military established a fort here in 1867 and stationed more than 100 men here at one time. What you're looking at now is a replica constructed as part of the Alaska Centennial in 1967.

Across Mission St from the fort is the **Russian Orthodox Church**, built in 1896 and today the oldest Orthodox church on mainland Alaska. West of the church is the blue-domed **St Nicholas Chapel**, built in 1906 on the burial site of Father Igumen Nicolai, Kenai's first resident priest. There are no regularly scheduled tours of either building but both are a photographer's delight.

Head south-east on Mission St and you will be traveling along **The Bluff**, a good vantage point from which to view the mouth of the Kenai River or the mountainous terrain on the west side of Cook Inlet. On the corner of Main and Mission streets is the **Beluga Whale Lookout**. From here it is possible to see groups of white whales in the late spring and early summer as they ride the incoming tides into the Kenai River to feed on salmon.

Places to Stay

Hotels in Kenai are expensive and tend to be filled during the king-salmon runs in June and July. If you're on a tight budget, either plan on camping in this area or head north where along Kenai Spur Hwy there are several motels that cater to the oil workers and offer lower rates. Within town the most affordable is *The Katmai Hotel* (☎ 283-6101) on the corner of Kenai Spur Hwy and Main St Loop Rd. Rooms during the peak season start at $79 for either a single or a double. Other places in town, such as *Uptown Motel* (☎ 283-3660) and *Kenai Merit Inn* (☎ 800-227-6131), are more than $100 a night.

Of the handful of motels in the North Kenai industrial district, the *North Star*

Canaries of the Sea

Of all the whales that inhabit Alaskan waters, the beluga is one of the most intriguing and certainly easiest to spot due to its unusual white color. The word beluga is actually Russian for sturgeon while Belukha was what the early Russians named the white whale they encountered in Alaskan waters. The animals have also been referred to as 'canaries of the sea' because of their noisy chatter.

Belugas are small, toothed whales with adults averaging 15 to 16 feet in length and reaching sexual maturity in four to five years. The beluga has no dorsal fin and this allows it to move easily under free ice. It's not unusual in the winter to see belugas sleeping under clear, newly formed ice.

The whale prefers the cold waters of the Bering Sea but is also found as far south as Cook Inlet and Yakutat Bay in Alaska and the Gulf of St Lawrence on the east coast of Canada. Belugas have also been spotted swimming 1240 miles up the Amur River in Asia, 600 miles inland in the Yukon River and in Lake Iliamna on the Alaska Peninsula.

There are three good spots to see the belugas in the Kenai Peninsula from June through September when the whales follow salmon runs during incoming tides. The best is at Beluga Whale Lookout near the corner of Main and Mission streets in the city of Kenai. Here on the edge of the bluff you have a view of the mouth of the Kenai River, where the white whales will be clearly visible even without binoculars.

They are also seen off Captain Cook State Recreation Area, at Beluga Point, which is 36 miles north of Kenai and 17 miles south-east of Anchorage along the Seward Hwy. At the point, which overlooks Turnagain Arm, you'll find picnic tables, benches, telescopes and an interpretive display. ∎

Lodge (☎ 776-5259) is the best, offering clean rooms with shared bath, on-site spa and sauna and a restaurant. The good news is that rooms are $55 a night for a single or a double and a bed in a bunkhouse is only $10. The bad news is that it's located at *Mile 21* of Kenai Spur Hwy, right across from the huge Unocal chemical plant.

Sadly there is no longer a public campground near Kenai. The city shut down the City Campground on Forest Dr and turned it into a picnic area after it was overrun by cannery workers. The nearest campground is now *Bernice Lake Recreation Area* (11 sites, $8) on Miller Loop Rd, six miles north of town off the Kenai Spur Hwy. Within town there are several commercial campgrounds that are geared for RVers. Both *Beluga Lookout RV Park* (☎ 283-5999) and *Overland RV Park* (☎ 283-4512) are within a five-minute walk of the visitor center and have laundry facilities, full hook-ups and showers. Expect to pay $15 a night for a site.

Places to Eat

For cheap food in town, there's the salad & soup bar at *Carr's* on Kenai Spur Hwy next door to Kmart. There's also an *Arby's* and a *McDonald's* but pass them up for *Burger-N-Brew* across from the visitor center on Kenai Spur Hwy. This small restaurant has a sunroom and a menu that features 40 types of hamburgers from $4 to $7 as well as sandwiches, seafood, salad and soup. Everything can be washed down with a pitcher of beer.

On Willow St, just off Kenai Spur Hwy, are three restaurants within walking distance of each other. The small *Thai Lotus* and the larger *Peking Chinese* both have lunch buffets for under $7 and dinners that range from around $10. Nearby is *Kitchen Express* which doubles up as an espresso shop, kitchenwares store and seafood saloon. Its menu includes Crabby Louie for $12.50 and salmon scampi for $10.50. Across from the visitor center is *Paradisos Restaurant*, a longtime favorite for Italian, Greek and Mexican dishes.

Getting There & Away

Air Kenai has the main airport on the peninsula and is serviced by ERA (☎ 283-3168). ERA has more than a dozen daily flights between Anchorage and Kenai. The one-way fare between the two cities costs around $60 for the 30-minute flight.

Bus Bus service to the west side of the Kenai Peninsula was suspended in 1994 when Homer Bus Lines went out of business. Ask around for any upstarts but this has been an unprofitable route for the handful of bus companies that have tried it over the years.

CAPTAIN COOK STATE RECREATION AREA

By following the Kenai Spur Hwy north for 36 miles, you will first pass the trailer parks and chemical plants of the North Kenai industrial district and then eventually reach this uncrowded state recreation area that encompasses 4000 acres of forests, lakes, rivers and beaches along Cook Inlet. The area offers swimming, camping and the beauty of Cook Inlet in a setting that is unaffected by the stampede for salmon to the south.

Kenai Spur Hwy ends in the park after first passing Stormy Lake, where there is a bathhouse and a swimming area along the water's edge. Also within the park is the *Bishop Creek Campground* (12 sites, $8) and the *Discovery Campground* (57 sites, $10). Both camping areas are on the bluff overlooking the Cook Inlet where some of the world's greatest tides can be seen ebbing and flowing.

The best hiking in the park is along the saltwater beach, but don't let the high tides catch you off guard. Those paddling the Swanson River Canoe Route (see the Paddling section in the Wilderness chapter) will find the park an appropriate place to end the trip.

If you're not keen on roughing it, eight miles south of the park in Nilkiski is *Moose Haven Lodge* (☎ 776-8535), with five rooms that range in price from $60 to $110 per night for two people. The rate includes a large

SOUTHCENTRAL

breakfast while an Alaskan seafood dinner is an extra $15. The lodge also features a jacuzzi tub, a large deck outdoors and laundry facilities.

SOLDOTNA

Soldotna (pop 3800) is strictly a service center at the junction of the Sterling Hwy and Kenai Spur Hwy. The town was born when both roads were completed in the 1940s and WWII veterans were given a 90-day preference to homestead the area. But what used to be little more than a hub for anglers hoping to catch an 80-pound-plus king salmon from the Kenai River, is now one of the fastest growing commercial areas on the peninsula. The main reason for the boom in business is tourism. The Alaska Department of Fish & Game reports the Kenai River to be the most heavily fished stream in the state, as hundreds of thousands of anglers flood the area annually and congest the waterway with powerboats.

Just about all of these people (anglers, RVers and hitchhiking backpackers) have to pass through Soldotna, the reason no doubt there's a McDonald's in town.

Information

Tourist Office Information on the area can be obtained at the Kenai Peninsula Visitor Information Center (☎ 262-9814) in the center of town on the Sterling Hwy, just south of the Kenai River Bridge. The impressive center, open to 7 pm daily during the summer, is built in a wooded setting along the banks of the river and outside there is a series of steps and landings that leads down to the water. Inside is a 94-pound king salmon that was caught in 1987 and is the fifth largest sport-caught salmon in the world.

Money First National Bank of Anchorage (☎ 262-9070) is at 44501 Sterling Hwy.

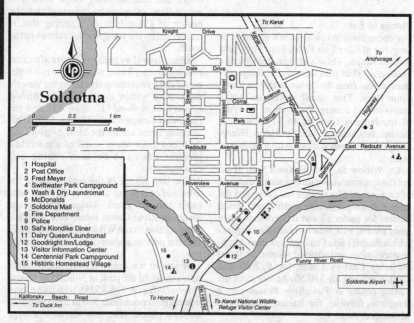

Soldotna

0   0.5   1 km
0   0.3   0.6 miles

1 Hospital
2 Post Office
3 Fred Meyer
4 Swiftwater Park Campground
5 Wash & Dry Laundromat
6 McDonalds
7 Soldotna Mall
8 Fire Department
9 Police
10 Sal's Klondike Diner
11 Dairy Queen/Laundromat
12 Goodnight Inn/Lodge
13 Visitor Information Center
14 Centennial Park Campground
15 Historic Homestead Village

To Kenai
To Anchorage
Knight Drive
Mary
Dale Drive
Corral
Park
Redoubt Avenue
Riverview Avenue
East Redoubt Avenue
Kenai River
Riverside Dve
Funny River Road
Soldotna Airport
Kalifonsky Beach Road
To Duck Inn
To Homer
To Kenai National Wildlife Refuge Visitor Center
Ski Hill Rd

Post The post office is on Corral Ave, just west of Kenai Spur Hwy and north of the Soldotna 'Y'.

Travel Agency The Travel Place (☎ 262-3992) is at 44096 Sterling Hwy.

Library The Joyce Carver Memorial Library (☎ 262-4227) is near the post office at 235 Binkley St and open Monday through Saturday, when at 2 pm Alaskan videos are shown.

Laundry Just up Kenai Spur Hwy at the Soldotna 'Y' is Wash & Dry, while on the Sterling Hwy next to the Dairy Queen is Alpine Laundromat. Both have showers.

Medical Services Central Peninsula General Hospital (☎ 262-4404) is on Mary Dale Dr, just west of Kenai Spur Hwy in Soldotna and serves both Soldotna and Kenai. For walk-in service there is Soldotna Medical Clinic (☎ 262-5115) nearby at 35251 Kenai Spur Hwy.

Things to See & Do
The most interesting thing to do in Soldotna is to drive on to Kalifonsky Beach Rd just after passing the bridge over the Kenai River. The road heads west at first and passes Centennial Park where in 1990 the Soldotna Historical Society opened **Historic Homestead Village** on six acres within the park. The village consists of six log buildings from early Soldotna, including a log schoolhouse, the former tourist information building and Damon Hall. Many of them now have historical displays, or in the case of Damon Hall wildlife exhibits. Hours are from 10 am to 4 pm Tuesday to Sunday in the summer.

Opposite Kalifonsky Beach Rd near the Kenai River is the junction with Funny River Rd. Turn left (east) here and turn right (south) immediately onto Ski Hill Rd, following it for a mile to reach the **Kenai National Wildlife Refuge Visitor Center** (☎ 262-7021). Open from 8 am to 4.30 pm weekdays and from 10 am to 5 pm weekends, the center features a series of wildlife displays, daily slide shows and wildlife films in its theater and naturalist-led outdoor programs on the weekends. There are also three short trails (maps available) that begin at the visitor center and wind into the nearby woods or to a viewing platform on Headquarters Lake. There is no admission fee.

Places to Stay
Camping There is the *Centennial Park Campground* (108 sites, $6 per night), on the corner of Sterling Hwy and Kalifonsky Beach Rd (near the visitor center), and the *Swiftwater Park Campground* (20 sites, $6), on East Redoubt Ave at *Mile 94* of the Sterling Hwy. Both are on the Kenai River which means from June through July you'd better be there before noon to stake out a site.

B&Bs There are more than 30 B&Bs in the area and rates range from $50 to $70 for a single. Stop at the visitor center for brochures and locations of them or call *Accommodations on the Kenai* (☎ 262-2139), which is a referral service for B&Bs, lodges and fish camps in central Kenai Peninsula.

Near Soldotna there is *Denise Lake Lodge* (☎ 262-1789 or (800) 478-1789 in Alaska). Located 2.5 miles from downtown Soldotna on Denise Lake, the log lodge features six rooms and a cabin along with a large fireplace and a kitchen available to guests at night. A double is $65 to $75. *Dudes Bunk & Breakfast* (☎ 283-9233 or 262-4221), on Kalifonsky Beach Rd 3.3 miles south of Bridge Access Rd, has an apartment for rent and three bunkrooms. A bunk is $35 a night, the apartment $75 and both include a full breakfast.

Hotels Most of the hotels are geared up for RVers and anglers and are lined up along Sterling Hwy and Kenai Spur Hwy – take your pick. Within town, the most affordable is *Goodnight Inn Lodge* (☎ 262-4584 or (800) 478-4584 in Alaska) on the Sterling Hwy across from the visitor center. Summer rates are $89/99 for a single/double. Slightly better is the *Duck Inn* (☎ 262-1849), 3.5

miles out on Kalifonsky Beach Rd, with singles or doubles for $79. Still cheaper is *4 Royale Parkers Motel* (☎ 262-4670) a couple of miles north on Kenai Spur Hwy. The place is a little run down but more than adequate and singles/doubles are $60/70.

Places to Eat

Chain restaurants include *McDonald's* and *Burger King* on the Sterling Hwy, while *Fred Meyer*, just before the Soldotna 'Y', has a deli, bakery and ready-to-eat food items. *Safeway* is open 24 hours and has a salad bar.

Sal's Klondike Diner near the bridge on the Sterling Hwy is open 24 hours and breakfast begins at $3.50. You can amuse yourself with the menu before the eggs and toast arrive. A wider selection of breakfasts, especially omelettes, is found at *Hog Heaven Cafe* next door to the Goodnight Inn. It has more than 20 types of omelettes that range in price from around $7.

In the Soldotna Mall on Sterling Hwy, there is a Chinese restaurant with a lunch buffet and *Le Croissant Shoppe* with espresso, salads and a variety of croissant sandwiches for about $7. There is also a couple of Mexican restaurants, practically across from each other. *Grand Burrito* on the 'Y' has quick Mexican food with enchilada and taco platters at $7 and a small lunch buffet. For something more authentic that can be enjoyed with a frozen margarita, try *Don Jose* across the street.

Getting There & Away

Without regular bus service, getting in and out of Soldotna is a little more challenging for those without a vehicle. You might call Day Breeze Shuttle (☎ 399-1168) in Homer. In 1996, the tour company began making the Homer-to-Anchorage run on Monday, Wednesday and Friday and would stop in Soldotna if it was pre-arranged.

STERLING HIGHWAY TO HOMER

At Soldotna, the Sterling Hwy rambles south, hugging the coastline and opening up to grand views of Cook Inlet every so often. This stretch is 78 miles long and passes through a handful of small villages near some great clamming areas, ending at the charming village of Homer. Take your time in this area; the coastline and Homer are worth every day you decide to spend there.

Kasilof

Kasilof (pop 1200), a fishing village, is at *Mile 108.8* of the Sterling Hwy. Turn west on Kalifonsky Beach Rd and travel 3.6 miles to reach the Small Boat Harbor on the Kasilof River. Sterling Hwy crosses a bridge over the Kasilof River a mile south of the Kalifonsky Beach Rd turn-off. On the other side of the bridge is the *Kasilof River State Wayside* (11 sites, $8 fee) on the riverbank. At *Mile 111.5* of the Sterling Hwy, the Cohoe Loop Rd heads north-west towards the ocean, passing *Crooked Creek State Recreation Area* along the way where there are rustic camp sites for $8 a night. Also along the road is *Kasilof River Kabins* (☎ 262-6348), with individual cabins that rent for $50/60 a single/double, a shared shower cabin and a short walk to the river itself.

South-east of the Cohoe Loop intersection is Johnson Lake Access Rd which quickly passes the *Johnson Lake Recreation Area* (43 camp sites, $10 fee). The lake itself is non-motorized and has rainbow trout. At the end of the seven-mile access road is the *Tustumena Lake Campground* (10 sites, $8 fee), which really lies on the Kasilof River, a mile from the large Tustumena Lake.

Clam Gulch

At *Mile 117.4* of Sterling Hwy, before reaching the hamlet of Clam Gulch (pop 120), you pass the junction of a two-mile gravel road. Just west on the road is *Clam Gulch State Recreation Area* which has covered picnic tables, outhouses and a campground (116 sites, $8 fee) on a steep bluff overlooking Cook Inlet. More importantly, the road provides access to the beaches below and the start of the area's great clam digging. Of all the beaches, the Clam Gulch beach is generally thought to be the best by clammers due to its easy access, the nearby campground

Digging for Clams

Almost all of the beaches on the west side of the Kenai Peninsula (Clam Gulch, Deep Creek, Ninilchik and Whiskey Gulch) have a good supply of razor clams, considered by mollusk connoisseurs to be a true delicacy from the sea. Not only do razors have the best flavor, but they are the largest of the mollusks gathered. The average razor clam is 3½ inches long but most clammers have their heart set on gathering clams five, six or even seven inches in length.

You first have to purchase a sport-fishing license (a one-day visitor's license is $15, and a 14-day license is $30). The daily bag limit is 60 clams but remember that's an awful lot of clams to clean and eat. Two dozen per person are more than enough for a meal. There is good clamming from April to August, though the best time is July, right before spawning. Wait for the tide to drop at least a foot from the high-water mark, or better still to reach its lower levels of four to five feet down.

Equipment consists of a narrow-bladed clam shovel that can either be purchased or, if you don't feel like hauling it around all summer, rented at many lodges and stores near the clamming areas. You also will want rubber boots, rubber gloves, a bucket and a pair of pants you're not terribly attached to.

Once you are on the beach, you have to play detective. Look for the clam's footprint in the sand, a dimple mark left behind when it withdraws its neck. That's your clue to the clam's whereabouts but don't dig directly below the imprint or you'll break its shell. Shovel a scoop or two next to the mark and then reach in the sand for the clam. You have to be quick, since a razor clam can bury itself and be gone in seconds.

Once you are successful, leave the clams in a bucket of sea water or, better yet, beer for several hours to allow them to 'clean themselves'. Many locals say a handful of cornmeal thrown in helps this process. The best way to cook clams is right on the beach over an open fire while you're taking in the mountain scenery across Cook Inlet. Use a large covered pot and steam the clams in salt water or, better still, in white wine with a clove of garlic.

Here's where to go:

Clam Gulch This is the most popular and many say most productive spot by far. The best razor clamming is April through August. The Clam Gulch Wayside is a half mile from *Mile 189* of the Sterling Highway, where there's a short access road to the beach from the campground.

Ninilchik Best bet is to camp at Ninilchik View Campground, located above the old village of Ninilchik. From there walk to beaches for clamming.

Deep Creek Just south of Ninilchik is Deep Creek Campground, where there's camping and plenty of parking along the beach.

Whiskey Gulch Look for turn-off about *Mile 154* of the Sterling Hwy. Unless you have a 4WD vehicle, park at the elbow-turn above the beach.

Mud Bay Located at the left side of the Homer Spit is Mud Bay, a stretch abundant with eastern soft shells, nuttals, cockles and blue mussels. Some surf clams (rednecks) and razor clams can also be found on the Cook Inlet side of the Spit.

Some other highly edible mollusks found on the western side of the Kenai Peninsula include:

Eastern Soft Shell Clam An introduced species from the Atlantic Ocean, the eastern soft shell clam is most likely to be found in muddy, sand or gravel bottoms where the salinity has been reduced by fresh water influx. Mud Bay is one good source for these clams.

Horse Clams These are the 'granddaddies' of the local mollusks, reaching a weight of 4.5 pounds in some cases. They are available on the south side of Kachemak Bay along the rocky beaches in the more protected bays.

Nuttals & Cockles These shellfish make a good chowder base. They are also prevalent in Mud Bay.

Blue Mussels Often overlooked, blue mussels are abundant throughout Kachemak Bay and Cook Inlet, attaching themselves to rocks and pilings. These mollusks can be delicious when prepared with care. ■

SOUTHCENTRAL

and gradual gradient that makes for wide beds.

The village of Clam Gulch is less than a mile south of the gravel road on Sterling Hwy and has a post office and gasoline station. More importantly, there's *Clam Shell Lodge* (☎ 262-4211), where you can rent a clam shovel for $5 and then, after a morning on the beach, take a shower and do some washing. If that sounds too much like work, the lodge restaurant serves clam chowder, razor clams and steamers (also a type of clam). Rooms are $70 for single or double in July and $60 in August.

Ninilchik

Halfway between Soldotna and Homer is Ninilchik, a scenic area with a Russian accent, some great clamming beaches and four state campgrounds of which three have a view of those impressive volcanoes across Cook Inlet. For many travelers, Ninilchik is merely a stop for gas and a quick look at its Russian church. But this interesting little village is well worth spending a night at if for no other reason than it has some of the most affordable accommodation on the west side of the Kenai Peninsula.

The community is actually the oldest on the Kenai Peninsula, having been settled in the 1820s by employees of the Russian-American Company. Many stayed even after imperial Russia sold Alaska to the USA and their descendants form the core of the present community.

Like so many other Kenai Peninsula towns, Ninilchik suffered heavily during the 1964 earthquake when the village sank three

feet and huge sections of land, including its landing strip, disappeared into the Cook Inlet. Subsequently, 'New Ninilchik' was built on the bluffs at *Mile 135.5* of the Sterling Hwy between the Ninilchik River and Deep Creek.

Information The Ninilchik Community Library (☎ 567-3333), on Sterling Hwy just north of Oilwell Rd, doubles up as a visitor information center.

Things to See & Do Head west on Beach Access Rd, just south of the bridge over Ninilchik River, and stop at the Village Cache Gift Shop to pick up a free *Tour of Ninilchik Village* brochure. **Old Ninilchik Village**, the site of the original community, is a postcard scene of faded log cabins in tall grass, beached fishing boats and the spectacular backdrop of Mt Redoubt. The walking tour of the old village points out a dozen buildings, including the Sorensen/Tupper

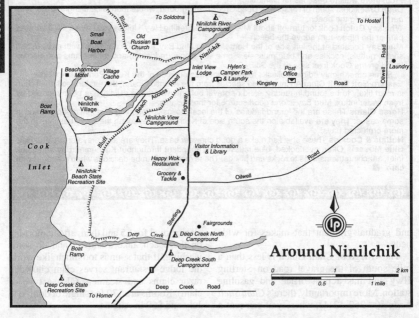

Around Ninilchik

Home built in 1895 with fir logs salvaged from fish traps and the town's first Russian school house.

The most spectacular building, however, is the **Russian Orthodox church**, built in 1901 and reached from a posted footpath in the village. The historic church, topped with the unique spires and crosses of the Russian Orthodox faith, is on a wide bluff and commands an unbelievable view of Cook Inlet and the volcanoes on the other side. A Russian Orthodox cemetery adjoins the church and together they make for a photographer's delight on a clear day.

Also spend some time at **Village Cache**, a log cabin that was built in the late 1800s and then completely dismantled and restored, log by log, in 1984. Inside is a gift shop featuring unusual Native Alaskan and Russian artwork and jewelry, not moose-nugget ear rings.

The other popular activity in Ninilchik is clamming. At low tide head to either Ninilchik Bear State Recreation Site or Deep Creek. You can either purchase a shovel at the Ninilchik General Store on Sterling Hwy or rent one from the Village Cache in the old village.

The main event in Ninilchik is the Kenai Peninsula State Fair, the 'biggest little fair in Alaska', which is held annually in town near the end of August.

Places to Stay – Campgrounds Sand-wiched around the town are a handful of state campgrounds with more just down the highway. Across the river from the old village is *Ninilchik Beach State Recreation Site* (50 sites, $8 fee), an open area along the shoreline. It can get windy here at times but the clamming is great. Just south of Beach Access Rd on Sterling Hwy is *Ninilchik View Campground* (12 sites, $10 fee) which has camp sites on a wooded bluff just above the beach campground. Most are in the trees but some have a great view of the village or Cook Inlet. A stairway leads down the bluff to the beach, the river and the village of Ninilchik.

Across Sterling Hwy from Coat Rd is *Ninilchik River Campground* (43 sites, $10),

in a wooded area away from the river. At *Mile 137.2* of Sterling Hwy is the *Deep Creek State Recreation Site* (100 sites, $6) on the beach near the mouth of the creek. The facility features a boat launch, information board about clamming, parking for 300 cars and boat trailers and a pay phone. It's heavily used by both campers, clammers and anglers who launch their boats in the creek. There is also camping on both sides of the Sterling Hwy Bridge across Deep Creek with sites for $8 a night.

If these are all full, continue south to *Stariski Creek State Recreation Site* (13 camp sites, $10 fee) on a bluff overlooking Cook Inlet at *Mile 152* of Sterling Hwy.

For a shower or laundry facilities, there's *Hylen's Camper Park* on Kingsley Rd or *Ninilchik Corners* just up the hill at Kingsley and Oilwell Rd.

Places to Stay – Hostel Ninilchik has one of the newest hostels in Alaska and it's well worth the effort to reach it. *The Eagle Watch* (☎ 567-3905) is three miles east of town on Oilwell Rd and features eight bunks, a kitchen, showers and laundry facilities. The rural setting is spectacular as the log home was built on a high bluff overlooking the Ninilchik River Valley. The rate is $10 for members, $15 for non-members and $2 for a bed sheet rental as the owners will not allow sleeping bags to be used.

Places to Stay – Motels & Cabins On Sterling Hwy, *Inlet View Lodge* (☎ 567-3330) is a restaurant, liquor store and has 11 cabins for rent. The cabins are very rustic and small with a shared shower area but are only $35 per night. Right on the beach in the old village is *Beachcomber Motel* (☎ 567-3417) with half-a-dozen small rooms that rent for $50/60 for a single/double.

Places to Eat There is a general store along the Sterling Hwy and an espresso shop (of course) but the best place for a bite to eat is the nearby *Happy Wok Restaurant*. A plate of fried rice begins at $7 while full dinners, which include soup, egg roll, two main dishes and fried rice, are $10 to $13.

Anchor Point

Twenty miles south of Ninilchik is Anchor Point (pop 1300) and, as a monument here notes, 'the most westerly point on the North American continent accessible by a continuous road system'. The town is a fishing hot spot during the summer with Anchor River renowned for its salmon, steelhead and Dolly Varden fishing. If you're bringing your rod and reel, make sure you pick up an Anchor River State Recreation Area brochure which lists the seasons and even shows the favorite fishing holes along the river. But be prepared for massive crowds here in July and through much of August.

Information At the junction of Sterling and Old Sterling highways is the Anchor Point Visitor Center, housed in a log cabin and staffed by volunteers. Summer hours are from 10 am to 4 pm weekdays.

Places to Stay & Eat Old Sterling Hwy, or Anchor River Rd, leads to the Anchor River State Recreation Area. Entrance into the state area is by a beach access road on the south side of Anchor River which leads past five campgrounds ($8 fee). The last one, *Halibut Campground*, has 30 sites and overlooks Cook Inlet beach, while the rest are on the river. In between them is a handful of RV parks and tackle shops, testimony to the king-salmon fever that runs through this place in July. Good luck in getting a site then.

The road ends at a beautiful stretch of beach with good views of Mt Redoubt and Mt Iliamna across the inlet, and an information display about 'the Ring of Fire' volcanoes on an observation deck with sighting scopes.

On the Sterling Hwy in town is *Anchor River Inn* (☎ 235-8531), which has small economy rooms for $45/50 a single/double and larger motel rooms for $80/85.

For a hamburger ($6) and a beer served on an outdoor deck, try *Teri Ann's* on the Sterling Hwy. For an espresso or deli sandwich

while you wait for your wash to finish, there's the delightful *Anchorage Point Roadhouse* just down the road.

HOMER

Arriving in Homer (pop 3900) is like opening one of those pop-up greeting cards – it's an unexpected thrill. From Anchor Point, Sterling Hwy ascends the bluffs overlooking Kachemak Bay and three miles before Homer provides a few teasers that whet your appetite but never fully prepare you for the charming, colorful fishing village that lies ahead. As the road makes a final turn east along the bluffs, Homer unfolds completely. It's a truly incredible panorama of mountains, white peaks, glaciers, and the beautiful Kachemak Bay into which stretches Homer Spit, a long strip of land.

History

In the beginning the Spit was Homer, and it has always played a prominent role in the development of the city. The town was founded, and picked up its name, when Homer Pennock, an adventurer from Michigan, landed on the Spit with a crew of gold seekers in 1896, convinced that Kachemak Bay was the key to their riches. It wasn't and in 1898 Pennock was lured away by the spell of the Klondike fields, failing to find gold there as well.

Coal first supported the fledging town and ·in 1899 the first dock on the Spit was built by the Cook Inlet Coal Field Company (CCC). It was later destroyed by ice. The second dock didn't come until 1938 when a combination of the CCC and local fund raising (including the efforts of the Homer Women's Club which raised enough to build a warehouse) reconnected the city to the sea. When the first steamship arrived that fall, the residents celebrated the end of an era of dismal isolation.

Despite the arrival of the first gravel road to Homer in 1951, the Spit continued to be the focal point of the town. Homer switched from a coal-based economy to fishing which is centered in the Small Boat Harbor on the Spit and today pumps $30 million a year into

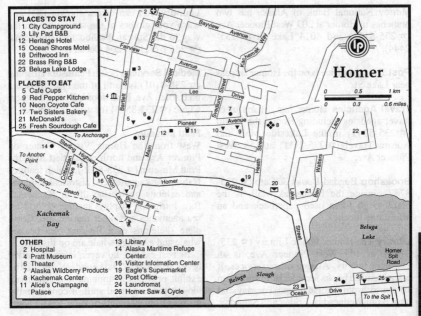

PLACES TO STAY
1 City Campground
3 Lily Pad B&B
12 Heritage Hotel
15 Ocean Shores Motel
18 Driftwood Inn
22 Brass Ring B&B
23 Beluga Lake Lodge

PLACES TO EAT
5 Cafe Cups
9 Red Pepper Kitchen
10 Neon Coyote Cafe
17 Two Sisters Bakery
21 McDonald's
25 Fresh Sourdough Cafe

Homer

OTHER
2 Hospital
4 Pratt Museum
6 Theater
7 Alaska Wildberry Products
8 Kachemak Center
11 Alice's Champagne Palace
13 Library
14 Alaska Maritime Refuge Center
16 Visitor Information Center
19 Eagle's Supermarket
20 Post Office
24 Laundromat
26 Homer Saw & Cycle

SOUTHCENTRAL

the area. The Spit and the town also survived the Good Friday Earthquake, which dropped the narrow peninsula by six feet and leveled most of the building. By high tide the Spit was no longer a spit but an island. Six years and almost $7 million later, the Spit and the road to it were reconstructed.

The Spit has also survived the ravages of fire and high water, political battles over land use and currently is being besieged by an onslaught of tourism. Nonetheless its unique character is still intact as is the rest of Homer.

The community is supported by both its fishing industries and a growing influx of tourism but is still recognized around the state as the arts capital of Southcentral Alaska and something of a retreat for the 1960s generation of radicals, artists and dropouts from mainstream society.

It is little wonder that the graying hippies choose Homer; the scenery is inspiring and the climate exceptionally mild. Homer is protected from the severe northern cold by

the Kenai Mountains to the north and east. Summer temperatures rarely go above 70°F, while winter temperatures rarely drop much below 0°F. Annual rainfall is only 28 inches, much of it snow.

This is a town that lures you to stay for a while. Between its half-dozen espresso shops, great scenery and interesting side trips to the other side of Kachemak Bay, you could easily spend a week here.

Information

Tourist Offices The Homer Visitor Center (☎ 235-7740) is at 135 Sterling Hwy or what is usually labeled as the Homer Bypass. The center is open daily during the summer and until 8 pm Friday through Sunday and has racks of information, free coffee and courtesy phones to book rooms or tours. There is also some limited tourist information at the Pratt Museum and the Alaska Maritime National Wildlife Refuge Visitor Center (see those individual sections).

Money National Bank of Alaska has two branches in Homer at 203 West Pioneer Ave (☎ 235-8151) and 4014 Lake St (☎ 235-2444).

Post The post office is on the Homer Bypass near Lake St.

Travel Agencies Homer has a handful of travel agencies including Round the World (☎ 235-5241) in the Lakeside Mall and Aurora Travel (☎ 235-2111) at 158 West Pioneer Ave.

Bookshop Bagdad Books & Cafe (☎ 235-8787), inside the Kachemak Mall, is the place to go for a used paperback and an affordable lunch.

Library The Homer Public Library (☎ 235-3180), at 141 West Pioneer Ave, is an excellent facility. Among other services, it often has used books for sale. Hours are from 10 am to 8 pm Thursday and Tuesday and until 6 pm Wednesday, Friday and Saturday.

Laundry You can take a shower ($3) and wash your clothes at the same time on the way to the Spit at Washboard Laundromat (☎ 235-6781) at 1204 Ocean Dr.

Medical Services South Peninsula Hospital (☎ 235-8101) is north of the Pratt Museum on Bartlett Ave. Next door is Homer Medical Clinic (☎ 235-8586) for walk-in service.

Pratt Museum

West from the Homer Visitor Center on Pioneer Ave and north on Bartlett St is the Pratt Museum (☎ 235-8635), which features Native Alaskan artefacts, historical displays, and exhibits on marine life in Kachemak Bay. Intriguing displays include octopuses, sea anemones and other marine life. Complete skeletons of a Bearing Sea beaked whale and a beluga whale are on display.

Its best exhibit, however, is on the lower level. Entitled 'Darkened Waters', the exhibit provides a stunning and emotional look at the Exxon oil spill. It considers the disaster from all points of view, has an hour-

The Literary Pride of Homer

It may be an artist colony in Alaska, but around the country Homer is best known as the home of Tom Bodett, the folksy voice that tells millions of Americans that 'Motel 6 has the lowest rates of any national chain'.

Born in Sturgis, Michigan, Bodett dropped out of Michigan State University and followed his wanderlust first to Oregon and eventually to Homer, where he was making a living as a construction worker. His literary career started when he tried to quit smoking and wrote a humorous piece about it for the *Anchorage Daily News*. That resulted in a Sunday column and commentaries on National Public Radio.

His life really changed when a Dallas advertising executive in charge of the Motel 6 account became infatuated with Bodett's accent listening to National Public Radio while driving. In 1986, Bodett, then just a nervous carpenter and fledgling radio commentator, wound up in a San Francisco recording studio doing the voice overs for the Motel 6 ads. With a couple of seconds to spare after reading the ad copy he ad-libbed the 'We'll leave the light on for ya' tag line. It was pure Heartland America and since has become one of the most noted advertising slogans of its time. Ten years and 300 Motel 6 advertising spots later, it's still being used.

The fame allowed Bodett to begin producing his *End of the Road* variety show from his Clearshot Studios in Homer in which he mixed his tales with home-grown musical talent. The show immediately drew comparisons to Garrison Keillor's *Prairie Home Companion*, though Bodett's humor tends to be simpler and more innocent. *End of the Road* aired for three years and, at its peak in 1990, reached listeners on 150 stations across the country.

After a follow-up show, *Bodett & Co*, Bodett stepped away from the radio shows in 1993 to concentrate on his writing. His humorous tales and 'aw-shucks' stories on National Public Radio resulted in four books of short stories, and in 1996 his first novel, *The Free Fall of Webster Cummings*, was released. ■

by-hour account of the effort to save just one oil-soaked seal, the radio tapes of Captain Joseph Hazelwood contacting the coast-guard, and displays on both protesters and 'spillionaires' – locals who made small fortunes from the spill. It is by far the best look at Alaska's worse environmental tragedy. The museum is open daily in summer from 10 am to 6 pm and charges $4 for admission.

Alaska Maritime National Wildlife Refuge Visitor Center

More natural displays can be seen nearby at the Alaska Maritime National Wildlife Refuge Visitor Center, on Sterling Hwy just before entering town. There is a small theater with regularly scheduled videos, a book and map counter and information on hiking and kayaking in Kachemak Bay. The center (☎ 235-6961) also hosts guided bird walks and children's programs throughout the summer. Opening hours are 9 am to 5 pm daily.

Galleries

The beautiful scenery has inspired numerous artists to gather here, and the handful of galleries in town display more than the usual ivory carvings and gold-nugget jewelry you see everywhere else. Most of the galleries are along Pioneer Ave, including Ptarmigan Arts (☎ 235-5345), which features a variety of jewelry, pottery and weaving from more than 40 artists in the area and Fireweed Gallery next door. Bunnell Street Gallery features 'explorative Alaskan Art' while the Pratt Museum also has an art gallery that exhibits work by artists from around the Kenai Peninsula. You can also visit a number of artists who maintain galleries in their studios, including Ahna Iredale, whose pottery is often decorated with Alaskan landscapes or fish. Her studio (☎ 235-7687) is 10 minutes from downtown on Bay Ridge Road.

For a map and descriptions of the galleries in town, pick up the *Downtown Homer Art Galleries* from the visitor center or *Homer Tourist Guide*, published by the *Homer News*.

Homer Spit

This long needle of land is a five-mile sand bar which stretches into Kachemak Bay; during the summer it is the center of activity in Homer and the heart of its fishing industry. The Spit draws thousands of tourists and backpackers every year, making it not only a scenic spot but an interesting mecca for fishers, cannery workers, visitors and charter-boat operators.

The hub of all this activity is the **Small Boat Harbor** at the end of the Spit, one of the best facilities in Southcentral and home base for over 700 boats. On each side of the harbor's entrance is a cannery. Nearby is the **Seafarer's Memorial**, a touching monument to the 27 residents who were lost at sea.

The favorite activity on the Homer Spit, naturally, is beachcombing, especially at dawn or dusk while viewing the sunset or sunrise. You can stroll for miles along the beach, where the marine life is as plentiful as the driftwood, or you can go clamming at Mud Bay on the east side of the spit. Blue mussels, an excellent shellfish overlooked by many people, are the most abundant. Locals call the clams and mussels 'Homer grown'.

Another popular activity on the Spit is a shrimp, clam or crab boil. Grab your camp stove and large metal pot, purchase some fresh seafood from the seafood markets around the Small Boat Harbor and buy a can of beer from the general store next door to the Salty Dawg Saloon. Then head down to the beach and enjoy your Alaskan feast while watching the tide roll in and the sun set. No beach fires are allowed between Land's End and the Whitney Fidalgo Access Rd.

If you're into catching your dinner rather than shoveling or buying it, try your luck at the **Fishing Hole**, signposted across the road from the visitor center. The small lagoon is the site of a 'terminal fishery' in which salmon are planted by the state and then return three or four years later to a place where they can't spawn. From mid-May to mid-September, anglers bait their hooks with colorful spoons, salmon eggs, or herring or shrimp under bobbers and then cast into the

SOUTHCENTRAL

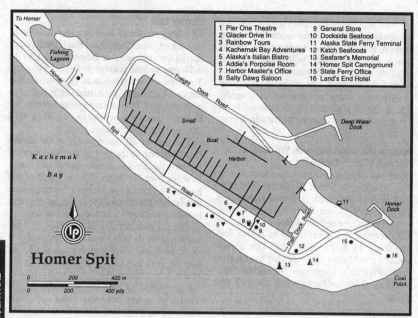

To Homer

1 Pier One Theatre	9 General Store
2 Glacier Drive In	10 Dockside Seafood
3 Rainbow Tours	11 Alaska State Ferry Terminal
4 Kachemak Bay Adventures	12 Katch Seafoods
5 Alaska's Italian Bistro	13 Seafarer's Memorial
6 Addie's Porpoise Room	14 Homer Spit Campground
7 Harbor Master's Office	15 State Ferry Office
8 Salty Dawg Saloon	16 Land's End Hotel

Fishing Lagoon

Homer

Freight Dock Road

Spit

Small Boat Harbor

Deep Water Dock

Kachemak

Bay

Road

Fish Dock Road

Homer Dock

Homer Spit

0   200   400 m
0   200   400 yds

Coal Point

lagoon. More than 15,000 salmon, ranging from 40-pound kings to five-pound pinks and cohos, are caught here by people from shore every summer.

Skyline Dr

North of town are bluffs, referred to by locals as 'the Hill', that rise gently to 1100 feet. These green slopes, broken up by colorful patches of wildflowers, on a clear day provide excellent views of the glaciers that spill out of the Harding Icefield across the bay. The best views are from Skyline Dr, which runs along the bluff above Homer.

Follow Pioneer Ave east out of town where it turns into East End Rd and then turn north onto East Hill Rd up the bluffs to Skyline Dr. At the west end of Skyline Dr is Ohlson Mountain Rd which ascends 1513 feet to the peak of Ohlson Mountain. Many roads, including East End Rd, are paved and ideal for cycling (see the Homer Cycling section).

Hiking

For all its natural beauty, Homer lacks good public trails. The best hiking is along the beaches, while most trails off the road system are private paths that usually lead to somebody's homestead or cabin.

Bishop Beach Hike This hike, which begins at Bishop Park, makes either an excellent afternoon stroll or an 11-mile trek north of Homer. The views of Kachemak Bay and the Kenai Mountains are superb, while the marine life seen scurrying along the sand at low tide is fascinating.

Check a tide book, available from most gasoline stations or sports stores, and leave before low tide and return before high tide. High tides cover most of the sand, forcing you to scramble onto the base of the nearby cliffs. Within three miles of the park you'll pass a sea-otter rookery a few hundred yards offshore. In seven miles you'll reach Diamond Creek which will lead you up to

SOUTHCENTRAL

the Sterling Hwy, four miles north of town. To reach Bishop Park head south on Main St, then left on Bunnell Ave and right on Beluga Ave.

Homestead Trail This relatively new trail, developed by the Kachemak Heritage Land Trust (KHLT), is a 6.7-mile trek from Rogers Loop Rd to the City Reservoir just off Skyline Dr on Crossman Ridge Rd. From Rogers Loop Rd it's a 2.5-mile walk to Rucksack Drive which crosses Diamond Ridge Rd. Along the way you pass through open meadows where there are panoramic views of Kachemak Bay and Mt Iliamna and Mt Redoubt on the other side of Cook Inlet. The trek continues another 4.2 miles by following Rucksack Dr and Crossman Ridge Rd to the reservoir. Cars are banned from both of these dirt roads.

To reach the west of the trail, head out of town on the Sterling Hwy and then turn right on Rogers Loop Rd across from Bay View Inn. The trailhead will be a half mile on your right. For an interpretive brochure on the trail stop at the KHLT office (☎ 235-5263) at 395 East Pioneer Ave.

Carl E Wynn Nature Center Located on the bluffs above Homer, this 126-acre reserve is managed by the Center for Alaskan Coastal Studies and features several short nature trails. One is a handicapped-accessible trail that takes visitors through a spruce forest and grassy meadow to an observation platform.

Due to a 30-acre wildlife refuge also located here, you can only visit the area with a naturalist from the center. Guided tours are conducted throughout the week during the summer at various times. Call the Center for Alaskan Coastal Studies (☎ 235-6667) for tour times. The nature center is reached from East Hill Road by turning right on Skyline Drive for 1.5 miles.

Cycling
The dirt roads in the hills above Homer lend themselves to some great mountain biking, Diamond Ridge and Skyline in particular, while an easy tour is to just head out East End Rd which extends 20 miles east to the head of Kachemak Bay. Homer Saw & Cycle (☎ 235-8406), at 1535 Ocean Dr on the way to the Spit, has mountain bike rentals for $25 a day or $15 a half day as well as maps of the area and a limited selection of parts.

SOUTHCENTRAL

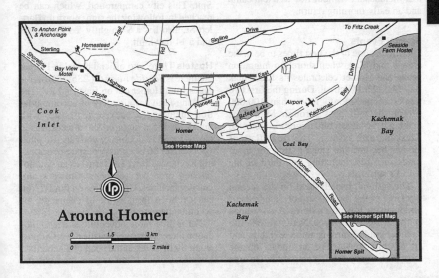

Around Homer

Rocky River The best mountain-bike adventures in the area are on the south side of Kachemak Bay where you can ride along the Jakolof-Rocky River Rd from Jakolof Bay all the way to Windy Bay. The 20-mile rough dirt road follows a river bed that cuts across the very tip of the Kenai Peninsula. There are numerous stream crossings. Beware of loggers, and thus logging trucks, in the Windy Bay area at the end of the road. Cyclists in good shape can reach Rocky Bay and return in one day, a 30-mile ride. Otherwise plan to camp. To reach the dock on Jakolof Bay there's Jakolof Ferry Service (☎ 235-2376) that departs the Spit daily during the summer at 10 am.

Horseback Riding

There are several ranches and outfitters along East End Rd that offer horseback-riding adventures in the valleys and hills that surround the upper portion of Kachemak Bay. You can undertake an hourly ride, an all-day ride or a pack trip where you spend the night camping in Fox River Valley. Trails-End Horse Adventures (☎ 235-6393) offers an overnight trip for $110 per person that includes a two-hour ride to a tent camp and an early morning return.

Special Events

For birders, one of the best times to be in the area is mid-May, when shorebird migration peaks and Homer celebrates its Kachemak Bay Shorebird Festival. During the first two weeks of the month more than 100,000 shorebirds will pass through Mud Bay, making it the largest bird migration along the Alaskan road system. The tidal flats of Homer become the staging area for thousands of birds, including one-third of the world's surfbirds.

The festival, usually held on the second weekend of the month, attracts hundreds of birders to the town for a series of workshops at the Alaska Maritime National Wildlife Refuge, guided birding tours, exhibits and art & craft shows. For an update on the migration or any birding activity in the area

call the Kachemak Bay Birdwatchers Hotline (☎ 235-7337).

Other events in Homer include the almost month-long Spring Arts Festival in May. This event began as an outlet for local artists to display their work and has since evolved into a festival with dancers, musicians and craftspeople.

The 4 July celebration is usually a three-day event that includes a parade, a foot race, various local contests such as a grease-pole climb, and art & craft booths.

Places to Stay

Camping Beach camping is allowed in designated areas on the west side of Homer Spit, a beautiful spot to pitch a tent. The nightly fee is $3 if you are pitching your tent in the city controlled sections near the end of the Spit, $7 if you are parking your RV. There are toilets next to the Harbor Master's Office and a shower costs $3 at the *Homer Spit Campground*. Keep in mind the Spit can get rowdy at times.

The *Karen Hornaday Hillside Campground* is on a wooded hill with an impressive view of the town and bay below, making it considerably more private than the Spit. This city campground, which can be reached by following the signs north up Bartlett St, also has a $3 nightly fee for tenters and a 14-day limit.

Hostels There's no official hostel in Homer but there is *Seaside Farm* (☎ 235-7850), five miles from Homer out on East End Rd. The working farm has a variety of accommodation including a backpacker hostel with bunks for $15 a night or $80 a week, rustic cabins for $55 a double, or you can also pitch your tent for $6 in a grassy pasture overlooking Kachemak Bay. The farm has an outdoor kitchen area for campers, showers and laundry facilities. Getting low on funds? You can even do farm work in exchange for accommodation.

For a little more adventurous accommodation there is also the Seaside Farm Outpost along Swift Creek at the head of Kachemak. Located another 15 miles from the farm, the bunkroom ($15 per night) and rent-a-tents ($5 per person per night) are a half-mile hike in from East End Rd.

Within downtown Homer at 358 East Lee St is *Sunspin Guest House* (☎ (800) 391-6677 or 235-6677) which has bunkrooms for $25 per person as well as private rooms for $40/60 a single/double. The rates include pick-up from the airport or ferry terminal and breakfast in the morning.

B&Bs These places have popped up in Homer like mushrooms in the spring and at last count there were more than 40 in the area. You can get a list or brochures for most of them at the visitor center and then use the courtesy phones to book a room. Remember there is a 5.5% tax on rooms in Homer.

In the heart of town is the *Lily Pad* (☎ 235-6630), at 3954 Bartlett St, with seven rooms above a beauty salon. Doubles cost $65. The *Beach House Bed & Breakfast* (☎ 235-5945) is near the airport with four rooms that begin at $60, good views of the Spit and a jacuzzi.

In the downtown area the *Spruce Acres Cabins* (☎ 235-8388), off Sterling Hwy just before Pioneer Ave, has individual cabins for $55 to $85 a night for two people. The *Brass Ring B&B* (☎ 235-5450), at 987 Hillfair Court, is a log-cabin home with five rooms where singles/doubles with shared bath are $65/70 and features, among other amenities, an outdoor hot tub.

The other option is to head out East End Rd where you will pass one B&B sign after another and practically all of them have a grand view of Kachemak Bay and the surrounding mountains. You'll quickly pass the *Road Runner B&B* (☎ 235-3678) with rooms that begin at $48 for two people as well as tent sites and free transport from the airport or ferry terminal. *Frontier Cottages* (☎ 235-8275) is 3.5 miles from Homer and features four new cabins, each with kitchen, living room and upstairs sleeping loft. The rate is $98 for up to three people, while children are free.

Head further east still to reach the *Chocolate Drop B&B* (☎ 235-3668). More of a lodge than a B&B, the Chocolate Drop is a stunning log inn overlooking the bay with an outdoor hot tub on the 2nd floor porch and a sauna inside. All rooms have baths and private entrance and range from $85 to $105 for two. There is also a family suite with a kitchen that is a bargain at $135 a night if there are four of you.

Hotels/Motels There are almost a dozen hotels/motels in the area with most single rooms ranging from $60 to $70. All of them are heavily booked during the summer. A delightful, small hotel is the *Driftwood Inn* (☎ 235-8019 or (800) 478-8019 in Alaska), on the corner of Main St and Bunnell Ave near Bishop Beach. Non-view rooms without bath are $60/70 a single/double, while others overlook Kachemak Bay and are $78/80 a single/double. In the lounge is a fieldstone fireplace, while overlooking the bay is a barbecue area and deck. Coffee and rolls are available in the morning.

Within walking distance of downtown Homer is *Ocean Shores Motel* (☎ 235-7775 or (800) 770-7775), at 3500 Crittenden Dr, with a variety of rooms. Economy rooms are $60 for a single or a double but are limited. Other rooms are $75/80 while new bayview rooms with kitchenettes are $120 a night. Right on Pioneer Ave is *Heritage Hotel* (☎ 235-7787 or (800) 478-7787 in Alaska), an historical log lodge where rooms with shared bath are $70/80 a single/double.

More upscale is *Beluga Lake Lodge* (☎ 235-5995 or (800) 478-8485 in Alaska), at 984 Ocean Dr, overlooking its namesake lake. Double rooms begin at $78 a night. At the end of the Spit is *Land's End Hotel* (☎ 235-2500 or (800) 478-0400 in Alaska) where doubles with an outdoor balcony and a spectacular view begin at $99.

Places to Eat
Sure, Homer has a *McDonald's* and even two *Subway* shops, but pass up the fast lane to fast food and try one of the charming and unique eateries. Spoon for spoon, no other town in Alaska has the variety in dining that Homer boasts with the exception of the big two – Anchorage and Fairbanks.

In town there is an assortment of cafes and bakeries, including a handful of espresso shops. It isn't who serves café latte in Homer, but who doesn't. This town of 3000 supports more than a half-dozen places where you can get a cup of cappuccino. The most interesting is *Cafe Cups* with its bizarre coffee cup exterior and its pleasant interior where each wall is an art gallery. Huge sandwiches, made with thick cuts of bread, are $6 and include several veggie models, while home-made soup is $5. The cafe opens up at 7 am for breakfast and serves several unusual egg dishes – just what you would expect in Homer.

Equally good café latte, baked goods, and that 1960s atmosphere can be enjoyed at *Two Sisters Espresso & Bakery* on the corner of Main and Bunnell streets. The shop is in the Old Inlet Trading Post Building and has a few tables inside and a few more outside on the porch overlooking the bay. On Pioneer Ave as you head out of town is *Espresso Express*, a small cafe with a coffee drive-thru window. It has the best prices along with muffins and sandwiches.

Interesting and affordable is *Neon Coyote*, a diner on Pioneer Ave that specializes in Southwest cooking. For dinner there's grande burrito filled with chicken and black beans that will fill you up for $7 or shrimp enchiladas for $16. Practically next door is *Red Pepper Kitchen*, a little more low key with pizza, salads or Mexican dishes and outdoor seating. An enchilada plate is $6 and includes beans, rice, chips and salsa. For $2 there's the bean burrito with chips and salsa that will hold you over until breakfast.

The best vegetarian is at *Smoky Bay Co-op* on Pioneer Ave. The Co-op is Homer's health-food store but also runs a small kitchen that serves filling vegetarian dishes for lunch for under $7 and soups and sand-wiches for even less. Inside is limited seating. The best baby back ribs are nearby at *Pioneer Barbecue*.

Homer has two Chinese restaurants next door to each other on Pioneer Ave with lunch and dinner buffets. It's a toss up between *The Thai & Chinese* or *Young's Oriental*, both featuring a $6.50 feast for lunch and an all-you-can-eat deal at dinner for just $1 more. There is also *Pioneer Pizza* on Pioneer Ave, which has all the pizza, salad and pop you can 'scarf' down from Monday to Saturday for $7.

On the way to the Spit at 1316 Ocean Dr is *Fresh Sourdough Express*, a good bakery and restaurant for breakfast. Eggs, potatoes and sourdough toast is $5, huge sourdough pancakes $5.75. Eight miles out of town along East End Rd is *The Homestead* (☎ 235-8723), Homer's finest restaurant. You must have a reservation but it's worth the effort as the food and view of the bay and mountains are excellent from the log lodge. Pasta dinners range from $14 to $18, seafood $17 to $21, and prime rib is $19.

Cheap eats at the end of the Spit consist of a *Subway* franchise, a fish & chips carry out, *Glacier Drive-In* and a couple of meals-on-wheels vans selling espresso and fresh bagels. For something a little more charm-ing, however, drop in at *Dockside Seafood Restaurant*. Bowls of halibut chowder, seafood gumbo or a fisherman's stew with a big slice of sourdough bread is $5. It has an interesting selection of imported beer and if the day is nice you can sit outside on a deck and watch the cannery workers ice down fish. Nearby is *Katch Seafood* for fresh, smoked and canned salmon, halibut, prawns and other delicacies from Kachemak Bay.

A step up is *Alaska's Italian Bistro* with an elegant dining room overlooking Kachemak Bay. A 12-inch pizza costs $12, a plate of pasta and salad $13, and most seafood dinners $18. Across the road is *Addies Por-poise Room*, which has a dining room and bar overlooking the Small Boat Harbor. Baked halibut dinner is $15, steamed tanner crab in the shell is $19 while most hamburg-ers are about $7 and a halibut burger is $8.

Entertainment

Homer's most famous drinking hole is on the Spit. The *Salty Dawg Saloon*, a log cabin bar with a lighthouse tower over it, has the same claim to fame as Juneau's Red Dog Saloon, right down to the sawdust on the floor and an amazing collection of orange life-rings on the walls, each stenciled with the name of the ship from which it came. Actually the saloon is three small log structures, including a tower that was originally a water tank, relocated here after the Good Friday Earthquake of 1964. It's worth at least a look at the life-rings collection, if not a few beers while you study it.

Downtown there is *Alice's Champagne Palace*, which rocks with bands and live music almost nightly while next door is the saloon of the *Heritage Hotel*, both on Pioneer Ave. There is also live music throughout the summer at *Moby Dick's Bar & Grill* in the Buluga Lake Lodge and rock-and-roll bands and a packed dance floor Wednesday through Saturday at *Waterfront Bar* on Bunnell St across from Driftwood Inn.

The Grog Shop, 369 East Pioneer Ave, is the place to pick up some brew to take back to the camp site. The shop has an excellent selection of beer, including most of the brands produced by the Alaskan microbreweries.

Homer is also blessed with entertainment that doesn't require a bar stool. *Pier One Theater* (☎ 235-7333) performs live drama and comedy in a 'come as you are' warehouse next to the Fishing Hole on the Spit. Performances are Friday and Saturday at 8.15 pm and Sunday at 7.15 pm throughout the summer. If possible, try to catch a performance of Fresh Produce, Homer's very funny alternative theater group. There is also *Homer Family Theater* (☎ 235-6728) on the corner of Main St and Pioneer Ave.

Getting There & Away
Air ERA Aviation (☎ (800) 426-0333), the contract carrier for Alaska Airlines, provides six daily flights between Homer and Anchorage from the Homer airport, 1.7 miles east of town on Kachemak Dr. The one-way fare is $65; a round-trip, advance-purchase ticket is $124. SouthCentral Air (☎ (800) 478-2550) also offers two flights daily Monday through Friday between the two cities. Homer Air (☎ 235-8591 or (800) 478-8591 in Alaska)

provides an air-taxi service to Seldovia. The one-way fare is $26, while round-trip is $47.

Bus Homer Bus Lines is gone but stepping in is Day Breeze Shuttle (☎ 399-1168) which began making the Homer-to-Anchorage run in 1996. The van service departs Homer at 9 am Monday, Wednesday and Friday and Anchorage from 8th St and G St at 3 pm. One-way is $45, round-trip $80, and always double check with a phone call to make sure the service is still available.

Car To obtain an affordable rental car, stop at Polar Car Rental (☎ 235-5998) at 455 Sterling Hwy or at its desk in the airport. The small dealer has subcompacts for $47 a day with the first 100 miles free or $282 for the week.

Hitchhiking Along with Bay Bushlines, a radio program in which messages are swapped back and forth between isolated neighbors, KBBI-AM 890 also has a 'Rideline' for people seeking either transportation out of town or passengers. Call the public radio station (☎ 235-7721) to leave a message for the show.

Boat The ferry MV *Tustumena* provides twice-weekly service from Homer to Seldovia and three times a week to Kodiak, including one run that continues onto Seward and the rest of the Southcentral ports. The ferry terminal (☎ 235-8449) is at the end of Homer Spit. The one-way fare from Homer to Seldovia is $18 and from Homer to Kodiak $48.

Rainbow Tours departs daily from the Spit to Seldovia at 11 am, and returns at 4 pm. The trip takes 1½ hours and the fare is $40 return or $25 one way.

Getting Around
Day Breeze Shuttle (☎ 399-1168) runs a van between the Spit and the downtown area, departing from the Land's End Hotel on the Spit at 11 am and 3 pm. The cost is $2 per person.

KACHEMAK BAY

This beautiful body of water extends 30 miles into the Kenai Peninsula and features a coastline of steep fjords and inlets with the glacier-capped peaks of the Kenai Mountains in the background. Marine and bird life are plentiful in the bay, but it is best known for its rich fishing grounds, especially for halibut.

A portion of the bay is preserved as Kachemak Bay State Park, a popular destination for backpackers and kayakers while within a few of the bays and long fjords are a handful of small villages and wilderness lodges.

Gull Island

For those who have no desire to hook an 80-pound halibut, there's Gull Island, a group of bare rock islets halfway between the Spit and Halibut Cove. The islands are the site of thousands of nesting sea birds: tufted puffins, black legged kittiwakes, common murres, cormorants and many more species. The stench is surpassed only by the opportunities to photograph the birds up close, even if you don't have a 300-mm lens.

Several tour-boat operators on the Homer Spit offer a cruise to the rookery including Rainbow Tours (☎ 235-7272), which departs daily at 9 am and 4.30 pm for a 1½-hour trip. The cost is $15 per person, making it possibly the best birding tour in the state.

Rainbow Tours also has a Natural History Tour, in which a full day is spent in Kachemak Bay to sight more wildlife and to include a visit to the **Center for Alaskan Coastal Studies**, a non-profit marine center in Peterson Bay. The tours depart daily at 9 am, return at 6 pm and are $55 per person, or less for seniors and kids.

Halibut Cove

Another interesting side trip is Halibut Cove, a small village of 50 people on the south shore of Kachemak Bay. In the early 1920s, the cove supported 42 herring salteries and had a population of over 1000. Today, the quaint community has a pair of art galleries

---

Hooking a Halibut in Homer

Homer may be the home of Tom Bodett and an intriguing arts community, but to thousands of tourists who come to Alaska every summer, Homer is the place where you go to catch a halibut.

Halibut is a bottom-dweller that, when first born, looks like any normal fish with an eye on each side of the head. But as a halibut feeds exclusively off the bottom, it flattens out and one eye moves to the other side, now the top of the fish. Females are larger than males, in fact, just about every halibut more than 100 pounds is a female. And almost without fail, a 300-pound halibut is hauled out of Kachemak Bay every summer. The Alaskan state record halibut is well over 400 pounds.

The average size fish, however, is closer to 30 or 40 pounds. Anglers use a large hook, usually baited with a chunk of cod or herring, and a 40-pound weight to take it 200 feet to the bottom of the bay where they proceed to 'jig' (raising and lowering the hook slightly) for a fish. Or as one writer described it, 'People put hunks of baits the size of footballs on hooks the size of trailer hitches to pull up the fish the size of barn doors.'

As you can imagine, reeling in a halibut can be quite a workout and many anglers find it exciting though these fish are not battlers or jumpers like salmon or trout. Actually getting the fish into the boat can be the most exciting part as charter captains often use a club or even a gun to subdue their catch and a gaff to haul it aboard.

There are more than two-dozen charter captains working out of the Spit and charging anywhere from $100 to $155 for a halibut trip. Most charter captains try to take advantage of two slack tides and often leave at around 6 am for a 12-hour trip on the bay. Pack a lunch or purchase one from a handful of restaurants that sell box lunches on the Spit. Also take warm clothing and rain gear and purchase a fishing license (non-resident licenses cost $15 for three days, $30 for 14 days).

Head to the Spit to book a charter. Just about all of them have an ad in the *Homer Tourist Guide* handed out free at the visitor center in town. ■

that produce 'octopus ink paintings', the noted Saltry Restaurant, some cabins for rent and boardwalks to stroll on but no roads.

Danny J is the ferry that will run you across to the cove from the Homer Spit. It departs at noon, swings past Gull Island and then at 1.30 pm arrives at Halibut Cove where you have 2½ hours to explore the 12 blocks of boardwalks and galleries or have lunch on the outdoor deck of the *Saltry Restaurant*. The ferry returns to the Spit by 5 pm and then makes an evening run to the cove for dinner at the Saltry, returning to Homer at 10 pm.

The noon tour of the *Danny J* is $35 per person, while its evening trip is $17.50. Dinner at the Saltry ranges from about $15 and is well worth it. To make Halibut Cove an even more interesting side trip, book a cabin at *Quiet Place Lodge* (☎ 296-2212) and spend the night. Cabins are $150 per couple and include breakfast. There is also *Halibut Cove Cabins* (☎ 296-2214) which offers a pair of cosy cabins that rent for $75 a night and sleep four people each (bring your own sleeping bags). You can book all of this at Central Charter Booking Agency (☎ 235-7847 or (800) 478-7847 in Alaska) which has an office on the Spit.

Tutka Bay

North of Seldovia is this remote bay, where Jon and Nelda Osgood run their *Tutka Bay Wilderness Lodge* (☎ 235-3905 or (800) 606-3909). The resort is a series of chalets, cottages and rooms surrounding the lodge house where guests enjoy their meals with a sweeping view of the inlet and Jakolof Mountain. The accommodation is very comfortable, the food is excellent and at your disposal is a sauna, deepwater dock, boathouse and hiking trails. Activities range from clamming to sea kayaking.

The isolated resort always gets high marks but is an experience rather than a place to stay. You have to book a room or cottage for at least two nights and the rates begin at $550 a person, which includes all meals and transportation from Homer as well as a room.

Kachemak Bay State Park

This park, along with the adjoining Kachemak Bay State Wilderness Park to the south, is 350,000 acres of mountainous and glacial wilderness that is only accessible by bush plane or boat. The most popular attraction of the park is Grewingk Glacier, which can clearly be seen across the bay in Homer. For most people the glacier is a boat trip to the park and a one-way hike of 3.2 miles to see it.

In recent years a controversy has erupted between helicopter operators, who have been running an increasing number of sightseeing trips to the glacier, and hikers who feel they are constantly being buzzed by the $300-an-hour flights.

Outside of the glacier, however, you can easily escape into the wilderness setting of this great state park by either hiking or kayaking. Visitor facilities include primitive camp sites, a rental cabin at the head of Halibut Cove Lagoon (reservations, $35 a night) and almost 20 miles of trails. For information on the park or to reserve the cabin, contact the Alaska Division of Parks & Outdoor Recreation office (☎ 235-7024) at *Mile 168.5* of Sterling Hwy, four miles north of Homer.

Hiking

Grewingk Glacier Trail The most popular hike in the Kachemak Bay State Park is this 3.5-mile, one-way trail from a trailhead near *Rusty Lagoon Campground* (five sites). It is a level, easy-to-follow trek across the glacial outwash and ends at a lake with superb views of Grewingk Glacier. Camping on the lake is spectacular and often the shoreline is littered with icebergs.

Alpine Ridge Trail At the high point of the mile-long Saddle Trail from Grewingk Glacier Trail is the posted junction for this two-mile climb to an alpine ridge above the glacier. The climb can be steep at times but manageable for most hikers with daypacks and on a nice day the views of the ice and Kachemak Bay are stunning.

Lagoon Trail Departing from the Alpine Trail is the mile-long Saddle Trail and this 5.5-mile route leads to the ranger station at the head of Halibut Cover Lagoon passing Goat Rope Spur Trail along the way, a steep climb into the alpine tundra. You also pass the signposted junction of Halibut Creek Trail. If Grewingk Glacier is too crowded for you, follow this trail to Halibut Creek to spend the night in a beautiful but much more remote valley.

Lagoon Trail is considered a moderately difficult hike and involves fording Halibut Creek which should be done at low tide. At the ranger station, more trails extend south to several lakes, Poot Peak and the Wosnesenki River.

Kayaking

You can also spend three or four days paddling the many fjords of the park, departing from Homer and making overnight stops at Glacier Spit or Halibut Cove. Think twice before crossing Kachemak Bay from the Spit. Although it's only 3.5 miles across, the currents and tides are strong and can cause serious problems for inexperienced paddlers.

Tour boats that run hikers across can also handle kayakers (see the following Getting Around section). The major headache for most travelers, however, is where to rent a boat. The best place to try is True North Kayak Adventures (☎ 235-0708) which has an office at 158 West Pioneer Ave. The small guiding company runs day trips on the south side of the bay that includes kayaks, a lunch, a guide and transportation. The cost is $140 per person and includes round-trip water taxi. True North also offers multi-day trips and will rent kayaks to experienced paddlers.

Getting Around

The state park makes an excellent side trip for anybody who has a tent, a spare day and wants to escape the overflow of RVers on Homer Spit. A number of tour boats offer drop-off and pick-up to the state park, charging about $60 for a round-trip ticket. St Augustine's Charters will drop you off at

Rusty Lagoon and pick you up at Saddle Trail as a way to avoid some backtracking. Book them through Inlet Charters (☎ 235-6126) on the Spit. You can also call Rainbow Tours (☎ 235-7272), while Jakolof Ferry Service (☎ 235-2376) provides transport to Jakolof Bay.

SELDOVIA

Across Kachemak Bay from Homer and in a world of its own is Seldovia (pop 400), a small fishing village. The town is slow moving, sleepy and lives up to its nickname, 'City of Secluded Charm'. Although in recent years tour boats have made it a regular stop, the village has managed to retain much of its old Alaskan charm and can be an interesting and inexpensive side trip away from Alaska's highway system.

History

Seldovia is one of the oldest settlements along Cook Inlet and may have been the site of the first coal mine in Alaska when the Russians began operating one in the late 1700s. Named after the Russian word *seldevoy*, meaning herring bay, the town grew into a year-round harbor for the Russians who gathered timber here to repair their ships. By the 1890s, Seldovia was an important shipping and supply center for the region and the town boomed right into the 1920s with salmon canning, fur farming and a short-lived herring industry. After the Sterling Hwy to Homer was completed in the 1950s, Seldovia's population and importance as a supply center began to dwindle but it was the 1964 earthquake that caused the most rapid change in the community.

The Good Friday Earthquake caused the land beneath Seldovia to settle four feet, allowing high tides to flood much of the original town. In the reconstruction of Seldovia, much of its waterfront and beloved boardwalk were torn out while Cap's Hill was levelled to provide fill material.

Information

Tourist Office An information cache is in the Synergy Art Works on Main St across from

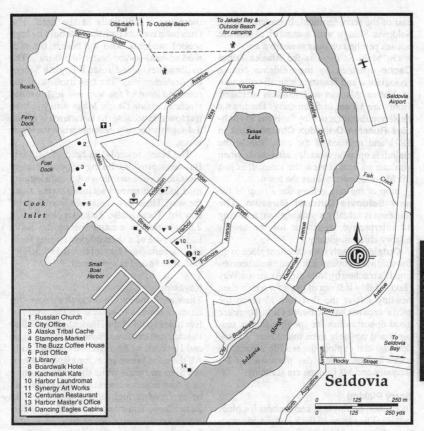

Map legend:
1 Russian Church
2 City Office
3 Alaska Tribal Cache
4 Stampers Market
5 The Buzz Coffee House
6 Post Office
7 Library
8 Boardwalk Hotel
9 Kachemak Kafe
10 Harbor Laundromat
11 Synergy Art Works
12 Centurian Restaurant
13 Harbor Master's Office
14 Dancing Eagles Cabins

Seldovia

0   125   250 m
0   125   250 yds

the boat harbor. The rustic log building is a co-op for local artists to display and sell their pottery, jewelry, prints and other handcrafted items. You can also call the Seldovia Chamber of Commerce (☎ 234-7612) for information.

Post The post office is near the corner of Main St and Anderson Way.

Bookshops Lost Horizon Books, on Main St above the boat harbor, has new and used books for sale.

Laundry Harbor Laundromat (☎ 234-7420) on Main St is a place to do your laundry, take a shower, play a game of pool, or have an ice cream. Owner Peggy Boscacci calls it diversification because 'when you're this small, you've got to cover your bases'.

Medical Services The Seldovia Medical Clinic (☎ 234-7825) is just up Anderson Way from Main St.

Things to See
A small remnant of the early boardwalk can be seen if you walk a short distance to the

east of the ferry terminal. It stretches along Seldovia Slough with a number of historic houses perched on pilings nearby.

On Main St there is the **Alaska Tribal Cache** operated by the Seldovia Native Association and featuring a small collection of Native Alaskan and Russian artefacts. Hours are 10 am to 5 pm daily. The town's most popular attraction by far is the **St Nicholas Russian Orthodox Church**. Built in 1891 and restored in the early 1980s, the church is open on weekday afternoons when you can go in and view the icons. It is just off Main St, overlooking the town.

Stop at the city offices for a map of the new **Seldovia Outdoor Museum**. The museum is actually a walking tour, featuring 12 interpretive signs that list the town's history chronologically.

Outside Beach is an excellent place to go for wildlife sightings and a little beachcombing. It's reached by following Anderson Way (Jakolof Bay Rd) out of town for a mile then heading left at the first fork to reach the picnic area at Outside Beach Park. There are good opportunities for spotting eagles, seabirds and possibly even otters here. At low tide you can explore the sea life among the rocks and on a clear day the views of Mt Redoubt and Mt Iliamna are stunning.

Berry Picking

In Homer, Seldovia is known best for blueberries. They grow so thick just outside town you often can rake your fingers through the bushes and fill a two-quart bucket in minutes. You'll also find good berry picking for low-bush cranberries and salmonberries, a species not found around Homer. But the blueberries are the best. They ripen from late August to mid-September and one of the best places to pick is **Blueberry Hill** between the airstrip and the slough. If you are in Homer on Labor Day weekend head to Seldovia for its **Blueberry Festival** which features, among other activities, a blueberry bake sale and a pick-a-cup-of-berries bicycle race.

Hiking

For those who spend a night in Seldovia, there are a few trails in the area. The Otterbahn is a foot path that was built by high school students who dubbed it the we-worked-hard-so-you-better-like-it trail. The trailhead lies behind Susan B English School off Anderson Way. The trail itself skirts the coastline most of the way and in 1.5 miles reaches Outside Beach. Make sure you hike it at low tide because the last stretch is across a slough that is only passable when the water is out.

The beach towards the head of Seldovia Bay also provides hiking opportunities at low tide or you can follow a 4.5-mile logging road to reach several secluded coves along the way. These two trails start from Jakolof Bay Rd. There is also Tutka/Jakolof Trail, a 2.5-mile trail to a camp site on the Tutka Lagoon, site of a state salmon-rearing facility. It departs from Jakolof Bay Rd 10.5 miles east of town and is signposted.

Kayaking

There are some excellent kayaking opportunities in the Seldovia area. To the north, or five miles south of the Homer Spit, is Eldred Passage and the three islands, Cohen, Yukon and Hesketh, which mark the entrance to it. All three are prime spots for viewing otters, sea lions and seals while the northern shore of Yukon features caves and tunnels that can be explored at high tide. Even closer are Sadie Cove, Tutka and Jackolof bays offering protected water, interesting geological features and numerous camping areas along their beaches.

In town, you can rent kayaks through Kayak'Atak (☎ 234-7425) and then contact Jakolof Bay Express (☎ 234-7479) at the Buzz Coffee House about transport out to Jakolof Bay dock as a way to skip the open stretch of Kachemak Bay. Kayak'Atak also offers guided trips in the area.

Places to Stay

The town's hotel, *The Boardwalk Hotel* (☎ 234-7816 or (800) 238-7862) is on Main St across from the Small Boat Harbor and charges close to $89 a double, or more if the room has a view of the harbor. The hotel also offers a package that includes a room for a night, a cruise to Seldovia and a flight back with Homer Air for $119 per person.

There are also several B&Bs in town with room rates around $75 a night. They include *Gerry's Place* (☎ 243-7471) a block from the harbor and *Seldovia Rowing Club Hotel* (☎ 234-7614) which has a suite for $95 a night for two or three people. The Rowing Club is located on the old boardwalk with a deck overlooking the water. *Dancing Eagles Lodge* (☎ 234-7627) has bedrooms for $45 per person, a chalet cabin for $125 per couple and, best of all, a hot tub. *Seldovia Seaport Cottages* (☎ 234-7483) overlooking the airport has cabins for $60 for two people.

For something a little different there's *Across the Bay Tent & Breakfast* (☎ 235-3633 summer or 345-2571 winter), located eight miles from town right on Jakolof Bay. Accommodation is in cabin-like wall tents for $38 per person, which includes a full breakfast and transportation from Seldovia. For $65 you get all your meals, and dinner could consist of fresh oysters, beach-grilled salmon or halibut stew. The offbeat resort also has mountain bikes for rent for $25 a day and organizes kayak trips.

The best option for many is to camp on spectacular Outside Beach, where the city maintains *Seldovia Wilderness Park*. The rustic facility has spots for both RVers for $8 a night and tent campers for $5. RVers have to stay in the park on the bluff but backpackers can also pitch their tent closer to the shore at one end of Outside Beach.

Places to Eat

At Harbor View and Main St is *Kachemak Kafe*, which opens at 7 am for breakfast and on Friday evening features pizza. Head to the *Centurian Restaurant* on Main St for a view of the harbor or book a reservation at *Harmony Point Lodge* (☎ 234-7858) before 4 pm for an excellent family style seafood dinner in a resort that is located 2.5 miles out Rocky St on Seldovia Bay.

A good place to start the day is *The Buzz Coffee House* on Main St. The coffee house opens at 6 am and doubles up as a bakery and restaurant serving quiches, muffins, croissants and pastries all served in tableware produced by a local potter. Stop by at lunch for home-made soup and bread for $5.50. You'll also find three bars and the *Stamper's Family Market* for groceries, beer and supplies.

Getting There & Away

The ferry makes a run to Seldovia twice a week from Homer. The boat to catch is the Tuesday run which leaves Homer around noon, arrives in Seldovia at 2 pm and stays in port for four hours before returning. The other services reach the town in the early hours of the morning. The ferry terminal (☎ 234-7886) is at the north end of Main St and the one-way fare from Homer to Seldovia is $18.

Several tour boats also offer trips to Seldovia and generally stay in port for two to three hours. Among them is Rainbow Tours (☎ 235-7272 in Homer) which departs daily and swings past the Gull Island bird rookery as well. The round-trip fare is $40.

You can also fly to Seldovia. A scenic 12-minute flight from Homer passes over the Kenai Mountains and Kachemak Bay. Homer Air (☎ 235-8591 or (800) 478-8591 in Alaska) offers several flights daily to Seldovia with a one-way fare of $26 and a round-trip fare of $47.

Getting Around

At the Buzz Coffee House you can rent a mountain bike for $15 for six hours or $20 for the day to see the sights and surrounding area. You also pick up the Jakolof Express Bus that makes the 10-mile run out to the dock in Jakolof Bay and will take you and your kayak or bike as well. The one-way fare is $6.

Kodiak Island

KODIAK

South-west of the Kenai Peninsula in the Gulf of Alaska is Kodiak (pop 15,575). The city is on the eastern tip of Kodiak Island, the largest island in Alaska at 3670 sq miles and the second largest in the country after the Big Island of Hawaii. Kodiak claims several other firsts. It has the largest fishing fleet in the state, with over 2000 boats, making it the second largest commercial fishing port in the USA. At one time fishers were hauling in so much king crab it made the city the top fishing port in the country. Residents proudly call their town the 'King Crab Capital of the World'.

Kodiak Island is home of the famed Kodiak brown bear, the largest terrestrial carnivore in the world. There are an estimated 2400 of these bears on the island and some males have reached 1500 pounds in weight.

Kodiak has some of the foggiest weather in Southcentral Alaska. Greatly affected by the turbulent Gulf of Alaska, the city is often rainy and foggy with occasional high winds. The area receives 80 inches of rain per year

and has an average temperature of 60°F during the summer. On a clear day, however, the scenery is equal to that in any other part of the state. Mountains, craggy coastlines and some of the most deserted beaches accessible by road are Kodiak's most distinctive features.

History

The island, especially the city of Kodiak, can also claim some of the most turbulent history in Alaska. The Russians first landed on the island in 1763 and returned 20 years later when Siberian fur trader Grigorii Shelikhov heard about the abundance of sea otters. Shelikhov sailed into Three Saints Bay on the south side of the island and brought with him his wife, the first White woman to set foot in Alaska. He also had 192 men and a cache of muskets and cannons. Shelikhov's attempts to 'subdue' the indigenous people resulted in a bloodbath near what used to be the village of Old Harbor in which more than

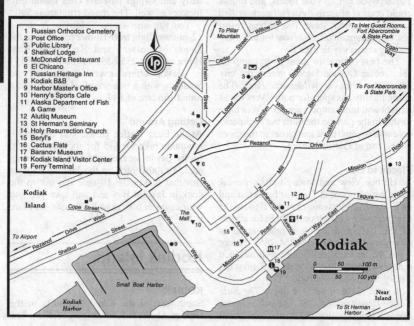

1 Russian Orthodox Cemetery
2 Post Office
3 Public Library
4 Shelikof Lodge
5 McDonald's Restaurant
6 El Chicano
7 Russian Heritage Inn
8 Kodiak B&B
9 Harbor Master's Office
10 Henry's Sports Cafe
11 Alaska Department of Fish & Game
12 Alutiiq Museum
13 St Herman's Seminary
14 Holy Resurrection Church
15 Beryl's
16 Cactus Flats
17 Baranov Museum
18 Kodiak Island Visitor Center
19 Ferry Terminal

To Pillar Mountain
Willow St
Cedar Street
Thorsheim Street
Lower Mill Bay Street
Carolyn
Wilson Ave
Rezanof Drive
Hillcrest Street
Center
Marine Way
The Mall
Mission Road
Katmai
Erskine Avenue
Mission Road
Tagura Road
Benny Benson Drive

To Inlet Guest Rooms, Fort Abercrombie & State Park
Egan Way
To Fort Abercrombie & State Park

Kodiak Island
Cope Street
West
To Airport
Rezanof Drive
Shelikof Street

Kodiak

Small Boat Harbor
Kodiak Harbor

0   50   100 m
0   50   100 yds

Near Island

To St Herman Harbor

Top: The ghost town of Portage (JD)
Bottom: Homer Spit & Kachemak Bay (JD)

Top: Nugget Pond at Camp Denali with Mt McKinley behind (CD)
Bottom: King Mountain & the Matanuska River (DS)

500 Alutiiq Indians were massacred and an equal number drowned in their effort to escape.

Shelikhov returned home the next year and in 1791 Alexander Baranov arrived as the manager of the colony and the Russian American Company. After an earthquake nearly destroyed the infant settlement at Three Saints Bay, Baranov moved his operations to more stable ground at a harbor at the north end which he named St Paul. Quickly it became a bustling port as the first capital of Russian America and today is the city of Kodiak. When the sea-otter colonies had been wiped out, Baranov moved again, this time to Sitka in 1804.

In 1912, Kodiak had its next disaster when Mt Katmai on the nearby Alaska Peninsula erupted. The explosion not only created the Valley of 10,000 Smokes, now part of Katmai National Park, but it blanketed the then sleepy fishing village with 18 inches of ash that blotted out the sun for two days. When a 20-room log cabin caught fire, people 200 feet away were unaware of the blaze it was so dark. Kodiak's 400 residents escaped to sea briefly on a ship that was in port fueling but soon returned to find ash drifts several feet high and spawning salmon choking in ash-filled streams.

Disaster struck again in 1964. The Good Friday Earthquake shook the entire island, and the subsequent sea wave, known as a tsunami, completely leveled the downtown area, destroying the boat harbor and wiping out the local fishing fleet. Processing plants, canneries and 158 homes were lost; damage cost was a sum unheard of back then of $24 million.

The natural disasters, however, are now part of Kodiak's turbulent history and today the city thrives as the fishing capital of Alaska with 15 fish-processing plants employing thousands of people during the summer. Kodiak Island is also the site of Alaska's largest US Coast Guard station, which occupies the old US naval base. Four large Coast Guard cutters patrol out of Kodiak, seizing foreign vessels that illegally fish in US waters and assisting distressed ships caught in the violent storms of the North Pacific.

Kodiak Island was also affected by the Exxon mishap but the oil spill's impact on the fishing pales compared with what over-harvesting did to several species, most notably the king crab.

This giant of crabs is taken from especially deep areas of the ocean and can easily exceed 10 to 15 pounds – enough to feed two or three people. The record king taken in Kodiak weighed a whopping 25 pounds and had a leg span of almost five feet. Kodiak began canning king crabs in 1949 and by 1966, the peak year of the catch, the town landed 90 million pounds. Two years later Kodiak, for the first time, topped all other ports in the country in the value of fish caught with an incredible $132 million, mostly from king crab and a lucrative shrimp fishery.

But the harvest of king crab went into a downward spiral after that until a moratorium halted the crab fishery in 1983. The drag fishery for shrimp was also halted two years later. The city has since rebuilt its seafood industry on bottomfish but the dock-side value of this fishery is a far cry from the golden days of king crab.

Information

Tourist Offices The Kodiak Island Visitor Center (☎ 486-4782) is next to the ferry terminal, on the corner of Center Ave and Marine Way, and open weekdays from 8 am to 5 pm and weekends from 10 am to 3 pm.

The Alaska Division of Parks & Outdoor Recreation maintains an office (☎ 486-6339) at Fort Abercrombie State Historical Park, 4.5 miles north-east of the city off Monashka Bay Rd. The office is open weekdays from 8 am to 5 pm and is the place to go for information on hiking trails, state campgrounds or renting recreation cabins.

The Kodiak National Wildlife Refuge office (☎ 487-2600) is four miles south-west of the city, near the airport at 1390 Buskin River Rd. Open from 8 am to 4.30 pm weekdays and from noon to 4.30 pm weekends, it has information on the public-use cabins.

Money National Bank of Alaska (☎ 486-3126) is on the corner of Mission Rd and Marine Way and features a king-crab display in its lobby.

Post The post office is on Lower Mill Bay Rd just north of the library.

Travel Agencies American Express Travel (☎ 486-6084) is at 202 Center Ave and US Travel (☎ 486-3232) is at 340 Mission Rd.

Bookshop & Library Shire Book Store (☎ 486-5001) is at 104 Center Ave and the Holmes Johnson Memorial Library is on Lower Mill Bay Rd and open daily.

Laundry Ernie's Laundromat (☎ 486-4119), on Shelikof St across from the Small Boat Harbor, has showers for $3.25.

Medical Services Kodiak Island Hospital (☎ 486-3281) is north of the downtown area at 1915 on East Rezanof Dr.

Baranov Museum
Across the street from the visitor center is the Baranov Museum in Erskine House, built by the Russians between 1792 and 1799 as a storehouse for precious sea-otter pelts. The museum contains many items from the Russian period of Kodiak's history and many fine examples of Aleut basketry. The museum is open from 10 am to 4 pm weekdays and noon to 4 pm weekends; admission is $2.

Holy Resurrection Church
Near the museum on Mission Rd is the Holy Resurrection Church, which serves the oldest Russian Orthodox parish in the New World. Established in 1794, the parish celebrated its bicentennial in 1994 with a visit from the Patriarch of the Russian Orthodox Church, Aleksy II. The present church was built in 1945 and is the third one at this site.

One of the original clerics was Father Herman, who was elevated to sainthood at Kodiak in 1970 during the first canonization ever performed in the USA. His relics are kept in a carved wooden chest near the altar.

Also within the church are polished brass-ware, several icons and rare paintings. The church doesn't keep set opening hours; enquire at the visitor center about tours of the interior. Its blue and white onion-domed features make a great photograph, if you can squeeze out the huge gas storage tank that flanks it. A better place to photograph the church is directly above it from Mill Bay Rd where there is an overview of the historical structure.

Alutiiq Museum & Archaeological Repository
Kodiak's newest attraction is the Alutiiq Museum & Archaeological Repository (☎ 486-7004). The museum, just up Mission St from the church, opened in 1995 and features displays, galleries and exhibits in an effort to explain and preserve the Alutiiq heritage of Kodiak's indigenous people. Inside, artefacts range from bone fish hooks and a spruce-framed kayak to a diorama of a traditional village. Hours are from 10 am to 4 pm Monday through Saturday and noon to 4 pm on Sunday. Admission is $2.

St Herman's Theological Seminary
More Russian Orthodox history can be explored still further along Mission Rd at St Herman's Theological Seminary which was founded in 1973 and opens its Veniaminov Research Institute Museum to the public from 1 to 4.30 pm daily. On display inside the museum are indigenous artefacts, icons and Bibles used by Orthodox missionaries on the Yukon River in the 1800s.

Boat Harbors
Follow Marine Way left (west) from the ferry terminal as it curves past the **Small Boat Harbor**, the heart and soul of Kodiak. Crab boats, salmon seiners and halibut schooners cram the city docks, while more boats dock across the channel at **St Herman Harbor** on Near Island. An afternoon on the docks can lead to friendly encounters with fishers and the chance to see catches unloaded or nets being repaired. Although no tours are available, canneries can be seen clattering and

steaming around the clock during the summer on nearby Shelikof St, or you can take the bridge across the channel to St Herman Harbor to view more boats and stop at the **Fish Industrial Technology Center** (☎ 486-1500). Known locally as the Fish Tech Center, this is an extension of the University of Alaska-Fairbanks specifically to provide research for the Alaska seafood industry. Its bayside setting on Near Island is beautiful and inside the lobby is a visitor information display. Hours are 8 am to 5 pm weekdays.

Fort Abercrombie State Historical Park

This military fort was built during WWII by the US Army and included a pair of eight-inch guns for a Japanese invasion that never came. In the end it was lousy Kodiak weather, not the army's superior firepower, that kept the Japanese bombers away from the island. Today, the fort is a state historical park, sitting majestically on the cliffs over wooded Monashka Bay.

Within the 143-acre state park is a small visitor center with natural history displays while a self-guided tour winds through the military relics on Miller Point. On Sunday, Tuesday and Thursday at 2.30 pm, the park staff give a guided historic tour, beginning at the visitor center. Just as interesting as the gun emplacements are the tidal pools found along the rocky shorelines of the park. It's best to have rubber boots if you can for an afternoon of searching for starfish and other sea creatures. The park is 4.5 miles northeast of Kodiak off Monashka Bay Rd.

Pillar Mountain

The placement of a Distant Early Warning (DEW)-line site (a series of radar towers across Alaska and northern Canada that were built primarily to detect an air attack on North America by the USSR) and later a communications saucer on top of this 1270-foot mountain has resulted in a road that climbs to a scenic overlook behind the city and provides excellent views of the surrounding mountains, ocean, beaches and islands. One side seems to plunge straight

down to the harbor below, while the other overlooks the green interior of Kodiak Island. Pick up the bumpy dirt road to Pillar Mountain by heading north up Thorsheim St and turning left on Maple Ave, which runs into Pillar Mountain Rd.

Buskin River State Recreation Site

Four miles south-west of the city on Chiniak Rd is this 90-acre state recreation area, containing 18 camp sites and access to the Buskin River. Anglers flock here for the salmon fishing, the best on this part of Kodiak Island, while nearby is the US Fish & Wildlife Service visitor center dedicated to Kodiak National Wildlife Refuge. The center has numerous exhibits and displays, as well as films on the island's wildlife including the brown bears that live there. Outside there is Buskin View Trail, a short, self-guided nature trail. The center is open from 8 am to 4.30 pm weekdays and from noon to 4.30 pm weekends.

Hiking

There are dozens of hiking trails in the Kodiak area but unfortunately very few are maintained and the trailheads are not always marked along the roads. Once on the path, windfall can make following the track difficult or even totally conceal it. Still, hiking trails are the best avenue to the natural beauty of Kodiak Island. Before starting out, contact the Kodiak area ranger of the Alaska Division of Parks (☎ 486-6339) for the exact location and condition of trails.

Pillar Mountain Trails Two trails depart from Pillar Mountain Rd. The first begins near the KOTV satellite receiver near the lower city reservoir and provides an easy walk north to Monashka Bay Rd. The second begins at the communications tower at the top of the mountain and is a descent of the south-west side. It ends at the Tie Substation, where a gravel road leads out to Chiniak Rd about a mile north-east of the Buskin River State Recreation Site. Plan on an afternoon for either trail.

SOUTHCENTRAL

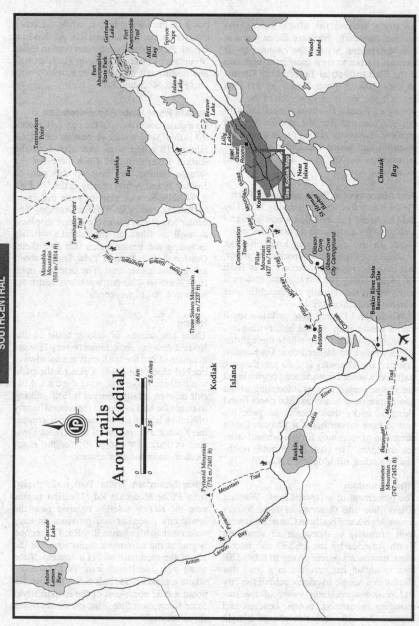

Trails
Around Kodiak

0   2   4 km
0   1.25   2.5 miles

Barometer Mountain Trail This popular trail is a steep climb of five miles to the 2452-foot summit. To reach the trailhead, follow Chiniak Rd south of the Buskin River Campground and turn right on the first road immediately after passing the end of the airport's runway. Look for a well-worn trail on the left. The trek begins in thick alder before climbing the hogback ridge of the mountain to provide spectacular views of Kodiak and the bays south of the city.

Termination Point Trail This is another popular hike along a five-mile trail that starts at the end of Monashka Bay Rd and branches into several trails near Termination Point. Most hiking is done in virgin spruce forest.

Cycling

Cyclists will find Kodiak's roads interesting to ride around, especially the 12-mile Anton Larsen Bay Rd that leads north-west from near Buskin River State Campground over the mountain pass to the west side of the island, where you will find quiet coves and shorelines to explore. Plan on two hours for the ride to Anton Larsen Bay. The ride down Chiniak Rd can be equally impressive while there is now a bike trail that begins on Beaver Lake Loop and ends at the entrance of Fort Abercrombie State Historical Park.

52 Degrees North (☎ 486-6249), at 326 Center Ave, is an outdoor shop that carries mountain bikes and parts, and will know if anyone in town has bikes for rent.

Kayaking

With its many bays and protected inlets, scenic coastline and offshore rookeries, much of Kodiak is a kayaker's dream. A scenic day trip from the downtown area is to paddle around Near and Woody islands (both of which have trails on them), then onto Monashka Bay. More extensive expeditions can be put together by flying into the long bays of Kodiak National Wildlife Refuge or Shuyak Island.

Just finding somebody to rent you a kayak might be tough but ask around. Both Kodiak Kayak Tours (☎ 486-2722 or email Fish2live@aol.com) and Wavetamer Kayaking (☎ 486-2604) offer guided trips, which include all the equipment. For a two to three-hour paddle to Near Island it's around $45 per person, while for a half-day outing to Monashka Bay it's $85.

Organized Tours

Island Terrific Tours (☎ 486-4777) offers tours of the island that include the coast guard base, wildlife refuge center, Baranov Museum and Fort Abercrombie State Historical Park among other sights. The cost is $75.

Special Events

Kodiak's best event, if you happen to be around in late May, is its week-long Crab Festival featuring a parade, a blessing of the fleet, foot and kayak races, fishers'-skills contests like a survival-suit race, and a lot of cooked king crab.

There is also the State Fair & Rodeo held on Labor Day weekend at the Bell Flats rodeo grounds, a 4 July celebration and a variety of foot races throughout the summer, including the Chad Ogden 43-mile Ultra-marathon, staged by Kodiak Parks and Recreation (☎ 486-8665).

Places to Stay

Camping There are no campgrounds in Kodiak and camping within the city limits is illegal. The closest campground is *Gibson Cove City Campground* two miles south-west of the city off Chiniak Rd. This is little more than an open gravel parking lot designed to handle the large influx of cannery workers during the summer. There are restrooms with showers for $3 a night.

Another two miles along Chiniak Rd on the way to the airport is *Buskin River State Recreation Site* (18 sites, $6 fee). The spot is much more pleasant than the cove and provides picnic shelters, pit toilets, trails through nearby wooded areas and good fishing on Buskin River or surf fishing in the ocean. Nearby is the Kodiak National Wildlife Refuge headquarters and visitor center.

The best camping is at *Fort Abercrombie State Historical Park* (14 sites, $6 fee) north-

SOUTHCENTRAL

east of Kodiak, the most scenic campground in which to pitch a tent, and at *Pasagshak River State Recreation Site* 45 miles from town. All three state campgrounds have a seven-day limit on stays.

B&Bs There are almost 20 B&Bs in Kodiak and most have rates ranging from $60 to $70. While not exactly budget accommodation, keep in mind these places provide breakfast, usually transport from the airport and sometimes laundry service. You can get a current list of them at the visitors center in advance that will include rates, facilities offered and other details.

In the downtown area, with rooms for $60/72 a single/double, are *Kodiak Bed & Breakfast* (☎ 486-5367) at 308 Cope St, just up the hill from the Small Boat Harbor, and *Lotus Inn* (☎ 486-4962) at 304 Wilson St. Many of the B&Bs are on Mission Rd towards the Coast Guard base but all of them provide pick-up service. There's *Star House B&B* (☎ 486-8823) with singles/doubles for $55/70, *Wintel's B&B* (☎ 486-6935) nearby with four rooms for $50 to $90 and *Shahafka Cove B&B* (☎ 486-2409) with four rooms at $55 to $95.

Hotels There is no hostel in Kodiak and hotels are expensive, partly because the city hits you with a 6% sales tax and a 5% bed tax. On a $60 room you can pay almost $7 in local taxes. The run-down Kodiak Star Motel has recently been renovated and is now the *Russian Heritage Inn* (☎ 486-5657), 119 Yukon St, featuring some rooms with kitchenettes and an on-site laundromat. Rates begin at $65 for a single or a double. In the same price range is *Shelikof Lodge* (☎ 486-4141) at 211 Thorsheim St. There's also *Inlet Guest Rooms* (☎ 486-4004 or (800) 423-4004), 10 blocks north of the downtown area on Mill Bay Rd. The six rooms are $55/65 for singles/doubles. All hotels tend to be heavily booked during the summer.

Places to Eat
For fast food there's *McDonald's* near the

busy intersection of Center Ave and East Rezanof Dr, while just down Center Ave towards the ferry terminal is *Subway* where small subs are $4 and a large seafood and crab sub is $7. There's also a *Pizza Hut* on Mill Bay Rd.

There's also *King's Diner* in the Lilly Lake Plaza on Mill Bay Rd. It opens daily at 5.30 am to serve sourdough pancakes while at night there are dinner specials and home-made pie. For Mexican food, there's *El Chicano* on Center St in the mall next to the Ford dealer. Open daily, the popular restaurant has small portions but 'grande' margaritas. It's up to you if you want to eat or drink.

All of the city's Asian restaurants are near Rezanof Dr and Center Ave. The best deal on Chinese, however, is at *Henry's Sports Cafe* on the mall in front of the Small Boat Harbor. It has a $7 Chinese-lunch special from 11 am to 3 pm, seafood, hamburgers for under $6, beer on tap and even espresso.

You'll find health food at *Cactus Flats* on the corner of Mission Rd and Center Ave and espresso and desserts at *Beryl's* down an alley just off Center Ave. Or have a night of adventure by driving 40 miles to the end of Chiniak Rd where you'll find *Road's End Restaurant* (☎ 486-2885).

Entertainment
Clustered around the city waterfront and Small Boat Harbor are a handful of bars that cater to Kodiak's fishing industry. At night they are interesting places, overflowing with fishers, deck hands and cannery workers drinking hard and talking lively. The *B&B* across from the harbor claims to be Alaska's oldest bar, having served its first beer in 1899. Another is the *Breakers* nearby on Center Ave which is almost as colorful inside as is its mural outside. For music at night there is *Mecca*, 302 Marine Way, with rock & roll music booming across its dance floor on most nights in the summer.

Getting There & Away
Air Both Alaska Airlines and its contract carrier, ERA (☎ (800) 426-0333), fly to

Kodiak to combine for six flights daily. The regular, round-trip fare is $300 to $380 but a 14-day advance purchase ticket with which you stay over on Sunday is only $199. Keep in mind that if you travel from Anchorage to Kodiak by going via bus to Homer and then taking the ferry, it's going to cost you $176 for the round trip and involve your spending 12 hours on a bus. The airport is five miles south of Kodiak on Chiniak Rd and the Airport Shuttle will run you into town for $5.

Boat The ferry MV *Tustumena* stops at Kodiak three times a week coming from either Seward or Homer, stopping first at Port Lions, a nearby village on Kodiak Island. The ferry terminal (☎ 486-3800) is right downtown where it's easy to walk around even if you're just in port for an hour or two. The one-way fare to Homer is $48 and to Seward $54.

Getting Around

Car There are a number of car-rental companies in Kodiak that will provide you with wheels to explore the island's outer edges. The cheapest is Rent-A-Heap where used cars cost $30 a day plus 29 cents a mile for a small two-door compact. The company has two locations: at the airport (☎ 487-4001) and at the Port of Kodiak Gift Shop (☎ 486-8550) downtown on the mall. If you're planning to drive around the island that 29-cents-a-mile rate will quickly drain your funds. In that case, rent a subcompact from Budget Rent-A-Car (☎ 487-2220) with unlimited mileage for $43 a day.

AROUND KODIAK
Kodiak Island Roads

More than 100 miles of paved and gravel roads head from the city into the wilderness that surrounds Kodiak. Some of the roads are rough jeep tracks, manageable only by 4WD vehicles, but many can be driven or hitched along to isolated stretches of beach, great fishing spots and superb coastal scenery.

To the south of Kodiak, Chiniak Rd winds 47.6 miles to Cape Greville, following the edge of three splendid bays along the way. The road provides access to some of the best coastal scenery in Alaska and opportunities to view sea lions and puffins offshore, especially at Cape Chiniak near the road's southern end. To spend a night this far out, there's *Road's End Lodge* (☎ 486-2885) at *Mile 42* where a single or a double is $60 a night.

Just past *Mile 30* of Chiniak Rd you arrive at the junction with Pasagshak Bay Rd that winds 16.4 miles due south to the *Pasagshak River State Recreation Site* near a beautiful stretch of rugged coastline. This small, riverside campground (seven sites, free) is famous for its silver and king-salmon fishing as well as for a river that reverses its flow four times a day with the tides. These scenic areas, and not the city, are the true attractions of Kodiak Island. Anybody who has the time (and patience) to hitchhike or the money to rent a car (see the previous Kodiak Getting Around section) should explore these roads.

Kodiak National Wildlife Refuge

This 1.8 million-acre preserve, which covers the southern two-thirds of Kodiak Island as well as Ban Island and a small section of Afognak Island, is the chief stronghold of the Alaska brown bear. An estimated 3000 bears reside in the refuge and the surrounding area, which is known worldwide for brown bear hunting and to a lesser degree for salmon and steelhead fishing. There are no maintained trails within the preserve and cross-country hiking is extremely hard due to thick bush. Nor can any part of the refuge be reached from the road system. Access to the park is by charter plane or boat out of Kodiak – either way can run you a tab as most of the refuge is at least 25 air miles away.

What most people really want to see in the refuge are the massive brown bears. Just about every air charter company in town offers a brown bear-viewing flight, in which you fly over remote shorelines in the refuge looking for bears. The length of flights and the number of times you land differ from one 'tour' to the next but generally you can count on paying from $200 to almost $400 per person for flights lasting from 90 minutes to half a day, and that price includes landing and photographing bears feeding on salmon. For those with only a day or two in Kodiak, this is really the only feasible way you have of seeing the famous bears. Among the air services that offer bear tours are Seahawk Air (☎ 486-8282 or (800) 770-HAWK), Island Air Service (☎ (800) 504-2337 or 486-6196) and Uyak Air Service (☎ (800) 303-3407 or 486-3407).

Places to Stay The US Fish & Wildlife Service administers seven cabins in the refuge that should be reserved in advance. The closest units to Kodiak are *Uganik Lake Cabin* and *Veikoda Bay Cabin*, which are on the ocean and features good beaches nearby. The rate is $20 a night. If you are planning your trip, write to the Kodiak National Wildlife Refuge (1390 Buskine River Rd, Kodiak, AK 99615) about reserving a cabin. If you're already in Kodiak, call the refuge

headquarters (☎ 487-2600) to check if any cabins are available.

Shuyak Island State Park

Covering almost a quarter of the most northern island in the Kodiak archipelago, this park, 54 air miles north of Kodiak, features a unique rainforest of virgin Sitka spruce, rugged coastline, beaches and protected waterways. Wildlife offshore includes otters, sea lions and dall porpoises, while on shore a modest population of the famous Kodiak brown bear.

Shuyak is not large – the island is only 12 miles long and 11 miles wide – yet it contains more sheltered waterways than any other part of the archipelago, making it a kayaker's delight. Most of the kayaking takes place in and around Big Bay, the heart of the state park. From the bay you can paddle and portage to all four public cabins and other protected bays including Skiff Passage and

The Bears of Kodiak

The Kodiak Archipelago is home to a wide range of land mammals, including river otters, Sitka black-tail deer, Roosevelt elk and mountain goats. But almost everybody arrives hoping to catch a glimpse of just one – the Kodiak bear.

This subspecies of the brown bear, or *Ursus arctos middendorffi* as the scientific community refers to it, is the largest land carnivore in the world. Males normally weigh in at more than 800 pounds but have been known to exceed 1500 pounds. Females usually weigh in at 400 to 600 pounds. From late April through June the bears range from sea level to mid-elevations and are seen feeding on grasses and shrubs. In July many are found grazing in alpine meadows. But from mid-July to mid-September, the bears congregate at streams to gorge themselves on spawning salmon. The runs are so heavy, the bears often become selective and many feast only on females and then eat only the belly portion containing the eggs. The carcass they toss aside is immediately devoured by such scavengers-in-waiting as red foxes, bald eagles and sea gulls.

Because of their overwhelming size and strength and their unpredictable personalities, Kodiak bears are potentially very dangerous animals. But they rarely live up to their 'killer' reputations. Only seven people were mauled between 1973 and 1992 and none of them died. In fact, no one has been killed by a bear on Kodiak in more than 35 years.

Biologists estimate there are 3000 brown bears living in the archipelago, or one bear per 1.5 sq miles, with more than 2500 on Kodiak Island itself. But you won't see any near the city of Kodiak or even from the road system itself. Like most wild animals, Kodiak bears are often secretive around humans. They are most active in early morning and late evening hours and spend much of their time in dense alder thickets.

The best time to see the bears is during the salmon-feeding period from July to September and the only practical way to do this is through the handful of air-charter operators who specialize in bear-sighting flights. A half-day flight usually includes 30 to 60 minutes in the air and a couple of hours on the ground watching the bears feed at a salmon stream. The cost can range anywhere from $300 to $500 a person. So how badly do you want to see the world's largest land carnivore? ■

Western Inlet, where there are numerous islands to explore at it's entrance as well as the opportunity to sight an occasional humpback whale.

The park's four *cabins* are on Big Bay, Neketa Bay and Carry Inlet, and are cedar structures with bunks for eight, a wood stove, propane lights and a cooking stove, but no running water. The cabins cost $50 per day or $35 before June. It's best to write for reservations before your trip to Alaska State Parks, SR Box 3800, Kodiak, AK 99615. But if you are passing through Kodiak give the Alaska Division of Parks (☎ 486-6339) a call to see if any of the cabins happen to be available.

Anchorage

Anchorage, the hub of Alaska's road system and home for almost half of the state's residents, is a city of prosperity and much debate. Those who live in the Anchorage area (pop 248,296) claim there is no other city like it in the world. In Alaska's Big Apple everything you could possibly want is only a short hop away; glaciers, mountains, hiking trails or whitewater rivers to raft are just a 30-minute drive from the city. And within a couple of hours there's the recreation paradise of the Kenai Peninsula and a handful of state and national preserves which offer unlimited camping, hiking and fishing.

Yet in Anchorage you can enjoy all the comforts and attractions offered by any large US city, including a modern performing arts center, enclosed shopping malls and major retailers such as Kmart, Wal-Mart and Computer City that bring the lowest cost of living in Alaska to Anchorage. At night, bars and nightclubs buzz into the late hours.

But many of the state's residents shake their head and say, 'Anchorage is great, it's only 20 minutes from Alaska'. To these people, everything that Alaska is, Anchorage isn't. The city is a mass of urban sprawl or, in down-to-earth terms, 'a beer can in the middle of the woods'. It has billboards, traffic jams, dozens of fast-food restaurants and, occasionally, smog and crime.

With the exception of New York, no other city provokes such a love-hate relationship. Without exception, no other city in any other state has such pull or gobbles up so much of the public funds as Anchorage, an Athens in Alaska. And if you're a traveler, it is inevitable that you'll pass through Anchorage at least once, if not several times.

Anchorage has the advantage of being north of the Kenai Mountains, which shield the city from the excess moisture experienced by Southcentral Alaska. The Anchorage Bowl – the city and surrounding area – receives only 14 inches of rain annually. Nor does the area have the extreme

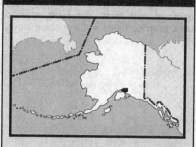

HIGHLIGHTS

- Gaze at Sydney Laurence's 10-foot painting of Mt McKinley
- Rent a bicycle and enjoy views of Cook Inlet and the Alaska Range
- Watch videos of brown bears, whales and other wildlife at the Alaska Public Lands Information Center
- Laugh at Alaskans making fun of Spam and themselves at *Mr Whitekey's Fly by Nite Club*
- Touch an iceberg at Portage Glacier's Begich-Boggs Visitor Center
- Visit an historic gold mine in a beautiful alpine setting at Independence Mine State Historical Park

temperatures of the Interior. The average temperature in January is 13°F, while at the height of the summer it's only 58°F. The area does, however, have more than its fair share of overcast days, especially in early and late summer.

History

Although Captain James Cook sailed up Cook Inlet in 1778 looking for the elusive Northwest Passage, Anchorage wasn't founded until 1914 when surveyors chose the site as the work camp and headquarters for the Alaska Railroad. In 1915 the 'Great Anchorage Lot Sale' was held when some 655 lots were sold for $225 and soon there was a tent city of 2000 people. From that point on the area's growth occurred in spurts caused by increased farming in the Matanuska Valley to the north in the 1930s, the construction of military bases during WWII, and the discovery of oil in Cook Inlet in 1957.

But two events literally reshaped and were responsible for Anchorage today. The first was the Good Friday Earthquake of 1964, the largest one ever recorded in the western hemisphere. It was originally measured at 8.4 on the Richter scale but years later was upped to 9.2. It lasted an unprecedented five minutes and when it was finished the north side of 4th Ave was 10 feet lower than the south side. In one neighborhood, more than 100 homes slid off a bluff into the Knik Arm, some as far as 1200 feet. Nine people were killed and a city lay in shambles. Then four years later, Atlantic Richfield discovered a $10-billion oil reserve at a place called Prudhoe Bay.

Though the Trans-Alaska Pipeline doesn't come within 300 miles of Anchorage, as the headquarters for the petroleum and service companies the city gushes with oil money. Prudhoe Bay oil revitalized Anchorage and turned its downtown area into a showpiece that would be the envy of many other cities.

When a barrel of crude was more than $20 during the late 1970s and Alaska couldn't spend its tax revenue fast enough, Anchorage received the lion's share. The downtown area was revitalized with such projects as the Sullivan Sports Arena, the Egan Civic Center and the stunning Alaska Center for the Performing Arts. As well, a 122-mile network of bicycle trails was paved and the Anchorage Historical & Fine Arts Museum was expanded.

The city that has stage plays and snowy peaks also has pork-barrel power. It comes from its residents, who make up 40% of the state's population. Translated into political muscle, nine of the 20 state senators and 17 of the 40 state representatives represent the municipality of Anchorage. This causes problems if you don't happen to live in Anchorage. The biggest rivalry exists between Anchorage and Fairbanks, the

second largest municipality with 70,000 residents. Fairbanks has long accused its sister to the south of trying to have major departments at the Fairbanks campus of the University of Alaska (the main one) moved to UA-Anchorage. Juneau, the third largest city (pop 30,000), has no love for Anchorage either, seeing it as the power broker in an effort to move the state capital north.

What can't be debated is that Anchorage is truly the heart of Alaska and the center of the state's commerce and financial communities. Though the wide Anchorage Bowl is boxed in by the Chugach Mountains to the east and Cook Inlet to the west, the city continues to sprawl and seems to be in a constant state of rebuilding. Although the decline of oil prices in the late 1980s has slowed its economy, Anchorage is still the fastest growing city in Alaska. Love Anchorage or hate it, one thing is certain – as long as oil gushes in Alaska, this city will prosper.

Orientation

If you fly into Anchorage, you'll arrive at the airport in the south-west corner of the city. If you drive in from the south on Seward Hwy or from the north on Glenn Hwy, the roads lead you to the downtown area, where they end less than a mile from each other.

Downtown Anchorage is a somewhat undefined area boxed in by 3rd Ave to the north, 10th Ave to the south, Minnesota Dr to the west and A St to the east. What is commonly referred to as Midtown Anchorage is an area that extends from east to west from Minnesota Dr to Seward Hwy and north to south from Fireweed Lane to International Airport Rd. The heart of it is the heavily commercialized area around Northern Lights and Benson boulevards. Finally, South Anchorage is generally considered to be the area south of Dowling Rd, including the Hillside Park residential areas on the doorstep of Chugach State Park.

Information

Tourist Offices There are several visitor centers in Anchorage. The main one is the Log Cabin Visitor Center (☎ 274-3531), on

ANCHORAGE

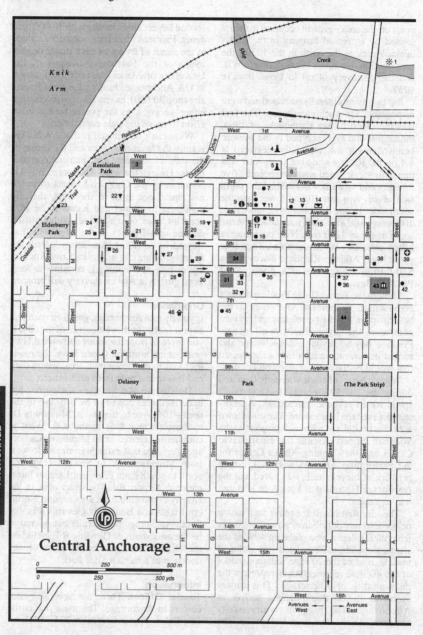

Central Anchorage

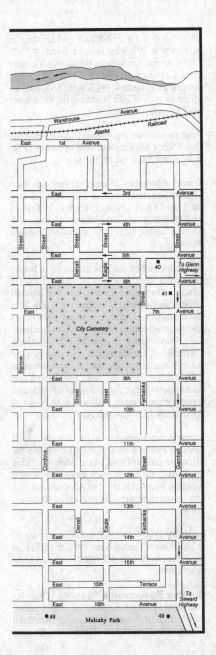

PLACES TO STAY
21 Hotel Captain Cook
25 Copper Whale Inn
26 Caribou Inn
29 Inlet Inn
38 6th & B Bed & Breakfast
40 Red Ram Motel
41 Alaskan Samovar Inn/Seward Bus Lines
46 Anchorage International (AYH) Hostel
47 Snowshoe Inn

PLACES TO EAT
11 Downtown Deli
13 Blondie's Cafe
15 Cyrano's Books & Cafe
19 Side Street Espresso
22 Alaska Adventures & Delights Espresso
24 Simon & Seafort's Saloon & Grill
27 Wings 'n Things/Muffin Man
32 Bear Paw Coffee
33 Humpy's Bar

OTHER
1 Ship Creek Salmon Viewing Platform
2 Alaska Railroad Train Station
3 State Court Building
4 Alaska Statehood Monument
5 Cadastral Survey Monument
6 Saturday Market
7 Alaska Airlines
8 Alaska Booking & Reservation Center
9 Old Federal Building & Alaska Public Lands Information Center
10 Gray Line & Columbia Glacier Tours
12 Post Office Mall
14 Post Office
16 Old City Hall
17 Log Cabin Visitors Center
18 Convention Center
20 Imaginarium
23 Oscar Anderson House
28 Oomingmak Musk Ox Producers Co-op
30 Transit Center
31 City Hall
34 Alaska Center for the Performing Arts
35 Library
36 Fire
37 Police
39 Open Door Clinic
42 Taheta Art & Culture Group Co-op
43 Anchorage Historical & Fine Arts Museum
44 Federal Building
45 ACRO Building
48 Mulcahy Ball Park
49 Sports Arena

ANCHORAGE

the corner of 4th Ave and F St, open daily from 7.30 am to 7 pm June to August, 8.30 am to 6 pm May and September, and 9 am to 4 pm the rest of the year. Along with many services and hand-outs, this center operates an Emergency Language Bank of 27 languages designed to help foreign travelers in distress. It also has a 24-hour All About Anchorage recording (☎ 276-3200) that lists current events taking place in the city that day.

There is another visitor center (☎ 266-2437) at the Anchorage international airport in the baggage claim level of the south (domestic) terminal. It is open from 9 am to 4 pm. You will also find self-service information areas in the north (international) terminal and the Alaska Railroad Depot downtown.

Backpackers and hikers should contact the Alaska Public Lands Information Center (☎ 271-2737) in the Old Federal Building on the corner of 4th Ave and F St (diagonally opposite the Log Cabin Visitors Center) for information and hand-outs on any national park, federal refuge or state park in Alaska. This is where to head for help when planning wilderness adventures and to purchase topographic maps and books. Visiting the center is like 'one-stop shopping' for information on outdoor activities and trips; 99% of your questions will be answered here. It is open from 9 am to 5.30 pm daily in the summer.

If the Public Lands office can't help you, there are several other centers that you can contact. Information on state parks can also be obtained from the Alaska Department of Natural Resources Public Information Center (☎ 269-8400) at 3601 C St. The Chugach National Forest office (☎ 271-2500) at Suite 206, 201 East 9th St, has details on any USFS national forest, trail or cabin. The US Fish & Wildlife Service (for the Kenai National Wildlife Refuge) (☎ 786-3487) also maintains an office at 1011 East Tudor Rd.

Money Banks and ATMs abound in Anchorage. Key Bank of Alaska has several locations including one downtown at 601 West 5th Ave (☎ 257-5500) and another in Midtown at 101 West Benson Blvd (☎ 562-6100). In the Anchorage Hilton is a Thomas Cook Currency Service (☎ 278-2822), while American Express (☎ 274-5588) has an office in the ACRO Building on the corner of G St and 7th Ave.

Post Downtown the main post office is at the Post Office Mall on 4th Ave opposite D St, with an entrance off of 3rd Ave.

Travel Agencies Werner Travel has two offices, one downtown at 444 West 7th Ave (☎ 276-5855). World Express Travel (☎ 786-3200), at 206 West 34th Ave, will arrange airline tickets to anywhere outside Alaska.

Bookstores For the best selection of books on Alaska, head to either the Alaska Public Lands Information Center (see the Tourist Offices section of this chapter) or Cook Inlet Book Store at 415 5th Ave, which always has autographed copies of titles by local authors. Title Wave Used Books, at 505 Northern Lights Blvd, carries a great selection of used but still readable paperbacks, most priced at half of what they cost new. For almost any Alaska newspaper and many out-of-state and foreign papers there is *Sourdough News & Tobacco* at 735 West 4th Ave.

Library Anchorage's main library is ZJ Loussac Public Library (☎ 261-2845) in the Midtown area at Denali St at 36th Ave. This impressive facility is open daily, has several lounges, Internet access, an Alaskana section and a complete set of topographic maps for the state.

Laundry Dirty clothes can be taken care of at Don Dee's Laundromat (☎ 279-0251) on the corner of Northern Lights Blvd and Minnesota Ave.

Outdoor Equipment & Supplies Whatever you need, a bicycle spoke or a tent stake, you'll find it somewhere along Northern Lights Blvd, between Minnesota Dr and

New Seward Hwy. For backpacking, kayaking or camping gear, there's an impressive REI (☎ 272-4565) at 1200 West Northern Lights Blvd in the Northern Lights Shopping Center or Gary King's Sports (☎ 272-5401) at East Northern Lights Blvd while across the street from REI is R&R Bicycle (☎ 276-8536). There is also the Sears Mall near New Seward Hwy with a Carrs Supermarket on one side of it and a Fred Meyers on the other to replenish your food bag.

Medical Services The Alaska Regional Hospital (☎ 276-1131) is on the corner of DeBarr Rd and Airport Heights near Mirrill Field. Medical Park Family Clinic (☎ 279-8486), at 2211 East Northern Lights Blvd, has walk-in service and is open on Saturday.

Walking Tour
Begin any visit to the city at the **Log Cabin Visitors Center** on the corner of 4th Ave and F St. Among the hand-outs and maps they provide is the *Anchorage Visitors Guide*, which describes among other things a three to four-hour walking tour of the downtown area.

The beautiful thing about getting around Anchorage is the simplicity of the street layout, especially in the city center. Numbered avenues run north to south and lettered streets east to west.

The city walking tour begins by heading over to the **Alaska Public Lands Information Center**, in the Old Federal Building, open from 9 am to 5.30 pm. Even if you're not into backpacking or camping, you will find the exhibits inside excellent. Among the wildlife displays, there is a series of individual monitors that shows videos on topics ranging from glaciers and salmon in the Kenai River to Inuit whaling.

By backtracking to E St and heading north, you pass the **Cadastral Survey Monument** on the corner of 2nd Ave and then swing around near the **Alaska Railroad Depot**. The monument notes the original 1915 town-site survey and has four etchings that trace the development of Anchorage

from its first auction of public land to a current city map. The railroad depot, at the base of the hill, features historical photos and a railroading gift shop in its lobby, totem poles outside and Engine No 1 on a platform.

The tour, however, misses the depot by turning west at 2nd Ave and passing the **Alaska Statehood Monument, Ship Creek Viewpoint** and the start of the **Tony Knowles Coastal Trail** (see the Cycling section of this chapter).

Back on 4th Ave, head west of the Log Cabin to K St and turn right. Half a block north on K St is the eye-catching large statue entitled **The Last Blue Whale**.

Nearby at the west end of 3rd Ave is **Resolution Park** and the **Captain Cook Monument**, which honors the 200th anniversary of the English captain's sailing into Cook Inlet with officers George Vancouver and William Bligh at his side. If not overrun by passengers of a tour bus or two, this observation deck has an excellent view of the surrounding mountains, including the Talkeetnas to the north-east and the snow-covered Alaska Range to the west. On a clear day you can see Mt McKinley and Mt Foraker to the north, while to the west is Mt Susitna, known as 'The Sleeping Lady', which marks the south-west end of the Alaska Range.

The tour continues south down to **Oscar Anderson House** (☎ 274-2336) in the delightful Elderberry Park on M St just north of 5th Ave. Anderson was the 18th person to set foot in Anchorage and his home was the first wood-frame house built in the city. Now it's the only home museum in Anchorage and is open from noon to 4 pm daily. Admission is $3.

On the corner of 6th Ave and H St is the **Oomingmak Musk Ox Producers Co-op** (☎ 272-9225). The co-operative handles a variety of garments made of arctic musk-ox wool, hand knitted in isolated Inuit villages. Outside, a mural depicts a herd of musk oxen, while inside the results of this cottage industry are sold.

At 725 5th Ave, near the Transit Center, is the **Imaginarium** (☎ 276-3179), a hands-on

The Art of Sydney Laurence

Of all the artists who have been inspired by Alaska – and the grandeur of this land has inspired a lot of them – none is more widely recognized than Sydney Laurence, the 'Painter of the North'. Born in Brooklyn, New York, in 1865, Laurence was exhibiting paintings by the time he was 22 and was involved in the founding of the American Fine Arts Society in 1889. But the lure of gold was a strong fever and in 1904 the painter left his wife and two children and made his way to Alaska.

For the next nine years Laurence did little painting and a lot of panning for gold in Southcentral Alaska but never found any great quantities of the precious metal. In 1913, he was commissioned by a group of Valdez businessmen to produce a painting of Mt McKinley for the Panama Pacific Exposition in San Francisco. The grand painting never made it to the expo but was added to the Smithsonian Institution collection in 1915, the same year Laurence set up a photography studio in a bustling little tent city called Anchorage.

The painter lived in Anchorage until his death in 1940 and during those years was enormously prolific. While the rest of the country may not have always recognized his name, in Alaska, Laurence has become an almost mythic figure and his paintings still mesmerize thousands of people each summer. As one art critic put it in an issue of *Southwest Art* magazine: 'The message of his work is clear; the Alaskan landscape was immeasurably greater than the deeds of the men and the women who inhabited it. Not so much hostile as indifferent, the northern landscape had the same mystique of unspoiled, seemingly limitless horizon that the American west had a half century earlier.'

Laurence's most impressive work, a six by 10-foot painting of Mt McKinley, is the centerpiece of the historical art collection of the Anchorage Historical & Fine Arts Museum which has a room devoted to oils by Laurence. You can also enjoy a half-dozen more of his works, including several smaller paintings of Mt McKinley (his favorite subject), at the fine Heritage Library Museum in the National Bank of Alaska building on Northern Lights Blvd. ■

science museum and a place to go if you have children tagging along. The award-winning center features more than 20 exhibits that explain the northern lights, earthquakes, oil exploration, bears and other Alaskan topics. You can even enter a polar bear's den or dabble your fingers in a marine-life touch tank. The museum is open from 10 am to 6 pm Monday to Saturday and noon to 5 pm on Sunday. Admission is $5 for adults and $4 for children.

Diagonally across from the Transit Center on the north side of 6th Ave is the new **Alaska Center for the Performing Arts**, one of only 22 such centers in the country. Alaskan artists designed the lobby and contributed a number of art pieces, including 23 Native American masks. During the summer, tours are given on Wednesday at 1 pm for a $1. Or you can just buy your lunch from a street vendor on 4th Ave and enjoy it on a hillside seat in **Town Square Park** that overlooks the arts center and surrounding flower beds.

Eventually, the tour leads to the **Anchorage Historical & Fine Arts Museum**

(☎ 343-4326) near the corner of 7th Ave and A St. In 1984, the museum was expanded to triple its original size and now is an impressive center for displays on Alaskan history and indigenous culture as well as an art gallery featuring work by regional, national and international artists. The Alaska Gallery upstairs traces the history and people of this land in three-dimensional exhibits. The museum is open daily from 9 am to 6 pm during the summer and the admission of $4 is well worth it.

Heritage Library Museum

A place to see fine Native Alaskan art work is the Heritage Library Museum (☎ 265-2834) on the 1st floor in the National Bank of Alaska Building on the corner of Northern Lights Blvd and C St. The center features an impressive collection of Native American tools, costumes and weapons, original paintings, including several by Sydney Laurence, and lots of scrimshaw. Much of the carved ivory is from the gold-rush days in Nome and was purchased by miners as proof they had been in Alaska despite not bringing any gold home. The museum is open weekdays from noon to 4 pm and admission is free.

Parks

Earthquake Park Among other things, the 1964 earthquake caused 130 acres of land on the west side of the city to slip 2000 feet towards the sea. The east end of that strip was Turnagain Heights, a neighborhood where 75 homes were destroyed and three people died. The other end was undeveloped and today is Earthquake Park at the west end of Northern Lights Blvd on the Knik Arm.

There is an interesting display at the park which details the earthquake while its power can still be seen in a jagged crease that runs through the middle. The best feature of the park is the panorama of the city skyline set against the Chugach Mountains. On a clear day you can see Mt McKinley and Mt Foraker to the north from the Tony Knowles Coastal Trail at the lower area of the park.

Delaney Park Within the city center there is Delaney Park, known locally as 'The Park Strip' because it stretches from A to P streets between 9th and 10th avenues. The green belt, the site of the 50-ton bonfire that highlighted statehood in 1959 and later where Pope John Paul II gave an outdoor mass in 1981, is a good place to lie down on a hot afternoon.

Russian Jack Springs This is a 300-acre park south of Glenn Hwy on Boniface Parkway that can be reached by Bus No 12. The city park features tennis courts, four miles of hiking and biking trails and a picnic area. Near the entrance is the **Municipal Greenhouse** (☎ 333-8610) with tropical plants, exotic birds and fish and is open from 8 am to 3 pm daily.

Far North Bicentennial Park This is 4000 acres of forest and muskeg in east central Anchorage. It features 20 miles of trails for hiking and mountain biking along with **Hilltop Ski Area**, whose chalet (☎ 346-1446) can provide you with a trail guide. In the center of the park is **BLM's Campbell**

Tract, a 700-acre wildlife oasis where it's possible to see moose and bears in the spring and brilliant fall colors in mid-September. To reach the Hilltop Ski Area, take O'Malley Rd east to Hillside Dr and follow the road to the parking area. Bus Nos 91 and 92 go past it.

Westchester Lagoon Waterfowl Sanctuary More wildlife, mostly ducks and geese, can be seen closer to the downtown area at this sanctuary. On the corner of Spenard Rd and 19th Ave, the small preserve is a year-round home for a variety of birds and features displays and a half-mile nature trail around the small lake. For information on park activities, call the city's Department of Parks & Recreation (☎ 343-4474).

Lakes

If the weather is hot enough, several lakes in

Goodbye to the 'Alaska Ear'

In 1996 a little bit of what was unique about Alaska was put to death by an Outsider and it irked many residents of Anchorage. For years the *Anchorage Daily News* ran a column that was called 'Alaska Ear: The Divine Appendage', a potpourri of local tidbits, political hearsay and good old fashioned gossip according to 'unnamed sources' and Alaskans everywhere loved it. As one reader wrote: 'It was an example of that irreverent we-don't-care-how-they-do-it-on-the-Outside attitude that drew most of us to Alaska in the first place'.

But after Howard Weaver, the longtime editor of the *Daily News*, went south for a new position and warmer weather in California, the company that owned the *Daily News* sent up an Outsider to take his place and he promptly axed the 'Alaska Ear'. Alaskans were either stunned or saddened. 'Can we vote on whether to keep the Ear or junk it?' asked one reader. 'After all, we get to vote on the comics'. ■

the area offer swimming or simply a place to sit and watch the water. The closest one downtown is **Goose Lake**, two miles southeast on Northern Lights Blvd near the UA-Anchorage campus (take bus No 3 or 45). It is connected to Goose Lake Park by footpaths. There is also swimming at **Spenard Lake**, three miles south of the downtown area on Spenard Rd and then west on Lakeshore Dr (take bus No 7 or 36), and at **Jewel Lake**, 6.5 miles south-west of the city center on Dimond Blvd (take bus No 7).

Military Bases
Elmendorf Air Force Base and Fort Richardson were established during WWII as the major northern military outposts for the USA, and continue today to contribute to Anchorage's economy. Due to military cutbacks, however, neither base offer tours but both still manage wildlife museums.

Elmendorf Air Force Base Wildlife Museum
This museum (☎ 552-2282) has more than 200 Alaskan mammals, fish, birds and a 10½-foot-high brown bear that misses the world record by an eighth of an inch, as well as hands-on exhibits. It is open from 10 am to 2 pm weekdays, and 1 to 5 pm on Saturday. Admission is free and can be reached by bus No 75 from the Transit Center.

Fort Richardson Fish and Wildlife Center
The center (☎ 384-0431), featuring 250 specimens in Building 600, is open from 9 am to 4.30 pm weekdays, except Wednesday when it is open only to 11.30 am. Admission is free and can be reached by bus No 75 from the Transit Center.

UA-Anchorage
This is the largest college campus in the state but there is not nearly as much to do here as there is at its sister school, UA-Fairbanks, to the north. Still the school is impressive and connected with bike paths to Goose Lake, Chester Creek Green Belt and Earthquake Park. Stop in at the Campus Center where you'll find an Olympic-size pool with open

swims, a small art gallery, and the UA-A Bookstore for some collegewear with Alaska on it. On the ground floor is the University Pub where there are affordable sandwiches and occasionally live music. Bus Nos 3, 11, and 45 swing past the campus.

Lake Hood Air Harbor
Those enchanted by Alaska's bush planes and small air-taxi operators will be overwhelmed by Lake Hood, the world's busiest float-plane base (and ski-plane base in the winter). Almost every type of small plane imaginable can be seen flying onto and off the lake's surface. The float-plane base makes an interesting afternoon trip when combined with a swim in adjoining Lake Spenard (take bus No 7 or 36).

Alaska Aviation Heritage Museum
On the south shore of Lake Hood at 4721 Aircraft Dr is the Alaska Aviation Heritage Museum (☎ 248-5325). In an effort to preserve Alaska's unique approach to aviation, the museum has films, displays on such pioneer pilots as Ben Eielson, Noel Wein and Russell Merrill, vintage aircraft and an observation deck. Summer hours are from 9 am to 6 pm. The admission is $5.75.

Reeve Aviation Picture Museum
If you're really into planes, you may also want to stop in at the Reeve Aviation Picture Museum, dedicated to Alaska pioneer-aviator Robert Reeve. Located downtown on the corner of 6th Ave and D St, the museum is actually a room with more than 1100 photos of the state's famous bush pilots and the story of Robert Reeve and Reeve Aleutian Airlines, which despite flying in one of the most turbulent places in the world has never lost a plane – amazing! The museum is open from 9 am to 5 pm weekdays and admission is free.

Ship Creek Salmon Overlook
From mid to late summer, king, coho and pink salmon spawn up Ship Creek, the historical site of Tanaina Indian fish camps. The overlook, a half-mile east from the Alaska

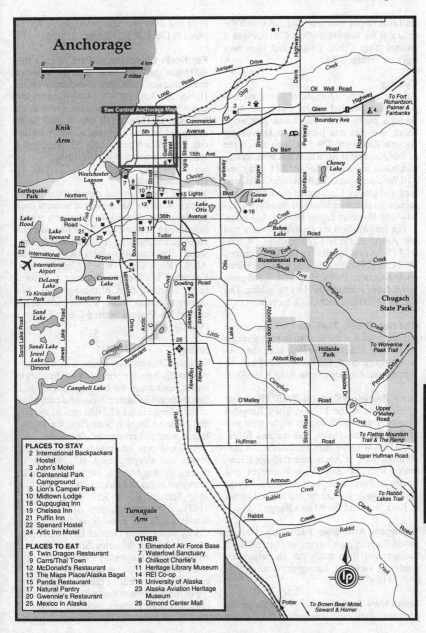

Anchorage

0   2   4 km

0   1   2 miles

Knik Arm

See Central Anchorage Map

Westchester Lagoon

Earthquake Park

Lake Hood

Lake Spenard

International Airport

DeLong Lake

To Kincaid Park

Sand Lake

Sundi Lake
Jewel Lake

Campbell Lake

Turnagain Arm

Juniper Drive

Loop Road

Ship Creek

Commercial

5th   Avenue

15th Ave

Chester

Northern

Spenard Road

Airport

Raspberry Road

Sand Lake Road

Dimond

Connors Lake

Minnesota Drive

Arctic Boulevard

Campbell

Oil Well Road

Glenn Highway

Boundary Ave

De Barr Road

Blvd

36th

Tudor Road

Dowling Road

Seward Highway

Alaska Railroad

C Street

Little Campbell Creek

Davis

Creek

To Fort Richardson, Palmer & Fairbanks

Cheney Lake

Goose Lake

Lake Otis Avenue

Behm Creek

Bragaw

Boniface

Muldoon Road

North Fork

South Fork

Bicentennial Park

Campbell Creek

Chugach State Park

To Wolverine Peak Trail

Abbott Loop Road

Hillside Park

Abbott Road

Campbell Road

O'Malley Road

Huffman Road

De Armoun Road

Rabbit Creek

Rabbit Creek Road

Birch Road

Hillside Dr

Upper O'Malley Road

To Flattop Mountain Trail & The Ramp

Upper Huffman Road

To Rabbit Lakes Trail

Clarks Road

Prospect Drive

Little Rabbit Creek

To Potter

To Brown Bear Motel, Seward & Homer

PLACES TO STAY
2   International Backpackers Hostel
3   John's Motel
4   Centennial Park Campground
9   Lion's Camper Park
10   Midtown Lodge
18   Qupqugiaq Inn
19   Chelsea Inn
21   Puffin Inn
22   Spenard Hostel
24   Artic Inn Motel

PLACES TO EAT
6   Twin Dragon Restaurant
9   Carrs/Thai Town
12   McDonald's Restaurant
13   The Maps Place/Alaska Bagel
15   Panda Restaurant
17   Natural Pantry
20   Gwennie's Restaurant
25   Mexico in Alaska

OTHER
1   Elmendorf Air Force Base
7   Waterfowl Sanctuary
8   Chilkoot Charlie's
11   Heritage Library Museum
14   REI Co-op
16   University of Alaska
23   Alaska Aviation Heritage Museum
26   Dimond Center Mall

ANCHORAGE

Railroad Depot, is where you can watch the return of the salmon. Follow C St north as it crosses Ship Creek Bridge and then turn right on Whitney Rd.

Cycling

Anchorage has 122 miles of paved bicycle paths that parallel major roads or wind through many of its parks and green-belt areas. You can rent bicycles at Downtown Bicycle Rental (☎ 279-5293), on the corner of 6th Ave and B St, which has both mountain bikes and road bikes for $14 a day and $10 for four hours. That includes a helmet, lock and gloves. Late-model mountain bikes are also available at Sunshine Sports (☎ 272-6444) on Northern Lights Blvd for $25 a day.

For information on organized tours call the Arctic Bicycle Club hotline (☎ 566-0177). Alaskan Bicycle Adventures (☎ 243-2329) offers six-day trips, including on the George Parks Hwy and a 360-mile pedal down Richardson Hwy to Valdez. The cost is $1700 and includes a bicycle.

Chester Creek Trail One of the more popular routes is the four-mile path through the Chester Creek Green Belt from the UA-Anchorage and Goose Lake Park to Westchester Lagoon overlooking Knik Arm.

Tony Knowles Coastal Trail The most scenic route is the 11-mile Tony Knowles Coastal Trail, which begins at the west end of 2nd Ave downtown and reaches Elderberry Park within a mile. From there it winds 10 miles west of Anchorage through Earthquake Park, around Point Woronzof and finally to Point Campbell in Kincaid Park. Along the way you are treated to good views of Knik Arm and the Alaska Range.

Turnagain Arm Bike Path This 14-mile paved bicycle path begins at Potter Marsh Refuge and then hugs the shoreline for sweeping views of Turnagain Arm until it ends at Bird Creek.

Glenn Hwy Trail Head north on this paved path out of the city. It begins at the Bartlett Pool and then parallels the highway for 14 miles to Chugiak Elementary School.

Far North Bicentennial Park Within this 4000-acre park are more than 20 miles of trails, many of them open to mountain bikes. Hilltop Ski Area (☎ 346-1446) rents mountain bikes daily during the summer for $12 a half day and $18 a full day. It also holds two-night lessons on Monday and Wednesday from 6 to 8 pm, where $30 gets you a rental and instruction in trail riding.

Rock Climbing

You can free climb and rappel a short drive from downtown Anchorage at several rock faces along the Seward Hwy, the most prominent known as Boy Scout Rock passed a few miles before reaching Alyeska Hwy at Girdwood. You can also climb indoors at the Alaska Rock Gym (☎ 562-7265) at 4840 Fairbanks St. The gym features a 30-foot-high, 5000-sq-foot climbing wall. For information on more serious climbing contact the Mountaineering Club of Alaska (☎ 272-1811).

Hiking

With the Chugach Mountains at its doorstep, Anchorage has excellent day hikes that begin on the outskirts of the city and quickly lead into the beautiful alpine area to the east. Most of them begin in the Hillside area of the city that borders Chugach State Park, the second largest state preserve at 495,000 acres.

You can rent equipment such as tents, stoves and sleeping bags at a variety of places in Anchorage, including Alaska Mountaineering and Hiking (☎ 272-1811) at 2633 Spenard Rd or REI Co-op (☎ 272-4565) on Northern Lights Blvd. Cheaper rentals might be possible at the Campus Center Information Desk at UA-Anchorage (☎ 786-1204) or Moseley Sports Center at Alaska Pacific University (☎ 564-8314) but sometimes they can be hard to deal with if you are not a student or faculty member.

For descriptions of the trails along Seward Hwy towards Portage, see the South of Anchorage section of this chapter. Also, for information on guide companies that run hiking trips see the Organized Tours section in this chapter.

Maps The USGS map center, which sells topos for the entire state, is in Grace Hall at Alaska Pacific University at the east end of Providence Dr. It is open from 8.30 am to 4.30 pm weekdays and can be reached on bus No 11 or 45. Upstairs from the map center is the headquarters of Lake Clark National Park. There's also Maps, Maps, Maps (☎ 562-6277), an excellent store on the corner of Arctic Blvd and 34th Ave that sells USGS topos and a variety of other recreational maps to the state.

To/From the Trailheads At $1 a ride, the People Mover bus is the cheapest way to get to within walking distance of a few of the trails. For others there is Backpacker Shuttle (☎ 344-8775) which provides transportation right to the trailheads. The van service picks up hikers at the international hostel, REI in the Midtown area and Centennial Camper Park and then continues on to a variety of trails including Bird Creek and Crow Pass along the Seward Hwy and Ship Creek, the Eagle River trails and Eklutna Lake. The fare is $5 one way for trails like Flattop Mountain and ranges up to $20 one way for Crow Pass and Eklutna Lake.

Flattop Mountain Trail Because of its easy access, this trail is the most popular hike near the city. The path to the 4500-foot peak is not difficult to walk and from the summit there are good views of Mt McKinley (to the north) and most of Cook Inlet. The trail begins at the Glen Alps entrance to the Chugach State Park.

Catch bus No 92 to the corner of Hillside Rd and Upper Huffman Rd. Walk 0.7 miles east along Upper Huffman Rd and then turn right on Toilsome Hill Dr for two miles. This switchback road ascends steeply to the Glen Alps park entrance, a parking lot where trailhead signs point the way to Flattop Mountain. The round trip is four miles with some scrambling over loose rock up steep sections near the top of the mountain. Plan on three to five hours for the entire hike.

Rabbit Lake Trail People Mover bus No 92 also provides transport to this trail, which leads to the beautiful alpine lake nestled under 5000-foot Suicide Peak. Leave the bus at the corner of Hillside Dr and De Armoun Rd. Extending to the east here is Upper De Armoun Rd. Follow it a mile and then turn right onto Lower Canyon Rd for 1.2 miles to reach the trailhead parking lot.

The trail begins by paralleling Upper Canyon Rd, a rough jeep track, for 3.5 miles and then continues another two miles from its end to the lake. The return trip from the corner of Hillside Dr and De Armoun Rd is 15.4 miles, or a six to nine-hour hike. You can camp on the lake's shore for a scenic evening in the mountains.

Wolverine Peak Trail This path ascends to the 4455-foot triangular peak that can be seen to the east of Anchorage. It makes for a strenuous but rewarding full-day trip resulting in good views of the city, Cook Inlet and the Alaska Range.

Take bus No 92 to the intersection of Hillside Dr and O'Malley Rd. Head east up Upper O'Malley Rd for a half-mile to a T-intersection and turn left (north) onto Prospect Dr for 1.1 miles. This ends at the Prospect Heights entrance and parking area of the Chugach State Park. The marked trail begins as an old homesteader road that crosses South Campbell Creek and passes junctions with two other old roads in the first 2.3 miles.

Keep heading east, and the old road will become a footpath that ascends above the bush line and eventually fades out. Make sure to mark its whereabouts in order to find it on the way back. From here it is three miles to the Wolverine Peak.

The return trip from the corner of O'Malley Rd and Hillside Dr is 13.8 miles, a nine-hour hike. Many people just trek to the good views above the bush line, shortening the trip to 7.8 miles.

ANCHORAGE

Rendezvous Peak Route The trek to the 4050-foot peak is an easy five-hour round trip, less from the trailhead, and rewards hikers with incredible views of Mt McKinley, Cook Inlet, Turnagain and Knik arms, and the city far below. Take bus No 75 for 6.5 miles north-east on Glenn Hwy to Arctic Valley Rd. Turn right (east) on Arctic Valley Rd (this section is also known as Ski Bowl Rd) and head seven miles to the Arctic Valley Ski Area at the end. From the parking lot, a short trail leads along the right-hand side of the stream up the valley to the north-west. It ends at a pass where a short ascent to Rendezvous Peak is easily seen and climbed.

The round trip from the ski area parking lot is only 3.5 miles, but it is a much longer day if you are unable to thumb a ride up Arctic Valley Rd.

The Ramp This is another of the many alpine summit hikes from the east side of the city that includes hiking through tranquil tundra valleys with good chances of seeing dall sheep during the summer. Begin at the Glen Alps entrance to the state park (see the previously mentioned Flattop Trail for directions to the entrance).

Instead of following the upper trail to Flattop Mountain at the parking lot, hike the lower one as it extends half a mile to the power line. Turn right and follow the power line for two miles, past 13 power poles, to where an old jeep trail crosses over from the left and heads downhill to the south fork of Campbell Creek.

The trail then crosses the creek and continues up the hill beyond it to a valley on the other side. Hike up the alpine valley to Ship Lake Pass, which lies between The Ramp at 5240 feet to the north, and The Wedge at 4660 feet to the south. Either peak can be climbed. The round trip from the Glen Alps entrance is 14 miles, or an eight to 10-hour hike.

Williwaw Lakes Trail This hike leads to the handful of alpine lakes found at the base of Mt Williwaw. The trail makes a pleasant overnight hike and many trekkers consider it the most scenic outing in the Hillside area of Chugach State Park. The hike begins on the same lower trail as The Ramp does, from the Glen Alps entrance parking lot (see the Flattop Mountain Trail for directions to the entrance).

Walk half a mile to the power line and then turn right. This time walk only about 300 yards and then turn left on a trail marked by a 'Middle Fork Loop Trail' sign. This trail leads down and across the south fork of Campbell Creek and then north for 1.5 miles to the middle fork of the creek. Here you reach a junction; continue on the right-hand trail and follow the middle fork of Campbell Creek until you reach the alpine lakes at its end. The round trip from Glen Alps is 16 miles, or seven to nine hours of easy hiking.

Organized Tours
City Tours The Anchorage Historical Properties conducts an hour-long walking tour of the downtown area Monday through Friday during the summer beginning in the lobby of the renovated Old City Hall at 1 pm. Admission is $5. Even cheaper is to hop on the People Mover's Downtown Anchorage Short Hop bus, which is free.

A number of companies offer a city bus tour of Anchorage. Almost all of these tours are three to four hours long and include Resolution Park, Lake Hood, and usually an hour or so at the Anchorage Historical & Fine Arts Museum. Just about everybody – Gray Line (☎ 277-5581), Alaska Sightseeing (☎ 276-1305), Far North Tours (☎ 272-7480) and Princess Tours (☎ 276-7711) – charge $25.

Perhaps a better deal is Alaska Sightseeing's full-day tour which also includes Portage Glacier and Alyeska Ski Resort. Book this trip within seven days and it's only $52.

Area Tours Gray Line offers a daily seven-hour Portage Glacier/Turnagain Arm tour for $57 which departs at 9 am and noon. The trip includes the USFS visitor center and a trip on Gray Line's *Ptarmigan* which cruises past the face of Portage Glacier. For a more personal tour, check out Killer Whale Tours (☎ 258-7999). Longtime marine biologist Tony Carter leads small groups along Turnagain Arm in a tour that includes birding at Potter Marsh and sighting beluga whales and bore tides in the inlet as well as Portage Glacier. The cost is $65.

You can also do Seward and Kenai Fjords National Park in a day from Anchorage. The Alaska Railroad (☎ 265-2494 or (800) 544-0552) has a day in Seward that includes the train ride down and a half-day cruise to Bear Glacier on the edge of the national park. The fare is $139 per person and the train pulls out daily at 7 am.

Far North Tours has a Matanuska Valley tour that includes the interesting Iditarod Headquarters, Musk Ox Farm and Eklutna Historical Village. You have to be hard pressed for something to do to take the farm tour, but it departs at 8 am during the summer and the fare is $65.

Several companies, including Far North Tours and Denali Express (☎ (800) 327-7651) offer a one-day tour to Denali National Park or Talkeetna. The Denali Express tour is $159 per person and includes round-trip van transportation, a ride on the park shuttle bus to Eielson Visitor Center (the best place to view the mountain) and lunch.

A better and much cheaper way to spend an afternoon is to hop on People Mover bus No 74, 76 or 102 for the scenic trip north of Anchorage along Eagle River, through Chugiak and to Peter's Creek. The 48-mile round trip takes about two hours and costs a mere $2. Those who take the first bus out in the morning have been known to occasionally spot moose between Fort Richardson and Eagle River.

Package Tours Travelers on a tight schedule will find a variety of package tours to other areas of the state available in Anchorage. They include accommodation, transport and meals, and are a way to cover a lot in a day or two if you are willing to pay the price.

The most popular trip out of the city is the cruise past Columbia Glacier to Valdez and returning to Anchorage along the scenic Richardson and Glenn highways. Both Gray Line (☎ 277-5581) and Alaska Sightseeing (☎ 276-1305) offer the tour as a two-day/one-night package with an overnight stay at a Valdez hotel. American Sightseeing's two-day trip is $345 per person, based on shared accommodation; Gray Line is cheaper at $295.

Gray Line and Alaska Sightseeing, along with a few other large tour companies, have package tours everywhere, shuffling tour groups to such unlikely places as Barrow and Kotzebue. This is a quick way to see an interesting slice of Alaska but not cheap. The Gray Line two-day/one-night tour of Kotzebue and Nome is $497 per person based on double occupancy.

Also offering a variety of package tours is Alaska Railroad (☎ 265-2494). Three of these tours are worth considering for those short on time. The Denali Overnight tour includes a return train trip to Denali National Park and a night's lodging in the park for $269 per person, based on double occupancy. It does not include, however, a bus ride through the park to Wonder Lake. Eagle Custom Tours also has a 'Denali Quickie', while Gray Line comes in with a four-day trip that includes two nights in the national park and two more in Fairbanks for $975, including travel on its private railcars on the Alaska Railroad.

If you don't book these package tours in advance and find yourself in Anchorage near the end of your stay with too much money in your pocket, try to cut a deal on 4th Ave. Along this downtown avenue there is a number of booking and reservation centers that might have better deals for you. Two places to try are Alaska Booking & Reservation Center (☎ 277-6228) on the corner of F St, and All Alaska Tours (☎ 272-8687) on G St next door to Darwin's Theory Bar.

Guide Companies Anchorage is home base for a large number of guide companies that run hiking, kayaking and rafting trips to every corner of the state. Check the Wilderness chapter for the complete list and descriptions of their expeditions, and don't be shy about calling them at the last minute. Often you not only get a place in the group but get a hefty discount as well for filling up a leftover spot.

Chugach Hiking Tours (☎ 278-4453) offers several guided hikes into the surrounding state park, including a sunset one that begins at 6 pm and returns at 11 pm. The treks often range from two to five miles in length and include a naturalist's perspective, trail snacks and opportunities for photography going to and from the trailheads. All trips depart from the Log Cabin Visitors Center downtown and are $45 per person.

The best whitewater in the Anchorage area is Eagle River, a 15-mile run of mostly Class I water but with short stretches of Class II and even Class III. Alaskan Whitewater (☎ 333-3001) runs the river daily in the summer. It also rents rafts and provides drop-off and pick-up services.

Special Events

In the summer months, festivals include a large 4 July celebration, a Renaissance Faire with Shakespearean-type costumes and plays in early June at the Hilltop Ski Area, and the Mayor's Midnite Sun Marathon (call Anchorage Parks & Recreation on ☎ 343-4474) which celebrates the summer solstice with a variety of foot races.

For a small town festival, head to Girdwood on the 4 July weekend for its Girdwood Forest Faire or to Eagle River in mid-July (call ☎ 694-4702 for exact dates) for the Bear Paw Festival. A number of smaller events, such as Kite Day in early June, Anchorage's annual eating fest called The Taste, free concerts and arts & crafts shows, are held throughout the summer in Delaney Park. Call the All About Anchorage recorded message (☎ 276-3200) to see if anything is happening while you're passing through town.

Places to Stay

Camping The Anchorage Parks & Recreation Department (☎ 343-4474) maintains two parks where there is overnight camping. The main one is *Centennial Park*, which has

89 sites, showers and rest rooms but is 4.6 miles from the downtown area on Glenn Hwy. In recent years there also has been a theft problem at the campground. Take the Muldoon Rd exit south of the highway and turn west onto Boundary Ave for half a block. Bus No 75 runs past the corner of Muldoon Rd and Boundary Ave. The cost is $12 per night and there is a limit of seven days. When Centennial is full, the city uses *Lion's Camper Park* in Russian Jack Springs Park as an overflow camping area. There is also *Ship Creek Landings* (☎ 277-0877) which offers 180 RV sites just off East 1st Ave. The tent rate is $15 per night, a full hook-up $27.

Chugach State Park, which practically surrounds Anchorage, also has public campgrounds but none of them is close and they always fill up fast. The nearest facilities are at Bird Creek on the Seward Hwy (see the South of Anchorage section of this chapter) and at Eagle River off the Glenn Hwy (see the North of Anchorage section). It is also a common practice among RVers to simply park overnight in the parking lot of stores such as Fred Meyer or Wal-Mart.

Hostels The *Anchorage International (AYH) Hostel* (☎ 276-3635) is downtown, one block south of the Transit Center at 700 H St. The cost is $15 per night for members and $18 for nonmembers and there are a few private rooms available for $40. There is a four-night maximum stay unless special arrangements are made. Along with sleeping facilities, there is a common room, kitchen, showers and even double rooms. Laundry facilities are available and you can store extra bags here for $1 per day. This hostel is busy during the summer, so many travelers reserve a bunk ahead of time by calling in advance and using either a Visa card or MasterCard to secure the reservation. You can also mail a money order for the first night's stay along with details of the number and gender of people arriving to Anchorage AYH, 700 H St, Anchorage, AK 99501.

A smaller but more personal hostel is *Spenard Hostel* (☎ 248-5036) situated near

Gwennie's Old Alaska Restaurant off Turnagain Rd at 2845 West 42nd Place (bus No 7). The four-plex apartment has couple and family rooms as well as a kitchen, laundry facilities and bike rentals. The cost is $12 a night. There is also *International Backpackers Hostel* (☎ 274-3870) on the east side of the city. The hostel is actually five homes in the same neighborhood that can accommodate up to 45 people a night with two to four people per room. Facilities include a coin-operated laundry, a fully equipped kitchen and a TV room. Rates range from $12 to $15 a night. To reach the hostel from the Transit Center take Bus No 45 to Bragaw St and Peterkin Ave and head west on Peterkin Ave for three blocks.

Alaska Pacific University (☎ 564-8238), at 4101 University Dr, also rents out dorm room bunks from late May through early August. Beds fill up quickly but it's $25 a night if you need sheets, only $15 a night if you have a sleeping bag.

B&Bs These have blossomed in Anchorage. There are now several hundred residents who have opened up their spare bedrooms to summer travelers. Most places are on the fringes or in the suburbs of the city and provide a clean bed, a good breakfast and local insight into both the city and the Alaskan way of life. The going rate is a bit steeper in Anchorage than in the rest of the state as you generally pay from $75 to $100 per couple a night. Stop at the Log Cabin Visitors Center for an entire rack of B&B brochures or you can call either Alaska Private Lodging (☎ 258-1717) or B&B Hotline (☎ 272-5909) to arrange such accommodation.

In the downtown area there is *6th & B Bed & Breakfast* (☎ 279-5293), located, you guessed it, on the corner of 6th Ave and B St. The three rooms range in price from $78 to $105 and there are complimentary bikes to use. At 440 L St, next door to Simon & Seafort's Saloon & Grill, is *Copper Whale Inn* (☎ 258-7999), with a great view of Cook Inlet. Rooms start at $100 in the summer and it puts you within easy walking distance of

most downtown restaurants, bars and delightful Elderberry Park. *Little Blue House B&B* (☎ 258-2653), 327 East 15th Ave, and *Walkabout Town B&B* (☎ 279-2918), 1610 E St, across from the Chester Creek park strip, have doubles priced from $75. Walkabout also provides courtesy pick-up from the airport or train station and has two rooms that share a small kitchen area.

In the Hillside area at 7501 Upper O'Malley Rd is *Aurora Winds B&B* (☎ 346-2533). This place is unbelievable with its mirror gym, billiards, sauna and huge hot tub. There's even a white grand piano in the living room. Rooms range from $100 to $150 a night.

Hotels & Motels Although Anchorage has more than 50 hotels and motels and 4000 rooms for rent, in the middle of the summer you must still plan on spending a few dimes on phone calls to find a bed. Trying to find a single room for under $75 is even more challenging. Passing through the city before June or after August saves you a bundle as room rates often drop as much as 30% to 40% a night in the off season. Remember that Anchorage has an 8% bed tax.

Airport Late night arrivals at the airport have a choice of motels that offer courtesy transportation and are nearby along Spenard Rd just north of International Airport Rd. But be prepared for Alaska-size rates of around $100 a night. *Puffin Inn* (☎ 243-4044), at 4400 Spenard Rd, is clean, will run out to the airport until 1 am and has complimentary muffins, coffee and newspapers in the morning. A double is $106 a night. Nearby is *Lake Shore Motel* (☎ 248-3485 or (800) 770-3000), at 3009 Lake Shore Dr. It has courtesy transport and a single/double is $94/104.

The alternative is *Arctic Inn Motel* (☎ 561-1328), at 842 West International Airport Rd. It's a $7 taxi ride away and has singles/doubles for $69/79. Each room has a small stove and refrigerator and there is a laundry room at the motel.

Downtown Try to avoid the shabby *Inlet Inn* (☎ 277-5541) across from the Transit Center even if singles/doubles are $60. A cleaner and safer choice downtown is *Caribou Inn* (☎ 272-0444) at 501 L St. It features 14 rooms that begin at $69 and includes a full breakfast and courtesy pick-up from the airport or train station. The Caribou fills fast so try to book a room in advance if you can. There's also the *Snowshoe Inn* (☎ 258-7669) on the corner of K St and 9th Ave with rooms with shared bath for $75 that includes a light breakfast and laundry facilities.

Entering the city from the Glenn Hwy, you end up on 5th Ave where there is a cluster of motels, among them *The Red Ram Motel* (☎ 274-15125) at 642 East 5th Ave. Rates are $70/80 for a single/double but the place is clean, has a communal kitchen for meals and free pick-up from the airport and train station. The nearby *Kobuk Motel* (☎ 274-1650) is $5 cheaper but considerably more run-down.

At the other end of the scale, if you want to spend your final night or two in Alaska in glorious comfort, there is *Hotel Captain Cook* (☎ 276-6000), with an ideal location downtown on the corner of 5th Ave and K St. Rooms start at $230 but you are pampered here. The *Inlet Tower* (☎ (800) 544-0786), 1200 L St, also has 1st-class service and spectacular views from its 180 suites. Rates in the summer range from $120 to $180.

Midtown To the south is log-lodge-like *Midtown Lodge* (☎ 258-7778) where the rooms are small and you share the bath, but there is a group kitchen. Rates are only $60/70 for a single/double which includes a light breakfast, soup and sandwiches later in the day and pick-up at the airport. The lodge is at 604 West 26th Ave, just off Spenard Rd near Chilkoot Charlie's Saloon. Even further south is *Qupqugiaq Inn* (☎ 562-5681), at 640 West 36th Ave between Arctic Blvd and C St. This is actually a group of houses where doubles with shared bath and a common kitchen begin at $22 a night. The rate is cheap but the rooms are small and a little shabby. Check the house before handing over your money to make sure you feel comfortable in the situation.

At the other end of the scale is *Chelsea Inn* (☎ 276-5002 or (800) 770-5002), nearby at 3836 Spenard Rd. Singles/doubles are $95/105 but the rooms are very clean and comfortable, a continental breakfast is provided and there are kitchen facilities. It also provides 24-hour pick-up service to the airport.

Elsewhere If you have a car, book a room on the outskirts of the city for better rates. If you're heading up from the Kenai Peninsula, *The Brown Bear Motel* (☎ 653-7000), in Indian 20 minutes south of Anchorage on the Seward Hwy, has clean rooms with a private bath and TV for $38 a night. They don't come any cheaper than this, folks. Also on site is the Brown Bear Saloon. Just off the Glenn Hwy before it becomes 5th Ave is *John's Motel & RV Park* (☎ 277-4332) where small rooms begin at $50 and full hook-ups on a gravel parking area are $22.

Places to Eat

Anchorage offers just about any kind of food you might desire at prices that range from budget to expensive. Because the restaurants are spread across the city they are divided here into areas. However, as there is a large number of Oriental-style restaurants and Espresso Shops in the city, these have been placed under there own headings at the end of this section.

Downtown For those on a strict budget there's a choice of fast-food places including *McDonald's* on the corner of 4th Ave and E St and *Burger King* at 520 West 5th Ave. Just as easy on the money pouch is the *Federal Building Cafeteria* off C St between 7th and 8th avenues, just across from the Anchorage Museum. It opens at 7 am weekdays and serves breakfast for around $5 as well as lunch in pleasant surroundings where you don't feel like gulping down your food. If the weather is nice, there is seating outdoors. On Saturday morning from 10 am to 6 pm there is the *Saturday Market* at 3rd Ave and E St where fresh produce and seafood is sold along with arts & crafts.

For food and surroundings that are a little more distinct, the downtown area of Anchorage has a wonderful selection of cafes, eateries and espresso shops. There's *Blondie's Cafe* open 24 hours on the corner of 4th Ave and D St. At the start of the Iditarod race, the bright and cheery cafe is loaded with sled-dog paraphernalia, including an entire sled hanging on the wall. An eggs breakfast is $4.25, a huge Blondie burger $6. Further west on 4th Ave is *Tito's Gyros* where you can get a medium cheese pizza for under $10 and gyros sandwiches stuffed with lamb for $6. Still further west on 4th Ave is the *Downtown Deli*, unquestionably the city's best known delicatessen. Breakfasts are great – eggs, potatoes and a lightly toasted bagel for $5 – large deli sandwiches cost from $7 to $9. Highly recommended is *Sack's Cafe*, 625 5th Ave, especially whatever fresh shellfish it has on the menu.

Other fine spots to enjoy lunch or dinner outdoors include *Phyllis's Cafe* on the corner of 5th Ave and D St. Art decorates the interior, while a sawdust-covered courtyard is out the back. The salmon dinner costs $18 and the hamburgers (from $5.50 to $8) are excellent. Try the Bristol Bay Buffalo Burger (yes, it is buffalo meat you're eating), the Rampart Reindeer Burger or the Moose Pass Mushroom Burger.

Cheap eats near the Anchorage International Hostel include *Wings & Things*, near the corner of I St and 6th Ave, which is open to 10 pm on the weekends. Chicken wings, vegetables and sauce (try their Nuke sauce if you want to burn your mouth) are $7, while whole subs start at $6.50. Next door is *Muffin Man Cafe* which opens for breakfast at 6 am. Muffins are 75 cents, a full breakfast $6 and, of course, there's espresso.

The best-known Thai restaurant in the city is *Thai Cuisine*, downtown on H St, between 4th and 5th avenues, where dinners range from $7 to $9 and seafood is around $17.

Those looking to make an evening out of dinner have a long list of places to choose from. One of the best is *Simon & Seafort's Saloon & Grill* (☎ 274-3502) at 420 L St between 4th and 5th avenues. The restaurant has the interesting décor of a turn-of-the-century grand saloon and a nice view of Cook Inlet where you can watch the sun set behind Mt Susitna. Dinners are expensive – plan on spending from $16 to $22 not counting your liquor. Reservations are a must. The liveliest pub with the best food is *Humpy's* at the corner of 6th Ave and F St. Pass up the burgers to try a halibut tacos for $7 or smoked-salmon scollops on pasta for $8. The place gets crowded so be prepared to wait for a table.

One other eatery that has to be mentioned is *Peggy's Place* on 5th Ave, right across from Merrill Airfield. While not exactly downtown, this restaurant is well worth the extra effort required to reach it. The longtime favorite is famous for Peggy's home-made pies, 20 different types that range from Nutdelight and boysenberry to a strawberry cream pie that is six-inches high. Breakfast ranges from $3.50 to $8 for Peggy's Special – ham, bacon, three eggs, toast and pancakes all smothered with a country gravy. If that doesn't give you a stroke, nothing will.

There's no shortage of cappuccino in this city. You can't walk more than a block or two downtown without passing a coffee shop. Drive-through espresso shacks seem to be on every corner. There's even an espresso bar in some Kinko's Print Shops. Have a cafe latte while waiting for your copies!

Relax at *Side Street Espresso*, just off 4th Ave on G St. There's an interesting selection of prints on the walls, a used-book shelf in the corner and, by the afternoon, a couple of copies of the *Daily News* spread across the tables. Also downtown on 4th Ave and K St is one of several *Cafe Del Mundos* in the city while nearby is *Alaska Adventures & Delights*. The latter doubles as a travel-book store with material on Alaska and the complete selection of Lonely Planet guides. Sip, read and dream about your next trip. A large 16-ounce cafe latte at any of them is $3.

Further east at F St and 7th Ave is *Bear Paw Coffee Co* where you can get blasted awake in the morning with its 20-oz latte with five shots of espresso ($5). The food here is very good – huge bagels with cream cheese ($1.50), giant Belgian waffles and quiche. Another interesting place is *Cyrano's Books & Cafe*, on the corner of 4th Ave and D St. The shop is an offbeat bookstore with an excellent Alaska section as well as an espresso shop with a variety of baked goods, sandwiches and lunches.

Midtown Head down Northern Lights Blvd or Benson Blvd, between New Seward Hwy and Minnesota Dr, for any fast-food restaurant you're craving for. On Benson Blvd near New Seward Hwy is one of four *Skipper's* in Anchorage where you can get all the fish, salad and chowder you can consume for $8 (or on Tuesday for only $5.50). The most affordable food, however, is at the *Carrs Aurora Village Store*, on the corner of L St and Northern Lights Blvd, the largest of the Carrs chain. The salad bar is great at $3 a pound while also inside is a deli, an Orient express for stir-fry, a bakery, an espresso shop and seating.

There are also two interesting, and very distinct, places in the center slice of the city. *Hogg Brothers Cafe*, near the corner of West Northern Lights Blvd and Spenard Rd, is a bizarre restaurant with a 'piggy' décor including a stuffed hog mounted on the wall. Breakfast is served all day and the selection is creative. You could order two eggs, home fries and toast for $3, but why when there are more than 20 omelettes like Mat-Zu-Mama (Canadian bacon, cheese and tomatoes). The place isn't as classic as the original that was next door to Chilkoot Charlie's but the food is still good and plentiful.

Also serving breakfast all day is *Gwennie's Old Alaska Restaurant*, at 4333 Spenard Rd, west of Minnesota Dr. The portions are big, the prices reasonable and the artefacts are so numerous that the place mat doubles up as a guide to what's on the walls. Order an omelette ($7 to $9) and then study the baleen sleds that Native Alaskans once used to haul freight, photos of the 1964 earthquake, pieces of the Trans-Alaska Pipeline

or the 45,000-year-old bison head found in the Lucky Seven Mine.

Along Spenard Road is *Java Joint* between Fireweed St and Northern Lights Blvd. This two-story coffee house not only has the usual espresso drinks but serves good breakfast in the morning and interesting pizzas ($10 to $12) in the evening.

To the south in the Plaza Mall, on the corner of 36th Ave and C St, is *Natural Pantry* (☎ 563-2727), a health-food store and a restaurant with a $5 lunch special of soup, sandwich and a drink. At 1406 West 31st Ave is *Crazy Croissants French Bakery*, a hard-to-find eatery between Spenard Rd and Minnosta Dr. The search is well worth the effort as bakery goods are excellent, salads and quiches wonderful and prices very reasonable.

A great selection of bagels (50 cents each) plus bagel sandwiches (about $7), breakfast bagels with eggs (about $4) and cafe latte is at *Alaska Bagel, Inc*, 113 West Northern Lights Blvd.

Good Greek and Italian food are combined at *The Greek Corner* at 302 West Fireweed Lane. The moussaka plate for $13 will fill you up while Italian dishes range from garlic-fetta spaghetti and rigatoni al forno to calzone. Beer and wine are also served here.

An interesting evening can also be enjoyed at *Flying Machine*, the restaurant inside the Regal Alaskan Hotel, at 4800 Spenard Rd. The dinners are excellent ($15 to $22) and from your table you can watch the float planes take off from Lake Hood.

Oriental restaurants, from Thai and Mongolian barbecue to Chinese restaurants, are found in this part of the city. One of the best for traditional Chinese is *Panda*, a small restaurant at 504 East Northern Lights Blvd. The Cantonese and Sichuan dinners are excellent and affordable, ranging from $7 to $10. Nearby on East Benson Ave across from the Sears Mall is *Peking Place* for spicy northern Chinese cuisine. Full dinners, including soup, egg rolls and three main courses begin at $10 per person.

Excellent Mongolian barbecue, where

you fill your bowl with raw vegetables, fish, chicken and beef and then hand it to the chef to cook on a round grill, is enjoyed at *Twin Dragon* at 612 East 15 Ave near Gambell St. If that's too far away, you can get the same thing at *Golden China* in a mall on Minnesota Dr south of Northern Lights Blvd. At both it's an all-you-can eat dinner for $10, or lunch for $6.

For Thai cuisine a good choice is *Thai Town* in the same mall as Carrs on Minnesota Dr and Northern Lights Blvd. Dinners range mostly from $6 to $9. There is an extensive selection of vegetarian main courses as well as seafood. Try the sir-fry shrimp curry in a coconut-milk sauce. Also highly recommended by locals is *Thai Kitchen* at 3405 East Tudor Rd. Most dishes are from $6 to $8 with all the steamed rice you can eat.

South Anchorage The best place for a burger south of Tudor Rd is the original *Arctic Roadrunner*, at the corner of International Airport Rd and Old Seward Hwy. The 'Local Burgerman' has been serving them for more than 30 years and you can enjoy the big hamburgers while looking at the restaurant's Customer Gallery. Among those enshrined are Norma Jean Saunders, the first

---

⚜⚜⚜⚜⚜⚜⚜⚜⚜

Email in Anchorage
Want to email your friends a wish-you-were-here message? There are a handful of places in the Anchorage area with free computer access to the Internet, including the ZJ Loussac Library (☎ 343-2975), at 36th Ave and Denali St. The public library has two computers that allow you to explore the Internet or send outgoing email. The drawback is the computers are set up for text-only. At ServCom Alaska (☎ 274-9472), an Internet provider in the Northland Mall, there are three computers capable of Internet access and email. Outgoing email is free, incoming email is $1 a message.

You can also surf the Net and sip a latte at Kaladi Brothers, 6921 Brayton Dr in Midtown Anchorage, and Sleepy Dog Coffee Co, on Old Glenn Hwy in Eagle River. Both coffee houses have one computer available on a first-come-first-use basis. ■

⚜⚜⚜⚜⚜⚜⚜⚜⚜

---

woman to climb Mt McKinley; Mark Scherath, the only Alaskan-born player in the National Football League; and Bob Henderson, who once landed a 26-pound northern pike with a muskrat in its stomach. Across Old Seward Hwy is the *Peanut Farm*, a bar with good food, cheap beer and an outdoor deck. At this place you can drink until staff start serving breakfast in the morning.

Nearby the tourists are bussed to the *Sourdough Mining Co* (☎ 563-2272), a half-block off Old Seward Hwy at International Airport Rd and Juneau St. For $19, you can enjoy the Sourdough Seafood Sampler (snow crab, salmon, halibut, prawns) and other dishes in the re-created miner's hall or head outside for an all-you-can eat buffet in a dinner tent. There is also a nightly Alaskan show while next door is the huge Alaska Wildberry Products store for dessert.

The best Mexican dishes are found in South Anchorage at *Mexico in Alaska*, 7305 Old Seward Hwy, just south of Dowling Rd. The menu covers traditional Mexican cuisine with dinners ranging from $9 to $13, the beer list from Mexico is impressive and there is an outdoor seating area if the weather is nice.

It's a long way from downtown but bus No 60 goes right past the restaurant. The best ribs are also on the south side of the city at *The Bar-B-Que Pit*, at 1160 West Dimond Blvd. A barbecue beef sandwich is $5 and includes beans and coleslaw, while the Polar Bear Delight for $13.50 is barbecue beef, ham *and* ribs with a ton of side dishes.

Entertainment
There's lots to do in Anchorage when the midnight sun finally sets. The best way to check out what's happening is to pick up a copy of *Anchorage Press*, which features bar and dance club listings, movie reviews and news about events and festivals in the Southcentral portion of the state. It's free and distributed at most tourist places in the downtown area. In the Friday edition of the *Anchorage Daily News* is the equally good weekend entertainment section called '8'.

Cinemas The city has numerous movie theaters, including *Capri Cinema* (☎ 561-0064) at 3425 Tudor Rd, *Fireweed Theater* (☎ 275-3139) at Fireweed and Gamble Rd, and *Totem Theater* (☎ 275-3188) at 3131 Muldoon Rd. *Denali Theater* (☎ 275-3106), just off Spenard Rd at 27th Ave, has late-run movies for $2 a seat. In the fall of 1996, ACT III Theaters, which already owns half the movie houses in Anchorage, opened the largest one with a nine-screen complex at the Dimond Center at Dimond Rd and Old Seward Hwy.

Or for something more touristy, head to the *Alaska Experience Theater* (☎ 272-9076) on the corner of G St and 6th Ave. The theater shows a 40-minute, 70-mm film that is projected on a huge domed screen and is entitled *Alaska the Great Land*. Admission is $7. For $10 you also get to watch a second film about the 1964 Good Friday Earthquake.

Theater Anchorage has a civic opera, a symphony orchestra, several theater groups and a concert association that brings a number of dance companies and art groups to the city every year. Big-name performers arrive more frequently now that the *Alaska Center for the Performing Arts* (☎ 263-2900) has been completed. Call the center for a schedule of who's in town and, if interested, then call its box office (☎ 263-ARTS) for the price and availability of tickets. Not so big names in music and other acts appear at *Hollywood Rock* (☎ 278-4900) downtown at 313 E St.

You'll also find live theater at the *Mainstage Theater* in the UA-Anchorage Arts Building (☎ 263-ARTS) as well as the *Off Center Playhouse* in Cyrano's Books & Cafe (☎ 274-2599), 413 D St. The unique coffee shop-bookstore-cafe also maintains a small stage for live theater and poetry readings throughout the summer.

Rock, Jazz & Blues Anchorage is a city where you can hike all day in the mountains and dance all night in the bars. One of the more colorful places is *Chilkoot Charlie's*, or 'Koots' as the locals call it, at 2435 Spenard Rd in the Midtown area. The bar hops at night and features three bands, dancing, horseshoes outside and a long bar with sawdust on the floor and rusty artefacts all over the walls. There is a cover charge and liquor prices are Alaskan but reasonable if you arrive before the bands do at 9 pm.

Other places for music are *Hot Rods*, a 50s nightclub with a DJ at 4848 Spenard Rd; *Rumrunner's Old Town Bar*, which has rhythm and blues in the Anchorage Hotel at 330 E St, and *The Whale's Tail*, a lounge with live entertainment in the Hotel Captain Cook.

There's lighter acoustic music at *Humpy's* at 610 6th Ave, while *Kaladi Brothers' Coffeehouse*, in the Brayton Mall at 68th Ave and Frontage St, often has jazz or folk music on the weekends. The *Last Frontier Bar* at 369 Muldoon Rd and *Buckaroo Club* at 2811 Spenard Rd feature country music and line dancing.

Then there is *Mr Whitekeys Fly by Nite Club* (☎ 279-SPAM) at 3300 Spenard Rd. The club plays jazz, blues and early rock but is best known for its 'Whale-Fat Follies', a fun and raunchy look at Alaska that teaches you all you'll ever want to know about duck tape, spawning salmon and Alaska's official state fossil, the woolly mammoth. The two-hour show is 8 pm Tuesday through Saturday, tickets are $12, $15 and $17, and reservations are a must.

Pubs & Bars Downtown there is a variety of low-key pubs and lively bars where you can go to cap off the evening. Locals head for *Darwin's Theory* where the popcorn is free. It's near the corner of 4th Ave and G St. *The Sports Edition Bar* in the Anchorage Hilton has 20 TVs of every size imaginable for viewing whatever game is being played that night. You could also try the *Lion's Den* in the best Western Golden Lion Hotel at 1000 East 36th St, while yuppie Anchoragites drink at *F Street Station* across from the Old Federal Building.

Great views of the area can be obtained for

the (steep) price of a drink in the *Crow's Nest,* at the top of the Hotel Captain Cook on the corner of 5th Ave and K St; or at the *Penthouse Lounge,* at the top of the Westmark Hotel at 720 West 5th Ave, where floor-to-ceiling windows let you marvel at Mt McKinley on a clear day.

Brewpubs & Microbreweries Always just a step behind the rest of the Pacific Northwest, Alaska now has a growing number of brewpubs and microbreweries with the vast majority concentrated in the Anchorage area, including *Bird Creek Brewery* (☎ 344-2473), 310 E 76th Ave.

The maker of Old 55, Anchorage Ale and Denali Ale offers free tours at 5.30 pm Thursday and also sells merchandise. There's also *Midnight Sun Brewing Co* (☎ 344-1179), the maker of such beers as Kodiak Brown Ale, Mammoth Extra Stout and Wolf Spirit Sparkling Ale, which has tours and T-shirts at 7329 Arctic Blvd.

The best brewpub in the city is *Cusack's* in the Ramada Inn on West Northern Lights Blvd. This is where serious beer drinkers come as there are more than 20 varieties on tap, including the five house brews (try MacGrooder's Scottish Ale). Can't make up your mind? Then try several at once via the sampler glass. Before you leave, check out the record moose on display in the lobby of the Ramada.

Other brewpubs in the city include the *Railway Brewing Co* in the historic Alaska Railroad Depot on 1st Ave and *Glacier Brew House,* which only started brewing in 1996 downtown at 737 West 5th Ave. Nearby *Humpy's Alehouse* on 6th Ave has almost 40 beers on tap including most of the Alaskan brews.

Things to Buy
The downtown area between 4th and 6th avenues is overrun with gift shops, many of them hawking the same tacky souvenirs; moose-nugget earrings, I-Kissed-a-Moose T-shirts, beer coasters in the shape of igloos. Among the better ones are Arctic Art at 5th Ave and D St for scrimshaw and soapstone

carvings, TJ Shirts on 6th Ave near E St which carries LA Gear clothing with quality embroidery, and the shops in the Hotel Captain Cook. For the cheapest stuff, the place to go for that souvenir you promised your six-year-old cousin (who is just going to lose it within a day anyhow) is Polar Bear Gifts on 5th Ave and E St.

Be careful when purchasing Native Alaskan art (see the Facts for the Visitor chapter).

An excellent place to check out is the Alaska Native Hospital's Gift Shop (☎ 257-1150), whose low commission for the items it sells keeps the prices very reasonable. The hospital is at 3rd Ave and G St. Across A St from the historical museum is Taheta Art & Culture Group Co-op (☎ 272-5829), which is a Native American arts cooperative, where you can watch artists work on ivory, soapstone and other materials.

Getting There & Away
Air Anchorage International Airport, 6.5 miles west of the city center, is the largest in the state, handling 130 flights daily from more than a dozen major airlines that serve it. From here you can catch a flight to anywhere in Alaska. Alaska Airlines (☎ (800) 426-0333) provides the most intrastate routes to travelers, many of them through its contract carrier, ERA, which services Valdez, Homer, Cordova, Kenia, Iliamna and Kodiak.

Reeve Aleutian Airways (☎ 243-4700 or (800) 544-2248) offers flights throughout south-west Alaska, including Pribilof Islands, King Salmon, Bethel and Unalaska. SouthCentral Air (☎ 283-3926 or (800) 478-0800) has two flights to Homer and 14 daily during the week to Kenai.

Bus There is now a variety of bus and van transport companies operating out of Anchorage and providing service to almost everywhere in the state. The biggies, like Alaskon Express, you can count on but double-check on many of the smaller companies by making a phone call.

ANCHORAGE

Tok & Haines Alaskon Express (☎ 227-5581) departs from its office on 745 West 4th Ave as well as from a handful of major hotels on Sunday, Tuesday and Friday at 7.30 am for Palmer, Glennallen, Tok and Beaver Creek in the Yukon Territory where the bus stops overnight. From Beaver Creek you can make connections to Whitehorse, Haines or Skagway. The one-way fare to Haines is $185 and to Glennallen $59. Alaska Direct (☎ 277-6652 or (800) 770-6652) offers a similar run for a slightly smaller fare. The bus departs Anchorage Sunday, Wednesday and Friday for Glennallen, Tok and Whitehorse.

Denali & Fairbanks Moon Bay Express (☎ 274-6454) has daily van service to Denali National Park and anything in between, including trailheads. The van leaves daily from the international hostel at 8 am, reaching the park at 1 pm.

The one-way fare is $35, the round trip $60. Alaska Backpacker Shuttle (☎ 344-8775) also makes the run to Denali for the same rate, while Parks Highway Express (☎ 479-3065), based in Fairbanks, departs the Egan Center in Anchorage at 4 pm daily, stopping at a variety of places, including Denali and Nenana, before reaching Fairbanks. The one-way fare to Denali is $20, and to Nenana and Fairbanks $40.

Kenai Peninsula Seward Bus Line (☎ 278-0800) takes on passengers at the Samovar Inn on the corner of 7th Ave and Gambell St and departs daily at 2.30 pm for Seward, reaching the town at 5.30 pm. The one-way fare is $30.

Valdez & Portage Alaska Backpacker Shuttle (☎ 344-8775) provides service to Portage, picking up at the downtown hostel and meeting three trains a day. The cost is $20 one way, while a bicycle is another $5.

Train The Alaska Railroad (☎ 265-2494) maintains its office in the depot at 421 West 1st Ave and provides services both north and

south of Anchorage. The most popular run is the *Denali Express* which departs Anchorage daily at 8.30 am for Denali Park and Fairbanks. The one-way fare to Denali is $95 and to Fairbanks $135. On Wednesday and Saturday a local 'Flag Stop' train departs Anchorage at 6.30 am and makes an all-stops trip to Hurricane Gulch. The return fare to Hurricane Gulch is $88. On Sunday the same train departs at noon.

The Alaska Railroad runs from Portage to Whittier and from late May to the first week of September to Seward along one of the most scenic rail routes in the country. For times and prices check the Getting Around chapter.

Hitchhiking Hitching out of Anchorage can be made a lot easier by first spending $1 and hopping on a People Mover bus. Travelers heading north should take bus No 76 or 102 to Peter's Creek Trading Post on Glenn Hwy. If you're heading to Portage, Seward or the rest of the Kenai Peninsula, take bus No 92 and get off at the corner of De Armoun Rd and Seward Hwy.

Boat The Alaska Marine Hwy (☎ 272-4482) doesn't service Anchorage but does have an office in the city at 333 West 4th Ave. Here you can obtain information, make reservations or purchase advance tickets.

Getting Around
The Airport For reasons I'll never understand, the People Mover bus service to the airport was eliminated. The closest stop is now across from the Regal Alaskan Hotel on Spenard Rd, a walk of more than a mile along a bike path. Alaska Backpacker Shuttle (☎ 344-8775) now runs out to the airport from 6 am to 10 pm daily, charging $5 for the ride to the hostel, $10 to Centennial Park Campground. Call when you arrive for the time of the next run.

Many hotels and B&Bs, mostly listed in the baggage claim area, also have courtesy van service. Finally there is an endless line of taxis eager to take your bags and your money. Plan on a $12 to $15 fare to the downtown area.

Bus Anchorage has an excellent public bus system in the People Mover with its clean buses and friendly drivers. All buses, except Nos 91 and 92, begin at the People Mover's downtown terminal in the Transit Center at the corner of 6th Ave and G St. Most buses pass by every half an hour and there's a time schedule posted at every stop. The fare is $1 a ride or $2.50 for an all-day, unlimited ticket. If the trip requires more than one bus, ask the driver for a transfer, which allows you to ride on the connecting bus for only an additional 10 cents.

A full service of 18 routes operates from Monday to Friday from 6 am to 10 pm, with a reduced service on Saturday from 8 am to 8 pm and on Sunday from only 9.30 am to 6.30 pm. For information on any route, call the Rideline on ☎ 343-6543.

Car For two or more of you, renting a used car is the most affordable way to see Anchorage, the surrounding area or the Kenai Peninsula. The cheapest deal is available from Affordable Car Rental (☎ 243-3370 or (800) 248-3765), at 4707 Spenard Rd, across from the Regal Alaskan Hotel. It advertises some cars for as low as $30 per day but never seem to have any vehicles available when you call.

There's also Rent-A-Wreck (☎ 562-5499 or (800) 478-5499 in Alaska) at 512 West International Airport Rd, which has subcompacts for $39 a day with 100 free miles. Both Rent-A-Wreck and Affordable will provide courtesy transport from your motel or to the airport before or after you rent the car. Other discounted car rental places include Anchorage Rent-A-Car (☎ 561-0350), Arctic Rent-A-Car (☎ 561-2990) and Denali Car Rental (☎ 258-8150).

All the national concerns (Avis, Budget, Hertz, Payless, National etc) maintain a counter in the ground transportation lobby of the south terminal at the airport. Reserve one if you can, as all car rentals in Anchorage are heavily booked in the summer.

South of Anchorage

Travelers who arrive in Anchorage and head south to the Kenai Peninsula will immediately be struck by Alaska's splendor; they no sooner leave the city limits than they find themselves following the edge of the spectacular Turnagain Arm. An extension of Cook Inlet, the arm is known for having some of the highest tides in the world while giving way to constant views of the Kenai Mountains to the south.

SEWARD HIGHWAY
The Seward Hwy, which runs along Turnagain Arm south of Anchorage, hugs the water and at times has been carved out of the mountainside; it runs side by side with the Alaska Railroad. A bike path shoulders much of the road and when completed will connect the bike trails in Anchorage with those in Girdwood.

The Seward Hwy begins as New Seward Hwy in Anchorage, on the corner of 5th Ave and Gambell St at a junction with the Glenn Hwy. It heads south and reaches the coast near Rabbit Creek Rd. From here the mileposts on the road measure the distance to Seward. Keep in mind that people who live in Anchorage often play on the Kenai Peninsula. Add the usual RVers of the summer and on Friday afternoon you have a major traffic tie-up heading south on Seward Hwy.

At *Mile 118*, or nine miles south of Anchorage city center, the highway passes the first of many gravel Turnagain Arm lookouts. In a mile, the highway reaches two lookouts and a massive boardwalk out onto the **Potter Marsh Waterfowl Nesting Area**, a state game refuge. There are display signs at the lookouts where you can often marvel at arctic terns and Canada geese nesting nearby. Some 130 species of birds and waterfowl have been spotted in this refuge at Anchorage's back door.

Two miles to the south you enter Chugach State Park and pass the **Potter Section House**. A home for railroad workers who maintained the tracks when locomotives were powered by coal, the house is now a state historic site and museum with displays and railroad exhibits, including a vintage snowblower and working model train. It's open from 8 am to 4.30 pm daily. Stop here for information on outdoor activities in Chugach State Park.

Across the street is the posted northern trailhead for the **Turnagain Arm Trail**, an 11-mile foot path. The route was originally used by Native Alaskans and later by Russians, trappers and gold miners at the turn of the century. It provides you with an easy hike and a 'mountain-goat's-view' of Turnagain Arm, alpine meadows and beluga whales feeding in the waters below. From Potter, the trail heads south-east and reaches McHugh Picnic Area in 3.5 miles; Rainbow (with access to Seward Hwy) in 7.5 miles; and Windy Corner at its southern end in 9.5 miles. Plan on five to seven hours for the entire walk.

In the next 10 miles, the highway passes numerous lookouts, many with scenic views of Turnagain Arm. Just beyond *Mile 112* of Seward Hwy is McHugh Creek Picnic Area (30 picnic tables) and the second access to the Turnagain Arm Trail followed by **Beluga Point**. The point has a commanding view of the Turnagain Arm and features telescopes and interpretive displays to assist travelers in

spotting the white whales in May and August. At *Mile 103.6* is **Indian**, consisting mainly of a couple of bars and a restaurant.

Just west of Turnagain House and Indian Creek is a gravel road that leads 1.3 miles past a pump station and ends near Indian Creek, where there is parking space and the posted trailhead for the **Indian Valley Trail**, a six-mile path to Indian Pass. The trail is easy, with only an occasional ford of Indian Creek, and leads to the alpine setting of the pass. In the alpine areas of the pass, more experienced hikers can continue north to eventually reach the Ship Creek Trail, which ends at Ski Bowl Rd north of Anchorage. Plan on five to seven hours for the 12-mile round trip on the Indian Valley Trail.

The **Bird Ridge Trail** starts near *Mile 102* of Seward Hwy – look for a large marked parking area to the north. From here the trail to the ridge begins with an uphill climb to a power-line access road, follows it for 0.3 miles and then turns left and climbs Bird Ridge, which runs along the valley of Bird Creek. The hike is steep in many places but quickly leaves the bush behind for the alpine beauty above. You can hike more than four miles on the ridge itself, reaching views of the headwaters of Ship Creek below. Viewing points of Turnagain Arm are plentiful and make the trail a good mountain hike.

The *Bird Creek State Campground* (19

Death in the Mud Flats

As you drive the Seward Hwy along the Turnagain Arm, the sand may looking inviting when the tide is out but *never venture out on it!* Cook Inlet has the second highest tides in North America, and with a range of nearly 40 feet, the mud flats they expose are a deadly quicksand. In the past 30 years three people have drowned after sinking into the ooze and many duck hunters and clammers have been pulled out in dramatic fashion with the water rushing in.

The saddest incident occurred in 1989 when an all-terrain vehicle (ATV) of a husband and wife driving across the flats became stuck. As the couple tried to push out the ATV, the wife, Adeana Dickison, also became mired in the mud. With the tide coming in, her husband rushed to the nearby Tidewater Cafe to call for help. The troopers arrived quickly but the 38˚F water was already at the woman's chest and she was begging them to save her. Rescuers fought against the mud and on-rushing water but to no avail. As the tide covered her head, Dickison was given a tube to breath through, but she was already suffering from hypothermia and could not hold it for very long.

Six hours later, when rescuers went out to retrieve the body, one of the legs was still firmly trapped in the mud. All of Anchorage was shocked at such a horrible death but nobody as much as the Girdwood rescuers, who later met with psychiatrists in an effort to come to terms with the ordeal. ∎

sites, $8) is just beyond *Mile 101*. The campground is scenic and known for its fine sunbathing, but is often full by early afternoon during the summer, especially on weekends.

The next 10 miles after Bird Creek Campground contain 16 turn-offs, all good spots to watch the **tidal bores**. Bores (barreling walls of water that often exceed 10 feet in height as they rush 15 mph back across the mud flats) are created twice a day by the powerful tides in Turnagain Arm.

There are more than 60 places around the world where tidal bores occur (the highest are the 25-foot bores on the Amazon basin) but the Turnagain and Knik arms are the only places in the USA where they take place on a regular basis. To avoid missing the turbulent incoming waves, get the time of low tide from the *Anchorage Daily News* and add two hours and 15 minutes. At that time the bore will be passing this particular point along the highway. Arrive early and then continue down the road after the bore passes your lookout to view it again and again.

Girdwood & Alyeska

At *Mile 90* of Seward Hwy is the junction with Alyeska Hwy, the access road which goes to Girdwood, a small hamlet of 300 residents, two miles up the side road. The junction itself now features a strip-mall housing a 7-Eleven, a taco shop and a video-rental store. For something less urban, pass this up for Girdwood. The town has a post office, grocery store and Kinder Park, site of the town's annual Forest Faire usually held in the first week of July.

Head 3.5 miles up Crow Creek Rd to see the handful of historical buildings at **Crow Creek Mine** (☎ 278-8060). Built in 1898, the camp includes a mess hall, a blacksmith's shop, a bunkhouse and several other restored buildings. Admission is $3 but for $5 you can also get a gold-panning demonstration and then can strike out on your own at a nearby creek. You can also camp here for $5 a night. An excellent way to reach the mine and continue up Crow Pass Rd is to rent a mountain bike from Girdwood Ski & Cyclery

(☎ 783-BIKE). Bikes are $20 a day or $5 an hour.

Another mile east of Girdwood is the **Alyeska Ski Area**. The ski resort hums during the winter and is also a busy place during the summer, when tour groups leave the buses to wander through the gift shops and expensive restaurants or participate in hot-air balloon flights and horse-drawn carriage rides. The best thing about the resort is the scenic ride up Mt Alyeska. In 1993, the ski resort replaced the open chair lift with a pair of 60-passenger trams. The trip up is now a five-minute ride that ends at the 2300-foot level of Mt Alyeska, where you enjoy a view of Turnagain Arm and seven area glaciers. At the top are two restaurants: fine dining at Seven Glaciers or something cheaper and quicker at Glacier Express. The ride up is $16 per adult but for an additional $2 Glacier Express will give you a ride-and-lunch combo.

Places to Stay During the summer there are rooms at the resort's *Nugget Inn* but they tend to be overrun by tour bus groups and rates reflect that. There is also the new *Alyeska Prince Resort* (☎ 754-2111 or (800) 880-3880), the only hotel in Alaska to receive a four-star rating from the American Automobile Association. The eight-story, 300-plus-room hotel opened in 1994 and features four restaurants, a 16-person whirlpool and an indoor pool that overlooks Mt Alyeska...as well as some steep rates. But if you want to be pampered, packages for $295 include accommodation for one night, tickets to the tram and dinner and champagne for two at the Seven Glaciers Restaurant.

A small but charming hostel in the area can be reached by turning right into Timberline Dr before the ski lodge and then turning right again into Alpine Rd for 0.4 miles. The *Alyeska Home Hostel* (☎ 783-2099 or 276-3635) is in a cabin with wood heating, gas lighting and a kitchen area, and includes the use of a wood-burning sauna. Unfortunately, the hostel only has eight beds, so you might want to call ahead to try to secure space. There is a three-night maximum stay and the nightly fees are $10 for members and $13 for nonmembers.

Places to Eat There are two good restaurants in Girdwood. *Chair 5 Restaurant* is right in town and features gourmet burgers for about $7, vegetarian sandwiches and salads as well as beer on tap and a friendly crew sitting at the bar. *Double Musky Inn* is just up Crow Pass Rd and is one of the outstanding restaurants in the Anchorage area, specializing in Cajun dishes and blackened steaks and fish. It's open only for dinner and no reservations are taken so be prepared for a long wait. Dinners are $16 to $26 but the food is well worth the wait and added expense to your budget.

At the strip mall along Seward Hwy, there is *Taco's*, where the menu is hand written in neon chalk on two large blackboards and the chunky salsa is made fresh daily. Burritos, tamales and nachos are all $3 to $5 or for $4.50 you can fill up on a chicken taco and a healthy portion of rice or beans.

Hiking
Just up the Alyeska Hwy from Seward Hwy is a Chugach National Forest ranger office (☎ 783-3242). The center is open daily during the summer and is a place to go for information on hiking trails not only in the Girdwood area but throughout the Kenai Peninsula.

Begin the **Alyeska Glacier View Trail** by taking the tram to the top and then scrambling up the knob behind the sun deck. From here, you follow the ridge into an alpine area where there are views of the tiny Alyeska Glacier. The entire return hike is less than a mile. You can continue up the ridge to climb the so-called summit of Mt Alyeska, a high point of 3939 feet. The true summit lies further to the south but is not a climb for casual hikers.

Winner Creek Gorge This is an easy and pleasant hike that winds 3.5 miles through a tall spruce and hemlock forest and ends in the gorge itself. The gorge is where Winter Creek flows through a small cleft in the rocks

and becomes a series of small falls and cascades on its way to emptying into Glacier Creek. You pick up the trail at Alyeska Ski Resort by parking on Arlberg Rd and walking along the bike path past the Alyeska Prince Hotel towards the bottom of the tram. Follow the edge of a ski trail above the tram and look for the footpath heading into the forest.

Crow Creek Trail Two miles up the Alyeska Access Rd and just before Girdwood is the junction with Crow Creek Rd, a bumpy gravel road. It extends 5.8 miles to a parking lot and the marked trailhead to the Crow Creek Trail, a short but beautiful alpine hike. It is four miles to Raven Glacier, the traditional turn-around point of the trail, and with transport, hikers can easily do the eight-mile round trip in four to six hours.

The trail is a highly recommended trek as it features gold-mining relics, an alpine lake and usually dall sheep on the slopes above. There are also many possibilities for longer trips and a USFS cabin three miles up the trail (it charges $25 per night and reservations are required). You can also camp around Crow Creek, turning the walk into a pleasant overnight trip. Or, you can continue and complete the three-day, 25-mile route along the Old Iditarod Trail to the Chugach State Park's Eagle River Nature Center (see the North of Anchorage section in this chapter).

Portage
From the Alyeska Access Rd, Seward Hwy continues south-east and at *Mile 81* reaches the **Wetland Observation Platform** which was constructed by the Bureau of Land Management. The platform features interpretive plaques on the ducks, arctic terns, bald eagles and other wildlife that can often been seen from it.

Portage, the departure point for passengers and cars going to Whittier on the Alaska Railroad, is passed at *Mile 80* of Seward Hwy. There is not much left of Portage, which was destroyed by the Good Friday Earthquake, other than a few structures sinking into the nearby mud flats. During the summer, the shuttle train departs the loading ramp several times daily, with one trip connecting with the MV *Bartlett*, the ferry that cruises from Whittier to Valdez (see the Getting Around chapter).

Portage Glacier

A mile south of the loading ramp in Portage is the junction with Portage Glacier Access Rd. The road leads 5.4 miles past three campgrounds to a visitor center overlooking Portage Glacier, which has surpassed Denali National Park as Alaska's most visited attraction. The magnificent ice floe is five miles long and a mile wide at its face and is the Southcentral's version of the drive-in glacier. It's impressive, but in 1880 it filled what is now Portage Lake. Native Alaskans and miners used the ice as a route or 'portage' between Turnagain Arm and Passage Canal. By 1890 the glacier had begun to retreat and today more than 2.5 miles of the lake has been exposed. Retreating at more than 300 feet per year, the glacier is now expected to reach the end of the lake by the year 2020. What it will do at this point is anybody's guess.

The glacier and the ice that clutters the west end of the lake is quite a sight and more than 700,000 people view it annually, with the number increasing sharply each year. This is evident during the summer as a stream of tour buses and cars is constantly passing through. But even if crowds are what you're trying to avoid, Portage Glacier is not to be missed, as it is classic Alaskan imagery. The **Begich-Boggs Visitor Center** (☎ 783-2326) is also well worth viewing. The center houses, among other things, a simulated ice cave you can walk through to reach the Glacier Exhibit room with its displays demonstrating the formation of crevasses, as well as glacial motion and the range of glaciers today. Elsewhere you can touch an iceberg, brought in fresh daily, take a close look at ice worms or take in the excellent movie *Voices From the Ice* shown every hour in a 200-seat theater. All around there are observation decks and telescopes from which to view the main attraction. During the summer the center is open from 9 am to 6 pm daily.

For those who want to get even closer to the glacier, Gray Line offers hour-long cruises on board its tour boat, *Ptarmigan*. Don't get this cruise confused with any glacier cruise along Tracy Arm in the Southeast or College Fjord in Prince William Sound; you simply motor around the lake and it's $21 per person.

Check with the rangers about a planned trail to the face of Portage Glacier. Otherwise, hiking in the area consists of the **Byron Glacier Trail**, an easy one-mile path to the base of Byron Glacier that begins on the road to the tour-boat dock. Once you reach the permanent snow in front of the glacier, look for ice worms in it. The worms, immortalized in a Robert Service poem, are black, thread-like and less than an inch long. They survive by consuming algae and escape the heat of the sun by sliding between ice crystals of glaciers and snowfields.

Places to Stay There are only two campgrounds in the area; *Black Bear Campground* (12 sites, $6 fee) and *Williwaw Campground* (38 sites, $6 fee). Williwaw is particularly pleasant as there is a salmon-spawning observation deck near it and a mile-long nature walk through beaver and moose habitat.

Keep in mind that you never get a site late in the day at these campgrounds. With more than 700,000 people coming to see Portage Glacier annually, the facilities always seem to be full.

From Portage, Seward Hwy turns south and heads for the scenic town of Seward on Resurrection Bay, 128 miles from Anchorage (see the Southcentral chapter).

North of Anchorage

GLENN HIGHWAY

The 189-mile Glenn Hwy begins on the corner of Medfra St and 5th Ave *(Mile 0)*, just west of Merrill Field Airport in Anchorage, and extends to Glennallen and the Richardson Hwy. The first 42 miles head north-east to Palmer, the trade center of the Matanuska Valley, and has been converted into a true highway, featuring four lanes which enable motorists to pass road hogs in their RVs. Just west of Palmer the Glenn Hwy forms a major junction with the George Parks Hwy. The George Parks Hwy heads to Fairbanks. Glenn Hwy curves more due east to Glennallen (see the Interior chapter). Mileposts on the highway show distances from Anchorage.

On the first eight miles north-east from Anchorage, you pass the exits to Elmendorf Air Force Base, Centennial Campground and Arctic Valley Rd to Fort Richardson (see the Anchorage section). At *Mile 11.5* of Glenn Hwy is the turn-off to *Eagle River State Campground* (58 sites, $15 fee), just up Hiland Rd. The scenic campground is in a wooded area on the south bank of the Eagle River. The spot is popular and has a four-day limit. Don't drink the glacier-fed water of the Eagle River. Also, don't depend on getting a tent space if you happen to arrive late. This is one of the busiest campgrounds in the state.

Eagle River
At *Mile 13.4* of Glenn Hwy is the exit to Old Glenn Hwy which takes you through the bedroom communities of Eagle River and Chugiak. Eagle River (pop 14,000) has a couple of plazas and just about every business you need. Chugiak is almost void of any commercial service and at times it's even hard to know when you have passed through the town.

The **North Anchorage Visitor Center** (☎ 696-4636) is in the Valley River Mall off Old Glenn Hwy and open during the mall business hours. There is also the **Southcentral Alaska Museum of Natural History** (☎ 694-0819), in the Parkgate Building across from McDonald's Restaurant on Old Glenn Hwy. Exhibits include Alaska dinosaurs, minerals, fossils and wildlife displays of black and brown bears. Admission is $3

and opening hours in summer are 10 am to 5 pm daily.

But the main reason to exit at Eagle River is to drive Eagle River Rd. This 12.7-mile road is paved and a beautiful side trip into the Chugach Mountains. It ends at the **Eagle River Nature Center** of the Chugach State Forest. The log cabin center (☎ 694-2108) is open daily from 10 am to 7 pm and features wildlife displays, hand-outs for hikers, naturalist programs and telescopes with which to view dall sheep in the surrounding mountains. There is also an outdoor picnic area with more telescopes and a stunning view of the Chugach Mountains.

Hiking Two trails depart from the Eagle River Nature Center. One is the easy **Rodak Nature Trail**, a loop of less than a mile that passes a series of interpretive panels and an impressive observation deck straddling a salmon stream. **Albert Loop Trail** is a three-mile hike through a boreal forest and along Eagle River.

The nature center also serves as the northern trailhead for the **Old Iditarod Trail**, a 26-mile historical trail. The route was used by gold miners and dog-sled teams until 1918, when the Alaska Railroad was completed from Seward to Fairbanks. It is a three-day hike through excellent mountain scenery and up to Crow Pass, where you can view nearby Raven Glacier and Crystal Lake. From here you hike down the Crow Creek Trail and emerge on Crow Creek Rd, seven miles away from the Seward Hwy (see the South of Anchorage section in this chapter).

Although this route involves fording several streams, including Eagle River itself, and some climbing to Crow Pass, it is an excellent hike – one of the best in the Southcentral and Anchorage regions. Backpackers in Anchorage can reach the junction of Eagle River Rd on People Mover bus Nos 74 and 76 and from there hitch to the visitor center. Or Alaska Backpacker Shuttle (☎ 344-8775) will transport you to the nature center for $12 and then pick you up at the Crow Pass Trailhead three days later for $20.

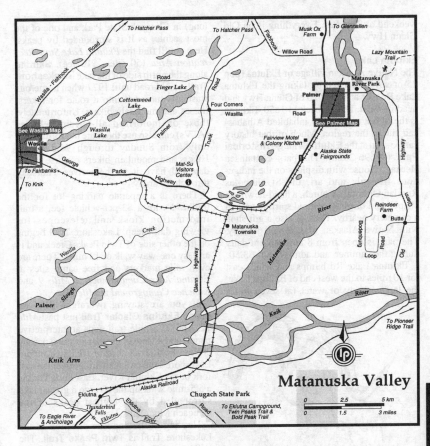

Matanuska Valley

Bring a stove as campfires are not allowed in the state park.

Northbound on Glenn Hwy, the Thunderbird Falls exit is reached at *Mile 25.2* and leads 0.3 miles to a parking area and the trailhead for the **Thunderbird Falls Trail**. The mile-long trail is a quick uphill climb to the scenic falls formed by a small, rocky gorge. At the end is a deck with benches overlooking the cascade, a great place to enjoy lunch.

Places to Stay & Eat If the public campgrounds are filled and you're too tired to hassle with Anchorage, there's the *Eagle River Motel* (☎ 694-5000), which includes a laundromat. A single/double is $76/$85.

In town, there is a *Carrs* with its salad bar and ready-to-eat items, and a *Sleepy Dog Coffee Co* for a latte and an opportunity to surf the Internet. There are also the usual fast-food chains of McDonald's, Taco Bell, Subway and Pizza Hut. The best eatery is *Bombay Restaurant* in the Eagle River Shopping Center. The Indian cuisine is good enough for locals to justify the drive from Anchorage. *North Slope Restaurant* includes a microbrewery while there's dancing on the weekend at *Tips Bar*. Everything is on Old Glenn Hwy.

Eklutna Lake

The Native Alaskan village of Eklutna (pop 25 or so) is reached by taking the Eklutna Lake Rd exit at *Mile 26.5* of Glenn Hwy and heading west. Dating back to 1650, Eklutna is the oldest continually inhabited Athabascan site in the region. Much of that history can be seen at the **Eklutna Village Historical Park** (☎ 696-2828). The park contains a Heritage House with displays on the indigenous lifestyle, the St Nicholas Russian Orthodox Church, a hand-hewn log chapel, and brightly colored spirit houses in a cemetery nearby. There is also a gift shop with Native Alaskan baskets and jewelry. The park is open from 8 am to 6 pm daily during the summer, and admission is $3.50.

Eklutna Lake Rd bumps and winds east for 10 miles to the west end of Eklutna Lake, the largest body of water (at seven miles long) in Chugach State Park and one of the most scenic, as it is surrounded by peaks. Here you'll find the *Eklutna Lake State Recreation Area* (50 sites, $10 fee). Skirting along the north side of the lake is **Lakeshore Trail**, an old road until 1977 when numerous washouts turned it into a route for hikers, horses and mountain bikers. Unfortunately, those on motorized all-terrain vehicles (ATVs) can also use the route but fortunately only from Sunday through Wednesday. Hikers and mountain bikers can use it any day and have it to themselves Thursday through Saturday.

There is a separate parking lot for the trailhead with a $3-per-vehicle fee, a trail information kiosk and telescopes for viewing dall sheep. Lakeshore Trail begins on the other side of Twin Peaks Creek and is an easy one-way walk of 13 miles. There are even mile markers and free camp sites at *Eklutna Alex Campground* at *Mile 9* and *Kanchee Campground* at *Mile 11*.

If you are staying overnight, plan on hiking **Eklutna Glacier Trail** just past *Mile 12*. The 0.75-mile trail ends at interpretive panels and a view of the glacier. Also nearby is **East Fork Trail** at *Mile 10.5*, just before Lakeshore Trail crosses a bridge over the east fork of the Eklutna River. East Fork Trail is a 5.5-mile walk up the river to a glacial lake surrounded by the highest peaks of the Chugach Mountains.

Heading in the opposite direction of the Lakeshore Trail is **Twin Peaks Trail**. The trail is another abandoned road that heads 3.5 miles above the tree line to the passes between Twin Peaks. It is well marked in the beginning and halfway up you can lie out and soak up the views of the lake and valley and some sun, if it's shining that day (chances are it won't be). Above the tree line, the trail becomes steeper and more challenging to follow. At this point, scrambling in the alpine area is easy and the views of Eklutna Lake below are excellent. Plan on several hours for the hike, depending on how far you go above the tree line, and keep a sharp eye out for dall sheep.

Bold Peak Trail is another good hike

Massive curling horns are the hallmark of a Dall ram.

which starts 5.5 miles along the Lakeshore Trail. The 3.5-mile trail is a moderately hard hike to the alpine area below Bold Peak (7522 feet) and begins with a steep ascent, reaching the bush line in 1.5 miles. Great views of the valley, Eklutna Glacier and even Knik Arm of Cook Inlet are obtained here, while people with the energy can scramble up nearby ridges. Plan on two hours to climb the trail and an hour for the return. To actually climb Bold Peak requires that you have mountaineering skill and equipment.

PALMER

From Eklutna Lake Rd, the Glenn Hwy continues north, crosses bridges over the Knik and Matanuska rivers at the northern end of Cook Inlet, and at *Mile 35.3* reaches a major junction with the George Parks Hwy. At this point, Glenn Hwy curves sharply to the east and heads into Palmer (pop 3500), seven miles away. If you're driving, a much more scenic way to reach Palmer is to leave Glenn Hwy just before it crosses Knik River and follow Old Glenn Hwy into town.

History

Although a train station was built here in 1916, Palmer was really born in 1935 when it was selected for an unusual social experiment during President Franklin Roosevelt's New Deal relief programs. Some 200 farming families, hit hard by the Great Depression in the US midwest, were moved north to raise crops and livestock in the Matanuska and Susitna valleys.

The failure rate was high within this transplanted agricultural colony, but somehow Palmer survived and today it is the only community whose economy is based primarily on farming. The farms of the Matanuska Valley grow the 60-pound cabbages and seven-pound turnips as a result of the midnight sun that shines up to 20 hours a day during the summer.

Information

Tourist Office Stop at the Palmer Visitor Center (☎ 745-2880), a rustic log cabin near the corner of Fireweed Ave and South Valley

Matanuska Valley is known to produce BIG cabbages.

Way in the center of town. Open from 9 am to 6 pm daily, the center has a small museum in the basement with relics from its 'colony' era. Outside is a picnic area and the **Matanuska Valley Agricultural Showcase**, a garden of flowers and the area's famous oversized vegetables. To see cabbages the size of basketballs or radishes that look like red softballs, you have to come from late July to late August. It is open from 8 am to 6 pm daily in the summer.

Money A Key Bank of Alaska (☎ 745-6100) is at 1150 South Colony Way.

Post The post office is at the corner of South Cobb St and West Cedar Ave.

Bookshop & Library The Book Nook (☎ 745-8863), at 105 East Arctic Ave, sells and trades used books. The library is on East Dahlia Ave just north of the visitor center.

Laundry Gateway Center (☎ 745-6161), at *Mile 6.5* of Fishhook-Willow Rd to Hatcher Pass, has a laundromat and showers as well as groceries and a beer store.

Medical Services Valley Hospital (☎ 746-8600) is at 515 East Dahlia, east of the library.

Alaska State Fairgrounds

The town's biggest attraction is its annual Alaska State Fair, held in the last week of August (see Special Events following). But even if you're not here when the fair is, the

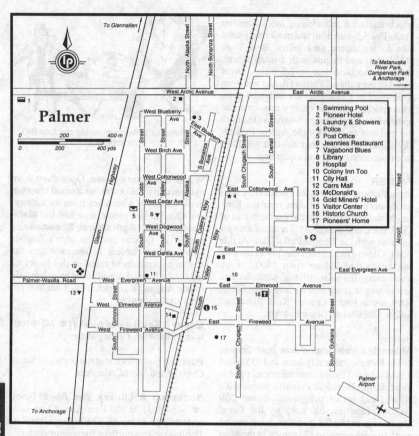

To Glennallen

Palmer

0   200   400 m
0   200   400 yds

To Matanuska
River Park,
Campervan Park
& Anchorage

West Arctic Avenue

East   Arctic   Avenue

1	Swimming Pool
2	Pioneer Hotel
3	Laundry & Showers
4	Police
5	Post Office
6	Jeannies Restaurant
7	Vagabond Blues
8	Library
9	Hospital
10	Colony Inn Too
11	City Hall
12	Carrs Mall
13	McDonald's
14	Gold Miners' Hotel
15	Visitor Center
16	Historic Church
17	Pioneers' Home

West Blueberry
Ave

East Blueberry
Ave

West Birch Ave

West Cottonwood
Ave

West Cedar Ave

Cottonwood   Ave

West Dogwood
Ave

West Dahlia Ave

East   Dahlia   Avenue

East Evergreen Ave

Palmer-Wasilla Road

West   Evergreen   Avenue

West   Elmwood   Avenue

Elmwood   Avenue

West   Dimond   Street

West   Fireweed   Avenue

East   Fireweed   Avenue

Palmer
Airport

To Anchorage

ANCHORAGE

Alaska State Fairgrounds are still the site of a number of events and the home of **Colony Village**, which began in 1975 as a Bicentennial project. The village attempts to preserve buildings from the area's 'colony' days of the late 1930s. Of the five buildings, four of them – two houses, a barn and a church – were part of the original Matanuska Valley Colony and built in either 1935 or 1936. Admission to the village is free, and it is open from 10 am to 4 pm Monday to Saturday.

Farms

If you have a vehicle, a drive around the back roads of the Palmer area and past the farms makes an interesting afternoon. To view a few of the colony farms that survived along with the original barns built, head north-east nine miles on Glenn Hwy and exit onto Farm Loop Rd. Keep an eye out for vegetable stands if you're passing through the area from mid to late summer. The Matanuska Farm Market is at *Mile 38* of the Glenn Hwy while Pyrah's Farm is a pick-your-own-vegetables farm just before *Mile 3* of Bodenberg Loop Rd south of Palmer.

At *Mile 11.5* of Old Glenn Hwy you pass near a farm of a different sort – one that raises reindeer. Turn onto Bodenberg Loop Rd and within a mile you'll reach the **Reindeer Farm** (☎ 745-4000). You view and photograph the Lapland animals as they graze or you can join a tour. The farm is open daily from 10 am to 6 pm from June to September and admission is $5.

At *Mile 50* of Glenn Hwy, just north of Palmer, is the **Musk Ox Farm** (☎ 745-4151), where you can see the only domestic herd of these prehistoric beasts in the world. Tours allow you to view and photograph more than 100 shaggy musk oxen while the guide explains how their qiviut (down hair) is combed and woven into the world's rarest cloth – probably one of the most expensive cloths at more than $60 per ounce. During the tour, you get so close to the oxen that you can pet and feed them. The farm is open daily from May to September from 10 am to 6 pm and admission is $7. Tours are given every half-hour and a gift shop displays and sells the finished products.

Hiking

Lazy Mountain The best hike near Palmer is the climb to the top of Lazy Mountain, elevation 3720 feet. The 2.5-mile trail is steep at times, but makes for a pleasant trek that ends in an alpine setting with good views of the Matanuska Valley and its farms below. From the Glenn Hwy in Palmer, head east on Arctic Ave, the third exit off the highway into town, which turns into Old Glenn Hwy. After crossing the Matanuska River, turn left into Clark-Wolverine Rd and then right after half a mile at a T-junction. This puts you on Huntly Rd, and you follow it for a mile to the Equestrian Center parking lot at its end. The trailhead, marked 'Foot Trail', is on the north side of the parking lot. Plan on three to five hours for the return hike.

McRoberts Creek Trail This is a backcountry hike up McRoberts Creek valley and provides an easy approach to climbing Matanuska Peak (6119 feet). The trail reaches the tree line in 2.5 miles and 3880-foot Summit Ridge in nine miles. The trek to Matanuska Peak would be an 18-mile hike. To reach the

trailhead, take Old Glenn Hwy from Palmer toward Butte and turn left onto Smith Rd at *Mile 15.5*. Follow Smith Rd for 1.4 miles until it curves into Harmony Ave. There is no parking at the South Fork Trailhead so leave the car at the bend in the road.

Pioneer Ridge Trail This is a 5.7-mile route from Knik River Rd to the main ridge that extends south-east from Pioneer Peaks, elevation 6400 feet. The first half of the climb is through birch and cottonwood and then alder thicket until you reach the alpine tundra at 3200 feet. Once on the ridge, South Pioneer Peak is a mile to the north-west and North Pioneer Peak is two miles away. To scale either one requires rock-climbing experience and equipment. To the south-east the ridge leads towards Bold Peak, Hunter Creek drainage and eventually Eklutna Lake. To reach the trailhead, turn into Knik River Rd just before crossing the river on Old Glenn Hwy and follow it for almost four miles.

Organized Tours

Want to see a glacier? Knik Glacier Adventures (☎ 746-5133) offers a four-hour air-boat tour of the three-mile-long glacier. It's $60 per person but includes a barbecue meal at the face of the glacier.

The Palmer area also boasts a number of riding stables. The Rafter T Ranch (☎ 745-8768), near *Mile 5* of the Palmer Fishhook Rd, offers both guided and unguided horseback rides through wooded trails along the Knik River. Rates range from $35 an hour per person; overnight rides can also be arranged.

Special Events

The best reason to stop in Palmer is the Alaska State Fair, an 11-day event that ends on Labor Day. The fair features produce and livestock from the surrounding area, horse shows, a rodeo, a carnival and the largest cabbages you'll ever see.

There is also more to eat at the fair than just corn dogs and cotton candy, as you can feast on fresh salads, home-made desserts,

Alaskan seafood and barbecue ribs and chicken.

Within the state fairgrounds is the outdoor Borealis Theater and during the 4 July weekend it is the site of a bluegrass festival, worth attending if you are passing through. Those in Anchorage should check with Far North Tours (☎ 272-7480) which runs a special Alaska State Fair Shuttle that departs the big city at 9 am and 1 pm. The round-trip fare is $25 but includes fair admission.

Places to Stay

Camping You can pitch a tent or park a trailer at *Matanuska River Park*, less than a half-mile east of town on Old Glenn Hwy. One half of the campground features wooded sites for $8 per night, showers and a series of trails that wind around ponds and along the Matanuska River. The other half is an open dayuse area that includes a large softball complex.

B&Bs Outside the Palmer Visitor Center is a rack for the local B&Bs and you'll find more than a dozen in the area. You can also call the Mat-Su Chapter of the B&B Association of Alaska (☎ 376-4461 or (800) 401-7444) in advance for a room in a B&B.

Hotels There is no hostel in Palmer, which also has an 8% bedroom tax. The cheapest hotel in town is the *Pioneer Motel* (☎ 745-3425) on the corner of North Alaska St and West Arctic Ave, where a double is $45 per night in rooms that are small but clean with some featuring kitchenettes. Also in Palmer is the *Goldminer's Hotel* (☎ 745-6160 or (800) 725-2752) on West Elmwood Ave and South Colony Way with doubles or singles for $65. The *Fairview Motel* (☎ 745-1505) across from the state fairgrounds has singles/doubles for $50/60 and rooms with kitchenettes for $5 more.

Places to Eat

Palmer has a *McDonald's* and a *Subway* near the intersection of the Glenn and Palmer-Wasilla highways and I'm sure other fast-food chains will begin appearing soon.

For something a little more personal, try *Colony Inn Too*, in the former teacher's dorm, one of the original Matanuska Colony buildings at 325 East Elmwood Ave. The food is excellent and most of it made from scratch, especially the desserts. Dinners range from $11 to $17.

Vegetarian dishes and other healthy stuff is available at *Jeannies – The Health Connection* at 610 South Bailey St. The restaurant is open for lunch and dinner and on the second Thursday of each month has a special dinner served from 5 to 8 pm by reservation only. For breakfast try *Colony Kitchen* next door to the Fairview Motel on Glenn Hwy. A skillet of eggs and potatoes or home-made biscuits and gravy is $5 and can be enjoyed in an interesting interior of stuffed birds suspended from the ceiling.

Vagabond Blues, at 642 South Alaska St in the heart of Palmer, doubles as a bakery & restaurant and coffeehouse with live music at night. The menu is limited but the home-made soup and bread is excellent.

HATCHER PASS

Just north-east of Palmer, via the Fishhook-Willow Rd off Glenn Hwy, is the Hatcher Pass area (see the The Interior map in the Interior chapter), an alpine paradise filled with panoramas of the Talkeetna Mountains, foot trails, gold-mine artefacts and even some unusual lodging possibilities. The area is probably the most photographed in the Mat-Su Valley and can be entered from either Wasilla, Willow or Palmer, but the drive from Palmer is the shortest and especially scenic as it follows the Little Susitna River through a vertical-walled gorge. It also has the most traffic, making hitching a lot easier for those without a set of wheels.

The pass itself is 22 miles out of Palmer and, at 3886 feet, is an alpine area of meadows, ridges, steep drops and a beautiful body of water known as Summit Lake. It's also a popular destination for parasailing and, on most calm evenings, you can sit on a ridge and watch the daredevils strap themselves to the colorful sails and glide with the wind.

Independence Mine State Historical Park

This fascinating 272-acre state historical park, 18 miles north of Palmer, is entirely above the tree line. Within the beautiful bowl-shaped valley of the park are the remains of 16 buildings that were built in the 1930s by the Alaska-Pacific Mining Company (APC) which for 10 years was second only to Juneau's A-J Mine as the leading hardrock gold mine in Alaska.

Gold was first discovered in the area by a pair of Japanese prospectors shortly after 1900 and the rough nature of the gold was an indication to many miners that there was a 'motherlode' waiting to be found higher in the Talkeetna Mountains. Robert Lee Hatcher discovered and staked the first lode claim in Willow Creek valley in 1906 and within a few years mining took off. From 1906 until 1950 more than 50 gold mines were worked in the Hatcher Pass area, but the two most productive were the Alaska Free Gold Mine on Skyscraper Mountain and Independence Mine on Granite Mountain.

In 1938, the two mines were consolidated by APC, which controls a block of 83 mining permits, 1350 acres and 27 structures. In is peak year of 1941 APC employed 204 workers, blasted almost 12 miles of tunnels and recovered 34,416 ounces of gold that was worth $1.2 million. Today that gold would be worth almost $18 million.

WWII shut down the Independence Mine in 1943. It reopened in 1948 and briefly in 1950 before being finally abandoned in 1955. It is now a state park, and seeing Independence Mine and the company town that was built around it makes for a fascinating afternoon in anybody's trip to Alaska. Admission is only $2 per vehicle.

Begin at the Manager's House, which has been converted into a visitor center. There are video interviews of the old miners, displays on the different ways to mine gold (panning, placer mining and hardrock) and even a simulated mining tunnel.

The visitor center (☎ 745-2827) is open from 11 am to 7 pm daily and can provide a walking-tour map of the park and a list of area hikes. Guided tours are conducted daily at 1.30 and 3.30 pm and are $3 per person.

From the center, you follow Hardrock Trail past the buildings, including bunkhouses and the mill complex that is built into the side of the mountain and looks like an avalanche of falling timber. Make an effort to climb up the trail to the water tunnel portal where you get a great overview of the entire complex and a blast of cold air pouring out of the mountain.

Hiking

Gold Mint Trail This is one of the easiest hikes in the Hatcher Pass area. It begins at a parking lot across from Motherlode Lodge at *Mile 14* of the Fishhook-Willow Rd. The trail follows the Little Susitna River into a gently sloping mountain valley. Within three miles you can spot the ruins of Lonesome Mine. Keep trekking and you will eventually reach the head of the river at Mint Glacier.

Reed Lakes Trail A mile past Motherlode Lodge, a road to Archangel Valley splits off from Fishhook-Willow Rd and takes you to the trailhead of Reed Lakes. The trail begins as a wide road and is soon climbing to the crest of the valley. Lower Reed Lake is reached within a quarter-mile after reaching the crest; Upper Reed Lake follows after a bit more climbing.

Craigie Creek Trail This trail, posted along the Fishhook-Willow Rd west of Hatcher Pass, actually starts out as a road that is occasional used by 4WD vehicles. The trail follows a valley up to the head of the creek where it's possible to cross a pass into the Independence Mine Bowl. The road climbs gently for four miles past several abandoned mining operations and then becomes a very steep trail for three miles to Dogsled Pass.

Places to Stay & Eat

At *Mile 14* of Fishhook-Willow Rd is *Motherlode Lodge* (☎ 746-1464), which was originally built in the 1930s as part of the local mining operation. Today it's been totally renovated and has rooms for $65 a night including breakfast. There is also a dining room here with superb views of the mountains from every table and a bar where you can sit out on the deck and take in more panoramas.

Closer to the pass itself and within Independence Mine State Park is *Hatcher Pass Lodge* (☎ 745-5897) where small cabins are $110 a night per couple and rooms cost $70. Both prices include breakfast. The lodge also has a restaurant and bar where you can enjoy your favorite brew at 3000 feet above sea

level as well as a sauna built over a rushing mountain stream.

Getting There & Around

Other than renting a car in Wasilla or hitching, the only way to get to Hatcher Pass and Independent Mine is to join a tour. Mat-Su Tours (☎ 376-3608) offers a full-day tour that begins in Wasilla and includes the Musk Ox Farm and the state park for $65. It also throws in lunch but the price still seems steep.

The Interior

At the Fairview Inn in Talkeetna the house rules are easy to understand and even easier to read. They're posted right above the hotel's horseshoe bar:

All firearms must be checked in with the bartender before drinks are ordered.

The bartender is the only one allowed to stoke the wood-burning stove.

Welcome to Interior Alaska, that 'great, big, broad land way up yonder' between Anchorage and Fairbanks that has been searched over by miners, immortalized by poets such as Robert Service, and is immediately visualized when somebody says 'the Last Frontier'.

The images of Alaska's heartland are of dog sleds and gold pans, roadhouses and fish wheels, a moose on the side of the road and a seemingly endless stretch of pavement that disappears into the mountains.

The Interior, in fact, is bordered by dramatic mountain chains, with the Alaska Range lying to the south and the Brooks Range to the north. In between is the central plateau of Alaska, a vast area of land that gently slopes to the north and is broken up by awesome rivers such as the Yukon, Kuskokwim, Koyukuk and Tanana.

It is the home of Mt McKinley, which is the highest peak in North America (20,316 feet), and of Denali National Park & Preserve, the best known attraction in the state for hiking, camping and wildlife watching. It is the stomping grounds for brown bear, moose, caribou and dall sheep, whose numbers here are unmatched anywhere else in the country.

The Interior can be enjoyed by even the most impecunious traveler because it's accessible by road. The greater part of Alaska's highway system forms a triangle which includes the state's two largest cities, Anchorage and Fairbanks, and allows cheap travel by bus, train, car or hitchhiking.

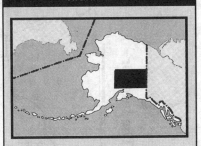

HIGHLIGHTS

- Belly up to the bar with mountain climbers and locals at the Fairview Inn
- Take a shuttle bus through Denali National Park to see brown bears, moose, caribou and other wildlife
- Hear Robert Service's poetry at its best at the Malemute Saloon in Ester
- Look for the Delta buffalo herd from an interpretive area at *Mile 241.3* of the Richardson Highway
- Camp at *King Mountain State Recreation Site* and take a whitewater raft trip down the Matanuska River
- Enjoy a walking tour with the Eagle Historical Society and relive this fascinating town's history

The George Parks Hwy leaves Anchorage and winds 358 miles to Fairbanks, passing Denali National Park along the way. The Glenn Hwy spans 189 miles between Anchorage and Glennallen and then continues another 125 miles to Tok in a section known as the Tok Cutoff.

The Richardson Hwy passes Glennallen from Valdez and ends at Fairbanks, 368 miles away. Dividing the triangle from east to west is the Denali Hwy, 136 miles long and at one time the only road to Denali National Park.

All four roads are called highways, though they are rarely more than two-lane roads. All of them pass through spectacular scenery,

INTERIOR

The Interior

offer good possibilities of spotting wildlife and are lined with turn-offs, campgrounds and hiking trails. For the most part, the towns along them are small, colorless service centers with gasoline stations, motels and cafés, although a few have managed to retain their rustic gold-rush and frontier flavor. The real attraction of the Interior is not these service centers but what lies in the hills and valleys beyond the highway.

Bus transport is available on every highway except the Denali, and there is a train service between Anchorage and Fairbanks. Bus routes and even the companies themselves change often in Alaska, so it pays to double-check bus departures with a phone call.

The hitchhiking is surprisingly good during the summer, as the highways are cluttered with the stream of RVs and summer tourists arriving from down south. Avoid backtracking if you can, even if it means going out of your way on an alternative route. All the highways offer their own roadside scenery that is nothing short of spectacular.

Climate

In this region of mountains and spacious valleys, the climate varies greatly and the weather can change appreciably from one day to the next. In the winter, the temperatures drop to -60°F for days at a time; in the summer, they can soar above 90°F. The norm for the summer is long days with warm temperatures from 60°F to 70°F. However, it is common for Denali National Park to experience at least one snowfall in the lowlands between June and August.

Here, more than anywhere else in the state, it is important to have warm clothes while still being able to strip down to a T-shirt and hiking shorts. Most of the area's 10 to 15 inches of annual precipitation comes in the form of summer showers, with cloudy conditions common, especially north of Mt McKinley. In Denali National Park, Mt McKinley is hidden by the weather for two out of three days.

George Parks Highway

Many travelers and most overseas visitors arrive in Alaska through Anchorage and venture north along the George Parks Hwy. The road, which was opened in 1971, provides a direct route to Denali National Park while passing through some of the most rugged scenery Alaska has to offer. The road begins at a junction with the Glenn Hwy 35.3 miles north of Anchorage. Mileposts indicate distances from Anchorage and not from the junction.

WASILLA

From its junction with Glenn Hwy, the George Parks Hwy heads west then north and, for the first 20 miles, passes through a jungle of tacky tourist stops, strip malls and as many fast-food restaurants as you'll see in all of the Southeast.

The ultimate in this stretch of seemingly out-of-place tourist traps can be found at the junction with Big Lake Rd where you have several discount fireworks stands, including one that has a huge gorilla balloon floating overhead.

The reason for the development is the caravan of RVers heading north to Denali National Park, a steady stream of consumerism that everybody is trying to tap into, and the town of Wasilla (pop 4500) just seven miles from the junction.

History

At one time, this community was a mining supply center and in the 1970s was little more than a sleepy little town servicing local farmers. From 1980 to 1983, the population of Wasilla doubled when Alaskans who wanted to work in Anchorage but live elsewhere began moving into the town making it an Anchorage dormitory community.

There was even talk of building a bridge across the Knik Arm to shorten the drive to Anchorage. Meanwhile, shopping centers and businesses have mushroomed along the highway.

INTERIOR

Wasilla

```
0        200        400 m
0        200        400 yds
```

1 Swimming Pool	6 City Hall & Police
2 West Valley Medical Center	Department
3 Laundromat	7 Bank
4 Post Office	8 Train Station
5 Library, Museum, Visitor	9 McDonald's Restaurant
Center & Historic Park	10 Pizza Hut

This is all a bit ironic because many feel that Wasilla, with its strip malls and convenience stores, is now just a slice of the big city that others were trying to escape.

Information
Tourist Offices Near the junction of George Parks Hwy and Trunk Rd is the Mat-Su Visitors Center (☎ 746-5000) open from 8.30 am to 6.30 pm daily during the summer. The log lodge sits on a small rise and, along with bathrooms and racks of brochures, it has a outdoor deck with a great view of the mountains surrounding Knik Inlet.

The Dorothy Page Museum (☎ 376-9071) in the town of Wasilla, just off the highway on Main St, doubles as the visitor center and is also open daily.

Money Wasilla has a half-dozen banks and credit unions in town with most of them along the George Parks Hwy.

Post The post office is three blocks north of George Parks Hwy on Main St near the Dorothy Page Museum.

Travel Agency Sanctuary Travel Services (☎ 373-1212) is at 1590 Financial Dr.

Bookshop A Waldenbooks is in the Cottonwood Creek Mall on the George Parks Hwy on the south side of town.

Laundry There are two laundromats; Wasilla Homestyle Laundry in the Wasilla Shopping Center on the highway and Wash Day Laundry behind the McDonald's Restaurant.

Medical Services The West Valley Medical Center (☎ 376-5028) is on East Bogard St just east of Crusey St.

Dorothy Page Museum
This is both a museum and an interesting historical village of preserved buildings,

each loaded with artefacts. Named after 'the Mother of the Iditarod', the museum is open daily year-round from 9 am to 6 pm and admission is $3. The museum is packed with artefacts, including tools and other relics from the early farmers, and mining displays in the basement. In the historical village there are a half-dozen buildings, mostly classic log cabins. One is Wasilla's first public sauna that was opened in 1942 with men and women using it on alternate days of the week. Another is the Capital Site Cabin, erected in Wasilla as a reminder of an issue that had split the state. If you have already traveled through Juneau you will have picked up the residents' fear at the thought that the state capital might move. Now you are in Wasilla where, for a brief time in the late 1970s, the residents were drooling in anticipation of all that political pork coming north.

Museum of Alaska Transportation & Industry

What was once a Palmer attraction is now part of Wasilla, as the Museum of Alaska Transportation & Industry (☎ 376-1211) moved from the Alaska State Fairgrounds to a location off the Richardson Hwy in 1992. Turn off at *Mile 47* and follow the signs for less than a mile to see such transportation relics as a C-123 plane, tractors of the first Mat-Su farmers, and the first diesel locomotive used in Alaska. There is also a picnic area and a mini-steam railroad for kids. The museum is open from 9 am to 6 pm daily and admission is $5 per adult or $12 for a family.

Sled Dogs & the Iditarod

Wasilla serves as the second starting point for the famous 1049-mile Iditarod race to Nome, while Knik, the home for many Alaskan mushers, is checkpoint No 4 on the route. For more on this uniquely Alaskan race, stop in at the **Iditarod Headquarters** (☎ 376-5155) at *Mile 2.2* of Knik Hwy. The log cabin museum is open daily during the summer from 8 am to 5 pm and has one room that is laden with historical displays, photos of past champions and racks of race para-

phernalia – jackets, hats and shirts for sale. The most unusual exhibit is Togo, the famous sled dog that lead his team across trackless Norton Sound on the last leg in delivering the serum to diptheria-threatened Nome in 1925, which gave raise to today's Iditarod. He's been stuffed and is now on display.

In another room, an excellent video on sled dogs and the race itself is shown. But almost as impressive is the checkpoint-by-checkpoint leader board of the last race that is posted on the wall, telling you who made it and whose team couldn't endure the challenge of 1049 miles. This is a small but interesting museum and, best of all, it's free.

If you want more information on dog mushing and racing, continue south along Knik Hwy to *Mile 13.7* and the **Knik Museum & Sled Dog Musher's Hall of Fame**. The museum, a pool hall at one time, is on the original townsite of Knik, which at the turn of the century had a population of more than 500 while Anchorage was nowhere to be found. Inside you'll find displays on the Iditarod Trail, early Alaskan mushers and, of course, the Canine Hall of Fame. Outside you can easily walk a portion of the historic Iditarod Trail which passes the museum. It is open from noon to 6 pm Wednesday to Sunday and admission is $2.

Places to Stay

Still want more on mushing? Can't get that Iditarod blood out of your system? Then book a room at *Yukon Don's Bed & Breakfast* (☎ 376-7472 or (800) 478-7472), 1.5 miles down Fairview Loop Rd and posted along George Parks Hwy. Within this converted barn are five guest rooms, including the Iditarod Room filled with memorabilia of the famous race including a dog sled above your bed. Nightly rates range from $65 to $105. B&Bs overlooking lakes include *Blodgett Lake B&B* (☎ 892-6877) at *Mile 50* of George Parks Hwy and *Lakeshore B&B* (☎ 376-1380), two miles from Wasilla on Lake Lucille. Both have canoes and paddleboats as well as a double room for $65.

INTERIOR

The most convenient place to stay is the *Windbreak Hotel* (☎ 376-4484), a mile south of town on George Parks Hwy. The hotel has singles/doubles for $55/$65 and a good cafe that isn't part of a national chain, a rarity in Wasilla. Also check the *Mat-Su Resort* (☎ 376-3228) on the shores of Wasilla Lake. The resort has rooms and cabins, some with kitchenettes if you plan to stay for a while, along with a restaurant, lounge and an assortment of rowboats and paddleboats for rent on the lake. Cabins are $85 a night.

The nearest place to camp is *Lake Lucille Park*, a Matanuska-Susitna Borough park near the Iditarod Headquarters on Knik Hwy. The park has a campground (46 sites) along with rest rooms, a shelter and a network of trails. There is also access to the lake which is stocked annually with silver salmon and rainbow trout.

Places to Eat

The variety of fast-food restaurants found in Wasilla is mind boggling, and most survive on the highway trade. In this town of under 4000 residents, you'll find a *Pizza Hut*, *McDonald's*, *Burger King* and *Taco Bell*. The only one missing from this group is the Colonel.

Head further north on the highway for restaurants that don't have a clown or play area for the kids. One of the best in town is *JD's Bar-B-Que Pit* on George Parks Hwy across from the Cotton Creek Mall. The ribs and catfish are spicy and the portions large. Equally big portions are at *Windbreak Cafe & Hotel* on the George Parks Hwy as you enter town. There are 20 types of hamburgers on the menu and 15 chicken sandwiches, all of which you can enjoy while admiring the impressive display of trophy fish mounted on the walls. Sandwiches are around $8, while dinners are from $9 to $15.

The *Kashim Inn* is a little run-down but is open 24 hours for typical road food. Nearby, *Chepo's* has decent Mexican dinners for $7 to $9 and lunch specials for $5.25. Just past *Mile 49* of the George Parks Hwy north of Wasilla is *Classic Cafe*, with good food and lots of 1950s memorabilia, including a yellow 1957 Chevy outside. At the Old Wasilla Town Site behind the Dorothy Page Museum is a farmer's market held every Wednesday from 4 to 7 pm for some of those oversized Mat-Su veggies.

BIG LAKE

From Wasilla, the George Parks Hwy continues in a westerly direction for the next 10 miles and then curves north, reaching Willow at *Mile 69*. Before entering the small village, you pass two side roads to the west that lead to state recreation areas offering lakeside campgrounds and canoe trails.

At *Mile 52.3*, where the George Parks Hwy curves north, is the junction with Big Lake Rd. Head 3.3 miles down the road and turn right at the gasoline station; in half a mile you will reach the *Rocky Lake State Campground* (10 sites, $10 fee). A few hundred yards further along Big Lake Rd is a fork known as 'Fisher's Y' where the town of Big Lake (pop 2300) has sprung up. The right fork leads 1.6 miles to the *Big Lake North State Campground* (150 sites, $10 fee), the left fork 1.7 miles to the *Big Lake South State Campground* (13 sites, $10 fee). Keep in mind that in the summer of 1996 the Big Lake area was engulfed by wildfire that burnt almost 40,000 acres and more than 300 homes, resorts and other buildings. At one point it even jumped across the George Parks Hwy near *Mile 59*, closing the highway briefly and backing up traffic for miles. Although businesses will rebuild quickly, the scars from this fire will be seen for years to come.

NANCY LAKE STATE RECREATION AREA

The George Parks Hwy continues north-west from Big Lake Rd, passes the village of Houston (pop 900) and *Little Susitna River City Campground* (86 sites, $6 fee), and reaches the junction with Nancy Lake Parkway at *Mile 67.2*. The parkway leads to the northern portion of the Nancy Lake State Recreation Area, one of Alaska's few flat, lake-studded parks that offers camping, fishing, canoeing and hiking.

Although it lacks the dramatic scenery of the country to the north, the 22,685-acre state park with its 130 lakes is still a scenic spot and one worth stopping at for a couple of days if you have the time. Within a mile or so on the parkway you come to the State Recreation Area office (☎ 495-6273). It's unmarked from the road so most people just pass it by but it is the place to stop for information or to reserve a cabin. Nancy Lake Parkway extends 6.6 miles to the west and ends at the South Rolly Lake Campground.

Hiking
Chicken Lake Trail For those without a canoe, you can still reach the backcountry by one of two trails. The Chicken Lake Trail is one of these and begins at *Mile 5.7* of the parkway and extends three miles south to the lake and another 2.5 miles to the east shore of Red Shirt Lake. A round-trip hike on the trail is an 11-mile overnight trek but count on wet conditions from time to time.

Twin Shirt Lakes Trail is the other trail into the backcountry and begins near the campground at the end of the parkway. This trail is more popular, and drier, than the Chicken Lake Trail. Built in 1986, the trail leads 3.5 miles south primarily on high ground and ends at the north end of Red Shirt Lake. Along the way you pass Red Shirt Overlook with its scenic views of the surrounding lake country and the Chugach Mountains on the horizon. You end at a group of backcountry camp sites with a vault toilet, situated along the lake.

Short Hikes There are also two short hikes in the park to stretch your legs. At *Mile 2.5* of the parkway is Tulik Trail, a one-mile, self-guided nature trail that takes you past ponds and bogs via boardwalks and viewing platforms. Near South Rolly Lake Campground there is also a half-mile trail to North Rolly Lake.

Paddling
Lynx Lake Loop This is the most popular canoe trail which is a two-day, 16-mile trip that passes through 14 lakes and over an equal number of portages. The trail begins and ends at the posted trailhead for the Tanaina Lake Canoe Trailhead at *Mile 4.5* of the parkway. The portages are well marked and many of them are planked where they cross wet sections. The route includes 12 backcountry camp sites, accessible only by canoe, but bring a camp stove because campfires are prohibited in the backcountry.

The largest lake on the route is Lynx Lake and you can extend your trip by paddling south on it where a portage leads off to six other lakes and two more primitive camp sites on Skeetna Lake. You can rent canoes at Tippecanoe Rentals (☎ 495-6688) which has an office on the George Parks Hwy just south of the parkway and a rental shed in South Rolly Lake Campground. Rates begin at $6 an hour or $41 for two days, $51 for three and $61 for four to seven days. The company will also provide free drop-off and pick-up transport within a 15-mile radius of Willow.

Places to Stay
Cabins The state recreation area has 12 cabins scattered along the shorelines of four lakes. They can be rented for up to three nights and most hold six people and cost $35 a night. Four of the cabins are on Nancy Lake, and three of these can be reached after a short hike in from the Nancy Lake Parkway. Four more cabins are on Red Shirt Lake which require a three-mile hike in and then a short canoe paddle. This is possible because Tippecanoe keeps some canoes stashed on the lake and rents them to cabin users. The other four cabins are on the Lynx Lake Canoe Route with three on Lynx Lake and one on James Lake.

The cabins have plywood sleeping platforms, a wood stove and screens on the windows. As you can imagine, they are very popular. Try to reserve them ahead of time through the Alaska Public Lands Information Center (☎ 271-2737) in Anchorage, or Division of Parks & Outdoor Recreation office (☎ 745-3975) in Finger Lakes.

INTERIOR

Camping The *South Rolly Lake Campground* (106 sites, $8 fee) is a rustic campground which has secluded sites and is so large that the chances are good that there will be an open site, even on the weekend. Within the campground is a canoe-rental shed if you're interested in an easy paddle on the small lake.

The only other vehicle campground in the park is *Nancy Lake Campground* (30 sites, $8 fee) just off the George Parks Hwy and just south of the entrance to the parkway. This is not nearly as nice as setting up your tent at South Rolly Lake.

Getting There & Away

The state recreation area can be reached from the Alaska Railroad by taking the local train from Anchorage to Willow and then hitch-hiking or walking 1.8 miles south on George Parks Hwy to the junction of the Nancy Lake Parkway. Various Denali van services (see the Anchorage chapter) will also drop you off on their way to the national park.

WILLOW

Willow (pop 500) at *Mile 69* of the George Parks Hwy is a sleepy little village that became famous in the 1970s as the place selected for the new Alaskan capital that was to be moved from Juneau. The capital-move controversy was put on the back burner in 1982, however, when funding for the immense project was defeated in a general state election.

To many travelers heading north, Willow is often their first overwhelming view of Mt McKinley. If the day is clear 'the Great One' dominates the Willow skyline. Actually just about anything would dominate the skyline of this sparse little village.

More Sled Dogs

Willow, like many towns along this stretch, owes it existence to gold and the Alaska Railroad that came through in the early 1920s to serve the Hatcher Pass mines. Today the town calls itself 'Dog Mushing Capital of the World', though Wasilla, Tok and a few other communities would surely

dispute that. The area does, however, have its share of mushers and, in the 1993 Iditarod, 13 teams from the Willow area competed and 10 finished the 1049-mile event. Five teams even finished in the top 20 to bring home a slice of the purse.

Several of the kennels offer informal tours. The Susitna Dog Tours B&B (☎ 495-6324) doubles as a place of lodging with a bunkhouse and cabin accommodation and the dog kennel of Bill Davidson and Rhodi Karella, both Iditarod finishers. Karella was a grandmother when she ran and finished the 1987 race. There's also Bomhoff's Alaskan Sled Dog Kennel (☎ 495-6470) at *Mile 80* which also has a gift shop and an Iditarod Checkpoint Display. You can tour the kennels here or for $12.50 take a short ride in a basket sled on wheels pulled by one of the teams. But be forewarned: Alaskan huskies are so friendly you might end up bringing one home.

Places to Stay & Eat

Any possible service you need is available at the *Willow Trading Post Lodge* (☎ 495-6457), just off the Parks Hwy across from the train platform. This is a classic Alaskan roadhouse, originally built for the Lucky Shot Mine and moved to Willow in 1945. You can get a shower, a sauna, a shot of whiskey and a beer to chase it down. The food is basic but plentiful in the restaurant with nightly specials ($12 to $14) which include everything from coffee to dessert. Cabins without baths are $45 for two, and rooms with baths are also available. There is a liquor store, laundry facilities and just about everything you need to recuperate from a week in the wilderness.

Two miles north of Willow is the junction to Fishhook-Willow Rd that leads 31.6 miles to the Independence Mine State Park, via Hatcher Pass, and eventually to Glenn Hwy. By driving just 1.3 miles up this road you reach the *Deception Creek State Campground* (17 sites, $10 fee).

To spend a night in a rustic cabin or for a great piece of home-made pie, stop at the *Sheep Creek Lodge* (☎ 495-6227) at *Mile 88* of the George Parks Hwy. The lodge has four log cabins, without any plumbing whatsoever, that are $30 a night for two people. Inside the main lodge is a restaurant, a lunch counter and a bar.

TALKEETNA

At *Mile 98.7* of George Parks Hwy, a side road heads off to the north 14.5 miles to Talkeetna (pop 600), the most interesting and colorful town along the highway. Located near the confluence of the Susitna, Talkeetna and Chulitna rivers, Talkeetna is a Tanaina Native word meaning 'river of plenty'.

History

Gold bought miners to the Susitna River in 1896 and by 1901 Talkeetna was a miner's supply center and eventually a riverboat station. But its real growth came in 1915 when Talkeetna was chosen as the headquarters of the Alaska Engineering Commission responsible for building the railroad north to the Tanana River at Nenana. When the railroad was finished in 1923, President Warren G Harding arrived in Alaska and rode the rails to the Nenana River, where he hammered in the golden spike. In Talkeetna, they swear (with a grin on their face) that he

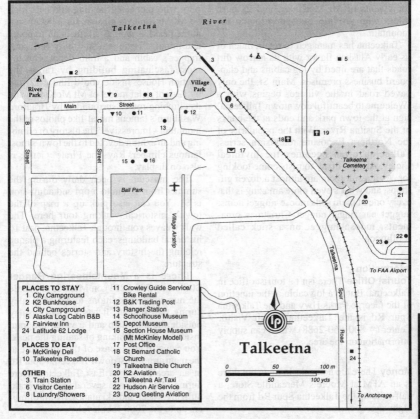

Talkeetna

```
PLACES TO STAY
1   City Campground
2   K2 Bunkhouse
4   City Campground
5   Alaska Log Cabin B&B
    Fairview Inn
24  Latitude 62 Lodge

PLACES TO EAT
9   McKinley Deli
10  Talkeetna Roadhouse

OTHER
3   Train Station
6   Visitor Center
8   Laundry/Showers

11  Crowley Guide Service/
    Bike Rental
12  B&K Trading Post
13  Ranger Station
14  Schoolhouse Museum
15  Depot Museum
16  Section House Museum
    (Mt McKinley Model)
17  Post Office
18  St Bernard Catholic
    Church
19  Talkeetna Bible Church
20  K2 Aviation
21  Talkeetna Air Taxi
22  Hudson Air Service
23  Doug Geeting Aviation
```

0   50   100 m
0   50   100 yds

To FAA Airport

To Anchorage

INTERIOR

stopped here on the way home, had numerous drinks in the local hotel and wound up dying in San Francisco less than a week later. For a long time residents of this off-beat little town boasted that 'President Harding had been poisoned at the Fairview Inn'.

Talkeetna's population peaked at 1000 residents before the mining slowed and WWI dramatically decreased its size. In 1964, new life flowed into Talkeetna when a 14-mile spur road connected the town to the George Parks Hwy, drawing the interest of anglers, hunters and others with the recreational opportunities of the area. But the people most interested in Talkeetna were climbers, who used the town as a staging area for ascents of Mt McKinley, and its bush pilots who provide transportation to the mountain.

Talkeetna has managed to retain much of its early Alaskan flavor with its narrow dirt roads that are lined by log cabins and clapboard business premises. Main St, the only paved road in the village, begins with a 'Welcome to beautiful downtown Talkeetna' sign at the town park and ends at the banks of the Susitna River. With the popularity of the Northern Exposure television series, Talkeetna often becomes the mythical Cicley, Alaska, many tourists come looking for. As a result there are almost a dozen gift shops, and what's even more amazing is that every one of them sells moose-nugget items: nugget ear rings, nugget Christmas ornaments, moose nugget on a stick called 'Lollipoop'.

Information

Tourist Office There isn't a tourist office in Talkeetna. But in a log cabin at the junction of the George Parks Hwy and the Talkeetna Spur Rd is the Talkeetna-Denali Visitor Center (☎ 800-660-2688) which can supply information on the area.

Money There are no banks in town but there is an ATM at Moore's Mercantile Store, a half-mile up the Talkeetna Spur Rd from the highway.

Post The post office is just off Talkeetna Spur Rd as you enter town.

Laundry There is a laundromat and public showers in the Talkeetna Tesoro on Main St.

Medical Services Sunshine Health Clinic (☎ 733-2273) is at *Mile 4.5* of the Talkeetna Spur Rd.

Things to See

A block south of Main St is the **Talkeetna Historical Society Museum** (☎ 733-2487), a small complex that consists of four restored buildings. In the town's 1936 schoolhouse is an exhibit devoted to Don Sheldon (the bush pilot who pioneered landing climbers high on Mt McKinley's glaciers for a better shot at the peak) as well as artefacts on trapping and mining. There is also a fully furnished trapper's cabin and a train depot. But the most fascinating building by far is the Section House. Inside you'll find a 12-foot by 12-foot relief model of Mt McKinley and its climbing routes surrounded by Bradford Washburn's famous mural-like photos of the mountain – impressive. The history of climbing and an exhibit devoted to the town's most famous climber, Ray 'the Pirate' Genet, is also on display.

The museum is open daily during the summer from 10 am to 5 pm and admission is $1. You can also pick up a map of the town's historical walking tour here. The walk weaves you through Talkeetna, past 16 historical buildings, each featuring a plaque relating the history and stories behind the structure.

There is a **Mountaineering Ranger Station** (☎ 733-2231) on Main St to handle the numerous expeditions to Mt McKinley during the summer. It has a small display outside the mountain and a video program inside for those thinking of scaling the peak. You can also get a sense of the adventure at the main airport just down Talkeetna Spur Rd in an area posted as East Talkeetna. Here during May and June several small aircraft, utilizing wheel-and-ski planes, fly the climbers up to the 7000-foot level.

INTERIOR

Scaling the Mountain

More than any other place in Alaska, much more than the entrance area of Denali National Park itself, Talkeetna is associated with climbing the highest peak in North America, Mt McKinley.

The first attempt to scale the mountain was undertaken by James Wickersham, the US District Judge in Alaska. After moving his court from Eagle to Fairbanks in 1903, the judge took a couple of months off that summer and trekked overland more than 100 miles to reach the 7500-foot mark of the 20,320-foot peak. Though his party was unsuccessful in its bid to be the first on top, it created a summit fever that would rage on for more than a decade until the peak was finally conquered.

In 1906, Dr Frederick Cook returned for his second attempt at the peak and this time attacked it from the south. His party disbanded after a month of slogging through the heavy brush and tussock but then in September, Cook and a companion sent a telegram to New York claiming that they had reached the peak and even sent along a photo showing the good doctor holding a flag at the top. The climbing world immediately disputed the claim and four years later Belmore Brown located the false peak and duplicated Cook's photo. Not only was the 8000-foot peak a lot shorter than Mt McKinley, it was more than 20 miles from the true summit. Despite all the evidence, the controversy over Cook continued right into the 1970s when his daughter wrote to Ray Genet for his opinion on the 1906 feat and photo. Both the letter and Genet's reply are now on display at the Talkeetna Museum.

The next serious attempt came in 1910 when four Fairbanks miners decided Alaskans should be the first to conquer the peak, not outsiders. Dubbed the Sourdough Expedition, they headed straight for the peak visible from Fairbanks. Remarkably they climbed the final 11,000 feet and returned to their base camp in 18 hours. Even more remarkably, they carried only a thermos of hot chocolate, a bag of donuts and a 14-foot spruce pole. Imagine then their shock when they reached the top of the North Peak only to realize that it was 850 feet lower than the South Peak and thus not the true summit.

Success finally came in 1913 when an expedition of Hudson Stuck, Henry Karstens, Robert Tatum and Walter Harper reached the top on 7 June. The foursome would have made it in May but they spent three weeks hewing a three-mile staircase through a mass of jumbled ice caused by the 1912 eruption and earthquake of Katmai 300 miles away. When they reached the top they saw the spruce pole on the North Peak to verify the claims of the Sourdough Expedition.

The most important date to many climbers, however, is 1951. That year Bradford Washburn, the director of the Boston Museum of Science, arrived and pioneered the West Buttress route, by far the preferred avenue to the top. Not long after Talkeetna's two most famous characters – Ray 'the Pirate' Genet and Don Sheldon – began to have an impact on the climbing world. Genet was an Alaskan mountain climber who made a record 25 climbs to the summit of Mt McKinley, including as part of the first successful winter ascent. Sheldon was a bush pilot who pioneered many of the routes used today to carry climbers to Mt McKinley.

The two men worked closely together in guiding climbers to the top and, more importantly, rescuing them when they failed. Their rescue attempts are legendary and a sample of these stories can be read in the Talkeetna Museum. Sadly, the town unexpectedly lost both men within four years. Sheldon, the most famous of all Alaskan bush pilots, died in 1975 at the age of 56 years due to cancer. Genet died at the age of 48 in Nepal. After reaching Mt Everest, the highest peak in the world, Genet froze to death in his sleeping bag on the descent and is still entombed on the side of that mountain today.

The Great One (as the Athabascan people called Mt McKinley) and the colorful legends of both these men add considerably to the mountaineering atmosphere that is felt, seen and heard in Talkeetna during the summer, especially during the climbing season of May and June. More than 80% of the climbers use the West Buttress route, which means flying in ski planes from the town's airstrip to a base camp on the Kahiltna Glacier. From here, at 7200 feet, they begin climbing for the South Peak, passing a medical/rescue camp maintained by mountaineering clubs and the National Park Service at 14,220 feet.

Roughly 1000 climbers attempt the peak each year, spending an average of three weeks on the mountain. Expeditions carry roughly 120 pounds of food and gear per person for the ascent. Ironically, due to the multiple trips required to shuttle gear to higher camps, successful climbers actually climb the mountain twice.

In a good season, when storms are not constantly sweeping across the range, 50% of those attempting the summit will be successful. (In 1995 a 12-year-old Anchorage girl became the youngest person to scale the mountain.) In a bad year, several people will die – in 1992 the mountain claimed the lives of 11 climbers. ■

Perhaps the most solemn way to appreciate the effect of the mountain on this town, and understand how the residents grieve when climbers are lost, is to visit the **Talkeetna Cemetery**, just off the Spur Rd across from the airport. The most impressive grave is Sheldon's with the mounted ice axe and his epitaph of 'He wagered with the wind and won'. There is also a Mt McKinley Climber's Memorial, including a stone for Genet despite the fact that his body was never removed from the slopes of Mt Everest. The most touching sight, however, is a simple bulletin board that lists the names and ages of all the climbers who have died on Mt McKinley over the years. Some were as young as 18.

The town also has two privately owned museums, attached to giftshops. **Museum of the Northern Adventure** (☎ 733-3999), right on Main St, consists of 24 large dioramas of historical events on two floors. It's open daily from 10 am to 6 pm but admission is $2.50 – a little steep for what you see. The other gift shop museum is at **B&K Trading Post**, Talkeetna's historical general store.

Even more interesting is the **Fairview Inn**, not an official museum but might as well be. The hotel was built in 1923 to serve as the overnight stop from Seward to Fairbanks on the newly constructed Alaska Railroad. Unfortunately, Anchorage, not Seward, was chosen as the start of the northerly trip so Curry, not Talkeetna, was the halfway point and overnight stop. Still the hotel survived and today is listed on the National Register of Historical Sites.

And it should be. The bar on the 1st floor is classic Alaska while the walls are filled with memorabilia. There's Deadman's Wall, covered with pictures of those who have fallen victim to the mountain, Talkeetna's only slot machine, a corner devoted to President Harding and the ad in which Ray Genet is promoting 'Hot Tang'. Most interesting, perhaps, is a photo labeled 'The Women of Talkeetna' that was taken in the Fairview Inn and appeared in a 1985 issue of Playboy magazine. The story behind it is hilarious. The only way to enjoy the inn is to belly up to the bar, order a schooner of beer and take in the décor.

Scenic Flights

With Mt McKinley in their backyard, scenic flights have become a staple for the handful of air-service companies in Talkeetna. At any time of the summer they will do scenic flights of the mountain and the Alaska Range and on a clear day it's the best bargain in this expensive state. At times, it is even possible to see climbing parties en route to the summit.

Check around with the handful of charter companies, but plan on spending from $75 to $150 for a flight, depending on whether you want to land on a glacier. And if it's a clear day, plan on waiting in line for a flight. Offering such trips are K2 Aviation (☎ 733-2291), Hudson Air Service (☎ 733-2333) and Doug Geeting Aviation (☎ 733-2366).

Cycling & Canoeing

Crowley Guide Service (☎ 733-1279) on Main St has mountain bikes for rent for $10 a half day or $18 a day. One possibility is to rent one for several days and then hop on the train to Denali National Park and explore the park road by pedaling.

Talkeetna Camp & Canoe (☎ 733-CAMP) rent canoes for $38 a day and will arrange drop-off and pick-up service.

Special Events

Talkeetna's love of moose scat can be traced back to 1974 when the town first began holding its annual Moose Dropping Festival on the second weekend of July. The three-day event has the usual: a parade, live entertainment and a beer tent they call a 'Tee Pee'. And then there are bizarre things you will only find in Talkeetna: a Moose Dropping Toss Game (or 'how far can you throw a moose turd?'), an opportunity to kiss a moose, and the Mountain Mother Contest in which single women compete in various skills: wood chopping, water hauling, fire building etc in front of a panel of eligible bachelors. The festival is a good time and

Talkeetna's annual Moose Dropping Festival attracts over 5000 people.

every effort should be made to attend it if you are in the area. But beware – more than 5000 people now pack Talkeetna during the event.

The town's other noted event is the Talkeetna Blue Grass Festival, which began in 1982. The four-day event is held in early August and is so large it has been moved to 142 acres of forested land at *Mile 102* of the George Parks Hwy. Admission is $25 whether you stay one day or all four.

Places to Stay

There are numerous hotels, motels, roadhouses and B&Bs in Talkeetna along with a public campground. The *City Campground* is split with sites at the end of Main St and others with a boat launch and a shelter across the tracks from the train shelter. The fee is $5 a night.

A block off Main St near the river is the *K2 Bunkhouse* (☎ 733-2291). The hostel-style bunkhouse is primarily for climbers but others are welcome to stay if there is room. Inside there are showers and a large kitchen

downstairs and 18 bunks upstairs. The rate is $15.75 a night.

There is also the *Fairview Inn* (☎ 733-2423), on Main St, where singles/doubles are $41/52 per night. There are seven rooms and a shared bath but remember that on the weekends the band in the bar just below you plays until 2.30 am. The *Talkeetna Roadhouse* (☎ 733-1351) is just up Main St with equally small rooms and shared bath for $47/63 a single/double and a bunkroom with single beds for $21. Of the handful of motels in town, try the *Latitude 62 Lodge* (☎ 733-2262) on the Talkeetna Spur Rd where singles/doubles with private bath are $57/68.

Talkeetna Camp & Canoe (☎ 733-CAMP), operates a small camp just outside Talkeetna and offers tent cabins, complete with cookstove, lights and a table, for $70 a night for two people or $65 a night for four.

How about renting a log cabin? Hey, why not, this is Alaska. Call *Alaska Log Cabin B&B* (☎ 733-2584), a private cabin two blocks from the Talkeetna River, or *Trapper John's B&B* (☎ 733-2354), a 1920s cabin and outhouse at the south end of the Village Airstrip where a double is $60.

Want a cabin that's more remote? *K2 Aviation* has three fly-in rental cabins on lakes in the Talkeetna Mountains. The closest at Katie Lake sleeps four and is 15 air miles north-east of Talkeetna. The round-trip airfare is $300 for the entire plane while the cabin costs $85 a night. If split among four people, which is what a Cessna 206 holds, a three-day/two-night wilderness escape into the mountains is less than $120 per person.

Places to Eat

The best place for a hearty meal is the *Talkeetna Roadhouse* on Main St, where the Red House special (eggs, toast, potatoes and sausage, fresh fruit, and so on and so on) is served in the morning for climbers and other hungry people for $8. Only one main course is available at dinner ($8 to $14) so ask before sitting down.

Across the street is *McKinley Deli & Espresso Bar*, open to 11 pm daily during the summer. Sandwiches and subs are priced

INTERIOR

from around $7, while a small pizza is $12. The cinnamon rolls are more than enough to keep you going in the morning.

Getting There & Away

The express train of the Alaska Railroad stops daily in Talkeetna from late May to mid-September on both its northbound and southbound runs between Anchorage and Fairbanks. The northbound train from Anchorage, heading for Denali National Park, arrives at 11.20 am; the southbound train arrives at 4.30 pm and reaches Anchorage that night at 8.30 pm. The one-way fare from Anchorage is $45. On Thursday, Saturday and Sunday during the summer, the local train passes through Talkeetna before it turns around at Hurricane Gulch.

DENALI STATE PARK

This 324,420-acre reserve, the second largest state park in Alaska and roughly half the size of Rhode Island, is entered when you cross the southern boundary at *Mile 132.2* of the George Parks Hwy. The park covers the transition zone from low coastal environment to the spine of the Alaska Range and provides numerous views of towering peaks, including Mt McKinley and the glaciers on its southern slopes. The park is largely undeveloped but does offer a handful of turn-offs, trails and one campground that can be reached from the George Parks Hwy which runs through the park.

It may share the same name and a border with the renowned national park to the north, but Denali State Park is an entirely different experience. Because of its lack of facilities, you need to be more prepared when you arrive for hiking and backpacking adventures. There are no rangers here describing routes nor an information center selling maps and guidebooks. But this may be the park's blessing for this preserve also lacks the crowds, long waits and tight regulations that irk many backpackers to the north in Denali National Park. At the height of the summer season, experienced backpackers may want to consider the state park as a

hassle-free and cheaper alternative to the national park.

South Denali Viewpoint

Less than three miles from the southern boundary of the park at *Mile 135.2* of George Parks Hwy is this viewpoint, where the Ruth Glacier is less than five miles to the northwest. Displays at the paved lookout also point out Mt McKinley, Mt Hunter, Moose Tooth and several other glaciers.

Hiking

There are several trails and alpine routes in the park and interested hikers should contact the Department of National Resources Public Information Center in Anchorage (☎ 269-8400) about possible closures (due to bears) and location of trails. Keep in mind that no fires are allowed in the backcountry so you must pack a stove.

Troublesome Creek Trail The trailhead is posted and in a parking area at *Mile 137.6* of the George Parks Hwy. The trail ascends along the creek until it reaches the tree line where you move into an open area dotted with alpine lakes and surrounded by mountain views. From here it becomes a route marked only by rock cairns as it heads north to Byers Lake.

Byers Lake Campground is a 15-mile backpacking trip of moderate difficulty or, if you are more adventurous, you can continue on to the Little Coal Creek Trail, a 36-mile trek above the tree line. The views from the ridges are spectacular. Keep in mind that the numerous black bears feeding on salmon is the reason for the creek's name and that often in July and August the trail is closed to hikers.

Byers Lake Trail This is an easy five-mile trek around the lake. It begins at the Byers Lake State Campground and passes six hike-in camp sites on the other side of the lake that are 1.8 miles from the posted trailhead.

Kesugi Ridge Trail This is actually a route that departs from the Byers Lake Trail and ascends its namesake ridge and then follows it to Little Coal Creek Trail at the north end of the park. The route is well marked with cairns and flags to provide a 27.4-mile route to George Parks Hwy via Little Coal Creek Trail.

Little Coal Creek Trail At *Mile 163.9* of the George Parks Hwy there is the trailhead and parking area for the Little Coal Creek Trail, which ascends to the alpine areas of Kesugi Ridge. From there, you continue to the summit of Indian Mountain, an elevation gain of about 3300 feet, or continue along the ridge to either Byers Lake or Troublesome Creek. Little Coal Creek is the easiest climb into the alpine area as you emerge above the tree line in three miles. It's a nine-mile round-trip trek to Indian Peak and 27.4 miles to Byers Lake.

Places to Stay
Lower Troublesome Creek State Recreation Site (10 sites, $6 fee) at *Mile 137.3* and *Byers Lake State Campground* (66 sites, $10 fee) at *Mile 147* of George Parks Hwy provide tables, outhouses and are close to nearby trails. Byers Lake Campground also has access to Byers Lake.

At *Mile 156* of Parks Hwy is *Chulitna River Lodge* (☎ 733-2521), the only facility within the state park. The lodge has a small cafe, gas and log cabins for $50 to $80 a night. It's also near the Ermine Hill Trailhead, an emergency trail that accesses the Kesugi Trail in the state park.

BROAD PASS TO DENALI NATIONAL PARK
The northern boundary of the Denali State Park is at *Mile 168.5* of George Parks Hwy, and nine miles beyond that is the bridge over Honolulu Creek where the road begins a gradual ascent to **Broad Pass**. Within 18 miles of the creek you begin viewing the pass and actually reach it at *Mile 203.6*, where there is a paved parking area.

Broad Pass (elevation 2300 feet) is the point of divide where rivers to the south drain into Cook Inlet and those to the north empty

into the Yukon River. The area is worth stopping in for some hiking. The mountain valley, surrounded by white peaks, is unquestionably one of the most beautiful spots along the George Parks Hwy or the Alaska Railroad, as both use the low gap to cross the Alaska Range.

From the pass, the George Parks Hwy begins a descent and after 6.3 miles comes to the Cantwell post office just before *Mile 210* at the junction with Denali Hwy. The rest of **Cantwell** (pop 100) lies two miles west on the Denali Hwy. Another scenic spot is reached at *Mile 234* on the east side of the highway, where there are fine views of **Mt Fellows**, which has an elevation 4476 feet. The mountain is well photographed because of the constantly changing shadows on its sides. The peak is especially beautiful at sunset.

The entrance to Denali National Park & Preserve is at *Mile 237.3* of George Parks Hwy and just inside the park are two campgrounds. The next public campground is in Fairbanks. The highway before and after the park entrance has become a tourist strip of private campgrounds, lodges, restaurants and other businesses, all feeding off Alaska's most famous drawcard.

Denali National Park

Call it the Dilemma in Denali: 'We love the wilderness and wildlife so much we're overrunning what is unquestionably Alaska's best known attraction'. In 1995, with the park attracting close to a million visitors a year, the National Park Service instituted the most sweeping change in the history of its management of the wilderness by allowing a concessionaire to implement fees for the shuttle buses and a reservation system for both a seat on the bus and sites in the campgrounds.

These and Denali's carefully imposed barriers such as backcountry zones should help reduce, but never eliminate, the long lines at the visitors center, the crowds at the entrance

Denali National Park

Brooker Mountain (1150 m/3774 ft)

Kantishna Wilderness Lodge

Busia Mountain (989 m/3246 ft)

Ranger Station

Wonder Lake Campground

McKinley River

Park Road

Polychrome Mountain (1764 m/5789 ft)

Polychrome Pass

Toklat River

East Fork Toklat River

Toklat Ranger Station

Divide Mountain (1583 m/5195 ft)

Highway Pass

Stony Hill

Thorofare Pass

Mile 65

Stony Dome (1432 m/4697 ft)

Eielson Visitor Center

Mt Eielson Loop

Mount Eielson (1768 m/5802 ft)

Muldrow Glacier

Bald Mountain (1586 m/5285 ft)

Pass Summit (1432 m/4700 ft)

Sunset Glacier

Castle Rock (1798 m/5900 ft)

area and the bizarre atmosphere of people hustling and pushing just for an opportunity to get away from it all in the wilderness. Backcountry bus fees now range as high as $30 while 40% of the seats and the sites are reserved.

If you can plan your trip in advance or have the patience to wait for permits and bus seats on a first-come-first-served basis, Denali National Park is still the great wilderness that awed so many of us 10 or 20 years ago. The entrance has changed, but the park itself hasn't, and a brown bear meandering on a tundra ridge still provides the same quiet thrill as it did when the Denali first opened in 1917.

History

Although generations of Athabascans had wandered through the area that the national park now encompasses, they never set up permanent settlements. This changed in 1905 when gold was discovered and a

miners' rush resulted in the town of Kantishna. A year later, naturalist and noted hunter Charles Sheldon was stunned by the beauty of the land and horrified at the reckless abandon of the miners and others in hunting the caribou and other big game. Sheldon returned in 1907 and with guide Harry Karstens traveled the area in an effort to set up boundaries for a proposed national park.

Sheldon then launched a campaign for a Denali National Park, but politics being politics and Ohio having a particularly strong delegation of senators, it emerged as Mt McKinley National Park. Karstens became the park's first superintendent and in 1923, when the railroad arrived, 36 visitors enjoyed the splendor of Denali.

As a result of the 1980 Alaska Lands Bill, the park was enlarged by four million acres, redesignated and renamed. Denali now comprises six million acres or an area slightly larger than the state of Massachusetts, and is

INTERIOR

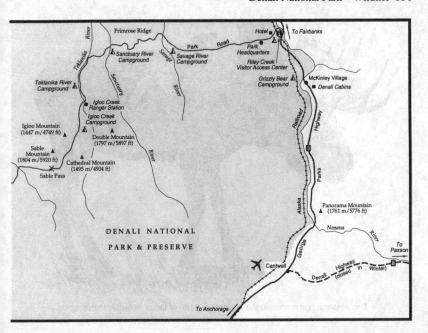

generally ranked as Alaska's second-most-visited attraction after Portage Glacier.

Wildlife

Situated on the north and south flanks of the Alaska Range, 237 miles from Anchorage and about half that distance from Fairbanks, Denali is the nation's first subarctic national park and a wilderness that can be enjoyed by those who never sleep in a tent. Within it roam 37 species of mammals, ranging from lynx, marmots and dall sheep to foxes and snowshoe hares, while 130 different bird species have been spotted, including the impressive golden eagle. Most visitors, however, want to see four animals in particular: the moose, caribou, wolf and brown bear. If you see all four from the shuttle bus you will have scored a rare 'grand slam', according to the drivers.

There are an estimated 200 to 300 brown bears in the park and another 200 black bears, most of them west of Wonder Lake.

It's everybody's favorite, the brown, or grizzly, bear, that is almost always seen while you're on the shuttle bus. Since Denali's streams are mostly glacially fed, the fishing is poor and consequently the diet of the bears is 85% vegetable materials. This accounts for their small size. Most males range from only 300 to 600 pounds while their cousins on the salmon-rich coasts can easily top 1000 pounds.

All the caribou in the park belong to the Denali herd, one of 13 herds in Alaska, which fluctuates in size between 2500 and 3000 animals. Since the park has been enlarged, the entire range of the herd, from its calving grounds to where it winters, is now in Denali. The best time to spot caribou is often late in the summer when the animals begin to band into groups of six to a dozen in anticipation of the fall migration. The caribou is easy to spot, as the racks of a bull often stand four feet high and look out of proportion with the rest of its body.

The Alaskan bull moose is the largest member of the deer family in the world.

Most visitors will sight their moose on the east half of the park road, especially along the first 15 miles. Moose are almost always found in stands of spruce and willow shrubs (their favorite food) and often you have a better chance of seeing a moose while you're hiking the Horseshoe Lake Trail than you do in the tundra area around Eielson Visitor Center. There are roughly 2000 moose on the north side of the Alaska Range and the most spectacular scene in Denali comes in early September when the bulls begin to clash their immense racks over breeding rights to a cow.

The wolf is the most difficult of the 'grand slam' four to see in the park. There is a stable population of 160 wolves and during much of the summer, when small game is plentiful, the packs often break down and wolves become more solitary hunters. The best bet for most visitors is witnessing a lone wolf crossing the park road.

Because hunting has never been allowed in the park, professional photographers refer to animals in Denali as 'approachable wildlife'. That doesn't mean you can actually approach them, though every year visitors and photographers alike try to in an effort to get that photo-of-a-lifetime. It means bears, moose, dall sheep and caribou are not nearly as skittish as in other regions of the state and tend to continue their natural activities despite 40 heads with camera lenses hanging out of a yellow bus 70 yards away on the park road.

Despite the excellent wildlife-watching opportunities, the park's main attraction is still Mt McKinley – an overwhelming sight if you catch it on a clear day. At 20,316 feet, the peak of this massif is almost four miles high, but what makes it stunning is that it rises from an elevation of 2000 feet. What you see from the park road is 18,000 feet (almost three miles) of rock, snow and glaciers reaching for the sky. In contrast, Mt Everest, the highest mountain in the world at 29,028 feet, only rises 11,000 feet from the Tibetan Plateau.

INTERIOR

Combine the park's easy viewing of wildlife and the grandeur of Mt McKinley with its wilderness reputation throughout the world and suddenly the crowds are easy to understand. From late June to early September, Denali National Park is a busy and popular place. Riley Creek Campground overflows with campervans, nearby Morino Campground is crowded with backpackers, and the park's hotel is bustling with large tour groups. The pursuit of shuttle-bus seats, backcountry permits and campground reservations at the Visitor Access Center often involves long Disney World-type lines.

Although crowds disappear once you are hiking in the backcountry, many people prefer to visit the park in early June or late September to avoid them. Mid-September can be particularly pleasant, for not only are the crowds thinning out but so are the bugs. This is also when the area changes color and valleys go from a dull green to a fiery red, while the willows turn shades of yellow and gold. The problem is that the shuttle buses (your ticket into the backcountry) stop running around 10 September. A four-day vehicle lottery follows when 400 private cars a day are allowed into the park and then the road is closed to all traffic until next May.

By late September, however, the snow has usually arrived for the winter and another backpacking season is over in the park. The crowds do begin to diminish in late August and early September but getting a campground site or backcountry permit can still be an agonizing challenge.

Without advance reservations, you have to include extra days for your trip. If all you want to do is camp at the entrance and take the shuttle bus out along the road one day, a minimum of four days is needed at the park, possibly five if you arrive at the height of the season. If you want to spend two or three days backpacking or staying in the interior campgrounds, you'll need from seven to 10 days.

There's no getting around it. You'll waste one day alone on the outside of the park waiting to get into the Riley Creek area. Another two days can be used up waiting for a campground or backcountry area to become available.

In the end, however, if you are patient and follow the system, you will get into the backcountry and then, thanks to the rules and permit limits you were cussing just a day before, you will enjoy a quality wilderness experience.

Information

Reservations & Fees If you can plan the exact days you will be in the park, booking bus seats and camp sites in advance saves an awful lot of hassle. The system worked so well the first year when reservations claimed a third of the bus seats and sites, that in 1996 the park management allowed advance bookings to claim 40% of what is available. To arrange a reservation call Denali National Park Reservation Service (☎ (800) 622-7275 or 272-7275). Outside the USA, you can't use the toll-free number. Reservations can be made for the buses five days in advance while for the campgrounds there is a one-time $4 reservation fee.

There is also an admission fee, though it should hardly stop anybody from visiting the park. A $3 per person or $5 per family fee is charged to all visitors traveling beyond the checkpoint at Savage River Campground. The fee is good for seven days in the park and is collected when you obtain a shuttle bus ticket at the Riley Creek Visitor Access Center. Keep in mind that this is an entrance fee and you will still have to pay to stay in the park's campgrounds.

Tourist Offices The Visitor Access Center, or VAC for short, near the entrance of the park is the place to organize your trip into the park and pick up permits and coupons as well as purchase topographic maps and books. The center is open daily during the summer from 7 am to 8 pm and lines begin forming outside the door at 6 am. At the height of the summer, there can be more than 100 people in line and it's something of a stampede when the door is opened. This is necessary because only 60% of the shuttle bus seats and camp

Denali National Park - Entrance Area

sites are available, while backcountry permits are only handed out one day in advance. That's why you can't arrive at the park at midday and plan your stay. It's almost imperative you be at the VAC before 7 am to be able to book anything at all.

Within the VAC there is a bookstore; staff counters for backcountry permits, shuttle buses and camp sites; a video theater with shows 10 and 40 minutes after the hour; and rest rooms. There is also an information area on other parks in Alaska in case the Denali hassle is too much for you. Outside there is an information board with all park activities,

a monitor that gives you a basic rundown on park procedures and storage lockers that are big enough to handle a backpack.

Eielson Visitor Center is a smaller center at *Mile 66* of the park road and features displays, a small bookstore and a great observation deck overlooking Mt McKinley. The rangers hold their own hikes and naturalist programs. Eielson is open daily during the summer from 9 am to 7 pm.

Post & Communications You can mail letters or make international phone calls from the Denali Park Hotel.

Medical Services The Healy Clinic (☎ 683-2211) is in the Tri-Valley Community Center, 13 miles north of the park and a half-mile east of George Parks Hwy on Healy Spur Rd.

Shuttle Bus

What makes the park and its wildlife so accessible is the park road that runs the length of the preserve and the shuttle buses that use it. The shuttle-bus service began in 1972 after the George Parks Hwy was opened and attendance in the park doubled in a single season. Park officials put a ban on private vehicles to prevent the park road from becoming a highway of cars and RVers and today the wildlife is so accustomed to the rambling buses that the animals rarely stop their activities when one passes by.

The buses also provide access for day hiking for which backcountry permits are not needed. Once in the backcountry, you can stop a bus heading east on the park road by flagging it down for a ride back. Some photographers ride the bus only until wildlife is spotted. Changing buses several times each day is a practice commonly referred to as 'shuttle bus surfing'. By all means get off the buses as it's the only way you will truly see and experience the park, but remember you can only get back on if there is an available seat. No one is ever left out in the backcountry against their will but it's not too uncommon at the height of the season to have to wait two or three hours because the first four buses that pass you are full.

While riding the buses, passengers armed with binoculars and cameras scour the terrain for wildlife. When something is spotted, the name of the animal is called out, prompting the driver to slow down and most often stop for viewing and picture taking. The driver also doubles as a park guide and naturalist for a more interesting trip.

Many of the old yellow school buses were replaced with much more comfortable tour buses when the fee system was implemented in 1995. Still, if you're planning just to spend the day riding the bus, pack plenty of food and drink. It can be a long, dusty ride and there are no services in the park, not even a vending machine at Eielson Visitor Center. Also carry a park map so you know where you are and what ridges or river beds appeal to you for day hiking later. The best seats to grab are generally at the front of the bus but if you end up in the back, don't be shy about leaning over somebody for a view out a window.

In 1995, 25 buses were added and buses now leave the VAC for Eielson Visitor Center on a regular basis from 6.30 am until 1.30 pm when the last bus departs. There are also several buses that go all the way to Wonder Lake. It's an 11-hour trip to ride out to the end of the road and back, which makes for a long day. The ride to Eielson is an eight-hour journey and passes the most spectacular mountain scenery by far. The only exception to this is when Mt McKinley is visible then the ride to Wonder Lake is 11 of the most scenic hours you'll ever spend on a bus of any kind.

Technically you pay for any travel west on the park road and get a free ride back to the Riley Creek area. The single-trip fare to Toklat is $12, to Eielson $20 and to Wonder Lake $26. There are youth fares, and a three-trip ticket which allows one person to ride the bus for three days. The multiple-trip ticket costs $40 to Eielson and $52 to Wonder Lake.

Tickets are available up to five days in advance of a particular bus departure. If you don't have a reservation, you most likely will have to wait two days to obtain a bus ticket. One way around this is to stop at the park and reserve one and then keep heading north to spend a few days in Fairbanks, backtracking to Denali when your reservations kick in.

Tour Bus

Denali Park Resorts operates two narrated, wildlife bus tours along the park road. The Tundra Wildlife Tour departs from the Denali National Park Hotel twice daily. The six-hour tour, designed primarily for package-tour groups, costs $54 per person and goes to Stony Hill when the mountain is visible, to the Toklat River when it isn't.

There is also a three-hour Natural History Tour that departs twice daily for Primrose Ridge for $30 a person. Reserve a seat for either tour the night before at the Denali National Park Hotel (☎ 276-7234) reservation desk or by calling in advance.

Along the Park Road

The park road begins at George Parks Hwy and winds 91.6 miles through the heart of the park, ending at Kantishna, an old mining settlement and the site of three wilderness lodges. Travelers with vehicles can only drive to a parking area along the Savage River at *Mile 14*, a mile beyond the Savage River Campground, unless they have a special permit that's nearly impossible to obtain.

Most of the free shuttle buses run from Riley Creek to the Eielson Visitor Center at *Mile 66* and then turn around. The round trip takes eight hours. Five buses drive all the way to Wonder Lake Campground, at *Mile 84*, which is an 11-hour round trip.

Mt McKinley is not visible from the park entrance or the nearby campgrounds and hotel. Your first glimpse of it comes between *Mile 9* and *Mile 11* of the park road, if you are blessed with a clear day. The park's weather, despite its Interior location, is cool, with long periods of overcast conditions and drizzle during the summer. The rule of thumb stressed by the National Park Service rangers is that Mt McKinley is hidden two out of three days. Keep in mind that, while 'the Great One' might not be visible for most of the first 15 miles, this is the best stretch to spot moose because of the cover of spruce and especially willow, the animal's favorite food.

From Savage River, the road dips into the Sanctuary and Teklanika river valleys, and Mt McKinley disappears behind the foothills. Both these rivers are in excellent hiking areas, and three of the five backcountry campgrounds are situated along them. Sanctuary River Campground is the most scenic of the three and at *Mile 22* it is a good base camp from which to explore Primrose Ridge, an excellent hiking area.

Equally scenic and just as small (seven sites) is the Igloo Creek Campground at *Mile 34* of the park road in spruce woods along the creek. This camp allows you to make an easy day hike into Igloo and Cathedral mountains to spot dall sheep.

After passing through the canyon formed by Igloo and Cathedral mountains, the road ascends to **Sable Pass** (elevation 3880 feet) at *Mile 38.5*. The canyon and surrounding mountains are excellent places to spot dall sheep, while the pass is known as a prime habitat for Toklat brown bears. From here, the road drops to the bridge over the East Fork Toklat River at *Mile 44*. Hikers will enjoy treks that lead from the bridge along the river banks both north and south. By hiking north, you can complete a six-mile loop that ends at the **Polychrome Pass Overlook** at *Mile 46.3* of the park road.

The pass is a rest stop for the shuttle buses and a popular spot for visitors. This scenic area has an elevation of 3500 feet and gives way to views of the Toklat River to the south. The alpine tundra above the road is good for hiking as you can easily scramble up ridges that lead north and south of the rest-area shelter.

The park road then crosses two single-lane, wooden bridges over the Toklat River and ascends near **Stony Hill** (elevation 4508 feet) at *Mile 61*. This is perhaps the finest place to view Mt McKinley in the stretch to Eielson Visitor Center. Another quarter-mile down the road is a lookout for viewing caribou and from here a short scramble north takes you to the summit of Stony Hill.

After climbing through Thorofare Pass (elevation 3900 feet) the road descends to the **Eielson Visitor Center** at *Mile 66*. The center is known for its excellent views of Mt McKinley, the surrounding peaks of the Alaska Range, and Muldrow Glacier. It offers a few interpretive displays and conducts a series of its own programs, including a tundra hike daily at 1.30 pm, an hour-long walk from the center. Catch a shuttle bus by 9 am at Riley Creek to make it to the Eielson Visitor Center for the walk. Several day and overnight hikes are possible from the center, including one around Mt Eielson (see the Hiking section in the Wilderness chapter) and another to Muldrow Glacier.

Past the Eielson Visitor Center the park road drops to the valley below, passing at *Mile 74.4* of the park road a sign for **Muldrow Glacier**. At this point, the glacier lies about a mile to the south, and the terminus of the 32-mile ice floe is clearly visible though you might not recognize it. The ice is covered with a mat of plant life. If the weather is cloudy and Mt McKinley and the surrounding peaks hidden, the final 20 miles of the bus trip will be a ride through rolling tundra and past numerous small lakes known as kettle ponds. Study the pools of water carefully to spot beavers swimming or a variety of waterfowl.

Wonder Lake Campground is at *Mile 84* of the park road. Here the beauty of Mt McKinley is doubled on a clear day, with the mountain's reflection in the lake's surface. Ironically, the heavy demand for the 28 sites at Wonder Lake and the numerous overcast days caused by Mt McKinley itself prevent the majority of visitors from ever seeing this remarkable panorama. If you do experience the reddish sunset on the summit reflecting off the still waters of the lake, cherish it as a priceless moment.

The campground is on a low rise above the lake's south end and is only 26 miles from the mountain. First the shuttle bus stops at a bus shelter near the campground and then drives to the edge of the lake for half an hour or so before turning around and heading back. Those who come on the early buses can gain another hour at the lake by getting off and picking up a later bus for the trip back. Keep in mind that those famous McKinley-reflected-in-the-lake photos are taken along the north-east shore two miles beyond the campground. The historic mining town of Kantishna is six miles from where the shuttle bus stops.

Visitor Programs

The Visitor Access Center offers a variety of programs during the summer, all of them free. One of the most popular is the **sled dog demonstration**. Denali is the only national park that keeps the sled dogs for winter maintenance and during the summer holds demonstrations daily at 10 am and 2 and 4 pm at the kennels, 3.5 miles west of the entrance on the park road. A free bus leaves the VAC half an hour before each demonstration, and the park hotel 20 minutes before.

The VAC also offers daily nature walks and longer hikes throughout the park (see the following Hiking section) while the auditorium behind the park hotel is the site of daily slide or film programs at 1.30 and 8 pm, which cover the history, wildlife or mountaineering aspects of the park. There are also daily campfire programs at Riley Creek, Savage River and Teklanika River campgrounds at 8 pm which are open to anybody.

Hiking

Even for those who have neither the desire nor the equipment for an overnight trek, hiking is still the best way to enjoy the park and to obtain a personal closeness with the land and its wildlife. The best way to undertake a day hike is to ride the shuttle bus and get off at any valley, river bed or ridge that takes your fancy. No backcountry permit is needed.

There are few trails in the park as most hiking is done across open terrain. You can hike virtually anywhere in the park that hasn't been closed because of the impact on wildlife. Popular areas include the Teklanika River south of the park road, the Toklat River, the ridges near Polychrome Pass and the tundra areas near the Eielson Visitor Center.

There are numerous guided walks in the park for those unsure of entering the backcountry on their own. The best is the Discovery Hike that departs at 8 am daily for a moderately strenuous, three to four-hour hike in the park's backcountry. The location of this trail-less adventure changes daily and you must sign up one to two days in advance. The VAC will have a list of all ranger-led hikes.

The few maintained trails in the park are

found around the main entrance area and are described below.

Horseshoe Lake Trail This trail is a leisurely 1.5-mile walk through the woods to an overlook of the oxbow lake and then down a steep trail to the water. The trailhead is 0.9 miles on the park road where the railroad tracks cross. Follow the tracks north a short way to the wide gravel path.

Morino Loop Trail This leisurely walk of 1.3 miles can be picked up in the back of Morino Campground as well as at the park hotel parking lot and offers good views of Hines and Riley creeks.

Taiga Loop Trail This is another easy hike that begins off the parking lot of the park hotel and loops 1.3 miles through the taiga forest.

Mt Healy Overlook Trail Veering off the Taiga Loop Trail is the trail for the steep hike up Mt Healy. The trail is 2.5 miles long, ascends 1700 feet and offers fine views of the Nenana Valley. Plan on three to six hours for the round trip.

Rock Creek Trail This moderate 2.3-mile walk connects the hotel area with the park headquarters and dog kennels area. However, it's far easier hiking the trail to the hotel than taking it from the hotel to the dog kennels, as all the elevation is gained with the drive up the park road. The trail begins just before the park road crosses Rock Creek but doesn't stay with the stream. Instead it climbs a gentle slope of mixed aspen and spruce forest, breaks out along a ridge with scenic views of Mt Healy and the Parks Hwy and then begins a rapid descent to the service road behind the hotel and ends on the Taiga Loop Trail.

Backpacking
For many, the reason to come to Denali, to endure the long lines at the VAC, is to escape

into the backcountry for a true wilderness experience. Unlike many parks in the Lower 48, Denali's rigid restrictions ensure that you can trek and camp in a piece of wilderness that you can call your own, even if it's just for a few days.

The park is divided into 43 zones and in 37 of them only a regulated number of backpackers is allowed into each section at a time. You have to obtain a permit for the zone you want to stay overnight in, and that usually means waiting two days or more at Riley Creek until something opens up.

All of this is done at the VAC where at the Backcountry Desk you'll find two wall maps with the zone outlines and a quota board indicating the number of vacancies in each unit. Permits are issued only a day in advance and at first glance backpackers are horrified to find most units full for two or three days in a row.

Like getting into the campgrounds, the key to obtaining a permit is first getting into the backcountry. Once you're in, you can book a string of other units throughout the park for the next 14 days. Units that are easier to obtain include Nos 1, 2, 3 and 24 because they surround the park entrance and are heavily wooded. Spend a night or two here and then jump on a camper bus for a more favorable place deeper in the park. At the opposite end of the park are the zones with unlimited access. These tend to be areas of extensive tussock where the trekking is extremely difficult or involves a major fording of the McKinley River, a difficult feat even when the river is low. Again, by camping here, you can enter the backcountry immediately and then book other units as they open, bypassing the one-day-in-advance restriction.

Although any regulated zone can be filled, you'll generally find the more popular ones to be Nos 12, 13 and 18 in the tundra area south of Eielson Visitor Center; Nos 8, 9, 10 and 11 which include both branches of the Toklat River and tundra area south of Polychrome Pass; No 27 north of Sanctuary Campground and No 15, the unit just west of Wonder Lake.

The first step in the permit process is to watch the Backcountry Simulator Program in a video booth in the VAC. It's an interactive video that covers such topics as dealing with bears and backcountry travel. Then check the quota board for an area that you can access within a day and finally approach the ranger behind the desk to outline your entire backcountry itinerary.

Along with your permit, you'll receive a Bear Resistant Food Container, free of charge, for food storage in the backcountry. The containers are bulky but they work. Since they were first introduced in 1986, bear encounters in the park have dropped by 90%. Next shuffle over to the shuttle bus counter and sign up for a camper bus and finally head over to the bookstore to purchase whatever topographic maps ($2.50) you will need.

It's important to realize that Denali is a trail-less park and the key to successful backcountry travel is being able to read a topographic map. You must be able to translate the contours (elevation lines) on the map into the land formations in front of you. River beds are easy to follow and make excellent avenues for the backpacker but they always involve fording. Pack a pair of tennis shoes for this.

Ridges are also good routes to hike if the weather is not foul. The tree line in Denali is at 2700 feet above that you usually will find tussock or moist tundra – humps of grass with water between to make for sloppy hiking. In extensive stretches of tussock the hiking has been best described as 'walking on basketballs'. Above 3400 feet you'll encounter alpine or dry tundra which generally makes for excellent trekking.

Regardless of where you are headed, five miles of backcountry in Denali is a full day for the average backpacker. For the best overview of the different units in the park purchase the book *Backcountry Companion for Denali National Park* by Jon Nierenberg (Alaska National History Association, 605 West 4th Ave, Anchorage, AK 99501; 94 pages). It's available at both the VAC and park hotel gift shop.

Cycling

An increasingly popular way to explore the park road is on a mountain bike. No special permit is needed to ride your bike on the road but you are not allowed to leave the road at any time. Most bikers book a camp site at the VAC and then carry the bike on the camper bus (see Camping in the Park in the Places to Stay section), using it to explore the road from there. You can even book sites at a string of campgrounds and ride with your equipment from one to the next. You can rent a bike from Denali Mountain Bike Rental (☎ 452-0580), next to the Denali Salmon Bake just north of the park entrance, for $25 a day.

Rafting

The Nenana River and the impressive gorge it carves is a popular whitewater rafting area. The most exciting stretch of the river begins near the park entrance and ends 10 miles north near the town of Healy. Here the river is rated Class III as rafters sweep through standing waves, rapids and holes with names like 'Coffee Grinder' that are situated in sheer-sided canyons. South of the entrance the river is much milder but to many it's just as interesting as it swings away from both the highway and the railroad increasing the opportunities of sighting wildlife.

Several rafting companies offer daily floats during the summer and the Nenana is easily one of the most rafted rivers in Alaska. Denali Raft Adventures (☎ 683-2234) has been around the longest and seems the most organized. Its office is at *Mile 238* of the highway but it will provide free transport from the train station inside the park. Both their Canyon Run through the gorge and the milder McKinley Run are offered three times daily and are $42 per person. The four-hour Healy Express is a combination of both for $62. It departs daily at 1.30 pm.

Places to Stay

Camping in the Park As with the bus seats, you can reserve a camp site in advance by calling ☎ (800) 622-7275 and paying a $4 reservation fee. The park will hand out 40%

of the sites this way, holding the rest for people who book them in person up to two days in advance at the VAC. If you have a vehicle but not a reservation (thus you can't stay at Morino), then count on finding a site the first night outside the park, as often there is a two-day wait for a site inside. All campgrounds charge $12 a night with the exception of Morino ($6 per person) and Igloo Creek ($6 per site).

The key to getting into the campground of your choice, like Wonder Lake, is just getting into a campground, any campground, including either Morino or Riley Creek. Once in, you can secure a guaranteed site for the next 14 days wherever there is an opening. With this system, you can still get to Wonder Lake even during the busiest time of the year if you are willing to camp elsewhere in the park for four or five days. This is especially easy for people walking in who can immediately pitch a tent in Morino then return to the VAC that afternoon to book other campgrounds as soon as there are openings. The limit on staying in one campground or a combination of them is 14 days.

Due to the popularity of the shuttle buses, there are camper buses with a third of the seats removed to facilitate hauling in backpacks and mountain bikes. There are a handful of these buses that charge a straight $15 fare to any point along the park road, including Wonder Lake.

Riley Creek The campground at the main entrance of the park is Riley Creek, the largest and nicest facility in Denali as well as the only one open year-round. A quarter-mile west of George Parks Hwy, Riley Creek has 102 sites, piped-in water, flush toilets and evening interpretive programs. Popular with RVers – in fact overrun by RVers – this is the only campground where you can not choose your own site. A site is assigned for you at the visitor center.

Morino Near the train station, Morino is a walk-in campground for backpackers without vehicles. It provides only two metal caches to keep your food away from the

bears, piped-in water and vault toilets. Though its capacity is listed at 60 persons, it's rare for anybody to be turned away. During much of the summer, however, this place can be packed and rangers are very strict about not allowing people to pitch a tent beyond the campground. You skip the VAC and self-register at Morino.

Savage River Despite its name, Savage River is at *Mile 13*, a mile short of the actual river. It is only one of two campgrounds with a view of Mt McKinley. It has 34 sites that can accommodate both RVs and tents and has water, flush toilets and evening interpretive programs. Those with a vehicle can drive to this campground.

Sanctuary River This is the next campground down the road, at *Mile 23* on the banks of a large glacial river. There are seven sites for tents only and no piped-in water. It's a great area for day hiking, however. You can either head south to hike along the Sanctuary River or make a day out of climbing Mt Wright or Primrose Ridge to the north for an opportunity to see and photograph dall sheep.

Teklanika River At *Mile 29*, Teklanika has 50 sites for either RVs or tents, piped water and evening programs. You must book this one for a minimum of three days due to the fact that you are allowed to drive to the campground. Registered campers are issued a road pass for a single trip to the facility and then must leave their vehicle parked until they are ready to return to Riley Creek.

Igloo Creek This is another waterless facility located at *Mile 34* with only seven sites limited to tents. The day hiking in this area is excellent, especially the numerous ridges around Igloo Mountain, Cathedral Mountain and Sable Pass that provide good routes into the alpine area.

Wonder Lake The jewel of Denali campgrounds is Wonder Lake, at *Mile 85* of the park road, due to the immense views of Mt

McKinley. The facility has 28 sites for tents only but does feature flush toilets and piped-in water. If you are lucky enough to reserve a site, book it for three nights and then pray that the mountain appears during one of the days you are there. Also pack plenty of insect repellent and maybe even a head net. In midsummer, the bugs are vicious.

Other Park Accommodation Those opposed to sleeping in a tent have few alternatives at the main entrance of the park. The *Denali National Park Hotel* (☎ 683-2215 in the summer) is the only lodging available in the entrance area of the park and rooms here are $145 for two people per night.

At the western end of the park road are three places that are as close to wilderness lodges as you'll ever find on a road. Their rates tend to shock most budget-conscious backpackers but include round-trip transportation from the train station, meals and guided activities.

Camp Denali (☎ 683-2290 or 603-675-2248 during the winter) offers several different types of accommodation, most with fixed arrival and departure dates. The camp is more of a resort and definitely not just a place to sleep as it offers a wide range of activities including wildlife observation and photography, rafting, fishing, gold panning and, of course, hiking. Plus your best view of Mt McKinley is obtained from here.

Rooms at both Camp Denali and it's North Face Lodge are $275 per person per night and include all meals, most guided activities and your transportation from the Denali train station, all meals, guided expeditions and trips and use of recreational equipment.

Nearby is the *Kantishna Roadhouse* (☎ (800) 942-7420) with 28 cabins that cost $550 for two people per night and $844 if there are four of you. Again this includes meals, activities and transport from the park entrance. The wilderness resort has gold panning, hiking, photographic activities during the day and a hot tub and sauna to enjoy at night. Keep in mind that these places will most likely be booked long before you arrive in Alaska. If you want to treat yourself

(and escape the crowds at Riley Creek), write to the lodges in advance – six months in advance is not overdoing it. Write to: Camp Denali, PO Box 216, Cornish, NH 03746, or Kantishna Roadhouse, PO Box 130, Denali National Park, AK 99755.

Also at the end of the road accommodation is the *Denali Backcountry Lodge* (☎ 683-1341 or (800) 841-0692) with 24 cabins for $530 for two people and a 'standby rate' when you book 72 hours before arriving of $390 per night. There is also hostel-like accommodation in Kantishna at *McKinley Gold Camp* (☎ (800) 770-7275). A night at the camp in cabin tents is $88 per person, which includes a bunk, an outhouse and the ride through the park.

Accommodation Outside the Park For a park of six million acres, Denali occasionally stuns visitors who arrive late in the afternoon or the early evening to find that there is no place to stay. They are informed by National Park Service rangers of individuals offering private accommodation outside the park, and these people can make a living just from the overflow.

Included among these are several private campgrounds where you can expect to pay from $15 to $20 for a camp site. Six miles south of the park entrance is the *Denali Grizzly Bear Campground* (☎ 683-2696) which offers camp sites for $17 a night, platform tents for $23, and cabins with cooking facilities and coin-operated showers. Near Healy, a small town 11 miles north of the park entrance, there is the *McKinley KOA* (☎ 683-2379 or (800) 478-2562), which has tent sites for $17, and RV sites for $23, along with bus transport to the VAC.

If there are three or four in your party, consider booking a cabin in advance. At *Denali Cabins* (☎ 683-2643 during the summer) you can get a large cedar cabin for one to four people with outdoor hot tub for $142 per night. The cabins are two miles south of the park entrance at *Mile 229* of George Parks Hwy but there is a free shuttle bus service to the entrance. Also south of the entrance at *Mile 224* of the George Parks Hwy is *Carlo Creek Lodge* (☎ 683-2576) with creekside cabins for $75 to $95 for two people and tent sites for $11, all located on 32 wooded acres. This is a great place if you have a vehicle but not if you don't, as the lodge doesn't supply transport to the park. Cabins closer to the entrance include *Denali River Cabins* (☎ 683-2500 or (800) 230-7275) and *Sourdough Cabins* (☎ 683-2773). At either one expect to pay close to $150 per night for a double.

There is a backpacker's hostel in Healy. *Denali Hostel* (☎ 683-1295) has bunks for $22 a night along with kitchen facilities, showers and transport back to the park. If you arrive on the train, there will be a Denali Hostel van at the depot. Also in Healy the *Stampede Hotel* (☎ 683-2242), where a double is only $50 a night, gets high marks.

For those with an RV, van or even a car who arrive late, there are large gravel pull-outs north of the park entrance on both sides of George Parks Hwy where you can stop and spend the night at a pinch. There are almost a dozen of them between Healy and the park entrance, and throughout the summer you'll see from eight to 10 vehicles there every night.

Places to Eat

Inside the Park There are two restaurants and one bar in the park, all off the lobby of the Denali National Park Hotel. The *Denali Dining Room* serves full meals in pleasant surroundings but is overpriced for most budget travelers. Breakfast after 7 am, however, can be a leisurely and reasonable $7 affair; it is pleasant to sit around drinking fresh coffee for a spell. The *Whistle Stop Snack Shop*, also off the lobby, is open from 5 to 7 am to provide early shuttle-bus passengers with breakfast or the opportunity to purchase a box lunch. It's then open from 8 am to 11 pm. Hamburgers and sandwiches are priced from $5 to $7, a cup of coffee and a large sweet roll around $4.

The *Gold Spike Saloon*, two lounge cars side by side, is the hotel's bar but an even more interesting gathering of travelers can be found in the hotel lobby itself whenever it rains or snows – you'll find retired couples dragging large suitcases, foreign tour groups being herded here and there, and backpackers munching on dried banana chips from their day packs.

McKinley Mercantile, a block from the hotel, sells a variety of fresh and dried food, some canned goods and other supplies. The selection is limited and highly priced. Your best bet is to stock up on supplies in Fairbanks or Anchorage before leaving for the park. The small park grocery store is open daily from 8 am to 11 pm and has showers behind it.

Outside the Park The best food outside the park is at *Lynx Creek Pizza* (☎ 683-2548) near the McKinley Chalets, north of the entrance at *Mile 238.6*. The log cabin restaurant has excellent pizza along with Mexican dishes, deli sandwiches and an impressive selection of beers. A small pizza that will feed two people or one backpacker just out of the mountains is $12.

Practically across the highway is *Denali Salmon Bake* where $15 gets you the usual Alaskan salmon dinner. You get a single serving of salmon but everything else is all-you-can-consume. South of the park entrance at *Mile 224* is *The Perch* (☎ 683-2523), one of the best restaurants in the area. Steak or seafood dinners begin at $15 but they also have a home-made soup and a salad for $7.50.

Getting There & Away

Bus Both northbound and southbound bus services are available from Denali National Park. If heading south, there is Moon Bay Express (☎ 274-6454 in Anchorage) whose van departs from the VAC daily in the summer at 3 pm, reaching the Anchorage International Hostel at 8 pm. The one-way fare to Anchorage is $35. Slightly cheaper is Alaska Backpacker Shuttle (☎ 344-8775) at $30 and Parks Highway Express (☎ 479-3065) at $20. Heading north is Fireweed Express (☎ 452-0521 in Fairbanks), which swings by both the VAC and park hotel at 4 pm and then arrives at the Fairbanks Visitor Center at 6.30 pm. The one-way fare is $25.

Train The most enjoyable way to arrive or depart from the park is aboard the Alaska Railroad (see the Getting Around chapter) with its viewing-dome cars that provide sweeping views of Mt McKinley and the Susitna and Nenana river valleys along the way. All trains arrive at the train station between the Riley Creek Campground and the park hotel, and only stay long enough for passengers to board.

The northbound train arrives in Denali at 4 pm and reaches Fairbanks at 8.30 pm. The southbound train arrives in Denali at 12.15 pm and in Anchorage at 8.30 pm. Tickets are not cheap; a one-way fare from Denali National Park to Anchorage is $95, to Fairbanks $50.

Getting Around
Courtesy Buses There is free transportation into and around the park entrance. The Front-Country Shuttle Buses run every half-hour, beginning at the VAC. The park also runs free buses to the sled-dog demonstrations that depart the VAC a half-hour before each show. There are also courtesy buses that transport people from the hotels, lodges and campgrounds outside Denali to the park hotel, where a schedule is usually posted. If you want to go to Lynx Pizza Parlor, the Salmon Bake or anywhere north of the entrance, grab the bus for the McKinley Chalets; to the south jump on the one for McKinley Village.

North of Denali National Park

Continuing north, the George Parks Hwy in the next 50 miles parallels the Nenana River, providing many viewing points of the scenic river. One of them is the June Creek Rest Area at *Mile 269*, where a gravel road leads

down to the small creek and a wooden staircase takes you up to fine views of the area.

Nenana
The only major town between Denali National Park and Fairbanks is Nenana (pop 540) which you reach at *Mile 305* of George Parks Hwy before crossing the Tanana River. Nenana was little more than the site of a roadhouse until it was chosen as the base for building the northern portion of the Alaska Railroad in 1916. The construction camp quickly became a boom town that made history on 5 July 1923 when President Warren G Harding arrived to hammer in the golden spike on the north side of the Tanana River.

The sickly Harding, the first president ever to visit Alaska, missed the golden spike the first two times, or so the story goes, but finally drove it in to complete the railroad. Less than a month later the president died in San Francisco, prompting the citizens of Talkeetna to claim he was 'done in' when he stopped at their Fairview Inn for a drink on the ride home.

In preparation for the president's arrival, the Nenana train station was built in 1923 at the north end of A St, extensively restored in 1988, and is now on the National Register of Historical Sites. It's an impressive building and includes the **Alaska State Railroad Museum** (☎ 832-5500), which houses railroad memorabilia and local artefacts. It's open from 8 am to 6 pm daily and admission is free. East of the train station, a monument commemorates when President Harding drove in the gold spike marking the completion of the Alaska Railroad.

An equally interesting building is the **Nenana Visitor Center** (☎ 832-9953), a log cabin with a sod roof that during the summer is planted with colorful flowers. It's on the corner of the George Parks Hwy and A St and features a few displays on the Nenana Ice Classic, the town's noted gambling event, as well as local information. Outside the visitor center is the *Taku Chief* river tug, which once pushed barges along the Tanana River. The

Nenana

1 Fish Wheels
2 Ice Classic Tower
3 Train Station
4 St Mark's Church
5 Post Office
6 Depot Cafe
7 City Police
8 Nenana Inn
9 Taku Chief Riverboat
10 Visitor Information Center
11 Nenana Valley Campground

center is open daily during the summer from 8 am to 6 pm.

Travel down Front St, parallel to the river in town, or cross to the north side of the bridge to view **fish wheels** at work, best seen in late summer during the salmon runs. The wheels, a traditional fish trap, scoop salmon out of the water as they move upstream to spawn.

Places to Stay & Eat *Nenana Inn* (☎ 832-5238), on the corner of 2nd and A St, is open 24 hours and has a laundromat and showers even if you're just camping off in the woods. Rooms are $65 for a single/double. Also within town is *Nenana Valley Campground* (☎ 832-5230), off 4th St, with tent sites for $10 which include showers.

At *Mile 302* of the Parks Hwy, 2.5 miles south of Nenana, is *Finnish Alaskan B&B* (☎ 832-5628), with three rooms and a Finnish log sauna for guests. Rates range from $60 to $80 per room.

For a bit to eat, try the *Depot Cafe* on the corner of 1st and A streets and open daily from 6 am to 10 pm. The giant cinnamon rolls are all you need for breakfast.

Ester

From Nenana, the George Parks Hwy shifts to a more easterly direction, passes a few more scenic turn-offs and arrives at the old mining town of Ester (pop 350) at *Mile 351.7*. The town was established in 1906 when a sizeable gold strike was made at Ester Creek, and at one time Ester was a thriving community of 15,000 with three hotels and five saloons. The town was revived in the 1920s when the Fairbanks Exploration Company began a large-scale mining operation. Most of Ester's historical buildings are from that era and were either built by the company or moved from Fox.

Gold mining still takes place in the hills surrounding Ester. But the town is best known as the home of the Cripple Creek

Breaking the Ice in Nenana

Railroads may have built Nenana but the town's trademark today is its annual gamble, the Nenana Ice Classic. The lottery event has Alaskans all over the state trying to guess the exact time of ice breakup on the frozen Tanana River. The first movement of river ice in April or May is determined by a tripod, which actually has four legs and stands guard 300 feet from shore. Any surge in the ice dislodges the tripod, which tugs on a cord, which in turn stops a clock on shore. The exact time on the clock determines the winner.

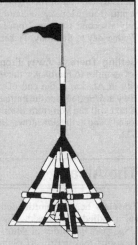

Crazy? Sure, but what else is there to do at the end of a long Alaskan winter? The tradition began in 1917 when Alaska Railroad surveyors, stir crazy with cabin fever, pooled $800 of their wages and made bets about when the ice would move out. That same excitement still swells in the small town, and through most of Alaska for that matter, as breakup in Nenana triggers visions of $100,000 payouts everywhere else.

Tickets are $2 for each guess, and guesses must be registered by 1 April. What you win is determined by how many other people had the same guess as you did. In 1993, the jackpot was $240,000 but only had to be split three ways after the tripod tripped at 1.01 pm on 23 April for the second earliest breakup ever. Often so many people have the same guess that the winners take home only a few hundred dollars.

You can see a replica of the Ice Classic tripod and the 1974 book of guesses – a 12 by 18-inch volume that is almost four inches thick – at the Nenana Visitors Center. You can see the real tripod even if you're not getting off the train. When not on the ice, it's on the banks of the Tanana River near the depot and can be seen from the left side of trains heading north.

You can enter the contest even if you are basking in the sun in southern California. Frostbitten toes are not a requirement to lay down your bets. Just send a $2 money order and include the date, hour and minute you think the ice will go out to: Ice Classic Office, PO Box 272, Nenana, AK 99760. The office will then send you a photocopy of your guess and keep the original in case you are the winner. ∎

Resort and its Malemute Saloon. The restored mess hall and bunkhouse of the mining camp is a regular stop for every tour bus out of Fairbanks. If you can hold off from rushing into Fairbanks, an evening here can be enjoyable, but only after 5 pm. Nothing happens in this town until the evening – even the two gift shops don't open their doors until the magic hour of 5 pm.

Places to Stay & Eat Rooms at the *Ester Gold Camp* (☎ 479-2500 or (800) 676-6925), an old miner's bunkhouse, are 'historically proportioned' (small) but affordable. Singles are $52 a night, doubles $65. There is also *Northern Exposure RV Park* (☎ (800) 428-8303) in town where tent sites are $12 a night.

Dinner is an all-you-can-eat feast at the Ester Gold Camp and is served in dining-hall fashion. The regular buffet is excellent and includes halibut, chicken, reindeer stew, corn-on-the-cob and great biscuits among other things. The price is $15, which is not cheap but worth it if you've just spent a week living off freeze-dried dinners at Denali.

Entertainment The *Malemute Saloon* is one of those classic Alaskan bars – sawdust on the floors; junk, err excuse me, mining artefacts in the rafters; patrons tossing peanut shells everywhere. You can go in there and have a beer any time but the saloon is famous for its stage show which combines skits, songs, Robert Service poetry and the Sawdust String Band. This is one of the best, and funniest, shows in Alaska, guaranteed to leave you rolling in the sawdust and peanut

INTERIOR

shells by the end of the night. Show time is 9 pm, from Monday to Saturday, while in July a second show at 7 pm is added from Wednesday to Saturday. Tickets are $11.

Getting There & Away From Ester, it is seven miles to Fairbanks, the second largest city in Alaska, at the end of George Parks Hwy at *Mile 358* (see the Fairbanks chapter). A taxi will run you from Ester to the airport for $13 and to the downtown area for around $22.

The Alcan

Travelers heading north along the Alcan (also called the Alaska Hwy) reach the US/Canadian border at *Mile 1189.5* from Dawson Creek in British Columbia. The spot is marked by an observation deck and plaque, while a half-mile further along the highway is the US customs border station. On the US side of the highway you will notice mileposts at almost every mile. These posts were erected in the 1940s to help travelers know where they were on the new wilderness road. Today, they are a tradition throughout Alaska and are still used for mailing addresses and locations of businesses. They measure the mileage from Dawson Creek, *Mile 0* on the Alcan.

Your first opportunity for information and free hand-outs comes at *Mile 1229*. The **Tetlin National Wildlife Refuge Visitor Center** (☎ 883-5312) is a sod-covered log cabin with a cache and a huge viewing deck overlooking the Scotty and Deeper creeks drainage areas with Mentasta and Nutsotin mountains in the distance. Inside, the cabin is packed with interpretive displays on wildlife and mountains and racks of brochures. It is open from 7 am to 7 pm daily during the summer.

You also pass two US Fish & Wildlife campgrounds (free!) along the Alcan before you reach Tok. At *Mile 1249.4* is the *Deadman Lake Campground* (18 sites) which has a boat ramp on the lake and a short

nature trail but no drinking water. At *Mile 1256.7* is the *Lakeview Campground* (eight sites) on beautiful Yager Lake, where on a nice day you can see the St Elias Range to the south. It's also a free campground with no piped-in water.

TOK

Although you enter Alaska just north of Beaver Creek in the Yukon, Tok serves as the gateway to the 49th State. The town of 1250 people, 125 miles beyond the US/Canadian border, is at the major junction between the Alcan that heads north-west to Fairbanks 206 miles away, and the Tok Cutoff, an extension of the Glenn Hwy that ends in Anchorage 328 miles to the south-west.

Tok was born in 1942 as a construction camp for the Alcan. Originally, it was called Tokyo Camp near Tokyo River, but WWII sentiment caused locals to shorten it to Tok. Today, the town is a trade and service center for almost 4000 residents in the surrounding area. If you're arriving in Alaska, this is your first chance to gather up information and brochures for the entire state.

Information
Tourist Offices If nothing else, Tok is a town of information, maps and brochures because of its role as 'the Gateway to Alaska'. Near the corner of the Tok Cutoff (Glenn Hwy) and the Alcan is the Tok Visitors Center (☎ 883-5887). The massive log building was built in 1992 to celebrate the 50th anniversary of the Alcan to the tune of $450,000. Inside there is regional and local information along with free coffee, while outside a sign shows the temperature extremes the town suffers every year. It is open from 7 am to 9 pm daily during the summer.

Next door is the Alaska Public Lands Information Center (☎ 883-5667), open daily in the summer from 8 am to 8 pm. The center offers a mountain of travel information and hand-outs along with free coffee, a large floor map and rest rooms. The small museum features wildlife displays. The most important item in the center for many backpackers is the message board. Check out the board or display your own message if you are trying to hitch a ride through Canada along the Alcan. It is best to arrange a ride in Tok and not wait until you reach the international border. In recent years, the Canadian customs post at the border has developed a reputation as one of the toughest anywhere. With a new 'zero tolerance' attitude, it's not unusual to see hitchhikers, especially Americans, turned back at the border. Directly across the highway from the visitor centers is the US Fish & Wildlife Service office (☎ 883-5312) with information about various USFW refuges in northern Alaska including Tetlin National Wildlife Refuge. It is open from 8 am to 4.30 pm Monday to Friday.

Money The only bank in Tok is Denali State Bank in the Frontier Foods Supermarket at *Mile 1314* of the Alcan.

Post The post office is on the Alcan, just west of the intersection with the Tok Cutoff.

Bookshops The best place to purchase Alaska books is at the Alaska Public Lands Information Center.

Laundry There are several places around town to do your laundry, including the Village Texaco at *Mile 1313.4* of the Alcan.

Medical Services The Public Health Clinic (☎ 883-4101) is at the opposite end of the Alaska Public Lands Information Center building.

Things to See
Tok, along with a half-dozen other towns, considers itself the 'Sled Dog Capital of Alaska' as it is estimated one of every three people in the area is involved with the sport in one way or another – most of them by raising dogs. Ask at the visitor center about local dog-sled demonstrations that are usually held in town throughout the summer.

Places to Stay
Camping The closest private campground is

the *Golden Bear Motel* (☎ 883-2561) just a quarter of a mile south of town on Tok Cutoff. The motel has tent spaces for $10 a night with showers, but it is the first of many tourist traps in the state set up to catch the steady stream of RVers passing through.

Hostels Probably the most affordable place to stay in town is at the *Tok International (AYH) Hostel* (☎ 883-3745), a mile south on Pringle Dr at *Mile 1322.5* of the Alcan. That puts it nine miles west of the town, but it provides 10 beds in a big army tent along with tent sites in a pleasant wooded area. Those cycling to Alaska should note that Tok's bike trails pass near the hostel before ending at Tanacross Junction at *Mile 1325.8* of the Alcan. The rate per night at the hostel is $7.50.

Hotels & Motels Those travelers bussing up north from Haines or Skagway will find themselves stopping overnight in Tok. There are eight hotel/motels in the area; many of them are around the junction of the two highways. The cheapest one is the *Snowshoe Motel* (☎ 883-4511 or (800) 478-4511 in Alaska or the Yukon) across the Alcan from the visitor center. The motel has doubles for $67 which includes a light breakfast. Just about everything else in town begins at $70.

Getting There & Away
Tok can be difficult for hitchhikers. If you can't score a ride, even after pleading with motorists at the visitor center, keep in mind that Alaskon Express is likely to have a bus headed where you want to go. The buses leave from the Westmark Inn (☎ 883-2291). On Sunday, Tuesday and Friday a bus leaves at 4 pm and stops overnight in Beaver Creek, reaching Whitehorse, Haines or Skagway the next day. On Monday, Wednesday and Friday a bus departs at 11 am and reaches Anchorage by 7.30 pm that day. The one-way fare from Tok to Anchorage is $105, to Fairbanks $67, to Glennallen $59, to Haines $145 and Skagway $159.

The Alaska Direct bus (☎ 883-5059) passes through Tok almost daily during the summer. Once on its way to Whitehorse and Haines, it pulls in Sunday, Wednesday and Friday at 2.30 pm and then continues on to Beaver Creek. Westbound buses depart at 2.30 pm on Wednesday, Friday and Sunday with one heading for Glennallen and then Anchorage and another going to Fairbanks. The one-way fare from Tok to Anchorage is $65, to Fairbanks $40.

TOK TO DELTA JUNCTION

Within 10 miles west of Tok on the Alcan you are greeted with views of the Alaska Range which parallels the road to the south. The *Moon Lake State Campground* (15 sites, $8 fee) is at *Mile 1332*, 18 miles west of Tok. This state wayside offers tables, outhouses and a swimming area in the lake where it is possible to do the backstroke while watching a float plane land nearby.

Although there are no more public campgrounds until Delta Junction, travelers often stop overnight at the *Gerstle River State Wayside*, a large lookout at *Mile 1393* of the Alcan. The scenic spot provides covered tables and outhouses but no piped-in drinking water. Nearby is the trailhead for the **Donna Lakes Trail**, a trek of 3.5 miles to Big Donna Lake and 4.5 miles to Little Donna Lake. Both are stocked with rainbow trout.

DELTA JUNCTION

This town (pop 800) is known as the 'End of the Alcan', as the famous highway joined the existing Richardson Hwy here to complete the route to Fairbanks. The community began as a construction camp and picked up its name from the junction between the two highways. Delta Junction was also home to Fort Greely, which at one point employed 250 civilians, but in 1996 the Army began transferring the base to Fairbanks and by 1998 it will be virtually closed. The town continues to serve as a service center not only for travelers but also for the growing agricultural community in the surrounding valleys.

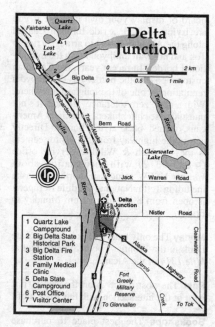

1 Quartz Lake Campground
2 Big Delta State Historical Park
3 Big Delta Fire Station
4 Family Medical Clinic
5 Delta State Campground
6 Post Office
7 Visitor Center

Information

Tourist Office The log cabin which houses the Delta Junction Visitor Center is in the 'Triangle', the area where the Alcan merges into the Richardson Hwy and the town's unofficial 'downtown'. Just outside the visitor center is the large white milepost for *Mile 1422* of the Alcan, marking the end of the famous highway.

The visitor center (☎ 895-9941), open daily from 8.30 am to 7.30 pm in the summer, is the usual source of local information, hand-outs and free coffee. There is also a display of local crafts and furs while those who have just completed the journey on the Alcan from Dawson Creek can purchase an End-of-the-Highway certificate.

Money You'll find a National Bank of Alaska and an ATM within the Diehl's Shopping Center, a half-mile north of the visitor center.

Post The post office is on the east side of the Richardson Hwy, two blocks north of the visitor center.

Library The public library (☎ 895-4102), behind the city hall in the center of town, runs a paperback swap for travelers if you have run out of reading material after the long haul on the Alcan. In the summer the library is open Wednesday, Thursday and Saturday.

Laundry Two blocks north of the Delta State Campground on the Richardson Hwy is Delta Self Service Laundry (☎ 895-4561) which has showers and is open to 10 pm daily.

Medical Services Just north of the Delta State Campground on Richardson Hwy is the Family Medical Clinic (☎ 895-5100).

Things to See
There isn't a lot to do in Delta Junction unless you wander in during the Deltana Fair (giant vegetables, livestock shows and parades) on the last weekend of July. To see a homestead farm or a large collection of early farming equipment, head to the **Alaska Homestead & Historical Museum**, six miles east of town on the Alcan. It is open from 10 am to 7 pm daily in the summer.

If you have the time, head three miles south of Delta Junction down Richardson Hwy to the scenic lookout across from the FAA facility. The mountainous panorama with the Delta River in the foreground is spectacular from this spot. On a clear day you can easily spot Mt Hayes (13,697 feet) in the center and Mt Moffit (13,020 feet) to the left, as well as several other peaks.

Places to Stay
Camping There are two public campgrounds in the area. The closest is the *Delta State Campground* (24 sites, $8 fee), a mile north of the visitor center.

The other campground is the *Clearwater State Campground* (18 sites, $8 fee), 13 miles north-east of town. Follow the Rich-

ardson Hwy and turn right on Jack Warren Rd, 2.4 miles north of the visitor center. Head 10.5 miles east along the road and look for signs to the campground, along Clearwater Creek, which has good fishing for grayling.

Hostels At one point Delta Junction had two hostels operating. At the time of writing there were none. Check with the visitor center to see if one is up and running.

Hotels & Motels There are several motels, including *Kelley's Country Inn* (☎ 895-4667) two blocks north of the visitor center on Richardson Highway, which has singles/doubles for $65/75. On the edge of town, four miles north from the visitor center on the Richardson Highway, is *Alaska 7 Motel* (☎ 895-4848) with singles/doubles at $54/60. Also consider the *Silver Fox Roadhouse* (☎ 895-4157), 18 miles south-east of Delta Junction on the Alcan, where there are cabins.

Places to Eat
There's a handful of restaurants in town and *Delta Shop-Rite*, a large supermarket that features bulk foods, bakery, home-cooked specials, ready-to-eat items and a salad bar. It's a half-mile north of the visitor center across from the post office on the Richardson Hwy. Also keep in mind that beginning in July many farmers set up stalls around the visitor center and sell their local produce.

Richardson Highway

The Richardson Hwy, Alaska's first highway, begins in Valdez and extends north 266 miles to Delta Junction, where the Alcan joins it for the final 98 miles to Fairbanks. The road was originally scouted in 1919 by Captain WR Abercrombie of the US Army, who was looking for a way to link the gold town of Eagle with the warm-water port of Valdez. At first it was a telegraph line and footpath, but it quickly turned into a wagon trail following the gold strikes at Fairbanks around the turn of the century.

Today, the road is a scenic wonder; it passes through the Chugach Mountains and the Alaska Range while providing access to Wrangell-St Elias National Park. Along the way it is highlighted by waterfalls, glaciers, five major rivers and the Trans-Alaska Pipeline, which parallels the road most of the way. Many say the most scenic stretch of highway in the state is the 100-mile drive from Gulkana to Delta Junction.

VALDEZ TO DELTA JUNCTION

The first section of the Richardson Hwy from Valdez, *Mile 0*, to the junction with the Glenn Hwy, *Mile 115*, is covered in the Richardson Hwy to Glennallen section in the Southcentral chapter. The next 14 miles from Glennallen to the junction of the Tok Cutoff, which includes the campgrounds at the Dry Creek State Recreation Site and Gulkana, is covered in the Tok Cutoff section following in this chapter. Mileposts along the highway show distances from old Valdez, four miles from the present city which is the new beginning of the Richardson Hwy.

Glennallen to Sourdough Creek

At *Mile 112.6* of the highway, just north of Glennallen, is a turn-off with an interpretive display on the development of transport in Alaska. Even more appealing is the view from a bluff nearby where you can see several peaks of the Wrangell Mountains which lie in Wrangell-St Elias National Park. The highest mountain is Mt Blackburn at 16,518 feet.

At *Mile 147.6* the road reaches the Bureau of Land Management *Sourdough Creek Campground* (60 sites, free), which provides access into the Gulkana River for canoeists and rafters. In 1994, the campground was reopened after a $2 million facelift and now includes a new boat launch and entrance, trails that lead to a river observation shelter and a fishing deck. Also in the campground is a set of interpretive panels detailing the history of the Sourdough Roadhouse, a col-

orful lodge and national historical site that burned to the ground in 1992.

Gulkana Canoe Route

This trip along the Gulkana River from Paxson Lake, *Mile 175* of the Richardson Hwy, to where the highway crosses the river at Gulkana is a popular canoe, kayak and raft route of 80 miles. The first 45 miles are only for experienced whitewater paddlers or rafters, as they involve several challenging rapids, including Canyon Rapids, Class IV whitewater. Although there is a short portage around Canyon Rapids, rough Class III waters follow. The final 35 miles from Sourdough Creek BLM Campground to Gulkana are a pleasant one or two-day paddle in mild water that can be enjoyed by less hard-core canoeists.

All land from the Sourdough Creek Campground south is owned by the Ahtna Native Corporation, which charges boaters to camp on it. The exceptions – three single-acre sites – are signposted along the river banks and have short trails leading back to the highway. Raft rentals and shuttle service for many area rivers, including the Gulkana River, can be arranged through River Wrangellers (☎ 822-3967) in Gakona.

Alaska Range Foothills to Black Rapids Glacier

Ten miles north of Sourdough Creek, the Richardson Hwy enters the foothills of the Alaska Range. Gradually sweeping views open up of not only the Alaska Range to the north but the Wrangell Mountains to the south and the Chugach Mountains to the south-west. More splendid views follow; you can see the large plateau to the west where the headwaters of the Susitna River form and the Glennallen area to the south. At *Mile 175* of Richardson Hwy is the gravel spur that leads 1.5 miles west to the recently upgraded *Paxson Lake BLM Campground* (50 sites, $6). The lakeshore campground now has walk-in sites for tenters that cost only $3 a night.

The junction with the Denali Hwy is at *Mile 185.5*, where the small service center of

Paxson is located. Five miles north of Paxson, look for the parking area by the Gulkana River on the west side of the highway, where there are litter barrels and picnic tables. This scenic spot provides views of Summit Lake and the Trans-Alaska Pipeline. From mid to late summer this is also a good spot to watch the salmon spawn.

After passing Summit Lake, the bridge over Gunn Creek is reached at *Mile 196.7* of Richardson Hwy and provides views of **Gulkana Glacier** to the north-east. From here, the highway begins climbing to its highest point at **Isabel Pass**, with an elevation of 3000 feet. The pass is at *Mile 197.6* and is marked by a historical sign dedicated to General Wilds Richardson, after whom the highway is named. From this point you can view Gulkana Glacier to the north-east and Isabel Pass pipeline camp below it.

Three miles north of the pass, at *Mile 200.5* of Richardson Hwy, a gravel spur leads 1.5 miles to *Fielding Lake Wayside*, where you can camp (seven sites, free) in a scenic area above the tree line at 2973 feet. This high up in the Alaska Range, the ice often remains on the lake until July. The highway and the pipeline parallel each other north from Fielding Lake, and there are several lookouts from which to view the monumental efforts to move oil. One of the best is at *Mile 205.7*, where the pipeline can be photographed on an incline up a steep hill.

At *Mile 225.4* of Richardson Hwy, there is a viewpoint with picnic tables and a historical marker pointing out what little ice remains of **Black Rapids Glacier** to the west. The glacier became known as the 'Galloping Glacier' after its famous three-mile advancement in the winter of 1936 when it almost engulfed the highway. Across from the marker, the easy **Black Rapids Lake Trail**, 0.3-miles long, winds through wildflowers to Black Rapids Lake.

Donnelly Creek to Delta Junction

The last public campground before Delta Junction is just before *Mile 238* of Richardson Hwy, where a short loop road leads west of the highway to the *Donnelly Creek State*

Campground (12 sites, $8). This is a great place to camp as it is seldom crowded and is extremely scenic with good views of the towering peaks of the Alaska Range. Occasionally, the Delta bison herd can be seen from the campground.

Two interesting turn-offs are passed in the final 25 miles before you reach the Alcan. The first is at *Mile 241.3* and overlooks the calving ground of the Delta buffalo herd to the west. Twenty-three bison were relocated here from Montana in 1928, for the pleasure of sportsmen, and today there are almost 400 bison. The animals have established a migratory pattern in the area which includes summering and calving along the Delta River. There is an interpretive display at the turn-off where often you can spot up to 100 animals. Since the herd is two to three miles away, binoculars are needed for clear views.

The other turn-off is just before *Mile 244* and has spectacular views of the pipeline and three of the highest peaks in the Alaska Range to the south-west. From south to west you can view Mt Deborah (12,339 feet), Hess Mountain (11,940 feet) and Mt Hayes (13,697 feet).

The highway passes Fort Greely just beyond *Mile 261* and then arrives at the Delta Junction Visitors Center on the 'Triangle', where the Alcan merges with the Richardson Hwy at *Mile 266*. From here it is 98 miles to Fairbanks.

DELTA JUNCTION TO FAIRBANKS

From Delta Junction, the Richardson Hwy merges with the Alcan for the remaining 98 miles to Fairbanks and passes the most interesting attraction in the Delta Junction area at *Mile 275*. **Big Delta State Historic Park** (☎ 895-4201), a 10-acre historical park, preserves Rika's Landing, an important crossroad for travelers, miners and the military on the Valdez-to-Fairbanks Trail from 1909 to 1947.

The centerpiece of the park is Rika's Roadhouse which has been renovated and now contains historical displays and a gift shop. The roadhouse began as little more than a cabin in 1904 when John Hajdukovich came along and constructed most of the buildings within the park before trading them with a young Swedish woman in 1923, reportedly for $10 and her back wages. The roadhouse is named after Erika Wallen, who ran it until the late 1940s and lived there until her death in 1969. Of the 30 roadhouses that once stretched along the rutted and muddy Valdez-to-Fairbanks Trail (now the Richardson Hwy), only Rika's and the one in Copper Center remain.

Today guides in period dress lead tours through the complex which includes a blacksmith's shop museum, Signal Corp station, and the Packhouse Pavilion where local artisans work on spinning, weaving, quilting and willow carving. The roadhouse is open daily during the summer from 8 am to 8 pm and admission and guided tours are free. There is also the Packhouse Restaurant open from 9 am to 5 pm for lunch and dinner.

Just beyond the state historic park, you pass through the farming village of **Big Delta** (pop 300) at *Mile 275.3*. From the town's bridge across the Tanana River you can look east for an impressive view of the Trans-Alaska Pipeline suspended over the water or look west for equally impressive views of the Alaska Range.

The junction to the *Quartz Lake State Campground* (16 sites, $8 fee) is at *Mile 277.7* of Richardson Hwy. Turn east at the posted road and head 2.8 miles to the campground along the shores of the scenic lake which provides good fishing for rainbow trout. A trail from the campground leads over to nearby Lost Lake, where there are two more camp sites.

For the next 20 miles, the highway passes a handful of lookouts where there are spectacular views of both the Tanana River in the foreground and the Alaska Range behind it.

The spur that leads to *Harding Lake State Campground* (89 sites, $8 fee) is at *Mile 321.5*. The campground, which has a ranger office near the entrance, has picnic shelters and drinking water as well as swimming and canoeing opportunities in the lake.

From the campground, it is 43 miles to Fairbanks, and there are two public camp-

grounds along the way. At *Mile 346.7* of Richardson Hwy is **Chena Lakes Recreation Area**. This facility opened in 1984 as the last phase of an Army Corps of Engineers flood-control project prompted by the Chena River's flooding of Fairbanks in 1967. Two separate parks, Chena River and Chena Lakes, make up the recreational area which is 18 miles south-east from Fairbanks off the Laurance Rd exit of Richardson Hwy. The Chena River park contains a 2.5-mile self-guided nature trail. The Chena Lakes park offers swimming as well as canoe, sailboat and paddleboat rentals. Between the two parks there are three campground loops providing 78 sites. The day-use fee is $3 and the overnight camping fee is $8. The Richardson Hwy reaches Fairbanks at *Mile 363*.

Tok Cutoff

The Tok Cutoff is often considered to be the northern half of the Glenn Hwy, but mileposts along the road show distances from Gakona Junction and not from Anchorage, as they do once you pass Glennallen.

TOK TO GLENNALLEN

From Tok, it is 328 miles to Anchorage or a full day's drive. You first travel 139 miles south-west along the Tok Cutoff to Glennallen at the junction of Richardson and Glenn highways and then another 189 miles to Anchorage via the Glenn Hwy.

The first of only two public campgrounds on the Tok Cutoff is reached at *Mile 109.3*. The *Eagle Trail State Campground* (40 sites, $8 fee) is near Clearwater Creek and provides drinking water, toilets, rain shelter and fire pits. The historical **Eagle Trail**, which at one time extended to Eagle on the Yukon River, can still be hiked for a mile from the campground. Look for the posted trailhead near the covered picnic shelters.

The second campground is another 45 miles south-west along the highway just before *Mile 64.2*. The *Porcupine Creek State Recreation Site* (12 sites, $8 fee) is set in a scenic spot along the creek and provides tables, toilets and drinking water. An historical marker and splendid views of Mt Sanford, a dormant volcano with an elevation of 16,203 feet, is a mile north along the highway.

Nabesna Road

At *Mile 59.8* of Tok Cutoff is the junction with Nabesna Rd. The 45-mile side road extends into the Wrangell-St Elias National Park (see the Wrangell-St Elias National Park section in the Southcentral chapter) and ends at **Nabesna**, a mining community of less than 25 residents.

Taking the side trip is a unique experience off the highways; the road is one of only two that lead into the heart of the national park. At the beginning of the road is **Slana**, a small village of 40 residents or so. Slana has a Native Alaskan settlement on the north banks of the Slana River and fish wheels can still be seen working during the salmon runs. The area around it was one of the last places in the USA to be opened to homesteading, as late as the early 1980s. There is a new National Park Service ranger station (☎ 822-5238) that can assist with information on Wrangell-St Elias National Park. It is open from 8 am to 5 pm daily from June to September.

There is some unique accommodation near Slana. *Huck Hobbit's Homestead* (☎ 822-3196 in Gakona) is a campground and wilderness retreat four miles off the Nabesna Rd with the last mile accessible only by hiking or ATVs. The cabins are relatively new and cost $25 a night. Camp sites are $2.50 and the hosts serve homestyle meals for $5 per person. Stay an extra day here – the scenery is beautiful – and splurge on a canoe trip down the Slana River for $35 per canoe (two people).

Also near Slana is *Natal Creek Hostel* (☎ 822-5028), where the hosts meet you at Nabesna Rd and then lead you to their place via a hike and a river crossing by canoe. The hostel includes a common kitchen, sauna, bunkroom and private cabins. A bunk is $15 a night, a cabin for two $40 and tent space

$5. Ask at the ranger station in Slana about how to reach either place.

The first 30 miles of Nabesna Rd is manageable gravel road but after that the surface is extremely rough with several streams flowing over it. There is a lodge with gas at *Mile 28.6* but no other tourist facilities beyond that or in Nabesna. There are also no public campgrounds along the way. Good camping spots, however, along with scenic lakes and inviting ridges for backpackers, lie from one end of this road to the other.

Gakona Junction

Officially, Tok Cutoff ends at Gakona Junction, 125 miles south-west of Tok, where it merges with the Richardson Hwy. The village of **Gulkana** (pop 200) is two miles to the south and you can camp along the Gulkana River by the bridge in town. There is also *Bear Creek Inn* (☎ 822-5095), a B&B with a sauna and a good view of the Wrangell Mountains, two miles south of Gakona Junction at *Mile 126* of the Richardson Hwy. Singles/doubles are $60/70. For an interesting meal, try the dining room of the *Gakona Lodge* (☎ 822-3482). The roadhouse opened in 1905 as Doyle's Ranch near the junction of the Eagle and Fairbanks cutoffs. In 1929, a larger lodge was added and the original one was made into a carriage house. Today it's listed on the National Register of Historical Places and the carriage house has been turned into a dining room. There is also a bar inside and a natural-food store. Rooms are available.

From the roadhouse at Gakona Junction, the eastern end of the Glenn Hwy is 14 miles south via Richardson Hwy.

Glenn Highway

The Glenn Hwy runs west from Glennallen to Anchorage with the mileposts along the road showing the distance from Anchorage, *Mile 0*.

GLENNALLEN

Glennallen (pop 1000), referred to by some as 'the Hub' of Alaska's road system, is a service center on Glenn Hwy, two miles west from the junction with the Richardson Hwy. Because of its strategic location, the town provides a wide range of facilities and services, and is the major departure point to the Wrangell-St Elias National Park. It is also the home base for many fishing and hunting guides; otherwise, it looks like a RV park and there is little reason to linger here.

Information

Tourist Office The Greater Copper River Valley Visitor Center (☎ 822-5555) is a log cabin at the junction of the Glenn and Richardson highways open from 8 am to 7 pm daily.

Money Glennallen has the only full-service bank in the Copper Valley region, a National Bank of Alaska at *Mile 187.5* of Glenn Hwy.

Post The post office is on Aurora Dr, just off Glenn Highway near the bank.

Library The public library is on Glenn Hwy as you enter town from the west and open from 1 to 6 pm Tuesday through Saturday.

Laundry The Glennallen Laundromat (☎ 822-3999) is located next to Park's Place Supermarket on Glenn Hwy in the downtown stretch of Glennallen.

Medical Services The Cross Road Medical Center (☎ 822-3203) near the corner of Glenn Hwy and Auroa Dr is a walk-in clinic and pharmacy, and offers 24-hour emergency service.

Places to Stay

Camping The closest public campground is the *Dry Creek State Campground* (60 sites, $8 fee), five miles north-east of town on the Richardson Hwy between the junction with the Glenn Hwy and the Tok Cutoff to the north. Within town is *Northern Nights Campground* (☎ 822-3199) where a tent site

is $10 a night but there are no showers. You might as well walk a half-mile out of town and camp for free in the woods.

Motels The *Caribou Motel* (☎ 822-3302) is right on Glenn Hwy and its lack of competition shows. The rooms are nice but run $95/105 a night singles/doubles. Four miles west of Glennallen on the Glenn Hwy is *Brown Bear Rhodehouse* (☎ 822-3663) with three cabins for $45 for two people.

Getting There & Away

Bus Glennallen is notorious among hitchhikers as a place for getting stuck in, especially at the Glenn Hwy junction when trying to thumb a ride north to the Alcan. Luckily a variety of buses are always passing through.

Gray Line's Alaskon Express passes through almost daily headed either for Anchorage or Tok. On Sunday, Tuesday and Friday a bus heads north at 12.30 pm while on Monday, Wednesday and Friday a bus heads south at 3 pm. The one-way fare to Anchorage is $59, to Haines $175. On Sunday, Wednesday and Friday there is also an Alaska Direct bus passing through in each direction.

The Caribou Cafe (☎ 822-3656), next door to the Caribou Hotel, serves as the pick-up point for these buses along with the vans from Backcountry Connection (☎ 822-5292 or (800) 478-5292 in Alaska). Backcountry Connection departs for McCarthy on Monday through Saturday at 7 am, reaching the historic town at 11.45 pm. The one-way fare is $49.

GLENNALLEN TO PALMER

The Glenn Hwy runs west from Glennallen through a vast plateau bordered by the Alaska Range to the north and the Chugach Mountains to the south. This is an incredibly scenic section that extends for almost 150 miles west; it is also a good area for spotting wildlife. Moose and caribou roam the lowlands and the timbered ridges are prime habitat for black bears and grizzlies. On the slopes of both mountain ranges, and often visible from the highway, are dall sheep.

Tolsona Creek to Little Nelchina River

The first campground west from Glennallen is the *Tolsona Wilderness Campground* (☎ 822-3865), a private facility with 45 sites that border the river at *Mile 173* of the Glenn Hwy. The fee is $10 to $15 a night for a site but here you have water, coin-operated showers and laundry facilities. In the morning, if you're really hungry, stop at the *Tolsona Lake Lodge* (☎ 822-3433) at *Mile 170.5* of Glenn Hwy for its all-you-can-eat sourdough-pancake breakfast.

The first public campground along the highway is the *Lake Louise State Recreation Area* (46 sites, $8 fee), which provides shelters, tables, water and swimming in the lake. The scenic campground is 17 miles up Lake Louise Rd, which leaves the Glenn Hwy at *Mile 160*. A mile up Lake Louise Rd from the Glenn Hwy is a turn-off with good views of Tazlina Glacier and Carter Lake.

The *Little Nelchina River Campground* (11 sites, free) is just off Glenn Hwy at *Mile 137.5*. The 35 miles between these three campgrounds is a hiker's delight, as several trails go from the highway to the nearby mountains and lakes.

A lookout with litter barrels marks the trailhead for the **Mae West Lake Trail**, a short hike at *Mile 169.3* of Glenn Hwy. This mile-long trail leads to a long, narrow lake fed by Little Woods Creek.

The trailhead for the **Lost Cabin Lake Trail** is on the south side of the highway at *Mile 165.8*, where a pair of litter barrels has been placed. The trail winds two miles to the lake and is a berry picker's delight from late summer to early fall.

At *Mile 138.3* of Glenn Hwy, or 0.8 miles east of the Little Nelchina River Campground, is the trailhead for the **Old Man Creek Trail**. This trail leads two miles to Old Man Creek and nine miles to Crooked Creek, where you can fish for grayling. It ends at the old mining area of Nelchina, 14.5 miles from the highway. Here it merges into the old Chickaloon-Knik-Nelchina Trail, a gold

miner's route used before the Glenn Hwy was built.

The **Chickaloon-Knik-Nelchina Trail** is an extensive system of trails that extends beyond Palmer, with many posted access points along the north side of the highway. The system is not maintained regularly and hikers attempting any part of it should have good outdoor experience and the right topographic maps. Also keep in mind you'll have to share the trail with off-road vehicles.

Eureka Summit to Palmer

From Little Nelchina River, the Glenn Hwy begins to ascend, and views of Gunsight Mountain (you have to look hard to see the origin of its name) come into view. At Eureka Summit, you can not only see Gunsight Mountain but the Chugach Mountains to the south, the Nelchina Glacier spilling down in the middle and the Talkeetna Mountains to the north. This impressive, unobstructed view is completed to the west, where the highway can be seen dropping into the river valleys separating the two mountain chains. Eureka Summit (elevation 3322 feet) is at *Mile 129.3* of the Glenn Hwy; it is the highway's highest point.

The trailhead for the **Belanger Pass Trail**, at *Mile 123.3* on Martin Rd across from the Tahneta Lodge, is marked by a Chickaloon-Knik-Nelchina Trail sign. For the most part it is used by miners and hunters in off-road vehicles for access into the Talkeetna Mountains, and at times the mining scars are disturbing.

The views from Belanger Pass, a three-mile hike, are excellent and well worth the climb. From the 4350-foot pass, off-road-vehicle trails continue north to Alfred Creek, another 3.5 miles away, and eventually they lead around the north side of Syncline Mountain past active mining operations.

Two miles west of the Belanger Pass trailhead is **Tahneta Pass** at *Mile 121* of the Glenn Hwy and half a mile further is a scenic turn-off where you can view the 3000-foot pass. To the east of the turn-off lies Lake Liela, and Lake Tahneta beyond it.

The **Squaw Creek Trail** is another miners'

and hunters' trail that begins at *Mile 117.6* of Glenn Hwy and merges into the Chickaloon-Knik-Nelchina Trail. It begins as an off-road-vehicle trail marked by a Squaw Creek Trail sign. It extends 3.5 miles to Squaw Creek and 9.5 miles to Caribou Creek after ascending a low pass between the two. Although the trail can be confusing at times, the hike is a scenic one with the Gunsight, Sheep and Syncline mountains as a backdrop.

From here, the Glenn Hwy begins to descend and the scenery becomes stunning as it heads towards the Talkeetna Mountains, passing an oddly shaped rock formation known as the Lion's Head at *Mile 114*. A half a mile beyond it, the highway reaches the first view of Matanuska Glacier. To the north is Sheep Mountain, properly named, as you can often spot dall sheep on its slopes.

At *Mile 113.5* of Glenn Hwy is the *Sheep Mountain Lodge* (☎ 745-5121), which is affiliated with Alaska Youth Hostels. The lodge is 70 miles east of Palmer and has no kitchen facilities but does feature a cafe, bar and liquor store along with 12 beds. There is also a sauna, hot tub and great hiking nearby. The hostel charges $12 a night for a bunk and is open from April to September. The lodge also has comfortable cabins for $95 a night if you're not up for a bunk. There's also a restaurant that serves excellent home-made soups and sandwiches for $6 to $7.

There is also inexpensive lodging just two miles west down the road at *Mile 111.5* of the Glenn Hwy, which raises the question of why good places to stay are always next door to each other? The *Bunk 'n' Breakfast* (☎ 745-5143) offers a bunk and light breakfast for $15 per night. Bring your sleeping bag and your binoculars to search for dall sheep on Sheep Mountain just across the highway.

At *Mile 101* you reach the *Matanuska Glacier State Campground* (12 sites, $8 fee). The area has sheltered tables, water, and trails and viewing decks along a nearby bluff that provide good views of the glacier. It is a beautiful campground but, for obvious reasons, a popular one, so there is a three-day limit here.

Matanuska Glacier is a stable ice floe that is four miles wide at its terminus and extends 27 miles back into the Chugach Mountains. Some 18,000 years ago, it covered the area where the city of Palmer is today. If you want to drive near the glacier's face, swing into the *Glacier Park Resort* (☎ 745-2534), *Mile 102* of Glenn Hwy, and pay $6.50 to follow its private road to within 400 feet of the ice. At this point some people just walk to the face, while others spend a whole day on the ice. For another $6 you can also camp at this 540-acre resort which features a cafe and limited supplies. A good view of the glacier is also possible from the *Long Rifle Lodge* (☎ (800) 770-5151), where you can gaze at ice from the dining room while enjoying a good bowl of chilli. The lodge-bar-motel is passed just before the entrance to Glacier Park Resort.

The **Puritan Creek Trail** is just before the bridge over the creek (also known as Puritan) at *Mile 89* of the Glenn Hwy. There is a short dirt road that heads north of the highway and then east, passing an off-road-vehicle trail that ascends a steep hill to the north. The trail is a 12-mile walk to the foot of Boulder Creek, though most of the final seven miles is a trek along the gravel bars of the river. The scenery of the Chugach Mountains is excellent and there are good camping spots along Boulder Creek.

In the next 13 miles, the Glenn Hwy passes three public campgrounds. The first is *Long Lake State Campground* (nine sites, free) at *Mile 85.3*. Along with toilets and fire pits, the campground offers access to a grayling fishing hole that is a favorite with Anchorage's residents.

Two miles west of the Long Lake State Campground is a gravel spur road that leads to the *Lower Bonnie Lake State Campground* (eight sites, free), a two-mile side trip from the highway. The third campground is the *King Mountain State Recreation Site* (22 sites, $8 fee) at *Mile 76* of the Glenn Hwy. This scenic campground is on the banks of the Matanuska River, with a view of King Mountain to the south-east. Just outside the campground is *King Mountain Lodge* for your burger and beer along with a small market for other supplies. Across the highway is the office for Nova (☎ 745-5753), a rafting company which runs the Matanuska River daily. It offers a mild 3½-hour run at 10 am for $60 per person, and a wilder one which features Class IV rapids around Lionshead Wall, at 9 am and 2 pm for $75. All this – the scenery, the rafting and the beer store – makes the state campground a good place to pull up, or stop hitching, for a day or two.

Just before passing through Sutton (pop 850) at *Mile 61*, you come to **Alpine Historical Park** (☎ 745-7000). The park has several buildings, including the Chickaloon Bunkhouse and the original Sutton post office which now houses a museum. Inside the displays are devoted to the Athabascan people, the 1920 coal-boom era of Sutton and the building of the Glenn Hwy. The park is open from 10 am to 6 pm daily during the summer and admission is $2.

Beyond Sutton, you come to the last public campground before Palmer. The *Moose Creek State Recreation Area* (12 sites, $8 fee) is a small campground on the creek at *Mile 54.5* of Glenn Hwy which has sheltered tables, outhouses and drinking water. There is also a trail that leads up the creek for anglers. Five miles beyond Moose Creek is the junction to the Fishhook-Willow Rd which provides access to the Independence Mine State Park (see the Hatcher Pass section in the Anchorage chapter). The highway then descends into the agricultural center of Palmer.

From Palmer, Glenn Hwy merges with the George Parks Hwy and continues south to Anchorage, 43 miles away (see the Anchorage chapter).

Denali Highway

With the exception of 21 miles that is paved at its east end, the Denali Hwy is a gravel road extending from Paxson on the Richardson Hwy to Cantwell on the George Parks Hwy, just south of the main entrance to Denali National Park.

When the 135-mile route was opened in 1957 it was the only road to the national park, but it became a secondary route after the George Parks Hwy was completed in 1972. Today, the Denali Hwy is only open from mid-May to October. Most of it runs along the foothills of the Alaska Range to the north and through glacial valleys where you can see stretches of alpine tundra, enormous glaciers and braided rivers. The scenery is spectacular but the road itself can be a disaster at times. This, say most travelers, is the worst road in Alaska. Plan on at least six hours to drive it from end to end. On the other hand, it's quickly becoming a favorite for mountain bikers.

There are numerous trails into the surrounding backcountry but none of them is marked. Also in the area are two popular canoe routes. Ask locals at the roadhouses for information and take along topographic maps that cover the areas you intend to trek or paddle.

There are no established communities along the way, but four roadhouses provide food and lodging and two of them, at *Mile 20* and *Mile 81*, have gasoline for sale. If driving, it is best to fill up with gasoline at Paxson or Cantwell.

Paxson to Tangle Lakes

From Paxson, *Mile 0*, the highway heads west and passes the mile-long gravel road to Sevenmile Lake at *Mile 7*. From here, the terrain opens up and provides superb views of the nearby lakes and peaks of the Alaska Range. Most of the lakes – as many as 40 in the spring – can be seen from a lookout at *Mile 13* of the Denali Hwy.

Swede Lake Trail This trail is near *Mile 17* of the highway and leads south three miles to Swede Lake after passing Little Swede Lake in two miles. Beyond here, it continues to the Middle Fork of the Gulkana River but the trail is extremely wet at times and suitable only for off-road vehicles. Anglers fish the lakes for trout and grayling. Enquire at

INTERIOR

Denali Highway

the Tangle River Inn (☎ 822-7304) at *Mile 20* for directions to the trail and an update on its condition. The inn has a cafe, gas, canoe rentals, showers and motel rooms that begin at $45/50 for a single/double.

Canoeing The **Delta River Canoe Route** is a 35-mile paddle which begins at the Tangle Lakes BLM Campground north of the highway and ends a few hundred yards from *Mile 212.5* of Richardson Hwy. Begin the canoe route by crossing Round Tangle Lake and continuing to Lower Tangle Lake, where you must make a portage around a waterfall. Following the waterfall is a set of Class III rapids that must either be lined for two miles or paddled with an experienced hand. Every year, the BLM reports of numerous canoeists who damage their boats beyond repair on these rapids and are forced to hike 15 miles back out to the Denali Hwy. The remainder of the trip is a much milder paddle.

The **Upper Tangle Lakes Canoe Route** is easier and shorter than the Delta River route but requires four portages, none of which is marked although they are easy to figure out in the low bush tundra. All paddlers attempting this route must have

topographic maps. The route begins at Tangle River and passes through Upper Tangle Lake before ending at Dickey Lake, nine miles to the south. There is a 1.2-mile portage into Dickey Lake.

From here, experienced paddlers can continue by departing Dickey Lake's outlet to the south-east into the Middle Fork of the Gulkana River. For the first three miles, the river is shallow and mild but then it plunges into a steep canyon where canoeists have to contend with Class III and IV rapids. Most canoeists choose to either carefully line their boats or make a portage. Allow seven days for the entire 76-mile trip from Tangle Lakes to Sourdough Campground on the Gulkana River off Richardson Hwy.

Places to Stay The paved portion of the Denali Hwy ends just beyond *Mile 21*, and in another half-mile the highway reaches the BLM *Tangle Lakes Campground* (13 sites, free) to the north, on the shores of Round Tangle Lake and features displays explaining the archaeological digs in the area. A second BLM campground, *Upper Tangle Lakes* (seven sites, free), is a quarter-mile down the road on the south side. Both camp-

INTERIOR

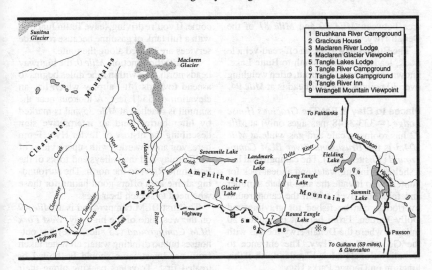

1 Brushkana River Campground
2 Gracious House
3 Maclaren River Lodge
4 Maclaren Glacier Viewpoint
5 Tangle Lakes Lodge
6 Tangle River Campground
7 Tangle Lakes Campground
8 Tangle River Inn
9 Wrangell Mountain Viewpoint

grounds serve as the departure point for two scenic canoe routes and nearby Tangle River Inn provides canoe rentals. Caribou are occasionally spotted in the surrounding hills.

Tangle Lakes to Denali National Park

At *Mile 25*, the Denali Hwy crosses Rock Creek Bridge, where the **Landmark Gap Trail** leads north three miles to Landmark Gap Lake, with an elevation of 3217 feet. You can't see the lake from the highway but you can spot the noticeable gap between the Amphitheatre Mountains.

A parking lot on the north side of the highway at *Mile 32* is the start of the three-mile **Glacier Lake Trail**.

From here, the highway ascends **Mac-Laren Summit** (elevation 4086 feet) one of the highest highway passes in the state. The summit is reached at *Mile 35.2* and has excellent views of Mt Hayes, Hess Mountain and Mt Deborah to the west and MacLaren Glacier to the north.

The MacLaren River is crossed at *Mile 42* of Denali Hwy on a 364-foot multiple-span bridge. Another bridge crosses Clearwater Creek at *Mile 56*, where nearby there are camp sites and outhouses. Beginning at *Mile*

69 is the first of many hiking trails in the area; all are unmarked and many are nothing more than old gravel roads. Enquire at the Gracious House Lodge, a roadhouse at *Mile 82*, for the exact location of the trails.

Hiking There are many hiking opportunities in the next 25 miles of the highway. The **Hatchet Lake Trail**, a five-mile walk, begins near Raft Creek just before *Mile 69* of Denali Hwy.

Denali Trail begins on the north side of the highway at *Mile 79*, a half-mile before the road crosses the Susitna River on a multiple-span bridge. It winds for six miles to the old mining camp of Denali, first established in 1907. A few of the old buildings still remain. Today, gold mining has resumed in the area. Several old mining trails branch off the trail, including an 18-mile route to Roosevelt Lake from Denali Camp. The area can provide enough hiking for a two to three-day trip, but only tackle these trails with a map and compass in hand.

The **Snodgrass Lake Trail** leads two miles south of the highway to Snodgrass Lake, known among anglers for its good grayling fishing. The trail starts at a parking area between *Mile 80* and *Mile 81* of the Denali Hwy.

The **Butte Lake Trail**, an off-road-vehicle track, leads five miles south to Butte Lake, known for its large lake trout, often weighing over 30 pounds. The trailhead is at *Mile 94.*

Places to Stay & Eat The *Gracious House Lodge* (☎ 333-3148 messages only) at *Mile 82* has rooms, a cafe and gas while at *Mile 104.3* is the *Brushkana River BLM Campground* (17 sites, free). The campground has a shelter, drinking water and a meat rack for hunters who invade the area in late summer and fall. The river, which the campground overlooks, can be fished for grayling and Dolly Varden. From here, it is another 20 miles to where the Denali Hwy merges with the George Parks Hwy. The entrance to Denali National Park is 17 miles north of this junction on George Parks Hwy.

Taylor Highway

The scenic Taylor Hwy extends 161 miles north from Tetlin Junction, 13 miles east of Tok on the Alcan, to the historic town of Eagle on the Yukon River. It is a beautiful but rough drive as the road is narrow, winding and ascends Mt Fairplay, Polly Summit and American Summit, all over 3500 feet in elevation.

The highway is the first section to Dawson City in the Yukon and offers access to the popular Fortymile River Canoe Route and much off-road hiking. As with the Denali Hwy, the problem of unmarked trailheads exists, making it necessary to have the proper topographic maps in hand. Many trails are off-road-vehicle tracks used heavily in late summer and fall by hunters.

By Alaskan standards there is light-to-moderate traffic on Taylor Hwy during the summer, until you reach Jack Wade Junction, where the majority of vehicles continue east to Dawson City. Hitchhikers going to Eagle have to be patient in the final 65 miles north of Jack Wade Junction, but the ride will come. If you're driving, leave Tetlin Junction with a full tank of gasoline because roadside services are limited along the route.

From Tetlin Junction, *Mile 0*, the highway heads north, and within nine miles begins to ascend towards Mt Fairplay which has an elevation of 5541 feet. A lookout near the summit is reached at *Mile 35* and is marked by litter barrels and an interpretive sign describing the history of Taylor Hwy. From here, you are rewarded with superb views of Mt Fairplay and the valleys and forks of the Fortymile River to the north. The surrounding alpine area offers good hiking for those who need to stretch their legs.

The first BLM campground is at *Mile 49* on the west side of the highway. *West Fork BLM Campground* (25 sites, free) has outhouses but no drinking water; all water taken from nearby streams should be boiled or treated first. Travelers packing along their gold pans can try their luck in West Fork River, which is the first access point for the paddle down Fortymile River.

CHICKEN

After crossing a bridge over the Fortymile River's Mosquito Fork at *Mile 64.4*, the Taylor Hwy passes the old **Chicken post office** on a hill beside the road, at *Mile 66.2*. The post office, still operating today, was originally established when Chicken was a thriving mining center. **Old Chicken**, the original mining camp, is now privately owned but can be viewed during a walking tour that begins at 1 pm daily at the Chicken Creek Cafe. Among the buildings you will see is the schoolhouse of Ann Purdy, who later wrote the novel *Tisha*, based on her days as a school teacher here.

The community of Chicken itself (population between 30 and 50) is 300 yards to the north on a spur road that leads to an airstrip, a grocery store, the *Chicken Creek Cafe* and a gasoline station. The town's name, according to one tale, originated at a meeting of the resident miners in the late 1800s. When trying to come up with a name for the new tent city, somebody suggested Ptarmigan, since the chicken-like bird existed in great

The ptarmigan (the 'p' is silent) was the inspiration for Chicken's name.

numbers throughout the area. All the miners liked it but none of them could spell it. The town's name has been Chicken ever since.

Just north of the spur to the village is Chicken Creek Bridge, built on tailing piles from the mining era. If you look back to the left, you can see the **Chicken Dredge** which was used to extract gold from the creek between 1959 and 1965. Most of the forks of the Fortymile River are virtually covered from one end to the other by active mining claims and often you can see suction dredging for gold from the highway. At *Mile 75.3* is the bridge over South Fork and the most popular access point for the Fortymile River Canoe Route.

FORTYMILE RIVER CANOE ROUTE
The historic Fortymile River, designated as the Fortymile National Wild River, offers an excellent escape into scenic wilderness for paddlers experienced in lining their canoes around rapids. It is also a step back into the gold-rush era of Alaska as paddlers will view such abandoned mining communities as Franklin, Steele Creek and Fortymile while undoubtedly seeing some present-day mining. The best place to start is the bridge over South Fork, because access points south of here on Taylor Hwy often are too shallow for an enjoyable trip.

A common trip is to paddle the 40 miles to the bridge over O'Brien Creek at *Mile 113* of Taylor Hwy. This two to three-day trip involves three sets of Class III rapids. A greater adventure is to continue past O'Brien Creek and paddle the Fortymile River into the Yukon River and from here head north to Eagle at the end of the Taylor Hwy. This trip is 140 miles long and requires seven to 10 days to cover, along with lining several sets of rapids in the Fortymile River. The planning and organizing for such an expedition has to be done carefully before you leave for Alaska (see the Eagle section later in this chapter for information about paddling the Yukon River).

WALKER FORK TO AMERICAN CREEK
At *Mile 82* of Taylor Hwy is the *Walker Fork BLM Campground* (18 sites, free) which lies on both sides of the highway and has tables, firewood and a short trail to a limestone bluff overlook.

A lookout is reached at *Mile 86* of the highway, where you can view the **Jack Wade Dredge**, which operated from 1900 until 1942. For most of its working days the dredge was powered by a wood-burning steam engine which required 10 to 12 cords of wood per day. The old Jack Wade mining camp is passed four miles north of the dredge; after being abandoned for 30 years the mine is now being reworked as the result of higher gold prices.

The Jack Wade Junction is at *Mile 95.7* of Taylor Hwy, and here the Top of the World Hwy (also known as the Dawson Hwy) winds 3.5 miles to the Canadian/US border and another 75 miles east to Dawson City.

INTERIOR

The Taylor Hwy continues north from the junction and ascends **Polly Summit**, with an elevation of 3550 feet. The summit is reached at *Mile 105*, and five miles beyond it is a scenic lookout where you can view the Fortymile River.

From the summit, Taylor Hwy begins a steep descent; drivers must take this section slowly. Along the way there are numerous lookouts with good views as well as a variety of abandoned cabins, old gold dredges and mine tailings. Primitive camping is possible at *Mile 134* of Taylor Hwy on the south side of a bridge over King Solomon Creek. This is a former BLM campground which has not been maintained in years. Holiday prospectors should try their luck in the nearby creek. Eagle is another 27 miles to the north.

EAGLE
History
The historic town of Eagle (pop 160) had its beginnings in the late 1800s and today is one of the best-preserved boom towns of the mining era in Alaska.

The original community, today called Eagle Village, was established by the Athabascan Indians long before Francois Mercier arrived in the early 1880s and built a trading post in the area. A permanent community of miners was set up in 1898. A year later, the US Army decided to move in and build a fort in its conviction to maintain law and order in the Alaskan Interior. A federal court was established at Eagle in 1900 by Judge Wickersham, and the next year President Theodore Roosevelt issued a charter that made Eagle the first incorporated city of the Interior.

Eagle reached its peak at the turn of the century when it had a population of over 1500 residents, and the overland telegraph wire from Valdez was completed in 1903. Some residents even went as far as to call their town the 'Paris of the North', though that was hardly the case.

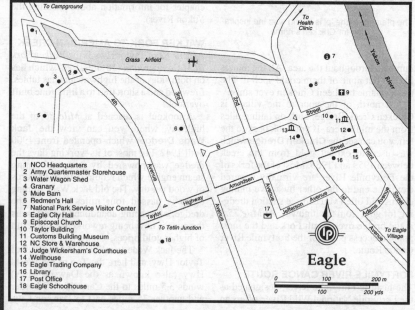

1 NCO Headquarters
2 Army Quartermaster Storehouse
3 Water Wagon Shed
4 Granary
5 Mule Barn
6 Redmen's Hall
7 National Park Service Visitor Center
8 Eagle City Hall
9 Episcopal Church
10 Taylor Building
11 Customs Building Museum
12 NC Store & Warehouse
13 Judge Wickersham's Courthouse
14 Wellhouse
15 Eagle Trading Company
16 Library
17 Post Office
18 Eagle Schoolhouse

Eagle

Other gold strikes in the early 1900s, most notably at Fairbanks, began drawing residents away from Eagle and caused the removal of Judge Wickersham's court to the new city in the west. The army fort was abandoned in 1911, and by the 1940s Eagle's population had dwindled to 10. When the Taylor Hwy was completed in the 1950s, however, the town's population increased to its present level.

Information

Tourist Office The best place for information is the National Park Service Visitor Center (☎ 547-2233), which is the headquarters for the Yukon-Charley Rivers National Preserve. Located on the banks of the Yukon River off 1st Ave, the center is open weekdays from 8 am to 5 pm.

Post The post office, on the corner of 2nd Ave and Jefferson Ave, also doubles as the US Customs office.

Bookshops You can purchase Alaska books in the National Parks Service Visitor Center or the Museum Store in Judge Wichkersham's Courthouse.

Library The public library (☎ 547-2334) is on Amundsen St just east of 1st Ave.

Laundry There is a laundromat within Eagle Trading Company at the end of Amundsen St on the banks of the Yukon River.

Medical Services The Eagle Health Clinic (☎ 547-2243) is in Eagle Township, three miles north along 1st Ave.

Things to See

If you're spending a day in Eagle, the best way to see the town and learn its history is to be in front of **Judge Wickersham's Courthouse**, on the corner of B St and 1st Ave, at 9 am. The courthouse, now a museum managed by the Eagle Historical Society, offers a walking tour of the town daily during the summer, beginning at the front porch. The tour is $3 per person and covers such

historical buildings as the **Eagle City Hall**, where the city council continues to hold regular meetings, the **Customs Building Museum** and the **Eagle post office**, where a plaque commemorates explorer Roald Amundsen's visit to Eagle.

The Norwegian explorer hiked overland to Eagle in 1905 after his ship froze in the Arctic Sea off Canada. From the town's telegraph office he sent word to the waiting world that he had just navigated the Northwest Passage. Amundsen stayed two weeks in Eagle and then mushed back to his sloop. Nine months later, the ship reached Nome completing the first successful voyage from the Atlantic to the Pacific Ocean across the Arctic Ocean.

To the north of town is **Fort Egbert**, which can be reached from Taylor Hwy via 4th Ave. The BLM has restored the old army fort, which once contained 37 buildings; several are now open to visitors during the summer, including the restored mule barn, carriage house, dog house and officers' quarters, which are clustered together in one section of the fort. There is a interpretive display explaining the renovation project.

Paddling

Yukon River Float During its heyday, Eagle was an important riverboat landing for traffic moving up and down the Yukon River. It is still an important departure point for the many paddlers who come to float the river through the Yukon-Charley Rivers National Preserve. The 150-mile Yukon River trip extends from Eagle to Circle at the end of Steese Hwy north-east of Fairbanks; most paddlers plan on six to 10 days for the float.

It is not a difficult paddle, but it must be planned carefully with air-taxi operators in order to shuttle boats, equipment and people from Circle. Floaters and paddlers should come prepared for insects and can usually camp on open beaches and river bars where winds keep the bugs down. Paddlers also need to be prepared for extremes in weather; freezing nights can be followed by daytime temperatures of 90°F.

For equipment, Eagle Commercial

INTERIOR

Company (☎ 547-2355) rents 14 and 16-foot rafts that come with rowing frames, oars, dry bags and coolers and carry four people and gear comfortably. Either size is $100 per day. Eagle Canoe Rentals (☎ 547-2203) provides canoes for travel between Dawson City or Eagle and Circle. You pick-up the boat at either the Dawson City River Hostel (☎ (403) 993-6823) or Eagle and then leave it in Circle. A four-day rental between Dawson and Eagle is $110; a five-day rental between Eagle and Circle is $160.

Check Warbelow's Air Ventures (☎ (800) 478-0812 in Fairbanks), which has offices in Fairbanks, Eagle and Circle, about a return flight. The cost for a flight between Circle and Eagle is $65 per person plus a $50 one-time flagstop fee of $50 per flight and a freight charge for any additional weight more than 40 pounds per person.

The National Park Service Visitor Center in Eagle (☎ 547-2233) has maps and books for sale and, on request, will show a video on the preserve. Write to the National Park Service (PO Box 167, Eagle, AK 99738) in advance for more information on traveling the Yukon River.

Boat Tours

There are no buses in or out of Eagle but there is the *Yukon Queen*, operated by Gray Line (☎ (403) 993-5599 in Dawson, the Yukon Territory). The tour boat makes the trip from Dawson as part of a package tour but the operators will also sell round-trip and one-way tickets in either town to fill up the empty seats.

Places to Stay

The *Eagle Trading Co* (☎ 547-2220) has rooms for $50/60 a single/double along with groceries, a cafe and public showers. The one-stop business is on Front St. Down the Yukon River at the public boat landing is *Yukon Adventure B&B* (☎ 547-2221) with doubles for $50 to $60 and spaces outside to pitch a tent. Most people camp at the *Eagle BLM Campground* (15 sites, free). To reach it, follow 4th Ave north 1.5 miles through Fort Egbert to the campground.

Top: Winter in Interior Alaska (DS)
Left: Fall colors, Mentasta Range, Interior Alaska (DS)
Right: Birch trees in winter, Fairbanks (DS)

Top: Taking a break during a midnight softball match at Talkeetna (JW)
Bottom: Junk Wagon, Fairbanks Golden Days Festival (DS)

Fairbanks

Fairbanks (pop 82,500) goes by a lot of names and descriptions. It's often referred to as the 'Golden Heart City' because of its location in the center of the state and, I suspect, the willingness of the residents to help each other out during those long, cold winters. It's also been labeled the 'Hub of the Interior' for the role it plays as the transportation center for the Bush. But perhaps the best description for Fairbanks was a slogan its Visitors Bureau came up with one summer. Fairbanks, according to the ad campaign, was 'extremely Alaska'. Oh, is it ever. Extremes are a way of life in the state's second largest city.

At first glance, Fairbanks appears to be a spread-out, low-rise city with the usual hotels, shopping malls, fast-food chains and a university tucked away on the outskirts of town. A second look reveals that this community is different, that the people and the place are one of a kind, even for Alaska.

Fairbanks has log cabins, lots of them, from the heart of town to those hidden among the trees on the back roads. It has a semiprofessional baseball team that plays games at midnight without the aid of artificial lights. It also has a golf course that claims to be the 'world's most northernmost', a college campus where if the day is clear students can view the highest mountain in North America and there are more sled dogs living here than there are horses in the bluegrass state of Kentucky.

'Extremely Alaska' is the only way to describe Fairbanks' weather. During the summer, it is pleasantly warm with an average temperature of 70°F and an occasional hot spell in August where the temperature breaks 90°F.

The days are long with more than 20 hours of light from June to August, peaking at almost 23 hours on 21 June. In the winter, however, Fairbanks is cold, when the temperature often drops to -60°F or even lower for days at a time.

HIGHLIGHTS

- Gaze at Mt McKinley from the University of Alaska-Fairbanks Campus, then visit the University Museum
- Spend an afternoon wandering through the historical buildings at Alaskaland in Fairbanks
- Rent a canoe and paddle the Chena River
- View the Midnight Sun from Eagle Summit, on or near the summer solstice on 21 June
- Marvel at the collection of gold nuggets at the District Museum in Central
- Soak in the hot tubs and pools at Chena Hot Springs

History

Consider the city's boom-or-bust economy for extremes. Fairbanks was founded in 1901 when ET Barnette was heading up the Tanana River with a boat load of supplies for the Tanacross gold fields. When the river became too shallow to travel, he convinced the riverboat captain to try the Chena. When that river was also too shallow he, his wife and his supplies, were left ashore at the present site of the corner of 1st Ave and Cushman St. Barnette could have been just another failed trading post merchant in the Great White North but the following year an Italian prospector named Felix Pedro struck gold 12 miles north of Barnette's trading post. A large boom town sprang to life amid the hordes of miners stampeding into the

Winter in Fairbanks

Summers in Fairbanks are often warm and sunny but the winters can be brutally cold. The temperature stays below 0°F for months and can drop to -60°F or even lower for days at a time. The days are short, as short as three or four hours, and the nights are cold. It's so cold in the winter that parking meters come equipped with electric plugs because cars have heaters around the transmission, oil pan and battery. When it's -60°F unprotected fingers become numb in seconds, beards and moustaches freeze and turn into icicles in minutes and a glass of water thrown out of a 2nd-floor window shatters as ice when it hits the ground.

When it's -60°F, planes don't fly into Fairbanks for fear that landing gear will freeze up, the mail isn't delivered, state employees are not required to go to work and, perhaps most unusual, tires freeze. This strange phenomenon is known as 'square tires' because the bottom of tires molds to the flat surface of the road. When you take off, they're simply pulled off the rims. ■

area and by 1908 there were more than 18,000 people residing in the Fairbanks Mining District.

But retrieving the gold proved far more challenging here than elsewhere in Alaska due to the permafrost. Gold pans and sluice boxes were of little use here because the ground firstly had to be thawed before the mineral-rich gravel could be recovered. Early miners cuts trees to thaw the ground with fires but timber was scarce this far north and eventually other gold rushes drained the city of its population. By 1920, Fairbanks had a population of a little more than a 1000.

Ironically, the city's gold mining industry outlasted any other in the state. After the Alaska Railroad reached Fairbanks in 1923, major mining companies, with money to invest in materials and machines, arrived and brought with them three-story mechanized dredges. But the key to reaching the gold was a new process that utilized needle-nose pipes to thaw the ground. Hundreds were driven into the ground by hand and then water was forced through an opening at the end of the pipes into the frozen ground. Once the ground was thawed, the dredges worked nonstop extracting the gold and turning the terrain into mincemeat.

More than $200 million in gold has been extracted from the mining district where dredges still operate today. The most famous one, however, was Gold Dredge No 8, that operated from 1928 to 1959 in recovering 7.5 million ounces of the precious metal. Eventually it was listed as a National Historical Site and today is probably the most viewed dredge in the state.

When mining activity declined, Fairbanks' growth slowed to a crawl. WWII and the construction of the Alcan and military bases produced the next booms in the city's economy, but neither affected Fairbanks like the Trans-Alaska Pipeline. After oil was discovered in Prudhoe Bay in 1968, Fairbanks was never the same. From 1973 to 1977, when construction of the Trans-Alaska Pipeline was at its height, the town burst at its seams as the principal gateway to the North Slope.

The aftermath of the pipeline construction was just as extreme. The city's population shrank and unemployment crept towards 25% through much of 1979. The oil industry bottomed out in 1986 with the declining price of crude and Fairbanks, like Anchorage, suffered through more hard times.

But like the weather, Fairbanks' residents endured all this, and will endure more busts or booms if oil companies are allowed to drill the Arctic National Wildlife Refuge. Perhaps more so than any town south of the Arctic Circle, Fairbanks' residents are a hardy and independent breed because they have to be. That, more than the log cabins or the midnight sun, is the city's trademark. The residents tend to be more colorful than most Alaskans, maybe a bit louder and a degree more boastful. They exemplify to the fullest the Alaskan theme of 'work hard, play hard, drink hard'.

Whether you enjoy Fairbanks or not depends on where you're coming from and your perceptions. If you've just spent 10 days paddling along the Noatak River in the Brooks Range, Fairbanks can be an extremely hospitable place to recoup. And an affordable one at that. Generally you'll find tourist-related businesses – hotels, taxis, restaurants etc – to be much more reasonably priced than in Anchorage. If, however, you've just arrived from such places as Homer or Juneau, the charming aspects of these towns surrounded by mountains, glaciers and the sea might blind you to what is so unique – and so extreme – about Fairbanks.

Orientation

Fairbanks, the transport center for much of the Interior, is a spread-out town that covers 31 sq miles. 'Downtown' is hard to describe and even harder to recognize sometimes. Generally, it is considered to be centered around Golden Heart Park on the corner of 1st Ave and Cushman St and spreads west to Cowles St, east to Noble St, north across the Chena River to the railroad depot and south along Cushman St as far as you want to walk. Cushman St is the closest thing Fairbanks has to a main street.

Several miles to the north-west is the university area, sprawling from the hilltop campus of UA-Fairbanks to the bars, restaurants and other businesses along University Ave and College Rd that make a living serving the college crowd. The city's other major commercial district is along Airport Way, between University Ave and Cushman St, where you'll find most of the fast-food chain restaurants, malls, and Fred Meyers store as well as many motels.

If you arrive by train, motels, B&Bs and restaurants in the downtown area are a 15-minute walk away. If you arrive by bus, you can usually get dropped off either along the Airport Way stretch or downtown. Fly in and the only way to get out of the airport (see Getting Around) is by taxi. The downtown area is a $8 fare away.

Information

Tourist Offices The main source of information is the Convention & Visitors Bureau Log Cabin (☎ 456-5774) which overlooks the Chena River near the corner of 1st Ave and Cushman St. The many services offered include a recorded telephone message (☎ 456-INFO) that lists the daily events and attractions in town; racks of brochures and information, courtesy phones to call up motels and B&Bs and a fairly knowledgeable staff. The log cabin is open daily during the summer from 8 am to 8 pm weekdays and 10 am to 4 pm Saturday and Sunday. Other visitor centers are in the Railroad Depot (open before and after each train arrival), Alaskaland and there's a limited one near the baggage claim of the Fairbanks International Airport.

Head to the Alaska Public Lands Information Center (☎ 456-0527) on Cushman St, two blocks south of the Chena River, for brochures, maps and information on state and national parks, wildlife refuges and recreation areas. The center has exhibits and video programs on a variety of topics along with a small theatre that shows nature films at 10 am, noon and 2 and 4 pm and interpretive programs daily at 3 pm. Hours for the center are from 9 am to 6 pm daily during the summer.

Money There are banks and ATMs scattered all over the city. Downtown, the Key Bank of Alaska (☎ 452-2146) is at Cushman St and 1st Ave and inside features an impressive gold nugget display.

Post The main post office is downtown on 4th Ave between Barnette St and Cushman St.

Travel Agencies Vista Travel (☎ 456-7888) is at 1211 Cushman St and US Travel (☎ 452-8992) is 609 2nd Ave.

Bookshops Gulliver's Books (☎ 474-9574, 456-3657) sells new and used books and Alaskan titles at two shops: in Campus Corner Mall on the corner of College Rd and University Ave near UAF, and at Shoppers Forum at Airport Way and Cowles St. There are also good selections of books at the Alaska Public Lands Information Center downtown and the UAF Bookstore on campus.

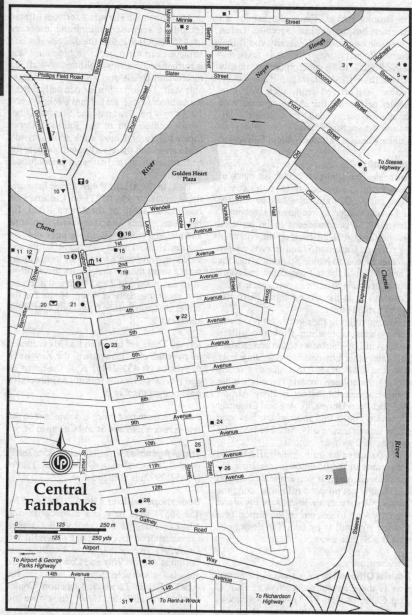

Central Fairbanks

PLACES TO STAY
1   Tamarac Inn
2   Minnie Street B&B
11 Bridgewater Hotel
15 Hotel Captain Hook
24 Westmark Fairbanks
25 Golden Nugget Motel

PLACES TO EAT
3   Burger King
5   Royal Fork Restaurant
8   June's Cafe
10 Souvlaki
12 Gambardella's Pasta Bella
17 Plate & Palette Gallery Cafe
18 Soapy Smith's
22 Thai House
26 Peking Gardens
31 Kentucky Fried Chicken

OTHER
4   Laundry/Showers
6   Graehl Landing
7   Train Station
9   Immaculate
     Conception Church
13 Key Bank of Alaska
14 Yukon Quest
     General Store & Museum
16 Visitors Bureau
     Log Cabin
19 Alaska Public
     Lands Information Center
20 Post Office
21 Woolworth's
23 Transit Park
27 Federal Building
28 Carr's Supermarket
29 Vista Travel
30 Gray Line Office

Library The excellent Noel Wien Library
(☎ 459-1020), on the corner of Airport Way
and Cowles St, is a long walk from the
Visitors Bureau (take the Metropolitan Area
Commuter Service (MACS) Blue Line bus).
Along with a large Alaskan section, the
library has a selection of more than 50 paintings and prints, many by Alaskan artists, and
a stone fireplace, so it can be a warm place
to be on a rainy day. It's open daily and until
9 pm Monday to Wednesday.

Laundry & Showers For those needing a
shower and some clean clothes, there's B&C
Laundromat (☎ 479-2696) in the Campus
Corner Mall on the corner of College Rd and

University Ave near UAF. It's open to 10.30
pm daily and showers are $2.50. In the
downtown area head north of the Chena
River to B&L Laundromat (☎ 452-1355), in
the Eagle Plaza on Third St, a block east of
Steese Hwy.

Medical Services Fairbanks Memorial Hos-
pital (☎ 452-8181) is at the corner of E
Crowles St and 14th Ave on the south side of
Airport Way.

Things to See
Downtown Next to the Visitors Bureau is the
Golden Heart Plaza, a pleasant riverside
park that is truly the center of the city. Show-
cased in the middle is the impressive bronze
statue, *The Unknown First Family*, that was
dedicated in 1986 and depicts an Athabascan
family struggling against all odds.

The **Immaculate Conception Church**,
just across the Chena River Bridge from the
plaza, was built in 1904 and was moved to
its present location in 1911. The church is a
national historic monument and features
beautiful stained glass windows. **St
Matthew's Episcopal Church**, at 1035 1st
Ave, is a unique log church built in 1905 and
rebuilt in 1947 immediately after it burned
down.

Don't overlook Fairbanks' outdoor art as
you walk around town. In 1979 local artists
painted murals, ranging from abstract art to
wildlife scenes, on 20 buildings as part of a
beautification program. Most of them can be
seen in a four-block section beginning at the
Visitors Bureau.

Alaskaland The city's largest attraction is
this 44-acre pioneer theme park created in
1967 to commemorate the 100th year of the
US possession of Alaska. Inside are such
historical displays as the *Nenana*, a former
sternwheeler of the Yukon River fleet, the
railroad car that carried President Warren
Harding to the golden spike ceremony in
1923, the home of Judge James Wickersham
and a century-old carousel that still offers
rides to the young and young-at-heart. You'll
also find here Gold Rush Town, a street of

relocated log cabins with many of them converted into giftshops, the Pioneer Air Museum and the Pioneers Museum which depicts the settlement of Alaska.

At the back of the park, you'll find the Native Village Museum and Mining Valley, with displays of gold-mining equipment. A miniature 30-gauge train, the Crooked Creek & Whiskey Island Railroad, will take the kids around the park, while at night there's entertainment at the Palace Saloon and one of the best salmon bakes in the state.

The entrance to Alaskaland is off Airport Way near Peger Rd. A free shuttle bus, made to look like a train, makes hourly runs each day between the Visitors Bureau and major hotels to the park from 4 am to 9 pm. You can also reach the park on a MACS Blue Line bus. Alaskaland (☎ 459-1087) is open daily from 11 am to 9 pm. Some visitors find a theme park in Alaska a little corny, while others think it is an enjoyable step back into Alaska's history. Whatever you may think, you can't beat the price – there is no admission fee.

University The University of Alaska-Fairbanks (UAF) is the original and main campus of the statewide college and an interesting place to wander around for an afternoon. It was incorporated in 1917 as the Alaska Agricultural College and School of Mines and began its first year with six students. Today it has more than 8,000 students and 70 degree programs despite the cold winters. The school is four miles west from the center of Fairbanks in a beautiful and unusual setting for a college; it is on a hill that overlooks the surrounding area, and on a clear day it is possible to view Mt McKinley from marked vantage points.

Stop first at the Wood Center in the middle of campus to pick up a map of the college. The building is the student center and general meeting place on campus, as it provides a cafeteria, pizza parlor, games rooms, outdoor patio, and an information desk for all activities on the campus. There is also a ride board here for those trying to hitchhike to other parts of the state or the Alcan.

Nearby is Constitution Hall where territorial delegates drafted a constitution for statehood. Now it's the site of, among other things, the University Bookstore where UAF and Nanook (school mascot) sweatshirts can be purchased.

The main tourist attraction of UAF is the excellent University Museum, which sits splendidly on top of a grassy ridge overlooking the Tanana Valley. The museum is generally regarded as one of the best in the state, rivaling the state museum in Juneau and definitely the best attraction in Fairbanks. Inside it is divided into regions of the state with each section examining the geology, history and unusual aspects of that area.

Its most famous exhibit is Blue Babe, the fully restored 36,000-year-old bison that was found preserved intact, thanks to the permafrost, by Fairbanks-area miners. Even more impressive, however, is the state's largest public gold display with nuggets large enough to make you run out and buy a gold pan. The museum is open daily in the summer from 9 am to 7 pm during the summer and to 5 pm in May and September. The admission fee is $5 – well worth it if you have the better part of an afternoon to thoroughly enjoy each exhibit.

There are free guided tours of UAF Monday through Friday at 10 am (meet at the museum) while on Wednesday you can take in free films on Alaska's mining heritage at 2 pm in the Brooks Building.

On the outskirts of the campus is the Agricultural Experiment Farm (☎ 474-7627), where the university dabbles in growing vegetables of mythical proportions as well as such small grains as barley, wheat and oats that seem best suited for the short Alaskan growing seasons.

Ironically because of the grain fields, the station is an ideal place to spot sandhill cranes, an endangered species in the rest of the country. The station is open for self-guided tours from Monday to Friday from 8 am to 8 pm and guided tours are offered at 2 pm on Friday. To reach the station take Tanana Dr west from the lower campus, bear left at the fork and continue for a mile on Sheep Creek Rd.

The UAF's Large Animal Research Station, which focuses on unique adaptations of animals to a sub-Arctic climate, is off Farmer's Loop Rd. Best known as a musk ox farm, the station also features colonies of reindeer, caribou and experimental hybrids of the two called 'reinbou' and 'carideer'. Platforms outside the fenced pastures provide visitors with a place to view the herds, but bring binoculars if you have them as the animals aren't always cooperative by grazing nearby. Viewing is free and there is a gift shop that sells, among other things, raw qiviut from the musk ox. To reach the station head north from the campus on Farmers Loop Rd, turn left on Ballaine Rd and then left again on Yanovich Rd.

Because of its lofty perch, the campus is the best place in Fairbanks to view Mt McKinley on a clear day. A turn-off and marker defining the mountainous horizon is at the south end of Yukon Dr. Call the UAF Relations office (☎ 474-7581) for more information on any UAF tour or attraction. Reach the campus by taking MACS Red or Blue Line buses right to Wood Center.

Pipeline The closest spot to view the Trans-Alaska Pipeline, where some 1.5 million barrels of oil flow daily on their way to Valdez, is at the Alyeska Visitor Center, eight miles north of the city on Steese Hwy. The turn-off is at Goldstream Rd. The center is open from Memorial Day to Labor Day from 8 am to 6 pm daily.

Sled Dogs Like a handful of other towns in Alaska, Fairbanks bills itself as the dog mushing capital of the world. It's hard to argue with them. Snow and temperatures begin dropping in early October and sled dog racers enjoy a season that often exceeds five months. The city even has a 'musher's race track'. Jeff Studdert Racegrounds is at *Mile 4* on Farmers Loop and consists of a system of groomed trails ranging in length from three to more than 20 miles.

Fairbanks is the home of the North America Sled Dog Championships, a three-day event where mushers, some with teams as large as 20 dogs, compete in a series of races. This is not the Iditarod. Speed, not endurance, is the key as the races range from 20 to 30 miles. The Alaska Dog Mushers Association, which hosts the championships, is in the process of relocating its Dog Mushers' Museum (☎ 456-6874), so give them a call to find out where it is located. Open daily from 10 am to 6 pm during the summer, the museum features exhibits on sled dog racing, of course, and videos of races and dogs in training. Among the equipment on display are the sleds used by Susan Butcher and Martin Buser to win the Iditarod.

Though the Iditarod is the best known dogsled event in Alaska, it's only one of two long-distance races. The other is the Yukon Quest, a 1000-mile run between Fairbanks and Whitehorse that was organized in 1983 along many of the early trails used by trappers, miners and the postal service.

Many will argue that the Quest is by far the tougher of the two races. Mushers climb four mountains more than 3000 feet in elevation and run along 200 miles of the frozen Yukon River. While the Iditarod has 25 checkpoints racers must stop at, the Quest has only six.

The race headquarters is at the Yukon Quest General Store (☎ 451-8985), just south of the Visitors Bureau on the corner of Cushman St and 2nd Ave. The store is open from 9 am to 7 pm daily and inside you'll find race memorabilia and souvenirs.

Gold Panning Those who are inspired by the huge gold nuggets at the University Museum, can try their own hand at panning in the Fairbanks area. If you're serious about panning, start out at Alaskan Prospectors & Geologists Supply (☎ 452-7398), at 504 College Rd, which stocks and sells all the necessary equipment for recreational prospecting. The store also has books, pamphlets and video tapes to help you strike it rich and even offers panning instructions. Hours are from 10 am to 5 pm Monday to Friday.

The next stop should be the Alaska Public Lands Information Center to research where you can pan and where you can't. Popular places in the area include Pedro Creek off the Elliott Hwy near the Felix Pedro monument and the Chatanika River off the Steese Hwy.

For the not so serious there are two gold-mining attractions that include a little panning as part of the tour. At *Mile 9* of Old Steese Hwy is Gold Dredge No 8 (☎ 457-6058), which includes gold panning as part of its $10 tour (see Steese Hwy in the Around Fairbanks section). Tours are held daily from 9 am to 6 pm. The El Dorado Gold Mine (☎ 479-7613) has a two-hour train tour on a mile-long narrow gauge track that winds through a reconstructed mining camp and culminates with visitors panning gold-laden dirt and helping the owner work a sluice box. The train departs daily from *Mile 1* of the Elliott Hwy and tickets are $25 per person.

Hiking

Unlike Anchorage or Juneau, Fairbanks does not have outstanding hiking on its door step. The best trail for an extended backpacking

The Northern Lights

Fairbanks' best attraction is also its highest one; the aurora borealis or better known as the northern lights. In the simplest of all explanations, the aurora is a phenomenon of physics that takes place 50 to 200 miles above the earth's surface. Solar winds flow across the earth's upper atmosphere, hitting molecules of gas so they light up much like the high-vacuum electrical discharge of a neon sign.

What you end up with is a solar-powered light show where waving, curtain-like light streaks across the night sky. In the dead of winter, the aurora often fills the sky with the dancing light lasting for hours. Other nights 'the event', as many call it, lasts less than 10 minutes with the aurora spinning into a giant green ball and then quickly fading. Milky green and white are the most common colors, red auroras are the rarest. In 1958, the northern sky was so bloody with brilliant red auroras that fire trucks were rushing out to the hills surrounding Fairbanks only to discover their massive forest fires were just the northern lights.

This polar phenomenon has been seen as far south as Mexico but Fairbanks is the undisputed aurora capital. Whereas somebody in upper Minnesota might witness less than 20 events a year and someone in Anchorage will see around 150, in Fairbanks you can see the lights on an annual average of 240 nights. Heading north the number begins to decrease. At the North Pole, somebody would see the lights less than 100 nights a year.

From May to mid-August, there is too much daylight in Alaska to see 'an event'. But generally by the second week of August, the aurora begins to appear in the Interior and can be enjoyed if you're willing to be awake at 2 am. By mid-September the lights are knocking your socks off and people are already asking 'did you see the lights last night'?

The best viewing in Fairbanks is in the outlying hills to distance yourself from the city lights. UAF is also a good spot to view the lights and you'll find a permanent aurora exhibit in the University Museum while its Geophysical Institute sells a informative booklet, *Understanding the Aurora* for $1.25.

If you're passing through during June or July, you're out of luck. In that case you might want to head to Ester where Leroy Zimmerman presents his *The Crown of Lights*. The photo symphony show features panoramic slides of the northern lights projected on a 30-foot screen and accompanied by classical music. It's the best view of the aurora you can get indoors. Shows are at 7 and 8 pm daily at the Firehouse Theater. Admission is $6. ∎

trip is the impressive **Pinnell Mountain Trail** at *Mile 85.5* and *Mile 107.3* of Steese Hwy (see the Hiking section in the Wilderness chapter). For a variety of long and short hikes head to the Chena River State Recreation Area. Neither area, however, is served by public transportation though hitching to the state recreation area would be fairly easy.

For information on Pinnell Mountain Trail or Summit Trail, part of the White Mountain Trail system, stop at the Public Lands Information Center or the Bureau of Land Management office (BLM; ☎ 474-2200) on the corner of Airport Way and University Ave. Practically next door to the BLM office is the Division of Parks office of Alaska Natural Resources (☎ 451-2695) with information on the Chena River State Recreation Area.

You can pick up topographic maps for anywhere in Alaska at the US Geological Survey office (☎ 456-0244) in the Federal Building at 101 12 Ave, east of Cushman St. Hours are from 8 am to 5 pm Monday to Friday.

Creamer's Field Trail A self-guided, two-mile trail winds through Creamer's Field Migratory Wildlife Refuge, an old dairy farm that has since become an Audubon bird-lover's paradise, as more than 100 species of bird pass through each year. The refuge is at 1300 College Rd (MACS Red Line bus) and the trailhead is in the parking lot adjacent to the Alaska Department of Fish & Game office (☎ 452-1531), where trail guides are available. The trail is mostly boardwalk with an observation tower along the way and lots of bugs.

Granite Tors Trail Along with the Chena Dome Trail, a 29-mile backpacking adventure (see the Wilderness chapter), there are several other good treks in Chena River State Recreation Area. The Granite Tors Trail is a 15-mile loop that provides access into the alpine area and to the unusual rock formations. The trailhead is across the road from Tors Trail State Campground, at *Mile 39* of the Chena Hot Springs Rd.

Tors are isolated pinnacles of granite popping out of the tundra. The first set of tors is six miles from the trailhead; the best group lies two miles further along the trail. The entire hike is a five to eight-hour trek and features a free-use shelter halfway along the way.

Angel Rocks Trail This 3.5-mile loop trail leads to Angel Rocks, large granite outcrops near the north boundary of the Chena River State Recreation Area. It's an easy day hike with the rocks less than two miles from the road. The posted trailhead is just south of a rest area at *Mile 49* of the Chena Hot Springs Rd. Practically across the street is the southern trailhead for the Chena Dome Trail.

Paddling

Fairbanks offers a wide variety of canoeing opportunities, both leisurely afternoon paddles and overnight trips, into the surrounding area. There are also several places to rent boats. The most convenient is 7 Bridges Boats & Bikes (☎ 479-0751) at Alaska's 7 Gables B&B, just off the river at 4312 Birch Lane. It provides canoes and a pick-up and drop-off service. Canoes are $30 a day, transport costs $1 a mile. You can even arrange to paddle down the Chena River and bike back to the downtown area.

For a guided paddle on area rivers, including the Chena, Tanana, Birch Creek and the Chantanika, call Bull Moose Canoe & Raft (☎ 474-9066). Custom trips for one to three people is $65 per person per day and includes equipment, transport and food.

Check the Wilderness chapter for a list of the Fairbanks-based outfitters that raft in the Brooks Range and Arctic National Wildlife Refuge. For a milder float, CanoeAlaska (☎ 479-5183) offers a daily four-hour float on the Upper Chena River for $40 per person including equipment, transport and lunch.

Around Town An afternoon can be spent paddling the Chena River; the mild currents let you paddle upstream as well as down. You can launch a canoe from almost any bridge crossing the river, including the Graehl

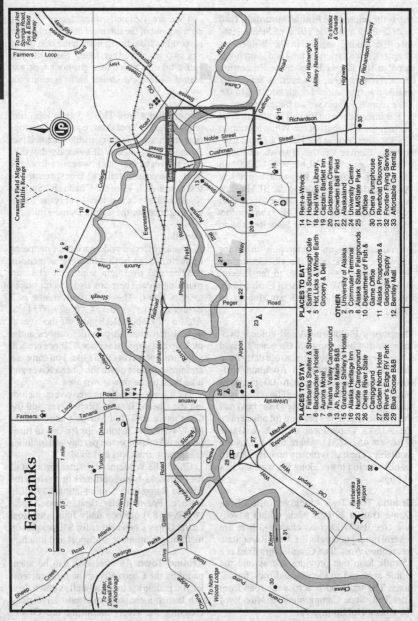

Fairbanks

To Chena Hot Springs Road, Fox & Elliott Highway

To Valdez & Canada

Creamer's Field Migratory Wildlife Refuge

Fort Wainwright Military Reservation

Old Richardson Highway

Noble Street
Cushman Street

Richardson

See Central Fairbanks Map

To Ester, Denali Park & Anchorage

Fairbanks International Airport

To North Woods Lodge

PLACES TO STAY
1 Fairbanks Shelter & Shower
6 Backpacker's Hostel
7 Aurora Motel
9 Tanana Valley Campground
13 Grandma Shirley's Hostel
16 Alaska Heritage Inn
23 Norlite Campground
26 Chena River State Campground
27 Golden North Hotel
28 River's Edge RV Park
29 Blue Goose B&B

PLACES TO EAT
4 Sam's Sourdough Cafe
5 Hot Licks & Whole Earth Grocery & Deli

OTHER
2 University of Alaska
3 Commuter Terminal
8 Alaska State Fairgrounds
10 Department of Fish & Game Office
11 Alaska Prospectors & Geologist Supply
12 Bentley Mall

14 Rent-a-Wreck
17 Hospital
18 Noel Wien Library
19 Captain Bartlett Inn
20 Goldstream Cinema
21 Growden Ball Field
22 Alaskaland
24 University Center
25 BLM/State Park Offices
30 Chena Pumphouse
31 Riverboat Discovery
32 Frontier Flying Service
33 Affordable Car Rental

Landing near the north side of Steese Hwy where locals like to paddle upstream and then float back down.

From 7 Bridges Boats & Bikes you can drop a canoe in the Chena River, head downstream and into the quiet Noyes Slough and complete the loop by paddling east back into the river. The round trip is a 13-mile journey.

Chena & Tanana Rivers Those looking for an overnight, or even longer paddle, should find out about a float down the Chena River from the Chena River Hot Springs Rd east of Fairbanks (see the Paddling section in the Wilderness chapter) or a pleasant two-day trip down the Tanana River. The popular Tanana River trip usually begins from the end of Chena Pump Rd and finishes in the town of Nenana, where it is possible to return with your canoe to Fairbanks on the Alaska Railroad. This 60-mile trip can be done in a single day but would require 10 to 12 hours of paddling.

Chatanika River The Chatanika River can be paddled for 28 miles west from Cripple Creek BLM Campground at *Mile 60* of Steese Hwy. The river runs parallel to the road to Chatanika River State Campground at *Mile 39*. From here, the trip can be extended another 17 miles to a bridge at *Mile 11* of Elliott Hwy.

The river is not a difficult paddle but this trip requires considerable driving because you have to shuttle boats and people between Fairbanks and the two highways. Many locals get around this by only paddling the upper portion of the river that parallels Steese Hwy and by leaving a bicycle chained at the end of the route so they can get back to their car.

Organized Tours
Grayline (☎ 456-7741), which has an office at 1980 S Cushman St, and Alaska Sightseeing, which departs from the Bridgewater Hotel (☎ 452-8518), offer a three-hour city tour that includes the university, Gold Dredge No 8 and the Trans-Alaska Pipeline.

The Gray Line tour is scheduled twice daily at 9 am and 2.30 pm and is $25 per person.

You can travel the Chena River on the historic sternwheeler *Riverboat Discovery* (☎ 479-6673) if you're up to parting with $37 for the four-hour trip. Along the way the boat stops at a replica of an Athabascan village and there's a demonstration with a dog musher and her team. The boat departs twice daily at 8.45 am and 2 pm in the summer from Discovery Landing, off the Dale Rd exit at *Mile 4.5* of Airport Way.

If for some strange reason you're not heading south but still want to experience Denali National Park, the Alaska Railroad (☎ 456-4155) has an overnight excursion to the park. The fare is $179 per person, based on double occupancy, and includes a return ticket, accommodation for one night and a three-hour tour along the park road.

The Arctic Circle may be an imaginary line, but it's fast becoming one of Fairbanks' biggest draws. Small air-charter companies are now doing booming business flying travelers across the Arctic Circle, landing in a small village for an hour or two and then heading back. Fort Yukon is probably the most popular destination for such a quick trip but such a tour can cost more than $200 per person. Call Larry's Flying Service (☎ 474-9169) if interested.

Special Events
Golden Days has grown to be Fairbanks' largest celebration of the summer. Staged during the third week of July, the festival commemorates Felix Pedro's discovery of gold with parades, games, booths, a boat parade on the Chena River and numerous special events such as the Hairy Legs Contest and locking up unsuspecting visitors in the Golden Days Jail. The summer solstice is also well celebrated on 21 June, when the sun shines gloriously for almost 23 hours. Events include foot races, speedboat races, art & craft booths and the traditional Midnight Sun baseball game pitting the Goldpanners against another Alaska rival in a night game in which no artificial lights are used.

Around the second week in August, the

Tanana Valley Fair is held at the fairgrounds on College Rd. Alaska's oldest fair features the usual sideshows, a rodeo, entertainment, livestock shows and large produce.

Places to Stay
Cabins Off *Mile 62* of Elliott Hwy, 10 miles before the junction with Dalton Hwy, a short spur leads from the road to **Fred Blixt Cabin**. This public-use cabin should be reserved in advance through the BLM office (☎ 474-2200) in Fairbanks. The rental fee is $20 per night.

An old trapper's cabin, **Cripple Creek Cabin**, was renovated by the BLM in 1972. It is between the Steese Hwy *(Mile 60.5)* and the Chatanika River and is reached by a short trail. The cabin, available only from mid-August to mid-May, does not offer a truly isolated setting because Cripple Creek Campground and a YCC Camp are nearby. Still, the surrounding area is scenic. The rental fee is $20 and the cabin should be reserved in advance through the Fairbanks BLM office.

In the White Mountains National Recreation Area, the relatively new **Lee's Cabin** is accessed from the Wickersham Creek Trail at *Mile 28* of the Elliott Hwy. It's a seven-mile hike in to the cabin, which features a large picture window overlooking the White Mountains and a loft that comfortably sleeps eight. Rental is $25 and the BLM is the place to reserve it in advance.

Camping The only public campground in the Fairbanks area is the *Chena River State Campground* (57 sites, $15 fee), off University Ave just north of Airport Way. The campground has tables, toilets, fire places and water, and being right on the river, a boat launch. It can be reached by MACS Blue Line bus.

If you just want to park the van or RV and don't need facilities or a hook-up, there's *Alaskaland* (☎ 459-1087) on the corner of Airport Way and Peger Rd, where spending the night in its parking lot costs $7. Even better is the *Fred Meyers* store just west along Airport Way. It's become a common practice since the store arrived for RVers and others to just spend the night in the parking lot. The store is open to 10 pm daily for restocking your supplies and there is no fee for spending the night.

Out in the university area is *Alfonsi Memorial Campground* (☎ 474-6027), in a wooded area in the north-west corner of the UAF campus. Sites are $4 a night and you can use the showers and laundry facilities in the basement of the Wood Center.

The other campgrounds in the city are private and charge from $15 to $20 per night to camp. They include the *Norlite Campground* (☎ 474-0206 or (800) 478-0206 in Alaska), on Peger Rd just south of Airport Way and the entrance to Alaskaland. Norlite has showers, laundry facilities, a small store and tent sites for $15 for two people with no vehicle, but its sites are open and close together. There's also *River's Edge RV Park* (☎ 474-0286 or (800) 770-3343), at 4140 Boat St near the corner of Airport Way and University Ave, which charges $15 for tents and $21 for hook-ups. The campground is on the Chena River and has showers, laundry facilities, shuttle service and access to the city's bike trail system. Finally *Tanana Valley Campground* (☎ 456-7956), near the fairgrounds on College Rd, has $12 tent sites, $6 if you walk or bike in.

Hostels The best thing to happen to Fairbanks is the arrival of backpackers' hostels that offer inexpensive, bunkroom-type lodging. There is an official international hostel here but it's been on the move ever since the local chapter was organized in the early 1980s. Presently the Fairbanks chapter (☎ 456-4159) is looking for a permanent location near UAF but call to double check its status.

Meanwhile there are five other hostels, all charging about $15 for a bunk. *Billie's Backpackers Hostel* (☎ 479-2034) is at 2895 Mack Rd which intersects Westwood Way (MAC Red Line). This hostel has a common kitchen, lounge area, a sun deck and an optional $5 breakfast which includes homemade sourdough bread or pancakes.

Also check out *Alaska Heritage Inn* (☎ 451-6587), an ex-bordello known as Ruthies Place, which has seven bunks as well as rooms that begin at $35. The inn is in the south Fairbanks area at 1018 22nd Ave, off South Cushman St. *North Woods Lodge* (☎ 479-5300 or (800) 478-5305 in Alaska), on Chena Hills Dr northwest of the city (for directions see under B&Bs below), has a hostel-style sleeping loft and tent sites for $8. *Grandma Shirley's Hostel* (☎ 451-9816), at 510 Dunbar near Fort Wainwright, has nine bunks in a large dorm room.

Fairbanks Shelter & Shower (☎ 479-5016), 248 Madcap Lane, is just north of UAF and has tent space, bunks and rooms. A tent space is $10, a shared two-person room is $15 and a private room is $18.

B&Bs Fairbanks has more than 100 B&Bs and most of them have a brochure in the Visitors Bureau downtown. A courtesy phone there lets you check who has a room and who's filled for the night. The Fairbanks Association of Bed & Breakfast also publishes a brochure with more than 50 members listed in it and a map showing their locations. Pick it up at the Visitors Bureau.

If you're arriving by train or bus, *Ah, Rose Marie* (☎ 456-2040) on the corner of Cowles St and 3rd Ave, within easy walking distance of the depot, has singles/doubles that start at $50/65. Even closer is *Minnie Street B&B* (☎ 456-1802), at 345 Minnie St on the same side of the river as the depot. The rooms range from $65 to $95.

If you have a vehicle, try the *North Woods Lodge* (☎ 479-5300) on Chena Hills Dr north-west of the city. It is reached from Chena Ridge Rd by turning south on Chena Pump Rd, then turning west on Roland Rd to Chena Hills Dr. Cabins and rooms are $35/40 for single/double and the lodge has laundry facilities, common kitchen and bike rentals. Nearby is the *Blue Goose B&B* (☎ 479-6973 or (800) 478-6973), at 4466 Dartmouth St off Chena Pump Rd, with rooms for $55 to $75 for two that includes a piece of Alaskan rhubarb pie with breakfast.

Hotels Most hotel/motel rooms in Fairbanks are not as expensive as those in Anchorage, but be prepared to pay $80 per night during the summer, especially when you add the 8% city bed tax. The few with reasonable rates are less than desirable or are a considerable distance from the city center.

Of the places clustered downtown on the east side of Cushman St check out the room before handing over your money. *Hotel Captain Hook* (☎ 452-4456), on 1st Ave across from the Visitors Bureau, often has rooms discounted at $70 for a single or double. If it doesn't, try *Alaskan Motor Inn* (☎ 452-4800) at 419 4th Ave, where rooms begin at $59 and those on the top floor are the best. The *Tamarac Inn* (☎ 456-6406), on the north side of the Chena River, is within easy walking distance from the railroad depot at 252 Minnie St. Singles/doubles cost $74/80; some units have cooking facilities.

By heading away from the city center you can find better rates and cleaner rooms. Try *Noah's Rainbow Inn* (☎ 474-3666) at 700 Fairbanks St, reached by heading west on Geist Rd from University Ave or by jumping on the MACS Blue Line. Rooms are small but are $40/45 for single/double and the inn features shared baths and a kitchen as well as having a coin-operated laundry on site. The *Golden North Motel* (☎ 479-6201 or (800) 447-1910) at 4888 Airport Way has rooms with cable TV, rolls and coffee in the office and free van service within the city. Rooms tend to be on the small side and begin at $69 for single or double. Closer to the downtown area at 1909 Airport Way is *Super 8 Motel* (☎ 451-8888) with clean, big rooms that cost $89/97 a single/double.

Finally, if you've just spent 10 days in the Bush and want to splurge, check into the *Bridgewater Hotel* (☎ 452-6661), downtown at 723 1st Ave. The hotel is one of the nicest in Fairbanks and certainly has the best location overlooking the Chena River. Singles/doubles cost $125/130 a night.

Places to Eat
Downtown A relatively inexpensive breakfast of two eggs and toast for $4, a hamburger

or even dinner is available at the grill in *Woolworth's* at 302 Cushman St. If you need to catch the morning train, there's *June's Cafe*, right in front of the railroad depot on Illinois St for good lunch-counter breakfasts served anytime and home-made soup. The cafe opens up at 6 am. Nearby, on the north side of the Chena River at 112 North Turner, is *Souvlaki* for gyros, spinach & cheese pie, stuffed grape leaves and lunch specials that start at $5.

More interesting places include *Soapy Smith's* at 543 2nd Ave. Despite the fact that Smith is a Skagway character and never set foot in Fairbanks, the restaurant has good hamburgers, including a half-pounder for $7, as well as deli sandwiches, salads and good clam chowder served in a saloon atmosphere. The full menu is often posted in Golden Heart Plaza. Next door to Bridge-water Hotel on 1st Ave but with an entrance on 2nd Ave is *Gambardella's Pasta Bella*, for home-made pasta dinners that begin at $11 as well as pizza. Its outdoor cafe is a delight during Fairbanks' long summer days. At the corner of 1st Ave and Noble St is *Plate & Palette Gallery Cafe* that specializes in veg-etarian dishes on the menu and local artwork on the walls. Sandwiches are $4 to $7, dinners $13 to $18.

By walking south on Cushman St, you'll reach several more restaurants, including *Thai House* on 5th Ave. *Peking Gardens* is on the corner of 12th Ave and Noble St and has a daily lunch buffet special for $7, dinners range from $8 to $11. Nearby on Gaffney Rd, just off Cushman St is *Carr's*, the city's best supermarket that is open 24 hours. Besides produce and groceries, you'll find an excellent salad and soup bar as well as a deli, bakery and the 'Orient Express' counter. The store also has seating inside and outside on an enclosed deck.

Airport Way This is Fairbanks' answer to your craving for fast food just like you eat at home. Between Cushman St and University Ave, you have *McDonald's*, *Pizza Hut* with a lunch buffet, *Burger King*, and a *Denny's* that will even give you a souvenir card

saying you ate in the 'Farthest North Denny's in the World'. Hungry souls should take in the *Alaskaland Salmon Bake* (free shuttle bus from major hotels, including the Bridgewater), where for $19 you not only get grilled salmon but halibut, spareribs and salad.

Along Airport Way is the *Food Factory* (other outlets in Bentley Mall and South Cushman St), which has cheap subs and other sandwiches that can be enjoyed with your favorite beer. Good soup, sandwiches and espresso drinks are also available at *Alaska Espresso & Chowder House* at 3226 Airport Way, east of University Center. The best Mexican restaurant is *Los Amigos*, near the corner of 28th Ave and Cushman St, south of Airport Way.

University Area More food chains can be found around UA-Fairbanks area but also some unique eateries. *Hot Licks* on the corner of College Rd and University Ave has delicious home-made ice cream, home-made soups and cinnamon rolls and an espresso bar. It's open until 11 pm from Monday to Saturday for that late-night cappuccino. Several blocks south at 1157 Deborah St is *Whole Earth Grocery & Deli* for natural foods, organic produce and a lunch menu of veggie sandwiches and salads. Just south on University Ave you can have good sour-dough pancakes anytime of the day at *Sam's Sourdough Cafe*, as well as lunch and dinner that can be enjoyed in an outdoor eating area. To the west at the fairgrounds on College Rd the *Tanana Valley Farmers' Market* is held throughout much of the summer from noon to 5 pm on Wednesday and 9 am to 4 pm on Saturday. Come in late August and you can buy a 20-pound cabbage, enough for a month's supply of coleslaw.

Fine Dining The best place around town to turn dinner into an evening is the *Pumphouse* (☎ 479-8452), two miles from downtown on Chena Pump Rd. The Pumphouse, once used in the gold-mining era, is now a national historical site that houses a restaurant and saloon. The atmosphere is classic gold rush;

inside and out there are artefacts and relics from the city's mining era. Dinners cost from $18 to $26, or you can go there simply to enjoy a drink while taking in the boat traffic on the Chena River. The MACS Blue Line bus includes the restaurant in its run.

Another enjoyable spot for fine dining is *Two Rivers Lodge* (☎ 488-6815), 16 miles out on Chena Hot Springs Rd. The lodge offers a rustic décor in a natural setting away from town with the drive out being almost as pleasant as the meal itself. The *Turtle Club* (☎ 457-3883), on Old Steese Hwy in Fox, also get high marks for its seafood and salad bar.

Entertainment
Cinemas Fairbanks' largest movie house is *Goldstream Cinema* (☎ 456-5113), on the corner of Airport Way and Lathrop St, and features eight screens. Shows that start before 6 pm are only $3.50.

Theater Interested in a little culture in the Far North? Then you must check out the *Fairbanks Shakespeare Theatre* (☎ 457-POET). During July the group performs a Shakespeare classic at the Birch Hill Ski Area north of Fairbanks. They call it 'Shakespeare amongst the aspens'. Performances are staged on various days throughout the month and begin at 9 pm. Tickets are $12 per person. Bring a lawn chair, blanket or sleeping bag to sit on.

Saloons The bar rooms are the best place to meet locals in Fairbanks, and it seems you never have to travel far to find one. Rowdy saloons that are throwbacks from the mining days are the area's specialty. The *Palace Saloon* (☎ 456-5960) at Alaskaland is alive at night with honky-tonk piano, turn-of-the-century can-can dancers and other acts in the 'Golden Heart Revue' performed on its large stage. Show time is at 8.15 pm nightly and admission is $11.

The *Malemute Saloon*, seven miles west of Fairbanks in Ester, also offers music, skits and vaudeville acts and its ritual of reading Robert Service poetry. The bar is a classic

while the show is perhaps one of the best locally produced acts in Alaska. They'll have you laughing in the sawdust by the end of the evening. Showtime is at 9 pm daily and during July a second show is added at 7 pm. Admission is $11 per person. There's free bus transport from Fairbanks that stops at major hotels, including the Bridgewater. Or you can make it an evening by booking a room or a tent site at Ester Gold Camp (see Ester in the Interior chapter).

Music Other lively establishments are *Dog Sled Saloon* in the Captain Bartlett Inn at 1411 Airport Way, whose motto is 'No Cover, No Dress Code, No Taste'; and the *Howling Dog Saloon* in Fox, at the intersection of the Steese and Elliott highways 12 miles north of the city center and practically across the street the *Fox Roadhouse*. All these places have live music or entertainment. The Howling Dog has rock & roll bands and as well as volleyball games and horseshoes played out the back under the midnight sun. Fox Roadhouse books country bands.

Pubs & Bars If you're here in September, live music and a college atmosphere is found at the *University Pub* in the Wood Center at UAF once classes are in session. In the city center, try *The Big I Bar*, the local hang-out for city workers and reporters from the *Daily News-Miner*. The bar is north of the Chena River near the railroad depot on North Turner Rd. Another spot to meet locals is *LA*, the bar downstairs from Los Amigos restaurant near the corner of 28th Ave and Cushman St south of Airport Way.

Spectator Sport
The Goldpanners baseball team is Fairbanks' entry in a semipro league made up of teams of top college and amateur players from around the country which compete each summer. More than 80 professionals, including Tom Seaver, Dave Winfield and Barry Bonds, have played in what began as an all-Alaska baseball league but now includes teams from Hawaii, Nevada and other states

as well. Games are played at Growden Memorial Park on the corner of Wilbur St and 2nd Ave. Games start at 7.30 pm and admission is $5.

Getting There & Away

Air The Fairbanks International Airport serves as the gateway for supplies and travelers heading into the Brooks Range and Arctic Alaska. The airport is almost four miles south-west of the city off Airport Way.

Alaska Airlines (☎ 474-0481) provides eight daily flights to Anchorage, where there are connections to the rest of the state, as well as a direct flight from Fairbanks to Seattle. The one-way standard fare to Anchorage is normally around $100 to $150 but air-fare wars have pushed it to as low as $40 at times, making it cheaper than taking the train or bus. Delta Air Lines (☎ (800) 221-1212) also offers a handful of flights between the two cities while Air North Canada (☎ (800) 764-0407 in Alaska) provides service to Dawson City with a connecting flight to Whitehorse.

For travel into Arctic Alaska, there's *Frontier Flying Service* (☎ 474-0014) and *Larry's Flying Service* (☎ 474-9169) with offices/terminals next door to each other off University Ave on the east side of the airport. There's a regularly scheduled flight to more than 30 villages, including Nome, Kotzebue and Galena. The round-trip fare to Bettles, to access Gates of the Arctic National Park, costs from $226; to Fort Yukon $150 and Nome $506.

Bus From Fairbanks, *Alaskon Express* (☎ 456-7741) stops at Delta Junction, Tok and then overnights at Beaver Creek in the Yukon. The next day you can make connections onto Haines or Whitehorse. Buses depart from the Westmark Fairbanks at 820 Noble St in the city center at 8 am Sunday, Tuesday and Friday during the summer. The one-way fare from Fairbanks to Tok is $67 and to Haines $180 (lodging at Beaver Creek is not included).

Alaska Direct Busline (☎ (800) 770-6652) makes the Fairbanks-Whitehorse run at 9 am on Sunday, Wednesday and Friday. It seems to move its pick-up point every summer so call to find out which hotel the buses depart from. The one-way fare to Whitehorse is $120.

Van service is the cheapest way to reach Denali National Park other than hitching. Both *Fireweed Express* (☎ 452-0521) and *Parks Highway Express* (☎ 479-3065) offer daily transport to the park with a van departing the Visitors Bureau between 7 and 8 am and arriving at the park's Visitor Access Center around 10.30 am, two hours before the train does. Parks Highway Express is slightly cheaper with a one-way fare of $20, round-trip $40. Fireweed Express is probably a little more dependable.

Train The Alaska Railroad (☎ 456-4155) has an express train that departs Fairbanks daily at 8.30 am from late May to mid-September. The train reaches Denali National Park around noon and Anchorage at 8.30 pm. The railroad depot is at 280 North Cushman St, a short walk from the Chena River. The one-way fare to Denali National Park is $50 and to Anchorage $95. If you plan to take the train, arrive at the depot a few minutes early to take in the model train that is maintained by the Tanana Valley Railroad Club. It's as extensive a model train as you'll see, complete with mountains, tunnels, entire towns and, this being Alaska, a glacier. The display fills a room of its own at the depot.

Hitchhiking Thumbing is made much easier by jumping on a MACS bus first. Hitchhikers heading towards Denali National Park and Anchorage on George Parks Hwy should take the Blue Line bus and get off on the corner of Geist St and the George Parks Hwy. To head down Richardson Hwy towards Delta Junction and the Alcan, jump on the Green Line Bus for the Santa Claus House on Richardson Hwy in North Pole.

Getting Around

The Airport There's no Metropolitan Area Commuter Service (MACS) bus to the airport; the closest stop is a 1.5-mile hike from the airport at the University Center on the corner of Airport Way and University Ave. GO Transportation Services (☎ 474-3847) or a taxi from the airport to downtown costs around $8.

Bus MACS provides local bus transport in the Fairbanks area from 6.25 am to 7.45 pm Monday to Friday with limited services on Saturday and none on Sunday. Transit Park, on the corner of Cushman St and 5th Ave, is the central terminal for the system as all buses pass through here. There are now three runs with a Green Line heading from the Transit Park downtown out to North Pole on the Richardson Hwy. The Blue Line runs from the Transit Park west via Airport Way and the university. The Red Line goes from the hospital on the south side of Airport Way, through the city and to the university via College Rd.

The fare is $1.50, although you can purchase an unlimited day pass for $3. For more information call the Transit Hotline (☎ 459-1011) which gives daily bus information.

There is also the Alaskaland Tram which runs daily from 11.30 am to 9 pm and passes the Visitors Bureau and a few of the major hotels (Westmark Inn, Golden Nugget) every hour. It heads west along 1st Ave to Alaskaland before heading back to the city center along Airport Way and Cushman St. It's limited transport but it's free.

Car For two or three travelers, a used-car rental is the cheapest way of getting around the city and outlying areas such as Chena Hot Springs. What the operators won't let you do, however, is drive the rough Steese, Elliott or Dalton highways, to visit such places as the Circle or Manley Hot Springs. In fact you might have to search around to find a place that will let you take a rental 'out on the road'.

The cheapest of the cheap rentals is *Affordable Car Rental* (☎ (800) 471-3101), at 3101 Cushman St, south of Airport Way, which has some small compacts for $30 a day. Nearby, *Rent-A-Wreck* (☎ 452-1606) at 2105 Cushman St has compacts for $42 per day with free pick-up. Also check with *Arctic*

Rent-A-Car (☎ 479-8044) at the airport which offers one-way rental between Anchorage and Fairbanks.

Bicycle Like so many other towns, Fairbanks is well on its way to putting together a fine network of signposted bike routes in and around the city. Bike paths begin at 1st Ave and Cushman St and extend all the way past Alaskaland, across the Chena River and to UAF and Parks Hwy. Shoulder bikeways lead you out of town.

You can pick up a free *Fairbanks Area Bicycle Map* at the Visitors Bureau and then rent a single or 10-speed for $10 a day from 7 Bridges Boats & Bikes (☎ 479-0751) at Alaska's 7 Gables B&B, 4312 Birch Lane. One of the more popular rides is to head north on Illinois St and then loop around on College Rd and Farmers Loop Rd for a ride of 17 miles.

Around Fairbanks

NORTH POLE
Back in the 1940s, a group of residents was kicking around names for their crossroad hamlet south-east of Fairbanks and somehow 'Mosquito Junction' just wasn't very appealing. So they settled on North Pole, Alaska. While the name hasn't brought in any Fortune 500 companies, a steady stream of camera-toting tourists has been wandering through ever since.

Today the funky little town (pop 1600) keeps up the Christmas theme year-round with holiday decorations and trimmings even if it's 80°F in July. You can wander down streets named Kris Kringle Dr and Mistletoe Lane or do your wash at Santa's Suds Laundromat. The town comes alive in December when radio stations from around the world call City Hall with disc jockeys asking what the temperature is or if 'Santa Claus really lives there'? And at the North Pole Post Office, at 325 South Santa Claus Lane, more than 400,000 pieces of mail arrive annually simply addressed to 'Santa Claus, North Pole, Alaska'.

The biggest attraction in town is **Santa Claus House**, a sprawling barn-like store that claims to be the 'largest theme gift shop in Alaska'. Here you'll find endless aisles of Christmas ornaments and toys, the largest Santa in the world and the 'North Pole' a candy-striped post. It's on the Richardson Hwy between the North Pole exits and is open until 8 pm daily. There's also **Jesus Town**, a sod-roofed log cabin community that surrounds KJNP, the 'Gospel Station at the Top of the Nation', off the Richardson Hwy off Mission Rd. A half-mile to the north is the Chamber of Commerce Log Cabin (☎ 488-2242) for information, and free tent camping is available at the *North Pole Public Park* on 5th Ave.

The town is about 15 minutes south of Fairbanks and reached on the MACS Green Line. Gimmicky? Sure, but if you have nothing else to do on an afternoon in Fairbanks, why not?

CHENA HOT SPRINGS ROAD
Chena Hot Springs Rd extends 56 miles east off Steese Hwy to the hot springs of the same

name. The road is paved and in good condition. The resort, the closest of the three hot-spring resorts to Fairbanks, is also the most developed as it has been turned into a year-round facility offering downhill skiing in the winter.

From *Mile 26* to *Mile 51*, the road passes through the middle of the **Chena River State Recreation Area**, a 254,080-acre preserve containing the river valley and the surrounding alpine areas. This is a scenic park that offers good hiking (see the Fairbanks Hiking section), fishing and two public campgrounds.

The first is *Roseship State Campground* (25 sites, $8 fee) at *Mile 27* of Chena Hot Springs Rd, whose large, flat gravel pads makes it a favorite with RVers. Further to the east at *Mile 39.5* is *Tors Trails State Campground* (20 sites, $8 fee) with large sites in a stand of spruce with a canoe launch on the Chena River. Across the highway is the trailhead for the Granite Tors Trail (see Hiking, Fairbanks). Both campgrounds tend to be popular during the summer but there are many gravel turn-offs along the road for the nights when they are full.

Just before the fifth bridge over the Chena

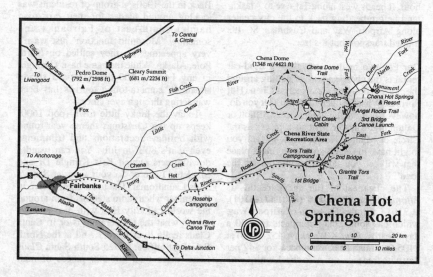

River at *Mile 49* of Chena Hot Springs Rd is the turn-off for the 3.5-mile Angel Rocks Trail (see Hiking, Fairbanks).

The trailhead for the **Chena Dome Trail** is at *Mile 50.5* of Chena Hot Springs Rd. The trail follows the ridge for almost 30 miles around the Angel Creek drainage area (see the Hiking section in the Wilderness chapter).

Chena Hot Springs

At the end of the Chena Hot Springs Rd is the Chena Hot Springs Resort (☎ 452-7867 or (800) 478-4681 in Alaska), which recently has added horseback riding to its many other facilities. The springs themselves were discovered by gold miners in 1905 and first reported by the US Geological Survey field teams two years later. By 1912, Chena Hot Springs was the premier place to soak for residents in the booming town of Fairbanks. It still is. The busy season for this resort, by far, is winter and often during midweek in the summer you can score on some impressive 'slow season discounts'.

The springs are at the center of a 40-sq mile geothermal area and produce a steady stream of water that's so hot, at 156°F, it must be cooled before you can even think about a soak. The most popular activity is hot-tub soaking, done indoors where there are two jacuzzis, a pool and a hot (very hot) tub. The resort has a restaurant, a bar and a huge fireplace in the lounge. Hotel rooms are $85 per couple per night, rustic cabins begin at $50. There are also large cabins with sleeping lofts that hold six for $110.

If there are only one or two of you, head for the campground, where a site is $10 per night. The use of the hot tubs is extra for campers; $8 for unlimited day use; $6 after 7 pm.

Getting There & Away

Call the resort to book shuttle-van service. Round-trip transport is $55 per person and a minimum of two people are needed. Hitchhiking is not the grand effort it is on the Elliott Hwy because of the heavy summer usage of the Chena River State Recreation Area.

STEESE HIGHWAY

Circle Hot Springs lies off the 162-mile long Steese Hwy, once a miners' trail, where today you can still see the signs of old mining camps as well as new ones. The road is paved for the first 44 miles and then consists of a good gravel base to Central then in the final 30 miles narrows and becomes considerably rougher. The excellent scenery along the highway and the good accommodation at Circle Hot Springs make this side trip well worth the time and money.

The Steese Hwy starts in Fairbanks, *Mile 0*, at the junction of Airport Way and Richardson Hwy. From there, it passes the beginning of Chena Hot Springs Rd at *Mile 4.6* and then Elliott Hwy at *Mile 11* near Fox, a small service center and your last opportunity to purchase beer, other supplies and gas at a reasonable price. The golden past of Steese Hwy can first be seen at *Mile 9.5*,

---

Hot Springs near Fairbanks

Back around the turn of the century, when gold prospectors were stooping in near-freezing creeks panning for gold, there was one saving grace in the area – the hot springs. There are three of them around Fairbanks and all were quickly discovered and used by the miners as a brief escape from Alaska's ice and cold. Today, the same mineral water, ranging in temperature from 120 to 150°F, soothes the aches and pains of frigid travelers passing by.

The hot springs include: Chena Hot Springs, 56 miles east of Fairbanks; Circle Hot Springs, 135 miles north-east of Fairbanks on Steese Hwy; and Manley Hot Springs, 152 miles west of Fairbanks on Elliott Hwy. Hitchhiking Chena Hot Springs Rd is possible, while Steese Hwy will require a little more patience and Elliott Hwy is a challenge to even the hottest thumb.

There is a shuttle service to Chena or you can rent a car (see the Fairbanks Getting Around section). If driving, you'll find Chena Hot Springs Rd a paved and pleasant drive; Steese Hwy paved for the first 40 miles and then a well-maintained gravel road beyond that; and Elliott Hwy a dusty long haul like the Denali Hwy or the road to McCarthy. ■

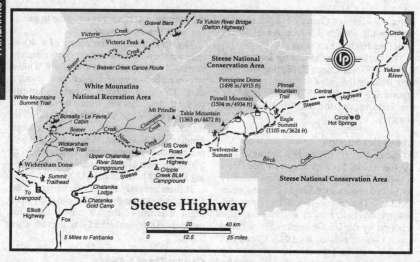

Victoria
Creek
Gravel Bars
To Yukon River Bridge
(Dalton Highway)
Circle
Victoria Peak
Creek
Beaver
Steese National
Conservation Area
Yukon
River
Beaver Creek Canoe Route
White Mounatins
National Recreation Area
Porcupine Dome
(1498 m/4915 ft)
Pinnell
Mountain
Trail
Central
Highway
White Mountains
Summit Trail
Pinnell Mountain
(1504 m/4934 ft)
Steese
Borealis - Le Fevre
Cabin
Mt Prindle
Table Mountain
(1363 m/4472 ft)
Eagle
Summit
(1105 m/3624 ft)
Circle
Hot Springs
Beaver
Creek
Champion
Creek
Nome
Wickersham
Creek Trail
Creek
US Creek
Road
Twelvemile
Summit
Wickersham Dome
Upper Chatanika
River State
Campground
Highway
Cripple
Creek BLM
Campground
Birch
Creek
Steese National Conservation Area
Summit
Trailhead
Steese
To
Livengood
Chatanika
Lodge
Chatanika
Gold Camp
Steese Highway
Elliott
Highway
Fox
5 Miles to Fairbanks
0   20   40 km
0   12.5   25 miles

where it passes the Goldstream Rd exit to **Gold Dredge No 8**, a five-deck, 250-foot dredge built in 1928 and named a national historical site in 1984. The dredge operated until 1959 and before it was closed had displaced 1065 tons of pay dirt from Pedro, Engineer and Goldstream creeks. No 8 is still making money, it's probably the most visited dredge in Alaska. Tours, which include actually stepping onto the dredge and panning for gold afterwards, are held daily from 9 am to 6 pm and are $10 per person.

At *Mile 16.6*, on the east side of the highway, is the **Felix Pedro Monument**, commemorating Felix Pedro whose discovery of gold nearby resulted in the boom town that was to become Fairbanks. Amateur gold panners are often in the nearby stream 'looking for color' or you can go another 10 miles to see a much more serious attempt at obtaining the metal. At *Mile 27.9* you take a sharp turn up a hill to reach the old gold camp at **Chatanika**. The support center was built in 1925 for the gold dredging that went on from 1927 to 1957 and removed an estimated $70 million in gold at yesterday's prices.

The *Chatanika Gold Camp* (☎ 389-2414) is another national historical site and lodge

with singles/doubles in the bunkhouse for $50/60 and small cabins for $65. The camp also has a great sourdough breakfast served from 10 am to 2 pm every Sunday. For $9 you get an all-you-can-eat buffet with sourdough pancakes (of course), sourdough biscuits, eggs, French toast, potatoes, sweet rolls – the list goes on – in a mining-camp dining room with a 12-foot-long wood stove.

Another mile up the road is *Chatanika Lodge* (☎ 389-2164), another log lodge with moose heads, bear skins and mining artefacts hanging all over the walls of the dining room and saloon. Single/double rooms are $45/50.

The first public campground along the Steese Hwy is the *Upper Chatanika River State Campground* (25 sites, $8 fee) on the river at *Mile 39*. Water and firewood are usually available, but have your bug dope handy – this is mosquito country. Those with a canoe can launch their boat here and the fishing for grayling is generally good. The next campground is the *Cripple Creek BLM Campground* (21 sites, $10 fee) at *Mile 60*, the site of the uppermost access point to the Chatanika River Canoe Trail (see Paddling, Fairbanks). The campground has tables, water and a nature trail nearby.

Access points for the Pinnell Mountain Trail (see the Hiking section in the Wilderness chapter) lie at *Mile 85.6* and *Mile 107* of the Steese Hwy. The first trailhead is Twelvemile Summit, and even if you have no desire to undertake the three-day trek, the first two miles is an easy climb to spectacular views of the alpine area and past some unusual rock formations.

The **Birch Creek Canoe Route** begins at *Mile 94* of the Steese Hwy, where a short road leads down to a canoe launch on the creek. The wilderness trip is a 140-mile paddle to the exit point at *Mile 147* of the highway. The overall rating of the river is Class II, but there are some Class III and Class IV parts that require lining your canoe. More details on the trip can be obtained from the Fairbanks BLM office (☎ 474-2200).

Eagle Summit (3624 feet) is at *Mile 107*, where you'll find a parking area and a display for the second trailhead of the Pinnell Mountain Trail. A climb of less than a mile leads to the top of Eagle Summit, the highest point along the Steese Hwy and a place where the midnight sun can be observed skimming the horizon around the summer solstice on 21 June. The summit is also near a caribou migration route. The next 20 miles, from Eagle Summit to the town of Central, is a scenic stretch of the Steese Mountains with the exception being the streams and creeks. Practically every one of these mountains has been marred and eroded to piles of rubble and tailings due to gold mining. Most of the operations are small and involve sluicing the rock with water from the creek. It's amazing how much of a creek bed or hillside the miners will chew up in their quest to find the precious metal. To environmentalists and others unaccustomed to active mining, it's repulsive.

Central
At *Mile 127.5*, the highway reaches Central (population 400 in the summer) where it's briefly paved and there are gasoline and groceries, a post office and various places to stay including a motel and cabins for rent.

History Originally referred to on maps as Central House, the town began as a supply stop on the trail from Circle City to the surrounding creeks of the Circle Mining District. Central became a town in the 1930s, thanks largely to the Steese Hwy that was built in 1927, and then in the late-1970s and early 1980s experienced something of a second gold rush.

With the price of the metal bouncing between $300 and $400 an ounce, miners were suddenly making a fortune sluicing the streams. One miner alone, Jim Regan, recovered 26,000 ounces of gold between 1979 and 1986 from the Crooked Creek area. Even more interesting was a diamond that was recovered by gold miners in 1982. Nicknamed 'Arctic Ice', it was the first diamond ever recovered from Alaska.

Although the mining activity has dwindled in recent years and most efforts are now small family operations, the miners' distrust of anybody or any agency threatening their right to make a living still looms throughout the town, especially at the bars.

Things to See & Do One of the best museums of any small Alaskan town is the Circle District Museum (%y520-1893), right on the Steese Hwy in Central. Established in 1984, the main portion of the museum is a large log lodge that houses a miner's cabin, exhibits on early mining equipment and dog-team freight and mail hauling and the Yukon Press, the first printing press north of Juneau which produced Interior Alaska's first newspaper.

But by far the most interesting display is the museum's collection of gold nuggets and gold flakes, recovered and donated by local miners. This, more than anything else, will help you understand why they continue to tear away at the hills and streams in an effort to find the precious metal.

Outside in a large barn is a collection of dog sleds and other large artefacts including an unusual covered wagon – covered with metal, not cloth. The museum also has a small video area with tapes on mining and a variety of topics, a gift shop, and a visitors' information area. Most amazing, it's open and staffed daily from noon to 5 pm during the summer. Admission is $1.

One of the things the museum sells is gold pans but before you go splashing around in the local creeks trying to find nuggets of your own, be aware that most streams are staked and to wander uninvited onto somebody's claim is asking for a nasty encounter with a miner or even worse – having a few pot shots aimed at your head. If you are swept up by the gold fever of this town, the safest place to pan is wherever the Steese Hwy crosses a creek or stream.

Places to Stay & Eat In town is the *Central Motor Inn* (☎ 520-5228) which has it all – rooms, camp sites, showers, cafe, gas, you name it. Rooms are $38 for a shared bath, $60 for a bath of your own and showers are $3 per person. The cafe is perhaps the best place to eat anywhere on the Steese Hwy. Three eggs with toast and potatoes is less than $5 and at night it often has specials for around $10. If the bugs are not too vicious you can enjoy the meal on an outdoor deck under the midnight sun.

Groceries and other supplies can be purchased at *Witt's End* which also has a cafe and laundromat.

Circle Hot Springs

Just beyond Central, the Circle Hot Springs Rd heads south and in six miles passes the site of a former BLM campground along Ketchem Creek. There are no facilities here but it' still the best place to pitch a tent in the area. Two miles beyond the creek is *Circle Hot Springs Resort* (☎ 520-5113), a popular spot with Fairbanks residents.

The springs were first used by Kutchin Indians and then miners began soaking in the naturally hot water at the turn-of-the-century. The resort followed 30 years later when Frank Leach arrived and made the development of the springs his lifelong obsession. Leach started by building Alaska's first runway specifically designed for airplanes in 1924 and then followed this

by building his impressive four-story hotel in the early 1930s, hauling most of the materials down the Yukon River to Circle City and then overland by wagon to the springs.

Now listed on the National Register of Historical Sites, the hotel is a classic. Inside the lobby and lounge there are artefacts everywhere including a safe where gold was once stored, photos and clippings on the wall illustrating the early mining era, and a poker table that looks as natural here as it would in Las Vegas. Outside is a string of small log cabins, each with some old mining equipment out the front and a moose rack over the doorway.

The water from the hot springs is 139°F but piped into an Olympic-sized pool at 103°F at a rate of 231 gallons a minute. Spend 20 or 30 minutes soaking here and you won't have sore muscles or a care in the world. There is also a restaurant and miner's saloon on site. The hotel rooms with shared baths begin at $48/74 for singles/doubles while on the 3rd floor are five sleeping cubby holes for $20/30 for singles/doubles but you need your own sleeping bag and pad. The rustic cabins, some with no running water, and other more deluxe cabins with kitchens and hot tubs, go for around $110 for two people. If you're camping down the road, it's $8 to soak in the pool that's open until midnight.

Circle

Beyond Central, the Steese Hwy passes the exit point of the Birch Creek Canoe Route at *Mile 147* and ends at Circle (pop 100) at *Mile 162*.

Circle is an interesting little wilderness town that lies on the banks of the Yukon River and was the northernmost point you could drive to before the Dalton Hwy was opened up. A large sign in the center of town still proclaims this fact. The town is 50 miles south of the Arctic Circle, but miners who established it in 1896 thought they were near the imaginary line and gave Circle its present name.

After gold was discovered in Birch Creek,

Circle was a bustling log-cabin city of 1200 with two theatres, a music hall, eight dance halls and 28 saloons. It was known as the 'largest log-cabin city in the world' until the Klondike reduced the town significantly and the Steese Hwy reduced its importance even more. For the most part, Central has now replaced Circle City as the supply center for area miners.

Much of the original town has been devoured by the Yukon River but you can get a feeling for the town's history by walking to **Pioneer Cemetery** which has headstones dating back to the 1800s. To find it, head upriver along the gravel road. Beyond a barricade is a trail that leads into dense underbrush and the graves are off to the left.

A city-operated *campground* at the end of Steese Hwy consists of tables, outhouses and a grassy area along the banks of the Yukon River where you can pitch your tent. Nearby is the *Yukon Trading Post* (☎ 773-1217), which includes a general store with Arctic Alaska prices, a cafe, bar and motel. The bar is an especially important spot because this is the only place you can go to at night (other than your car) to escape the maddening wave of mosquitoes.

Getting There & Away

Needless to say, hitchhiking is more difficult on Steese Hwy than on Chena Hot Springs Rd but it's not as difficult as it might appear. There is a fair amount of traffic moving between the communities and Fairbanks, and people this far north are good about stopping. Still, you have to consider your time schedule and patience level before attempting this road.

You can also reach the area renting a vehicle in Fairbanks but will have to look around. Most car-rental companies, including the discount ones like Rent-A-Wreck, do not allow their vehicles to be driven on the Steese Hwy. Flying into Circle Hot Springs is not that expensive and the area is well worth it. *Warbelo Air* (☎ 474-0518) in Fairbanks has regular flights to the hot springs airstrip for $134 per person round trip.

ELLIOTT HIGHWAY

From the crossroad with the Steese Hwy at Fox north of Fairbanks, the Elliott Hwy extends 152 miles north and then west to Manley Hot Springs, a small settlement near the Tanana River. This is by far the roughest road out of Fairbanks. The first 28 miles of the highway are paved and the rest is gravel; sections past the junction with Dalton Hwy are so narrow and steep you could get stuck behind an RV for days. At *Mile 28* of Elliott Hwy is the trailhead, parking lot and information box for the White Mountain Trail to Borealis-Le Fevre and Lee's cabins (see the Hiking section in the Wilderness chapter, and Cabins in Fairbanks' Places to Stay). Lee's is a seven-mile hike in and Borealis-Le Fevre is a hike of 19 miles over the Summit Trail.

An old Bureau of Land Management (BLM) campground, no longer maintained, is passed at *Mile 57* of Elliott Hwy where a bridge crosses the Tolovana River. There is still a turn-off here and the fishing is good for grayling and northern pike, but the mosquitoes are of legendary proportions. Nearby is the start of the **Colorado Creek Trail** to Windy Gap BLM Cabin. Check with the BLM office (☎ 474-2200) in Fairbanks about use of the cabin during the summer.

At *Mile 71* is the service center of **Livengood**, where you will find a small general store. At this point Elliott Hwy swings more to the west and in two miles passes the junction of the Dalton Hwy (see the Dalton Hwy section in the Bush chapter). From here, it is another 78 miles south-west to Manley Hot Springs.

Manley Hot Springs

The town, which has a summer population of 150 or so, is on the west side of Hot Springs Slough and provides a public *campground* ($5 per night) near the bridge that crosses the slough. The town was first homesteaded in 1902 by JF Karshner just as the US Army Signal Corps arrived to put in a telegraph station. Frank Manley arrived a few years later and built a four-story hotel at the trading center which was booming with miners from the nearby Eureka and Tofly mining areas. Most of the miners are gone now but Manley left his name on the village and today it's a quiet but friendly spot known for its lush gardens, a rare sight this far north.

Just before entering the village you pass the *Manley Hot Springs Resort* (☎ 672-3611) up on a hill, where most of the serious bathing is done. The resort has 24 rooms that range from $65 to $90, a restaurant, a bar and, of course, a mineral hot springs pool. It's $5 just to walk and use the hot springs. There are showers and a laundromat, and

organized tours up the Tanana River to see a fish camp or to go gold panning.

In town is the *Manley Roadhouse* (☎ 672-3161) offering singles/doubles for $55/$60 and cabins that sleep up to four people for $65. This classic Alaskan roadhouse was built in 1906 and features antiques in its restaurant, bar and lounge. You will find groceries, gas, liquor and the post office at the *Manley Trading Post* or you can wander around town and usually purchase vegetables from some of the residents. The produce here is unbelievable.

The Bush

The Bush, the wide rim of wilderness that encircles Anchorage, Fairbanks and all the roads between the two, constitutes a vast majority of the state's area, yet only a trickle of tourists ventures into the region for a first-hand look at rural Alaska.

Cost, more than mountains or rivers, is the barrier that isolates the Bush. For budget-minded travelers who reach the 'Great White North', what lies out in the Bush is usually beyond the reach of their wallets. Apart from a few exceptions, flying is the only way to reach a specific area. Once you're out there, facilities can be sparse and very expensive, especially if you don't arrive with a tent and backpacker's stove.

Those who do endure the high expense and extra travel are blessed with a land and people that have changed far less than the rest of the state. The most pristine wilderness lies in the many newly created national parks and preserves found away from the road system – parks where there are no visitor centers, campgrounds or shuttle buses running trips into the backcountry. Only nature in all its grandeur is encountered. Traditional villages, where subsistence is still the means of survival, and hearty home-steaders, as independent and ingenious as they come, lie hidden throughout rural Alaska.

There are three general areas in Bush Alaska. Southwest Alaska consists of the Alaska Peninsula, the Aleutian Islands and the rich salmon grounds of Bristol Bay. The Alaska Peninsula extends 550 miles from the western shore of Cook Inlet to its tip at False Pass. From there the Aleutian Islands, a chain of over 200 islands, curve another 1100 miles west into the Pacific Ocean.

Southwest Alaska is characterized by more than 60 active and dormant volcanoes, a treeless terrain and the worst weather in the state. Alaska's outlying arm is where the Arctic waters of the Bering Sea meet the warm Japanese Current, causing consider-

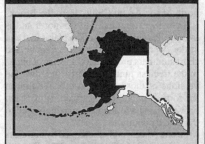

HIGHLIGHTS

- Hike up Unalaska's Bunker Hill to view gun turrets, Quonset huts and other WWII military remains
- Watch giant brown bears feed on salmon from an observation platform in Katmai National Park
- View the Valley of 10,000 Smokes on a bus tour in Katmai National Park
- Splurge on a package tour to see the amazing seal and bird colonies on the Pribilof Islands
- Pan for gold on Nome's beaches
- Take a bus tour to the Arctic Circle along the Dalton Highway

able cloudiness, rain and fog. Violent storms sweeping across the Pacific Ocean contribute to high winds in the area. The major attractions of the region are Katmai National Park and McNeil River State Game Sanctuary at the beginning of the Alaska Peninsula, Lake Clark National Park & Preserve across Cook Inlet from Homer and the Aleutian island of Unalaska.

Western Alaska is a flat, treeless plain that borders the Bering Sea north of the Alaska Peninsula to beyond Kotzebue and the Arctic Circle. This flatland is broken up by millions of lakes and slow-moving rivers such as the Yukon, while the weather in the summer is cool and cloudy with considerable fog and drizzle. The most visited parts of this region are the towns of Nome and Kotzebue, and the Pribilof Islands, north of the Aleutian Islands in the Bering Sea and the location of seal-breeding grounds and bird rookeries.

The third area in the Bush is Arctic Alaska, also known as the North Slope, which lies north of the Arctic Circle. Here the Brooks Range slopes gradually to the north and is eventually replaced by tundra plains that end at the Arctic Ocean. The harsh climate and short summers produce 400 species of plants in the treeless tundra that are often dwarfed versions of those further south. Wildlife in the form of polar bears, caribou, wolves and brown bears have adapted amazingly well to the rough conditions.

Arctic Alaska is characterized by nightless summers and dayless winters. In Barrow, Alaska's northernmost village, the midnight sun doesn't set from May to August. Surprisingly, the Arctic Alaska winters are often milder than those in the Interior. The summers, however, are cool at best and temperatures are rarely warmer than 45°F. Barrow attracts a small number of tourists each summer, and backpackers have discovered that the Gates of the Arctic National Park & Preserve, an intriguing place for a wilderness adventure, is becoming more accessible and more affordable with every passing summer.

Don't just pick out a village and fly to it. It is wise to either have a contact there (someone you know, a guide company or a wilderness lodge) or to travel with somebody who does. Although the indigenous people, especially the Inuit, are very hospitable people, there can be much tension and suspicion of strangers in small, isolated rural communities.

Southwest Alaska

There are two ways to see a part of the Bush without flying. One of them is to drive the Dalton Hwy to Prudhoe Bay. The other is to hop onto the Alaska Marine Hwy ferry when it makes its special run six times each summer along the Alaska Peninsula to the eastern end of the Aleutian Islands. Once in May, June, July and August and twice in September, the MV *Tustumena* continues west to Sand Point, King Cove, Cold Bay and Dutch Harbor/Unalaska, and possibly several other small villages, before backtracking to Kodiak.

This is truly one of the best bargains in public transportation. The scenery is intriguing. You'll pass the perfect cones of Pavlof and Pavlof's Sister (a pair of volcanoes on the Alaska Peninsula), the treeless but lush green mountains of the Aleutians, and distinctive rock formations and cliffs. The wildlife is even better.

Passing through Barren Islands on the way to Kodiak, passengers often spot two-dozen whales at a time. Sea lions, otters and porpoises are commonly sighted and then there are the birds. More than 30 species of seabirds nest in the Aleutians and 250 species of bird pass through. Diehard birders are often on board sighting such species as albatrosses, auklets, cormorants and puffins. Even if you don't know a puffin from a kittiwake, naturalists from the US Fish & Wildlife Service ride the ferry, pointing out birds and giving programs through the trip on other aspects of the Aleutians.

All the wildlife and scenery are very dependent, however, on the weather. This can be an extremely rough trip at times, well deserving of its title 'the cruise through the cradle of the storms'. On the runs in fall, 40-foot waves and 80-knot winds are the norm and no matter when you step aboard, you'll find 'barf' bags everywhere on the ship – just in case.

The smoothest runs are from June to August. A state room is nice but not necessary. There are no lounge chairs in the solarium but a sleeping pad and bag work out nicely. You'll find free showers on board, and free coffee and hot water. The hot water is especially nice, allowing you to stock up on cup-a-soup and tea to avoid spending a small fortune in the dinning room where lunch will cost $7 and dinner from $9 to $14. And bring a good book. On days when the

BUSH

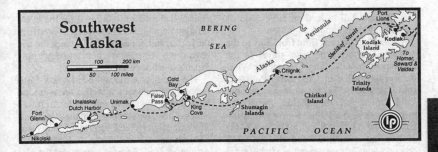

fog surrounds the boat there is little to look at but the lapping waves along the side.

The MV *Tustumena*, a 290-foot vessel which holds 230 passengers, is the only ferry in the Alaska Marine Hwy fleet rated as an ocean-going ship, thus its nickname, 'Trusty Tusty'. It leaves Kodiak on Wednesday, returns early Monday morning and continues on to Seward that day. The boat docks at the villages only long enough to load and unload (from one to two hours), but in Dutch Harbor/Unalaska it stays in port from five to six hours. Still, spending just an hour in most of these villages is more than sufficient time to get off for a quick look around.

The round-trip fare for walk-on passengers to Dutch Harbor from Kodiak is $404; if you begin in Homer and end in Seward, it is $492. For those who want to spend more time in Dutch Harbor/Unalaska, Reeve Aleutian Airways (☎ 243-4700 in Anchorage) and Peninsula Airways (☎ 243-2323 in Anchorage) provide services to the Aleutian Islands as well as the Pribilof Islands and other destinations on the Alaska Peninsula.

The other way to spend more time on land and reduce the cost of the trip is to leave the ferry early and then wait for it on its return run. King Cove is ideally situated for this but the place is little more than a company town. The best place by far is False Pass, a small village surrounded by snow-covered peaks. But carefully check to see if the ferry is stopping at the town both on the way out and back. If it doesn't, it could be a long wait until the next time the MV *Tustumena* is passing through.

KING COVE

This town of 700 residents is a commercial fishing base at the western end of the Alaska Peninsula near the entrance of Cold Bay. Surrounded by mountains, King Cove supports a hotel, a restaurant and a busy harbor during summer as well as a market and a laundromat. Those wishing to step off and just pitch a tent out on the road, beware. Brown bears wander into town frequently here. Reeve Aleutian Airways charges $405 for a one-way ticket to King Cove from Anchorage purchased 14 days in advance.

COLD BAY

On the west shore of Cold Bay is the town of the same name. The 160 residents are mostly government workers as the town is a major refueling stop for many flights crossing the Pacific to or from the Orient. Russian explorers also used the bay and most likely spent the winters here on their first trips along the coast. Before they departed, Count Feodor Lutke named Izembek Lagoon in 1827 after a doctor aboard one of his ships.

A huge airstrip was built in the area during WWII; today it's the third longest in the state and is why the town serves as the transport center for the entire Aleutian chain. You can still see Quonset huts and other remains from the WWII military build-up.

The town also serves as the gateway to the **Izembek National Wildlife Refuge**, which was established in 1960 to protect some 142 species of bird, primarily the black brant. Almost the entire North American population of brant, some 150,000 of them, arrive in spring and fall to feed on large eelgrass beds during their annual migration.

A 10-mile road runs from Cold Bay to the Izembek Lagoon; otherwise, travel in the refuge is by foot or plane. Contact the Wildlife Refuge office in Cold Bay (Pouch 2, Cold Bay, AK 99571) for more information. Within town, accommodation, meals and groceries are available. Reeve Aleutian Airways (☎ 532-2380 or (800) 544-2248) services the community and charges $345 for a one-way, advance-purchase ticket from Anchorage.

UNALASKA & DUTCH HARBOR

Unalaska on Unalaska Island and its sister town Dutch Harbor on Amaknak Island, are at the confluence of the North Pacific Ocean and the Bering Sea, one of the richest fisheries in the world. Dutch Harbor is the only natural deep-water port in the Aleutians and more than 400 vessels call there each year from as many as 14 countries. The two towns lie deep into Unalaska Bay and are connected to each other by a 500-foot bridge. During the summer, the population of the area can easily exceed 4300 due to the influx of cannery workers who process seafood, most notably crab. Dutch Harbor also serves as a transport center for much of the Bristol Bay salmon fishery. In 1993, the towns led the nation in both volume and value of seafood processed, with almost 800 million pounds produced for export that were valued at $161 million.

History

Unalaska was the first headquarters for the Russian-American Company and a cornerstone in the lucrative sea-otter fur trade in the 1700s. It was also an important harbor for miners sailing to the golden beaches of Nome. In 1939, the USA built navy and army installations here, and at one time there were 60,000 servicemen stationed here.

In June 1942, the Japanese opened their Aleutian Islands campaign by bombing Dutch Harbor, and then took Attu and Kiska islands in the only foreign invasion of US soil during WWII. The attack on Dutch Harbor had a silver lining in it for the USA. A fallen Zero fighter plane was retrieved near the harbor and, for the first time since the war began, the Americans could closely study Japan's most devastating weapon.

The bombing also resulted in heavy fortification of the islands as well as areas around Kodiak and Seward, in anticipation of future attacks and to regain control of the Aleutians. The campaign to retake the two islands was a bloody one and included a 19-day battle on Attu in which US forces recaptured the plot of barren land but only after suffering 2300 casualties and 549 deaths. The Japanese lost even more lives.

Dutch Harbor is the site of the canneries and fish-processing plants, something of an industrial park. Unalaska is where everybody lives and, despite the large influx of transient workers, can be a charming and friendly town, if you have the time to enjoy it. Unfortunately, those returning on the ferry really don't. To stay longer you can either splurge on an expensive airline ticket or be reckless and arrive hoping to pick up a cheaper one in town. Either way, a few days in Unalaska can be a refreshing cure for anybody who is suffering from an overdose of RVers and Alaska crowded with tourists and tour buses.

Information

Tourist Office The Unalaska/Dutch Harbor Visitors Bureau (☎ 581-2612) is at the Grand Aleutian Hotel on Airport Beach Rd in Dutch Harbor. Hours in the Summer are 8 am to 5 pm Monday through Saturday.

Money Key Bank of Alaska (☎ 581-1300) is in the Intersea Mall near the Grand Aleutian Hotel in Dutch Harbor.

Post There is a post office in Dutch Harbor, in the Intersea Mall, and in Unalaska at 82 Airport Beach Rd.

Travel Agencies USTravel (☎ 581-3133) is located at the Unalaska Airport and is open daily during the summer.

Unalaska/Dutch Harbor

0	400	800 m
0	400	800 yds

1 Grand Aleutian Hotel
2 Ziggy's
3 Intersea Mall
4 Carl's General Store
5 Church of the Holy Ascension
6 Stormy's
7 Health Clinic
8 Post Office
9 Parks, Recreation & Cultural
   Department
10 Library
11 Community Pool
12 USS Northwestern Memorial

Unalaska
Airport

Ballyhoo Rd

Dutch

Harbor

Ferry
Dock

Road

Sitka
Spruce
Park

Amaknak
Island

Dutch Harbor

Biorka

Street

Airport

Beach

East

Point

Road

Salmon
Way

Margaret
Bay

Iliuliuk

Bay

Iliuliuk Harbor

Gilman St

Small Boat Harbor

Expedition
Island

Bunker Hill

Airport

Beach

Road

Captain

Bay

South
Channel

Unalaska

Bayview

Broadway

Road

*Unalaska
Island*

Captain Bay Road
To OSI Bunkhouse

Unalaska
Lake

BUSH

Bookshops Books and topographic maps
are available at Nicky's Place (☎ 581-1570)
located on Front Beach in Unalaska.

Medical Services The Iliuliuk Family &
Health Services (☎ 581-1202), at 34 LaVelle
Ct just off Airport Beach Rd near the post
office, has walk-in and 24-hour emergency
service.

Things to See
Unalaska is dominated by the **Church of the
Holy Ascension**, the oldest Russian-built
church still standing in the country. It was

first built in 1825 and then enlarged in 1894
when wings were attached to change its floor
plan from a 'vessel' to a 'pekov' or one in the
shape of a crucifix. On Broadway and overlooking the bay, the church with its onion
domes is a photographer's delight. Outside
is a small graveyard with the largest marker
belonging to Baron Nicholas Zass. Born in
1825 in Archange, Russia, he eventually
became bishop of the Aleutian Islands and
all of Alaska before dying in 1882. Next door
is the **Bishop's House**; both buildings are
undergoing extensive renovation work. To
see the church's collection of more than 700

Russian Orthodox icons, books and paintings, call the Visitors Bureau (☎ 581-2612) and inquire about possible tours.

Nearby is the **Henry Swanson Visitors Center** (☎ 581-1483), on West Broadway between 2nd and 3rd St, the former home of one of Unalaska's most popular residents. Swanson was a fox farmer and fisherman, who grew up in Unalaska and as a child watched ships depart from the harbor for the Nome Gold Rush. He died in 1990. His home, open from 1 to 4 pm on Saturday, contains books, maps, and tourist information as well as a few displays.

Military relics still remain around Dutch Harbor and Unalaska, though in recent years the communities have begun an effort to clean them up. On the road from the ferry terminal and airport to Unalaska, you pass one concrete pillbox after another. **Bunker Hill** is an easy place to see the remains of the Aleutian campaign. Known to the military as 'Hill 400', it was fortified with 155-mm guns, ammunition magazines, water tanks, 22 Quonset hut bunkers and a concrete command post at the top. You can hike to the peak of Bunker Hill along a gravel road, picked up just after crossing the bridge to Amaknak Island. At the top are the gun turrets along with the ammunition magazines and the command post.

More war history can be found in Unalaska by following Front Beach Rd to the south end of town. There's a picturesque hillside graveyard along the bay with the **USS *Northwestern* Memorial**. Launched in 1889 as a passenger and freight ship for the Alaska Steamship Company, the vessel was retired in 1937 then repaired by the military in 1940 to serve as a floating bunkhouse. It was bombed during the attack of Dutch Harbor and burned for five days. In 1992, as part of the 50th anniversary of the event, the propeller was salvaged by divers and is now part of the memorial to those who died during the Aleutian campaign.

If it's raining in Unalaska, and it does more than 250 days of the year, head to the Community Pool (☎ 581-1649) in the school complex on Broadway. A number of swim periods are offered daily and the facility also includes a sauna.

Hiking

Within Dutch Harbor there is the Sitka Spruce Park, a national historical landmark where six trees planted by Russians in 1805 have somehow survived where all other foliage can't. That's it for trees on Unalaska Island and because of the treeless environment, hiking is easy here. Nor do you have to worry about bears – there are none.

There are few developed trails in the area, but an enjoyable day can be spent hiking to Uniktali Bay, a round trip of eight to 10 miles. From Captain Bay Rd, turn east on a gravel road just before passing Westword Cannery. Follow the road for a mile to its end where a foot trail continues along a stream. In two miles, the trail runs out and you'll reach a lake in a pass between a pair of 2000-foot peaks. Continue south-east to pick up a second stream that empties into Uniktali Bay. The bay is an undeveloped stretch of shoreline and a great place to beachcomb. From time to time even glass floats from Japanese fishing nets wash ashore.

You can also trek to the top of 1634-foot high Mount Ballyhoo behind the airport to look at more artefacts from the military build-up, including tunnels that allowed gunners to cart ammunition from one side of the mountain to the other. Hiking is like camping away from town as most of the land is owned by the Ounalashka (☎ 581-1276) and you need to obtain a permit first before heading out.

Places to Stay & Eat

In 1993, the *Grand Aleutian Hotel* (☎ 581-3844) opened up in Dutch Harbor near the airport, but unless you're willing to pay $175 a night for a double, you might want to look elsewhere for accommodation. There are actually a number of lodges in the towns, most catering to the cannery workers and fishers. The best rates are at *OSI Bunkhouse* (☎ 581-1515) near the end of Captain Bay Rd, the first intersection after crossing the bridge to Unalaska Island. The lodge is three miles from Unalaska but has singles/doubles for $81/106 a night. There is also a restaurant where fishers, construction workers and others feast on an all-you-can-eat breakfast for $8 and dinner for $13.

Most of the land outside of town is owned by the native corporation Ounalashka (☎ 581-1276) and you need to obtain a permit before setting up a tent. The corporation office is at Margaret Bay near the Grand Aleutian Hotel in Dutch Harbor.

In Unalaska on Broadway Ave, is *Stormy's* which serves everything from Mexican, Chinese and good old American pizza to sushi. Your cafe latte is at *Nicky's Place* on Front Beach in Unalaska. In Dutch Harbor, *Peking Restaurant* is in the Intersea Mall and *Ziggy's*, for breakfast and burgers, is on East Point Rd. Finally, fast food has reached this remote corner of Alaska: *Burger King*, *Pizza Hut* and *KFC* opened stalls recently in the AC Value Center on Salmon Way in Dutch Harbor.

For groceries, supplies or a deli counter there's *Carl's* on Broadway in Unalaska and the previously mentioned *AC Value Center* in Dutch Harbor. Both are large general stores.

Getting There & Around
The ferry terminal and the airport are on Amaknak Island, about three miles from Unalaska. The most amazing thing about this place is the number of taxi vans available. There are literally dozens of them running around on the dirt and gravel roads. You can't walk more than five minutes here without a taxi driver asking if you need a ride. It doesn't matter where you go or how far; all rides are $5 per person.

If you arrive on the ferry and are returning on it, the $10 you dish out for two taxi rides is money well spent to see as much of Unalaska as possible. If you're staying for a day or two, however, it's easy enough to hitchhike.

Another way to get around is to rent a mountain bike from the Unalaska Parks, Recreation & Cultural Department (☎ 581-1297), in the back of the community center

on Broadway. Bikes are $10 for the day or $3 an hour.

Other than the once-a-month ferry, the only other way of getting out of Unalaska/Dutch Harbor is flying. The town is serviced by Reeve Aleutian Airways (☎ 581-1202) and Peninsula Airways (☎ 581-1383). Reeve charges $355 for an advance purchase, one-way ticket to Anchorage and $710 for the round-trip.

WOOD-TIKCHIK STATE PARK
At 1.6 million acres, Wood-Tikchik is the largest state park in the country. It's 30 miles north of Dillingham, the service and transport center for Bristol Bay. The park preserves two large systems of interconnecting lakes that are the important spawning grounds for Bristol Bay's salmon which enter the area through the Wood River.

With the exception of five fishing lodges which only offer packaged stays at $2000 to $3000 a week, the park is totally undeveloped. There are no campgrounds, trails, ranger stations or shelters. In short, it is an ideal place for a wilderness canoe or kayak trip. Traditional trips include running the Tikchik or Nuyakuk rivers or floating from lake to lake.

Information
For park information contact Wood-Tikchik State Park (☎ (907) 842-2375); PO Box 3022, Dillingham, AK 99576.

Wood River Lakes These are the lakes in the southern half of the park connected to one another by shallow, swift moving rivers. For that reason most parties are flown in and paddle out, returning to Dillingham via the Wood River. A popular spot to put in is Lake Kulik and then you paddle to Dillingham, a trip of close to 140 miles requiring from seven to 10 days in a kayak or canoe.

These lakes are attractive to many as they eliminate the additional air time you need to be picked up. They also are an easy paddle for most intermediate canoeists. But keep in mind that three of the five fishing lodges are here and all use their powerboats extensively to get around the lakes.

Lake, requires a series of portages around Class V rapids. Likewise the upper Nuyakuk River, just below the Tikchik Lake outlet has a white-water stretch that will require you to make a portage. The upper lakes are more challenging and more costly to experience. But the scenery – mountains, pinnacle peaks and hanging valleys surrounding the lakes – is the most impressive in the park and there will be far less motorboat activity if any at all.

The paddling season is from mid-June, when the lakes are finally free of ice and snow, until early October when they begin to freeze up again. Be prepared for cool and rainy weather and pack along plenty of mosquito repellent. On the open lakes you have to be cautious as sudden winds can create white-cap conditions, and white water may exist on many of the streams connecting the lakes.

Highlights of any such adventure, besides the wilderness, are the possibilities of spotting brown and black bears, beavers, moose, foxes and maybe even wolves. The fishing for arctic char, rainbow trout, Dolly Varden, grayling and red salmon is excellent in late summer.

Dillingham Services

There are a number of hotels and lodges in Dillingham but you'll find the price of accommodation here on the high side, partly because of the 9% bed tax. At the top end is *The Bristol Inn* (☎ 842-2240) at $120/147 for singles/doubles, while slightly more affordable and in the center of town is *Dillingham Hotel* (☎ 842-5316) with singles/ doubles for $100/125.

Near the airport in the Tackle Shop is *Bristol Bay Rafters* (☎ 842-2212). This outfitter specializes in unguided trips into the state park and will provide canoe or raft rentals as well as other camping equipment. It also has a drop-off and pick-up service.

Getting There & Away

To reach Dillingham from Anchorage, try to book an air ticket 14 days in advance through

Tikchik Lakes In the northern half of the park, and much more remote, are these six lakes. The most common trip consists of being dropped onto Nishlik or Upnuk lakes and leaving them by traveling along the Tikchik River into Tikchik Lake. You can be picked up here or you can continue your journey by floating the Nuyakuk River and then the Nushagak River to one of several Native Alaskan villages where air charter is available back to Dillingham.

Keep in mind the Allen River, which drains from Chikuminuk Lake into Lake Chauekuktuli on another route to Tikchik

Top: Trans-Alaska Pipeline crossing, Tanana River (DS)
Bottom: Rock formations, Pinnell Mountain Trail, near Fairbanks (JD)

Top left: Chignik, Alaska Peninsula (DP)
Top right: Kayaker, Katmai National Park (JD)
  Bottom: Setting up camp after rafting in the Gates of the Arctic National Park (JD)

Alaska Airlines (☎ (800) 426-0333); a round-trip ticket costs from $300 to $350.

A 24-mile road extends from Dillingham to the village of Aleknagik on the south end of the Wood River Lakes system. Otherwise Contact Yute Air (☎ 842-5333) in Dillingham about chartering a float plane, but expect to pay around $300 an hour for the flight in. At such a rate that means flying into Upnuk Lake in the northern half of the park will be about $570 for two people and gear and being picked up at Tikchik Lake will be another $370.

KING SALMON

King Salmon and its runway is the transportation hub that you pass through on your way to Katmai National Park (see Getting There & Away in the following Katmai National Park section). Most people see little more than the terminal building where they pick up their luggage and the float dock where they catch a flight to Brooks Camp in the park, which is fine. King Salmon is a village of 600 residents, almost all of them either federal employees (National Park Service or US Fish & Wildlife Service).

Occasionally you get stuck in King Salmon for a few hours or even a day. If that's the case, head to the **King Salmon Visitor Center** (☎ 246-4250), right next door to the terminal and open daily during the summer from 8 am to 5 pm. The center is staffed by both the NPS and USFWS and inside there is an excellent selection of books and maps for sale, a growing number of displays and a small video room where you will be shown a variety of videos on subjects ranging from brown bears to the creation of the park.

Just up the road from the terminal, on the way to the town of Naknek, is the King Salmon Mall (no kidding, it even has a Radio Shack) with the headquarters of Katmai National Park on the 2nd floor. It's open from 8 am to 5 pm Monday to Friday and is a good place to ask questions, but there is little else for visitors there.

Nearby in the mall is a bar and restaurant, a large general store that also sells groceries and *King Ko Inn* (☎ 246-3377) where rooms run from $60 to $80 for a single in case, heavens forbid, you need to spend a night here. Better but more expensive accommodation can be found at *Quinnat Landing Hotel* (☎ 246-3000) where a single/double is $180/205. Or you could just wander down the road away from town and set up camp on the banks of the Naknek River. Just remember that winds can be murderous here, the real reason for the lack of trees in the region, so you'd best have a tent that can withstand strong gusts.

If you are struck for a day in King Salmon, consider giving Bristol Bay Tours (☎ 246-4218) a call. It offers a personalized van tour of the area, including the village of Naknek for a look at rural Alaska, a salmon cannery and a hike along the Bering Sea. The tours run from three to four hours and cost $35 per person, a minimum of two people.

KATMAI NATIONAL PARK

In June 1912, Novarupta Volcano erupted violently and, along with the preceding earthquakes, rocked the area now known as Katmai National Park & Preserve. The wilderness was turned into a dynamic landscape of smoking valleys, ash-covered mountains and small holes and cracks (fumaroles) fuming with steam and gas. In only one other eruption in historic times, on the Greek island of Santorini in 1500 BC, has more ash and pumice been displaced.

If the eruption had happened in New York City, people living in Chicago would have heard the explosion; it was 10 times greater than the 1980 eruption of Mt St Helens in the state of Washington. For two days, people in Kodiak could not see a lantern held at arm's length and the pumice, which reached half the world, lowered the temperature in the Northern Hemisphere that year by two degrees. In history books, 1912 will always be remembered as the year without a summer. But the most amazing aspect of this eruption, perhaps the most dramatic natural event in the 20th century, was that no-one was killed.

The National Geographic Society sent Robert Grigg to explore this locality in 1916,

BUSH

BUSH

and standing at Katmai Pass the explorer saw for the first time the valley floor with its thousands of steam vents. He named it the Valley of 10,000 Smokes. Robert Grigg's adventures revealed the spectacular results of the eruptions to the rest of the world and two years later the area was turned into a national monument. In 1980, it was enlarged to 3.9 million acres and redesignated a national park and preserve.

Although the fumaroles no longer smoke and hiss, the park is still a diverse and scenic wilderness, unlike any in Alaska. It changes from glaciated volcanoes and ash-covered valleys to island-studded lakes and a coastline of bays, fjords and beaches. Wildlife is abundant with more than 30 species of mammals including large populations of brown bears, some of which weigh over 1000 pounds. Katmai is also a prime habitat for moose, sea lions, arctic foxes and wolves. The many streams and lakes in the park are known around the state for providing some of the best rainbow trout and salmon fishing.

The weather in the park is best from mid-June to the end of July. Unfortunately, this is also when mosquitoes, always heavy in this part of the state, are at their peak. The best time for hiking and backpacking trips is from mid-August to early September, when the colors of fall are brilliant, the berries ripe and juicy, and the insects scarce. However, be prepared for frequent storms. In fact be ready for rain and foul weather any time in Katmai and always pack warm clothing. The summer high temperatures are usually in the low 60s°F.

The summer headquarters for Katmai National Park is **Brooks Camp**, on the shores of Naknek Lake, 47 miles from King Salmon. The camp is best known for Brooks Falls where thousands of red sockeye salmon attempt to jump every July, much to the interest of both bears and tourists. In the middle of the wilderness, this place crawls with humanity during July, when sometimes as many as 300 people will be in Brooks Camp and the surrounding area in a single day.

When you arrive at the camp, you are immediately given a 'bear orientation' by a ranger as the bruins are frequently seen – often strolling down the beach, between the lodge and cabins and the float planes pulled up the sand. From here you can head straight to a visitors' center, open from 8 am to 6 pm daily, to find out the status of available sites in the campgrounds or to fill out backcountry permits. You can also purchase books or maps at the center while rangers here run a variety of interpretive programs, including a daily walk to an Inuit pit house at 1 pm. At 8 pm nightly there are programs or slide shows at a nearby auditorium.

Information

Katmai is not a place to see at the last minute. Because of the cost involved in reaching the park, most visitors plan to spend at least four days or more to justify the expenses.

To contact the park beforehand write to: Katmai National Park, PO Box 7, King Salmon, AK 99613; or call on ☎ (907) 246-3305. In the USA, use the toll-free numbers to Katmailand (☎ (800) 544-0551) for advance reservations. Katmailand is the concessionaire that handles the lodge and canoe rentals.

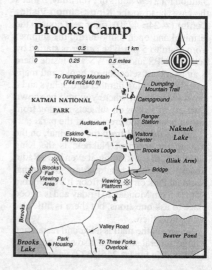

Brooks Camp

Bear Watching

Katmai has the largest population of non-hunted brown bears in the world – more than 2000 live in the park. At Brooks Camp they congregate around Brooks River to take advantage of the easy fishing for salmon. Most of this takes place in July when it is almost impossible to get a camp site, a cabin or sometimes even a spot on the observation decks without planning months in advance. The bear activity then tapers off in August when the animals follow salmon up into small streams but it increases again in September as the bears return to congregate in the lower rivers where they then feed on spawned-out fish. In reality, a few brown bears can be spotted in the Brooks Camp area through much of the summer as there always seem to be a couple of younger ones hanging around.

There are two established viewing areas. From Brooks Lodge a dirt road leads to a bridge over the river and a large observation deck.

From here you can spot the bears feeding in the mouth of the river or swimming in the bay. Continue on the road to the Valley of 10,000 Smokes and in half a mile a marked trail winds to Brooks Falls. It's another half-mile walk to the falls where there is a second observation deck. This is a prime viewing area. Right above the falls, you can photograph both salmon making those spectacular leaps or a big brownie at the top of the cascade waiting with open jaws to grab the fish.

At the peak of the salmon run, there are usually eight to 12 bears, two or three of them on the falls themselves. The observation deck, however, will be crammed with 30 to 40 photographers.

You can imagine how heated it gets there with people trying to squeeze in their open tripods for the photo-of-a-lifetime and professionals with two-foot-long lens battling it out with amateurs and their instamatics. For those reasons the NPS institutes a number of rules and limits your stay at the site to an hour or less. It's the only way to keep a 35-mm war from breaking out on the deck.

Bus Tours

The only road in Katmai is 23 miles long and ends at Overlook Cabin, where there is a sweeping view of the Valley of 10,000 Smokes. Katmailand, which runs the lodge, also has a bus that makes a daily run out and back, usually leaving at 9 am and getting back at 4.30 pm. Each bus carries a ranger who describes what you're looking at and then leads a short hike from the cabin to the valley below. You have a three-hour layover at Overlook Cabin, more than enough time to get a close view of this barren valley and its moon-like terrain.

The fare for the tour is $50 per person. Believe it or not, if the weather isn't too bad, most people feel it's money well spent at the end of the day. If you want a box lunch thrown in, it's $57 per person. Sign up for the tour at the Katmailand office across from the lodge as soon as you arrive. The bus is filled most of the summer and you often can't get a seat without reserving one a day or two in advance.

Hiking

Hiking and backpacking are the best way to see the park's unusual backcountry. Like Denali National Park, Katmai has few formal trails; backpackers follow river bars, lake shores, gravel ridges and other natural routes. Many hiking trips begin with a ride on the park bus along the dirt road to the Valley of 10,000 Smokes (see the Hiking section in the Wilderness chapter). The bus will also drop off and pick up hikers along the road but it is not a free shuttle system like at Denali National Park. The return fare is $60.

Dumpling Mountain Trail The only developed trail from Brooks Camp is a half-day trek to the top of Dumpling Mountain, elevation 2520 feet. The trail leaves the ranger station and heads north past the campground, climbing 1.5 miles to a scenic overlook. It then continues another two miles to the mountain's summit, where there are superb views of the surrounding lakes.

Paddling

There is some excellent paddling in the area (see the Savonoski River Loop in the Paddling section of the Wilderness chapter). The park concessionaire rents kayaks for $55 per day or canoes for $30 per day or $5 per hour. *Life Time Adventures* (☎ 333-4626 in Anchorage) also rents kayaks for $50 a day or $220 a week. Keep in mind that the winds are strong here and the lakes big. That's okay for sea-touring kayakers but can be a dangerous combination when you're in a canoe.

Bay of Islands

A group of dozens of islands lies at the east end of Naknek Lake's North Arm, a one-way paddle of 30-miles from Brooks Camp. Kayakers can make it in a long day, canoers best plan on two days to reach them. You'll find the islands scenic and the water exceptionally calm. The fishing for rainbow trout is also good, while at the very end of the lake is a ranger cabin. If the ranger is not in, paddlers are welcome to use the cabin and it makes a nice break from your tent. This is a good four to five-day paddle, depending on how much time you want to spend in the islands.

Margot Creek

Along the south shore of the Iliuk Arm of Naknek Lake is the mouth of this creek where you will find good fishing and lots of bear activity. It's a 10-mile paddle from Brooks Camp and, in ideal conditions, you can reach it in under five hours. But for most people it's a good overnight trip as you can camp on islands nearby to minimize encounters with bears.

Places to Stay & Eat

You have to reserve a site in the free *campground* but it might be easier winning the New York lottery. Reservations are accepted only by telephone (☎ 246-3305) beginning on the first working day of January and often the sites for the prime bear-viewing month of July are filled within three or four days. Camping is limited to a maximum of seven nights and if you don't have a reservation, you don't get a site. Park officials no longer try to squeeze in walk-in campers.

Within Brooks Camp is *Brooks Lodge*, where a basic cabin for two costs $274 per night, including three full meals. It's best to book a cabin in advance through Katmailand (☎ (800) 544-0551 outside Alaska or (800) 478-5448 inside Alaska).

A store sells limited supplies of freeze-dried food and camp-stove fuel, fishing equipment, flies and other odds and ends like beer for $3 a can. You can also sign up for the all-you-can-eat meals at Brooks Lodge without being a cabin renter; it's $10 for breakfast, $12 for lunch and $22 for dinner. Also in the lodge is a lounge with a huge stone fireplace, soft couches and bar service in the evening.

Getting There & Away

The vast majority of visitors to Katmai go through King Salmon due to regular jet service by Alaska Airlines. This makes it a lot cheaper. You can get there from Kodiak or Homer but this would involve chartering a bush plane, and I can't imagine what the cost of that would be. There are a variety of ways to reach the park. A round-trip ticket on Alaska Airlines to King Salmon is $310. Also check with Peninsula Airways (☎ 243-2323 in Anchorage) which offers service from Anchorage to King Salmon.

Once you're in King Salmon, a number of air taxi companies will fly out to Brooks Camp, including Katmai Air (☎ 246-3079 or (800) 478-3079 within Alaska) which charges $120 for a round trip. You can also take a jet boat from King Salmon to Brooks Camp on the *Katmai Lady*. The daily service is run through Quinnat Landing Hotel (☎ 246-3000) with the boat departing in the morning and then making a return trip to King Salmon in late afternoon. The round-trip fare is $125 per person.

McNEIL RIVER STATE GAME SANCTUARY

The McNeil River State Game Sanctuary, just north of Katmai National Park on the Alaska Peninsula, 200 miles south-west of Anchorage, is famous for its high numbers of brown bears from July to August. The majority of the bears gather a mile upstream from the mouth of the river where falls slow down the salmon and provide an easy meal. This spot is world renowned among wildlife photographers and every great bear-catches-salmon shot you've ever seen was most likely taken from either here or the Brooks River. Often there are 20 or more brown bears feeding together below the McNeil River Falls and up to 80 have been seen congregated here at one time.

The fishing is so easy, that by the end of the summer, the bears get picky. Many feel for the egg sack of a female salmon, eat the raw caviar and then discard the rest of the fish to waiting seagulls, eagles and other birds. Male salmon are often just dropped back in the river.

The Alaska Department of Fish & Game has set up a viewing area and allows 10 visitors per day for a four-day period to watch the bears feed. From a camp, park guides lead you on a two-mile hike across sedge flats and through thigh-deep Mikfik Creek to the viewing area on a bluff. There you can watch the bears feed less than 20 yards away in what is basically a series of rapids and pools where the salmon gather between leaps. Though an expensive side trip for most visitors, viewing and photographing giant brown bears this close is a once-in-a-lifetime experience.

That's the reason for the permit system. You need to pull a permit – lottery style – to be one of the 190 people who state officials allow into the park from early June to late August, the prime season for bear watching. Usually more than 2000 applications are received from around the world.

Permits

Visits to the game sanctuary are on a permit basis only and your odds of drawing a permit from the lottery are less than one in 10. Write to the Alaska Department of Fish & Game, Wildlife Conservation Division, 333 Raspberry Rd, Anchorage, AK 99518 for an application; or call (907) 267-2180. You can also request one via a fax (☎ 265-2885). Return your application with a $20 non-refundable fee, by March 1 for the lottery drawing. Permits are drawn for 10 people a day for four-day periods and you must be self-sufficient with camping equipment and food. If your name is drawn, by all means take advantage of this rare opportunity in wildlife photography.

Getting There & Away

Most visitors depart for McNeil River from Homer. Kachemak Air Service (☎ 235-8924) is based in Homer and offers a return fare of $309 to McNeil River. It makes the trip whether the plane is filled to capacity (12 seats) or carries only one passenger – the plane lands in a tidal area during high tide. Even if you don't have a permit, check with the air service as they stay in constant touch with rangers at the state game area. On some occasions, cancellations or no-shows will lead to last-minute openings in the sanctuary's permit system.

LAKE CLARK NATIONAL PARK

Apart from backpacking enthusiasts and river runners in Southcentral Alaska, few people knew about Lake Clark National Park & Preserve, 100 miles south-west of Anchorage, until recently. Yet it offers some of the most spectacular scenery of any of the newly created parks in the state. It is within this 3.6 million-acre preserve that the Alaska and Aleutian ranges meet. Among the many towering peaks are Mt Iliamna and Mt Redoubt, two active volcanoes clearly seen from Anchorage and the western shore of the Kenai Peninsula.

Much of the park's obscurity changed in January 1990 when Mt Redoubt erupted. After 25 dormant years, the volcano roared back to life sending ash into the air and creating a cloud that could be seen along the western shore of the Kenai Peninsula. The spreading ash closed the Anchorage International Airport and oil terminals in the area, while 10,000 face masks were distributed to the residents of central Kenai Peninsula worried about inhaling the fine powder.

Along with its now famous volcanoes, the park also features numerous glaciers, truly spectacular turquoise lakes (including Lake Clark, the park's centerpiece) and three designated wild rivers that have long been havens for river runners.

Wildlife includes brown and black bears, moose, red foxes, wolves and dall sheep on the alpine slopes. Caribou roam the western foothills, while the park's watershed is one of the most important producers of red salmon in the world, contributing 33% of the US catch. The weather in the western section of the preserve, where most of the rafting and backpacking takes place, is generally cool and cloudy with light winds through much of the summer. Temperatures range from 50 to 65°F from June to August, with an occasional heat wave of 80°F.

Information

There is a summer ranger station at Port Alsworth (☎ 781-2218), but it is best to contact the park headquarters (☎ 271-3751) in Anchorage regarding desirable places to hike and camp. You can also write to them before departing for Alaska at: Lake Clark National Park, 4230 University Dr, Suite 311, Anchorage, AK 99508.

Hiking

Lake Clark is another remote park exclusively for the experienced backpacker. Most extended treks take place in the western foothills north of Lake Clark, where the open and relatively dry tundra provides ideal conditions for hiking. Less experienced backpackers are content to be dropped off at the shores of the many lakes in the area to camp and undertake day hikes.

Telaquana Trail This 50-mile, historic trail, first used by Dena'ina Athabaskans and later by fur trappers and miners, is the best cross-country route in the park. It begins on the north shore of Lake Clark near the Dena'ina Athabaskan village of Kijik and ends near Telaquana Lake. In between, you pass through boreal forests, ford glacial rivers and cross the fragile alpine tundra when the route skirts the western flank of the Alaska Range.

Keep in mind that you still need route finding and backcountry wilderness skills to follow what is basically an unmarked route. Also, the Kijik River is a difficult ford throughout the summer and at times impossible to cross. For this reason backpackers begin or end their trip north of the river. Although a few people follow the entire route, most are satisfied with hiking just a portion of it. One of the most popular sections is from Turquoise south to Twin Lakes, where there is usually a ranger stationed. Experienced backpackers can travel between the two lakes in a day.

Rafting

Float trips down any of the three designated wild rivers are spectacular and exciting since the waterways are rated from Class III to IV. Raft rentals are usually available in Port Alsworth. Contact the ranger to ask who is providing the service.

Chilikadrotna River Beginning at Win Lakes, this river offers a good adventure for intermediate rafters. Its steady current and narrow course winds through upland spruce and hardwood forest, draining the west flank of the Alaska Range. From the lakes to a take out on the Mulchatna River is a 60-mile, four-day float with some Class III stretches.

Tlikakila This fast but small glacial river flows from Summit Lake to upper Lake Clark through a narrow, deep valley within the Alaska Range. The 46-mile trip requires three days and hits a few stretches of Class III water. The hiking in tundra around Summit Lake is excellent and from there you make a portage to the river.

Mulchatna River Above Bonanza Hills, this river is a shallow, rocky channel from its headwaters at Turquoise Lake with stretches of Class III rapids. Below the hills the Mulchatna is an easy and leisurely float. Plan on two days to float from the lake to the end of Bonanza Hills. The entire river is a 220-mile run to the Nushagak River.

Places to Stay

Iliamna, a small village 30 miles south of the park, is the jump-off spot for most trips into Lake Clark National Park. Located at the airport is *Airport Hotel* (☎ 571-1276) that has a restaurant, taxi service and rooms for $85 per person per night, including all meals. There is also *Roadhouse Inn B&B* (☎ 571-1272) near downtown Iliamna, which charges $75 per person for a room with breakfast and $100 if you want all three meals.

Getting There & Away

Access into the Lake Clark region is by small charter plane which makes the area tough to visit on a limited budget. The cheapest way to reach the park is to book 14 days in advance through Alaska Airlines (☎ (800) 426-0333). A return ticket between Anchorage and Iliamna is $216. ERA Aviation, a contract carrier of Alaska Airlines, makes the flight twice a day. From Iliamna, you have to charter a plane to your destination within the park through air-taxi operators such as Iliamna Air Taxi (☎ 571-1248).

Western Alaska

PRIBILOF ISLANDS

The Pribilof Islands are in the Bering Sea, 300 miles west of Alaska's mainland and 900 miles from Anchorage. They are desolate, wind-swept places where the abundance of wildlife has made them tourist attractions despite the inhospitable weather. The four islands have two communities: St Paul (pop 600) and St George (pop 200) consisting mostly of Aleut Indians and government workers.

Although the Pribilof Islands are the home of the largest Aleut villages in the world, seals are the reason for the tourist trade. Every summer the tiny archipelago of rocky shores and steep cliffs becomes a mad scene when a million fur seals swim ashore to breed and raise their young. The seals spend most of the year at sea between California and Japan, but each summer they migrate to the Pribilofs, becoming the largest group of mammals anywhere in the world.

Many visitors also venture to the islands to view the extensive bird rookeries. About 2.5 million birds, made up of 200 species, nest at the Pribilofs, making it one of the largest seabird colonies in North America. The cliffs are easy to reach and photograph, and blinds have been erected on the beach to observe seals.

Because of strict regulations and limited facilities, most travelers choose package tours in order to visit the Pribilof Islands. Gray Line (☎ 277-5581 in Anchorage) offers a three-day tour of St Paul that departs Anchorage on Tuesday and Thursday. The tour, which includes accommodation, meals, air fares and transport to the beaches and rookeries, costs $764 per person. Reeve Aleutian Airways (☎ (800) 544-2248) also runs tours to St Paul and offers longer stays including three days for $736, four days for $887 and six days for $1191. This includes round-trip air fare, hotel and sightseeing transport but not meals.

If you do have an extra $1000 to spend, a more unique experience, while still seeing the immense amount of wildlife, is to travel independently to St George, a smaller and much less visited island. You can stay at the *St George Hotel*, a designated national historical landmark, where rooms are $89 a person per night and you can cook your own meals in the kitchen downstairs.

Since the island isn't that big (only five miles wide) hiking to within view of the wildlife is possible. Call St George Tanaq Corp (☎ 272-9886) in Anchorage to reserve

A fur seal pup

a room at the hotel. Then contact Peninsula Airways (☎ 243-2323) to book a flight to St George; the return fare is around $940.

NOME

Nome (pop 4500) serves as the transport center for much of Western Alaska, and during the summer, ocean-going barges unloading offshore are a common sight. A surge in gold prices in the late 1980s gave new life to the mining industry, and the lure of gold still draws people to Nome. However, it's summer tourists rather than miners who contribute to Nome's economy these days, especially with the growing tours of Eastern Siberia.

Some tourist see Nome as a grimy, treeless town of unpainted houses each with a forsaken refrigerator in the front yard. But you'll find the residents are extremely friendly and the gold-rush fever contagious. From the prospectors on the beach to the weather-beaten sourdoughs in the saloons, this place on the edge of the continent is as Alaskan as a town can get.

History

In 1898, the 'Three Lucky Swedes' Jafet Lindberg, Erik Lindblom and John Brynteson found gold in Anvil Creek. By that winter the news reached the gold fields of the Klondike and the following year the tent city that miners initially called Anvil City had a population of 10,000. More gold was found on the beaches nearby that summer and when the news finally made its way to Seattle in 1900 it set off yet another stampede of hopeful miners to Alaska. By the end of that year, there were 20,000 people in the town that was now called Nome – a place that would forever be associated around the world with gold and quick fortunes. At the height of the gold rush, Nome was declared Alaska's largest city in 1900 when the US Census recorded a permanent population of

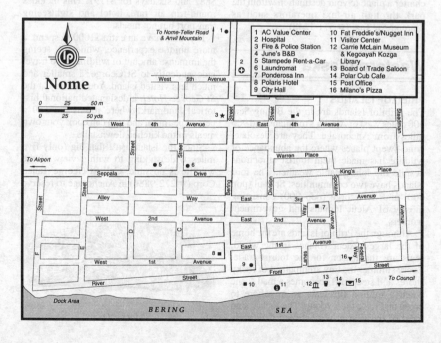

Nome

0   25   50 m
0   25   50 yds

To Nome-Teller Road & Anvil Mountain

To Airport

To Council

BERING   SEA

Dock Area

1 AC Value Center
2 Hospital
3 Fire & Police Station
4 June's B&B
5 Stampede Rent-a-Car
6 Laundromat
7 Ponderosa Inn
8 Polaris Hotel
9 City Hall
10 Fat Freddie's/Nugget Inn
11 Visitor Center
12 Carrie McLain Museum & Kegoayah Kozga Library
13 Board of Trade Saloon
14 Polar Cub Cafe
15 Post Office
16 Milano's Pizza

12,488 and listed one-third of all non-native Alaskan residents as living in the city.

Nome has had its fair share of natural disasters, like much of Alaska, as fires all but destroyed the town in 1905 and 1934 and a Bering Sea storm overpowered the sea walls in 1974. Though little of its gold-rush architecture remains, the city survived as did a little frontier facade along historical Front St.

Information
Tourist Office The Nome Visitor Center (☎ 443-5535) is on Front St across from the city hall and open from 9 am to 9 pm daily.

Money The National Bank of Alaska (☎ 443-2223) is at the corner of Front St and Federal Way.

Post The post office is on Front St next to the National Bank of Alaska.

Travel Agencies American Express Travel (☎ 443-2211) is on Front St across from the post office.

Library The Kegoayah Kozga Public Library (☎ 443-5133) is on Front St and includes a section of rare and first-edition books. It is open Tuesday through Saturday.

Laundry Blizzard Laundromat is on the corner of West C St and Seppala Dr, four blocks north of Front St.

Medical Services Norton Sound Hospital (☎ 443-3311), a 19-bed facility with 24-hour emergency medical service, is at the corner of 5th Ave and Bering St.

Things to See & Do
Nome's sights are along Front St and most travelers have little desire to venture any further into town.

Behind the Visitor Center is a wooden platform on the rock sea wall that provides views of the Bering Sea and Sledge Island. To the east of the center on Front St is the **Carrie McLain Museum** (☎ 443-2566) which is in the basement of the Kegoayah

Kozga Library. The museum features exhibits on the Bering Land Bridge, Inuit culture and gold-rush history, including more than 6000 photos from that era. It is open 10 am to 8 pm Monday through Friday and noon to 8 pm on Saturday and Sunday. There is no admission charge.

Also at the museum you can pick up a self-guided walking tour map that describes the city's few remaining historical buildings, noteworthy saloons and the old red-light district. Among the buildings listed is the **Nome City Hall**, west on Front St from the Visitor Center. In a lot next to this historical building is the **Iditarod finish-line arch**. The huge wooden structure is raised above Front St every March in anticipation of the mushers and their dog-sled teams ending the 1049-mile race here. Actually, the race is just the high point of a month-long celebration that includes such activities as golf tournaments on the frozen Bering Sea and softball games in which players wear snowshoes. All of it, of course, is merely a cure for cabin fever.

Nome's **public beach** is nearby, and in the height of the summer a few local children may be seen playing in the 45°F water. On Memorial Day (in May), 20 to 30 residents participate in the annual Polar Bear Swim by plunging into the ice-choked waters. A warmer swim can be obtained in the public pool (☎ 443-5717) at the Nome Public School. The admission charge is $2 per session.

Gold Dredges There are 44 gold dredges in the area surrounding the city, some of which are still being used, while many others lie deteriorating. The closest ones to Nome are the reactivated dredges near the northern end of the Nome Airport, two miles north of town. You can't walk near the dredges but you can view them and photograph the mining machinery from half a mile away.

Those fascinated by these relics of the gold-rush era might consider renting a car to explore the roads that extend into the Seward Peninsula from Nome. It is believed that there are close to 100 dredges scattered throughout the peninsula, many visible from the road.

Kayaking Inua Expedition Co (☎ 443-4994) offers river trips in sea kayaks. The trip down the Pilgrim River from the Kougarok Road to Pilgrim Hot Springs is $150 per person and includes transportation and lunch. Four-hour trips down the Nome and Snake rivers is $75 and multi-day paddles are available as well.

Organized Tours
City Tour Nome Tour & Marketing uses large vans to visit such sights as the golden beaches of Nome, the camp of Howard Farley, an original Iditarod musher, and Little Creek Mine. The price is $25 per person. Tours are booked and begin at the Nugget Inn (☎ 443-2651) on Front St.

Nome Area Nome Custom Adventures (☎ (800) 443-5134) runs a day-long tour to

Teller, 75 miles north-west of Nome, that includes a traditional lunch of moose, reindeer or salmon and an opportunity to purchase crafts at this Native Alaskan village. The cost is $125 per person.

Soviet Far East In 1988, Bering Air (☎ 443-5464) was the first commercial carrier to be granted permission for flights across the Bering Straits to the Russian city of Provideniya and today offers tours and charter flights to the Chukotka Region.

The Bering Air tour is for three days and two nights with a host family and includes a picnic on the tundra, cultural entertainment and a visit to a nearby hot springs. The cost is $999 per person for the flight, lodging, meals and ground transport.

Places to Stay
The Visitor Center has information about camping on the public beach which is a common practice in Nome. There are also 16 hotels and B&Bs and an 8% bed tax in Nome. The old section of the *Polaris Hotel* (☎ 443-2000) has singles with shared bath at $40 per night and doubles with private bath at $80. The *Ponderosa Inn* (☎ 443-5737) has

Only in Nome
To this day the Nome *Nugget* and the Wrangell *Sentinel* fight over which is Alaska's oldest newspaper. Regardless whether the *Nugget* is the oldest fish wrapper in the state, it's always been a good read. Even if you don't get to Nome, you can pick up a copy in the terminal of the Anchorage International Airport when you're passing through. One of it's best features is called 'Only in Nome' which once included a typical daily duty list for a woman in north-west Alaska:
- Order purple feathers for Miners & Mushers Ball dress.
- Buy fiberglass repair kit.
- Sell baby's outgrown snowmachine helmet.
- Mail dry cleaning to Anchorage.
- Buy skin sewing needles and rick-rack.
- Pull crap trap.
- Pay bills.
- Clean up spare bedroom for Iditarod guests.

singles/doubles for $65/75 and is nicer. Just a little more upscale is *Nugget Inn* (☎ 443-2323) on Front St with singles/doubles for $85/92. There is also a handful of B&Bs that generally charge $55/65 a single/double. Try *Betty's Igloo* (☎ 443-2419), *June's B&B* (☎ 443-5984) or *Oceanview Manor* (☎ 443-2133).

Places to Eat

Locals eat at the *Polar Cub Cafe* on Front St and *Fat Freddie's Spotted Owl Cafe* attached to the Nugget Inn. In a dig at environmentalists, Fat Freddies features boxes of 'Spotted Owl Helper' above the cash register as well as a menu with steak and eggs in the morning and Philly cheese steak sandwhich later in the day. Either is around $7 and most dinners cost from $11 to $15.

For pizza there's *Milano's Pizzeria*, on Front St. *AC Value Center*, seven blocks up Bering St from Front St, has a bakery, deli and even a Burger King outlet as well as groceries.

Entertainment

There are seven restaurants in Nome and eight bars, clear indication of what is important in this town. Even by Alaskan standards, drinking in Nome is legendary. Among the early bar owners in Nome was Wyatt Earp, the former marshal and noted gunslinger at the OK Corral. Earp was attracted by the Nome Gold Rush and ran the Dexter Bar during an era when it was said that 'a three-foot-thick glacier of urine ran between the saloons in the winter.'

All but two of the bars are clustered around each other on Front St with the *Board of Trade Saloon*, claiming to be the oldest bar on the Bering Sea, the most colorful.

Getting There & Away

Air Nome is serviced by Alaska Airlines (☎ (800) 468-2248), which offers three daily flights to the town from Anchorage. A return ticket, booked two weeks in advance, costs $358. Remember that three times a week Alaska Airlines also flies from Nome to Kotzebue and a round-trip, advance-purchase

ticket from Anchorage that includes both Bush communities is only $462.

Tours Many people visit Nome and Kotzebue on package tours, which, depending on the airfare, may not be as cheap as purchasing your ticket and lodging separately. Gray Line (☎ 277-5581 in Anchorage) offers a two-day package tour that begins in Anchorage, spends a day in Kotzebue and then overnights in Nome for $497. Alaska Airlines (☎ (800) 468-2248) has the identical trip for $447 plus one with a night each in Nome and Kotzebue for $495.

AROUND NOME

Extending from Nome are three major roads that are maintained by the state and well traveled during the summer. Each is an adventure in itself but they offer absolutely no services whatsoever, especially gas stations. There are four places in Nome to rent a car, all of them offering unlimited mileage in an area of the state where there is very limited mileage. *Stampede Rent-A-Car* (☎ 443-3838) has Ford Escorts for $55 a day, *Bonanza* (☎ 443-2221) has 4WD vehicles for $80 and *Budget Rent-A-Car* (☎ 443-2221) has campers that sleep four for $125 a day.

Nome-Council Road

This is a 72-mile route that heads north-east to the small Native Alaskan village of Council. For the first 30 miles the road follows the coast, where during the salmon season you'll see fish drying from driftwood racks. At *Mile 13* the road reaches Cape Nome, which offers a panoramic view of the Bering Sea, and then heads inland and passes through Solomon at *Mile 34*. The community was once prosperous and even boasted of having its own railroad. Today it's a ghost town and what's left of the Solomon Railroad will be seen before entering the town. Council is a town of 30 to 40 people during the summer and can only be reached after fording a small river. Otherwise head downriver to a launch and catch a ride with a resident crossing over in a boat.

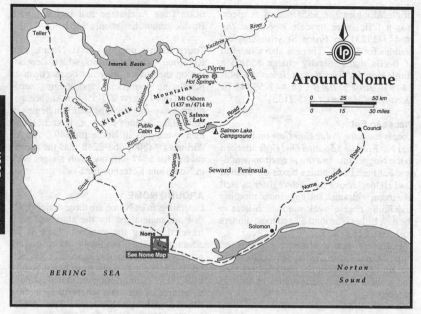

Kougarok Road

This is also known as Nome-Taylor Rd and leads 83 miles north through the heart of the Kigluaik Mountains. The drive will allow you to see more artefacts from the gold-rush days, including old miners' cabins, dredges and railroad bridges and tracks. At *Mile 40* you pass Salmon Lake Campground while a mile trek inland from the road is a public cabin managed by the city of Nome in the Mosquito Pass area. In the summer you can hike into the pass by leaving the road near the confluence of the Hudson Creek and the Nome River and heading west. The cabin is at the confluence of the Windy Creek and Sinuk River. Another 19 miles north of Salmon Lake at *Mile 65* is Pilgrim River Rd which leads west to Pilgrim Hot Springs.

Nome-Teller Road

This road leads 73 miles to Teller, a village of 200 with a gift shop and a small store but no other tourist facilities.

KOTZEBUE

Situated 26 miles north of the Arctic Circle, Kotzebue has one of the largest communities of indigenous people in the Bush; 90% of its 3600 residents are Inupiaq Eskimo. Kotzebue is on the north-west shore of the Baldwin Peninsula in Kotzebue Sound, near the mouths of the Kobuk and Noatak rivers. Traditionally, it serves as the transport and commerce center for Northwest Alaska.

The city also enjoys a steady flow of tourists in the summer, mostly through the efforts of NANA, a Native American corporation, and as the departure point into the new national preserves and parks nearby. NANA also manages a reindeer herd, numbering over 6000 head, on the Baldwin Peninsula. Many residents still depend on subsistence hunting and fishing to survive.

More recently Kotzebue has received a boost from the Red Dog Mine, the largest economic project in north-west Alaska located 90 miles north of the city. Red Dog

Mine holds some of the richest zinc deposits in North America and at peak production is expected to produce 5% of the world's supply of zinc and provide 360 direct jobs.

The majority of travelers to Kotzebue are either part of a tour group or are just passing through on their way to a wilderness expedition in the surrounding parks. The community is extremely difficult to visit for an independent traveler on a limited budget.

Information

Kotzebue doesn't have a visitor center or tourist office. The best place to call for advance information is the City Hall (☎ 442-3401).

Things to See & Do

The town is named after Polish explorer Otto von Kotzebue, who stumbled onto the village in 1816 while searching for the Northwest Passage for the Russians. Much of the town's history and culture can be viewed at the **Museum of the Arctic** (☎ 442-3747), where 2nd and 3rd avenues meet at the western end of town. The center is owned and operated by NANA, which offers two-hour programs (daily at 3 and 6 pm) of indigenous culture, demonstrations in Inuit handicrafts, a visit to the adjoining jade factory and a traditional blanket toss. Afterwards you can join a tour of the town and surrounding area. The shows are $20 per person and $55 when you add the city tour.

Perhaps the most interesting thing to do in Kotzebue is just stroll down **Front St** (also known as Shore Ave), a narrow gravel road only a few yards from the water at the northern edge of town. Here you can see salmon drying out on racks, fishing boats crowding the beach to be repaired and locals preparing for the long winter ahead. This is also the best place to watch the midnight sun roll along the horizon, painting the sea reddish gold in a beautiful scene of color and light reflecting off the water. Beginning in early June, the

BUSH

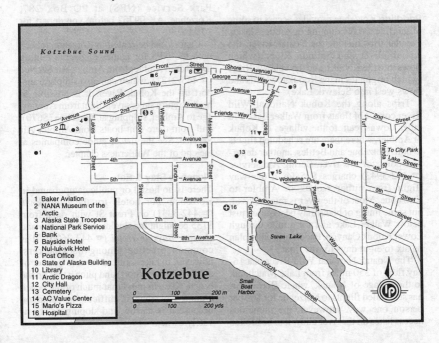

Kotzebue

Kotzebue Sound

Front Street
(Shore Avenue)
George Fox Way
2nd Avenue
Friends Way

1 Baker Aviation
2 NANA Museum of the Arctic
3 Alaska State Troopers
4 National Park Service
5 Bank
6 Bayside Hotel
7 Nul-luk-vik Hotel
8 Post Office
9 State of Alaska Building
10 Library
11 Arctic Dragon
12 City Hall
13 Cemetery
14 AC Value Center
15 Mario's Pizza
16 Hospital

To City Park
Wanda Lake Street

Swan Lake

Small Boat Harbor

0   100   200 m
0   100   200 yds

BUSH

Raising Money in Arctic Alaska
When public radio and television stations around the country raise money through tele-a-thons and auctions, they generally give away T-shirts, coffee mugs, wildlife prints, or lunch with local celebrities.

Not KOTZ, the public radio station in Kotzebue. At the 1995 fund-raising auction for this Arctic station the most popular items by far were a caribou with a couple of whitefish tucked into the carcass, 10 pounds of muktuk (whale blubber), two seals and a husky-wolf puppy. The caribou and puppy each drew bids of $200, the seals went for $100 each, and the muktuk sold for $175. ■

sun does not set for almost six weeks in Kotzebue.

In the center of town there is a large **cemetery** where spirit houses have been erected over many of the graves.

Paddling Kotzebue provides access to some of the finest river running in Arctic Alaska. Popular trips include the Noatak River, the Kobuk River and Salmon River (which flows into the Kobuk), and the Selawik River (which originates in the Kobuk lowlands and flows west into Selawik Lake).

Trips along the Kobuk National Wild River consist of floats from Walker Lake 140 miles downstream to the villages of Kobuk or Ambler, where there are scheduled flights to both Kotzebue and Bettles, another departure point for this river. Bering Air Service (☎ 442-3943) charges $95 for a one-way flight from either Kobuk or Ambler to Kotzebue. Most of the river is rated Class I, but some lining of boats may be required just below Walker Lake and for a mile through Lower Kobuk Canyon. Paddlers usually plan on six to eight days for the float.

The Noatak National Wild River is a 16-day float of 350 miles from Lake Matcharak to the village of Noatak, where Bering Air has scheduled flights to Kotzebue for $60 per person one way. However, the numerous access lakes on the river allow it to be broken

down into shorter paddles. The entire river is rated from Class I to II.

The upper portion in the Brooks Range offers much more dramatic scenery and is usually accessed from Bettles (see the following Gates of the Arctic section). The lower half, accessed through Kotzebue, flows through a broad, gently sloping valley where hills replace the sharp peaks of the Brooks Range. The most common trip here is to put in at Nimiuktuk River where, within an hour of paddling, you enter the 65-mile-long Grand Canyon of the Noatak, followed by the seven-mile-long Noatak Canyon. Most paddlers pull out at Kelly River where there is a ranger station with a radio. Below the confluence with the Kelly River, the Noatak becomes heavily braided.

For more information contact the National Park Service office (☎ 442-3890) in the Museum of the Arctic at Kotzebue, which is open Monday to Friday from 8.30 am to 5.30 pm in the summer, or write to the National Park Service (NPS) at PO Box 287, Kotzebue, AK 99752 before you depart for Alaska.

Canoes can be rented in Kotzebue (check with the NPS for names of people renting them) or in Ambler from Ambler Air Service (☎ 445-2121), which can also supply transport up the Kobuk River. It is possible to book a return supersaver flight from Anchorage to Ambler, stopping at Kotzebue ($670), and from there rent boats from Ambler Air Service. See the list of guide companies at the end of the Wilderness chapter.

Places to Stay & Eat
There is no hostel or public campground in Kotzebue. For hotels try the *Nul-luk-vik* (☎ 442-3331) on Front St with rates from $135 per night for singles, or the nearby and cheaper *Bayside Hotel* (☎ 442-3600). It is common practice among backpackers, however, to hike south of town (a quarter of a mile past the airport) and pitch a tent on the beach. Keep in mind that much of the beach around Kotzebue is difficult to camp on because it is narrow and sloping or is privately owned.

For a meal in Kotzebue try *Mario's Pizza*, the *Arctic Dragon* for Chinese, or one of the restaurants in the hotels.

Getting There & Away
Alaska Airlines (☎ (800) 426-0333) offers a round-trip ticket to Kotzebue, if booked two weeks in advance, for $348 from Anchorage. You can also purchase a round-trip ticket from Anchorage with stopovers in both Nome and Kotzebue for $462. See Getting There & Away in Nome for the tours offered by Gray Line and Alaska Airlines.

Arctic Alaska

DALTON HIGHWAY
Although officially called the Dalton Hwy, for years this road was best known simply as the 'haul road' because of its origins as a rough truck supply route during the construction of the Trans-Alaska Pipeline. This stretch of gravel winds 416 miles north from the Elliott Hwy to Deadhorse at Prudhoe Bay, the community that houses the workers of what was once the largest oil reserve in the USA. Prudhoe Bay is the start of the pipeline that carries oil 800 miles to the ice-free port of Valdez on Prince William Sound.

After the road was completed in 1978, all but the first 56 miles of the highway to the Yukon River was kept closed to the public. In 1981, after a bitter battle in the state legislature, the public was allowed to drive 211 miles to Disaster Creek along a section of the highway that takes you into the Brooks Range and near the border of the Gates of the Arctic National Park & Preserve. In 1994, the entire road was opened and the requirement to secure a permit from the Department of Transportation was dropped.

The Dalton Hwy is the northernmost extension of the US highway system but definitely not a trip for the misinformed or ill prepared. In the summer the 28-foot-wide truck route of course gravel is dusty, punctuated with potholes and littered with the

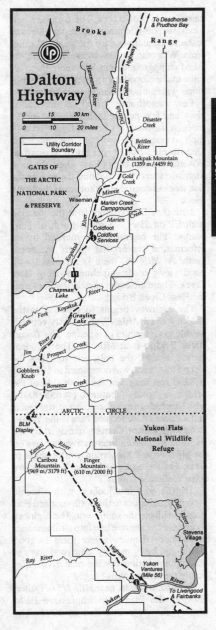

BUSH

carcasses of blown tires. There are few services, such as telephone, tire repair, fuel and restaurants, and none for the final 225 miles from Wiseman to Deadhorse. Beyond the BLM campground near Wiseman, there are only undeveloped camp sites and turnouts, some with outhouses and picnic tables.

Few motorhomes travel up the Dalton Hwy and few people manage to exceed 55 mph on the road. It's best to figure on a 40 mph average and two hard days to reach Deadhorse. Better yet, turn around at Wiseman or the Atigun Pass where the most dramatic scenery is. Beyond the pass is the flat, treeless coastal plain known as the North Slope.

Mile 0 of Dalton Hwy is at the junction with Elliott Hwy, 73 miles north of Fairbanks. The beginning is marked by an information center that covers the route north. At *Mile 25*, there is a lookout with good views of the pipeline crossing Hess Creek. There are camp sites in the trees near the Hess Creek Bridge.

The highway begins to descend to the Yukon River at *Mile 47*, and shortly you will be able to view miles of pipeline. The **Yukon River Bridge** is at *Mile 56*. The wooden-decked bridge, the only one to cross the Yukon in Alaska, was completed in 1975 and is 2290 feet long. On the north side of the bridge is Yukon Ventures (☎ 655-9001), which includes a motel, restaurant, tire repair and a phone. Also located here is the **Yukon Crossing Visitor Center**, managed by the BLM and featuring interpretive displays on the pipeline and the terrain you're about to enter. On the east side of the highway are some rustic camp sites.

At *Mile 86.5* is a lookout with a scenic view of granite tors to the north-east and Fort Hamlin Hills to the south-east. The highway ascends above the tree line into an alpine area in another 10 miles where there is good hiking and berry picking. The road stays in this alpine section for the next five miles before the terrain turns rugged.

The **Arctic Circle**, near *Mile 115* of Dalton Hwy, is the site of an impressive BLM display that was installed in 1992. The

exhibit includes a large, brightly colored circumpolar map of the imaginary line and four information panels explaining the basis for the seasons and what it means to Arctic plants and animals. There is also a viewing deck, picnic tables and a road leading a half mile to rustic campsites.

Keep in mind, however, that you can't really see the midnight sun here because it ducks behind the mountains on the northern horizon at that magical moment. To view the sun all night long (having driven this far north you might as well do it) continue on **Gobbler's Knob**, a hilltop viewpoint at *Mile 132* where there is a pullover and an outhouse.

From this turn-off, the road passes six streams and small Grayling Lake in the next 50 miles, all of which offer superb grayling fishing. *Coldfoot Services* (☎ 678-5201), a lodge and restaurant that also sells gasoline and groceries, is at *Mile 175*. The restaurant is open 24 hours and the food is surprisingly good. There is a laundromat, where a shower is $6, and a motel with single/double rooms for $95/125. If you want to camp, head another five miles north to the very pleasant *Marion Creek Campground* (27 sites, free) at *Mile 180*. The campground is situated in an open spruce forest with stunning views of the Brooks Range.

The road is now near the boundaries of Gates of the Arctic National Park and the scenery is at its best. Wildlife is plentiful, especially dall sheep high on the mountain slopes. After passing *Mile 186* there is a lookout where you can view the historical mining community of **Wiseman**, west of the highway across the Koyukuk River, which can now be reached by an improved road at *Mile 188.6*. The town's heyday was in 1910 when it was a service center for gold miners, and many buildings from that era still stand. Among them **Wiseman Trading Company**, which doubles as the general store and the town's museum with historic photos and mining equipment. Wiseman also has a public phone and a *campground*.

More spectacular mountain scenery begins around *Mile 194* of the Dalton Hwy, with the first views of Sukakpak Mountain to the north and Wiehl Mountain to the east, both over 4000 feet in elevation. Poss Mountain (6189 feet) comes into view to the east after another 2.5 miles, and the Koyukuk River, a heavily braided stream, is seen near *Mile 201*.

Just before *Mile 204* is a lookout with a half-mile trail leading to Sukakpak Mountain. The mounds between the road and the mountain were formed by ice pushing up the soil and vegetation.

Another lookout is passed after *Mile 206*, where there are good views of Snowden Mountain (5775 feet), 10 miles to the north-west. Six miles north of the lookout is Disaster Creek and the turnaround point before the road was open.

You are now allowed to drive the remaining 208 miles to Deadhorse. Even if you have no desire to see the Arctic Coastal Plain, continue another 40 miles to **Atigun Pass**. At an elevation of 4,800 feet, this is the highest highway pass in Alaska and marks the Continental Divide. You begin the steep climb to the pass at *Mile 242.5* and reach it within two miles where there is a pullover at the top. To the east are the Phillip Smith Mountains, to the west Edicott Mountains. Straight ahead is the descent into the North Slope, the arctic plains beyond the treeline.

Rustic *camp sites* are located at Galbraith Lake at *Mile 275*, where both BLM and USFWS maintain field stations. Three more scenic pull-overs are passed on the way to Deadhorse, the last being the **Coastal Plain Overlook** at *Mile 365*.

Deadhorse, reached at *Mile 414*, is the end of the highway and is a few miles short of the Prudhoe Bay oilfields and the Arctic Ocean. Surprisingly the service center has a population that ranges from 3000 to more than 8000 as well as three motels, including the *Arctic Caribou Inn* (☎ 659-2840), where rooms are $85 to $175 a night. There are also restaurants, fuel, supplies and a post office. Send mom a post card from the top of the world! For security reasons, you can't drive into the massive oil complex but must join a commercial tour of it through *Prudhoe Bay*

Hotel (☎ 659-2449). What disappoints most people, however, is to discover, after driving 400 miles north, they can't camp on the shores of the Arctic Ocean.

Tours
There are now a number of tours available in Fairbanks for a trip up the highway. Northern Alaska Tour Company (☎ 474-8600) offers three, including a daily bus tour to the Arctic Circle and back for $99 and another with a flight back to Fairbanks for $159. The company also has a three-day trip to Prudhoe Bay for $599 that includes lodging at Wiseman and Deadhorse, some meals and a flight back.

Princess Tours (☎ 479-9660) and Gray Line (☎ 456-5816) have three-day, two-night tours to the oil fields priced at $696.

Getting There & Away
Car Finding somebody to rent you a car in Fairbanks for travel on the Dalton Hwy would be a major challenge if not an impossible one. So don't even bother with the used-car rentals (see the Getting Around section in the Fairbanks chapter). If you're driving, remember that the road is used by tractor-trailer rigs driving at high speeds. Never stop in the middle of the road to observe wildlife or scenery, as trucks have limited braking ability. Gasoline at about $2 a gallon, tire-repair services and limited food supplies are available where the road crosses the Yukon River, Coldfoot, and Deadhorse.

GATES OF THE ARCTIC NATIONAL PARK
The Gates of the Arctic National Park & Preserve, one of the finest wilderness areas in the world, straddles the Arctic Divide in the Brooks Range, 200 miles north-west of Fairbanks.

The entire park covering 8.4 million acres, extends 200 miles from east to west and lies totally north of the Arctic Circle. The park extends from the southern foothills of the Brooks Range, across the range's ragged peaks and down onto the North Slope. Most of the park is vegetated with shrubs or is tundra. It is a habitat for grizzly bears, wolves, dall sheep, moose, caribou and wolverines. Fishing is considered superb for grayling and arctic char in the clear streams and for lake trout in the larger, deeper lakes.

Within this preserve you have dozens of rivers to run, miles of valleys and tundra slopes to hike and, of course, the Gates themselves. Mt Boreal and Frigid Crags are the gates that flank the North Fork of the Koyukuk River. It was through these landmark mountains that Robert Marshall found an unobstructed path northward to the Arctic coast of Alaska. That was in 1929 and Marshall's naming of the two mountains has remained ever since.

Hiking in the Arctic

The park is a vast wilderness containing no National Park Service facilities, campgrounds or trails. Many backpackers follow the long, open valleys for extended treks or work their way to higher elevations where open tundra and sparse shrubs provide good hiking terrain.

Regardless of where you hike, trekking in the Arctic is a challenge and not for anybody who's only used to the signposted trails of the Lower 48. Hiking across boggy ground and tussock, inevitable on any trip in the Gates of the Arctic, has been described by one guide as 'walking on basketballs'. A good day's travel in the Arctic is covering five or six miles.

It's also important to remember how fragile the Arctic ecosystem is. Its delicate balance of tundra, tussock plains and spruce boreal forests can be easily damaged by the most sensitive backpackers and require years to regenerate because of the permafrost and the short growing season. For these reasons the NPS puts a six-person limit on trekking parties. Try to avoid forming trails by traveling in a fan pattern whenever possible and by never marking routes.

Camp site selection is your most important decision when trying to minimize impact. Gravel bars along rivers and creeks are the best choice due to their durable and well-drained nature.

If you must choose a vegetated site, select one with a hardier species such as moss or heath rather than the more fragile lichens. And avoid building fires at all costs. Tree growth in the Arctic is extremely slow, a spruce only inches in diameter may be several hundred years old.

Most backpackers enter the park by way of charter air-taxi out of Bettles, which can land on lakes, rivers or river bars. Extended treks across the park require outdoor experience and good map and compass skills. One of the more popular treks is the four to five-day hike from Summit Lake through the Gates to Redstar Lake.

Less experienced backpackers often choose to be dropped off and picked up at one lake and from there explore the surrounding region on day hikes. Lakes ideal for this include Summit Lake, the Karupa lakes region, Redstar Lake, Hunt Fork Lake or Chimney Lake.

The lone exception to chartering a plane is the trek beginning from the Dalton Hwy into several different areas along the eastern border of the park. First stop at the Coldfoot Information Center for advice and assistance in trip planning. Then you continue north to your access point into the park. The further north you travel on the highway, the quicker you get into the tundra and the truly spectacular scenery. Many backpackers stop at Wiseman, however, which provides access to several routes including the following two.

Nolan/Wiseman Creek Area Just before *Mile 189* of the Dalton Hwy, head west at the Wiseman exit and continue hiking along the Nolan Rd which passes through Nolan, a hamlet of a few families, and ends at Nolan Creek. This will provide access to Wiseman Creek and Nolan Creek Lake which lies in the valley of Wiseman and Nolan creeks at the foot of three passes: Glacier, Pasco and Snowshoes.

Any of these passes provides a route to Glacier River which can be followed to the north fork of the Koyukuk for a more extensive hike. The USGS topographic maps that cover this area are Wiseman B-1, B-2, C-1 and C-2.

Lower Hammond River Area From Wiseman continue north by hiking along the Hammond Rd which can be followed for quite away along the Hammond River. By following the river, you can further explore the park by following one of several drainage areas including Vermont, Canyon and Jenny Creek, which heads east to Jenny Creek Lake. The USGS maps that cover this area are Chandlar C-6 and B-6 and Wiseman C-1 and B-1.

Paddling
Floatable rivers in the park include the John, the north fork of the Koyukuk, the Tinayguk, the Alatna and the middle fork of the Koyukuk River from Wiseman to Bettles. The headwaters for the Noatak and Kobuk rivers are in the park.

The waterways range from Class I to III in difficulty. Of the various rivers, the north fork of the Koyukuk River is one of the most popular because the float begins in the shadow of the Gates and continues downstream 100 miles to Bettles through Class I and II waters. Canoes and rafts can be rented in Bettles and then floated downstream back to the village.

Upper Noatak The best known river and the most popular for paddlers is the upper portion of the Noatak. Part of the reason is the excellent scenery as you float through the sharp peaks of the Brooks Range, and also because it is a relatively mild river that can be handled by many canoeists on an unguided trip.

The most common trip is a 60-mile float that begins with a put-in near Portage Creek and ends at a riverside lake near Kacachurak Creek, just outside the park boundaries. This float is often covered in five to seven days but does involve some Class II and possible Class III stretches of rapids towards the end. Also keep in mind that during the summer you will most likely see other canoeing or rafting parties on the water.

Guide Companies A number of guide companies run trips through the Gates of the Arctic National Park, including Sourdough Outfitters (☎ 692-5252 in Bettles) which charges $1350 for a seven-day canoeing expedition on the north fork of the Koyukuk River and $1950 for a 10-day paddle on the headwaters of the Noatak River. Also check the Wilderness chapter for Fairbanks outfitters that offer trips in the Brooks Range region.

Canoes and rafts can be rented from Sourdough Outfitters which offers unguided expeditions with arranged drop-off and pick-up air services for independent backpackers. A six-day backpacking adventure from Summit Lake to Chimney Lake is $441 per person for a party of two, and to turn that into a two-week adventure with a paddle down the north fork of the Koyukuk is $625. The company has a wide range of other unguided trips and rents canoes for $25 a day and rafts for $35 to $50 depending on their duration. Bettles Lodge (☎ 692-5111) also rents rafts/canoes for $45/35 a day.

Getting There & Away
Access to the park's backcountry is usually accomplished in two steps, with the first being a scheduled flight from Fairbanks to Bettles. Check out Frontier Flying Service (☎ 474-0014), or Larry's Flying Service (☎ (800) 478-5169) in Fairbanks which makes regular flights to Bettles for $200 round trip.

The second step is to charter an air-taxi in Bettles to your destination within the park. A Cessna 185 on floats holds three passengers and costs around $225 per hour. Most areas in the park can be reached in under two hours of flying time from Bettles. If you're in Bettles, check with Brooks Range Aviation (☎ 692-5444) or Bettles Air Service (☎ 692-5111) for air charters.

The alternative to expensive air chartering is to begin your trip from the Dalton Hwy. Travelers with time but little money can hitchhike the highway. Trucks will rarely if ever pick you up but a trickle of cars use the road daily in the summer.

BETTLES

This small village of 40 residents serves as the major departure point to the Gates of the Arctic National Park. Originally Bettles was six miles down the middle fork of the Koyukuk River. It was founded by Gordon C Bettles in 1900 as a trading post. Riverboats would work their way up the Koyukuk and unload their supplies in Bettles from where it was transported to smaller scows and horse-drawn barges. The smaller boats would then take the cargo to the mining country further upriver.

WWII brought a need for a major airstrip in Arctic Alaska and the Civil Aviation Agency (now the FAA) chose to construct one on better ground upriver. Eventually the entire village moved to the airstrip and today has the distinction of being the smallest incorporated city in Alaska.

Information

The National Park Service maintains a ranger station (☎ 692-5494) at Bettles, just beyond the airstrip next door to Sourdough Outfitters. During the summer the station is open daily and inside there are a stack of hand-outs and a small library of books and videos relating to the park.

Hiking

If you find yourself with an unexpected day in Bettles, something that can easily happen in August, take a hike up to Birch Hill Lake. The trailhead is unmarked but located by first heading to the Evansville Health Clinic. Next to it is a small brown house, and the trail can be found just to the right of it. It's a three-mile trek to the lake and can get swampy. It's best to wear rubber boots.

Places to Stay & Eat

Camping is allowed behind the Bettles Flight Service building, off the runway and at the north edge of the aircraft parking area, where you'll find barbecue grills. It would also be just as easy to pitch a tent on the gravel bars along the Middle Fork of the Kuyukuk River that the town overlooks.

A variety of lodging is available at *Bettles*

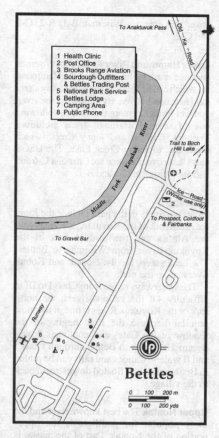

Bettles

1 Health Clinic
2 Post Office
3 Brooks Range Aviation
4 Sourdough Outfitters
  & Bettles Trading Post
5 National Park Service
6 Bettles Lodge
7 Camping Area
8 Public Phone

Lodge (☎ 692-5111), just off the runway. (Actually everything in Bettles is just off the runway.) It is a classic Alaskan log lodge with accommodation, a restaurant, a small tavern and bush pilots constantly wandering through in their hip boots. Singles/doubles are $85/110 a night, and a bed in a bunkhouse is $15. *Sourdough Outfitters* (☎ 692-5252) also has a bunkroom and showers for rent, and charges $15 a night for a bunk.

The restaurant is open from 8 am to 7 pm and has breakfasts for $8, hamburgers $7 and the single main course at dinner for $12. Sign up for dinner if you plan to eat there. The

This child is one of 42,000 Inuits living in Alaska.

1935. The plane carrying Rogers and Wiley Post stalled and crashed into a river, 15 miles south of Barrow, during their trip from Fairbanks to Siberia.

Most people visit the town to say they've been at the top of the world or to view the midnight sun, which never sets between 10 May and 2 August. There is little other reason to make the expensive side trip to Barrow.

The return air fare from Fairbanks can be as low as $360 if you book it 14 days in advance on Alaska Airlines, but rooms in the *Top of the World Hotel* (☎ 852-3900) range from $149 to $209 during the summer. Barrow is not geared for tourism as much as Nome and independent travellers can feel a bit of tension between themselves and the locals.

Getting There & Away
The best way to see Barrow is to book a package tour. Gray Line (☎ 456-5816) offers a 12-hour trip to the community for $411

other option for food is the *Bettles Trading Post*, which is run by Sourdough Outfitters and has the usual Bush Alaska selection and prices to match.

Getting There & Away
See Getting There & Away in the earlier Gates of the Arctic section

BARROW
Barrow (pop 4000) is the largest Inupiat Inuit community in Alaska and one of the largest in North America.

Although residents can enjoy such modern-day conveniences as a local bus system and gas heating in their homes courtesy of the nearby oil fields, they remain traditional in their outlook; this is symbolized by the spring whale hunts.

The town, the northernmost community in the USA, is 330 miles north of the Arctic Circle and less than 1200 miles from the North Pole. Barrow is close to the place where US humorist Will Rogers died in

---

Freeing the Whales

Barrow became front-page news around the world in the fall of 1988 after several residents discovered that three grey whales had become entrapped by ice during their migration south to warmer waters off the coast of Mexico. The Inuit, wielding chainsaws, spent long hours cutting holes in the ice to allow the mammals to breathe.

When the media caught wind of the story, Barrow was flooded by reporters and television crews. The Top of the World Hotel was booked solid, there was a 30-minute wait to be seated at Pepe's North of the Border Mexican Restaurant and somebody was selling souvenir T-shirts (your choice of commemorative logos) on the streets of Barrow.

The unusual ordeal lasted almost two weeks and more than a $1 million was spent keeping the whales alive before a Soviet icebreaker finally cleared a path through the ice to open water. Two whales swam to freedom, one died and Barrow returned to its normal lifestyle after the media left. 'It was a good experience,' said an employee of a local restaurant, 'but we're glad to see it over with.' ∎

from Fairbanks and $581 from Anchorage. Even better, Alaska Airlines (☎ (800) 468-2248) offers the same day trip from Fairbanks for $383 per person and an overnight trip with accommodations in the Top of the World Hotel for $427 base price.

Glossary

Alcan or **Alaska Hwy** – the main overland route into Alaska. Although the highway is almost completely paved now, completing a journey across this legendary road is still a special accomplishment that earns you a slash mark on the side of your pick-up truck. The Alcan begins at the *Mile 0* cairn in Dawson Creek in north-eastern British Columbia, Canada. It then heads north-west through Whitehorse, the capital of the Yukon Territory, to Fairbanks in Alaska. Actually the highway officially ends at Delta Junction (*Mile 1422*) 101 miles south-east of Fairbanks (*Mile 1523*). Between the two you follow the Richardson Hwy which comes north from Valdez in Prince William Sound.

aurora borealis or **northern lights** – a spectacular show on clear nights, possible at almost any time of the year. The mystical snakes of light that weave across the sky from the northern horizon are the result of gas particles colliding with solar electrons. The northern lights are best viewed from the Interior, away from city lights, between late summer and winter

bidarka – a skin-covered sea kayak used by the Aleuts

blanket toss – an activity originating with the Inuit in which a large animal skin is used to toss a hunter into the air to look for whales offshore

blue cloud – what Southeasterners call a break in the clouds

break-up – a phrase applied to rivers when the ice suddenly begins to melt, breaks up and flows downstream. Many residents also use it to describe spring in Alaska when the rain begins, the snow melts and everything turns to mud and slush

bunny boots – large, oversized and usually white plastic boots used extensively in subzero weather to prevent the feet from freezing. Much to the horror of many Alaskans, the company which manufactured the boot announced in 1995 it would discontinue the style

The Bush – any area in the state neither connected by road to Anchorage nor part of the Alaska Marine Hwy

cabin fever – a winter condition in which cross-eyed Alaskans go stir-crazy in their one-room cabins because of too little sunlight and too much time spent indoors

cache – a small hut or storage room built high off the ground to keep supplies and spare food away from roaming bears and wolves. The term, however, has found its way onto the neon signs of everything from liquor stores to pizza parlors in the cities

capital move – the political issue that raged in the early 1980s which concerned moving the state capital from Juneau closer to Anchorage. The issue was somewhat laid to rest in a 1982 state election when residents rejected the funding for the move north

cheechako – tenderfoot, greenhorn or somebody trying to survive their first year in Alaska

chum – not your mate or good buddy but a nickname for the dog salmon

clearcut – a hated sight for environmentalists, this is an area where loggers have cut every trees, large and small, leaving nothing standing. A traveler's first view of one, often from a ferry, is a shocking sight

d-2 – a phrase that covers the lands issue of the late 1970s, pitting environmentalists against developers over the federal government's preservation of 100 million acres of Alaskan wilderness as wildlife reserves, forests and national parks

developers – those residents of Alaska who favor development of the state's natural resources and land through such endeavors as logging and mining, as opposed to preserving it in national parks

Eskimo ice cream – a traditional food made of whipped berries, seal oil and snow

fish wheel – a wooden trap that scoops salmon or other large fish out of a river into a holding tank by utilizing the current as power

freeze-up – that point in November or December when most rivers and lakes ice over, signaling to Alaskans that their long winter has started in earnest

glacier fishing – picking up flopping salmon along the Copper River in Cordova after a large calving from the Childs Glacier strands the fish during the August spawning run. Practised by both bears and people, neither group needs a state fishing license to participate

greenies – a nickname for environmentalists and others who celebrated the passage of the Alaska Lands Bill

humpie – a nickname for the humpback, or pink salmon, the mainstay of the fishing industry in the Southeast

ice worm – a small, thin black worm that thrives in glacial ice and was made famous by a Robert Service poem

Iditarod – the 1049-mile sled-dog race held every March from Anchorage to Nome. The winner usually completes the course in under 14 days and takes home $50,000

Lower 48 – an Alaskan term for the continental USA

moose nuggets – hard, smooth little objects dropped by moose after a good meal. Some enterprising resident in Homer has capitalized on them by baking, varnishing and trimming them with evergreen leaves to sell during Christmas as Moostletoe

mukluks – lightweight boots of seal skin trimmed with fur, made by the Inuit

muskeg – the bogs in Alaska where layers of matted plant life float on top of stagnant water. These are bad areas in which to hike or pitch a tent

no-see-um – nickname for the tiny gnats found throughout much of the Alaska wilderness, especially in the Interior and parts of the Brooks Range

Outside – to residents, any place that isn't Alaska

Outsider – to residents, anyone who isn't an Alaskan

permafrost – permanently frozen subsoil that covers two-thirds of the state

petroglyphs – ancient rock carvings

potlatch – a traditional gathering of indigenous people held to commemorate any memorable occasion

qiviut – the wool of the musk ox that is often woven into garments

scat – animal droppings, however the term is usually used to describe those of a bear. If it is dark brown or bluish and somewhat square in shape, a bear has passed by. If it is steaming, the bear is eating blueberries around the next bend

solstice – the first day of summer on 21 June and the first day of winter on 21 December. In Alaska, however, solstice is synonymous with the longest day of the year and is celebrated in most towns

sourdough – any old timer in the state who, it is said, is 'sour on the country but without enough dough to get out'. Newer residents believe the term applies to anybody who has survived an Alaskan winter. The term also applies to a 'yeasty' mixture used to make bread or pancakes

stinkhead – an Inuit 'treat' made by burying a salmon head in the sand. Leave the head to ferment for up to 10 days, then dig it up, wash off the sand and enjoy

Southeast sneakers – also known as Ketchikan tennis shoes, Sitka slippers, Petersburg pumps and a variety of other names. These are the tall, reddish-brown rubber boots that Southeast residents wear when it rains, and often when it doesn't

taku wind – Juneau's sudden gusts of wind

that may exceed 100 mph in the spring and fall. Often the winds cause horizontal rain which, as the name indicates, comes straight at you instead of falling on you. In Anchorage and throughout the Interior, these sudden rushes of air over or through mountain gaps are called 'williwaws'

tundra – often used to refer to the vast, treeless Arctic plains

ulu – a fan-shaped knife that indigenous people traditionally used to chop and scrape meat, but the gift shops now use to lure tourists

Index

LONELY PLANET PHRASEBOOKS

Nepali phrasebook

Ethiopian Amharic phrasebook

Latin American Spanish phrasebook

Ukrainian phrasebook

Greek phrasebook

Vietnamese phrasebook

Building bridges,
Breaking barriers,
Beyond babble-on

Listen for the gems

Speak your own words

Ask your own questions

Master of your own image

- handy pocket-sized books
- easy to understand Pronunciation chapter
- clear and comprehensive Grammar chapter
- romanisation alongside script to allow ease of pronunciation
- script throughout so users can point to phrases
- extensive vocabulary sections, words and phrases for every situations
- full of cultural information and tips for the traveller

'...vital for a real DIY spirit and attitude in language learning' – Backpacker

'the phrasebooks have good cultural backgrounders and offer solid advice for challenging situations in remote locations' – San Francisco Examiner

'...they are unbeatable for their coverage of the world's more obscure languages' – The Geographical Magazine

---

Arabic (Egyptian)
Arabic (Moroccan)
Australia
 Australian English, Aboriginal and Torres Strait languages
Baltic States
 Estonian, Latvian, Lithuanian
Bengali
Burmese
Brazilian
Cantonese
Central Europe
 Czech, French, German, Hungarian, Italian and Slovak
Eastern Europe
 Bulgarian, Czech, Hungarian, Polish, Romanian and Slovak
Egyptian Arabic
Ethiopian (Amharic)
Fijian
French
German
Greek

Hindi/Urdu
Indonesian
Italian
Japanese
Korean
Lao
Latin American Spanish
Malay
Mandarin
Mediterranean Europe
 Albanian, Croatian, Greek, Italian, Macedonian, Maltese, Serbian, Slovene
Mongolian
Moroccan Arabic
Nepali
Papua New Guinea
Pilipino (Tagalog)
Quechua
Russian
Scandinavian Europe
 Danish, Finnish, Icelandic, Norwegian and Swedish

South-East Asia
 Burmese, Indonesian, Khmer, Lao, Malay, Tagalog (Pilipino), Thai and Vietnamese
Spanish
Sri Lanka
Swahili
Thai
Thai Hill Tribes
Tibetan
Turkish
Ukrainian
USA
 US English, Vernacular Talk, Native American languages and Hawaiian
Vietnamese
Western Europe
 Basque, Catalan, Dutch, French, German, Irish, Italian, Portuguese, Scottish Gaelic, Spanish (Castilian) and Welsh

---

LONELY PLANET JOURNEYS

JOURNEYS is a unique collection of travel writing – published by the company that understands travel better than anyone else. It is a series for anyone who has ever experienced – or dreamed of – the magical moment when they encountered a strange culture or saw a place for the first time. They are tales to read while you're planning a trip, while you're on the road or while you're in an armchair, in front of a fire.

JOURNEYS books catch the spirit of a place, illuminate a culture, recount a crazy adventure, or introduce a fascinating way of life. They always entertain, and always enrich the experience of travel.

'Idiosyncratic, entertainingly diverse and unexpected . . . from an international writership'
– The Australian

'Books which offer a closer look at the people and culture of a destination, and enrich travel experiences'
– American Bookseller

FULL CIRCLE
A South American Journey
Luis Sepúlveda
Translated by Chris Andrews

Full Circle invites us to accompany Chilean writer Luis Sepúlveda on 'a journey without a fixed itinerary'. Whatever his subject – brutalities suffered under Pinochet's dictatorship, sleepy tropical towns visited in exile, or the landscapes of legendary Patagonia – Sepúlveda is an unflinchingly honest yet lyrical storyteller. Extravagant characters and extraordinary situations are memorably evoked: gauchos organising a tournament of lies, a scheming heiress on the lookout for a husband, a pilot with a corpse on board his plane . . . Part autobiography, part travel memoir, *Full Circle* brings us the distinctive voice of one of South America's most compelling writers.

Luis Sepúlveda was born in Chile in 1949. Imprisoned by the Pinochet dictatorship for his socialist beliefs, he was for many years a political exile. He has written novels, short stories, plays and essays. His work has attracted many awards and has been translated into numerous languages.

'Detachment, humour and vibrant prose' – El País

'an absolute cracker' – The Bookseller

This project has been assisted by the Commonwealth Government through the Australia Council, its arts funding and advisory body.

LONELY PLANET TRAVEL ATLASES

Lonely Planet has long been famous for the number and quality of its guidebook maps. Now we've gone one step further and in conjunction with Steinhart Katzir Publishers produced a handy companion series: Lonely Planet travel atlases – maps of a country produced in book form.

Unlike other maps, which look good but lead travellers astray, our travel atlases have been researched on the road by Lonely Planet's experienced team of writers. All details are carefully checked to ensure the atlas corresponds with the equivalent Lonely Planet guidebook.

The handy atlas format means no holes, wrinkles, torn sections or constant folding and unfolding. These atlases can survive long periods on the road, unlike cumbersome fold-out maps. The comprehensive index ensures easy reference.

- full-colour throughout
- maps researched and checked by Lonely Planet authors
- place names correspond with Lonely Planet guidebooks
  – no confusing spelling differences
- legend and travelling information in English, French, German, Japanese and Spanish
- size: 230 x 160 mm

Available now:
Chile & Easter Island • Egypt • India & Bangladesh • Israel & the Palestinian Territories •Jordan, Syria & Lebanon • Kenya • Laos • Portugal • South Africa, Lesotho & Swaziland • Thailand • Turkey • Vietnam • Zimbabwe, Botswana & Namibia

LONELY PLANET TV SERIES & VIDEOS

Lonely Planet travel guides have been brought to life on television screens around the world. Like our guides, the programmes are based on the joy of independent travel, and look honestly at some of the most exciting, picturesque and frustrating places in the world. Each show is presented by one of three travellers from Australia, England or the USA and combines an innovative mixture of video, Super-8 film, atmospheric soundscapes and original music.

Videos of each episode – containing additional footage not shown on television – are available from good book and video shops, but the availability of individual videos varies with regional screening schedules.

Video destinations include: Alaska • American Rockies • Australia – The South-East • Baja California & the Copper Canyon • Brazil • Central Asia • Chile & Easter Island • Corsica, Sicily & Sardinia – The Mediterranean Islands • East Africa (Tanzania & Zanzibar) • Ecuador & the Galapagos Islands • Greenland & Iceland • Indonesia • Israel & the Sinai Desert • Jamaica • Japan • La Ruta Maya • Morocco • New York • North India • Pacific Islands (Fiji, Solomon Islands & Vanuatu) • South India • South West China • Turkey • Vietnam • West Africa • Zimbabwe, Botswana & Namibia

The Lonely Planet TV series is produced by:
Pilot Productions
The Old Studio
18 Middle Row
London W10 5AT UK

For video availability and ordering information contact your nearest Lonely Planet office.

Music from the TV series is available on CD & cassette.

PLANET TALK

Lonely Planet's FREE quarterly newsletter

We love hearing from you and think you'd like to hear from us.

*When...*is the right time to see reindeer in Finland?
*Where...*can you hear the best palm-wine music in Ghana?
*How...*do you get from Asunción to Areguá by steam train?
*What...*is the best way to see India?

For the answer to these and many other questions read PLANET TALK.

Every issue is packed with up-to-date travel news and advice including:

- a letter from Lonely Planet co-founders Tony and Maureen Wheeler
- go behind the scenes on the road with a Lonely Planet author
- feature article on an important and topical travel issue
- a selection of recent letters from travellers
- details on forthcoming Lonely Planet promotions
- complete list of Lonely Planet products

To join our mailing list contact any Lonely Planet office.

Also available: Lonely Planet T-shirts. 100% heavyweight cotton.

LONELY PLANET ONLINE

Get the latest travel information before you leave or while you're on the road

Whether you've just begun planning your next trip, or you're chasing down specific info on currency regulations or visa requirements, check out Lonely Planet Online for up-to-the minute travel information.

As well as travel profiles of your favourite destinations (including maps and photos), you'll find current reports from our researchers and other travellers, updates on health and visas, travel advisories, and discussion of the ecological and political issues you need to be aware of as you travel.

There's also an online travellers' forum where you can share your experience of life on the road, meet travel companions and ask other travellers for their recommendations and advice. We also have plenty of links to other online sites useful to independent travellers.

And of course we have a complete and up-to-date list of all Lonely Planet travel products including guides, phrasebooks, atlases, Journeys and videos and a simple online ordering facility if you can't find the book you want elsewhere.

www.lonelyplanet.com
or
AOL keyword: lp

LONELY PLANET PRODUCTS

Lonely Planet is known worldwide for publishing practical, reliable and no-nonsense travel information in our guides and on our web site. The Lonely Planet list covers just about every accessible part of the world. Currently there are eight series: *travel guides, shoestring guides, walking guides, city guides, phrasebooks, audio packs, travel atlases* and *Journeys* – a unique collection of travel writing.

EUROPE

Amsterdam • Austria • Baltic States phrasebook • Britain • Central Europe on a shoestring • Central Europe phrasebook • Czech & Slovak Republics • Denmark • Dublin • Eastern Europe on a shoestring • Eastern Europe phrasebook • Estonia, Latvia & Lithuania • Finland • France • French phrasebook • German phrasebook • Greece • Greek phrasebook • Hungary • Iceland, Greenland & the Faroe Islands • Ireland • Italian phrasebook • Italy • Mediterranean Europe on a shoestring • Mediterranean Europe phrasebook • Paris • Poland • Portugal • Portugal travel atlas • Prague • Russia, Ukraine & Belarus • Russian phrasebook • Scandinavian & Baltic Europe on a shoestring • Scandinavian Europe phrasebook • Slovenia • Spain • Spanish phrasebook • St Petersburg • Switzerland • Trekking in Greece • Trekking in Spain • Ukrainian phrasebook • Vienna • Walking in Britain • Walking in Switzerland • Western Europe on a shoestring • Western Europe phrasebook

Travel Literature: The Olive Grove: Travels in Greece

NORTH AMERICA

Alaska • Backpacking in Alaska • Baja California • California & Nevada • Canada • Florida • Hawaii • Honolulu • Los Angeles • Mexico • Miami • New England • New Orleans • New York City • New York, New Jersey & Pennsylvania • Pacific Northwest USA • Rocky Mountain States • San Francisco • Southwest USA • USA phrasebook • Washington, DC & the Capital Region

CENTRAL AMERICA & THE CARIBBEAN

Bermuda • Central America on a shoestring • Costa Rica • Cuba • Eastern Caribbean • Guatemala, Belize & Yucatán: La Ruta Maya • Jamaica

SOUTH AMERICA

Argentina, Uruguay & Paraguay • Bolivia • Brazil • Brazilian phrasebook • Buenos Aires • Chile & Easter Island • Chile & Easter Island travel atlas • Colombia • Ecuador & the Galápagos Islands • Latin American Spanish phrasebook • Peru • Quechua phrasebook • Rio de Janeiro • South America on a shoestring • Trekking in the Patagonian Andes • Venezuela

Travel Literature: Full Circle: A South American Journey

ANTARCTICA

Antarctica

ISLANDS OF THE INDIAN OCEAN

Madagascar & Comoros • Maldives • Mauritius, Réunion & Seychelles

AFRICA

Africa - the South • Africa on a shoestring • Arabic (Moroccan) phrasebook • Cape Town • Central Africa • East Africa • Egypt • Egypt travel atlas • Ethiopian (Amharic) phrasebook • Kenya • Kenya travel atlas • Malawi, Mozambique & Zambia • Morocco • North Africa • South Africa, Lesotho & Swaziland • South Africa, Lesotho & Swaziland travel atlas • Swahili phrasebook • Trekking in East Africa • West Africa • Zimbabwe, Botswana & Namibia • Zimbabwe, Botswana & Namibia travel atlas

Travel Literature: The Rainbird: A Central African Journey • Songs to an African Sunset: A Zimbabwean Story

MAIL ORDER

Lonely Planet products are distributed worldwide. They are also available by mail order from Lonely Planet, so if you have difficulty finding a title please write to us. North American and South American residents should write to Embarcadero West, 155 Filbert St, Suite 251, Oakland CA 94607, USA; European and African residents should write to 10 Barley Mow Passage, Chiswick, London W4 4PH; and residents of other countries to PO Box 617, Hawthorn, Victoria 3122, Australia.

NORTH-EAST ASIA

Beijing • Cantonese phrasebook • China • Hong Kong • Hong Kong, Macau & Guangzhou • Japan • Japanese phrasebook • Japanese audio pack • Korea • Korean phrasebook • Mandarin phrasebook • Mongolia • Mongolian phrasebook • North-East Asia on a shoestring • Seoul • Taiwan • Tibet • Tibet phrasebook • Tokyo

Travel Literature: Lost Japan

MIDDLE EAST & CENTRAL ASIA

Arab Gulf States • Arabic (Egyptian) phrasebook • Central Asia • Iran • Israel & the Palestinian Territories • Israel & the Palestinian Territories travel atlas • Istanbul • Jerusalem • Jordan & Syria • Jordan, Syria & Lebanon travel atlas • Middle East • Turkey • Turkish phrasebook • Turkey travel atlas • Yemen

Travel Literature: The Gates of Damascus • Kingdom of the Film Stars: Journey into Jordan

ALSO AVAILABLE:

Travel with Children • Traveller's Tales

INDIAN SUBCONTINENT

Bangladesh • Bengali phrasebook • Delhi • Hindi/Urdu phrasebook • India • India & Bangladesh travel atlas • Indian Himalaya • Karakoram Highway • Nepal • Nepali phrasebook • Pakistan • Rajasthan • Sri Lanka • Sri Lanka phrasebook • Trekking in the Indian Himalaya • Trekking in the Karakoram & Hindukush • Trekking in the Nepal Himalaya

Travel Literature: In Rajasthan • Shopping for Buddhas

SOUTH-EAST ASIA

Bali & Lombok • Bangkok • Burmese phrasebook • Cambodia • Ho Chi Minh City • Indonesia • Indonesian phrasebook • Indonesian audio pack • Jakarta • Java • Laos • Lao phrasebook • Laos travel atlas • Malay phrasebook • Malaysia, Singapore & Brunei • Myanmar (Burma) • Philippines • Pilipino phrasebook • Singapore • South-East Asia on a shoestring • South-East Asia phrasebook • Thailand • Thailand travel atlas • Thai phrasebook • Thai audio pack • Thai Hill Tribes phrasebook • Vietnam • Vietnamese phrasebook • Vietnam travel atlas

AUSTRALIA & THE PACIFIC

Australia • Australian phrasebook • Bushwalking in Australia • Bushwalking in Papua New Guinea • Fiji • Fijian phrasebook • Islands of Australia's Great Barrier Reef • Melbourne • Micronesia • New Caledonia • New South Wales & the ACT • New Zealand • Northern Territory • Outback Australia • Papua New Guinea • Papua New Guinea phrasebook • Queensland • Rarotonga & the Cook Islands • Samoa • Solomon Islands • South Australia • Sydney • Tahiti & French Polynesia • Tasmania • Tonga • Tramping in New Zealand • Vanuatu • Victoria • Western Australia

Travel Literature: Islands in the Clouds • Sean & David's Long Drive

THE LONELY PLANET STORY

Lonely Planet published its first book in 1973 in response to the numerous 'How did you do it?' questions Maureen and Tony Wheeler were asked after driving, bussing, hitching, sailing and railing their way from England to Australia.

Written at a kitchen table and hand collated, trimmed and stapled, *Across Asia on the Cheap* became an instant local bestseller, inspiring thoughts of another book.

Eighteen months in South-East Asia resulted in their second guide, *South-East Asia on a shoestring*, which they put together in a backstreet Chinese hotel in Singapore in 1975. The 'yellow bible', as it quickly became known to backpackers around the world, soon became *the* guide to the region. It has sold well over half a million copies and is now in its 9th edition, still retaining its familiar yellow cover.

Today there are over 240 titles, including travel guides, walking guides, language kits & phrasebooks, travel atlases and travel literature. The company is the largest independent travel publisher in the world. Although Lonely Planet initially specialised in guides to Asia, today there are few corners of the globe that have not been covered.

The emphasis continues to be on travel for independent travellers. Tony and Maureen still travel for several months of each year and play an active part in the writing, updating and quality control of Lonely Planet's guides.

They have been joined by over 70 authors and 170 staff at our offices in Melbourne (Australia), Oakland (USA), London (UK) and Paris (France). Travellers themselves also make a valuable contribution to the guides through the feedback we receive in thousands of letters each year and on our web site.

The people at Lonely Planet strongly believe that travellers can make a positive contribution to the countries they visit, both through their appreciation of the countries' culture, wildlife and natural features, and through the money they spend. In addition, the company makes a direct contribution to the countries and regions it covers. Since 1986 a percentage of the income from each book has been donated to ventures such as famine relief in Africa; aid projects in India; agricultural projects in Central America; Greenpeace's efforts to halt French nuclear testing in the Pacific; and Amnesty International.

'I hope we send people out with the right attitude about travel. You realise when you travel that there are so many different perspectives about the world, so we hope these books will make people more interested in what they see. Guidebooks can't really guide people. All you can do is point them in the right direction.'

– Tony Wheeler

LONELY PLANET PUBLICATIONS

Australia
PO Box 617, Hawthorn 3122, Victoria
tel: (03) 9819 1877 fax: (03) 9819 6459
e-mail: talk2us@lonelyplanet.com.au

USA
Embarcadero West, 155 Filbert St, Suite 251,
Oakland, CA 94607
tel: (510) 893 8555 TOLL FREE: 800 275-8555
fax: (510) 893 8563
e-mail: info@lonelyplanet.com

UK
10 Barley Mow Passage, Chiswick,
London W4 4PH
tel: (0181) 742 3161 fax: (0181) 742 2772
e-mail: lonelyplanetuk@compuserve.com

France:
71 bis rue du Cardinal Lemoine, 75005 Paris
tel: 1 44 32 06 20 fax: 1 46 34 72 55
e-mail: 100560.415@compuserve.com

World Wide Web: http://www.lonelyplanet.com
or *AOL* keyword: lp